Adversaries of Dance

Adversaries of Dance

From the Puritans to the Present

Ann Wagner

University of Illinois Press
Urbana and Chicago

© 1997 by the Board of Trustees of the University of Illinois
Manufactured in the United States of America
1 2 3 4 5 C P 5 4 3 2 1

This book is printed on acid-free paper.

Library of Congress Cataloging-in-Publication Data

Wagner, Ann Louise.
      Adversaries of dance : from the Puritans to the present
/ Ann Wagner.
            p.   cm.
      Includes bibliographical references and index.
      ISBN 0-252-02274-2 (cloth : alk. paper). —
ISBN 0-252-06590-5 (pbk. : alk. paper)
      ISBN 978-0-252-02274-6 (cloth : alk. paper). —
ISBN 978-0-252-06590-3 (pbk. : alk. paper)
      1. Dance—Moral and ethical aspects—United States—
History. 2. Dance—Social aspects—United States—
History. 3. United States—Moral conditions. I. Title.
GV1623.W25   1997
792.8'0973—dc20   96-25187
                                                              CIP

Contents

Preface vii

Introduction xi

Part 1: European Antecedents

1. The Pre-Reformation Tradition 3
2. The Voices of Protestant Reformers 19

Part 2: American Attitudes

3. The Puritans in New England: The Seventeenth Century 47
4. The Gentry and the Awakening: The Eighteenth Century 70
5. Early Evangelicals and American Etiquette: 1800–1839 106
6. The Evangelical Mainstream and Radical Reformers: 1840–60 141
7. Conservatives, Liberals, and the City: 1865–89 193
8. Embattled Fundamentalists and the Rhetoric of Moral Panic: 1890–1929 236

9. Urban Reformers and the Dance Hall: 1908–40   292
10. The Polemic Upstaged: 1930–69 and Beyond   320

Part 3: Critical Variables and Cultural Context
11. The Nature of Dance and the Polemic in Reprise   363
12. Aesthetics, Morality, and Gender   383

Appendix
A. Bible Verses on Dance   401
B. Known European Adversaries of Dance   407
C. Lesser-Known Adversaries Mentioned in the
   Text   413

Index   423

Preface

My interest in American opposition to dance developed initially during my undergraduate years at St. Olaf College (Minnesota) and Augustana College (Illinois)—both Lutheran schools that proscribed social dancing. Curiosity later turned into a serious research interest when my dissertation work revealed intense antagonism to dancing on the part of sixteenth-century Protestants. The bicentennial publication of Joseph E. Marks's *The Mathers on Dancing* contained a lengthy "Bibliography of Anti-Dance Books," which further stimulated my desire to understand the scope and sequence of American opposition. The beginning of a dance major curriculum at St. Olaf College in 1979, where I have taught since 1961, brought with it an opportunity to initiate a series of dance history courses, and that experience served as a catalyst to my work.

The present book results from a decade of summer research plus a half-year leave, all of which was funded in part by grants from St. Olaf College. The initial writing was made possible by a sabbatical supported by a National Endowment for the Humanities Fellowship for College Teachers. I am grateful to both St. Olaf and NEH for this invaluable financial support.

Because the amount of printed evidence that could be analyzed in an historical study of this scope is vast, I limited my research primarily to the arguments printed in American books and tracts. As a general rule, I included eighteenth- and nineteenth-century British publications found in American libraries and archives only if the books had been reprinted in this country. Due to the nature of the topic, my work on dance halls depended in part on articles from popular American periodicals.

The final analysis derives from my study of more than 350 primary source books and tracts in addition to the periodical literature. While Marks's bibliography provided my initial working tool, I found many additional books in the numerous public and private libraries I visited at colleges and seminaries. Interlibrary loan service proved invaluable for securing some publications.

In addition to the efficient and ongoing help provided by Connie Gunderson and Gretchen Hardgrove, interlibrary loan staff at St. Olaf College, I am grateful for the expert assistance of staff at the following libraries and archives I visited in the course of my research: American Antiquarian Society; American Baptist Historical Society; Andover-Harvard Theological School Library; Andover-Newton Theological School Library; Asbury Theological Seminary Library; Augustana College (Illinois); Beinecke Rare Book Library, Yale University; Bethel College; Billy Graham Archive; Boston Public Library; Boston University School of Theology Library; British Library; Carleton College; Chicago Historical Society; Concordia Historical Society; Concordia Theological Seminary Library; Congregational Church Archives; Disciples of Christ Historical Society; Emmanuel College Library, Cambridge University; Houghton Library, Harvard University; Lexington (Kentucky) Theological Seminary; Lutheran Theological Seminary at Philadelphia; Luther-Northwestern Seminary Library; Massachusetts Historical Society; Methodist Church Archives, Drew University; Moody Bible Institute; New York Public Library Dance Collection, Lincoln Center; New York State Library; Northwestern College; Oberlin College; Presbyterian Historical Society; Princeton Theological Seminary Library; Queens College Library, Oxford University; Rensselaer County (New York) Historical Society; South Carolina Historical Society; Southern Baptist Historical Society and Archives; Southern Baptist Theological Seminary Library; Southwestern Baptist Theological Seminary Library; Springfield, Massachusetts, City Library; St. Olaf College; Union Theological Seminary Library; University of Iowa; Walter Library, University of Minnesota; Widener Library, Harvard University; Wilson Library, University of Minnesota; and Worcester (Massachusetts) Free Public Library.

In quoting from the material I discovered in these repositories, I have made editorial changes in the orthography of sources from the sixteenth century or earlier, substituting the letters "v" and "j" for "u" and "i," respectively, and using the modern "s" throughout. Otherwise, I have retained original spellings even when the same word is spelled differently within a single quotation. I have retained the ampersand in direct quotations, although modern computer type does not quite duplicate the elaborate configuration of that symbol in earlier centuries.

Many people contribute ideas to a research project of this scope; though their help is invaluable, they become too numerous to mention. However, I am particularly indebted to several individuals. Erling Jorstad, professor emeritus of history and American studies at St. Olaf, provided thoughtful and detailed comments following an early reading of the entire manuscript and has given ongoing moral support. Susan Lindley, a professor in St. Olaf's religion department and also an active teacher-author in women's studies, read revised manuscripts and provided comprehensive, critical insights for further revision. My faculty colleagues Anne von Bibra and Anne Groton assisted with German and Latin translations. Jowane Howard, a friend and coworker, typed the manuscript and sundry revisions with keen interest, a careful eye, and expert computer skills. Janet Collrin, of St. Olaf's Academic Computer Center, provided timely consultation on manuscript preparation. Jude Tomac, my student assistant, proved invaluable in proofreading. My husband, Axel Bundgaard, has given continued moral support, listened to many laments and to many pages I read aloud, and accompanied me to all of the libraries I visited.

Introduction

Dance and dancing have encountered strong opposition throughout history, but the scope, substance, and cause of that opposition are not widely known or understood. Queen Elizabeth I delighted in the skilled dancing of her courtiers and, reportedly, danced several galliards daily for the sake of her health. Nevertheless, that famous Elizabethan preacher William Perkins admonished Christians about the evils of such an exercise, which he labeled "the very bellowes of lust." The devout, conservative Catholic courtier Sir Thomas Elyot told the English in 1531 that the virtue of prudence could be learned through dancing; yet within fifty years his countryman, the Protestant minister John Northbrooke, loudly proclaimed that "Dauncing is the vilest vice of all!"

A century later in America, the Puritan cleric Increase Mather, on behalf of several Boston clergymen, penned a treatise against "mixt" or "gynecandrical" dancing. In 1700 his son, Cotton Mather, continued writing stern admonitions to church members, emphasizing the temptations in the "Dancing Humour, as it now prevails, and especially in Balls." Yet by 1714, the Anglican Church in Boston had hired Edward Enstone from England to be its organist and gave him permission to supplement his salary by giving dancing lessons.

Though antidance voices subsided during the remainder of the eighteenth century, they did not fall silent. In fact, the voices rose again, growing louder and increasing in number, by the middle of the following century. Not only dancing but the circus, the theater, and cards all provoked the wrath of devout evangelicals across denominational lines. In fact, the "amusement" question claimed the attention of clergy and evangelists from 1840 through the opening decades of the twentieth century, when "movies" were added to the list of proscribed entertainments.

By the second decade of this century, Americans in urban areas had gone "dance-mad" as hundreds of new fad dances appeared in hotels, cabarets, and dance halls around the country. Although Vernon and Irene Castle demonstrated that even the imported, seductive tango could look refined and graceful, Billy Sunday, America's premiere evangelist during the teens, thundered with a ferocity that recalled John Northbrooke's over three centuries earlier. According to Sunday, even swinging corners in square dances brought the bodies of men and women into positions that shouldn't be tolerated in "decent society." Despite such warnings, the popularity of dancing continued unabated.

As Americans matured in outlook, developed more cosmopolitan tastes, and became widely attuned to events throughout the country via radio, movies, and television, the opposition to dancing died down. By the early 1960s, the latest fads—such as the twist, the monkey, and the Watusi—seemed as ubiquitous as had the grizzly bear, the turkey trot, and other dances from the ragtime era. As the twentieth century draws to a close, one rarely hears attacks on dancing except in isolated pockets of the country. Never in the history of America has dance been so widely embraced and studied as a serious art form—in universities and theaters, and even in some churches. Yet vestiges of the old notions sometimes appear—as in the small community of Purdy, Missouri, where a legal battle arose not long ago over whether or not the school board could prohibit dancing. In 1987, Hollywood produced *Dirty Dancing,* a film set in the early 1960s, about young people who struggled to overcome rules forbidding dancing. Some conservative groups still send out antidance tracts, and some private colleges continue to require students to sign a pledge that they will not dance.

Even the mildly curious mind must wonder at the tenacity of dance opponents for half a millennium. Is dancing so evil that it has merited the constant barrage of allegations for centuries? Is there something in the nature of dance that provokes such fierce attacks? Or, are there cultural characteristics that evoke antidance sentiment? Do all kinds of dance elicit antagonism? What happens when music and dances change from one decade or century to the next? The answers do not come easily.

Central to understanding the antidance tradition is an awareness that the art of dance has some essential characteristics that, historically, have been variously interpreted. First and most obvious, dancing involves the human body. Even the person untrained in dance knows that the human body is subject to wide-ranging perceptions and values. The body can be thought beautiful or ugly, good or evil. It is personal, sensual, sexual, and powerful. When issues of gender and race are added to the mix, views of and values assigned to the body become ever more complex. Television commercials and magazine ads make the point with varying degrees of sophistication on a daily basis. Second, music, rhythm, and movement can range from quiescent to wild, from soothing to energizing to erotic. They evoke emotions with equally broad ranges. When bodily motion is accompanied by rhythmic sound, powerful sexual stimuli can come into play. Finally, people usually dance in time free from work. As a kind of recreation, entertainment, art, amusement, and/or exercise, dancing provides no necessary material goods or services. Therefore, the issue of whether or not people can or should dance becomes intertwined with other basic values—especially those pertaining to study, work, worship, family, and friends.

The same kind of complex interpretation applies to values surrounding the use of money—a necessary exchange for dance lessons, admission to dances and concerts, or mounting a dance production. Should one spend money on dancing or watching dances when shelter, clothing, food, and other survival goods require so much of the family budget? Should money be spent to produce dances when so many homeless and hungry people exist in the country? Should capital be used to add dance studios to public school buildings when science laboratories lack new equipment? Should dance teachers be hired when math classes demand more instructors to provide more effective learning to smaller groups of students? The questions could continue. Although the centuries-long historical polemic has virtually ended, issues related to the valuing of dance remain vital in American culture today.

Yet most Americans have practically no objective knowledge about the history and status of dance in our culture. Compared with the study of music, for example, dance has been little researched and studied. Many people have inherited biases against dancing. Uninformed and unexamined attitudes can evoke strong behaviors that serve to perpetuate ancient antagonisms. It is my hope that this book will help to dispel some of the myth and untruth surrounding the valuing of dance by providing new insights and information and by stimulating further research.

My goal has been to lay out both the scope and substance of American opposition to dance, as that antipathy emerged out of sixteenth-century Reformation fervor, and to present an analysis of why such antidance attitudes existed. I believe that students of dance history will be interested in this material, as will scholars in women's studies and American studies, especially those focusing on religion in America. They will find that my subject inevitably involves an interdisciplinary perspective and that I have tried to maintain a balance of information and perspective that is reasonably sufficient for readers from these backgrounds.

To understand the adversaries of dance and the substance of their opposition, one has to know something of the dancing and the dance advocacy that fueled that opposition. I deemed the two best sources for such information to be the dance manuals, or "how-to" books, and the courtesy manuals of much earlier centuries, which continued as etiquette books in the nineteenth and twentieth centuries. The former provide information about the importance of dancing from the perspective of dance masters and teachers. Courtesy and etiquette books lend insight into the valuing of dance in relation to social class, gender, ethnicity, and race. Both kinds of primary sources exist in a continuous line of development, paralleling the writings of dance opponents, from the sixteenth century to the twentieth.

In shaping this book, I have purposely not given a definition of dance, for the precise reason that adversaries themselves did not define it. Nonetheless, they focused their opposition narrowly. They invariably talked about "dance" or the "dance of modern society" and used the terms to refer to the social dances and balls of their own day. In a few instances, opponents spoke about folk dancing; occasionally they referred to stage dancing. What is universally indicted over the centuries is dancing in which men and women moved and mixed together, sometimes with partners and sometimes without; sometimes in square, circle, or line formations; and sometimes traveling around a room, one among many couples, as in a waltz. The dancing regularly denounced came from European courts and assembly halls, until the early twentieth century, when Latin American and African American rhythms, steps, and styles became popular. Dancing occurred in this country in contexts ranging from home parlor, to public hall, to commercial "palace" and sleazy dive. These facts make issues of gender, race, and socioeconomic status central to the discussion.

In effect, the American tradition of dance opposition has emanated from white, male, Protestant clergy and evangelists who argued from a narrow and selective interpretation of biblical passages and who persisted in seeing dancing only within a moral and spiritual frame of reference. The fact that not all professing Christians, or clergy, or evangelists adhered to the antidance sentiment will be demonstrated by interpretations expressed in other writings, including the courtesy literature, etiquette books, and dance manuals. Ultimately, the degree to which American dance opposition existed and flourished has depended upon shifting configurations of the following: (1) the power of conservative, evangelical denominations and dogma in America; (2) the existence of a unified identity and calling of denominational clergy; (3) the pervasiveness of traditional gender roles with their attendant assumptions about women; (4) a sense of the body and sex as taboo subjects; and (5) the popularity of dancing as a leisure and artistic activity. For example, a powerful configuration of all five forces produced an outpouring of antidance literature, across denominational lines, in the middle decades of the nineteenth century. Variations in the strength and/ or pervasiveness of one or more of the five forces has resulted in a more limited dance opposition for other decades and centuries.

The adversaries, their views and shifting denominational positions, must be seen within the context of a changing American church that has responded to a changing culture, from the seventeenth to twentieth centuries. The most helpful frame of reference I have found for understanding that shifting context, as it pertains to the subject at hand, is the perspective developed by William G. McLoughlin in his book *Revivals, Awakenings and Reform*. He posits "Five Awakenings" or reorientations in cultural values and beliefs—from the Puritan Awakening in the seventeenth century to a Fourth Great Awakening in the late twentieth century. The American adversaries of dance emerge from the Puritan culture to march through and beyond the Third Great Awakening, from 1890 to 1920, before effectively meeting their demise by the 1960s. Revivalists and evangelistic clergy in these awakenings fueled dance opposition; their themes of conversion and a reformed life, based on biblical principles, have been central to the antidance literature.

I have organized the chapters in this book by centuries initially and then later, as the material becomes more voluminous, by decades. Most chapter titles highlight the core of dance opposition that continued over centuries. I have intended each chapter to be complete in itself, for a reader interested only in a particular time period. Throughout, I have tried to let primary sources speak for themselves. People and their arguments are set within historical contexts of time, place, and events. Therefore, exposition of scope, substance, and analysis proceeds in chronological, episodic, and inductive fashion. Chapter 11 deals with the nature of dance and offers a longitudinal summary of arguments from all centuries. In the final chapter I analyze the dance opponents collectively in terms of their focus on morality and spiritual growth, and then suggest an alternative view.

Readers will find arguments pertaining to time, place, scope, substance, and context in each chapter. However, each chapter will also reveal some recurring themes. The fact that adversaries came primarily from the ranks of male clergy, whose views emanated from the "evangelical" perspective, will inevitably mean that certain themes reappear, for example, personal conversion and behavioral reform; the authority of selected biblical passages (quoted in this book from the Good News version, unless noted otherwise); the practice of piety and separation from the world; the stewarding of time, money, and health; and the assumed ideals in religious/social roles for men and women. Variations on these themes in each time period pertain to tone and language, logic of reasoning, the objects of attack, and the authors of such attacks.

To research the adversaries of dance over the centuries is to cover the broadest possible scope yet all the while trying to steward time and focus evidence. The search for information has been comprehensive but can never be exhaustive. Myriad sources—unpublished committee reports, synod minutes, correspondence among clergy, and the like—remain tucked away in libraries and archives awaiting examination. Some individual adversaries merit further analysis. Additional work also remains to be done in comparing contemporary movements like temperance and prostitution reform with the antidance tradition; associations of drinking, dancing, and brothels figure prominently in the antidance literature. My hope is that the present study will offer other scholars tantalizing views of the opposition to dance and that they will extend their own research into new paths.

Part 1

European Antecedents

1

The Pre-Reformation Tradition

Amongst the Papists, some of their more grave Writers,
decry such a practice as a great Immorality.

Increase Mather, 1685

When Increase Mather penned "An Arrow Against Profane and Promiscuous Dancing," the first extant antidance treatise written in America, he drew on a long tradition of authority from Continental and British scholars. One of the latter had established the single most comprehensive catalog then available, which listed authors constituting the European heritage. William Prynne's *Histrio-Mastix* appeared in 1633; Mather characterized it as a "large discourse on this subject." Although Mather himself presented scholarly and ecclesiastical authorities extending back several centuries, his list by no means compares with Prynne's in length. And, almost all of Mather's pre–sixteenth-century sources are also found in Prynne's work. To understand the origins of American opposition to dance, the tradition that succeeded from the Reformation era and then from Mather, it is important to begin with European antecedents, that is, with a broad picture of Catholic opposition to and support of dancing. The Old World perspective can be most concisely summarized through a sampling of Mather's and Prynne's citations.

Like Mather a scholar and a Puritan, William Prynne (1600–1669) graduated from Oxford, studied law at Lincoln's Inn, and was called to the bar in 1628. He began his *Histrio-Mastix* in 1624 and it was first published in 1632. Prynne's discourse on the evils of dancing appears among the "adjuncts" to his disputation on stage plays. However, neither he nor Mather delineated the kind of dancing they opposed. They objected to all "mixt," "lascivious," and "immoral" dancing, but both men denigrated the art as though all dancing were the same. Neither Prynne nor Mather clarified whether or not they had first-hand knowledge of the activity they railed against. Yet as devout Puritans, their viewpoints were clear. Both men intended to keep the church pure and orthodox, as they saw that direction. To that end, they aimed to show that dance opponents constituted a lengthy and venerable tradition.

Prynne confronted his readers with a catalog of both pagan and Christian writers, as well as church councils, who opposed dancing. Both he and Mather concentrated on the opposition to dancing based on its unlawfulness for Christians. Pagan opposition served merely to reinforce their stance. They reasoned that, since even the pagans opposed dancing, it must be evil indeed. Prynne's major premise, stated early in his section on dancing, declares that: "all mixt effeminate, lascivious, amorous dancing . . . is utterly unlawfull unto Christians, to chaste and sober persons; as sundry Councels, Fathers, moderne Christian, with ancient Pagan Authors and Nations have resolved; though it bee now so much in use, in fashion and request among us, that many spend more houres (more dayes and nights) in dancing, then in praying, I might adde working too."[1] To support this assertion, Prynne listed numerous church councils from the early Christian era through the sixteenth century. His second battery of opposition included names of some forty church fathers and ancient authors. Bringing the tradition of ecclesiastical opposition up to his own time, Prynne cited writers from the Middle Ages through the seventeenth century, and emphasized contemporary Englishmen. Even more than Mather, Prynne appears to have assumed that the longer his list of authorities, the stronger and more credible would be his position. At least six pages of his text consist merely of citations plus additional notes with names and sources.

Although Prynne does not identify authors' works in all instances, a review of his sources reveals that the medieval and Renaissance authorities consisted of churchmen, reformers, university scholars, and humanists. As Prynne's major premise implies, these men did not write as a mere rhetorical exercise; they wrote against the dancing found in the society in which they lived. The fact that dancing existed prior to the Reformation points to the reality that, under Roman rule, dancing was permitted or sponsored by the Catholic church as well as opposed at various times by councils or individual churchmen.

Medieval Traditions

In his detailed study *Religious Dances in the Christian Church and in Popular Medicine,* E. Louis Backman, an early twentieth-century researcher who was also a pharmacologist, divides dances from the medieval and early modern eras into the sacred and the popular. The former were those performed by clerics or others involved in official church functions, that is, dances by bishops, priests, choirboys, and nuns. Popular dances were those performed by laity. Special celebrations such as the Children's Festival and the Festival of Fools were recognized occasions for dancing. Specific dances such as the pelota, bergerette, and los seizes have been identified as sacred dances performed during the later Middle Ages. Other occasions for dancing included the induction of monks or nuns into order, though such practice apparently became too disorderly and was prohibited after 1385.[2]

Church Councils and Popular Dancing

Church councils regularly pronounced against dancing and the undesirable behavior it allegedly elicited. Prynne cites nineteen councils that censured immoral, "effeminate," and "mixt" dancing. Violators, he says, were subject to excommunication. Backman's chronology of church sanctions begins with the fourth century and continues through the sixteenth. His list includes no sanctions against dancing per se but targets the time and place when dancing occurred or the undesirable behavior accompanying it, for example, shameless singing, drunkenness, and fornication. Such proscriptions evidenced the councils' clear intent to curb specific forbidden behaviors and, by extension, to control social conduct.

Although some of the proscriptions specifically named women, the degree to which they were targeted is not clear from Backman's list of sanctions. Yet the practice of blaming women for alleged evil and immorality was commonplace. For example, Bede Jarrett, in his *Social Theories of the Middle Ages,* writes: "There are denunciations in all medieval literature of the evil effects of women upon mankind, of the unhappy snares they spread for the destruction of poor innocent men. . . . it is hard to find a theologian, or a scriptural commentator, or a preacher, or a poet, who did not denounce these and similar practices."[3] A more specific and ancient example of such practice involved the biblical Salome and her mother. The medieval church fostered miracle and morality plays, in which dancing constituted a part of the presentation. Such plays included the dancing of follies and portrayed devils and Salome as personifications of vice. According to the scriptural account, Salome's dancing proved so enchanting to King Herod that he agreed to grant her any wish. Her mother, Queen Herodias, told her to ask for the head of John the Baptist on a platter.[4] Generations of dance opponents used the incident as proof of the wickedness of dancing. The charge also reinforced the belief that women as dancers and women per se were perpetrators of evil.

Popular dancing by the laity would have encompassed a range of activities. The ubiquitous folk dancing of any century is difficult to research because much of it was conveyed through the oral tradition. However, sufficient evidence exists to substantiate a medieval tradition of professional dancing/entertainment under the broad category of minstrelsy.[5] In addition, distinctions in social rank and the advent of dance masters, who wrote instructional manuals, gave rise to the art of courtly dancing in Italy and Burgundy by the fifteenth century.

In sum, dancing had existed under active church sponsorship or passive permission for centuries prior to the Reformation. But during that lengthy period, the church also issued regulatory edicts. In addition to proscriptions by church councils, another kind of official document pertained to the act of confession.

Summas for Confessors

One might argue that, in the Middle Ages, when the literacy rate was low and the printing press had not yet come to the West, any written document held considerable importance. However, given the power of the medieval church, ecclesiastical documents would have carried more authority than would poetry, for example. Foremost among church literature, with respect to seriousness and control over individual lives, were the books called summas for confessors, or summas of cases of conscience, a genre identifiable between the early thirteenth and early sixteenth centuries. The institution of confession had been mandated by a papal bull of 1215, which required all persons at or over the age of discretion to make an annual confession to their priests. The summas, which originated between 1220 and 1245, served to define and explain sins or forbidden behavior, penance or punishment, and restitution. So thorough were these books that the historian Thomas Tentler calls them "ecclesiastical and theological encyclopedias." Sin was the subject of confession, and the summas classified sins in detail. They told the confessor what kinds of behavior constituted sins, how serious they were, how they should be confessed, and why and when such behavior should be forgiven. In effect, Tentler argues, the summas also served as a means of social control. To have the knowledge and power to control confession—that is, to offer forgiveness and to prescribe penance—is to wield substantial authority over a person's earthly life and eternal future. Into this body of serious and authoritative literature fall some of the proscriptions of dancing.[6]

Prynne cites two authors of popular summas, the entire genre of which numbered between twelve and twenty-five, depending on how they were defined. Astesanus de Asti (died c. 1330), a Franciscan, wrote a summa around 1317 that, if frequency of reprinting is the criterion, enjoyed great popularity and importance. It appeared ten times in incunabular editions and once in the sixteenth century.[7] The other summa cited by Prynne constituted one of the two most popular from the late Middle Ages and Renaissance, according to Tentler. The *Summa Angelica* was written by another Franciscan, Angelus Carletus de Clavasio (1411–95), who attained fame as a moral theologian for this work. Published first in Venice in 1486, it was issued in twenty-four incunabular printings, from the major publishing cities in Europe, and had at least nineteen printings between 1501 and 1520, the year when Martin Luther burned it.[8]

Prynne's citation of a portion of the *Summa Astensis* provides an example of the detailed classification of sins common to the genre. This work is organized into eight books, the second of which addresses virtues and vices. Within that book, each title treats a particular subject. Thus, title 53 discusses varying degrees of and contexts for sinning with respect to outward movements of the body. Astesanus reasons in tight deductive fashion, by posing a general question, giving an answer, and then posing a more specific question, until he covers the range of possibilities for sinning under this specific heading. His key themes for determining culpability are motive and frequency of participation. He asserts that there can be virtue in pastimes or recreational activity (*ludi*) if they are performed for the sake of healthful renewal of the body. There can also be vice in an excess of recreation, that is, in participation beyond moderation. In discussing spectators of such activity, Astesanus declares that watching the dancing "of lascivious women" can progress from venial to mortal sin if one studiously fixes attention on the dancers. Treating female dancers (*c[h]oreatrices*) as participants, he asserts that they would be sinning mortally if they intended to incite themselves or others to lust, or if they danced habitually, even though free of corrupt intention. Astesanus remained uncertain about whether or not a woman would sin mortally if she rarely, and without corrupt intention, engaged in dances. However, such behavior still proved questionable because she could be exposing others to lust and would be setting a bad example for them.[9]

Manuals of Pastoral Care

Manuals of pastoral care were similar to the summas in popularity and practicality, though less encyclopedic in scope. Prynne refers to a writing of John de Burgh (fl. 1370–86) titled *Pupilla Oculi,* compiled between 1380 and 1385. Its preparation partially coincided with the author's terms as chancellor of Cambridge University in 1384 and 1386. Quoting from this "widely used" text,[10] Prynne notes that Burgh had declared dancing a mortal sin on the grounds of its incitement to lust and its setting a bad example for others. Those who danced "out of custome," though with innocent intent, still provided an undesirable example for others to follow. Thus, the themes of motive, frequency of participation, and consequences of participation, which Astesanus had detailed, continued half a century later. In Prynne's words: "That those who dance to incite themselves or others unto lust, yea those likewise who dance out of custome, sin mortally, though they do it not with a corrupt intent. Neither dare I (saith he) to excuse these from a mortall sinne, since by dancing they plunge themselves into this danger, of provoking others unto lust, and ipso facto seeme to approve of dancing, and by their example give authority to others to doe the like."[11]

Tentler's comprehensive analysis of sin and of the practice of confession at the beginning of the sixteenth century provides insight into the ultimate seriousness of classifying some dancing as a mortal sin, as Astesanus and John de Burgh did. Tentler points out that the difficulty in assessing the degree of culpability for an individual sinner lay in determining the difference between mortal and venial sins. The latter were slight offenses, but the former could earn one a fall from grace and eternal damnation.[12] Thus, both Astesanus and Burgh declared it a mortal sin to dance habitually even though with innocent intention. To be responsible for providing an example that could lead another into eternal damnation was a matter of utmost seriousness.

Although Mather had read Prynne and knew that author's sources, he does not mention that John de Burgh or Astesanus assigned dancing to the category of mortal sins. In fact, Mather laments that "corrupt Schoolmen" made light of dancing by calling it merely a venial sin. Though he does not name particular scholastics, the reference applies generally to those teachers of philosophy and theology who flourished prior to John de Burgh, from the eleventh through the thirteenth centuries, at Europe's great universities. Mather also asserts that "Popish Casuists" tended "generally" to justify dancing as they did "many other moral evils."[13]

Contrary to Mather's biases against the "corrupt Schoolmen," the written tradition—the edicts by church councils, the confessional summas, and the pastoral care manuals—makes clear that the pre-Reformation church did not give unqualified support to dancing. In addition to these institutional attempts by the church to regulate dancing, the medieval era gave rise to some radical reformers who pronounced unequivocally against dancing as the devil's own activity.

Early Reformers

Both Mather and Prynne approved of the sentiments of Alexander Fabritius, whom they labeled "a Learned man, though Popishly affected." Little is known about Fabritius, whose Anglicized name was Alexander Carpenter and who flourished in the early fifteenth century. The author of *Destructorium Vitiorum,* begun in 1429, Fabritius may have been a fellow at Balliol College, Oxford, and/or he may have been a follower of Wycliffe. The *Destructorium* enjoyed a "considerable popularity in the fifteenth and sixteenth centuries."[14] The text was cited by Mather as well as by Prynne, who quoted Fabritius at length. What must have appealed to Mather and Prynne was the focus of Fabritius's arguments. Fabritius charged that dancing offended against sacraments of the church, those rites understood to be instituted or recognized by Christ. His allegations, therefore, struck at the heart of Christian worship and ritual. Mather quotes the following charge made by Fabritius: "The entring into the Processions of Dances, hinders men from ingress into the heavenly Procession; and those who Dance, offend against the Sacraments of the Church. First, against Baptism; They break the Covenant which they made with God in Baptism; wherein they promised, to renounce the Devil and his Pomps; but when they enter into the Dance, they go in the Pompous Procession of the Devil."[15]

Fabritius's assertion that dancing belonged to the "Pompous Procession of the Devil" reiterated a notion long held by dance opponents. Precisely where and when the charge originated is not clear. Prynne credits Chrysostom and other early church fathers with declaring the devil to be the original author of "mixt, effeminate, lascivious, amorous dancing." Mather, who also credits the church fathers, considered the connection of dance with the devil to be a strong indictment against dancing. In further support of the point, he quotes at some length from Jean Paul Perrin's *History of the Doctrine and Discipline of the Waldenses,* a study of a sect Mather considered among the "great Reformers of Religion and Opposers of Antichristianism."[16] Although Mather quotes from Perrin's history, Prynne includes a fuller excerpt drawn from a "Censure of Dancing" by the Waldenses and another heretical sect, the Albigenses. Both Prynne and Mather include in their own catalogs the following indictment: "A Dance (as I finde their words in their Treatise against Dancing) is the Devils procession, and he that entreth into a Dance, entreth into his possession. The Devill is the guide, the middle, and end of the Dance. As many paces as a man maketh in Dancing, so many paces doth he make to Hell. A man sinneth in Dancing divers wayes: as in his pace, for all his steps are numbred: in his touch, in his ornaments, in his bearing, sight, speech, and other vanities."

The detailed charges against dancing made by the Waldenses and Albigenses reveal two fundamental premises: first, dancing is evil because it is the work of the devil, who is ever out to tempt the devout Christian to sin or forbidden behavior; and second, as inheritors of the opprobrium of the creation story, women are agents of the devil. Prynne cites the charge that the devil's "most powerfull armes are women." Especially when painted, adorned, and dancing, women entice men by touch, sight, and hearing. The allegation that dancers broke the Ten Commandments indicated the seriousness of the activity; such behavior would have been a mortal, not a venial, sin. The charge that dancers also broke their baptismal vows would have been equally serious, since those vows pledge allegiance to God and renunciation of the devil.[17]

Two other voices critical of dancing, and of the morals of the clergy, belonged to Antoninus de Forciglioni (1389–1459), archbishop of Florence, and Nicholas de Clamanges (1360–1437), rector of the University of Paris and later archdeacon of Bayeux. Prynne cites both men but does not quote from their works. However, both men are also cited by modern scholars. Antoninus, famed in his own day for his devout faith and compassion, as well as for his work toward rigorous reform in the church, prepared his *Chronicles* as a supplement to his *Summa Theologica.* As a compilation of writings from the lives of pious and eminent men, the *Chronicles* apparently used history as a moral discipline, to show by example how people should live.[18] Johan Huizinga, in his book *The Waning of the Middle Ages,* cites Nicholas de Clamanges as an authoritative chronicler of the era. In particular, the French ecclesiastic refers to vigils being "kept with lascivious songs and dances, even in church." Further, according to Huizinga, "On festal days, exclaims Nicolas de Clemanges, people go to visit distant churches, not so much to redeem a pledge of pilgrimage as to give themselves up to pleasure. Pilgrimages are the occasions of all kinds of debauchery; procuresses are always found there, people come for amorous purposes."[19] Though not acknowledged by Mather, both Antoninus and Clamanges would seem to qualify as two of the "more grave" writers among the "Papists," to use the Puritan's expression.

Apart from the reforming voices and the church's institutional opposition, Prynne also cites a selected body of writing by learned men. Nothing appears to unite his citations except the fact that these authors were early humanist scholars who opposed dancing. However, their backgrounds indicate that at least some of them wrote specifically in opposition to dancing at courts. Thus, the possibility of dance opposition as a part of social class criticism becomes apparent.

Early Renaissance Humanist Traditions

Early Humanists looked to the ancient Greek tradition that valued the body, dance, sports, and games as an integral part of education. Yet, within that positive configuration, Renaissance educators were divided on the value of dance in training young gentlemen.

Humanist Scholars

Vittorino da Feltre (1378–1446), often called the first "modern schoolmaster," included both dancing and music in his school at Mantua, Italy. However, both Mapheo Vegio (1406/7–58) and Aeneas Silvius de Piccolomini (1405–64), the latter of whom became Pope Pius II, omitted dancing from their prescribed curricula for a liberal education. Their opposition stemmed from moral concerns. Aeneas's experience at the court of Frederick III in Germany led him to conclude that the atmosphere surrounding dancing provided too many temptations to lust. Similarly, Mapheo Vegio considered dancing the source of evils that could undermine the development of virtue in young men.[20] Other opponents struck at the essential nature of dancing.

Francesco Petrarch (1304–74) charged that dancing not only tempted to immoral conduct but was, in fact, an absurd activity. That is, without the covering power of music, the movements of dancers appeared totally ridiculous. The objection suggests that contemporary dance involved movements and shapes not aesthetically pleasing in and of themselves. In fact, Petrarch's point may not be original but merely a variant on Cicero's frequently quoted indictment, which Mather translated as "if a Man be a Dancer, he is doubtless either a Drunkard or a mad man."[21] Similarly, Sebastian Brant (1458?–1521), whose widely popular poem *Ship of Fools* satirized the folly and decadence of the age, charged that no game on earth was so "damnable" as foolish dancing. The people who pursued it appeared to have unstable minds; that is, they seemed like "mad folke."[22] Brant's description clearly suggests a disorderly kind of dancing, an activity that was vigorous, unrefined, and bawdy. Even allowing for the satirical nature of the poem, Brant's background makes it unlikely that he was referring to the highly artistic dancing prevalent in Italian and Burgundian courts.[23]

Courtly Dancing

The humanist tradition and its flowering during the quattrocento in Italy gave rise to the flourishing of dance as a courtly art. Two significant developments—the emergence of the dance master and the development of the dance manual—ensured that the ideal of the art would forever remain a formal, ordered event requiring both practice and instruction. The figure of the dance master, the professional teacher and choreographer who also wrote manuals of instruction, emerged fully distinct before the middle of the fifteenth century in both Burgundy and Italy. He belonged to the aristocracy and his authority was final in matters of dancing. The dance historian Ingrid Brainard writes: "All the leading courts of 15th century Italy had their dancing master in residence and it is not surprising that we find the great names of the 15th century choreography taking turns as *maestri del ballo* at Ferrara, Urbino, Mantua, Milan, Bologna, Venice, Florence and Naples."[24] The manuals that these men wrote tell of formal *basse danses,* with set steps and rhythmic patterns, which were to be performed with grace and perfection. The aim of the accomplished dancer was to present an artless, unaffected performance on the dance floor, a feat that could be accomplished only after daily lessons and practice, provided one also possessed the necessary talents of memory, measure, a sense of lightness and space, and an overall quality derived from good coordination. Moreover, good behavior, or the art of courtesy, went hand in hand with good dancing. Thus, the notion of dance as a courtly art, full of grace and perfection, provided dramatic contrast to perceptions of dancing as a sinful activity inviting damnation, or as a downright absurd activity, the province of "mad folke."

The contrasting views also point to clear distinctions of social class and gender. Dances choreographed for Italian and Burgundian courts remained the province of ladies and their courtiers. The privileged ranks of society possessed time and money to study dancing as well as great halls in which to practice and perfect the art. Dancing could serve not only as a popular pastime but also to distinguish people of power and privilege from the com-

mon folk. The dancing engaged in by the lower ranks of society had to occur in time free from work and, when weather permitted, on the village
green. Given such limited opportunities, country dancing could only have
been unrefined and spontaneous, probably often bawdy and boisterous.

Prelude to Late Sixteenth-Century Denunciations

Among the "more grave Writers" whom Increase Mather cited in his list of
Catholic opponents to dance, Juan Luis Vives (1492–1540) traveled in
courtly circles and indicted the art of dancing as well as schools of dancing.
A Spanish Catholic scholar, Vives went to England in 1523 and served as
counselor to Catherine of Aragon during her struggles to maintain the validity of her marriage to Henry VIII. The *Instruction of a christen woman,*
written by Vives and dedicated to Catherine in the year of his arrival in
England, speaks strongly about the loss of chastity in both body and mind
that followed the sights of dancing and the devil's temptings. Vives accounted
the eyes an open window for the entrance of lust. Through sight, the mind
became incited to sinful behavior. Vives quoted Ambrose, the early church
father, who urged that all virgins avoid dancing. He also quoted Cicero on
the point that no sober person danced. Elaborating his argument, Vives
stressed the absurdity of dance movements—hopping and shaking—carried
on until fatigue prevented the dancers from even going to church unless
carried there.

In his indictment of dancing schools, Vives introduced a new theme in
opponents' attacks. He does not say whether he is referring to schools in
England or elsewhere, but the existence of dancing schools clearly suggests
an urban context, not just a courtly or country setting. Vives's charge carried sufficient weight to be quoted by the Protestant minister John Northbrooke (fl. 1570s) some fifty years later: "But wee now in christian countries have schools of dauncing, howbeit that is no wonder, seeing also we
have houses of baudrie. So much the Paganes were better and more sadde
than we be, they never knew this newe fashion of dauncing of ours; and
uncleanly handlings, gropings, and kissings, and a very kindling of lechery."[25]

Northbrooke's indictment of dancing appeared as the first in a series of
extensive and often vitriolic outpourings against dancing by English Protestants during the later sixteenth century. However, Northbrooke did not
originate all the charges he levied. In addition to Vives, Northbrooke quoted at length from the German-born knight and scholar Henri Cornelius
Agrippa (1486–1535). Agrippa's famous book *Of the Vanitie and uncertaintie*

of Artes and Sciences appeared first in Cologne in 1527; thereafter it was issued regularly until 1714 from cities on the continent.[26] As the title implies,
the intent of the book was to detect and question the evil uses to which the
arts and sciences had been employed.

The section in Agrippa's *Vanitie* on music and dancing declares that the
two arts go together, yet the author bears down strongly on the immorality
of dancing. He clearly echoes Petrarch and Brant in his assertions. Like the
former, Agrippa declares that there would be no sight "more ridiculous, nor
more out of order" than that of dancers were their actions not tempered by
the sound of instruments. Their movements helped to create what he viewed
as disorderly sights: "Therefore it must needes be, that daûsing is the vilest
vice of all: and truly it cannot easily be sayde what mischiefes the sighte and
the hearing doth receyve hereby, which afterwarde be the causes of cômmu-
nication and embracing. They daunce with disordinate gestures, and with
monstrous thumping of the feete, to pleasante soundes, to wonton songes,
to dishonest verses." In this passage, which was quoted by Northbrooke,
Agrippa seems to have been impelled to wrath by the flagrant immorality
that allegedly accompanied the dancing; such baseness could have originated
only with the "Devils of Hell" who also tempted the people of Israel to
worship a golden calf.[27]

Agrippa also indicts "gentlewomen and ladies of the court" who had been
"nourished from their infancie" in dancing, idleness, and "all super-fluitie."
He perceives them to be idle, vain, proud, and arrogant. Thus, he clearly
attacks dancing as an undesirable pastime within his criticism of social class.[28]
Because Agrippa traveled extensively for several years and also taught in Italy, it is possible that he had been exposed to the Italian court dance, but
his graphic description of immoral conduct by dancers, as well as their reported "disordinate gestures" and "monstrous thumping" of feet, suggests
that he was not denouncing the courtly version of the art.

In a separate section of his book, Agrippa alleges the immorality of dancing, by "Stage Players." He calls their dancing the "Arte of Imitation and
Demonstration." In itself, that definition sounds harmless. But in the past,
such gestures and movements had included the "actes of Harlottes" and were
therefore condemned.[29]

Despite the fact that biographers have called Agrippa one of the "most
learned, original and remarkable men of his time," his ideas on dancing
appear unoriginal in the line of Catholic and humanist opponents from
Petrarch to the sixteenth century. Nonetheless, the vigor of his denunciations held appeal for Northbrooke. Since the English translation of Agrip-

pa's *Vanitie* was issued from a London press in 1569 and 1575, it is not surprising that Northbrooke knew it. What does seem surprising is that Northbrooke, as a zealous reformer, would have chosen to quote a Catholic. Although Agrippa remained a Catholic to the end, his biographers asserted, he insisted on the primacy of the Bible in matters of faith. Like the Protestant reformers, he taught the importance of change in behavior through the agency of the Holy Spirit.[30] Such credentials fit with those of sixteenth-century Protestant dance opponents such as Northbrooke.

Notes

1. William Prynne, *Histrio-Mastix* (London: E. A. and W. I. for Michael Sparke, 1633), 221.

2. E. Louis Backman, *Religious Dances in the Christian Church and in Popular Medicine,* trans. E. Classen (Stockholm: P. A. Norstedt och Söner, n.d.; rpt., London: George Allen and Unwin, 1952; rpt., Westport, Conn.: Greenwood Press, 1977), 50, 91.

3. Bede Jarrett, *Social Theories of the Middle Ages, 1200–1500* (London: Frank Cass, 1968), 90.

4. Margaret Fisk Taylor, *A Time to Dance,* rev. ed. (North Aurora, Ill.: The Sharing Company, 1976), 89. Basing her opinion on a bas-relief of Salome in Rouen, Taylor concluded: "It is evident that the dancing connected with these religious dramatizations was mainly theatrical and not devotional." See biblical accounts of Salome's dancing in Matt. 14, Mark 6, and Luke 3. The biblical account of Salome initially entered the argument of dance adversaries via the writings of the church fathers, who, themselves, constituted the earliest opponents in the Christian tradition. See brief explanation in H. P. Clive, "The Calvinists and the Question of Dancing in the 16th Century," *Bibliothèque d'Humanisme et Renaissance* 23, no. 2 (1961): 306–8.

5. E. K. Chambers, *The Mediaeval Stage* (Oxford: Clarendon, 1903), 1:44, 25. According to Chambers, the minstrels can be traced but "obscurely" from the sixth to the eleventh centuries and then more clearly to the sixteenth century. See also Pierre Aubry, *Trouvères and Troubadours* (New York: Cooper Square, 1969), and Constance Bullock-Davies, *Menestrellorum Multitudo* (Cardiff: University of Wales Press, 1978).

6. Thomas Tentler, *Sin and Confession on the Eve of the Reformation* (Princeton: Princeton University Press, 1977), 3–39; idem, "The Summa for Confessors as an Instrument of Social Control," in *The Pursuit of Holiness in Late Medieval and Renaissance Religion,* ed. Charles Trinkaus and Heiko A. Oberman (Leiden: E. J. Brill, 1974), 103, 108, 134–35; Mary F. Braswell, *The Medieval Sinner* (Madison, N.J.:

Fairleigh Dickinson University Press, 1983), 24–35. The proscriptions of dancing predate the summas in the penitential literature, though the early medieval handbooks on penance did not carry the authority of the later summas for confessors. Neither Prynne nor Mather mentions the earlier literature on penance. John T. McNeill identified three penitential texts from the eighth, ninth, and eleventh centuries that specifically mention dancing. But, like the medieval church council sanctions, these texts do not indict dancing per se. They indict and prescribe penance for certain times, places, and occasions of dancing—as, for example, dancing that endured as part of a pagan ritual. The same kinds of proscriptions and penance applied to singing. See John T. McNeill and Helena M. Camer, *Medieval Handbooks of Penance* (1938; rpt., New York: Columbia University Press, 1990), 46–50, 273, 289, 318f, 333, 419n.

7. Tentler, *Sin and Confession,* 35; idem, "Summa for Confessors," 103, 122.

8. Tentler, *Sin and Confession,* 34–35; *New Catholic Encyclopedia,* s.v. "Angelo Carletti Di Chivasso."

9. Astesanus, *Summa Astensis,* book 2, title 53, "De modestia in exterioribus motibus corporio" (Lyons, [1519]).

10. A. B. Emden, ed., *A Biographical Register of the University of Cambridge to 1500* (Cambridge: Cambridge University Press, 1963), s.v. "Burgh" (Borough, Burghe, de Burgo); J. R. Tanner, ed., *The Historical Register of the University of Cambridge . . . to the year 1910* (Cambridge: Cambridge University Press, 1917), s.v. "Burgh, John de."

11. Prynne, *Histrio-Mastix,* 238–39.

12. Tentler, *Sin and Confession,* 145.

13. Increase Mather, "An Arrow Against Profane and Promiscuous Dancing Drawn out of the Quiver of the Scriptures" (Boston, [1685]; rpt. in *The Mathers on Dancing,* ed. Joseph E. Marks III (Brooklyn, N.Y.: Dance Horizons, 1975), 39. The casuists Mather cites include Sylvester II, pope from 999 to 1003; Thomas de Vio, an Italian otherwise known as Cardinal Cajetan (1469–1534), an analyst of the writings of Thomas Aquinas and the church official who summoned Luther to Augsburg in 1518; and Juan Azor, or Azorius (1533–1603), a Spanish Jesuit and moral theologian. Mather probably referred to Azor's work titled *Institutions Morales.* See *Nouvelle Biographie Universelle* (Paris, 1852), vol. 3: s.v. "Azor ou Azorius (Jean)."

14. *Dictionary of National Biography,* s.v. "Carpenter, Alexander." The *DNB* says the name was Latinized as "Fabricius." I have retained the spelling "Fabritius" used by Mather and Prynne. Fabritius is incorrectly identified by Joseph E. Marks III as "Andreas Fabricius," who lived in the sixteenth century; see *The Mathers on Dancing,* 39.

15. Mather, "Arrow," 39. Mather may have copied this passage from Prynne. There is no substantial difference in the two translations, other than a few words omitted by Mather.

16. Ibid., 41. Originating in the later twelfth century and also called the Poor of Lyons, the Waldenses were inspired by an ideal of "evangelical poverty." Though condemned as heretics in 1184, probably for preaching without authority, the group attracted believers and expanded rapidly throughout France, Switzerland, Bavaria, Austria, and Bohemia. The French Waldenses later gave allegiance to the Reformation churches. See *New Catholic Encyclopedia*, s.v. "Waldenses."

17. Prynne, *Histrio-Mastix*, 229–32.

18. For an analysis of the sources and methods of Antoninus, see James Bernard Walker, "The Chronicles of Saint Antoninus" (Ph.D. diss., Catholic University of America, 1933).

19. Johan Huizinga, *The Waning of the Middle Ages* (Garden City, N.Y.: Doubleday Anchor, 1949), 160–61. Huizinga provides an interesting explanation for the irreverence of daily life and the "insolent mingling of pleasure with religion"; see 156–65. See also biographical sketch for Nicholas of Clamanges in the *New Catholic Encyclopedia*.

20. Vittorino understood that both music and dancing could produce positive or negative behavior. He included them in his curriculum, with some constraints, in order to achieve a positive development of the whole person. See William Harrison Woodward, *Vittorino Da Feltre and Other Humanist Educators* (Cambridge: Cambridge University Press, 1897), 43, 241. For discussions of Aeneas and Vegio, see Vincent J. Horkan, *Educational Theories and Principles of Maffeo Vegio: A Dissertation* (Washington, D.C.: Catholic University of America Press, 1953), 5–7, 10, 52–53, 89–93; and Joel S. Nelson, trans., *Aeneae Silvii De Liberorum Educatione* (Washington, D.C.: Catholic University of America Press, 1940), first section, on physical and moral training.

21. Mather, "Arrow," 44–45. For Petrarch's discussion, see the 23d Dialogue, "Of Daunsing," in his *Phisicke against Fortune* (London, 1579; rpt., Delmar, N.Y.: Scholars' Facsimiles and Reprints, 1980).

22. Sebastian Brant, *The Ship of Fools*, trans. Alexander Barclay (London, 1509; rpt., New York: D. Appleton, 1874), 291, 293–95.

23. Stanley Kunitz and Vineta Colby, eds., *European Authors, 1000–1900* (New York: Wilson, 1967), s.v. "Brant."

24. Ingrid Brainard, "The Role of the Dancing Master in 15th Century Courtly Society," in *Fifteenth Century Studies* 2 (1979): 22.

25. John Northbrooke, *A Treatise against Dicing, Dancing, Plays and Interludes* (London, c. 1577; rpt., London: The Shakespeare Society, 1843), 166; Juan Luis Vives, *A Very Fruteful and Pleasant Boke Called the Instruction of a christen woman* (London: Rychard Hyrde, 1557), 46–48.

26. John M. McClintock and James Strong, *Cyclopedia of Biblical, Theological, and Ecclesiastical Literature* (1873; rpt., Grand Rapids, Mich.: Baker Book House, 1968), s.v. "Agrippa."

27. Henri Cornelius Agrippa, *Of the Vanitie and uncertaintie of Artes and Sci-*

ences (London: Henrie Bynneman, 1575), 30–32. See also Northbrooke, *A Treatise,* 170–71.

28. Agrippa, *Of the Vanitie,* 115–16.
29. Ibid., 32–33.
30. McClintock and Strong, *Cyclopedia,* s.v. "Agrippa."

2 The Voices of Protestant Reformers

I have devised howe in the fourme of daunsinge . . . the hole
description of this vertue prudence may be founden out.

Sir Thomas Elyot, 1531

Dauncing is the vilest vice of all, and truly it cannot easily
be saide what mischiefes the sight and the hearing doe
receive thereby.

John Northbrooke, c. 1577

At least since Plato's time, people have held opposing views of dance and dancing, some seeing it as orderly, others as disorderly. Usually those who have perceived dancing to be an ordered form have also considered it moral. Conversely, those who have considered dancing to be disordered movement have declared it immoral as well. Nowhere was the contrast between these two perceptions more vividly propounded than among sixteenth-century English clerics and courtiers. In 1531, Sir Thomas Elyot (1490?–1546), adviser to Henry VIII, confidently announced that he had devised a means by which young gentlemen could be taught the virtue of prudence through learning to dance. Four and a half decades later, John Northbrooke (fl. 1570s), a Protestant minister under Elizabeth I, quoted Henri Cornelius Agrippa as he exclaimed: "Dauncing is the vilest vice of all!"

Northbrooke sounded no solo censure. He simply heralded the era's renewed fervor of English opposition and echoed the loud clamor of voices that issued from press and pulpit across the channel. Men of Calvinist, Puritan, Anglican, Lutheran, and Huguenot persuasions, from England, Holland, Germany, France, and Switzerland, taught, preached, and wrote against "dauncing." The great majority were "divines" and theologians—many associated with Oxford, Cambridge, and continental universities.

Meanwhile, more than fifty years after Elyot wrote about the virtue of dancing, Thoinot Arbeau (1520–95), a Catholic canon of Langres, France, produced his *Orchesographie,* the most complete collection of dances in the century, to that point.[1] Reiterating the classical emphasis on order, he urged his readers to present polite behavior and to practice their dancing diligently so that they might become fit companions for the planets, which dance naturally and perpetually in an ordered pattern.

A century later, in Boston, Increase Mather probably did not know about *Orchesographie,* but he was familiar with both English and continental churchmen who opposed dancing. For Mather, as for John Northbrooke, "mixt" dancing held no positive value. Yet, Elyot had asserted that the association of a man and woman dancing together signified concord and marriage and expressed "the figure of very nobility." There was no question of Elyot's being morally loose or a nonbeliever. He was as devout a Christian as Mather, despite the fact that Elyot remained conservative rather than turning reformer.[2] How then does one understand the diametrically opposite views about dancing promulgated by Elyot and Northbrooke?

During the sixteenth century, religious beliefs about dancing were intermingled with aesthetic, social, and moral views. All four combined in producing a tension between two reigning concepts—the ideal for the Christian and the ideal for the gentleman, the latter usually extending by implication to the lady. The former ideal emerges from the writings of dance opponents as a result of their instructions for right living and attendant efforts to prove the sinfulness of dancing and other idle pastimes. The ideal for the gentleman or lady developed by design in the works of courtesy authors who intended to educate and distinguish members of the upper ranks of society.

Order and the Ideal for the Gentleman and Lady

Central to the Elizabethan era and to the aesthetic ideal for dancing was the notion of order. In 1529, the Spanish Catholic Juan Luis Vives (1492–1540) clearly and concisely enunciated the accepted hierarchical schema: "This is the order of nature, that wisedome governe al things, & that al creatures, whiche wee see, obey unto man, & that in man, the body be obedient to the soule, and the soule unto god. If any thyng breake this order, it offendeth."[3] More than sixty years later, Sir John Davies (1569–1626), a lawyer and poet, composed the long poem *Orchestra,* in which he painted a picture of coherence in the universe by portraying the cosmic dance as the image of order and morality. An orderly Creation gave rise to an orderly dance both

in the heavens and on the earth. Whether or not the actual practice of dancing always achieved the ideal did not detract from Davies's image, which
fancifully depicted the prevailing views of the century held by those who
wrote courtesy treatises, including the dance manuals.

Courtesy literature was intended for the privileged ranks of society. In
general, these didactic treatises told gentlemen and, less directly, ladies how
to behave as well as what learning and recreational skills to acquire. The
sixteenth-century ideal required that gentlefolk be orderly in appearance and,
especially, in moral conduct. To that end, courtesy writers admonished the
gentleman to maintain his position in society apart from the commoner so
that the entire society would be neatly ordered according to the separate
functions of each social rank. Personal control was to be maintained by disciplining the mind to rule over passion. Thus, gentlemen were exhorted to
seek virtue and to shun vice. To fall into sin—to cultivate vice instead of
virtue—inevitably produced disorder both within oneself and within society at large. As Vives noted, "it offendeth." Accordingly, gentlemen were to
be wary of any occasion that might stimulate the emotions or passions, which
were constantly at war with the mind for supremacy in the individual. Order and morality went hand in hand with courtesy and polish on the dance
floor. The ideal for the gentleman was none other than the Renaissance *vir
perfectus,* the complete or "finished" man. To achieve this ideal required not
only moral, religious, and social distinction but learning, physical training,
a pleasing countenance, a well-proportioned body, and a graceful manner
in dancing.

The gentleman's civic duties suggest why such perfection was required.
He might be called to advise king or prince, to bear arms in defense of country, perhaps to govern estates, but always to set an example—whether in
public duties, play, or pastime—for those whose station ranked beneath his.
Though common folk danced, they had neither leisure nor wealth to perfect the skills of good dancing. Gentlemen and their ladies had the advantage of dance masters and dance manuals as well as the time and money for
the requisite instruction and practice. They aimed to present an artless,
unaffected yet perfectly ordered and graceful exhibition of dancing—in the
classical tradition of the noble amateur, not the virtuosic dance master.

Women danced, but their roles remain incompletely drawn by most courtesy writers. One exception is Baldassare Castiglione, who, in his *Book of the
Courtier* (1528), paints the ideal gentlewoman in some detail. Though the
qualities he requires of her differ from those demanded of the ideal courtier,
they seem no less formidable. Accordingly, a lady was to avoid haughtiness,

envy, contention, and ill speaking; sustain the good will of her ladies at court; be more circumspect in her behavior than men; yet possess the same wisdom and nobility of courage necessary for the gentleman. Ideally, she possessed beauty and a "certaine sweetnesse in language" to entertain men in worthwhile conversation. She exhibited "sober and quiet manners." She was to "bee esteemed no lesse chaste, wise and courteous, than pleasant, feate conceited and sober; and therefore muste she keepe a certaine meane verie hard." That is, she should approach the limits of a mean but not surpass them. Like the gentleman, the lady was instructed not to praise herself "undiscretely" or to assume affectations. She performed physical exercises that were "comely for a woman" with "exceeding good grace." Exercises considered "sturdie and boisterous" were not recommended. In dancing, "swifte and violent" movements were to be eschewed. In music, comeliness dictated avoiding performances on tabor, flute, and trumpet. Dignity required a lady to approach music and dancing with due modesty: "Therefore when she commeth to daunce, or to shew any kind of musicke, she ought to be brought to it with suffring her selfe somewhat to be prayed, and with a certain bashfulnesse, that may declare the noble shamefastnesse that is contrarie to headinesse." Concluding his portrait of the ideal lady at court, Castiglione summarizes her attitude and repertoire of skills: "And to make a briefe rehersall in few wordes of that is already saide, I will that this woman have a sight in letters, in musicke, in drawing, or painting, and skilful in dauncing, and in devising sports and pastimes, accompanying with that discrete sober moode, and with the giving a good opinion of her selfe, the other principles also that have been taught the Courtier."[4] In effect, the gentleman and, by extension, his lady were each to appear as nothing less than "a work of art."[5]

Dancing as Ordered Form: A Virtue

Although the sixteenth century's social and aesthetic valuing of dance was inextricably linked to the privileged ranks of society, such valuing depended on notions of dance as ordered form and motion.

Court Dance

The art of courtly dancing as ordered structure and aesthetically pleasing form emerged in documents written in the fifteenth century by Italian and Burgundian dance masters. The literature from the continent spread to England at least by 1521 in the form of an instructional manual printed by Robert Coplande and titled *The Manner To Dance Bace Dances*. Appended to a French grammar, the short treatise on dancing gave directions for the then ubiquitous basse danse, a slow processional dance performed low to the ground. The treatise concluded with the comment that such an orderly art enabled dancers to "rejoice somewhat their spirits honestly in eschewing of idleness the portress of vices."[6]

The outstanding example of dance as virtue appeared ten years later in Elyot's publication called *The Boke Named The Governour,* the first treatise written in English that told how to educate the sons of gentlemen for their future roles as advisers, counselors, or governors for the commonwealth. Because Elyot knew that moral lessons could be tedious for young people, he resorted to a method of camouflage, based on a rule of correspondence: "And by cause that the studie of vertue is tediouse for the more parte to them that do florisshe in yonge yeres, I have devised howe in the fourme of daunsinge, nowe late used in this realme amonge gentilmen, the hole description of this vertue prudence may be founden out and well perceyved, as well by the daunsers as by them whiche standinge by, wyll be diligent beholders and markers."[7] Elyot then described all the branches of prudence, aligning them with each of the steps in the basse dance. The significance of this connection rests on the importance of prudence. Widely recognized as the "mother" of all virtue, prudence headed the list in Cicero's catalog of Four Cardinal Virtues, a prominent authority for the century's courtesy writers. Prudence enabled men to distinguish good from evil, truth from falsehood, the honest from the dishonest. As such, prudence depended on the governing power of reason to maintain order by ruling over the passions. Elyot reinforced the notion of morality and order by stipulating a correspondence between dancing and the sacrament of matrimony. In his view, the several distinct qualities of men and women combined to produce concord when the sexes joined in a partner formation to dance.[8]

The concept that dance could signify concord in marriage is not unique to Elyot. Davies's poem *Orchestra* includes the same correspondence. Yet Davies goes beyond Elyot to stipulate that the rule in dancing provides the criterion for harmony in marriage: "For whether forth or back or round he go, As doth the man, so must the woman do."[9] The correspondence could not reveal more pointedly the moral essence of dancing. Lust, lechery, and adultery work against an orderly marriage. Any discord between man and wife militates against harmony. Thus, Davies portrays dancing as the model, the very image of concord. Though roles and positions may change for a time, the ideal wife, ultimately, follows her husband just as the female dancer always finally bows to the leading of her male partner.

Davies also connects dancing with chastity via the image of the Three Graces. By associating orderly, gracious dancing with virgins, he dramatically counters
the strongest contemporary criticism of dance as immoral. Davies depicts the
virgin, the century's youthful ideal of feminine virtue, as the perfect dancer. No
"disgrace" is found among the three virgins who dance with "moderation," "decent order," and "seemly modesty." Thus, both Davies and Elyot—by connecting
dancing with prudence, the mother of all virtue; with marriage, a church sacrament; and with chastity, the Christian ideal for women—place the art on the
highest moral plane. The fact that Davies wrote as an Elizabethan Protestant
and Elyot as an earlier Catholic demonstrates that Englishmen of both religious
persuasions held a positive view of the courtly dance.[10]

Similarly, the late sixteenth-century dance manuals of Arbeau and the
Italian dance master Fabritio Caroso make clear that courteous, ordered, and
graceful dancing continued as the ideal in Catholic lands. Although the
authors did not make the detailed moral correspondences of Elyot and
Davies, their directions for correct performance leave no doubt in the reader's
mind that good behavior and good dancing were linked.[11] The fact that these
manuals were aimed at literate individuals who had time to study indicates
that social rank, rather than religion or country, served to distinguish those
who practiced dancing as a courtly art and pastime.

Court Ballet and the Jesuit Stage

The point is further substantiated when one looks at the rise of ballet in
France under the sponsorship of Catherine de Medici. Her family lineage
and her experience with dancing in Italy led, in 1581, to her importing
Balthazar de Beaujoyeulx to choreograph and stage the now-acknowledged
"first ballet"—renowned for its unity of dance, music, poetry, and design.
The Ballet Comique de la Reine functioned allegorically at several levels of
meaning—mythical, metaphysical, political, and social—an example of the
popular taste for drawing correspondences in the sixteenth century.[12] To
understand the complex significance of such a performance required knowledge of history and an awareness of current events—requisite qualities of a
courtier and gentleman. Although succeeding ballets did not equal the splen-
dor of the 1581 Ballet Comique, the genre continued at the court of Ver-
sailles through much of the seventeenth century.

The court ballet, in turn, influenced the development of theater productions in Jesuit colleges on the continent. From the mid-sixteenth century,
the Society of Jesus began building a group of colleges in Austria, Italy,
France, and Germany where theater and ballet curricula contributed to the

education of the whole person through training in carriage, poise, gesture, and speech.[13] Artur Michel, writing about dance among the Jesuits, contrasts the purpose of Baroque court ballet with that of the Catholic stage: "While the court ballet was an accepted vehicle for flattering and glorifying the ruler, drama and dance on the religious stage had quite a different purpose. Here their mission was to make visible the fundamental tenets of Catholicism, to act as a weapon in the war waged for the Faith. As the prologue of a tragedy by one of the Jesuit fathers puts it, the audience was to experience 'Christian virtues, battles and victories.'" Michel notes that the intention was frequently fulfilled; after one performance in 1609, fourteen courtiers left their "worldly ways in abject repentence and sought shelter in the arms of the Church. Nor was this an isolated instance. Many of these performances exercised a great influence, even an irresistible spell upon the minds and emotions of their audiences."[14] Clearly, both Jesuit ballets and court ballets had to be ordered form to communicate complex meanings to audiences. Yet those who urged dance as a courtly art, in the education of gentlefolk, were mindful of potential problems.

The Dance Controversy and Mulcaster's Analysis

In the 1530s, Elyot understood the long conflict about orderly and disorderly dancing, but he maintained that not all dancing was to be reproved. For Arbeau, some dances seemed potentially more hazardous than others. He specifically wondered if a lady did not damage both health and honor when performing the turning dance called la volta. It is not clear whether that was the same German turning dance that Martin Luther reported made women bare in both front and back as they performed it. In any event, such a dance involved rapid turning, during which a woman's skirts flew up and she was required, in Arbeau's words, to make "large steps and separations of the legs." Although Queen Elizabeth's tutor, Roger Ascham (1515–68), asserted the importance of dancing for those at court, like Arbeau he qualified his approval. For Ascham, to "daunce cumlie" was not merely desirable for a gentleman but essential to his training. Nonetheless, Ascham limited his program of exercises to those that involved physical activity and were done "in open place" as well as in daylight. Dancing had to serve as one of the activities that distinguished the gentleman from the commoner in "vertue, wisedome and worthinesse."[15] However, a full analysis of the dance controversy awaited the pen of Ascham's contemporary, the Anglican churchman and schoolmaster Richard Mulcaster (1530?–1611).

Mulcaster's analysis of the conflict surrounding dance in the early 1580s clarifies implications of the century's dominant Christian ontology for the valuing of the art. Because the human body is the instrument of performance and because there is continual warfare within the individual between reason and passion, the very nature of dancing presents difficulty in maintaining order and virtue:

> To keepe thinges in order, there is in the soule of man but one, though as verie honorable meane, which is the direction of reason: to bring thinges out of order there be two, the one strong-headed, which is the commaundement of courage, the other many headed, which is the enticement of desires. Now daunsing hath properties to serve eche of these, exercise for health, which reason ratifieth, armour for agility which courage commendeth, liking for allowance, which desire doth delite.

According to Mulcaster, if dancing is not done for the sake of health, which reason can approve, then it is done for less worthy ends, such as sensual delight. He declares that critics opposed contemporary dancing because they could not discern in it any "honest and profitable" features. Mulcaster further declares that criticisms focused primarily on two specific "blames"; namely, that dancing was used at the wrong time for good health and that it "serveth delite to much, whereat good manners repine." Of the two faults, the latter offended more; when people danced to satisfy "delite" or desire, the faculty of reason held little importance. He concludes that "daunsing is healthful, though the daunsers use it not healthfully."[16]

Unlike many dance opponents, Mulcaster asserts that the abuse of an activity does not argue for its abolition: "if abuse of a thing, which may be well used, and had her first being to be well used, be a sufficient condemnation to the thing that is abused, let glotonie forbid meat, distempering drinke, pride apparell, heresie religion, adulterie mariage, and why not, what not? Nay which of all our principles shall stand, if the persons blame, shal blemish the thing?" Mulcaster would rather correct abuses than abolish the practice altogether. Accordingly, he advocates seeking masters who will fashion dancing "with good order in time, with reason in gesture, with proportion in number, with harmonie in Musick, to appoint it so, as it may be thought both seemely and sober, and so best beseeme such persons, as professe sobrietie: and that with all it may be so full of nimblenesse and activitie, as it may prove an exercise of health." Mulcaster thus reaffirms that the health value of dancing depended upon the aesthetic features of order, proportion, and harmony.[17] He also underscores the importance of reason, which helped to create order, so that dancing behavior would appear "both seemely and sober" and the activity itself would prove healthful.

Since the essential nature of dancing as a physical and heterosexual activity provoked delight and desire, as Mulcaster observed, and since dancing occurred in work-free time that could easily become wasted time, dancing had to be approved as healthful exercise if dance opponents were to be convinced of its value. Even the staunchest of antidance writers could not deny the importance of bodily health so that one could better serve the Lord and so that the body could more effectively function as the "temple of the Holy Spirit."[18] Given that the criterion of utility governed the valuing of pastimes in the sixteenth century, courtesy treatises did not speak about aesthetic satisfaction per se. Thus, if Christians did not approve dancing as an exercise for health, they had to ascribe moral virtue to it, as did Elyot, or social utility, as did Ascham; or they had to condemn it, as did many Protestant reformers.

Dancing as Disorderly Motion: A Vice

In the second half of the sixteenth century, Calvinists from across the English Channel held forth with strong denunciations and graphic illustrations about the absurd behavior and sinful conduct that dancers presented.

Continental Writers

John Calvin (1500–1564), the great reformer of Geneva, in his Sermon 79 on the twenty-first chapter of Job, sounded much like Sebastian Brant, who asserted that dancers resembled "mad folke": "Therfore wheras nowadaies we see many men seeke nothing but to royst it, in so much as they have none other countenance but in seeking to hoppe and daûce like stray beasts, and to do such other like things: let us understand that it is not of late beginning, but that the Divell hath raigned at all times."[19] Thus, Calvin also continued the centuries-old belief that the devil enticed people to sin through their fleshly nature. In addition, he decried provocative song lyrics that prompted people to dance. In such cases, dancing became nothing more than an "inticement to whoredome."[20]

Perhaps the single most comprehensive exposition of Calvinist opposition to dance appeared in the 1579 *Traite Des Danses,* printed by François Estienne in Geneva and attributed to Lambert Daneau (1530–95), who was writing on behalf of the Reformed church ministers. At the time of publication, Daneau served as pastor and professor of theology in Geneva and was a close colleague of Theodore Beza, head of the city's academy.[21]

With respect to the essence of dancing, Daneau declares that the activity is not suited to persons who ought to be modest, sober, and of sound mind. He reiterates Calvin's charge that dancers resemble nothing more than wild beasts, and cites for comparison the specific images of monkeys and goats. Daneau also likens dancers to drunkards, frantic persons, or those seized by folly. By so doing, he recalls the ancient dictum of Cicero. Since dance movement is not automatic but willed, such gyrations in no way contributed to the kind of sober demeanor considered seemly for a Christian. Daneau's description of dance movements also recalls Petrarch's charge about the absurd sight dancers create when one sees them but hears no music: "Mais ce sont tousiours mouvemés & agitations du corps, & gesticulations contre l'ordinaire de nature. . .: lon recule, lon s'aváce, puis deça, puis dela: l'un se guinde en l'air, l'autre fait la roüe, l'autre des pieds bat la terre: c'est merveilles des inventions." Allowing that exercising by the young makes their bodies more agile, especially when movements are somewhat artistic, Daneau declares that the type of dancing he criticizes does not fall into that category. He objects to adults' taking time to learn and perfect dancing skills. In his opinion, to go to school to learn such ridiculous movements is surely the vanity of vanities. He believes that a Christian has enough to do, attempting to renounce the world and its lusts, without studying the art of publicly making an ass of oneself.[22]

Daneau's arguments against the incidental characteristics of dancing stress that the activity has always been the result or accompaniment of great vices like drunkenness, debauchery, and idolatry. Because the Sabbath is also a day of rest, to dance on the Sabbath becomes a double sin by profaning the Lord's day as well as by not resting and meditating on the Lord's word. Since dancing had been introduced at weddings, the solemnity of the marriage ceremony had been destroyed. To recite vows before God in one hour and then to engage in an enticement of the devil during the next simply outraged Daneau.[23] Like medieval writers, he cites the incidents of the Israelites dancing around the golden calf and the story of Salome as proof that dancing is evil. Such examples proved that the end of dancing was not health but sensual pleasure. In addition, dancing robs the body of sleep and works against digestion since one usually dances after large meals. Because of these ill effects and because the only end is pleasure, dancing is therefore profane and not acceptable recreation for the Christian, who must exercise soberly without too much enjoyment. Thus, Daneau's view confirms the analysis by Mulcaster that opponents saw dancing as serving "delite" too much and health too little.[24] Unlike Mulcaster, Daneau argued that abuses were so serious that no reform in dancing was possible. Therefore, the true Christian ought to abstain from the activity.

Although Daneau's treatise appeared only in French, much of the substance of his arguments was published in an English translation before the end of the century, in a book by Jean Taffin the Elder, who may have studied under Calvin and Beza at Geneva, perhaps contemporary with Daneau's student days there. Taffin states that he copied much of his discussion against dance from a larger treatise printed by Francis Stephens in 1579. Since Daneau's name is not affixed to his treatise and since the English translation of the name F. Estienne, the printer, is Francis Stephens, Taffin could have referred only to the Daneau work. Although Increase Mather does not mention Taffin, the Calvinist position received wide circulation through Taffin's writing. Taffin's *Amendment of Life* appeared first in French in 1594 when he served as pastor in Amsterdam. Other editions were published in English in 1595; Dutch in 1595; Latin in 1602; and Dutch again in 1628 and 1659.[25]

Taffin devoted about twenty pages to the evils of dance in the second book of his lengthy courtesy treatise. He counts dancing among those areas of life wherein all men ought to amend their sinful behavior, including: sumptuousness and excess in apparel, excess and superfluity in feasts, voluptuousness, drunkenness, fornication, and adultery. Analysis of his text indicates that Taffin, indeed, borrowed heavily from Daneau. He too views dancing as disorderly and absurd. The themes of devotion to Christ and purity of soul and body remain dominant. Yet, according to Taffin, it was not enough for the Christian to separate himself from evil; he was also to join the church, hear the word of God, and receive the sacraments regularly.[26] The church to be joined, of course, meant the Reformed church. Taffin declares that immoral dancing and music were "usual in the Church of Rome, in their confraries, dedications and holy daies, wherein they apply themselves to dancing."[27]

At least one contemporary observer thought that the ban on dancing by the French Reformed church may have prevented more people from converting to that religion. Sir Robert Dallington, a Cambridge graduate and an English schoolmaster and author, recorded his views about the French people following his extended travels through their country. He found dancing to be very popular; even the old women, who he said had more toes than teeth, loved to dance. Writing in 1598, Dallington concluded: "And I am persuaded, were it not for this, that they of the Reformed Religion may not Dance, being an exercise against which their strait-laced Ministers much inveigh, that there had long since many of the Catholics turned to their side."[28]

Protestant reformers aimed to return to what they viewed as the purity and authenticity of the early Christian church. As a guide to that end, they looked to the primacy of the Bible, rather than custom and tradition, in matters of right living. To educate the laity, "divines and theologians" wrote numerous *Loci Communes,* or "Commonplaces" of the Christian religion, which told readers, among other things, how to follow the Ten Commandments. This literature regularly proscribed dancing under the Seventh Commandment. However, one writer also focused on the responsibility of parents to prevent dancing.

Of all of the Protestant antidance writers of the era, the Lutheran divine Andreas Gerardus Hyperius (1511–64) is the only one who proscribed dancing under the Fifth Commandment (by a different numbering, the Fourth Commandment). Hyperius declares that this commandment prescribes certain responsibilities for parents and guardians, including their duty to correct children "when thou hast seene them use pretie sleights, craftie devises, slie shifts, vain songs, wanton daunces, and unseemly gestures, yea to utter filthy tearmes beastly words, and odious deedes." Thus, dancing falls among behaviors that need to be corrected, not reinforced.

Hyperius also labels dancing under the Seventh Commandment. Here the context is that of "sinnes outward" or observable, for example, addiction to idleness, banqueting, and drinking, or intentionally luring partners to lechery to satisfy one's own desires, via gestures, looks, immoral songs and music, nocturnal wanderings, and "purposely appointed daunces." In spelling out the implications of the Seventh Commandment for each social rank, Hyperius declares that magistrats must not tolerate "enterludes," stage plays, or games that include lewd talk, actions, and the like. "Musitians" and "Stageplaiers" are charged to avoid any action that would move the "beholders and hearers, to lascivious dancing, wanton thoughts, or unchaste actions."[29] The decade of the 1580s, when Hyperius's publication appeared in London, marked a time of intense Puritan opposition to stage plays and dancing.

Emigrés to England

The reliance on biblical principles and commandments, in addition to a strongly evangelical stance, characterized the Reformed church opponents on the continent, and these traits also were carried to England. The printing press made the arguments of continental reformers easily accessible across the channel. In addition, when Marian exiles fled to Geneva, Zurich, Strasbourg, and other cities in the early to mid-1550s, they would have learned firsthand the arguments against dancing, which they then brought back to England after 1558, when Elizabeth ascended the throne. Travel by scholars, such as the peripatetic Pietro Martire Vermigli (1500–1562), who taught at several universities in England and on the continent, also helped to spread antidance attitudes. And, as the persecution of French Huguenots continued later in the sixteenth century, many of them fled for safety to England. Robert Le Maçon (fl. 1562–1603), for example, who pastored the French Reformed church in London, edited Vermigli's writing on dance and published it under the title *Concerning the Use and Abuse of Dauncing*. It appeared in English about 1580. The anonymous translator, T.K., attributed his motive for the translation to "seeing these disordered and daly daunsings in the rude Countrey, marring mennes manners, breeding much beastly behaviour; and being desirous to have such rudenesse reformed."[30] T.K. was not alone in calling for repentance and reform.

A French Protestant grammarian can be credited with circulating antidance views broadly in England. Claudius Holyband, originally Claude DeSainliens (fl. 1566–97), presumably a gentleman, made his reputation in London as the author of a French grammar and as a teacher of language. His biographer, L. E. Farrer, infers that Holyband fled to London about 1564 or 1565, thus escaping from his native Moulins, a Protestant stronghold, before Charles IX and Catherine de Medici arrived in December 1565 to deal with the Huguenot heretics. Farrar notes that Holyband was a convicted Protestant and never missed any occasion to scoff or jeer at the Catholics.[31] His antidance treatise appeared anonymously in his grammar, *The French Littelton,* first published in London in 1576. The book enjoyed enormous popularity, coming out in at least fifteen editions by 1639. Consequently, the appended *Traicte Des Danses, auquel est monstre qu'elles sont comme accessoires et dependences de paillardise,* received extensive circulation in England. An anonymous publication of the *Traicte* was also issued separately from *The French Littelton,* presumably about the same time. In addition, a *Treatise of Daunces,* published anonymously in English in 1581 and cited by Prynne, proves to be a translation of both the Holyband *Traicte* and the anonymous French *Traicte.* The 1581 edition apparently differs only in that it places plays in the same category of objectionable activities as dances, while the French *Traictes* treat gambling along with objections to dancing. It is possible that both the French and English treatises derived from an earlier French source on the continent.[32]

Thus, the antidance arguments originally published in London as part of Holyband's grammar also circulated in separate publications. The 1576 date for the first printing of the French grammar marks the beginning of more than a decade when several publications denouncing dancing, theater, and other recreations rolled off London presses.

English Writers

John Northbrooke and his contemporaries decried the general disorder and breakdown of society in the 1570s and 1580s. Their objections focused on the city and on professional performers. In 1576, Stephen Gosson (1554–1624) went to London with an Oxford degree and made a reputation as a poet, actor, and dramatist. By 1579 his presumably liberal views had radically changed. In his *Schoole of Abuse,* published in August of that year, Gosson laments the passing of the "olde discipline of Englande," when worthy exercises requiring physical skills had been practiced. "But the exercise that is nowe among us, is banqueting, playing, pipyng, and dauncing, and all suche delightes as may win us to pleasure, or rocke us a sleepe." The evil that Gosson witnessed in the abuses of poets, pipers, and players brought citizens to sloth, sin, sleep, and, without repentance, to death and the devil. In Gosson's view, London was so overrun with such entertainers "that a man can no soner enter a taverne, but two or three caste of them hang at his heeles, to give him a daunce before he departe."[33] Similarly, John Northbrooke, writing perhaps two years earlier, lamented the disorderly class of people who loitered about the streets instead of engaging in honest work. Those who found time to dance joined a long list of undesirables in Northbrooke's writing. He grouped dancers, fiddlers, minstrels, maskers, jugglers, and interlude players with thieves, drunkards, dice players, beggars, fencers, and whoremasters.[34] In 1583, Phillip Stubbes (fl. 1581–95) added football playing, May games, usury, gluttony, church-ales, and the manner of keeping wakes, among other ills, to his *Anatomie of Abuses* that weakened England as a Christian nation.

Common to all of these critics is a perception of dancing as fundamentally immoral. Holyband, in fact, defines it as an activity that consists merely of immodest and dissolute movements by which the lust of the flesh is awakened and inflamed in both sexes.[35] But the attacks by Gosson and Northbrooke also aim at professional entertainers, hence, those in the lower ranks of urban society. Their indictments, as well as Stubbes's list of abuses, clearly imply that large groups of Londoners were wasting time in idle and unprofitable pursuits. Further, Stubbes singled out the city's schools of dancing. Vives had denounced dancing schools as "schools of Baudrie" in 1523 but did not specify whether he meant those in England. Northbrooke quoted Vives in the late seventies but, again, did not clarify whether he applied the indictment to the schools of his day. Stubbes's attack fell on the teachers at schools of singing and dancing for their effeminate and immoral character. Both male and female bore the brunt of his wrath:

> If you wold have your sonne softe, womannish, uncleane, smoth mouthed, affected to bawdrie, scurrilitie, filthie rimes, and unsemely talking; briefly, if you would have him, as it weare, transnatured into a woman, or worse, and inclyned to all kind of whordome and abhomination, set him to dauncing school, and to learn musicke, and then shall you not faile of your purpose. And if you would have your daughter whoorish, bawdrie, and uncleane, and a filthie speaker, and such like, bring her up in musicke and dauncing, and, my life for youres, you have wun the goale.[36]

Stubbes, Northbrooke, and Sir Thomas Lovell (d. 1567) all expressed additional concern that the existence of so many immoral pastimes profaned the sacredness of the Sabbath. Railing against abuses in dancing, stage plays, interludes, feasts, piping, and similar pursuits, Stubbes beseeched the Almighty: "Lord, remoove these exercises from thy Sabaoth!" The proper use of the Lord's day consisted in hearing the word of God, singing psalms, receiving the sacraments, collecting for the poor, and praying.[37] Christopher Fetherston (fl. 1583–1616) added to the list the duties of clothing the naked, helping the needy, producing peace, repenting of sin, and amending one's life.[38]

Honoring the Lord's day did not mean engaging in recreation. True recreation was to refresh both mind and body, but dancing fell far short of the mark. Those who read Stubbes learned that he knew people who had suffered broken legs from "skipping, leaping, turning and vawting." Fetherston told readers that he had heard "of those whiche have daunced one halfe day for pleasure and have laide in bedde two whole dayes for payne. Cal you this recreation?" Whether pain and broken legs actually resulted from the disorderly motion of dancers is not clear, but Fetherston and Lovell agreed with continental writers that dancers resembled animals in their antics and looked completely ridiculous, like men "not wel in wit."[39]

Not only did personal trauma accompany dancing; public consequences befell the country as a result of profaning the Lord's day. In the middle of the century, the early Puritan leader, speaker, and writer Robert Crowley (1518?–1588) had decried London's Parris Garden as the setting for bearbaiting and other Sunday amusements. Then in 1583 John Field (d. 1588) penned *A godly exhortation*, wherein he attributed the cause of a major accident at Parris Garden to God's judgment on Londoners. Seating stands at the park collapsed and people were maimed and killed. Field laments that Sunday found theaters full and churches empty.[40] He strongly believed that God speaks in and through present acts to the people of any age. Accordingly, the incident at Parris Garden was to be construed as retribution from God. Such an event, in Field's mind, called for repentance and reform by the people of England.

Only a year earlier Fetherston had sounded a similar note in his *Dialogue agaynst light, lewde, and lascivious daucing*. Not just one incident but the tenor of the times indicated that the whole country had been "lulled" into a sinful path with no thought for the judgment day to come: "Our fasting is tourned into feasting, our mourning into mumming, our praying into playing, our almes deedes into misdeedes. High and low, rich and poore, one with another are lulled on sleepe in the bedde of securitie, and no man thinketh on the day to come."[41] Northbrooke had issued a call for repentance and reform five years earlier in a statement telling readers clearly that the seriousness of the times derived from the Catholic-Protestant tensions of the century:

> Indeede, if they doe consider the daungerous times that we are in, they have little cause to use those follies, for instead of playing, they would use praying; insteade of daucing, repenting; for joye, sorrowe; for laughing, mourning; for myrth, sadnesse; for pride, patience; for wantonnese, wofulnesse, &c. Is it now . . . a time to be mery, dice, daunce, and playe, seeing before our eyes howe the blouddie Papistes murther and slaughter in all places rounde aboute us our poore brethren that professe the gospell of Jesu Christ? . . . God graunte to open the eyes of Englande, that it maye see his sinnes, and be ashamed thereof, and fall to repentaunce, and to rent their heartes, and not their garmentes, and turne to the Lorde God, for he is gracious and mercifull, &c.[42]

That antidance sentiment became entangled with anti-Catholic feeling becomes clearer when one looks at the assertions by Fetherston and Lovell. More than a decade before Taffin impugned the Church of Rome for permitting dancing, both English writers had pointed to the fact that dancing had been allowed, and sometimes sponsored, by Catholic authority on the basis of longstanding custom. Apparently unaware of prior Catholic opposition to dancing, Fetherston alleged that "the papistes" never found fault with the activity, that they "did suffer men to use all kind of sensuality, so did they never finde fault with this same vanitie, I mean daucing." He asserted that the Catholics reasoned from custom and antiquity in permitting pastimes like dancing. For Calvinist sympathizers like Fetherston, that criterion no longer carried weight, because the conduct of the masses constituted no fit guide for a Christian's life. Fetherston wrote that "though dauncing or any other exercise whatsoever, have bin used never so long, or though it be used in never so many places: yet if it be contrary to the worde and will of God, and forbidden by the same, it is detestable, and of all men to be eschewed." As if to reinforce his views with Protestant sentiment, Lovell closed his *Dialogue Between Custom and Veritie* with the wish that Queen Elizabeth would reign long days "to purge out clean all popish dregs."[43]

Thus, the concern of Stubbes, Northbrooke, Fetherston, Lovell, and others, regarding what they considered to be rampant immorality, arose from their Protestant evangelical beliefs. What they judged to be the ubiquitous presence of immoral behavior accompanying dancing simply proved that the activity attracted the carnally or fleshly minded person who had not repented of sin and been "born anew in Christ." In Stubbes's words,

> that whatsoever a carnall man, with uncircumcised heart, either desireth or taketh pleasure in, is most abhominable & wicked before god. As, on the other side, what the spirituall man regenerat, & borne anew in Christ, by the direction of God his spirit, desireth or taketh delight in, is good, and according to the will of God: And seeing mans nature is too proclive of it selfe to sinne, it hath no need of allurements & allections to sin (as dauncing is) but rather of restraints & inhibitions from the same, which are not there to be found.[44]

Although the Christian became a new person in Christ, he or she still had to guard continually against temptations from the world, the flesh, and the devil. Thus, repentance and reform went together. Those who feared a loss of control and a headlong rush into sin tended to proscribe dancing completely, in the manner of Calvin and his followers. Moderates like Mulcaster and Luther argued that dances and dancing could be reformed and that abuse of an activity by some did not mandate abstinence by all. However, by the turn of the seventeenth century, most English Puritans continued their fervent and focused opposition to dancing. Their views became well known across the Atlantic.

Mather's Cloud of Witnesses

"Amongst our English Divines there is a cloud of Witnesses," wrote Increase Mather in 1685, quoting from the phrase found in Hebrews 12:1. To add authority to his list, he hastened to point out that his "Witnesses" included three bishops and one archbishop, "tho we confess a Puritannical one."[45] Although Mather does not cite works of these men, it seems clear that, in most instances, he referred to their expositions of the Commandments.

William Perkins (1558–1602) was among the best known of the "cloud of Witnesses." Credited with being the "mightiest preacher of Elizabethan times" as well as "the most famous and influential spokesman for Calvinism of his day," Perkins experienced during his Cambridge years the kind of dramatic conversion that Augustine had undergone. Subsequently, Perkins pioneered the development of what his biographer, Thomas F. Merrill, calls a "uniquely Protestant science of casuistry." In that science, Perkins spelled out two rules that applied to the "lawfull" use of recreation for the Christian. First, approved recreation pertained only to "things indifferent," that is, things neither expressly commanded nor forbidden by God. Neither category required any human debate. Second, the extent of time spent in recreation had to be sparing and moderate. Dancing, as well as cards, plays, and interludes, fell outside the bounds of these rules. As proof, Perkins quotes almost verbatim both Daneau and Taffin with respect to the fruits of dancing and the ridiculous motions of dancers:

> This exercise cannot be numbred among things indifferent: for experience sheweth, that it hath beene usually either a fruite or a follower of great wickednesse, as idolatrie, fornication, drunkenesse: hereupon, one well compared it to a circle, whose center was the devill. Againe, if we must give an account of every idle word, then also of every idle gesture and pace: and what account can be given of these paces backward & forward, of caprings, jumpes, gambols, turning, with many other friskes of lightnesse and vanitie, more beseeming goates and apes, of whom they are commonly used, then men.[46]

Applying the criterion of adiaphora—the rule of "things indifferent"—was not unique to Perkins, but others could conclude differently. For example, another Puritan, Dudley Fenner, preached the same point of view as Perkins, but, as noted earlier, Martin Luther held that dancing in itself was not sinful.[47]

In addition to Perkins, the Oxford scholar John Rainolds stands out among the "cloud of Witnesses," as the author of a lengthy 1599 publication titled *Th'overthrow Of Stage-Playes*. In the preface, even the printer laments the continued "flocking and gadding that we see daily" to the theaters and other "ydle places of entercourse" by people who have no respect for the Sabbath as well as for their daily responsibilities.

Rainolds specifies that his objections pertain to stage dancing, all of which he believes savors of dishonesty. However, he particularly decries the dancing of men with boys attired like women or maidens. Underlying his concern lay strong adherence to a passage in Deuteronomy 22:5 that directs women to avoid wearing clothes normally worn by men, and vice versa. Rainolds stresses that he does not denounce all dancing out of hand but that he agrees with Ambrose, who denigrated "all histrionicall motions and playings on the stage." Rainolds declares that if dancers followed Elyot's direction and remembered that the steps of dancing corresponded to the various branches of prudence, then others besides Elyot would laud the art.[48]

With the exception of William Prynne, the remaining "cloud of Witnesses" wrote against dancing in their explanations of the Seventh Commandment. They excluded biblical examples as proof of the legitimacy of dancing, and they indicted stage dancing and mixed dancing as practiced in their day.[49] Expositions make clear that the command, "Thou shalt not commit adultery," encompasses far more than a single act. In effect, the intent is that Christians avoid all occasions for temptations to the sin of adultery.

The Ideal for the Christian and the Ideal for Gentlefolk

Dance opponents and courtesy writers embraced reigning concepts of the sixteenth century, such as the importance of worship, order, virtue, and health, but they differed in degree on critical points concerning these subjects. While courtesy writers aimed to delineate the ideal for the gentleman or lady, Protestant reformers who opposed dancing were concerned with formulating their ideal for the Christian. As portrayed in the antidance writings, the Christian owed allegiance solely to God. By contrast, the gentleman owed homage to God and king. The Bible served as the primary guide to right living for Protestant reformers, but courtly tradition weighed heavily in the training of a gentleman and a lady. Although dance opponents' strong emphasis on repentance and reform agreed with courtesy writers' exhortations to seek virtue and shun vice, Calvinist and Puritan detractors often demonstrated a more narrow, legalistic, and militant opposition to dancing. An emphasis on repentance, salvation, and eternity for the Christian could result in minimal attention to physical health. However, the gentleman could not escape the humanistic and courtly traditions that required an aesthetically pleasing body—one trained for distinction in warfare or in dance. The gentleman could never be an ascetic; he had to display a "work of art" in his own person and be able to defend king and country at a moment's notice. Similarly, the lady had to appear graceful and aesthetically pleasing in her person and behavior. The ideal for gentlefolk held importance for Catholic and Protestant members of the privileged ranks of society in England, France, and Italy. The ideal for the Christian as delineated by dance opponents drew support particularly from Calvinists and Puritans, including both commoners and courtiers, on the continent and in England.

These differing emphases produced varying perceptions of dancing. Courtesy writers, by definition, tended to see it from an aesthetic, social, and moral point of view. Calvinist and Puritan reformers did not usually specify the kind of dancing they opposed but their writings leave no doubt that they saw dancing exclusively from a moral and religious point of view. Those who perceived virtue in dancing, that is, the courtesy authors, ascribed that positive value only to the art as ordered form, governed by reason and producing healthful exercise. The reformers who denounced dancing viewed it as disorderly and immoral, serving "delite" rather than reason or health.

Antidance attitudes and the Puritan ideal for the Christian were transported to seventeenth-century Massachusetts via England and the continent. Mather's references to continental authorities point to the growth of Calvinist opposition during the century following the publication of Daneau's *Traite Des Danse*. As with his English divines, Mather's French, Dutch, and German authorities were learned men in the reformed tradition.[50] Thus, by the time he wrote against dancing in New England, Mather could draw from a widely established and lengthy tradition of dance opposition.

Notes

1. "Thoinot Arbeau" is an anagram for the author's real name, Jehan, or Jean, Tabourot. Some sources list his birth date as 1519, based on his known age at death, 76. He entered the chapter at Langres about 1542, following study in Paris and Poitiers. After occupying several positions, he finally became vicar general. See *Dictionnaire des Lettres Françaises, Le Seizième Siècle*, s.v. "Tabourot."

2. Elyot's biographer, Pearl Hogrefe, calls him a "conservative" and indicates that the label distinguishes followers of the "old religion" from the reformers. Elaborating on the strength of Elyot's religious and moral beliefs, Hogrefe states: "Thomas Elyot was a conservative in politics and in religious beliefs; he clung to the theology of the old religion all his life. It seems probable then, that his repeated emphasis upon the strength of carnal desires and the need for the governor or ruler to master them had some relation to Henry VIII. No other manual on the education and

the resulting virtues of the gentleman, so far as this writer knows, puts such stress upon continence." Hogrefe asserts that Northbrooke copied Elyot in attacks on idleness, playing dice, and accompanying oaths, as well as blaspheming. The fact that Northbrooke did not cite Elyot but instead Agrippa, on the evils of dancing, suggests that Northbrooke had not seen the moral and orderly basse dance, which Elyot employed for his correspondence with the branches of prudence. Northbrooke may have considered the basse dance out of vogue and, therefore, inappropriate as a correspondence. When Arbeau wrote from France in 1588, he said the basse dance had been out of fashion for about fifty years. See Pearl Hogrefe, *The Life and Times of Sir Thomas Elyot, Englishman* (Ames: Iowa State University Press, 1967), 140, 167, 124–25.

3. Johannes Ludovicus Vives, *Introduction to wissedome,* trans. Richarde Morisine (N.p.: N.p., 1563), sig. Dv. See also a discussion of the concept and images of order in E. M. W. Tillyard, *The Elizabethan World Picture* (New York: Vintage, n.d.).

4. I have selected courtesy treatises from those identified in two extensive bibliographies. See Virgil B. Heltzel, *A Check List of Courtesy Books in the Newberry Library* (Chicago: Newberry Library, 1942), and Ruth Kelso, *Doctrine for the Lady of the Renaissance* (Urbana: University of Illinois Press, 1956). Instructions for the gentleman far exceed any descriptions of the "lady" during the period. See also Ann Wagner, "The Significance of Dance in Sixteenth-Century Courtesy Literature" (Ph.D. diss., University of Minnesota, 1980), 10–13 and 149–51; Baldassare Castiglione, *The Book of the Courtier,* trans. Thomas Hoby (1561; rpt., London: J. M. Dent, 1928), 189–95.

5. Joseph A. Mazzeo coins the phrase "the self as a work of art" with reference to the ideal courtier depicted by Baldassare Castiglione in 1528. According to Mazzeo, a cluster of characteristics, which epitomized the artistic ideal of the age, defined the aesthetic appearance and performance of the courtier. "Gravità," he says, "is virtually synonomous with dignity." The courtier was to possess a "modest or measured greatness," at once "unstudied" and "'artless.'" Hence, the courtier did nothing in haste; he avoided "fast dances and when he rode, presumably even to war, he did so in a relaxed way." Secondly, *sprezzatura* described the quality that connoted "the art of concealing art." The courtier was to display a kind of "detachment" or "coolness" and, thereby, avoid that affectation of the dancing master, which was antithetical to the gentlemanly ideal. Finally, *grazia* connoted the grace that embodied the true amateur spirit; it indicated an easy effortlessness, a "skillful spontaneity." Though proper instruction aided the acquisition of this elusive quality, the courtier had to possess, innately, "at least the germ of it." *Grazia* included the grace that produced a harmony of parts in the person and, in Mazzeo's words, "makes the self into a work of art." Mazzeo deals only with the gentleman even though Castiglione gives one of the most complete portraits for the lady found in the courtesy literature. See Joseph A. Mazzeo, *Renaissance and Revolution: The Remaking of European Thought* (New York: Pantheon, 1965), 143–48.

6. Coplande's treatise resembles an anonymous instructional manual printed in 1488 and cataloged under the name of the Parisian printer Michel Toulouze. Both deal with the basse dance; moreover, both *L'Art et Instruction de Bien Dancer* and *The Manner to Dance Bace Dances* appear to have a common antecedent in a mid-fifteenth-century manuscript from the Burgundian court. See analysis of the evidence in: Daniel Heartz, "The Basse Dance," *Annales Musicologiques* 6 (1958–63): 296, 305–6; Artur Michel, "The Earliest Dance Manuals," *Medievalia et Humanistica* (1945): 127; Kathi Meyer, "Michel de Toulouze," *Music Review* 7 (1946): 182; and Margaret Dean Smith, "A Fifteenth-Century Dancing Book," *Journal of English Folk Dance and Song Society* 3, no. 2 (Dec. 1937): 100–109.

7. Sir Thomas Elyot, *The Boke Named The Governour* (London, 1531; rpt., New York: E. P. Dutton, n.d.), 97.

8. Ibid., 94–95.

9. Sir John Davies, *Orchestra, or A Poem of Dancing* (London, 1596; rpt., London: Chatto and Windus, 1947), stanza 111.

10. Ibid., stanzas 74–75. The Three Graces—Aglaia, Euphrosyne, Thalia, daughters of Zeus—were first identified by Hesiod in the eighth century. Presumably, Davies belonged to the Church of England. He served as a member of Parliament and subsequently as Attorney General for Ireland. In the latter capacity he was cited for his efforts to banish the Roman Catholic priests and establish the Protestant religion. See *Dictionary of National Biography* (hereafter *DNB*), s.v. "Davies, Sir John."

11. Thoinot Arbeau, *Orchesographie* (Langres, 1588; rpt., trans. Cyril W. Beaumont, Brooklyn: Dance Horizons, n.d.); Fabritio Caroso, *Nobiltà di Dame: A Treatise on Courtly Dance . . .* (1600; rpt., trans. Julia Sutton, music transcribed by F. Marian Walker, Oxford: Oxford University Press, 1986).

12. For an analysis of the allegorical meanings in the "Ballet Comique," see Camille Hardy, "Ballet Comique de la Reine: A Primer on Subtext and Symbol," in *Proceedings, Society of Dance History Scholars,* Fifth Annual Conference, Harvard University, 13–15 Feb. 1982, 137–47. Catherine de Medici was the niece of Lorenzo de Medici, fifteenth-century ruler of Florence and the choreographer of the *bassadanza* "Lauro."

13. *New Catholic Encyclopedia,* s.v. "Jesuit Drama"; John J. Walsh, S.J., "Ballet on the Jesuit Stage in Italy, Germany and France" (Ph.D. diss., Yale University, 1954), 16. One conservative estimate puts the total number of Jesuit colleges at about five hundred during the period 1650–1700. Intended for gentlemen's sons, the liberal arts curricula aimed to educate the whole person. Productions also assisted in the religious instruction of audiences as well as the actors, thereby helping to counter heresies of the day.

14. Artur F. Michel, "The Dance on the Jesuit Stage," *Historical Bulletin* 23, no. 3 (Mar. 1945): 51–52.

15. Elyot, *The Boke Named The Governour,* 85; Arbeau, *Orchesographie,* 106;

Luther's Works, ed. Helmut T. Lehman (Philadelphia: Fortress Press, 1975), vol. 50, 279; Roger Ascham, *The Scholemaster* (London: John Paye, 1570; rpt. in *English Reprints,* ed. Edward Arber, London: N.p., 1869), vol. 1, 64. In 1545, Luther wrote to his wife about a turning dance; he also preached against it. As early as 1511 the Leipzig city council had prohibited such dancing; so did the University of Wittenberg in 1540.

16. Richard Mulcaster, *Positions* (London: Thomas Vautrollier, 1581; rpt., London: Harrison and Sons, 1887), 58–60.

17. Ibid., 61–63. Martin Luther argued, using similar logic, that the dance was not to blame for the fact that people sinned while dancing. In fact, people sin at the table and in church. And eating and drinking are not to be forbidden because some folks turn into pigs. In Luther's view, if people were decent and moderate in their conduct, they could not dance away their faith. See *What Luther Says: An Anthology,* comp. Ewald M. Plass (St. Louis: Concordia Publishing House, 1959), vol. 3, 1562–63.

18. 2 Corinthians 3:16–18.

19. *Sermons of Maister John Calvin upon the Booke of Job,* trans. Arthur Golding (London: Thomas Woodcocke, 1584), 373.

20. Ibid., 373–74.

21. Eug. and E. M. Haag, *La France Protestante: ou, Vies des Protestants Français . . . ,* vol. 4 (Paris, 1853), s.v. "Daneau." His authorship has been questioned because the title page of *Traite Des Danses* says "Par François Estienne." However, Estienne was a printer, and the cataloger at Harvard's Houghton Library noted that Estienne's name was in the place on the title page normally used for the printer's name. *The National Union Catalogue of Pre-1956 Imprints* lists Daneau as author. For an analysis of the Calvinist opposition to dancing, based on sources other than those cited by Mather, see H. P. Clive, "The Calvinists and the Question of Dancing in the 16th Century," *Bibliothèque D'Humanisme Et Renaissance* 23, no. 2 (1961): 296–323.

22. [Daneau, Lambert], *Traite Des Danses, Auquel est amplement resolve la question, asavoir s'il est permis aux Chretiens de danser* ([Geneva]: François Estienne, 1579), 10–11, 12–13.

23. Ibid., 133, 140–41.

24. Ibid., 15–16, 18–19; Phil. 2:12 is the biblical authority cited for the importance of sobriety and gravity.

25. *The New Schaff-Herzog Encyclopedia of Religious Knowledge,* s.v. "Taffin." As a general rule, the dance opponents cited in this chapter are those mentioned by Mather and/or William Prynne.

26. Jean Taffin, *The Amendment of Life* (London: George Bishop, 1595), 70, 229–31, 77–78.

27. Ibid., 228.

28. Sir Robert Dallington, *The View of Fraunce* (London: Symond Stafford,

1604; rpt., Oxford University Press, Shakespeare Association Facsimiles No. 13, 1936), V2.

29. Andrew Gerard Hyperius, *The True Tryall And Examination of a Mans owne selfe* . . . , trans. Tho. Newton (London: John Windet, 1587), 67, 93–96, 101, 105–6.

30. Pietro Vermigli, *A briefe Treatise, Concerning the use and abuse of Dauncing*, comp. Rob. Massonius, trans. T.K. (London: John Jugge, n.d.), sig. Aii ff.

31. L. E. Farrer, *La Vie et Les Oeuvres de Claude de Sainliens* (Paris, 1908), 9. See also Claudius Holyband, *The French Littelton,* intro. M. St. Clare Byrne (1609; rpt., Cambridge: Cambridge University Press, 1953), viii–xi. Holyband was not cited by either Mather or Prynne; he was included in the bibliographies of courtesy books for the sixteenth century. I have included him here because his antidance treatise is the same as an anonymous treatise cited by Prynne and dated 1581.

32. Holyband, *The French Littelton,* xxiii, 213. According to the bibliographer Jacques-Charles Brunet, in his *Manuel du Libraire* (rpt., Copenhagen, 1966), a treatise with a similar title, *Traité des danses, auquel il est demontré qu'elles sont accessoires et dependances de paillardises* . . . , came from the pen of "frère Antoine Estienne, minime," and was published in Paris in 1564. Because the titles are similar and because the book appeared at about the time that Holyband left France for England, it seems possible that the treatise appended to *The French Littelton* actually represents the work of the French Catholic writer. Professor F. H. Stubbings, former librarian of Emmanuel College, Cambridge, has verified that the anonymous publication of the *Traicte,* which circulated about 1576–80 and is now held by Emmanuel College, has the same title, text, and typesetting as the 1576 Holyband work. After examination of colophons and printers' marks, Stubbings concludes that the anonymous Emmanuel *Traicte* came from the press of Thom. Vautrollier (Personal correspondence with F. H. Stubbings, 30 Aug. 1984, and personal interview, 4 Apr. 1985). The *Short Title Catalogue* indicates that all editions of Holyband's treatise between 1576 and 1609 issued from the press of Vautrollier and his inheritor, Richard Field.

The 1581 anonymous *Treatise of Daunces* was reprinted by Garland Publishing in 1974. In the preface to the Garland edition, Arthur Freeman writes that the *Treatise* was known to E. K. Chambers and that it is held by the British Museum as well as by Lambeth Palace. The Garland reprint was prepared from the latter copy. Freeman states that the *Treatise* had not been previously reprinted.

33. Stephen Gosson, *The Schoole of Abuse And A Short Apology of the Schoole of Abuse* (London, 1579; rpt., *English Reprints,* ed. Edward Arber, London: Alex. Murray, 1869), 7, 10–11, 34, 42; *Apology,* 87; *DNB,* s.v. "Gosson."

34. John Northbrooke, *A Treatise Against Dicing, Dancing, Plays, and Interludes. With Other Idle Pastimes* (London, c. 1577; rpt., London: Shakespeare Society, 1843), 76.

35. Holyband, *The French Littelton,* 130. Part of the way in which lust was in-

flamed derived from the paint, adornment, and dress of women. Although Holyband does not detail this theme in the antidance treatise, a contemporary publication spells out in great detail the style of attire for French women of the era. Frère
Antoine Estienne Mineur, who might be the author of the Holyband *Traicte,* has
been clearly credited with the authorship of *A Charitable Remonstrance Addressed
to the Wives and Maidens of France,* printed in Paris in 1570 or 1571. As a Franciscan friar, Frère Antoine relied heavily on the authority of early church fathers,
in addition to the Bible. He charges French females with going to excess in the
number of ornaments they added to their bodies—including false hair, pads, ear-
rings, masks, plaits, hair combs, tiaras, braids, fringes, feathers, fans, and busks. Rich
fabrics, flounces, ruffs, paint, and suggestive stockings, together with low-cut bod-
ices that bared the breasts, completed an appearance that "made war on God." Such
alterations of God's natural creation simply aligned women with the devil. More
specifically, it is the wanton woman, the prostitute, who chooses to alter and adorn
her natural creation so as to attract men.

36. Phillip Stubbes, *The Anatomie of Abuses* . . . (London: Richard Jones, 1584;
rpt., Vaduz, Liechtenstein: Kraus Reprint, 1965), 171.

37. Ibid., 137.

38. Christopher Fetherston, *A Dialogue agaynst light, lewde, and lascivious
dauncing* . . . (London: Thomas Dawson, 1582), sig. B4.

39. Stubbes, *Anatomie of Abuses,* 156; Fetherson, *Dialogue,* sig. B, D3–D4, D5;
Sir Thomas Lovell, *A Dialogue between Custom and Veritie concerning the use and
abuse of Dauncing and Minstrelsie* (London: John Alde, [1581]), sig. D–Dii.

40. John Field, *A godly exhortation, by the occasion of the late judgement of God,
Shewed at Parris-garden* . . . (London: Robert Walde-grave, 1583; rpt., intro. Peter
Davison, New York: Johnson Reprint, 1972), 2.

41. Fetherston, *Dialogue,* sig. A5.

42. Northbrooke, *Treatise,* 179–80.

43. Fetherston, *Dialogue,* sig. B5ff and C3; Lovell, *Dialogue between Custom and
Veritie,* last page.

44. Stubbes, *Anatomie of Abuses,* 155.

45. Increase Mather, "An Arrow Against Profane and Promiscuous Dancing
Drawn out of the Quiver of the Scriptures" (Boston, [1685]: rpt. in *The Mathers
on Dancing,* ed. Joseph F. Marks III, Brooklyn: Dance Horizons, 1975), 43.

46. William Perkins, *A Discourse of Conscience,* 2d ed. (Cambridge, 1608; rpt.,
William Perkins English Puritanist, ed. and intro. Thomas F. Merrill, Nieuwkoop:
B. De Graaf, 1966), x, 46; and William Perkins, *The Whole Treatise of the Cases of
Conscience* (N.p., n.d.; rpt., *William Perkins English Puritanist*), 221–22.

47. Dudley Fenner (1558?–1587), judged one of the "ablest exponents of Puritan views," addressed the matter of "things indifferent" in his publication of 1590
about lawful recreation. Quoting the apostle Paul that all things are lawful to the
Christian, but not all things profit him or her, Fenner agrees with Calvin that danc-

ing falls outside the boundaries of activities considered morally neutral. The dancing of men with women automatically precludes that shamefastness and gravity required in the Christian. Like Vives earlier in the century, Fenner argues that sight provokes to lust, therefore avoidance of dancing proved the only lawful path for the Christian. See Dudley Fenner, *A short and profitable Treatise, of lawfull and unlawfull Recreations, and of the right use and abuse of those that are lawfull* (Midleburgh: Richard Schilders, [1590]), 2d and 5th pages after sig. A3. By contrast, Martin Luther, argued that dancing in itself was not sinful. If it were, children could not be allowed to dance; and he thought that youngsters certainly danced without sinning. Rather than abstinence, Luther advocated supervision of dances to prevent immoral conduct. Reflecting his path of moderation, he urged the Christian to follow the "royal middle," avoiding the Epicurean on one side and the sad monk on the other. See *What Luther Says,* vol. 2, 787.

48. John Rainolds, *Th'overthrow Of Stage-Playes* . . . (1599; rpt., intro. J. W. Binns, New York: Johnson Reprint, 1972), Introduction, sig. A2 and 132, 133, 137.

49. William Ames (1576–1633) enlarged the context to "common revellings" and "sportly dancings." See William Ames, *Conscience With The Power And Cases Thereof* (1639; rpt., Amsterdam: Theatrum Orbis Terrarum, 1975), 214. For a more detailed discussion of English Puritan attitudes toward dance prior to the 1620s, see Jeremy Goring, *Godly Exercises or the Devil's Dance? Puritanism and Popular Culture in Pre–Civil War England* (London: Friends of Dr. Williams's Library, 1983).

50. André Rivet (1572?–1651), a French pastor and celebrated Protestant theologian, taught at the universities of Leyden and Oxford in the 1620s. Both Rivet and Pierre Ravanel (d. 1680), author of *A Complete Christian Dictionary* (Geneva, 1650), objected to the artificial and proud carriage learned in schools of dancing, according to Mather. The travel of individuals, as well as the circulation of books, was bound to spread antidance attitudes. For example, Fenner left England for Antwerp and later served the Reform church in Midleburgh. Ames studied under Perkins at Cambridge but left for Holland when suspended by university officials for some of his views. See Mather, "Arrow," 42–43; Haag et Haag, s.v. "Junius," "Marlorat," "Ravanel," "Rivet," "Tilenus"; McClintock and Strong, s.v. "Alting," "Lavater"; *Die Religion in Geschicte und Gegenwart,* s.v. "Polanus," "Zepper"; *Nouvelle Biographie Universelle,* s.v. "Aretius."

Part 2

American Attitudes

3

The Puritans in New England: The Seventeenth Century

> But our question is concerning Gynecandrical Dancing.
> . . . Now this we affirm to be utterly unlawful, and that it
> cannot be tollerated in such a place as New-England,
> without great Sin.
>
> Increase Mather, 1685

When Increase Mather (1639–1723) penned the first extant American an-tidance treatise, "An Arrow Against Profane and Promiscuous Dancing Drawn out of the Quiver of the Scriptures," he wrote with the same kind of zeal that had inspired the Puritan migration to Massachusetts. Address-ing descendants of the original Puritans in Boston, Mather exhorted with the intensity of the biblical Jeremiah, who prophesied doom to the ancient Israelites because they had forsaken the ways of God. Similarly, Mather de-clared that "for persons to Dance at a Time when God calls them to mourn, is certainly unlawful. But such is the case at this Day." He reminded his read-ers of Jeremiah's admonition, "Hear the Word of the Lord, O ye Women, and teach your daughters wailing." Like Fetherston and Northbrooke a century earlier, Mather argued that dancing was incompatible with mourn-ing. To dance at such a time was certainly a "great provocation." The church in the world at large suffered much "Affliction," a fact that called for New Englanders to sympathize and evidence their union with the "Mystical Body of Christ." Like the sixteenth-century English divines, Mather saw God's judgments at work in the world, but other citizens in Boston simply did not take their religion as seriously.[1] Their behavior demonstrated that fact.

The immediate incident that outraged Mather and other Boston clergy appears to have been the effrontery of a dancing master, one Francis Stepney, who, reportedly, "by one Play" could teach more "Divinity" than either the Old Testament or "Mr. Willard." In response to Stepney's alleged declaration, the clerics went to court on 12 November 1685 to "complain against a Dancing master who seeks to set up here and hath mixt Dances, and his time of Meeting is Lecture-Day," according to Judge Samuel Sewall. Thus Stepney, with either confidence or antagonism, challenged the preaching skill of the Reverend Mr. Willard, a Puritan cleric, and also proposed to desecrate the midweek day for church. Sewall recorded in his diary for 17 December that Stepney requested a jury, so the dance master was bound to January court for fifty pounds, ordered not to keep a dancing school, and warned that he would be held in contempt if he did so. Sewall's next entry on the matter mentions that "Mr. Francis Stepney has his Jury" and indicates the seriousness of the charge, namely, that the dance master would be tried for speaking "Blasphemous Words; and Reviling the Government." On 4 February, the court fined Stepney one hundred pounds to be settled as follows: "10£ down, the rest respited till the last of March, that so might go away if he would. He appeals." Twelve days later Sewall notes: "The Arrow against dancing comes out." In his diary the judge does not record the payment of Stepney's fine but on 28 July 1686 he reports succinctly: "Francis Stepney the Dancing Master runs away for Debt. Several attachments out after him."[2] In fleeing from debt, the Boston clergy, and the court, Stepney could only have reinforced the common notion that dancing masters generally proved to be of poor character.

Prior to Stepney's arrival in Boston, several other dance teachers had appeared in and near the Puritan center. During the early 1670s a dancing school may have been set up but it was put down. Then in 1678 a Charles Cleate, or Clete, an itinerant dancing master, was not allowed membership in the city by the town selectmen and was warned to get out of town. In 1681 a French dancing master, Henry Sherlot, was ordered out of both town and colony due to his ill-fame, namely, his having been prosecuted for rape in Ireland and having scoffed at religion.[3] Despite the abortive careers of these men, the fact that they appeared at all in the Puritan citadel suggests that they anticipated some prospect of earning a living. Their immigration to New England further supports Mather's contention that the colony was becoming ever more worldly.

With a population of about seven thousand by 1685,[4] Boston had grown well beyond the level of subsistence living that would have permitted citizens virtually no time for socializing and recreation. In the five decades since the great Puritan migration began, economic expansion and commerce with

Europe had brought some amenities and even luxuries to the colonists' daily lives. Evidence of increasingly worldly attitudes and practices comes from Mather's *Testimony Against several Prophane and Superstitious Customs,* written in October 1686, many months after the "Arrow" against dancing appeared.

The title page of the *Testimony* echoes themes from Jeremiah and Isaiah— "The Customs of the People are Vain." In particular, Mather remonstrates against health-drinking, dicing, cards, games, Christmas-keeping, New Year's gifts, and the like. His preface elaborates on the context:

> Since the Composure whereof, there is much discourse of beginning of Stage-Plays in New-England. The last Year Promiscuous Dancing was openly practised, and too much countenanced in this Degenerated Town. . . . If we should now behold things as bad or worse coming in upon us, and be altogether silent, I know not how we should be able to answer it to him, who has set us as Watchmen to the House of Israel, and most solemnly charged us to shew unto them their Iniquities.[5]

Moreover, Mather had heard talk of setting up a May pole, so he felt compelled to write briefly on the early history of that activity, noting that May games were not only pagan but connected with harlots. That such associations might prevail in Massachusetts struck him as nothing less than "abominable": "It is an abominable shame, that any Persons in a Land of such Light and Purity as New-England has been, should have the Face to speak or think of practising so vile a piece of Heathenism."[6]

At the time Mather wrote the treatise against "Prophane customs," John Cotton the Younger acknowledged that Mather held the "chief Rank" among the colony's modern authors.[7] Thus, it is not surprising that Mather has been identified as the author of the now famous "Arrow Against Profane and Promiscuous Dancing . . . ," which appeared the year before from the Boston press of Samuel Green. The essay carried no author's name, only the collective attribution, "By the Ministers of Christ at Boston in New-England." However, both Mather's bibliographer and his son, Cotton, list the "Arrow" as one of his works.[8]

Increase Mather's Analysis

Mather's knowledge of previous authorities and works opposing dance and theater bespeaks his great learning, but the organization, arguments, and style of the "Arrow" evidence no originality of thought. The entire treatise points back across the Atlantic and, ultimately, to classical antiquity. In effect, Mather merely reiterated for New Englanders the arguments that had been expounded in the sixteenth and seventeenth centuries. Typical of many Protestant reformers, Mather clarifies that he does not oppose all dancing; neither does he oppose dancing in and of itself. His complaint pertains to "mixt" dancing, men with women, because it falls into the category of activities that could entice participants to temptation, more specifically to the adultery forbidden in the Seventh Commandment. Even though some people might assert that they themselves are not tempted by dancing or watching dancers, Mather declares that if any person is so drawn into sin, then mixed dancing is evil. As proof, he invokes no contemporary evidence from Massachusetts, citing instead the work of the second-century Roman satirist Juvenal.[9] Interestingly, the remainder of Mather's arguments follow the same pattern, namely, using references to dancing in prior centuries as evidence to oppose the activity found in New England.

Arguments against Dancing

Mather divided the "Arrow" into six arguments against dancing followed by counters to five pleas for its legitimacy. As an orthodox Calvinist, Mather held to the primacy of Scripture as the bulwark for his stand against dancing. Thus, Mather's first argument asserts: "That which the Scripture condemns is sinful." Accordingly, he goes beyond the Seventh Commandment to argue his case. But, since the Bible nowhere expressly prohibits dancing, Mather has to rely on passages that stipulate a generalized behavior forbidden to the Christian.

The biblical passages used against dancing come from both Old and New Testaments. Isaiah 3:16 describes the daughters of Zion walking vainly and proudly in mincing steps, with wanton eyes. Mather says that the continental Reformed church theologians Junius, Rivet, and Ravanel interpret that Scripture to prohibit the artificial postures learned in dancing schools. The fact that Mather cites no examples in Boston of trained or artificial carriage could suggest that no dancing school had yet flourished in the city or that Mather had never observed those who studied dancing. But, since his entire treatise provides no descriptions of any contemporary dancing, such conclusions would seem unwarranted.

Mather's second scripture against dancing refers to rioting or reveling. He argues that 1 Peter 4:30 forbids dancing on the grounds that reformers as well as ancient classical writers interpreted rioting and reveling to include dancing. In similar fashion, Mather refers to historical accusations about the disorderliness of dancers: "And truly such affected Levity, and Antick Behaviour, when persons skip and fling about like Bedlams, as they say, Dancers are wont to do; is no way becoming the Gravity of a Christian." Although he cites Vives, Mather's description also recalls passages by Calvin, Daneau, and Cicero, which indict dancers for disorderly motion. Extending his arguments even more tenuously, Mather cites two more verses that, he asserts, prohibit dancing. In Philippians 4:8, Paul admonishes Christians to think on whatsoever is of good report; in 1 Corinthians 10:32, he urges believers to give no offense to Jew, Gentile, or the church of God. According to Mather's logic, since both Christian and non-Christian men who were grave and wise have indicated that dancing is of "evil report," the practice is, therefore, forbidden by the Scripture. In addition, Mather tells his readers that many passages in the Bible exhort Christians to sobriety and gravity, hence, dancing is unbecoming to a believer.[10]

As if assigning guilt by association, Mather subsequently declares that, because dancing was invented and patronized by the devil, heathens, and "Popish casuists," it has proved "highly provoking to the Holy God." By contrast, those who have proved themselves faithful reformers in the church have testified against dancing. Moreover, when even the "Graver sort of Heathen" have condemned dancing, Christians most assuredly should view the activity as sinful.

Moving from patrons of dancing to piety, Mather argues in his fourth assertion that any practice not sanctified by prayer "is surely an evil Practice." Using a rhetorical device later adopted by nineteenth-century dance opponents, he asks: "But who can seriously pray to the Holy God to be with him when he is going to a Promiscuous dance?" The strategy suggests the polemical nature of Mather's writing and characterizes later treatises: a rhetorical question is posed that contains no possible answer, but an implied negative response is meant to make the respondent feel guilty.

In a natural corollary, Mather's fifth argument speaks to an environment conducive to piety: "For Persons to Dance at a Time when God calls them to mourn, is certainly unlawful. But such is the case at this Day."[11] The reference points to Ecclesiastes 3, which begins: "Everything that happens in this world happens at the time God chooses," an idea that continues in verse 4: "He sets the time for sorrow and the time for joy, the time for mourning and the time for dancing." Mather asserts that the passage does not legitimate dancing by declaring that there is a lawful time to dance; rather, the biblical writer means merely that there is a limited time to dance.[12] Elaborating on the importunity of the present time, Mather declares that the judgments of God are abroad in the world. He quotes the late Reverend John

Cotton with respect to dancing, even at marriages, for the activity is "un-meet in N.E. and that now when the Churches of England are in such distresse, Ezek. 21:10."[13]

Finally, Mather returns full circle to his original argument, that dancing produces evil effects and fruits, which, in this case, refer to the judgments of God. For proof, Mather, like the late sixteenth-century English writers, cites the biblical story of Salome and John the Baptist as well as Thomas Beard's *Theater of God's Judgment* (1597).[14] In the tradition of earlier opponents, Mather's thorough analysis then moves to refute those who argued in favor of dancing.

Response to Dance Advocates

Countering the typical pleas by dance advocates, Mather first asserts that dancing in the Bible did not justify the contemporary practice. He excludes Old Testament examples on the usual grounds of their being single-sex activities performed for religious purposes. Interestingly, Mather declares that the only example of "mixt" dancing in the entire Bible pertained to that "accursed and damned Harlot the Daughter of Herodias." The outburst is unusual for Mather; he goes no further than this brief characterization and then moves on to the next point. His second response speaks to the plea that dancing served to teach polite behavior and carriage. Mather does not object in principle to the proposition but wants the teacher to be a "Grave Person." He then hastens to imply that dancing does not actually teach the alleged good behavior. "Why should Pantomimical Gestures be named good Carriage?" Referring back to the passage from Isaiah cited at the beginning, he declares: "If the Holy Prophet Isaiah were alive in these dayes, he would not call a stretched forth neck, and wanton eye, a Mincing as they go, by the name of good carriage." In fact, he asserts, that the devil likes to give "Golden Names" to corrupt behavior; in "this debauched Age," he adds, "frequent Osculations" among those not married is called by the term of "good Breeding." He quickly dispenses with the third plea. To the assertion that children are pleased with dancing, Mather responds that this is no surprise. Any activity that agrees with the corrupt natures of children is clear evidence of the evils of the activity. As a corollary, the fourth plea argues that dancing has become customary among Christians. Equally quickly, Mather declares that Christians ought to keep themselves separated from worldly customs, "pure from the sins of the Times."[15]

In a further variation on the theme of preference and custom, some people have argued that good men think dancing is lawful. With alacrity, Mather pronounces that Christians must walk by the authority of Scripture, not by the wisdom or example of good men. Clarifying this historical point of view, he declares: "But we cannot call to mind one Protestant Author who has been real for the interest of Reformation, that has set his Pen on work to plead for a practice so vile and infamous." Emphasizing his Bible-based view, Mather asserts that Scripture also teaches the duty of churches to discipline those members who offend. As testimony to the importance of this admonition, he cites the practice of disciplining dancers by the National Synod at Dort (1578); by several provincial assemblies in Holland; and by synods of the French Reformed church. Given such precedent, Mather queries incredulously: "And shall Churches in N.E. who have had a Name to be stricter and purer than other Churches, suffer such a scandalous evil amongst them?" Further, those church members who sent their children to be dancers or viewers of mixed dancing "have cause to be deeply humbled." Reminiscent of Calvin's sermon on Job, Mather alleges that such action typifies the behavior of the vain and wicked men whom the prophet laments. "The Catechism which Wicked men teach their Children is to Dance and to Sing. Not that Dancing, or Musick, or Singing are in themselves sinful: but if the Dancing Master be wicked they are commonly abused to Lasciviousness, and that makes them to become abominable."[16]

Mather's emphasis on parental responsibility recalls the charge to parents issued in the sixteenth century by the Lutheran Hyperius. Those who solemnly promised on behalf of their children to renounce the devil and all his pomps must not turn around and send them to learn dancing, the tool of the devil. To New England parents, Mather admonishes: "If you resolve not on Reformation, you will be left inexcusable." Softening his final exhortation, he urges the reader to carefully consider these words and the Lord will provide understanding.[17]

Mather's Position among Dance Opponents

In asserting that Scripture takes precedence over custom and the judgment of good men, Mather stands fully in the mainstream of Protestant reformers who elevated the Bible over dicta of popes and church councils. To reformers, the Bible provided the one essential means for knowing God in Christ as well as for understanding the nature of sin and its consequences. The Reformation had been launched on the basis of biblical interpretation. Thus, reformers knew their Bible well and skillfully separated the positive examples of dancing recorded in the Old Testament from those found in contemporary practice. In their role as ministers and theologians called to

interpret Scripture for the laity, reformers deduced from principles and generalizations to specific warnings and prohibitions. That is, where specific do's
and don'ts are absent from the Bible, sixteenth- and seventeenth-century
clerics produced expositions in the greatest detail to inform the laity of right
moral conduct. Though not writing a "case of conscience," Mather stands
squarely within this Reformation era tradition.

The timing of Mather's treatise and his references to dancing masters and
artificial postures acquired in dancing indicate that he aimed the "Arrow"
after the fleeing Stepney. His lack of contemporary descriptions of dancing
suggests that the practice of dance that existed in Boston may not have been
highly visible. Unlike Brant, Calvin, Daneau, Stubbes, and Northbrooke,
who provide short but graphic passages about the disorderly performance
of dancers, their immoral gestures, and the wanton ditties accompanying
the dances of their day, Mather remains silent on the subject. One could
almost surmise that he had written the treatise as a rhetorical exercise, giv-
en the fact that his proofs and evidence rely only on historical information,
European authors, and Scripture. Yet the treatise against "Prophane customs"
witnesses to the prior existence of "Promiscuous Dancing," and the grammatical tense Mather uses in indicting parents—"Such Church-Members
in N.E., as have sent their Children to be Practitioners"—indicates apparently recent action by parents.[18] Mather's tone clearly establishes that he, as
a pastor, wrote to persuade people that it was sinful to dance. Therefore, he
could only have been writing against a perceived threat to the life and faith
of the church.

That threat did not seem to be gender-specific. Mather opposes "mixt"
dancing but does not denigrate women in particular as temptresses or as
agents of the devil. The strongest attack on women, in terms of argument,
would be his Isaiah 3:16 reference, regarding vain and proud carriage by the
daughters of Zion, as a Bible verse that prohibits dancing. But Mather does
not elaborate or dwell on the point; he simply refers to European authors
who asserted that the passage pertained to artificial postures acquired at
dancing schools. The few references to women that Mather cites as part of
his historical authorities and examples do not unduly blame females for the
alleged immorality and/or heresy surrounding dancing. The references are
simply more citations in a series. In this context, only one reference to "Indians," witches, and the devil appears. The burden of Mather's arguments
points to the sinfulness of "mixt" dancing, for both men and women. Argument 5, for example, begins, "For *Persons* to Dance at a time when God
calls them to mourn, is certainly unlawful. But such is the case at this Day"

(emphasis mine). He also addresses church members, Christians, parents, young persons, and dancers. No admonition speaks only to women. Neither does Mather refer to seductive dress; to elaborate hair, jewelry, or painted faces; to wanton songs; or to wasting money. Yet, the indictment of parents who sent children to dance masters and the charges against the fleeing Stepney suggest that dancing parties for men and women existed at that time.

Evidence of Dancing

What then is the external evidence for dancing in New England? In fact, there is very little. Taken together, the bits and pieces of information form a picture that testifies that the Puritans did indeed dance in the seventeenth century. In an analysis of early dance music, Joy Van Cleef posits that the dancing occurred informally and spontaneously in homes and taverns, perhaps out of doors.[19] Puritan opinion on the subject of dancing and the fact that the Massachusetts Bay Colony had a strong, established church make it unlikely that there would have been formal, organized gatherings specifically aimed at dancing, at least not prior to the advent of dancing masters.

That dancing occurred informally in homes and taverns is indicated by laws for its regulation. Percy Scholes's analysis of Puritan music and dance shows that in 1631 and again in 1651 laws were passed forbidding dancing in taverns, where the activity apparently happened to celebrate weddings. The legislation sought to remedy abuses and disorders that had occurred. Another law that attempted to maintain civil order applied to the night watchman who was to report noise or disorderly behavior at the time of his ten o'clock rounds. Court records indicate that laws were enforced. For example, in 1641 at Salem, David Owls had to pay a fine of twenty shillings or sit in the stocks for leaping and dancing in his house. Twelve years later the same court fined Thomas Wheeler for "profane and foolish" dancing as well as immoral speech. Scholes also cites court cases for the 1670s that indicate people were cited for dancing and disorderly behavior as well as for breaking curfew. Though court records are not always comprehensive, there is no lack of clarity regarding the prohibition against dancing with Indians. For example, Scholes declares that a compendium of New Haven blue laws reveals that citizens of Connecticut, as of October 1678, were forbidden to frequent Indian meetings and dances because it encouraged the natives in their "Divill worship."[20] The sum of this sparse and negative evidence suggests that legislation against dancing per se did not exist. Rather, laws seem intended to forbid dancing where it provoked civil disorder and perceived pagan practices. Had there been no dancing, there would have been no need for such legislation.

Other evidence from diaries and biographies suggests that attitudes toward dancing varied among individual Puritans. For example, as early as the mid-1620s a group of troublesome fellows led by Thomas Morton had set up a May pole at Merry Mount and entertained themselves for several days by drinking and dancing with Indian women. William Bradford's account of the incident reports that they resembled "madd Bachinalians."[21] Samuel Sewall wrote in his diary for 26 May 1687 that the May pole at Charleston had been cut down the preceding week and then a bigger one replaced it. The next day's notes reveal that, in conversation with Father Walker, Sewall learned the other man had heard conversation about the practice in England of dancing about a May pole and "that 'twas to be feared such practices would be here."[22]

In contrast, Scholes reports that Oliver Cromwell had a wedding dance to celebrate the marriage of one of his daughters. The possibility of another context for dancing occurs in the citation by Henry Bamford Parkes, a biographer of Jonathan Edwards, regarding the latter's father. Parkes records that when the senior Edwards was ordained in 1694 in Connecticut, he held a dance in his house to celebrate the occasion. Then, in perhaps typical student fashion, Joseph Green, Harvard class of 1665, records in his diary that at school he "wasted much time in various sports and dancing."[23] The context of both sports and dancing suggests that Green would not have participated in them alone. The recreational propensities of college students also suggest that such participation would not have been an isolated incident. Given the influx of more tolerant Anglicans in the latter part of the century, as well as continued immigration and natural increase of the population, it is highly probable that dancing would have continued. Certainly by the turn of the century Cotton Mather was greatly exercised by the existence of dancing.

Cotton Mather's Analysis

Not all Puritans considered dancing a sign of worldliness and falling away from the true faith, but Cotton Mather (1663–1728), the son of Increase Mather, surely did. Educated at Harvard, the recipient of a divinity degree from the University of Glasgow, Cotton Mather was his father's assistant at the North Church and became perhaps the most learned man of his day in America.[24]

The Magnalia Christi

In his *Magnalia Christi Americana,* a comprehensive ecclesiastical history complete to the year 1698, the younger Mather catalogs the several evils in New England that, in his opinion, had provoked God's judgment on the populace. Those evils pointed to the people's lack of piety as well as their particular sins and worldly behavior.

Specifically, Mather noted that parishioners demonstrated great pride by refusing to submit to order and by wearing "strange Apparel, not becoming serious Christians, especially in these Days of Affliction and Misery, wherein the Lord calls upon Men to put off their Ornaments, Exod. 33:5 Jer. 4:30." Church fellowship was neglected, God's name profaned, and the Sabbath broken—apparently on a regular basis. Family order and discipline had dissipated, and intemperance had become much too common. According to Mather, town-dwellers and church members spent too much time in taverns or "publick Houses" intended only for the accommodation of strangers. Mather placed dancing in his catalog of temptations to breaking the Seventh Commandment: "immodest Apparel, Prov. 7:10 laying out of Hair, Borders, naked Necks, and Arms, or which is more abominable naked Breasts, and mixed Dancings, light Behaviour, and Expressions, sinful Company-keeping with light and vain Persons, unlawful Gaming, an abundance of Idleness." He concluded his enumeration of evils with charges of idolatry, that is, loving the world too much and lacking sufficient public spirit to improve the community and its schools.

Though women are clearly indicted in the description of immodest apparel and appearance, the remainder of Mather's complaint is aimed at both sexes, perhaps more pointedly at men. Contemporary church historians note, for example, that it was the Puritan men who fell away from the church but the women who continued to join. Thus, Mather condemns the worldliness of both men and women in Boston at the end of the century.[25]

The "Cloud of Witnesses"

Probably two years after completing the *Magnalia Christi,* Mather felt compelled to write specifically against dancing, "the Dancing Humour, as it now prevails, and especially in Balls, or in circumstances that Lead the Young People of both Sexes, unto great Liberties with one another."[26] Mather clarifies at the outset that the question is not whether "people of Quality" can employ a grave and circumspect dancing master to teach children proper carriage but whether the custom of dancing was a vanity forbidden to Christians. The phrase "People of Quality" would have referred to those who had sufficient time and money to afford amenities such as lessons from a dance master and attendance at balls. The argument suggests, perhaps, that there had been an increase in wealth and leisure during the fifteen years since Increase Mather had written. The senior Mather had stipulated that "to learn a due Poyse and Composure of Body" was not unlawful, provided the teaching was modest—that it did not foster pride or vanity—and the teacher was "some Grave Person." He could have been speaking to actual practice or he could have been theorizing in such a statement. By contrast, Cotton Mather's caveat implied that lessons in posture and carriage, from a dance master, had become customary. Thus he hoped to stem the tide of balls as fashionable and regular events. His attack points to a criticism of social class as well as dancing.

Unlike his father, Cotton Mather presents a defensive posture. It is as though he had been criticized and perhaps anticipated much outcry for his stance. Indeed, the more his opposition became a minority point of view, the greater the probability that he would have been criticized. Accordingly, he stipulates at the outset of his "Cloud of Witnesses": "Wherefore that the Reader may have no pretence to be Angry at any One such Minister, in the World, we will only bring some other Authorities." At the end, he poses the question whether or not a nonconformist minister can be "justly Reproached" for faithfully trying to exhort parishioners to guard their own and their children's virtue. Both the title of his work and the qualifiers he invokes suggest his desire to justify his position against the behavior of the majority, a contrast to the assertive and confident tone of Increase Mather, who had the backing of several Boston clergy. Although Cotton Mather's name is not affixed to the "Cloud of Witnesses," bibliographers have clearly established his authorship.[27]

The younger Mather presents nothing new in substantive arguments. In analysis, title, and most of the authorities he cites, he borrows from his father. The title of his work repeats the somewhat picturesque phrase from Hebrews 12:1 that Increase had used to describe the large number of English divines who had written against dancing. The authorities he mentions fall into the same categories mentioned by the elder Mather: church fathers, ancient pagan writers, Reformed church councils, English bishops, and Roman Catholics. Though his citations are shorter than those his father gave, and, in some cases include more recent writers, his analysis follows the same general line of reasoning though it lacks in degree of specificity.

He begins by noting that Scripture opposes dancing on the grounds of the Seventh Commandment and the linguistic translations that render rioting and reveling to encompass dancing. Like his father, he urges that Christians think only on that which is "of Good Report."[28] In typical style for the era, he calls forth historical witnesses to substantiate his position. However, he omits most of the sixteenth- and seventeenth-century continental reformers cited by his father and many of the latter century's English divines and theologians. Forbearing to copy the ancient Fabritius, Cotton Mather quotes at some length from two seventeenth-century French Catholic dance opponents, neither of whom are mentioned in the "Arrow." Probably this singular departure from his father's arguments occurred because both Frenchmen argued against balls as well as against dancing in general.

Quoting first and most extensively from Father Le Jeune (1592–1672), a member of the French Oratory of Jesus and a man known for his sanctity, Mather selected passages that speak to the traditional arguments that align dancing with the devil and remind the Christian reader about baptismal vows, which renounced the devil as well as all attendant pomps and vanities. The passages also emphasize the importance of stewarding time and cultivating a spirit of piety, charity, and repentance. Though not in an exact translation, Mather also describes how Father Le Jeune, like Calvin, reminded readers of Job's lament about the vain and wicked men whose children danced. Recalling Vermigli's sixteenth-century verdicts on marriages and dancing, Father Le Jeune, in Mather's translation, declared that no man of common sense would prefer a dancer, "a giddy, and an idle Damsel," to a "Modest, Reserv'd, and Retired" gentlewoman. However, the passage also includes the proviso that if young gentlewomen wanted to be well provided for, they would surely choose a man of "Sense and Judgment."[29]

The statement is the only one in both Mathers' analyses that contrasts two views of women, the negative one of the "idle Damsel" and the positive view of the modest and retiring gentlewoman. Cotton Mather offers no elaboration and no clue as to whether or not poor marriages had resulted from men and women meeting at balls. His including that part of Father LeJeune's testimony is the only thing that hints at any gender specificity in the younger Mather's writing.

Concluding his selection from the "Papist" churchmen, Mather adds testimony from a courtier, as though to clinch the case against dancing. Count Roger de Bussy-Rabutin (1618–93) confesses that his own experience testifies to the evils of balls, because that is where desires of even the "coldest Constitutions" are ignited. Mather continues his translation by asserting, in capital letters, that "A CHRISTIAN OUGHT NOT TO BE AT A BALL."[30]

Further, he includes Bussy-Rabutin's view that all those who are responsible for developing the conscience of children and adults ought to feel duty-bound to prohibit dancing for people under their direction. As a staunch Puritan, Mather stood in the line of those who believed that the minister was to guide and direct the lives of parishioners by instruction, exhortation, and admonition. Lest his own laity think him eccentric, he had in Bussy-Rabutin the support of one who came from groups considered especially worldly—namely, the French, the Catholics, and the courtiers. The citation suggests a broader frame of reference in which the Mathers must be viewed.

The Larger Context

Often unjustly maligned for what later American generations have considered puritanical attitudes, New England Puritans of the seventeenth century were not alone in their opposition to dancing. Research by Judith Rock demonstrates that the Jansenists vigorously opposed dancing. Similar to the Calvinists in theological outlook, members of this French Catholic order were inclined perhaps to be even more otherworldly, that is, to advocate withdrawal from the distractions of a world that turned people away from God. In particular, they opposed the Jesuit ballet and theater for being too costly and too closely aligned with the secular theater and its personages.[31] On the English side of the channel, Joseph Bentham (1594?–1671), a clergyman with royalist sympathies, wrote against mixed dancing in 1656. His treatise reads remarkably like those of sixteenth-century reformers in both substance and tone.[32] The fact is not surprising for his authorities include Vermigli, Rainolds, and Perkins, as well as early church fathers.

Courtesy Books

One can also find attitudes inimical to dancing among the seventeenth-century English books on piety and civility that were widely read in the colonies. For example, Henry Peacham (1576?–1643?), in his 1622 treatise, *The Compleat Gentleman,* advocated drawing, painting, music, and physical exercise but made no mention of dancing as a polite accomplishment. However, his 1642 essay "The Art of Living in London" identified dancing, fencing, riding, and painting as among those arts taught for money. Since it is his only mention of dance or dancing, the reference seems rather disparaging. The son of a clergyman, Peacham studied at Cambridge while William Perkins preached there, but Peacham sympathized with the royalist cause.[33]

Similarly, Richard Brathwait (1588?–1673), who also favored the royalist side, authored courtesy books popular in the colonies. Although the historian Lawrence Cremin reports that the colonists did not read Brathwait's *The English Gentlewoman* (1631) as avidly as they studied his manual *The English Gentleman* (1630), Brathwait's advice to the lady is, nevertheless, illuminating.[34] He spells out detailed instructions for the Christian gentlewoman—admonitions that were generally absent from similar sixteenth-century courtesy books but that foreshadow the outpouring of instructions on character and piety to the American lady of the nineteenth century. Notable also is the fact that Brathwait, unlike the Mathers, continues the centuries-old avowal that the devil fostered dancing and that those who revel in it are both immodest and imitative of the pagans. Thus, the gentlewoman reader learned that:

> To lead a dance gracefully; to marry your voyce to your instrument musically; to expresse your selves in prose and verse morally; are commendable qualities, and enforcing motives of affection. Yet I must tell you, for the first, though it appeare by your feet to be but a meere *dimension,* in the opinion of the Learned it is the *Divels procession;* Where the *Dance* is the *Circle,* whose *centre is* the *Devil,* Which may be restrained by a more easie or moderate glasse to such wanton and immodest *Revels,* as have anciently been used in the Celebration of their prophane feasts by Pagans, and are to this day by Pagan-christians; who, to gaine applause from the Spectator, care not what shamelesse parts they play in the presence of their Maker. But what are these worth, being compared with those inward Ornaments or beauties of your *mind;* which onely distinguish you from other creatures, and make you soveraignesses over the rest of Gods creatures? . . . Hold it no such necessary poynt of *Complement,* to shew a kinde of majesty in a *Dance;* and to preferre it before the Complement of a Religious taske.[35]

In exhorting the reader to a life of holiness, Brathwait draws a sharp contrast between the ideal for the Christian gentlewoman and the negative model in the tradition of the biblical Eve. Brathwait's ideal emphasizes mind over body and religious duties over social or artistic accomplishments such as dancing. The lady is to make virtue her ornament and the practice of piety her highest aim. Brathwait concludes with the admonition that one is to be guided by goodness and, reminiscent of the apostle Paul, to put on the "armour" of "righteousnesse," to demonstrate lowliness, and to be complete in holiness.

By contrast, Brathwait warns that the courtesan who delights in song will wail in hell. The unvirtuous woman knows how to dance a "Morrice" and

a "Pavin," while her looks entice to lasciviousness. In effect, the sensual crea-
ture focuses on vanity instead of fixing her gaze on eternity. Exhorting the
gentlewoman to the Christian ideal, Brathwait declares that a woman's honor
"is of higher esteem" than such "light and uncivill appearances."[36]

Pointing up the clear gender differences current in the century, Brathwait's book on *The English Gentleman* devoted nothing to apparel, an extensive subject for the lady, but gives over separate chapters to topics not
included for the lady, such as education, vocation, and recreation. His views
on dancing appear under the last heading. Brathwait allows dancing to be
a recreation that fits a gentleman for court. Yet, as in the sixteenth century,
the gentleman was to hold to moderation and to avoid affectation. Interestingly, Brathwait does not address the unspoken problem of a partner for
the gentleman to whom dancing is recommended. Since the book for the
gentlewoman was written a year later, he may have conveniently forgotten
that he had approved the art for the gentleman when he wrote to the lady
that it was the "Divels procession."[37]

Less problematic was the royalist sympathizer and minister Richard Allestree (1619–81), who wrote both courtesy and piety literature in which
he gave clear counsel respecting idleness and pastimes. Cremin calls Allestree's *The Whole Duty of Man* (1658) one of the three most popular piety
handbooks in the American colonies.[38] In that book as well as in his conduct books, *The Gentleman's Calling* (1660) and *The Ladies Calling* (1668),
Allestree sets a clear and strict context for recreations in which "the well
husbanding of this time" becomes all important for the Christian who considers his or her venture on earth but a "Prologue to Eternity elsewhere."
Though he does not single out dancing or other pastimes except for hunting and hawking, the context Allestree spells out clearly excludes a questionable activity like dancing: "for as for Sports and Pastimes, the best of them
come so near to Idleness, and the worst of them to Vice, that as the one is
not to be allowed any, so the other no considerable part of their time." Like
Renaissance writers, he considered idleness the mother of all vice, or in his
words, "the one fertile Seminary of most other Sins." In addition, the gentlewoman reader learned, as she had with Brathwait, that she must make
modesty, meekness, compassion, affability, courtesy, and piety her duty as
well as her ornament.[39]

Given this sampling of the larger context, neither Increase Mather nor
Cotton Mather can be considered eccentric in their opposition to dancing
and balls. However, they both stood with a diminishing minority of New
Englanders at the end of the seventeenth century. Fragmented evidence

testifies to the futility of their pleas and exhortations to proscribe dancing. Preaching a funeral sermon in Boston in 1708, upon the death of Ezekiel Cheever, former principal of the Latin School, Cotton Mather seemed to reflect back on concern he expressed in the *Magnalia Christi* ten years earlier, namely, that people were not sufficiently community-minded to improve the schools. On Cheever's death, Mather laments that adults counted no expense too much to put children into clothing or to have them learn "'some trifle'" at a dancing school, yet the same people remained unwilling to pay schoolmasters to train their children's minds and impart the riches of knowledge. Three years later Mather's diary records that he deplored an incident wherein several young people under his charge had celebrated Christmas night in reveling and a ball.[40]

By 1708 Boston's population numbered close to nine thousand people.[41] To expect uniformity of Puritan belief in a city of such size would have been unrealistic. Almost a century had elapsed since the start of the great migration. In the interim, not only had third- and fourth-generation Puritan descendants grown to adulthood, but people of other faiths and countries had landed in New England as well. Heterogeneity was becoming the norm despite the warnings and exhortations of the Mathers, who aimed to call people from worldliness to holiness.

The Ideal for the Christian and the Ideal for Gentlefolk

The Puritan ideal for the Christian, which derived from Scripture as well as from the sermons and writings of Protestant Reformers, particularly those of the Calvinist persuasion, depicted a person separated from the world in appearance and behavior. The Puritan concentrated on business, industry, and honest callings. The ideal stressed church, Bible reading, and Sabbath keeping but avoided the fashionable, often corrupt, customs of the world that served no useful purpose.[42] In Increase Mather's words: "But shall Christian [sic] follow the course of the World? They ought to swim against the stream, and to keep themselves pure from the sins of the Times of which this of *mixed dancing* is none of the least." The Puritan was to appear pious, sober, and grave, as Scripture admonished. The ideal also emphasized being civil, polite, and poised but these traits were not to be acquired through the instruction of a dancing master: "Religion is no Enemy to good Manners." To learn good carriage and "Composure of Body" was appropriate so long as the lessons did not foster pride and vanity.[43] Preachers, parents, Bible, and catechism, therefore, proved the best and essential instructors.

Every Christian needed right teaching, because human nature was born in sin. John Cotton's catechism for "Boston Babes in either England" taught that the notion of total depravity should be inculcated early in life so that temptation to sin could be resisted. To engage in pastimes such as dancing, which fostered pride and vanity, only nourished that which ought to be killed. Ever mindful of one's own depraved nature and the unfathomable sovereignty of a God who would ultimately render a final judgment, the devout Puritan understood that the doctrine of predestination translated into uncertainty about one's eternal salvation. When a final judgment would call for an accounting of every idle deed as well as word, decisions to spend time in dancing took on the consequences of eternity.

In the New World the Puritan ideal did not encounter competition with the ideal for the gentleman, as sixteenth-century writers had depicted. Allegiance to king and courtly tradition did not carry the weight that it had in the Old World. Moreover, the New England settling of towns varied dramatically from the centuries-old pattern of landed estates owned by the nobility. The tradition of landed wealth and aristocratic arts or pastimes flourished in southern colonies where the European concept of the gentleman took hold. But as large urban centers became more cosmopolitan, with an increase of wealth and leisure, the number of dance masters, schools, and assemblies also increased throughout the colonies. And, in Puritan Boston, a dance master even became associated with the Anglican church.

An Anglican Organist and Dancing Master

Perhaps the death knell for Puritan attitudes toward dancing was sounded in the early eighteenth century by the Anglican church in Boston. King's Chapel had been paid for, through the efforts of Governor Andros, and dedicated in 1689. In 1713 its vestrymen voted to install an organ, a gift from Thomas Brattle. The gift caused some distress, because traditionally Puritans did not approve of musical instruments in their church worship. Though Cotton Mather approved singing to praise God, he had written in the *Magnalia Christi* that to use instruments as was done in cathedrals tended "too much to Judaize . . . as well as to Paganize."[44] Nonetheless, the proponents of the organ won out, and it was duly installed. The problem then remained to find a competent organist.

In February 1714 the vestrymen asked their representative in London to inquire after the qualifications of one Edward Enstone and to see if he would be willing to sail for Boston. As Norman Arthur Benson observes in his recording of this incident, the fact that the Boston church knew of Enstone suggests a very early intercultural exchange with respect to music. After negotiations over pay, the vestrymen offered Enstone a salary as organist and gave him permission to augment that salary by teaching dancing and music lessons. According to Benson's account, when Enstone arrived in Boston, he took seriously the offer to teach dancing. But not so the Boston selectmen who, sometime before 1 April 1716, refused Enstone permission to keep a dancing school in town. Enstone, however, opened his school anyway, on 16 April 1716. His advertisement noted that dancing would be taught by an "'easier method'" than had heretofore been used. Samuel Sewall notes in the same year that Enstone gave a ball on 29 November. Sewall and other Puritans feared that the governor's presence at the ball would be a sign of royal, as well as Anglican, patronage.[45]

Enstone's contract was renewed and he continued for some years in his dual roles as organist for King's Chapel and dancing master. Benson reports that a 1720 advertisement in the *Boston Gazette* announced that Enstone had moved to larger quarters and that Thursdays henceforth were public days when visitors might come to watch the dancing. Benson speculates that the latter was a promotion drive to increase students for Enstone. Whether or not the King's Chapel vestrymen thought that Enstone was moonlighting too much is not clear. But by the early 1720s they were interested in training new organists for their church. Enstone's behavior certainly contributed to his alienation from the church. On 1 April 1724 the General Court charged him with unlawful cohabitation with a single woman during the previous June and July. Five days later the vestrymen and the entire congregation voted on Enstone's replacement.[46] Though dismissed as organist from the Anglican church, Enstone was not the last of the dancing masters in Boston.

Notes

1. Increase Mather, "An Arrow Against Profane and Promiscuous Dancing Drawn out of the Quiver of the Scriptures" (Boston, [1685]; rpt. in *The Mathers on Dancing*, ed. Joseph E. Marks III, Brooklyn: Dance Horizons, 1975), 47–49.

2. Samuel Sewall, *The Diary of Samuel Sewall 1674–1729*, ed. M. Halsey Thomas, 2 vols. (New York: Farrar, Strauss, and Giroux, 1973), 1:83, 88, 95, 96, 118. Thomas notes in the preface that the Julian calendar under which Sewall wrote began a new year on 25 March. Accordingly, he dates the publication of the "Arrow" as "Feb. 16, 1685/6."

3. Marks mentions the 1670s school in his introduction to *The Mathers on Dancing* (12–13), as does Norman Arthur Benson in his "Itinerant Dance and Music Masters of the Eighteenth Century" (Ph.D. diss., University of Minnesota, 1963), 323–24; but Marks and Benson cite different years. However, Barbara Lambert reports that a careful search of the records revealed no original source for a school in the 1670s. See Barbara Lambert, Appendix C: "Music Masters in Colonial Boston," in *Music in Colonial Massachusetts, 1630–1820* (Boston: Colonial Society of Massachusetts, 1985), vol. 2.

4. Marks, *Mathers on Dancing*, 7.

5. Increase Mather, *A Testimony Against several Prophane and Superstitious Customs* . . . (London, 1687; rpt., Charlottesville: University of Virginia Press, 1953), 10, 13. Cotton Mather explains, in his *Magnalia Christi,* that health-drinking was a pagan custom originally. To drink as part of an invocation was considered idolatry. See *Magnalia Christi Americana: Or, The Ecclesiastical History of New England* . . . (London: Thomas Parkhurst, 1702), 55.

6. Ibid., 5, 18.

7. Ibid., 7.

8. Marks, *Mathers on Dancing*, 23. Increase Mather's education and status among contemporaries no doubt accounted for his attributed authorship of the anonymous treatise against dancing. Not only was Mather an ordained clergyman, he was also president of Harvard College. The outpouring from Mather's pen continued from 1669 until 1722 and testifies to a learned mind as well as prodigious effort.

9. Mather, "Arrow," 32–33.

10. Ibid., 32–36.

11. Ibid., 37–44, 46–47.

12. For this distinction, Mather was indebted to his father-in-law, the Reverend John Cotton, a popular preacher and prime intellectual of his day in New England, who wrote *A Briefe Exposition With Practicall Observations Upon The Whole Book of Ecclesiastes* (London: T.C., 1654). In his initial clarification, Cotton points out that the opening passage in Ecclesiastes means simply that all things under heaven "are subject to a variety and vicissitude of changes, and that by the determinate appointment and limitation of God." More specifically, in reference to verse four, Cotton writes that one use of the text is: "To take off the plea for dancing hence. For it is not said there is a lawful time to dance, but a limited time." To have "a set or limited time or a determinate period" does not mean that there is a fit season for any of the several activities listed in the chapter. Cotton asserts that the entire passage speaks to the sovereignty of God; that is, the several changes and estates that befall men come by the divinely appointed hand of God. See Cotton, *Briefe Exposition,* 56, 58, 57.

13. Ibid., 58; Mather, "Arrow," 49.

14. Mather, "Arrow," 49–50.

15. Ibid., 51–54.

16. Ibid., 55, 57–58; 2 Thess. 3:6. The French Reformed church, begun in 1559, included many ministers who had trained under Calvin or at his academy in Geneva. The Genevan Catechism of 1545 proscribed dancing under the Seventh Commandment. The 1579 and 1581 synods of the French Reformed church referred to discipline of dancers. See Eug. and E. M. Haag, *La France Protestante: ou, Vies des Protestants Français . . . ,* vol. 10 (Paris, 1858), s.v. "National Synods"; George Rothrock, *The Huguenots: A Biography of a Minority* (Chicago: Nelson-Hall, 1979), 63; J. K. S. Reid, ed., *Calvin: Theological Treatises,* vol. 22, Library of Christian Classics (Philadelphia: Westminster Press, 1954), 115, 81.

17. Mather, "Arrow," 59. See my discussion in chapter 2, above, regarding the charges of Andreas Gerardus Hyperius, Lutheran homiletician, that dancing breaks the Fourth Commandment.

18. Ibid., 57. Samuel Sewall's diary makes clear that Mather's "Arrow" appeared twelve days after the court fined Francis Stepney, the dance master.

19. Joy Van Cleef and Kate Van Winkle Keller, "Selected American Country Dances and Their English Sources," in *Music in Colonial Massachusetts, 1630–1820* (Boston: Colonial Society of Massachusetts, 1980), vol. 1, 1, 5.

20. Percy Scholes, *The Puritans and Music in England and New England* (New York: Russel and Russel, 1962), 78–79, 375–76.

21. Cotton Mather, *On Witchcraft, being the Wonders of the Invisible World* (1693; rpt., Mt. Vernon, N.Y.: Peter Pauper Press, [1950?]) 120; Perry Miller and Thomas H. Johnson, eds., *The Puritans,* rev. ed. (New York: Harper Torchbooks, 1963), vol. 1, 108.

22. Sewall, *Diary,* vol. 1, 140–41.

23. Scholes, *Puritans,* 60; Henry Bamford Parkes, *Jonathan Edwards, the Fiery Puritan* (New York: Minton-Balch, 1930), 28, 83; Joan English, "Dance in Seventeenth-Century Massachusetts with Particular Reference to Indian, Puritan, and Anglican Cultures" (Ph.D. diss., University of Wisconsin, Madison, 1969), 39.

24. William B. Sprague, *Annals of the American Pulpit* (New York: Robt. Carter and Bros., 1857), vol. 1, 189–95.

25. Cotton Mather, *Magnalia Christi,* 88–91. See also the discussion on the decline of New England in Larzer Ziff's *Puritanism in America* (New York: Viking, 1973), 191ff. See analysis of gender and the church in Susan Hill Lindley, *"You Have Stept Out of Your Place": A History of Women and Religion in America* (Louisville: Westminster/John Knox Press, 1996), ch. 3, "Puritanism."

26. Cotton Mather, "A Cloud of Witnesses; Darting out Light upon a Case, too Unseasonably made Seasonable to be Discoursed on" (Boston: [B. Green and J. Allen], [1700]); rpt. in *The Mathers on Dancing,* ed. Marks, 65, 87.

27. Ibid., 65, 75; Marks, *Mathers on Dancing,* 23.

28. Cotton Mather, "Cloud of Witnesses," 66.

29. Ibid., 72–73.

30. Ibid., 73–74.

31. Judith Rock, "The Jesuits Go for Baroque: Theatrical Dance on the Old Order College Stage," *Proceedings, Society of Dance History Scholars,* Seventh Annual Conference, Goucher College, 17–19 Feb. 1984, 85–86.

32. Joseph Bentham, *ΧΟΡΟΘΕΟΛΟΓΟΝ Or Two Briefe but Usefull Treatises . . . The Other Of the Nature and . . . The Accidents of Mixt Dancing* (London: Thomas Roycroft, 1657).

33. Lawrence A. Cremin, *American Education: The Colonial Experience 1607– 1783* (New York: Harper Torchbooks, 1970), 68–70; Stanley J. Kunitz and Howard Haycraft, *British Authors before 1800* (New York: Wilson, 1952), 397; Henry Peacham, *The Complete Gentleman, The Truth of Our Times, and the Art of Living in London* (Ithaca: Cornell University Press, 1962), viii, 245.

34. Cremin, *American Education,* 71.

35. Richard Brathwait, *The English Gentlewoman . . .* (London: B. Alsop and T. Fawcet, 1631; rpt., Amsterdam: Theatrum Orbis Terrarum, 1970), 76–77.

36. Brathwait, *Gentlewoman,* 77–79, 29. Further emphasizing an apparent dislike of dance for the Christian gentlewoman, Brathwait stresses the importance of modesty in dress: "Let May-games and Morrices beautifie themselves with Anticke dressings, to captivate the vulgar eye; your breeding hath beene better . . . than to stoope to such base Lures" (7). His entire chapter on apparel stresses modesty and natural appearance in contrast to artificial, vain, and fashionable attire and adornment.

37. Richard Brathwait, *The English Gentleman* (London: John Haviland, 1630; rpt., Amsterdam: Theatrum Orbis Terrarum, 1975), 204–5, 221–23.

38. Cremin, *American Education,* 44. Gerald Carson observes that a list of all the owners of this book during America's first two hundred years would read like a register of first families of the South. See *The Polite Americans* (London: Macmillan, 1967), 50.

39. Richard Allestree, *The Gentleman's Calling* (London: R. Norton, 1668), 92, a3. Arthur Schlesinger characterizes Allestree's *The Ladies Calling* as the "mainstay" for colonial women, though they also read other imported civility books. See Schlesinger, *Learning How to Behave* (New York: Macmillan, 1946), 6. Richard Baxter, whose *The Poor Man's Family Book* (1674), was another of the most widely read piety books, agrees on the overriding importance of stewarding time. Dancing, stage plays, and worldly honors are specifically mentioned as outside the boundaries for wise use of time. See a complete exposition in his monumental summa of Christian ethics, *Christian Directory* (1673), 282, 272.

40. Scholes, *Puritans,* 65; English, "Dance in Seventeenth-Century Massachusetts," 38.

41. Carl Bridenbaugh, *Cities in the Wilderness* (New York: Ronald Press, 1938), 143.

42. Ziff, *Puritanism in America,* 19.

43. Mather, "Arrow," 54, 52.

44. Benson, "Itinerant Dance and Music Masters," 332–33; Cotton Mather, *Magnalia Christi*, 55.

45. Benson, "Itinerant Dance and Music Masters," 334–38; Sewall, *Diary*, vol. 2, 838.

46. *Music in Colonial Massachusetts, 1630–1820*, vol. 2, 977; Benson, "Itinerant Dance and Music Masters," 339–40.

4 The Gentry and the Awakening: The Eighteenth Century

And since nothing appears to me to give Children so much becoming Confidence and Behavior . . . as *dancing;* I think they should be taught to Dance, as soon as they are capable of learning it.

John Locke, 1693

It grieves me to find that in every little town there is a settled dancing-master, but scarcely anywhere a settled minister.

George Whitefield, 1739

Eighteenth-century writings on dance display a fully developed tension that continued from the sixteenth century, between the ideal for the gentleman and the ideal for the Christian. John Locke's *Thoughts Concerning Education,* widely read in the colonies, represented the former, maintaining the tradition begun for Englishmen by Sir Thomas Elyot's *Governour* some 160 years earlier. But Locke espoused dancing for different reasons than had Elyot. Whereas Elyot had urged that young boys learn to dance for the sake of learning prudence, Locke stressed the social value of dance lessons for men and women.[1] Surprisingly, Locke's ideas sound similar to those of Increase Mather, yet they stand in dramatic contrast to the views on dance held by the eighteenth-century English evangelist George Whitefield.

Increase Mather had disdained the artificial postures learned at dancing school but permitted the study of "that which may be truly Ornamental, or a desireable Accomplishment," provided that children are instructed by some "Grave Person that will teach them Decency of Behaviour," with the sexes learning separately.[2] Neither Locke nor Mather advocated an agreeable posture and a pleasing carriage for their intrinsic aesthetic value. Instead, both men argued a utilitarian merit. Mather allowed good manners to be no enemy of religion; civility simply represented that courtesy which was required of a sober and grave Christian.

By contrast, Locke considered carriage and motion central to the good breeding of a gentleman, who was also a Christian. Civility required that people of gentle rank present a pleasing carriage and agreeable motion of the body coupled with good manners. Locke meant by the term "civility" no slavish attention to outward details of behavior merely for the sake of fashion. True courtesy, in his opinion, undergirded the outward portrayal of civility. He valued dancing because it presented a pleasing outer appearance but also because it seemed to promote some inner value:

> And since nothing appears to me to give Children so much becoming Confidence and Behaviour, and so to raise them to the conversation of those above their Age, as *dancing;* I think they should be taught to Dance, as soon as they are capable of learning it. For though this consist only in outward gracefulness of Motion, yet, I know not how, it gives Children manly Thoughts, and Carriage more than any thing. But otherwise, I would not have little Children much tormented about Punctilios, or Niceties of Breeding.

Because Locke's treatise on education was written for a gentleman's son, his thoughts on the value of dancing for girls are not recorded there. They appear instead in a letter to Mrs. Clarke, whose husband had first requested Locke's advice on the rearing of a son. Offering additional advice to Mrs. Clarke, at her request, Locke said that girls should "have a dancing master at home early." Young girls would thus acquire both "fashion and easy comely motion." Locke even suggested that bashful girls could benefit from going "to dance publicly in the dancing schools." But he cautioned that the latter could be overdone, for "too much shamefacedness better becomes a girl than too much confidence." Modesty plus beauty would better suit the feminine gender. Accordingly, Locke tells Mrs. Clarke to take care of her daughter's beauty as much as her health by having the girl exercise in shaded areas, thus keeping the hot sun from her young skin.[3]

While strongly recommending dance training, Locke warned that it must be taught by a fit dancing master. One who did not teach "what is graceful and becoming, and what gives freedom and easiness to all the Motions of the Body" was worse than no dance teacher at all. A natural posture and motion, though not fashionable, was preferred to "apish, affected Postures." Locke thought it "much more passable to put off the Hat, and make a Leg, like an honest Country Gentleman, than like an ill-fashion'd Dancing-Master." He considered affectation of any kind invariably offensive, because its display "in any part of our Carriage, is lighting up a Candle to our Defects; and never fails to make us be taken Notice of, either as wanting Sense, or wanting Sincerity." Accordingly, Locke preferred even a "Plain and rough Nature left to it self" over and against "an Artificial Ungracefulness, and such studied Ways of being ill fashion'd."[4]

The *Thoughts Concerning Education* spelled out Locke's four aims of education: virtue, wisdom, breeding, and learning. They establish him in the tradition of educating a Christian gentleman whose character and demeanor were beyond reproach. Virtue, the most important quality, derived from a foundation in and knowledge of God, "from whom we receive all our Good, who loves us, and gives us all Things." Wisdom corresponded somewhat to Elyot's prudence, the ability to manage practical affairs wisely. Good breeding or civility required an internal attitude opposed to offending others and a corresponding external expression of "that decency and gracefulness of Looks, Voice, Words, Motions, Gestures, and of all the whole outward Demeanour, which takes in Company, and makes those with whom we may converse, easie and well pleased." Locke's emphasis on both an inner civility and an outer presentation of good manners reflects an organic connection producing true courtesy in contrast to mere politeness, an affectation displaying the fashionable mannerisms of the age. Locke placed learning in last place among his aims of education; though important, it was subservient to the development of character in a gentleman. But, as a part of learning, Locke, like Mather, would have the young gentleman learn by heart the Lord's Prayer, the Creeds, and the Ten Commandments.[5]

Given Locke's concept of breeding, it is not surprising that the philosopher cared little for the skill of dancing per se. "For as for the jigging part, and the Figures of Dances, I count that little, or nothing, farther, than as it tends to perfect *graceful Carriage*."[6] It was not steps and figures but the individual's total demeanor—words, motions, and gestures—that conveyed the desired internal civility of character that Locke considered the mark of good breeding. Less than a decade earlier, Increase Mather had expressed similar thoughts, though for different reasons, when he rhetorically asked New Englanders if it were then the time for jigs and galliards. Unconcerned with the social value of dancing, he voiced concern about the morality of stewarding time.

At the dawn of the eighteenth century, Mather was becoming an anachronism, with his hard-line views of what the ideal Puritan ought to represent, whereas Locke was in vogue. Also in vogue by midcentury was the preaching of the grand itinerant evangelist George Whitefield. As will be demonstrated, the views of Locke and Whitefield illustrate the fact that the valuing of dance in colonial America depended not on the art for its own sake but on a complex of ideas and assumptions that pertained to denominational affiliation, morality, race, gender, and social class. The prevalence of dancing was tied, to a great degree, to the presence of dance masters, settled towns and cities that fostered the art, and the century's awakening. Given the popularity of dancing, it seems at first amazing that so few published antidance writings survive.

Southern Colonies

Nowhere in the colonies did the English ideal for the gentleman seem to take hold with more tenacity than in the South. Settled primarily by Anglicans, Virginia, the Carolinas, and Georgia came to be "civilized" without the overarching religious zeal prominent in Puritan New England. In some instances, commercial motives outstripped any other reasons for colonizing. The types of rural-urban communities that developed played a vital role in perpetuating the ideal for gentry and dancing.

In his book *The First Gentlemen of Virginia,* Louis B. Wright records that as early as 1670 four prominent planters combined resources and talents to erect a "banqueting house" so that each man's family might have a place in which to entertain large groups of friends and relatives. On one recorded occasion late in the century, the popularity of dancing carried the activity through the night to eleven o'clock the next morning. Interestingly, that particular event had been sponsored by the daughter of a wealthy clergyman. Wright opines that the Reverend Mr. Teakle, a liberal Anglican, would no doubt have forgiven the all-night dance held in his absence, but it continued into the next morning—the Sabbath—and would have tried even his patience.[7]

That dancing continued to be extraordinarily popular in the eighteenth century is demonstrated by the historian Rhys Isaac in his Pulitzer Prize–winning book, *The Transformation of Virginia, 1740–1790.* Acknowledging the significance of dancing to a culture, Isaac writes: "In Virginia it was not in words but in vivid dance forms that the meaning of life was most fully expressed." The minuet and country dances displayed formal, ordered patterns. Yet jigs were also popular. Apparently borrowed from the blacks, these dances contributed elements of spontaneity to an evening of dancing. The fact that blacks usually served as attendants and musicians at the assemblies in great houses suggests the likelihood of exchange and modification of dances and music between the races.[8] Dances in Virginia occurred in the unusual town of Williamsburg as well as on plantations.

Williamsburg

In marked contrast to Boston, with its town life, Williamsburg developed as a county seat within the plantation culture of Virginia. As a focal point for the decentralized southern culture, Williamsburg during most of the year was a town of about a thousand people, according to a midcentury estimate. But when court was in session several times a year, the town's population ballooned to perhaps five thousand or six thousand. Balls constituted a part of the social life at periodic urban gatherings; those held at the governor's palace were important and select.[9] The itinerant dance and music master was needed in town during these "Publick Times," but during the remainder of the year he rode a circuit from one plantation to another.

Norman Arthur Benson's detailed analysis of the role of the itinerant dance master in these and other selected locales provides a useful perspective concerning the extent to which the art flourished. Benson identifies a total of six dance and music masters in the Williamsburg vicinity between 1716 and 1775. The earliest teacher, Charles Stagg, continued the line of European professionals who had first emerged as distinct personages in fifteenth-century Italy. An itemization of his estate in 1735 revealed that at his death he owned two instructional dance manuals by well-known eighteenth-century English dance masters, John Weaver and John Essex.[10] Stagg and William Levingston, an entrepreneur to whom the dance teacher was contracted, secured permission in March 1716 to teach dancing at the College of William and Mary until Levingston's own building was completed. In the interim, Levingston began to build the first theater in America, which was completed by 1718.

At Stagg's death, his wife, Mary, who had long assisted him, continued to teach dance in Williamsburg. But by 1737 she encountered a rival female teacher. Hugh Rankin's analysis of colonial theater records reveals that Madame Barbara de Graffenried advertised a dancing school and "sometime ballroom" in her townhouse next to the governor's mansion. Rankin observes that the two women competed in sponsoring balls and assemblies for the next two years, making them the earliest female dance teachers known in the colonies.[11] Their success did not result from lack of competition. In addition to managing balls and assemblies, William Dering opened a school at William and Mary in 1737 and advertised that he would teach gentlemen's sons in the latest French manner. Apparently after a busy decade of teaching and of playing the French horn at musical events and balls, Dering decided to move to Charleston in 1749.[12]

Not surprisingly in a colony with plantations distributed throughout, the business of teaching dancing did not center exclusively on town life. An active teacher among the plantations of northern Virginia, Francis Christian, appeared at Mount Vernon in 1770. As with the other circuit-riding dance masters, his typical day's activity consisted of lessons for children followed by an evening of dancing for both adults and children. A violinist, Christian could provide music for the dancing as well as instruct in steps, figures, styling, and deportment.[13] About the same time, another female teacher emerged in Williamsburg. Sarah Hallam, formerly of the Hallam theatrical company, an English troupe that toured the colonies, announced that she would open a dancing school. Rankin records that she operated the school successfully from 1775 until her death in 1793.[14] Neither Rankin nor Benson indicates that these female teachers rode the circuit to plantations. Nor do they comment on whether the women taught both male and female students.

As with the European tradition of the gentleman, the most apparent characteristic denoting the Virginia gentleman was good manners. No mere veneer, manners developed out of a person's conscious desire to maintain position and dignity in society. Morals, Louis B. Wright observes, were less distinctive than manners. A gentleman would not lie, steal, or cheat at cards, but he might be forgiven occasional sins of the flesh so long as the actions were not gross and he provided for illegitimate offspring. The accomplishments that constituted part of his dignity and manners included dancing, fencing, and riding, as well as ability in conversation and music. The gentleman in Virginia, like his European counterpart during the Renaissance, was to be proficient in the terpsichorean art but was not to display the skill of a dancing master. Isaac observes that "dancing was at the center of the [social] action and was evidently one of the most meaningful expressions of the soul of this entire people."[15]

Thus, dancing and dance instruction flourished throughout the century in Williamsburg and throughout Virginia due to a congenial atmosphere that provided space for the activity plus sufficient wealth to pay and sustain dance masters. Perhaps most important, the established Anglican clergy did not ban dancing.

Charleston

No formal or legal ban on dancing existed in Charleston, even though anti-dance sermons preached in the city testify to the cosmopolitan atmosphere that fostered dancing. Established in 1670 by planters from Jamaica and Barbados, Charleston represented a different type of culture from that in either Williamsburg or Boston. Because of intense heat and other climatic extremes from July through October or November, wealthy plantation owners moved into the city itself during those months. In Charleston they lived graciously in large houses and supported a musical and theatrical culture that attracted dance and music masters as well as actors. Well-to-do town merchants joined with the planters in sponsoring arts activities and in building Charleston into one of the most cosmopolitan of American cities. Cultural diversity derived from a mix of British and European immigrants as well as a pluralistic religious milieu. In 1708 Charleston's population numbered about three thousand; by 1763 it had grown to about four thousand whites and an equal number of blacks.[16] A combination of cultural diversity, money, leisure, a taste for European fashions, and the prevailing ideal for the gentleman led men in Carolina and Virginia to set the mold in fashion and elegance.[17] Such an atmosphere fostered the growth of dancing and the theater.

The first dancing master Benson identified in Charleston was an anonymous French teacher who reportedly settled in Craven County in 1708. He taught country dances to the Indians and also instructed them in the flute and hautboit. Other researchers found that George Brownell apparently worked as a dance master in Charleston in 1703 and then again from 1744 to 1750. The fact that he flourished in northern cities during the intervening decades typifies the careers of many peripatetic eighteenth-century dance and music masters.[18]

The first notice of a musical performance in Charleston appeared in 1732 when John Salter gave a concert. Subsequently, a pattern was established wherein such an event was presented in tandem with a ball.[19] Salter, like Edward Enstone in Boston, served as a church organist in addition to his duties as a dancing master, which included managing assemblies and balls, performing at concerts, accompanying dances, and teaching both dance and music. One of the more unusual of Charleston's dancing masters appears to have been a Mr. Boulson, who kept a "'Dancing School, Ball, Assembly, Concert Room, Etc.'" but then abandoned his profession after hearing the evangelist George Whitefield.[20]

Charleston's theater seasons originated in 1735, although the first theater building was not erected until 1736. After two years of scattered theatrical performances, a lull in both Charleston and Williamsburg preceded a midcentury resurgence. Rankin speculates that the revival preaching of Whitefield and John Wesley during 1737 in Charleston may have served to turn attention away from the theater and onto religion.

Eighteenth-century theatrical performances typically included dancing of various kinds in the plays and between acts. By the early 1750s, traveling troupes such as the Hallam Company from England entertained Charleston and Williamsburg audiences as well as those in New York and Philadelphia.[21] Tours by other companies continued theatrical events through the decades of the sixties and seventies. Following the war years, dancing again revived with extended seasons of dramatic performances and dancing during the 1790s. Benson records that in 1794–95, with two theaters operating and the ballad opera in vogue, Charlestonians were treated to a total of 270 plays, with performances three nights a week.[22]

In addition to stage performance and practice under the instruction of dance masters, subscription assemblies enjoyed great popularity. As early as 1735 an "Assembly of Dancing and Cards" met regularly. By 1763, one Charleston observer noted that a dancing assembly occurred once every two weeks. Nothing suggests that this schedule was atypical. Dancing assemblies were popular in several colonial towns and cities. Surviving records of the rules for these dance events indicate that they were formal and ordered affairs.[23]

Savannah

The popularity of dances and the orderly fashion in which they were conducted is well illustrated in the case of Savannah, Georgia, where the Savannah Assembly met once every two weeks, beginning at exactly 6:30 in the evening. A broadside from 19 November 1790 gives the "Rules and Regulations for the Dancing Assembly of Savannah," examples of which demonstrate the degree of decorum governing formal dances among the gentility and the special privileges reserved for female participants. As with most of these organized, regular dance associations, the Savannah Assembly held events for members only on a subscription basis. Each evening opened with minuets, though country dances comprised the majority of the dancing. The governor's lady always carried the privilege of dancing first without "drawing"; all other ladies had to draw for the numbers they would dance. "Brides and strangers" were exempt from this restriction and could dance second without drawing. The assembly rules do not define such procedures, since everyone at the time would have understood. The exemption for "brides and strangers" presumably accorded them a special status that guaranteed them the opportunity to dance at the beginning of the evening. The practice of drawing for numbers suggests that not all women could engage in every dance. Undoubtedly, the size of the room restricted the number of couples performing each dance.

Ladies also had the privilege of calling the figures for a dance, and the figures were to be followed unless the ladies agreed to some alteration. Ladies and gentlemen could engage their own partners, though the manager of the evening was responsible for seeing that everyone had a partner. No gentlemen in boots were permitted, but no specifications in attire or appearance existed for the ladies. Specific rules for ladies stipulated that they had to stand when their dance number was called, "and no Lady shall sit down til every couple shall have gone through the Dance."[24]

Middle Colonies

New York

Although there is no known publication of rules for the first dancing assembly in New York, it is known that an assembly was organized there in 1758.[25] Other evidence reveals that both colony and city provided an atmosphere where dancing was not restricted, as it had been in Massachusetts, even though the Dutch immigrants came from a Calvinist background. New Amsterdam had been founded by Dutch settlers interested in commercial gain; the city came under English control by 1664 and became New York. By the end of the seventeenth century, a religious pluralism prevailed, despite the prominence of the Dutch Calvinists. In general, Benson claims that the artistic activity of New Amsterdam followed the form and taste set by the Dutch Republic from which the majority of immigrants had come. Thus, New Amsterdam fostered an artistic climate dominated by an urban middle class, with aesthetic tastes dictated by men prominent in commerce and religion.[26]

The first dancing master to appear in New York turns out to have been none other than the fugitive Francis Stepney, after whom Increase Mather shot his "Arrow." When the unfortunate man arrived in the city by January 1687, he found his reputation had preceded him. Dutch magistrates informed Stepney that he had to post certain "sureties" or else get out of town. They understood that Stepney had "'been of loose carriage'" and that he had demonstrated no manual skills by which he could earn an honest living. Accordingly, they resolved that he would never teach dancing in their province. Clearly the magistrates did not consider the teaching of dancing to be an honest livelihood.[27]

By the early eighteenth century, dancing had been popular for several years, so later dancing masters fared better than Stepney. Benson notes that the *New York Gazette* in 1729 reported the sale of a house commonly called the "dancing school." Two years later, George Brownell appeared in the city to start a dancing school near the fort. After teaching there for about four years, he moved on to Boston where the selectmen permitted him to set up what was then the second dancing school in their city. The popularity of public balls beginning in about 1735 would have increased the call for dancing masters in New York. However, Benson's research reveals something of a cultural apathy toward theater and music in New York compared with the active encouragement of those arts in Charleston. In part, he attributes that apathy to unsophisticated tastes and to greater concern for commercial success. Opposition seems to have emanated from the Dutch burghers who jealously guarded civil control, including the licensing of theaters, and reluctantly permitted strolling players to perform.[28] One consequence of these attitudes was that theater did not secure a permanent foothold in New York until after the Revolution.[29]

Philadelphia

In contrast to the apathy to dancing and theater-going found in New York, active opposition to both was expressed in the city of Philadelphia from the beginning. There, as in Boston, religious motives had prompted the establishment of city and colony. Founded in 1682, Philadelphia grew quickly under William Penn's policy of religious tolerance. By 1742, the city numbered thirteen thousand people; by comparison, Boston's population just exceeded sixteen thousand.[30] According to Benson, the prominent cultural characteristic of Philadelphia in the late seventeenth century and for much of the eighteenth was its cluster of separate religious communities, including Quakers, Moravians, and Swedish Lutherans. In his opinion, the strongest single factor that served to retard musical activities was the Quakers' hold on civil and political power. From the outset, Penn's concern for maintaining civil order agreed with the basic beliefs of a rising middle class who saw such order as necessary for economic growth. Significantly, the "Great Law of the Colony," passed by the Provincial Assembly of Philadelphia in the city's year of founding, proscribed those kinds of amusements that sixteenth-century English reformers like Northbrooke and Stubbes had railed against, for example, stage plays (including dancing), cards, dice, May games, bearbaiting, and cockfights. The penalty for those who introduced or participated in such activities was a fine and imprisonment at hard labor.[31] The impact of the Great Law and subsequent versions lasted until the final decade of the eighteenth century.

Not only law but Quaker beliefs served actively to discourage dance and theater. The Quakers' Twelve Questions, as listed by Benson, clearly specify that the devout believer would not frequent "dancing and gaming" and would avoid excess in strong drink as well as elaborate apparel and speech. In effect, these basic principles emphasized personal piety, morality, planning, frugality, and independence. Benson mentions that one of the first recorded lapses from these basic tenets occurred in 1702 when a woman was found dressed in men's clothes and "walking and dancing" at ten at night in another's house. It seems unlikely that this was an isolated incident. After 1705, the Yearly Meeting specifically warned young people against dancing, music, lotteries, plays, and games.[32] The reference to dancing that appears in the Twelve Questions suggests that dancing existed in the colony and that authorities believed it needed to be restricted.

Evidence of ongoing dance activity in Philadelphia, despite laws and beliefs against it, comes from data on dance masters and an assembly. The earliest dance master appeared in 1710 and is identified as a Mr. Staples.[33] In 1729 Samuel Pierpont openly advertised a dancing school where he provided country dances every Thursday evening for the recreation of ladies and gentlemen. By 1735, Thomas Deering apparently had so many dance students that he divided them into beginners and advanced "Scholars."[34] The opportunity to practice one's dance skills came with the subscription assembly. The gentry of Philadelphia organized a dancing assembly in the winter season of 1748–49. Aside from those at Boston and Charleston, this seems to have been one of the earliest formed; the assembly of Washington, D.C., did not originate until fifty years later. Fifty-nine individuals joined Philadelphia's assembly the first year, at $5.25 per person.[35]

Theater dance also occurred in Philadelphia at an early date despite laws repeatedly enacted against it. Rankin mentions that itinerant entertainers arrived in 1723 and that a professional "roap" dancer advertised in 1724 but performed outside the city limits. With little more than sporadic expressions of concern for theater by local citizens, the next professional troupe to perform in the area was formally organized in 1749 under Walter Murray and Thomas Kean and made its first appearance in the city. In the face of renewed criticism to theater, the company left Philadelphia in February 1750 and headed for New York, where a new company member performed several dances as a part of the show. Subsequently the troupe moved on to Annapolis, Williamsburg, and other towns. Touring groups played sporadically in Philadelphia in the 1750s and 1760s despite Quaker opposition.[36] They all included some dancing as part of their performances.

Another indication of the popularity of theatrical events is the effort by the Continental Congress to restrict such activity. Federal attempts at suppression of theatrical entertainment came after the Revolutionary War began. The Continental Congress, meeting in Philadelphia, passed a resolution in October 1774 that attempted to encourage frugality and industry and to discourage idleness, extravagance, and dissipation. The resolution specifically named gaming, cockfighting, and plays, as well as other expensive diversions.[37] Since the recommendation tended to be ignored by military and civil personnel, the Congress passed another resolution in October 1778, which specified that any office holder who promoted or attended "such" plays would be dismissed from said office.

After the war, theater returned to Philadelphia. In 1789 a petition signed by nineteen hundred citizens asked that the law proscribing theatrical entertainments be repealed. A theater building appeared within the city limits by 1791.[38] Theater activities in Philadelphia grew in frequency and variety during the 1790s, as would befit the nation's capital. Anna Gardie, perhaps the first "real ballet star" to perform in the United States, made her debut in Philadelphia in 1794; John Durang, the first American to become a professional dancer, had debuted there ten years earlier.[39]

New England

Boston

Despite Boston's continuing to register the largest urban population of any city in the colonies during most of the eighteenth century, it did not develop the cosmopolitan context that would foster dance and theater. The Murray-Kean touring company played in Boston by midcentury, but opposition to it spurred the passage of an "Act for Preventing Stage Plays and other Theatrical Entertainments," in April 1750. The opening paragraph of the act spells out reasons for the law; namely, that plays occasion many mischiefs, unnecessary expense, immorality, and contempt for religion as well as serving to discourage industry and frugality. As in Philadelphia, the law continued until the end of the century, when it was allowed to expire; the first approved theater opened in 1794.[40] Apparently the Boston law proved more effective than that in Philadelphia, where companies simply performed outside the city limits when the law was in force. The Boston act carried penalties of twenty pounds for those who produced plays and five pounds each per actor and spectator. Rankin surmises that the threat to pocketbook probably proved more effective than any moral sanctions. He records no instances in which the other touring companies then operating in the colonies also traveled to Boston.[41]

Dancing masters fared somewhat better in the Boston environs. After the initial hiring and firing of Edward Enstone, at least nineteen other persons taught in Boston between 1730 and 1794.[42] In nearby Salem by 1739, Charles Bradshaw was teaching French and had permission to teach dancing so long as he maintained order. By 1755 a Protestant Parisian visited the town and taught the young people both dancing and manners. As in Boston, it seems that dancing and assemblies became very popular in Salem after midcentury. However, the 1750 act proscribing stage plays applied in Salem just as in Boston since the law had been passed by the General Court.[43] Not just legislation but citizen anger could fuel opposition to dance. When Peter Pelham Sr. announced a series of dancing assemblies in 1732, the notice touched off the wrath of one unidentified Boston citizen, who predicted that the assemblies would encourage immorality, cost too much money, and foster pride, envy, and prodigality.[44]

Other Towns

The popularity of dancing extended into other New England colonies as well. Extant evidence about a 1769 wedding in New London, Connecticut, reveals that 92 gentlemen and ladies attended and engaged in 92 jigs, 52 contra-dances, 45 minuets, and 17 hornpipes. They retired at 12:45 A.M., presumably exhausted. In Hartford in 1787, John Griffiths announced that he would open a dancing school to teach ladies in the mornings and gentlemen from six to nine in the evenings. Weekly balls would permit spectators. Griffiths proposed to teach four different kinds of minuets, cotillions, country-dances, and a hornpipe. Assemblies began there as early as 1790. Portsmouth, New Hampshire, newspapers report no fewer than fourteen dance masters from 1765 to 1800.[45]

In Rhode Island, an early assembly began in Newport in 1747, when, according to the historian Carl Bridenbaugh, a "committee of thirteen bachelors . . . sent a general invitation to thirty-two single ladies to attend assembly cotillions for the season. Other persons were invited only on specific occasions." Bridenbaugh does not indicate whether the cotillions continued more than one season. Nor does he comment on the numbers of women who may actually have attended the dances. By contrast, a broadside titled "The Rules for the Providence Assembly 1792" indicates that that town's assembly was well established. Similar to the regulations of the Savannah and Philadelphia assemblies, the rules for the Providence Assembly suggest that evenings were strictly ordered affairs concerned with civility as well as pleasure.[46] The social rules that ensured this civility and courtesy were typically part of the dance master's instruction.

Dance Masters and the Ideal for Gentlefolk

The presence of so many teachers in the colonies during the eighteenth century provides clear testimony to the popularity of dancing and the desire for instruction in one of the polite accomplishments. Altogether, at least eighty dance masters and mistresses have been identified by name in the geographical area ranging from Maine to Georgia and from the coastal states west to Pennsylvania and Kentucky.[47] However, these instructors tended to cluster in the urban areas. Many taught music and other subjects as well as dancing; some wrote music, but John Griffiths also wrote instructions on manners as a part of his music and dance manuscript.[48] His advice points to an ideal for gentlefolk of both genders.

A Collection of the Newest Cotillions and Country Dances, which Griffiths published in 1794, included "Instances of Ill manners, to be carefully avoided by *Youth of both sexes*"(emphasis mine). His instructions support Locke's contention that a dancing master could teach youth about carriage as well as good behavior and ease of motion. The admonitions of Griffiths clearly extend beyond manners for the dance floor. They represent something of that civility Locke expected of a well-bred gentleman and lady. Griffiths stresses directions for entering and exiting a room, including attentions to be paid to those already present. For example, youth were to avoid "leaning on the shoulder, or chair of another person, and overlooking persons who are writing or reading." Similarly, they were never to loll on a chair when speaking or being spoken to; whisper or point in company; laugh loudly when in company or drum the feet or fingers; or sit still when parents, instructors, or strangers entered the room. Moderation in carriage dictated that youth should avoid swinging the arms and "all other awkward gestures, especially, in the street, and in company." Thus, Griffiths wanted youth of both sexes to appear at ease, to display grace, and to move with that freedom of motion that reflected command of the body governed by moderation. Good manners dictated that "all actions that have the most remote tendency to indelicacy" should be avoided. In sum, Locke's sense of genuine courtesy, reflected in a concern for others, underlies the instructions by Griffiths.[49]

According to Locke's ideal of good breeding, true courtesy undergirded the exterior appearance of a gentleman well schooled in carriage, motion, and manners. Yet, the teaching of manners could easily become an end in itself. That is, a person could develop a brilliant facade with no depth of character. As Edwin Cady has pointed out in *The Gentleman in America,* the "fine" gentleman came to denote the fop, the rake, the snob, the clotheshorse, and the bully. Although Lord Chesterfield did not invent the "fine" gentleman, that model informed his advice to his son. The Englishman's recommendations conjured an image of an individual who cared more for himself and for getting ahead in society than for being truly considerate of others. Chesterfield's advice, while not totally devoid of redeeming value, eventually was expurgated and reappeared in America in some thirty-one volumes between 1775 and 1800. By contrast, the model of the well-bred gentleman carried the best of the ancient courtesy tradition and opposed the "fine" gentleman at every point. Further, the well-bred gentleman was widely considered to be a Christian. In Cady's words: "No one ever really pretended that every Christian man was automatically a gentleman. But it was held, most strongly at the popular level, that the true gentleman began by being a Christian."

No single treatise for women, comparable to Chesterfield's advice to his son, appears among American etiquette or courtesy publications for the eighteenth century. Indeed, the great volume of such advice to women does not appear until after 1820.[50] However, portraits of the ideal Christian lady are found in the writing of English evangelical dance opponents.

By at least the middle of the century, English proponents of the true Christian gentleman had begun to try to win the gentry to an evangelical Christianity, in part by emphasizing the strength of virtue in the courtesy tradition and by opposing deism as well.[51] That English assault on the brilliant manners, balls, and assemblies of "fine" gentlemen and ladies came to America in the person of George Whitefield and in the book titled *An Address To Persons Of Fashion, Relating To Balls . . .* , by Sir Richard Hill.

George Whitefield and the Ideal for the Christian

A fierce opponent of nominal or lukewarm Christianity, the Reverend George Whitefield (1714–70) contributed perhaps more than any other single individual to the spread of that religious fervor known in America as the Great Awakening. He rode up and down the eastern seaboard preaching to hundreds of thousands of people in a total of seven visits from England to this country between 1737 and 1770.[52] A fiery, indefatigable evangelist, he recorded in his *Journals* that he preached repentance and salvation; these, in turn, demanded reformed behavior, particularly the turning away from worldliness.

For Whitefield, a reformation in behavior included abstinence from dancing, balls, and assemblies. His *Journals* indicate that he found these worldly fashions to be as popular throughout the country as the evidence of dancing masters and assemblies confirms. On 9 January 1740, he recorded: "In

North Carolina there is scarcely so much as the form of religion. Two churches were begun, some time since, but neither is finished. There are several
dancing-masters, but scarcely one regular settled minister." On the prior
Christmas, he had written to a clergyman of Newborn, in that state, and
chastised the cleric for permitting his son to take dancing lessons. Whitefield
lamented:

> It grieves me to find that in every little town there is a settled dancing-master,
> but scarcely anywhere a settled minister to be met with; such a proceeding must
> be of dreadful consequence to *any,* especially a *new settled* province. All Gov-
> ernors, if it were only from a policy of human policy [*sic*], ought to put a stop
> to it; for such entertainments altogether enervate the minds of people, insen-
> sibly leading them into effeminacy, and unfitting them to endure those hard-
> ships, and fatigues, which must necessarily be undergone, to bring any prov-
> ince to perfection.[53]

Not only did dancing and like entertainments tend to soften a people in
Whitefield's view, but they also diverted the mind and soul from God and
lulled it "asleep as much as drunkenness and debauchery." He believed that
every minister ought to declare that such "innocent entertainments of the
polite part of the world" are the entrapments of the devil. In particular, he
declared from Annapolis in December 1739 that women became enslaved
to "their fashionable diversions" equally as much as men were bound to the
bottle and their hounds. The evil in each case derived from the focus on
pleasing self. Not indicting colonists alone, Whitefield lamented in April
1739 when preaching in England, "Oh the polite world! How are they led
away by lying vanities!" His lament applied to local ladies who sponsored
balls and assemblies.[54]

Yet, during his evangelistic tours, at home and abroad, Whitefield
preached to all classes of people, delivering essentially the same message. On
New Year's Day 1740, he entered a tavern five miles from the South Carolina border and found people celebrating. "By the advice of my companions, I went in amongst them whilst a woman was dancing a jig." Though
the woman attempted to "outbrave" the evangelist for some time, eventually she and the fiddler sat and listened to his discourse on the nature of
baptism and the need for being born again. Though Whitefield baptized one
of the children present, he observed that when he went to bed, he again heard
the music and dancing.[55]

Despite his apparent failure with the folk in the tavern, Whitefield recorded some examples of radical reformation in behavior following his ser-

mons. In Charleston on 17 March 1740 he "was more explicit than ever in exclaiming against balls and assemblies." After speaking again in the evening, he requested money for his orphans in Georgia and received "upward of £70 sterling, the largest collection I ever yet made on that occasion." The amount may not have been sacrificial giving, but it apparently signaled a "vast alteration" in several areas. Back in Charleston, Whitefield noted on 20 July:

> One, well acquainted with their manners and circumstances, told me that they spent more on their polite entertainments than the amount raised by their rates for the poor. But now the jewellers and dancing masters begin to cry out that their craft is in danger. A vast alternation is discernible in ladies' dresses; and some, while I have been speaking, have been so convinced of the sin of wearing jewels, that, I have seen them and, with blushes, put their hands to their ears, and cover them up with their fans. But the reformation has gone further than externals. Many moral, good sort of men, who before were settled on their lees, have been awakened to seek after Jesus Christ.[56]

Additional and perhaps unusual transformations in behavior occurred with two dancing masters. The historian Carl Bridenbaugh tells us that the only effort at providing education for Charleston's black population began in 1740 when Mr. Boulson, a dancing master, became converted, gave up his former life, and began a school for children. He soon had enrolled fifty-three students, before being hauled into court for violating the Slave Code by teaching young blacks to read. However, the authorities permitted him to continue. Whitefield also observed that rooms in Charleston that had formerly been used for balls and assemblies had been turned into meeting places for his gatherings. The transformation was not unique to Charleston. The previous April, Whitefield had pleaded so effectively that "Philadelphia's most prominent dancing master," Robert Bolton, had turned his school over to the education of young blacks. These brief accounts offer no insight as to why or how Whitefield persuaded the dance masters to give up their profession in order to assist in the education of black children. However, Harry Stout's biography of Whitefield, *The Divine Dramatist,* provides a vivid picture of the evangelist's persuasive convictions conveyed by dramatic presentations.[57]

Ideal for the Lady

Whitefield's attacks on dancing, as recorded in his *Journals,* generally focused on balls and assemblies. In his criticisms these polite entertainments seem more connected with women than with men. To what degree his remarks were aimed at gender or at social class is unclear. Both came to be accused of worldliness in his portrait of the "fine" lady with unregenerate heart.

Whitefield's *Law Gospelized; Or An Address To All Christians Concerning Holiness of Heart and Life* provides selected paragraphs that contrast the "fine" lady with the true Christian lady whose focus rests solely on God. Whitefield speaks particularly to those gentry who possessed sufficient wealth and time to qualify them for gentle rank and who also professed Christianity. He charges them at the outset with the scriptural admonition that to whom much has been given, of them much shall be required. Accordingly, those who profess Christianity are under greater obligation to live a life "wholly devoted unto God" than are those who do not give such lip service to their beliefs. The great sin of nominal believers among polite society, Whitefield asserts, is not gross sin but the misuse of things considered in themselves to be lawful and innocent. For example, a gentleman who spends his time in sports and a lady who spends all her money on clothes will not devote their attention to God. Yet these are typical "fine" folk. Clarifying further, Whitefield paints a portrait of Flavia, a fashionable lady who spends more time on her body than on her soul. The totality of her life is consumed in "eating, drinking, dressing, visiting, conversation, reading and hearing plays and romances, and attending at opera's [*sic*], assemblies, balls and diversions." By contrast, he holds up the ideal model of Miranda, a "sober reasonable Christian," whose sole aim is to do God's will. Miranda "has renounced the world, to follow Christ in the exercise of humility, charity, devotion, abstinence, and heavenly affections; and that is Miranda's fine breeding." The contrast with Miranda's former life, as Whitefield paints it, could hardly be more pronounced. Prior to her reformation, she spent her time in hearing "profane speech" at theaters, listening to "wanton songs" and romances at the opera, and dancing at "public places, that fops and rakes might admire the fineness of her shape, and the beauty of her motions."[58]

Once Miranda's heart had been transformed by Christ, she elected a life that Whitefield depicts as the ideal for the pious Christian woman: "She seems to be as a guardian angel to those that dwell about her, with her watchings and prayers blessing the place where she dwells, and making intercession with God for those that are asleep." She works all day doing what is necessary for herself and for others. Unlike Flavia, she has no idle time on her hands. "Her wise and pious mind neither wants the amusement, nor can bear with the folly of idle and impertinent work; she can admit of no such folly as this in the day, because she is to call herself to an account for all her actions in her secret retirement at night." In addition to performing the necessary tasks of household and family, Miranda reads her Bible and devotional literature daily, says prayers before and after meals, and performs many charitable works for others.[59] Miranda is Whitefield's model of the "fine" lady who places holiness before worldliness, recalling the ideal that guided Richard Brathwait and Richard Allestree in exhorting seventeenth-century English and colonial women. Interestingly, Whitefield does not paint a detailed portrait of the "fine" gentleman.

Underlying Whitefield's opposition to wasting time by following fashion lay a fundamental belief that the true Christian should renounce the world with all its pomps, vanities, and customs. Reacting to what he saw about him, Whitefield charged that the lives "of the moral and better sort of people" who professed Christianity fell short of this ideal of holiness, because they were "destitute of a true living faith in Jesus Christ." Whitefield ascribed fashionable folk's lack of faith to two primary factors. They feared the contempt of the world if they did not follow its customs. And, they had received an improper education. Men are trained, he writes, to develop the worldly traits of pride, ambition, envy, glory, desire for distinction, and the like. Women are trained to "pride, affectation, a delight in beauty, and fondness of finery." As a consequence of their training in worldliness, Whitefield declared that women were not to blame when they chose for their husbands men with only the veneer of polish. "If they are often too ready to receive the first fops, beaux, and fine dancers for their husbands, it is no wonder they should like that in men, which they have been taught to admire in themselves." Instead, the ideal education for youth would stress that "pious reading and religious conversation" are better than plays and operas. "What music, dancing, and diversions are to the people of the world, that holy meditation, fervent prayers, and other acts of devotion" are to the true Christian.[60]

Whitefield's exposition of the ideal for the Christian emphasizes a more detailed reformation in women's education and behavior than it does in that of men, because women would have the primary care for forming the bodies and minds of children. Though emphasizing a traditional domestic role, Whitefield does not ascribe lesser faculties to the female gender. He asserts that women are not naturally inferior but are rather encouraged and cultivated to be "so many painted idols." He argues that, if women are trained to piety, they will automatically reject the polite accomplishments of the world: "Let but a woman feel her heart full of this faith, and she will no more desire to shine at balls and assemblies, or to make a figure among those that are most finely dressed, than she will desire to dance upon a rope to please

spectators. For she will then know that the one is as far from the true nature, wisdom, and excellency of the christian spirit, as is the other."[61]

Thus, Whitefield's attacks on dancing, balls, and assemblies come as a
part of his larger emphasis on seeking holiness rather than worldliness, true
piety rather than vain fashion. Interestingly, he does not allege that dancing gives rise to lust, adultery, and drunkenness. This may suggest that he
never actually witnessed any balls or assemblies firsthand. It may also suggest that all such dance events were entirely circumspect, and that the rules
governing assemblies indeed provided for true courtesy and civility.

An Address to Persons of Fashion

Not surprisingly, Whitefield's portrait of the "fine" lady resembles one painted by his follower Sir Richard Hill (1732–1808) in the latter's *Address To
Persons of Fashion, Relating to Balls* . . . . Written presumably when Hill studied at Oxford between 1750 and 1754, the publication became popular at
home and in America. The second, third, and fourth editions, all from 1761,
were published in London. Two 1767 editions issued from a Boston press;
the final edition, in 1807, came from a Baltimore publisher. The subtitle
given in the last edition provides the reader with a fuller explanation of the
book's contents, which describe "the Character Of Lucinda, A Lady Of The
Very Best Fashion, And Most Extraordinary Piety." Like Whitefield, Hill
draws a detailed portrait specifically of the ideal Christian lady.

No author's name appears on the title page of Hill's book but a claim that
it is "by a Member of the Church of England" is included. As a baronet and
member of Parliament, Hill was well placed to address the members of polite
society in England about perceived failings in their behavior. The publication
of Hill's book in this country indicates a continuation of that English evangelical fervor ignited in the sixteenth century, transported across the Atlantic
in the seventeenth century, and rekindled again in the eighteenth century.[62]

Like Whitefield, Hill fears the lukewarm Christian more than the professed atheist or most wicked profligate. The latter present an obvious threat
to the true Christian; the former only seems harmless on the surface. Lucinda, for example, is well thought of, observes communion, hears her children recite Catechism, and says prayers regularly. However, she also goes to
the theater, plays cards occasionally, and takes lessons from a dance master.
Like many in society, Lucinda thinks she is saved. Hill observes that, although humans judge by outward appearance, Christ looks into the individual's heart.

Hill, like earlier dance opponents, attempts to base his opposition on biblical evidence. Because there is no specific scriptural injunction against balls, he uses general principles such as the admonition in 1 Corinthians 10:35, "Whatsoever ye do, do all to the glory of God." He concludes his line of argument with the assertion: "til it can be proved that Balls and Plays tend to promote the glory of God; how can it possibly be thought lawful for us to go to them, who are so solemnly called upon to imitate him and to make the glory of God the end of all our actions."[63] Since Hill views balls as worldly activities and since the Christian is to be separated from the world, his assertion makes perfect sense. True Christianity, for Hill, consists of continual growth in personal temper and spirit toward conformity with Jesus Christ. Like Whitefield, Hill stresses that such a development results only from God's spirit at work within the individual. Moreover, the change must be total; the true Christian cannot "stand up for a moderate share of worldliness." Extending the argument to induce fear, he asks rhetorically: What if one were at a ball and then seized by death? Would the person not then be excluded from fellowship with the communion of the saints as well as with the Father and the Son in eternity?[64]

That kind of question did not characterize the style of Increase Mather and Cotton Mather, who followed their earlier counterparts in using a thoroughly documented argument and almost ponderously heavy intellectual tone to speak against dancing and balls. Hill, though not a minister or theologian, writes in a fairly straightforward manner but begins the pattern of posing a rhetorical question calculated to induce guilt and to persuade by eliminating any other options. The technique characterizes American dance opponents in the nineteenth and early twentieth centuries. But the appeal to emotion more than to intellect also characterizes two of the known American adversaries from the eighteenth century.

American Opposition amid Religious and Political Awakening

Either by active dissent from established churches or by initial provisos for toleration, the colonies in the eighteenth century were decidedly pluralistic. Puritans remained strong in New England, and the Anglican church held the position of primacy in the South. However, Quakers, Dutch Calvinists, Baptists, and Methodists, as well as Catholics, Lutherans, Presbyterians, and Moravians, plus lesser-known sects, all had active churches in this country. The degree to which they influenced peoples' lives varied with denomination, sect, and region. In the South, the Anglican church never dominated the lives of the people with the same kind of control exerted by the Puritans in early New England. Other denominations made inroads. Baptists developed an early stronghold in Charleston and flourished throughout the eighteenth century. Following in the wake of George Whitefield in that city, the Baptist cleric Oliver Hart (1723–95) combined religious and political fervor in his preaching. He also wrote the first extant antidance sermon in the colonies since Cotton Mather's "Cloud of Witnesses." The fact is not surprising, given the wealth, early cosmopolitan milieu, and development of dancing and music in Charleston.

Reverend Oliver Hart

Born in Pennsylvania, Oliver Hart joined the church at age eighteen, having been accustomed to hearing the revival preaching of Whitefield as well as that of two American evangelists, William Tennent and his son, Gilbert Tennent.[65] Licensed to preach in 1746 and ordained in 1749, Hart was one of those men who, irrespective of their schooling, felt "called" to preach. The year of his ordination Hart received a request to take over the Baptist church in Charleston, where members had been trying unsuccessfully for years to get ministers either from the northern colonies or from Europe. He preached in Charleston for the next thirty years.[66]

When Hart went to Charleston the city had at least four Baptist churches, the first having been established in the 1680s and the last organized in 1746.[67] Hart's eminence within his denomination earned him the title "Bishop of the Baptists." In 1775 the South Carolina Council of Safety appointed him to travel to the interior or back country of the colony, along with William Tennent, to reconcile some of the disaffected citizenry to the importance of the war effort and enlist their support. Hart's sermon against dancing, delivered on 22 March 1778, was reprinted in 1860 in Frank Moore's *The Patriot Preachers of the American Revolution, 1766–1783*. It became the best known of his Charleston sermons.[68]

In the opening passages of his sermon, Hart sounds like the sixteenth-century English reformers John Northbrooke and Christopher Fetherston, who argued that the times in which they lived called for praying, not playing, and for mourning, not dancing. Hart argues that his decade calls for piety, sobriety, and militant devotion to the cause of liberty and God. He also observes that his sermon, "Dancing Exploded," might have languished in oblivion had not the practice of dancing been revived in a "frantic manner." He describes the state of affairs at a time when every thing in Providence is calling us to different exercises. The judgments of God are now opened over the land, and the inhabitants ought to learn righteousness. The alarm of war; the clangor of arms; the garments rolled in blood; the sufferings of our brethren in the northern states, and of others in a state of captivity; together with the late dreadful conflagration in this town; are so many loud calls to repentance, reformation of life, and prayer that the wrath of God may be turned away from us. Instead of which, we are smothered up in pleasure and dissipation. It will hardly be credited that the fire was scarcely extinguished in Charleston, before we had balls, assemblies, and dances in every quarter; and even in some of those houses which miraculously escaped the flames. . . . Is it thus we requite the Lord for our deliverance?[69]

Hart's call for discernment of God's judgment sounds no different than the exhortations of Increase Mather or John Cotton in the seventeenth century. But it is not possible to distinguish where Hart's evangelical motive ends and his patriotic motive begins. The tenor of his sermon stresses the need for individual behavioral reform. The substance of his remarks recalls sixteenth-century antidance arguments more than it points to a new American opposition.

Hart employs the same text John Calvin used to indict dancing, Job 21:11, in which the prophet laments that the wicked people of the world have fun, their children dance, and parents seem not to suffer for their wickedness. Like the sixteenth-century reformers and Increase Mather, Hart distinguishes the approved biblical examples of dancing from the type practiced in Charleston. However, he aligns the disapproved examples, such as the incident of Salome dancing before Herod, with the "profane" dancing in his day. In further support of his position, Hart quotes from a history of evangelical churches the passage that Increase Mather cited on the Waldensians, that is, the devil is the leader, the middle, and the end of the dance.[70]

Hart's arguments speak to the incidental characteristics of dancing rather than to its essential nature. Major themes revolve around stewarding time and money and developing piety. Declaring that the chief end of man is to glorify God, Hart pronounces that dancing is sinful because it contributes nothing to this end. He focuses not only on this life but also on eternity, reminding readers that diversions once thought delightful in time of health and youth will afford no comfort in a dying hour. "It behooves us to live each day and hour as we would wish to die, and not to engage in any thing that would alarm us, in case death should overtake us in the act." Faced with the prospect of a final accounting, the wise Christian will follow the biblical injunction to redeem time. In strident tones, Hart declares that time spent at balls and assemblies is time not redeemed but "murdered." Similarly, Hart charges that dancing and balls occasion extravagant waste of money on dresses, lessons at dancing school, and the like. In his view, such money could be better used to relieve the distress of the poor and orphans. He reminds the well-to-do in particular of a Last Judgment to come: "Our merry gentry, who delight so much in frolicking and dancing, would do well to consider how they will answer for all their filthiness, foolish talking, jesting and such like things when they come to stand at the bar of God."

Unlike Whitefield and Hill, Hart alleges that many dances "are extremely immodest, and incentive to uncleanness." Musical accompaniment is often vulgar and obscene, with "tunes being adapted to the most vulgar and filthy songs." In marked contrast to both Whitefield and Hill, Hart does not single out women for special vilification, other than making the charge about money wasted on dress. Neither does he paint a portrait of the ideal Christian lady.[71]

Because of the great popularity of dancing in Charleston, Hart no doubt thought that his sermon would be incomplete without refuting prevailing arguments that dance advocates advanced in its favor. To the obvious statement that dancing is a necessary part of good breeding, Hart counters that the disadvantages outweigh any possible advantages. That is, not only will carriage and posture be learned but the undesirable traits of vanity, self-importance, and the like will be fostered. To the argument in favor of dancing as good recreation, Hart responds that walking, riding, or manual labor can be equally beneficial without exposing the participant to the hazards of "night-damps and inclement air." To the time-honored assertion that Ecclesiastes says there is a time to dance, Hart replies that the biblical statement applies only if it can be proved that the dancing refers to contemporary practice. Devotees of dancing also declared its legitimacy by noting that many Christians dance; Hart stresses that the guide for true Christians is not the behavior of other "professors" but the model of Christ. Finally, like Cotton Mather, Hart stresses the responsibility of parents to bring up children in the fear and admonition of the Lord. He exhorts parents to use the money that would have been spent on dancing lessons for some charitable purpose; otherwise, "Think how dreadful it will be to have the blood of your dear children's souls crying against you, in the day of judgement."[72]

John Phillips and Bishop Francis Asbury

Hart's emphasis on a personal faith in Jesus Christ also characterized the thinking of Reverend John Phillips, who denounced dancing in Charleston two decades after Hart's sermon. Phillips flourished between 1792 and 1798, but little is known of his background. There is enough information to link him with the Methodists but also to mark him perhaps as a theological maverick. He penned his *Familiar dialogues on dancing, between a minister and a dancer* from Charleston and dated the preface 4 February 1797. However, the book was published in New York by T. Kirk in 1798. That same year Phillips's book opposing slavery, as well as other worldly evils such as dancing, cards, and theater, also appeared from the same New York press. Information from the prefaces of these and two other books by Phillips, plus church records and the *Journal* of Bishop Francis Asbury, provide the known, scant biographical information extant.

John Phillips first appears in 1793 in New York. By his own account, he was a Methodist on Long Island when he received a note from Bishop Thomas Coke in November 1792. Presumably Phillips was also a minister at that time, though the point is not clear. He attended the New York Methodist conference of 1793 and was admitted to membership in the denomination by its usual pattern of initially being "on trial." He says that he did not ask to become affiliated but had no objection to it, though he did not understand that he had been taken in only "on trial." Church records indicate Phillips remained "on trial" into 1794, but they give no subsequent explanation of any affiliation or withdrawal. At some point in 1793 or early 1794, Phillips reports that he was "ejected from among the Methodists" and went to live in New Brunswick.[73] Sometime after April 1794, Phillips, by request, went to Charleston to join a Rev. William Hammet who had sailed from England in 1785 with Bishop Coke and had gone to Charleston in 1791 to head up the first Methodist church in the city. Apparently a popular figure who eventually produced a schism in the local church, Hammet also parted ways with Phillips by early 1795.[74] From that point, until we cease to have information about him, Phillips remained in Charleston, apparently as a free-lance preacher and author. His *Familiar Dialogues* makes clear that he shared the evangelical viewpoint of Hart and Whitefield.

Journal entries by Bishop Francis Asbury show that Phillips was not alone in lamenting the lack of piety among Charleston's inhabitants. On 20 January 1795, Asbury wrote: "The desperate wickedness of this people grieves and distresses my soul, so that I am almost in continual heaviness." By 5 February his dejection had become critical:

I have been lately more subject to melancholy than for many years past; and how can I help it: the white and worldly people are intolerably ignorant of God; playing, dancing, swearing, racing; these are their common practices and pursuits. Our few male members do not attend preaching; and I fear there is hardly one who walks with God: the women and Africans attend our meetings, and some few strangers also. Perhaps it may be necessary for me to know how wicked the world is, in order that I may do more as a president [sic] minister.

The worldly diversions of the citizens, the contentiousness of church members, and the lack of worship attendance among Charleston's white and male populations all made Asbury feel that the city was "one of the most serious places I ever was in."[75]

Phillips's preface to *Familiar Dialogues,* dated 4 February 1797, indicates the same concern as Asbury's: "I have written the following with a view to facilitate the downfall of Satan's Kingdom, and with a sincere desire to assist unhappy beings in escaping out of the snares of the devil in which they are taken captive that they may come to Christ for life and salvation." The body of his text follows a pattern common in the writings of earlier dance opponents, namely the use of dialogue whereby the dance advocate puts the questions in favor of the activity and, in this case, the minister responds with arguments of opposition.

Phillips's opposition points to contemporary dancing, which he labels "artificial," as did Increase Mather in his day. Such dancing results either in pay for the dancing master or "vain" and "idle" amusement for the participants. Phillips calls the true purpose of amusement to "relieve the body, or mind"; thus, he likens amusement to recreation. Dancing, however, only "fatigues and dissipates our powers," in his opinion. Those most addicted to dancing, he asserts, are either those who have nothing to do or else those who have work to do but are too idle to do it.[76] Like Hart, Phillips refutes the typical arguments in favor of dancing, namely, that it promotes health and good breeding, by asserting that other exercises can provide the same benefits but without the disadvantages.

Resembling some of the sixteenth-century writers such as Philip Stubbes and Christopher Fetherston in his occasional statements of excess, Phillips declares that "for every single person who suffered in his health for want of learning to dance, there have been thousands who have lost both health and life together by means of dancing: to say nothing of the ABORTIONS caused thereby, in Adults." Also like Hart and the Mathers, Phillips puts serious charges to the parents. He points out that parents are duty-bound to teach their children the principles of Christianity, but children cannot focus on God when distracted by balls and dancing lessons.[77]

Phillips reminds the reader that, since the chief end of man is to glorify

God and to redeem time, there is really no time free for dancing. He goes on to indict the character of dancing masters and to impugn their art by asking, "Of what use is dancing?"[78] Moreover, he counts it "shocking" to think that people would begin to dance by praying in Christ's name. Since such a prayer would be ridiculous and absurd, if not profane, he also concludes that dancing does not contribute to Christian growth and piety. Such circular logic becomes typical of antidance writers in the nineteenth century.

Noteworthy in the writing of both Phillips and Hart is the absence of any reference to dancing by blacks. Charleston had a substantial black population, and dancing was part of that heritage. But the degree to which that tradition continued and/or was perceived as an opposition to Christianity is not clear from the antidance arguments discussed here. Bishop Asbury's comment that "women and Africans attend our meetings" remains the lone reference to blacks.

Dance Opposition during the Eighteenth Century

Given the popularity of dancing, balls, and assemblies throughout the colonies, as well as the awakening of evangelical and patriotic fervor during the period, it seems surprising that only three eighteenth-century antidance treatises—those by Hill, Hart, and Phillips—should survive. No single reason can account for the apparent paucity of published opposition, but several factors probably contributed to it.

An obvious assumption undergirding any type of polemic is that the practice inveighed against is seen as a threat to a particular established order. Clearly, the Mathers, Whitefield, Hill, Hart, and Phillips all perceived dancing and balls as impediments to the development of true Christianity. The absence of additional antidance treatises in the eighteenth century may mean that many other people did *not* believe dancing to be inimical to true Christianity. Those who held to Locke's ideal for the gentleman surely did not oppose dancing. Those who revered Chesterfield's model of "fine" gentlemen and ladies certainly did not consider dancing an evil. By contrast, those who lived in frontier settlements would have experienced little dancing and probably no formal balls. The plain folks who were unchurched would have had no religion-based reason to oppose the practice. Thus, by a process of elimination, a majority of the population probably would not have written against dancing.

The field of potential authors of antidance treatises narrows still further when education, locale, and motivation are considered. Those persons most likely to write treatises would have been the educated elite, namely college professors and clergy. Of that small group, only those considered to be "evangelical" Christians, such as Whitefield and Hart, would probably have opposed dancing. Among the latter category of clergy, some might have followed a course like Whitefield's, choosing to speak out against dancing but not to write for publication on the topic. For example, Isaac notes the objection to dancing by Baptists in Virginia but he does not cite extant sermons. Given the passion for dancing among Virginians and the powerful upsurge of Baptist evangelicalism in the decade before the Revolution, it is surely plausible that preachers opposed dancing in their sermons. Yet, these sermons may never have been written down, or, if written, simply may not have survived.[79]

Among those clergy who wrote extensively, some eminent divines concentrated on theological treatises rather than polemical prose. They may not have treated the issue of dancing at all, or perhaps they addressed it as part of a larger topic. For example, Nathanael Emmons (1745–1840) spent his entire ministry in Franklin, Massachusetts, in intellectual study and theological exposition. A review of his six-volume *Works* reveals that his whole theology emphasizes duty rather than diversion. He does not mention dancing at all and refers only twice to balls or ballrooms.[80] Joseph Bellamy (1719–90) was another eminent clergyman who spent his entire ministry in one city, in this case, Bethlem, Connecticut. An ardent disciple of Jonathan Edwards, Bellamy studied in the great theologian's home in the later 1730s. In turn, both Bellamy and Emmons trained innumerable young divinity students in the days before seminaries. Bellamy's *Works* was published in two volumes. Nothing in the detailed table of contents for both volumes mentions dancing, balls, amusements, or vanities. However, Bellamy wrote approximately eight pages on opposition to dancing under the larger subject of "Early Piety Recommended," a discourse given at Stratfield, Connecticut, in 1747.[81]

The substance of Bellamy's objections to dancing reinforces the assumption that those who opposed the activity would have come from the ranks of the evangelicals. Those ministers, like Whitefield, preached a direct encounter with Jesus Christ and a life that subsequently renounced worldliness and focused on the development of personal piety. In his Stratfield discourse, Bellamy lamented the decline in piety among young people, which had followed the awakening in New England in the early 1740s. He pointed out that one of the greatest hinderances [*sic*] to serious piety among young people, in most towns and societies, is the habit of attending places of vain and fashionable amusements. This is a habit of long standing in the country; one generation after another has been trained up in the practice of it, whereby a spirit of seriousness and sobriety has been almost rooted out of the land, though a land once famous for religion, for sobriety and universal temperance. Indeed, a few years ago this practice was generally laid aside, throughout all the country. When the Spirit from on high was poured out, when the great things of the eternal world were realized, when conscience was enlightened, awakened, in multitudes; then this practice was judged to be sinful. And no doubt there were hundreds, yea, thousands and thousands of vows and solemn resolutions, made among young people in New England, forever to lay aside the pernicious and insnaring practice of dancing. But since the Spirit of God has withdrawn, . . . the old practice is set up anew.

His challenge to youth to forsake the vain amusements of the world rests not on fear but, ultimately, on joy. Bellamy continued, "There is an unspeakable pleasure in religion itself, antecedent to all other considerations; yea, joy unspeakable and full of glory."[82] His admonitions make no mention of gender. Nor do they specify particular sins of lust, time and money wasted, or the like. His focus seems to be on the positive value of God and religion and on the negative side of worldly, vain amusements or activities that detract one from a total concentration on and devotion to loving God above all things and one's neighbor as oneself.

Bellamy's account of abstinence from dancing in the wake of revival fervor fits with testimony of other clergy. Whitefield's own journal entries about reformed behavior among Charleston gentry imply that he was equally successful in the other urban centers. Jonathan Edwards's report of his congregation in Northampton, Massachusetts, when revival broke out in 1734, declares that people totally changed their lives and their topics of conversation for about a year. Thus, it seems very probable that, with an increase in pious behavior, dancing diminished for periods of time during the successive waves of the Great Awakening.

Attention would also have been diverted from balls and dancing, to some extent, in time of feverish political activity and warfare. The Philadelphia Assembly, for example, met irregularly during the Revolutionary War and revived its normal schedule only in 1783, when hostilities had ceased.

Thus, it would seem that, for a variety of reasons, a relatively small number of dance adversaries wrote during most of the eighteenth century. That would change dramatically in the nineteenth century.

Notes

1. By the middle of the seventeenth century, thoughts on the social value of dancing had been elaborated upon by England's Lord Herbert of Cherbury. See *The Life of Edward First Lord Herbert of Cherbury written by himself*, ed. J. M. Shuttleworth (rpt., London: Oxford University Press, 1976), 31–32. Both Cherbury and Locke are cited in American etiquette books of the nineteenth century. Locke specifically states that the aim of his *Thoughts* is "'how a young gentleman should be brought up from his infancy; which in all things will not so perfectly suit the education of daughters.'" He allows that where the genders require different treatment, "'twill be no hard matter to distinguish." See John Locke, *Some Thoughts Concerning Education* (1693); rpt., ed. and intro. F. W. Garforth (Woodbury, N.Y.: Barron's Educational Series, 1964), 9.

2. Increase Mather, "An Arrow Against Profane and Promiscuous Dancing Drawn out of the Quiver of the Scriptures" (Boston, [1685]; rpt. in *The Mathers on Dancing*, ed. Joseph E. Marks III, Brooklyn: Dance Horizons, 1975), 52.

3. James L. Axtell, *The Educational Writings of John Locke* (Cambridge: Cambridge University Press, 1968), 162, 344–45.

4. Ibid., 310, 161.

5. Ibid., 241, 246, 253, 261–62.

6. Ibid., 310–11.

7. Louis B. Wright, *The First Gentlemen of Virginia* (San Marino, Calif.: Huntington Library, 1940), 81–82.

8. Rhys Isaac, *The Transformation of Virginia 1740–1790* (Chapel Hill: University of North Carolina Press, 1982), 81–85.

9. Norman Arthur Benson, "Itinerant Dance and Music Masters of the Eighteenth Century" (Ph.D. diss., University of Minnesota, 1963), 27, 29, 35.

10. Ibid., 46, 50.

11. Hugh F. Rankin, *The Theater in Colonial America* (Chapel Hill: University of North Carolina Press, 1960), 12–14, 17–18.

12. Benson, "Itinerant Dance and Music Masters," 52, 54.

13. Ibid., 58, 63.

14. Rankin, *Theater in Colonial America*, 200.

15. Wright, *First Gentlemen*, 8–13; Isaac, *Transformation*, 81.

16. Benson, "Itinerant Dance and Music Masters," 116–18, 128, 120–22.

17. Though a European education proved popular among Virginia families, South Carolinians sent a greater number of sons to Inns of Court than did all other American colonies (Benson, "Itinerant Dance and Music Masters," 128). See also Edwin Harrison Cady, *The Gentleman in America* (Syracuse: Syracuse University Press, 1949), 85.

18. Benson, "Itinerant Dance and Music Masters," 129; Barbara Lambert, ed., *Music in Colonial Massachusetts, 1630–1820* (Boston: Colonial Society of Massachusetts, 1985), vol. 2, 954.

19. Rankin, *Theater in Colonial America*, 25.

20. Carl Bridenbaugh, *Cities in the Wilderness: The First Century of Urban Life in America, 1625–1742* (New York: Ronald Press, 1938), 451.

21. Rankin, *Theater in Colonial America*, 27, 29, 63–64, 196, 50–73.

22. Benson, "Itinerant Dance and Music Masters," 147–48.

23. Ibid., 123; Bridenbaugh, *Cities in the Wilderness*, 441.

24. See "Rules and Regulations for the Dancing Assembly of Savannah . . ." (19 Nov. 1790), ([Savannah: James and Nicholas Johnston, 1790]), broadside; see also Charles Evans, *American Bibliography,* #22873. In researching the century's dances, Kate Van Winkel Keller found that English country dances, or "longways" dances, for as many couples as space permitted were the ones that were most often mentioned and best documented. The French cotillion, also danced, engaged only four couples in a square formation. The size of the room would have limited the number of squares. See Kate Van Winkel Keller, *"If the Company Can Do It!" Technique in Eighteenth-Century American Social Dance* (Towson, Md.: Goucher College International Early Dance Institute, 1989), 5.

25. Carl Bridenbaugh, *Cities in Revolt: Urban Life in America, 1743–1776* (New York: Capricorn Books, 1964), 165.

26. Benson, "Itinerant Dance and Music Masters," 263, 259.

27. Ibid., 271–72. Reinforcing the seriousness of their concern, the Dutch magistrates required Stepney to post the equivalent of about $1,250 for good behavior and two years' time plus another amount equivalent to $2,500 for good behavior and one year's time. Failure to put up this money meant that he had to leave the province within six days. As Benson observes, it would have been most surprising if Stepney had possessed this kind of money. No later record of this dancing master exists in the annals of any other city, according to Benson.

28. Ibid., 289, 287, 292–93, 312, 306, 309.

29. Lillian Moore, *Echoes of the American Ballet* (Brooklyn: Dance Horizons, 1976), 50. As in Charleston, the 1790s proved fruitful with respect to dance and theater in New York. The city experienced its first extended season in 1792 when twenty-seven performances of ballets and pantomimes were given between January and May. When the New York season closed, Alexander Placide and company moved on to Philadelphia, Boston, and finally to Charleston, where they settled in 1794.

30. Bridenbaugh, *Cities in the Wilderness,* 303.

31. Benson, "Itinerant Dance and Music Masters," 183, 194–97.

32. Ibid., 199; Bridenbaugh, *Cities in the Wilderness,* 279.

33. Benson, "Itinerant Dance and Music Masters," 213.

34. Bridenbaugh, *Cities in the Wilderness,* 438–39. In the same decade, George Brownell and Theobald Hackett also taught successfully. The latter conducted a boarding school so that students might come from beyond the city to learn good dancing and proper deportment.

35. Benson, "Itinerant Dance and Music Masters," 351, 215; Thomas Willing Balch, *The Philadelphia Assemblies* (Philadelphia: Allen, Lane and Scott, 1916), 14–15, 39–42, 101–2. Rules for the 1794 Philadelphia Assembly were similar to those of the Savannah Assembly. The success of the Philadelphia Assembly apparently inspired similar groups in smaller towns. Lynn Matluck Brooks, a dance historian, has found evidence of balls and assemblies in Lancaster, Pennsylvania, at least by the 1770s, with a regular subscription assembly organized by 1780. See Lynn Matluck Brooks, "The Philadelphia Dancing Assembly in the Eighteenth Century," *Dance Research Journal* 21, no. 1 (Spring 1989): 5.

36. Rankin, *Theater in Colonial America*, 30–33, 41, 38.

37. Ibid., 187. Rhys Issac clarifies that the resolution derived from article eight of the "code of conduct prescribed in the non-importation association." He says that in parts of Virginia, the patriot committees assumed dancing was forbidden as well, although "it had not been specifically listed in the terms of the association." See *Transformation of Virginia*, 247.

38. Benson, "Itinerant Dance and Music Masters," 208–11.

39. Lillian Moore, *Echoes of the American Ballet*, 60; Lillian Moore, "John Durang: The First American Dancer," in *Chronicles of the American Dance*, ed. Paul Magriel (New York: Holt, 1948), 16. Another indication of the cultural cosmopolitanism in end-of-the-century Philadelphia comes from the first edition of the *Encyclopaedia; Or, A Dictionary of Arts, Sciences and Miscellaneous Literature*—in effect, the first edition of the current *Encyclopedia Americana*, modeled after its predecessor, the *Encyclopaedia Britannica*. Appearing in 1798 from a Philadelphia publisher, the book contained fourteen pages on "Dance, or Dancing" that indicate the author's fairly sophisticated knowledge of the art but also his indebtedness to European dance masters.

40. Benson, "Itinerant Dance and Music Masters," 356–57, 368; Lambert, *Music in Colonial Massachusetts*, vol. 2, 846ff.

41. Rankin, *Theater in Colonial America*, 92–93, 201. Interestingly, not a touring company but the British Red Coats commandeered Boston's Faneuil Hall for a playhouse at some point during the Revolution, according to Rankin.

42. Benson, "Itinerant Dance and Music Masters," 351–52; Lambert, *Music in Colonial Massachusetts*, vol. 2, 941–43.

43. James Duncan Phillips, *Salem in the Eighteenth Century* (Boston: Houghton Mifflin, 1937), 182.

44. Benson, "Itinerant Dance and Music Masters," 351–52.

45. J. Hammond Trumbull, *The Memorial History of Hartford County, Connecticut, 1633–1884* (Boston: Edward L. Osgood, 1886), 357, 585–86; Louis Pichierri, *Music in New Hampshire* (New York: Columbia University Press, 1960), 139–44.

46. Bridenbaugh, *Cities in Revolt*, 164; Providence, Rhode Island, "Rules for the Providence [Dancing] Assembly" (Providence: [Bennett Wheeler], 1792), broadside; see Charles Evans, *American Bibliography*, #24723.

47. No single source contains a list of all eighteenth-century dance masters. My count derives from a search of the following sources, in addition to those cited above: Ann Barzel, "European Dance Teachers in the United States," *Dance Index* 3, nos. 4, 5, 6 (Apr., May, June 1944), 56–100; Mary Caroline Crawford, *Social Life in Old New England* (New York: Grosset and Dunlap, 1914); Joseph E. Marks III, *America Learns to Dance* (New York: Dance Horizons, 1957); Richard Nevell, *A Time to Dance: American Country Dancing from Hornpipes to Hot Hash* (New York: St. Martin's Press, 1977); Joy Van Cleef and Kate Van Winkel Keller, "Selected American Country Dances and Their English Sources," *Music in Colonial Massachusetts, 1630–1820* (Boston: Colonial Society of Massachusetts, 1980), vol. 2, 941–43.

48. Research by Van Cleef and Keller reveals eleven New England dance manuscripts, with 212 titles, from approximately 1780 to 1795. See *Music in Colonial Massachusetts,* vol. 1, 12.

49. *A Collection of the Newest Cotillions and Country Dances; Principally Composed by John Griffiths, Dancing Master. To Which Is Added, Instances of Ill manners, to be carefully avoided by Youth of both sexes* (Northampton, Mass.: N.p., [1788]), 11–12.

50. Cady, *Gentleman in America,* 12–13, 55; Arthur M. Schlesinger, *Learning How to Behave* (New York: Macmillan, 1946), 9, 11. Brilliant manners and wisely planned liaisons with well-chosen women could, Chesterfield advised, advance a man in court affairs and enhance social standing. Cady notes that it was Chesterfield's "historical misfortune" to encounter the devotees of the Christian gentleman who were restoring worship of women and chastity. They castigated and caricatured him for the ideal he portrayed. For a review of etiquette books for women and men, see Mary Reed Bobbitt, *A Bibliography of Etiquette Books Published in America before 1900* (New York: New York Public Library, 1947).

51. For a recent analysis of eighteenth-century English society, with attention to gender issues, see G. J. Barker-Benfield, *The Culture of Sensibility* (Chicago: University of Chicago Press, 1992), especially chaps. 2 and 5.

52. Whitefield's second trip to America, from 1739 to 1741, represented the height of the Great Awakening, of which he was a prime mover. In his lifetime he preached over eighteen thousand sermons. Reportedly, he could be heard outside, unamplified, by thirty thousand people. See *The Wycliffe Handbook of Preaching and Preachers,* ed. Warren W. Wiersbe and Lloyd M. Perry (Chicago: Moody Press, 1984), 298.

53. *George Whitefield's Journals (1737–1741),* intro. Wm. V. Davis (Gainesville, Fla.: Scholars' Facsimiles and Reprints, 1969), 387, 376.

54. Ibid., 363–64, 240.

55. Ibid., 379–80.

56. Ibid., 400, 444.

57. Bridenbaugh, *Cities in the Wilderness,* 451; Harry S. Stout, *The Divine Dramatist* (Grand Rapids, Mich.: Eerdmans, 1991), 108.

58. George Whitefield, "Law Gospelized; Or An Address To All Christians Concerning Holiness of Heart and Life . . . ," in *The Works of the Reverend George Whitefield* (London: Edw. and Charles Dilly, 1772), vol. 4, 383, 385, 387–89.

59. Ibid., 390–91.

60. Ibid., 404, 402, 407–8, 417, 419.

61. Ibid., 421–22, 395.

62. Sir Richard Hill, *An Address To Persons Of Fashion, Relating To Balls: With a Few Occasional Hints Concerning Play-Houses, Card-Tables, etc. In Which Is Introduced The Character Of Lucinda, A Lady Of The Very Best Fashion, And Most Extraordinary Piety* (Baltimore: J. Robinson, 1807), 68–69, 72, 74–75. The 1807 edition carries the same arguments as the 1761 third edition from London, which appears in the microform collection *Library of American Civilization,* #40027. See also the microform collection, *American Culture Series,* s.v. "Hill, Sir Richard," for the 1807 edition. See the Boston 1767 edition in Charles Evans, *American Bibliography,* #10644. See also *Dictionary of National Biography,* s.v. "Hill, Sir Richard." In his maiden speech to Parliament in May 1781, Hill spoke to a "Bill for the Better Regulation of the Sabbath." In his 1761 edition he observed that Sunday in "Popish countries" was devoted to horse racing, plays, balls, and cards. This observation did not appear in the 1807 edition. Though a member of the Anglican church, Hill became a defender of the "evangelical clergy" in his area as well as a champion of George Whitefield. He was also a supporter of the British and Foreign Bible Society.

63. Hill, *Address,* 34.

64. Ibid., 38, 54, 46.

65. William Tennent Sr. (1673–1746) and his son, Gilbert Tennent (1703–64), were Presbyterians. Hart preached a sermon in Charleston, published in 1777, "on the Death of the Rev. William Tennent," a fellow cleric and patriot.

66. Wm. B. Sprague, *Annals of the American Pulpit,* vol. 5, s.v. "Hart, Oliver." Charleston Baptists took an active interest in the education of the clergy. Church members gave a large amount toward the establishment of Rhode Island College in 1755 (later known as Brown University); the college conferred an honorary M.A. on Oliver Hart at its first commencement.

67. William Cathcart, *The Baptist Encyclopedia* (Philadelphia: Louis H. Everts, 1881), 1074b.

68. Sprague, *Annals,* vol. 6, s.v. "Hart, Oliver"; *American Writers before 1800,* s.v. "Hart, Oliver."

69. Oliver Hart, "Dancing Exploded. A Sermon showing the unlawfulness, sinfulness and bad consequences of balls, assemblies, and dances in general; preached in Charleston, S.C., 22 March 1778"; rpt. in *The Patriot Preachers of the American Revolution, 1766–1783,* ed. Frank Moore (N.p., 1860), 234. See also Charles Evans, *American Bibliography,* #15848. The military situation in Charleston in 1778, during the Revolutionary War, is not clear. Morison and Commager write that the year

was one of "incompetence and failure on all sides." No French arrived until July. Still, in the absence of any clarification by Hart, we do not know if the fire in Charleston was war-related or not. It seems safe to assume that Hart's patriotic fervor continued after his 1775 assignment by the South Carolina Council of Safety. See Samuel Eliot Morison and Henry Steele Commager, *The Growth of the American Republic* (New York: Oxford University Press, 1952), vol. 1, 218–20.

70. Hart, "Dancing Exploded," 241, 250.

71. Ibid., 240–47.

72. Ibid., 253–55.

73. John Phillips, *A Narrative Shewing Why The Rev. J. Phillips Is Not In Connection With The Episcopalian Methodists. With A Defense Of The Doctrines Held And Taught By The Author* (Charleston, S.C.: J. M'Iver, 1796), preface. See also Charles Evans, *American Bibliography,* #31007; *Minutes of the Annual Conferences of the ME Church For the Years 1773–1828* (New York: T. Mason and G. Lane, 1840), vol. 1, 48, 53.

74. Rev. F. A. Mood, *Methodism in Charleston,* ed. Thomas O. Summers (Nashville: Stevenson and Evans, 1856), 53–58.

75. Francis Asbury, *Journal of Rev. Francis Asbury in Three Volumes* (Cincinnati: Jennings and Pye, n.d.), 2:254–55. Methodist church records indicate that in 1795 there were 65 white members but 280 "Negro" members. Membership among whites grew by only a few people for the next three years but black membership increased by some 140 people. *Minutes,* vol. 1, 60, 80.

76. John Phillips, *Familiar Dialogues on dancing, between a minister and a dancer; taken from matter of fact with an appendix containing some extracts from the writings of pious and eminent men against the entertainments of the stage, and other vain amusements recommended to the perusal of Christians of every Denomination* (New York: T. Kirk, 1798), preface, 6–7; see Charles Evans, *American Bibliography,* #34373.

77. Ibid., 15, 21–22.

78. Ibid., 22–24.

79. See Isaac, *Transformation,* chap. 8, "Popular Upsurge: The Challenge of the Baptists."

80. The substance of Emmons's views on dancing will be treated in the following chapter, because those writings were presented and published in the early nineteenth century. In three talks during the 1790s, delivered to the Society for the Reformation of Morals in Franklin, Massachusetts, Emmons decried "frolicking" and the rage for foreign fashions, customs, and manners. I found no specific mention of dance or theater in these talks. That these pursuits would be indicted under a general theology is not at all in question. For example, Emmons declared in 1792: "Diversions, properly so called, have no foundation either in reason or religion. They are the offspring of a corrupt heart, and nourished by vicious example. God requires duties, and nothing but duties. And the duties which he requires are so various, and so well adapted to our present state, that in the performing of them, we may

find all the relaxation of body and mind, which either can ever require." See "The Force of Example," in *The Works of Nathanael Emmons,* ed. Jacob Ide (Boston: Congregational Board of Publications, 1862; rpt., New York: Garland, 1987), vol. 5, 50. See also sermons titled "The Evil Effects of Sin" (1790), and "Sinful Customs" (1793), in volume 5 of Emmons's *Works.*

81. A researcher sometimes learns of dance opposition through secondary references. For example, I was led to the *Works* of Emmons and Bellamy through writings by nineteenth-century dance opponents who quoted them. But in each instance I had to skim their *Works* and search likely subjects since the nineteenth-century writers cited no specific titles or publications.

82. *The Works of Joseph Bellamy, D.D.,* vol. 1 (Boston: Doctrinal Tract and Book Society, 1853; rpt., New York: Garland, 1987), 551–52 and 562.

5 Early Evangelicals and American Etiquette: 1800–1839

> When we contemplate the Americans . . . there seems
> nothing wanting but the graces of personal behaviour, and
> when these are added, what a glorious picture will they
> appear in the great spectacles of the world?
>
> Saltator, 1807

> The question now to be determined is, whether rational
> and accountable beings . . . have a right to spend their
> precious time, in dancing for mere amusement.
>
> Jacob Ide, 1818

When writing his *Treatise on Dancing,* the anonymous author known only as Saltator lamented a serious deficiency in American education. While citizens displayed bravery in war, enterprise in commercial relations, prudence in domestic spheres, "wisdom in council," and a good taste in "literary knowledge," they neglected the polite arts and accomplishments. Like Locke and the earlier European courtesy writers, Saltator valued dancing as an accomplishment that taught ease of motion and carriage as well as civility. Believing in the importance of good breeding, he urged that serious attention be given to including the "ornamental" part of education in the training of all young men and women. Yet, Saltator's views encountered serious opposition.

As the nineteenth century unfolded, increasing numbers of clergy, especially Congregational and Presbyterian ministers, declared it inappropriate for rational people to spend time in a merely mechanical exercise such as dancing. Some wrote individual sermons in opposition; many supported an organized opposition to dancing and other amusements that developed into the American Tract Society. In addition, organized revivals helped to spread the evangelical fervor, spawned by Whitefield in the eighteenth century, that emphasized separation from worldly vanities. Although few extant treatises opposing dance appeared before 1840, those that were published represent a rising disapproval emanating from different parts of the settled states and territories. The opposition grew as dancing became more prevalent.

The popularity of dancing became far more widespread than in the previous century. People gained entrée into middle- and upper-class balls and assemblies as they learned polite behavior and acquired both money and leisure time, in contrast to earlier eras when access came in the European manner, through an emphasis on birth and lineage. Itinerant dance masters opened schools, wrote instructional manuals, and helped to spread the art into smaller towns in areas away from the major urban centers.

As Americans struggled to define themselves, tensions developed between European ideals for gentlemen and ladies, on the one hand, and republican, as well as denominational, ideals for citizens and Christians, on the other. The definition of such ideals affected women in particular. They could read about dancing and etiquette as American publications addressing these topics grew in number after 1820, and they could heed the advice of female authors in the realm of polite behavior. The new publications gave clear prescriptions concerning the roles of one's social class and gender. But young ladies who also read conduct books written by male clergy encountered conflicting advice. In New England, the struggle between ideals of worldliness and holiness was waged in print by settled clerics and dancing masters.

Controversy in New England:
The Ministers and the Dance Masters

Early evidence for the popularity of dancing in smaller towns comes from Connecticut and Maine. The Reverend William Lyman (1764–1833) delivered his public discourse against dancing in East Haddam, Connecticut, on 24 December 1800. Published under the title *Modern Refinement* in 1801, Lyman's lecture reflects his frustration at the spread of dancing schools beyond the large cities. Finding that there were attempts being made to start "among us a school of modern refinement," he wrote, "I cannot content myself to remain silent on such an occasion. So long as people have been satisfied with having these things confined to cities or places of opulence and grandeur, the friends of virtue have had less reason to be alarmed." However, the schools spread "like foul and noxious weeds," calling for some action to check what Lyman viewed as a growing evil that was "sapping the foundations of sobriety and godliness." Although these schools were variously labeled "Manners' Schools" or "Schools for Morals and Good Manners," Lyman remained convinced that they all amounted to dancing schools. Recalling George Whitefield's lament that every small town had a settled dancing master, Lyman decried the schools' "receiving an establishment in almost every town, society and village." Evidence that Lyman probably did not exaggerate comes from the 1804 *Discourse*, on "Fashionable Amusements," by Kiah Bayley (1770–1857), a pastor in New-Castle, Maine. Though preaching against all worldly amusements, Bayley concentrated particularly on "dancing schools, balls, and assemblies." Like Lyman, he believed it his sacred duty to warn parishioners against threats to the development of a Christian life. Bayley wrote, "The minister, who neglects to warn his people of their danger . . . must answer for the blood of souls."[1]

Lyman considered the dancing schools "as branches or twigs of the general system of anti-christianism which is, at present, demoralizing the world. They serve to unhinge the mind from seriousness and prepare the way for a settled inveteracy against all vital, experimental and practical godliness." While Lyman does not count the exercise of dancing among the greatest of all worldly evils or label it a moral evil in itself, he opposes it on the ground of its tendencies to profaneness and impiety. He argues that the atmosphere at dancing schools leads to giddiness and an attitude of triviality. Moreover, such schools did not foster "rational, solid and useful improvements." Rather, they encouraged only "decorations and mechanical movements of the body." He objects not only to the lack of piety and serious mental development attendant upon dancing, but also to the waste of time and money engendered by dancing schools. Like Cotton Mather and Whitefield, Lyman and Bayley both argue that dancing serves to undermine the authority and importance of the family and that it breaks a covenant made in baptism to "'renounce the devil and his pomps.'"[2]

Taking issue with such views, Francis D. Nichols, a Boston dance master, demonstrated that the New England controversy over dancing schools and the values of dancing was waged among men of literacy with a concern for morality. Nichols's 1810 publication, *A Guide to Politeness: Or, A System of Directions for the Acquirement of Ease, Propriety and Elegance of Manners . . .* , contains forty-six pages on the merits of the art and on rules for deportment but only twelve pages describing new cotillions and country dances. This volume's emphasis on correct behavior contrasts with the content of late eighteenth-century manuals, which stressed instructions on dances but included few rules on polite conduct.

Nichols's emphasis suggests—and his preface acknowledges—that he was responding to arguments of those who denigrated dancing. He may have been overly effusive in his apology. Nonetheless, his manual points to some critical issues. When spelling out the values that dancing holds for both genders, Nichols cites the rise of cities, with men in service jobs, coupled with a decline in the country atmosphere that had provided a natural climate for exercise, particularly for the ladies: "Dancing is peculiarly beneficial to those men, who are engaged in sedentary employments, and who have few opportunities for exercise, and especially for those ladies of our populous cities, who are not engaged in the delightful cares of a family, and have no pleasant and wide-extended plains, over which they may ramble in a cool and cheerful morning, before the rising of the sun."[3] Nichols was convinced that dancing put a bloom to the ladies' cheeks and "perhaps" prevented the dread consumption, which regularly claimed so many victims.

Nichols sought to counter the argument of those who might say that dancing provided merely a physical activity but offered no improvement for the mind. He asserts that a good dancing master would consider it his primary responsibility not only to teach how to move the body with skill and grace but also to instruct youth in "those thousand little items of character and behaviour, which are so far from being trifles, that they decide and stamp the man; they procure for him future reception and favor among mankind; and too often determine through life his prosperity and fortune in the world." Harking back to antiquity for authority, as did certain sixteenth-century courtesy writers, Nichols quotes Cicero on the assertion that an outer calm and grace reflect an inner calm and serenity of mind. Nichols's ontological perspective leads him to declare the superior value of dancing because it develops both mind and body. The claim is unusual for the era: "so very intimately are connected the body and the mind, (the most beautiful with the most noble part of man,) that he, who has elegance of motion, ease and gracefulness of person, will perform every action and every duty that may fall to his lot in life, with the greatest propriety."[4]

Since dancing holds so many crucial values for the man who would be successful in life, and since the good dancing master considers it his duty to instruct youth in character as well as steps and styling, Nichols argues that the dancing school, when well ordered, is both important and necessary. Like Locke, he asserts that the young boy will learn "a becoming and manly civility to his inferiors," a comfortable mien toward equals and superiors, and a "becoming and highly important regard to his parents." Nichols's well-run school would prohibit young men from wearing boots and would discourage uncouth behavior such as smoking, spitting, talking during instruction, laughing at mistakes, or any "uncivil mode of using authority" by the teacher.[5] The contrast with Lyman's notion of the dancing school as an evil resembling "foul and noxious weeds" could hardly be more dramatic.

Other extant sermons indicate that the struggle in New England over the values of dancing continued into the second decade of the century. By December 1818, the Reverend Jacob Ide (1785–1880) of West Medway, Massachusetts, was preaching against balls, which had "become prevalent in this place." His quarrel reiterates the concern for piety and rational living preached by Lyman and Bayley in Connecticut and Maine at least fourteen years earlier:

> My business is with Balls as they are practised at the present day. The question now to be determined is, whether rational and accountable beings, capable of the exalted pleasure of serving and enjoying God, and destined to a future and an eternal existence, in which they are to receive according to the deeds done here in the body, have a right to spend their precious time, in dancing for mere amusement; in circumstances too, where they are exposed to peculiar temptations; where the mind is necessarily dissipated; where health and property are often wantonly sacrificed; devoted to hilarity and mirth; and where, by common consent and the laws of fashion, serious reflection and fervent piety have no place.[6]

Writing in a scholarly style reminiscent of that displayed by Increase Mather and Cotton Mather, Ide elaborates on the above themes by arguing that balls are either "very good things, or they are very bad things." If the former, then they will produce good effects; if the latter, they will produce bad effects. But, whereas the Mathers denounced dancing on the grounds of scriptural and historical authority, Ide stresses the bad effects produced by balls, which, in turn, prove that they are not worthy activities. In particular, he emphasizes the late hours, which rob sleep; the "ardent feelings" excited in youth; the dissipation of mental faculties engendered by the trivial spirit at balls; and the waste of participants' time and money. Just as Cotton Mather commented on parents who were willing to spend huge amounts on dancing lessons but little to improve their children's minds and community spirit, Ide asserts that the cost of a single ball is "often sufficient, and more than sufficient to defray the whole expense of a common District-School a month." Further, he declares that some individuals have spent more on a ball than it would cost to pay a student's tuition at one of the country's best academies for three months. Stressing the importance of home and family, Ide also argues that balls tend to make youth desirous of large gatherings and glamour rather than leaving them content with home as the center of entertainment. Sounding what becomes a common theme later in the century, he declares that familiarity with the ballroom leads many to the card table and later in life from the contentment of home to the intemperance of the "grog-shop."[7] By his logic, the sum of the bad effects produced by balls proves that they are by "nature and tendency" proscribed for Christians.

Ide's focus on "whether rational and accountable beings . . . have a right to spend their precious time, in dancing for mere amusement" reflects a new emphasis in dance opposition, that is, the notion that dancing was evil because it was anti-intellectual. Earlier dance opponents judged the atmosphere at balls to be trivial, but Ide's stress on humans as rational creatures appears symptomatic of the new era, his locale, and his denominational affiliation. Ministerial training among the Congregationalists stressed university preparation and further instruction. The early decades of the nineteenth century found much of New England engulfed by the Second Great Awakening as well as by a tide of rationalism and Unitarianism that swept eastern Massachusetts in particular. More specifically, both Ide and Bayley were influenced by the eminent divine, Nathanael Emmons (1745–1840), an "almost eccentric theological genius."[8] Ide married Emmons's daughter Mary in 1815 and later edited his father-in-law's *Works* in six volumes, published in 1842. Kiah Bayley and his wife both studied with Emmons during 1793–94 before going on to parish work in Maine and founding the Bangor Theological Seminary.[9]

Emmons's Calvinist stance leaves no doubt of his strict moral code and stern emphasis on duty, as against diversions. His 1819 sermon titled "A Warning to Youth" also addresses parents and specifically attacks "vain and sinful amusements," including dancing. In it he asks,

> If it be right to teach youth that their hearts are totally depraved, that they live in an evil and dangerous world, that they are already under a sentence of condemnation and the wrath of God abideth upon them; that they are exposed every day to sickness and death, that death will close their probationary state, and that after death is the judgment; can it be right to provide superb theatres and elegant ball-rooms, at a great expense, for their entertainments and vain amusements?

Emmons's clear and logical thought processes are revealed in his own memoirs and sermons and in additional memoirs by Ide. Though an independent thinker and theologian, Emmons did not stand alone in his opposition to vain amusements or in his concern for moral reform.[10]

The New England Tract Society and the Influence of Hannah More

A moral reform society existed at Yale University as early as 1797; soon such groups became statewide and then national in scope. The first of the American moral crusades waged by such groups focused on temperance. Other early efforts sought to reestablish the sanctity of the Sabbath.[11] These voluntary societies not only sought specific reforms, they also worked to spread the gospel via missions, education, and published tracts. The New England Tract Society, an organization begun in 1814 at Andover, Massachusetts, by a group of Congregationalists, was inspired by the Religious Tract Society organized in London in 1799. The Andover group aimed to distribute tracts that would interest serious Christians across denominational lines.[12]

This evangelical organization exhorted readers to a life of piety and what members believed to be the ideal for the Christian. As a part of that focus, the society issued a treatise, *Fashionable Amusements,* published at the Andover press of Flagg and Gould, in 1815. According to records of the American Antiquarian Society, the first edition ran to six thousand copies. A second edition appeared in 1816 and a fifth by 1823, testifying to the popularity of the topic among a certain segment of the country's population. The publication reiterated themes put forth by Ide, Emmons, Lyman, and Bayley.

Fashionable Amusements addresses pastimes such as cards and plays, but it focuses particularly on the dancing seen at balls or assemblies in the early part of the century. The anonymous author acknowledges the arguments of dance advocates but dismisses them quickly on the grounds that the Bible proscribes many activities in general rather than specific terms; that Christians must follow the guidance of the Bible; and that only the testimony and lives of "genuinely pious" believers can serve as models to follow. The burden of the treatise is summed up in the following: "that fashionable amusements are not consistent with the general tenour of scriptures; that they are expensive; that they occasion loss of time; that they hinder the acquisition of valuable accomplishments, and unfit the mind for communion with God. Other arguments might be brought, but they are thought unnecessary. It is deemed a sufficient reason for relinquishing any pleasure, that it hazards life or health."[13]

In what becomes a common gender-specific argument later in the nineteenth century, the author cites early deaths among females, especially from consumption, as traceable to "vain amusements." By threatening life, amusements also "alienate the soul from God, and thus prepare it for aggravated ruin." Clearly the life of the soul holds preeminence over the body and this earthly life, as the final exhortation indicates: "Reader, you have a soul of infinite value. Shall this soul be wantonly sacrificed? Will you for a single moment hazard its loss, for the sake of vain amusements?"[14]

The emphasis on practical piety was reinforced in an extract from the writing of Hannah More (1745–1833), an Englishwoman who wrote extensively on matters of religion from 1772 until well into the following century. A portion of More's writing was appended to the tract society's publication on amusements. It points to those evils of the polite world that Whitefield had decried, such as the lack of a personal religion and the amount of time and energy wasted in following the customs of society. More was known in America well before extracts of her essays appeared in *Fashionable Amusements*. For example, Bayley quoted her in 1804 with respect to female education and modesty. The eventual popularity of her writing in this country is suggested by the fact that her collected works were published in two volumes in an 1841 American edition.[15] Thus, More becomes the first female author to join the American dance opponents.

Presbyterian Opposition

The themes of the New England Tract Society publication were soon echoed by Presbyterian writers and thinkers. In fact, among the orthodox denominations with a well-educated clergy, Presbyterians proved to be early and active opponents of dancing. Their concern was expressed formally by 1818 in a "Pastoral Letter to the General Assembly."[16] A few years earlier an anonymous treatise had appeared from a Philadelphia press that addressed young ladies on the issue of dancing. Published around 1814–15 and probably authored by a Presbyterian, the *Essay on Dancing* stressed the implications of the mind-body dualism that Ide had assumed. The writer reasoned that, since dancing is merely a "mechanical art which requires but little exercise of the understanding," proficiency in it indicates virtually no intellectual excellence or improved understanding. Dancing "conveys no useful ideas to the mind," unless one considers the ideas pertaining to the art itself as useful. Because the sole purpose of dancing is pleasure, it represents only the lowest of human faculties—animal sensuality. Dancing, thus, becomes criminal, an animal pleasure elevated to the chief object of human desire. Because dancing is a carnal activity and because carnal activities are proscribed by the Bible under Paul's exhortation to avoid all "works of the flesh," including "revellings and such like" (Gal. 5:16–25), dancing is therefore prohibited by the Bible.[17] Such views are reiterated in books by later Presbyterian clergy.

Parish Pastors

Both Thomas Charlton Henry (1790–1827) and Joseph Penney (1790–1860) represent the tradition of well-educated ministers. Their careers reflect the Presbyterians' geographical spread and a rise in denominational membership. Henry wrote from Charleston in 1825; Penney, from Rochester, New York, in 1829.[18] Their publications offer a more complete understanding of the theological reasoning behind the dance opposition evidenced by both Presbyterians and Congregationalists.

Following the Pauline prescription, "Do not conform yourselves to the standards of this world, but let God transform you inwardly by a complete change of your mind" (Rom. 12:2), Penney and Henry assert that the true Christian must be separated from the world and dedicated to serving God, not humans. To be separate from the world does not mean "an ascetic retirement" but rather abstinence from anything that would make the Christian appear like the "worldling." Participation in amusements simply renders the Christian indistinguishable from the person of the world. Moreover, amusements provide temptations to sin that the Christian must, in good conscience, avoid. Dancing, for example, tends to tarnish the natural bashfulness of females; it wears down "that retiring feeling, which to the unsophisticated taste constitutes a principal charm of the female sex." To be vain and flippant runs counter to the virtues of piety and purity.[19]

An attitude of separation from the world developed naturally from the process of conversion and salvation, according to the Presbyterians. The converted sinner possessed a new heart and mind. He or she focused on glorifying God and on reaching the ultimate goal of eternal life, whereas the person with the unrenewed heart looked only to the present moment and to personal gratification. In stressing personal and total commitment, Henry sounds exactly like Whitefield, who declared that Christianity is most assailed by those outwardly professing religion but not inwardly renewed. Henry writes, "It is not when Christianity is openly assailed, and its defenders subjected to persecution, that evangelical truth is most in danger. It is when religion is outwardly respected—when no temporal affliction follows a profession—when thousands make it without counting the cost—and when, accordingly, the distinguishing traits of piety are crowded out by a temper of worldliness." Henry declares that those who advocate amusements are not known for their "spirituality" and "holy zeal." Moreover, he argues that amusements induce a spirit contrary to religious devotion; they divert the mind from God, prayer, and meditation on the Word.[20]

The truly pious soul will focus on good stewardship of time. Every day is important "to secure the essential objects for which one was sent into the world—sanctification of the soul, and advancement of the Redeemer's cause." To believe that humans were sent into the world merely to enjoy themselves amid momentary pleasures is, in Henry's view, tantamount to heresy.[21] While God does not forbid the enjoyment of pleasures, Penney declares that worldly amusements are nothing but the "avowed carnivals of the pleasures of sense, where pleasure is pursued for its own sake, and from which a regard to the great ends of life is professedly excluded."[22]

Emphasizing the importance of rationality, as Ide and Lyman did, Penney asserts that the nature of humans is such that they possess several faculties: a sensual or animal faculty, a rational soul, and a moral faculty. The first they hold in common with brute beasts. The second functions to govern the animal passions. The third raises humans still higher in the order of being. Since the moral faculty is "perverted and depraved," the restraints of reason and conscience must be sensitized and constantly used. If not, animal sensuality will rule, and the result will be self-gratification rather than God-glorification.

Though Bible-centered in their authority for opposition to dancing, the Presbyterian writers acknowledge that Scripture nowhere specifically prohibits dancing. Henry provides an explanation for those who would ask why dancing is not specifically condemned in Scripture, if it is evil. He says that the Bible could not precisely forbid all customs "inimical to religion" or the Scriptures would have become unwieldy. Hence, the "inspired writers" described the "relative duties of a pious life" required of a Christian.[23]

The Professional Evangelist

An emphasis on piety and holiness as counters to vanity and worldliness came from the first American to become nationally known as a professional evangelist. Between 1825 and 1830 Charles Grandison Finney (1792–1897) gained a widespread reputation for his successful revivals in cities along the Erie Canal, from Troy to Rochester, an area termed the "burnt district" because of the successive waves of revivals that swept the territory. Converted by the Presbyterian preacher George W. Gale in 1821, Finney left his law practice because he felt he had received a "retainer" from Christ to be his advocate. Ordained by the Presbyterians, Finney antagonized many members of that denomination, as well as traditional Congregationalists, because of his theology and his introduction of new revival techniques such as the "anxious bench" (a place for the "almost saved" so they could receive special attention), prayer and exhortations by women, and extended nightly meetings.[24] In effect, Finney declared that men motivated revivals by using successful methods.

Finney's opposition to dancing and amusements followed from his Americanized theology. A product of Jacksonian America, Finney repudiated traditional Calvinistic doctrine, which had proclaimed the moral depravity of man. He held that anyone who repented could gain immediate assurance of salvation. The contrast of his ideas with the orthodox Calvinistic belief in predestination was marked. When sin became a voluntary act, rather than an inheritance of original sin, then it became avoidable, and entire sanctification or holiness became possible.[25]

Usefulness coupled with temperance in all things proved the critical basis for right living. Christians had to learn to practice self-denial and to say no to temptation, separating themselves from worldly companions, tobacco, coffee, fashion, and the like. Finney would indict persons who spent money on such stimulants and diversions when that money could be better allocated for missionary efforts that would redeem the world: "Sit down and talk with many persons, and they will strenuously maintain that they cannot get along without these stimulants, these poisons, and they cannot give them up—no, not to redeem the world from eternal damnation. . . . O, how long shall the church show her hypocritical face at the Monthly Concert, and pray God to save the world, while she is actually *throwing away* five times as much for sheer intemperance, as she will give to save the world."[26] Finney's argument assumed that all people should spend their money in the same manner. It points to a legalistic brand of Christianity, based on piety and duty.

Not surprisingly, Finney sometimes attacked women from the pulpit for what he considered luxurious dress and slavish adherence to the rules of fashion. In his instructions on how to grow in grace, he declared: "Guard against pride and vanity in all their forms. Be very careful never to purchase an article of dress, or furniture, or any thing calculated to foster vanity in your mind. Woman, you are going to buy a bonnet, be careful not to get one that will make you think of it when you wear it. Alas! how much pains some people take to foster their own bad passions." Echoing the same theme in his lecture on "means to be used with sinners," Finney invoked the apostle Paul, who exhorted women to avoid costly array (1 Tim. 2:9). Finney advised women specifically to give up ribbons, jewelry, feathers, "broidered hair," and hoop skirts. Of course, the truly converted no longer had any desire for such vanities of the world. Like Whitefield, Finney asserted that serious believers willingly turned from such temptations. "Instead of lusting after the flesh-pots of Egypt, and desiring to go into their former circles, parties, balls, and the like, they find their highest pleasure in obeying God."[27]

In characterizing Finney's attitude toward polite society, the historian William G. McLoughlin writes that Finney carried a distrust for the diversions of the city and the refinements of social class. They tended to clash with duty, self-denial, and evangelism. Dancing and balls, of course, existed for people who had free time to indulge in recreations and to cultivate the manners of the polite world. According to McLoughlin, Finney considered dancing and other popular diversions only "slightly less heinous" than breaking the commandments against adultery and murder.[28]

Some later dance opponents argued that dancing was wicked because it worked in opposition to revivals. Finney sensibly recognized that any "diverting excitements" could have the same effect:

> Diverting excitements, if strong and permanent, will prevent a revival. Hence, it has always been the policy of Satan to keep the church, and if possible the ministry, in a state of worldly excitement. It is not very material what particular form these excitements take on, whether a pressure of business, of politics, of worldly amusements, of balls, or parties, or theatres, or games, or clubs. Whatever strongly excites the masses to the extent of diverting their attention, will prevent a revival of religion.[29]

Though Finney gained national prominence during the late 1820s and very early 1830s due to his enormous evangelistic successes in the cities of western New York, he quit the circuit in 1832 to pastor the Second Free Presbyterian Church in New York City. Three years later he went to Oberlin, Ohio, where he remained for the rest of his long life. He served first as professor of theology, then as president, at Oberlin College. He was also pastor of the First Congregational Church in Oberlin. It was from Ohio that Finney wrote in 1873 against "Innocent Amusements." Those essays and sermons, written in the twilight of his career, will be discussed in chapter 7.

Frontier Revivals and the "Dancing Exercise"

The camp-meeting revival, wherein settlers gathered from miles around to hear preachers exhort them to repentance and reform, was critical to the successful evangelizing of the frontier. The excesses of enthusiastic fervor that reportedly emanated from these meetings included so-called "dancing" as well as other examples of movement behavior. The more staid, rational, and better-educated Presbyterian and Congregational clergy looked with horror upon such disorderly physical manifestations of encounters with the Holy Spirit. Nonetheless, it was a Presbyterian who announced a camp meeting that has become famous as the greatest spiritual outpouring since Pentecost.[30]

In 1800 Barton Warren Stone (1772–1844) served the small churches at Cane Ridge and Concord in Bourbon County, Kentucky. His announcement of a meeting to be held at Cane Ridge on 6 August 1801 drew people by the thousands—by some estimates from ten thousand to twenty-five thousand—including both laity and ministers of Baptist and Methodist denominations. Typically, camp meetings served social as well as religious functions, since many folks came several miles by foot and horse. The Cane Ridge meeting lasted for six or seven days and nights. Of its significance to later generations, Ahlstrom writes: "It marks a watershed in American church history, and the little log meetinghouse around which multitudes thronged and writhed has become a shrine for all who invoke the 'frontier spirit' in American Christianity."[31]

Stone's autobiography includes an entire chapter devoted to the various bodily manifestations that seized the multitudes at Cane Ridge. In his account of these "remarkable religious exercises," Stone describes the "falling exercise," in which a subject emitted a piercing scream and fell like a log, only to appear as though dead on the floor or ground. Apparently such manifestations were common among "saints and sinners" of every class and age at the meeting, and Stone reports that he saw thousands of these displays. People who succumbed to the "jerks" endured apparently uncontrollable jerking in one part of the body or throughout the entire body. Some were thrown to the ground by the violence of the motion. Those who displayed the "jerks" but at the same time made a barking or grunting noise demonstrated the "barking exercise." Other people involuntarily broke into uncontrollable laughter. "The subject appeared rapturously solemn, and his laughter excited solemnity in saints and sinners. It is truly indescribable," Stone reported. Still others ran or attempted to run from the gathering. Before they got very far, they fell to the ground or became so agitated that they could not continue. Finally, some fell into the "dancing exercise," which Stone describes:

> This generally began with the jerks, and was peculiar to professors of religion. The subject, after jerking awhile, began to dance, and then the jerks would cease. Such dancing was indeed heavenly to the spectators; there was nothing in it like levity, nor calculated to excite levity in the beholders. The smile of heaven shone on the countenance of the subject, and assimilated to angels appeared the whole

person. Sometimes the motion was quick and sometimes slow. Thus they continued to move forward and backward in the same track or alley till nature seemed exhausted, and they would fall prostrate on the floor or earth, unless caught by those standing by. While thus exercised, I have heard their solemn praises and prayers ascending to God.[32]

Stone does not comment on the exercises beyond describing what he saw. There is no way of knowing if subjects had been somehow primed for such behavior by the preaching they heard. It seems plausible that the untamed frontier setting, the generally uneducated status of Baptist and Methodist clergy and settlers, and the size of the gathering produced a climate conducive to emotional excess. Although Stone's account of the "dancing exercise" at Cane Ridge may be the only known first-hand description in this country of such so-called "dancing," other historical accounts have been preserved.[33] It seems likely that such phenomena occurred at other camp meetings in the early nineteenth century.

The "dancing exercise" Stone described obviously contrasted dramatically with the fashionable and refined dancing at contemporary balls and assemblies. Given the emphases on rational and moral behavior preached by eastern Congregational and Presbyterian parish pastors such as Ide and Henry, one can understand that these ministers would eschew the frontier fervor as much as the polite assemblies—on the grounds that both activities were nonrational or nonintellectual. A different basis for dance opposition emerged in two other published primary sources.

Patriotic Opposition

In 1828 an anonymous writer from Philadelphia, calling himself "A Representative of Thousands," penned *A Few Reflections upon the Fancy Ball, Otherwise Known as the City Dancing Assembly.* The title clarifies that he aimed his arguments at the Philadelphia Dancing Assembly, begun in the winter of 1748–49. His opposition arises mainly from democratic-republican assumptions, which were typical of the country's attempt to distinguish an American identity during the first third of the nineteenth century. The self-styled "Representative of Thousands" spells out antiaristocratic and anti-European attitudes in specific language:

When we first learnt that the Fancy Ball . . . was about to take place, we could not, as rational beings, as republicans, as Americans! credit so unreasonable, though not unpopular, a report. . . .

For what is obtained by mingling in so grand a Carnival? Is it, gentlemen, we ask ye, for the pleasure of imitating those things ye would scorn to bow down before?—Kings?—To strut about a ball-room for an hour or two, in the character of a nobleman! to be introduced to the "King of _____" as "My Lord _____ of _____?" And the Ladies too!—Fie! for shame!—Has modesty lost her blush? dressed out in "robes of state," to please the greedy eyes of the opposite sex.[34]

Apart from his objections to the courtly attire and etiquette apparently to be represented at the ball, the author argues strongly against the excessive cost of admission. The initial ticket price was evidently $15 but was raised to $40 due to demand. The Philadelphian's objection, like that of Jacob Ide, centers on how such money could be better spent in society. For example, the Philadelphian declares that if 150 people each paid only $15, the total of $2,250 would be enough to supply 450 destitute families with wood for the winter. Moreover, making such a contribution would, he asserts, prove far more satisfying to the donor than would purchasing tickets for an evening of idle pleasure. Further, the reported demoralizing effect on the city's poor who heard about the proposed ball had apparently been widespread: "The Fancy Ball has been a source of unparalleled aggravation to the poor, and cannot but arouse them to a deeper sense of their own poverty, wretchedness and misery, thereby adding another agonizing pang to their sufferings; and also, to reflect upon the conduct of those whose object it should be to alleviate (as far as in their power lies) their condition; instead of giving them new cause to regret their deplorable fate."

Although the "Representative's" advocacy of noblesse oblige could reflect humanitarian or socialist sympathies, his other arguments suggest that he held a Christian bias. Apparently several tailoring establishments in Philadelphia remained open on the Sabbath to construct garments for an upcoming ball. The author declares that those who work on Sunday break an important commandment. Yet he appears not to be a typical evangelical Christian, for he declares theater to be more profitable to participants than would dancing since the former provides "more rational" and "truly instructive" amusement.[35]

Clearly, not all Americans agreed with the author of *A Few Reflections* concerning the merits of the theater. The Reverend Jeremiah Bell Jeter (1802–80) delivered "A Discourse on the Immoral Tendency of Theatrical Amusements" in the First Baptist Church of Richmond, Virginia, on 25 March 1838. His sermon was part of a series organized by the city's clergy. They felt that the theater had become too offensive to the "refinement and the virtue of the community." Though Jeter had become pastor of the First Baptist Church just two years earlier, his sermon was so successful that several men, including state legislators, asked for copies of it, resulting in its publication.

The biblical texts Jeter cites—for example, Paul's admonition to "abstain from all appearance of evil" (1 Thess. 5:22)—are typical of those used by evangelicals of all denominations. But Jeter introduces patriotic concerns as well. He cites the resolution during the Revolutionary War by which the Continental Congress tried to suppress theatrical entertainments as well as gaming and other diversions productive only of idleness and dissipation.[36] Jeter does not quote the entire resolution but rehearses the preamble, which asserts that "'true religion and good morals, are the only solid foundation of public liberty and happiness.'" His specific objections to theatrical entertainments concentrate on the immoral influence they spread, which serves to subvert "national prosperity and independence." He contends that the subject and dialogue of plays contain profanity; vice is "artfully . . . instilled." In fact, the latter proves its allure: "The comedy, the farce, the buffoonery, the merry song, the brilliant scenery, the vulgar jest, the indelicate dance, the profanity and obscenity of the low comedians—these are its grand attractives."

On a national level, Jeter believed, such demoralizing influence militates against the development of patriotism, public spirit, industry, enterprise, and economy. Theater fosters idleness, luxury, and dissipation. These charges emanate not only from a concern for national prosperity and independence, but also from the authority of the Bible and the evangelical belief that the true Christian must be separated from the demands of the flesh and the world.[37] Thus, Jeter's fundamental position as a Baptist objecting to theatrical entertainments differs little from the basic viewpoint of contemporary Presbyterians and Congregationalists who opposed balls and assemblies. Although Jeter's stance recalls eighteenth-century laws against theatrical entertainments in Pennsylvania and Massachusetts, which attempted to foster frugality and industry, not until the early twentieth-century tirades of Billy Sunday would patriotism and dance opposition again be so closely linked.

American Tract Society

By the time that Jeter wrote his antidance views, the burgeoning American Tract Society had been vigorously active for over a decade. In the early 1830s this group published a brief tract titled *A Time to Dance*. It purports to summarize the biblical references to dancing and establish that the passage from

Ecclesiastes quoted in its title did not give approval to contemporary dancing at balls, assemblies, or schools of dancing. The importance of this organized opposition and the widespread circulation of the tract can hardly be
overestimated.

Formed on a national scale in 1825, the American Tract Society grew
rapidly in its early years and distributed its materials in all sections of the
country. Stephen Slocum's study of the association from 1825 to 1975 shows
that it initially printed titles inherited from the earlier New England Tract
Society. However, the American Tract Society added about fifteen new titles each year between 1827 and 1850. By 1832, a summary of titles then
in print included a total of 280 different tracts. Of that number, about 20
were devoted to fighting popular vices.

The leaflet on dancing appeared probably in 1833. Its circulation can be
judged by the scope of contacts that the society had established. Slocum's
research indicates that by 1830 the American Tract Society claimed to be
affiliated with "some 2,606 auxiliaries located in towns and villages of every state and territory of the union." The success and solvency of its publishing efforts are attested to by the fact that the annual budget increased
from just over $10,000 in the first year of operation to over $308,000 by
1850. The interdenominational makeup of the society's board surely contributed to the universal popularity of its publications. Known dance opponents on its original national board included Charles P. McIlvaine, an
Episcopalian bishop of Ohio who was widely quoted in later decades by
antidance authors, and Henry Ward Beecher, the Congregational preacher
in Indiana and New York City who, among other things, became an outspoken critic of the ballet dancer Fanny Elssler's success in this country in
the early 1840s.[38]

Despite the persuasive power of such a well-organized national opposition
to dancing, many Americans continued to enjoy balls and assemblies. Some
thought dancing to be an artistic activity. Others valued it as a social pursuit.
Some also defended it as a rational art that involved the whole person.

Social and Aesthetic Values of Dancing

Just months before Jacob Ide preached against dancing in West Medway in
1818, an old resident of Concord—unnamed—wrote a *Short and Hasty
Essay in Favour of Dancing and Musick*. A conflict raged in Concord over
the closing of a local dancing school and the character assassination of the
dancing master. The anonymous author comments that he almost had been

"compelled to write in self-defence [*sic*]," presumably because some of the students at the dancing school had been his relatives. He does not tell readers why the school closed, but he says he was prompted to write because of numerous "illiberal remarks" he had heard concerning dancing, the school, and the "Master and Scholars." Having personally attended the school by invitation on several occasions, the author testifies to the decorum and modesty practiced between the sexes and to the "excellent good order" kept by the dancing master.[39]

The remarks against dancing that irritated the author had appeared in the *Middlesex Gazette* from the pen of one "Timothy Rightrate." Rushing to aid the art, the Concord citizen responded in effusive terms about the benefits of dancing as a polite art:

> Dancing, if considered merely as a recreation is, perhaps, the most innocent, brilliant, and captivating pastime that man ever did, or can invent; sometimes imparting to the participators, sensations of the most exquisite delight, approaching even to rapture! Yet, after all, what makes me an advocate and promoter of this diversion, is, a belief of its great utility to mankind. . . . How is the contour of this beautiful, majestic, and godlike structure, man, shown to the best advantage? He bears an indubitable stamp of divinity in all positions; but is more particularly graceful when in motion; and the almost infinite variety of dances invented, are, no doubt, the happiest mean, whereby he can display the symmetry of his form to the best possible advantage.[40]

The "utility" of dancing pertains to the grace and carriage of the body. By linking the human form with divine creation, the Concord defender casts the value of dancing in terms far greater than merely social advantage. The ascribed aesthetic value reinforces similar imputations by Nichols and Saltator years earlier.

Whether or not the Concord writer had read the treatises published in Boston by dance advocates is not clear, but Saltator particularly stressed the aesthetic aspect of dancing and choreographing. He quoted extensively from the 1798 *Encyclopaedia,* which cites Jean Georges Noverre, a French ballet master, and Andrea Gallini, an Italian dance master at the Haymarket Theater in London. Like Locke, Saltator declared that dancing gives a "respectful and manly address." He also stressed the importance of knowing the "true harmony and composure of the limbs."[41] The aesthetic and the socially useful became intertwined in his apology for dancing just as those values had been since the sixteenth century, when authors of courtesy books wrote similarly for the instruction of gentlemen and ladies.

For defenders of dancing, such as the Concord resident and Saltator, aesthetic valuing also becomes intertwined with an ontological view that sees dancing as an art involving the whole person. Reinforcing the opinion that dancing was no mindless or mechanical activity, Saltator asserted that the true aim in dancing is "to make the mind and body improve together; and if possible, to make gesture follow tho't, and not let thought be employed upon gesture." Pursuing the point on dancing as a total art, Saltator continues:

> It has been an error in the wiser and soberer part of mankind, to think that the art of dancing gave the mind a turn to levity, which is prejudicial to the Christian religion; but under favor of the soberer and wiser part of mankind, it is believed to be quite the reverse: It teaches persons a fit and suitable conduct of their carriages and behaviour, while their minds are engaged in the solemn duties of devotion. It teaches them those reverential attitudes of their person and aspect, which the sentiments of the heart wish to express and which are required of all, when engaged in that solemn performance.

Not only must mind and body be harmonized in dancing, movement must fit the musical accompaniment so that the dancing displays "the highest summit of grace and beauty, that the human figure is capable of."[42]

Despite his unreserved admiration for the art of dancing, Saltator does not extol its virtues in unqualified terms. He actually decries the general run of dance masters:

> The instructors of this polite accomplishment are in general, men of the most illiterate class, whose only knowledge is contained in their heels and fiddle. They know nothing of the true harmony of motion and jesture, understand but little, if any thing at all of good-breeding; and all that recomends them, is, they will keep cheaper than the accomplished instructor. They generally make their own music, and in their own schools, there is no kind of moral deportment inculcated, nor actions expressive of moral dignity.

Saltator's charges would seem to contradict the emphasis on good breeding in Nichols's 1810 manual. It is not clear when Nichols went to Boston to teach, hence if Saltator had the opportunity to know him. Saltator could not have spoken so highly of dancing in aesthetic terms unless he had encountered some of the better dance masters. Nonetheless, in addition to stressing the need for high-quality dance masters, Saltator advises that amusements must be pursued temperately. Dancing too often and too late at night deprived the art of its "moral beauty."[43]

Vigorous support for dance also came from a surprising contemporary source abroad. The Reverend G. Oliver, D.D. (1781–1861), an Anglican cleric in England, wrote *A Vindication of Rational Amusements,* which, though published in England in 1818, found its way to Yale University, ultimately to be included in a volume called *College Pamphlets*. In his preface, Oliver decries the Methodists who were then widely circulating several publications, including George Burder's *Village Sermons*. Oliver scorns such reading as "senseless ribaldry" whose sole aim is to save souls. In defending amusements, he points out—as did Luther and Mulcaster in the sixteenth century—that men may often abuse an activity, but the fact of abuse by some ought not to prevent all Christians from engaging in what is in itself neither harmful nor sinful. Oliver makes a critical point by declaring that evil has often been ascribed to an activity whereas the evil actually lies in those who participate from wrong motives. If the Christian's only goal in taking part is "innocent" amusement or recreation, Oliver maintains that such activities are permissible.[44] Motive, therefore, becomes the key variable in distinguishing lawfulness.

This valuing of dance on combined moral, rational, social, and aesthetic grounds recalls the themes of dance advocates among sixteenth-century courtesy writers who emphasized that well-ordered form and motion resulted from dancing governed by reason. Such dancing served as an aesthetically pleasing and socially useful pastime for gentlefolk. But, whereas courtesy writers and philosophers such as Locke had advocated the art in prior centuries, the early nineteenth-century advocacy, Oliver's excepted, came from anonymous writers and from dance masters, descendants of those who had been run out of seventeenth-century Boston.

However, advocacy of dancing also came to the new American and republican citizenry from etiquette writers, an emerging group of authorities, some of whom were native-born and others of whom continued the English tradition of gentility. Though many of these authorities were male, increasing numbers of women began to prescribe a code of conduct for polite Americans, which included dancing, balls, and assemblies. The kind of dancing they advocated was formal, ordered, and rule-governed, according to the literature of the day.

Assemblies and Dances

That evening assemblies continued in the early nineteenth century is evident from an 1810 broadside stating the rules of the Salem Assembly. Similar in content to rules for the Providence and Savannah subscription assemblies published in the 1790s, the Salem regulations admitted no gentleman unless he had attained the age of twenty years and subscribed to the Assembly. No woman under the age of sixteen could attend. Dancing evenings began at six o'clock, though it is not clear if the dancers followed Saltator's advice and concluded at a prudent hour. Managers governed the evening's choice of partners, order of dances, and the like. They also granted permission for couples to leave their sets, and they generally maintained strict order. No particular attire was prescribed for ladies, but gentlemen were forbidden to dance in leather boots or pantaloons.[45]

J. H. Trumbull's history of Hartford County in Connecticut confirms that assemblies and cotillion parties remained popular in New England but also suggests that war, as well as outspoken preaching, may have put an end to some occasions for dancing. Trumbull asserts that the War of 1812 probably would have caused the demise of the Hartford Assemblies even if nothing else had happened. But apparently the company also grew less exclusive, and the behavior of some gentlemen brought reproach upon the assembly. Cotillion parties continued there until 1817, when assemblies were revived for two years; local preaching and revivals seem to have put a stop to regular assemblies in Hartford from that time on.[46]

At the beginning of the century, Saltator had stated that country dances were the most common of all forms then practiced. Though not so elegant as some dances, they provided an "agreeable party," in his opinion. Cotillions also proved popular, as Nichols's 1810 dance manual demonstrates. Both kinds of group figure dances depended upon communal participation and spirit; they did not require individual or group virtuoso performances. Yet, to be danced well, they necessitated some instruction and practice, according to contemporary dance and etiquette manuals. The dance instructional manual of E. H. Conway, titled *Le Maitre de Danse or, The Art of Dancing Cotillons: By Which Every One May Learn to Dance Them without a Master . . .* (1827), confirms the continued popularity of the communal dances through the first quarter of the century. Conway, a New York dancing master, presents figures for nineteen sets of cotillions as well as the French terms and definitions for necessary patterns, directions, and steps.

Conway's manual continued the centuries-old tradition of dance masters' publishing instructional books for the reading public. Unlike some eighteenth-century publications containing music with figures for country dances, Conway's book concentrated on dance terminology, directions for dancers, and some remarks on the value of the art. The reader understands from the title page that the book permits one to learn dancing without a "master." The subtitle may have been only a ploy to sell books, but the author's instructions are in fact fairly explicit. The traveling steps in vogue for the country dances and cotillions might indeed have been learned without the services of a dance master, provided a dancer knew the figures. Conway supplied drawings of the figures for just that reason.

In extolling dancing, Conway emphasizes its health value, the graceful agility it teaches, and the social accomplishment it imparts, calling it one of the "principal graces."[47] In the course of his writing Conway cites Quintilian's treatise on the education of orators, suggesting that the New Yorker was quite literate and not unfamiliar with classical literature. This seems to counter Saltator's indictment that the general run of dance masters possessed all their knowledge in their "heels" and "fiddles."

A review of other American imprint titles for the 1820s indicates that new dances were then beginning to edge into popularity. Waltzes appeared from the presses of music publishers after 1820. They represent the new closed couple traveling dances, which would draw the sustained fire of dance opponents after 1840. The ubiquitous nineteenth-century group figure dances, the quadrilles, appeared in print by 1825.[48]

More information about the dancing then in vogue and the quality of contemporary assemblies appears in the *Encyclopaedia Americana*. The first edition of that reference book is dated 1829–33. However, the same information on "Dancing" that appears there is repeated in the 1836 and 1857 editions. After discussing the impression that dancing is merely instinctive, the anonymous author declares that, in the course of time, "Grace became one of its chief objects, and it was much cultivated as an elegant amusement in the intercourse of society, and an elegant spectacle in public entertainments." The reader also learns that dancing "has always been cultivated among Christians, as an agreeable amusement and elegant exhibition." But acknowledgment follows that at the present day, polite assemblies are "too much crowded to leave room for graceful dancing, and, in England and the U. States, one kind of dance, being kept up during a whole evening, of course tends to produce tediousness."[49]

American Etiquette and Character Books

Very few etiquette books appeared from American presses in the eighteenth century, but the almost feverish outpouring of these volumes after 1820 demonstrates that citizens of the new republic became avidly concerned with acquiring the polite graces demanded in a genteel world. Despite some continued English influence in the first half of the century, Americans eventually developed their own authorities and their own rules. Arthur Schlesinger, in his analysis of this genre, reports that an incomplete count found twenty-eight different manuals published in the 1830s.[50] The majority of the books came from the pens of women or anonymous authors. However, some were written by male clergy. The distinctions drawn by the two kinds of authors, with respect to dance, shed light on the controversy surrounding the art in the first third of the century.

Some etiquette books primarily provided a discussion of rules for behavior. Early publications in this category highlight the American character of the author and/or the prescriptions. For example, an expurgated and final volume of Chesterfield appeared in 1828 under the title *The American Chesterfield . . . with Alterations and Additions Suited to the Youth of the United States.* Its advice on dancing merely followed the original volumes, in which Chesterfield advised his son to know how to dance because the practice prevailed in society. To dance well pleased others, just as wearing a wig and good clothes was fashionable and pleasing.

The anonymous author of the *Ladies and Gentlemen's American Etiquette,* published in Andover, perhaps in the 1820s, quotes Chesterfield on dancing's being one of the "established follies" to which sensible people conform. But the book proves more illuminating with respect to behavior in the "Ball-Room," a topic meriting a short chapter. The prescribed accoutrements for ladies include white kid gloves; small, well-fitting shoes; and a perfumed, snowy white handkerchief. Beyond that, the author declines to prescribe appropriate dress, since fashion changes constantly. As for her conduct, the lady is advised to avoid staring and loudness, to make up her own party when going to a public ball, and to dance little when giving her own ball. The gentlemen reader is told to wear gloves, lead gently, avoid performing with the skill or style of a dancing master, engage a lady for a dance well ahead of the scheduled number, and avoid quarreling in a ballroom. He is reminded that meeting a lady at a ball does not give him license to greet her as a friend on the street the following day unless she chooses to recognize him as an acquaintance. Heralding a later controversy about the permissibility of waltzing, the author advises the gentleman: "If you cannot waltz gracefully and well, do not venture at all. The gentleman is shown more in his waltzing than any other dance. He will exercise the utmost delicacy in touching the waist of his partner." When dancing a quadrille, the gentleman was told to know something of the figure before standing up in the dance.[51]

Several books from early in the century specifically addressed one sex or the other. Those for men continued the long tradition of the ideal gentleman, reiterating the distinctions between the true gentleman and the man of fashion that had been drawn in the eighteenth century. For example, an 1836 publication titled *The Laws of Etiquette,* "By a Gentleman," cautions that the two kinds of men must never be confused: "Men of fashion are to be seen everywhere: a pure and mere gentleman is the rarest thing alive." According to the American author, a model of the "pure gentleman" could be found in the English Lord Herbert of Cherbury, not Chesterfield. *The Laws of Etiquette* discusses rules for public meetings and occasions, including introductions, dress, visits, the drawing room, dances, and the like. The rules for dance parties show that opponents of such activities were not wrong in their claims that they involved late hours. The etiquette manual tells the gentleman that an invitation to an evening, if begun at eight or nine o'clock, inevitably meant dancing, but arrival by ten o'clock was "quite early enough." Many guests, in fact, would come later.[52]

More important perhaps, the 1836 *Laws of Etiquette* told the gentleman how to perform on the dance floor. Skill was important lest he put his partner in a disadvantageous position or cause "bystanders" to be filled with anxiety:

> No man should attempt to dance without being well acquainted with the figures; for his blunders place the woman who does him the honour to dance with him in an embarrassing situation, and he will make quite a different figure from what he intends. But they are learned without any difficulty, being very simple and generally unvarying. As to the *steps,* that is quite another affair. Unless a man has a very graceful figure and can use it with great elegance, it is better for him to walk through the quadrilles, or invent some gliding movement for the occasion. To see an awkward or grave man going with pious scrupulosity through the 'one, two, three, and four' of a balancez, and shaking a vast frame in a manner to fill the bystanders with reasonable dread lest it should fall to pieces, is ludicrous enough.

After sundry other comments about the availability of cards, the gentleman is told that, if he takes his wife to a dance, he must be careful not to dance with her. "Such are some of the canons of the ball." No rationale for the neglect is offered.[53] The point becomes significant later in the century when opponents attack dancing for the immoral displays of men on the dance floor with partners other than their wives.

Advice to the Lady

Books for the lady present similar advice about rules for behavior, but in the pre–Civil War period they more often include recommendations for character traits that define the role of the true lady in American society. Common titles for such manuals are *The Young Lady's Book: A Manual of Elegant Recreations, Exercises and Pursuits* (1830) and *The Young Lady's Own Book: A Manual of Intellectual Improvement and Moral Deportment* (1833). Both of these books for young readers were written anonymously. Both also include the same chapter headed "Moral Deportment" and stress that character becomes more important than accomplishments. The lady learned from these and similar books that home was her "sphere" or "empire." To govern it well, she was to cultivate the following virtues: "Piety, integrity, fortitude, charity, obedience, consideration, sincerity, prudence, activity, and cheerfulness, with the dispositions which spring from, and the amiable qualities which rise out of them, may, we presume, nearly define those moral properties called for in the daily conduct and habitual deportment of young ladies." An array of accomplishments also fell within the realm of the young lady's necessary competence, including painting, writing, embroidery, music, archery, riding, flowers, birds, mineralogy, and entomology. Yet the list was incomplete without dancing. The young reader learned that Locke and Lord Herbert of Cherbury had praised dancing and that the art was "now universal," hence essential in the education of a gentlewoman.[54]

Like the gentleman, the lady was advised that public and private dancing skills were vastly different: "it is the ambition of the *artiste* to astonish and delight; the lady who joins in a quadrille, aspires only to glide through the figure with easy and unobtrusive grace." It would be in extremely bad taste for a ballroom dancer to attempt the brilliant embellishment of the stage dancer. Nonetheless, the lady who aspired to perform well in the ballroom was advised to practice her dancing. It was not "easy of acquirement." The lady learned that carriage of the body was critical and that all affectation was to be avoided.[55] The "vulgar, indelicate or boisterous" were also to be avoided. Such advice followed the time-honored tradition passed on from the Renaissance courtesy books. Because dancing was an imitative art, the lady needed a good teacher and regular practice. Etiquette books cautioned the lady to avoid excess in dancing, however, reminding her that any pursuit can be abused, even those that most people approved. Some authors even urged her not to dance in public assemblies because that practice diminished her "lovely bashfulness." Yet dancing in private circles, with due regard for health and with older folks present, could be salutary.[56]

"Salutary" effects generally referred to the health benefits of dancing as an exercise. Yet the ideal for the lady restricted her to hearth and home and encased her in a corset of steel and whalebone, rendering her relatively inactive, hence physically unfit, by today's cardiovascular standards. A woman thus confined may have experienced some physical stress when first exposed to lively dancing. Under such circumstances, dance opponents may not have been overstating their charge that disease and death from exposure to cold followed vigorous or extensive dancing at an evening ball.

By the 1830s, female authors in particular became concerned about the health of women. Among the early women writers on etiquette, Eliza Farrar (1791–1870) addressed not only conduct but also health issues for women, yet she advised no radical reforms such as throwing away corsets. Her *Young Lady's Friend* (1837) stresses that good or "pure" air is essential to well being. "Heated rooms and crowded assemblies" produce "vitiated air" harmful to health. For proof she tells the reader to observe the pallor of young girls who have been engaged for the winter in a round of the fashionable amusements in a city. "You may read, in those pallid cheeks and hollow eyes, in that languid air and shrunk form, a lesson on the evil influences they have been under." She recommends daily washing and regular riding or walking; she proscribes tight lacing and tight shoes.[57] True to her role as an etiquette writer, Farrar also advises young ladies on use of time, domestic economy, dress, behavior toward parents, nursing the sick, female companions, treatment of domestics, conversation, visits, and evening parties.

The ill effects induced by women's preparations for a ball are spelled out in *A Manual of Politeness* (1837). The anonymous author writes that young women often have gone with no food since breakfast on the day of a ball. Though presenting no evidence other than, presumably, personal observation, the author remains "fully persuaded that long fasting, late dining, and the excessive repletion then taken into the exhausted stomach, with the tight pressure of steel and whalebone on the most susceptible parts of the frame then called into action, and the midnight, nay, morning hours, of lingering pleasure, are the positive causes of colds taken, bilious fevers, consumptions, and atrophies." Like Farrar, the writer urges daily exercise in the open air and regular baths, in addition to temperance at the table and in dancing. Yet, the counsel to moderation does not minimize the value of dance; the manual quotes both Locke and Herbert of Cherbury on the benefits of the art.[58]

With regard to dancing, Farrar in her manual instructed the young lady in both modesty and carriage: "All unmeaning and unnecessary movements are contrary to the rules of grace and good breeding. When not intentionally in motion, your body and limbs should be in perfect rest." Farrar advises the lady to be so self-possessed and disciplined that she presents the appearance of total self-control. Self-possession is the first prerequisite to good manners, and good manners and beauty prove the chief attractions at a party. Instructing the young lady how to behave at a ball, Farrar advises her to be neither elated nor depressed by attention or the lack of it. When not asked to dance, the young lady should engage someone in conversation or study a painting or other art object in the room. Although not opposed to dancing, Farrar seemed to tolerate evening parties only as a necessary evil then in vogue. She thought it a great waste of time to go too often and again reminded the young reader that frequent attendance could damage her health. Although low-cut gowns, worn in the cold night air, could prove hazardous to health, Farrar counseled against such attire on moral grounds: "Whatever the fashions may be, never be induced by them to violate the strictest modesty. No woman can strip her arms to her shoulders and show her back and bosom without injuring her mind and losing some of her refinement; if such would consult their brothers, they would tell them how men regard it." How many young ladies took Farrar's advice is, of course, unknown, but several generations of women were exposed to her ideas. *The Young Lady's Friend* was widely read in this country and England as late as 1880.[59]

Imputing superior moral values to the woman who would be a true lady became a commonplace in America after the 1820s. The ideal held that the lady's piety and devotion to religion shielded her from the temptations of the world and kept her pure and moral. In the words of the father who wrote *My Daughter's Manual* (1838), which contained advice for his offspring and other young women, "Your superior delicacy, your modesty, and the usual severity of your education, preserve you, in a great measure, from any temptation to those vices to which we are most subjected." The manual advised the young lady that religion provided the only solace for the suffering that women have to bear and tended to check any hint of dissipation. It counseled her to read only the Bible to form her opinions about religion, to attend church regularly, to have her own private devotions with equal regularity, and to avoid any books or conversation that would threaten her faith. The author asserted further: "Women are greatly deceived, when they think they recommend themselves to our sex by their indifference about religion. Even those men who are themselves unbelievers dislike infidelity in you. . . . Besides, men consider your religion as one of their principal securities for that female virtue in which they are the most interested." Despite his strong emphasis on piety and morality, the father permitted dancing for young women, advising them to practice so that they performed well but not with the brilliance that would attract undue attention. Regarding quality of performance, he urged: "I would have you to dance with spirit; but never allow yourselves to be so transported with mirth as to forget the delicacy of your sex. Many a girl dancing in the gaiety and innocence of her heart, is thought to discover a spirit she little dreams of."[60]

Thus, one antebellum model for the ideal lady prescribed that she be protected, pure, and pious yet at the same time accomplished in dancing and the other polite arts. Other writers advised a more stringent upbringing for young ladies, one that included absolutely no dancing or fashionable amusements. Two books by Congregational clergymen provide a sampling of this latter model, drawn from the character or conduct literature of the era. The authors emphasize the development of Christian piety for a lady, as did contemporary sermons against dancing.

William Buell Sprague's (1795–1876) *Letters on Practical Subjects, to a Daughter* appeared first in 1822 and thereafter in eleven editions through 1855. The eleventh edition was published by the American Tract Society. Educated and well known in his day, Sprague first published his *Letters* in his youth, when he was serving as a Congregational minister in West Springfield, Massachusetts. The third edition, from 1834, evidences a stern, evangelical point of view; it is doubtful that his advice mellowed much over the years. Sprague's opening remarks on the subject of amusements sound not just serious but threatening:

> Many a young female, who might have been an ornament to her sex, and a blessing to the world, has, by yielding to the dictates of a wayward inclination, and setting aside the decisions of sober reason on this subject, not only rendered herself of no account in society, but clouded all her prospects both for this world and another. In contemplating this subject, I wish you to feel that you are standing by the grave of female character and hopes, and to heed the monitory voice that issues from it, charging you to beware how you tread in the footsteps of the fallen and ruined.[61]

Sprague continues by pointing out that many females have mistakenly fallen in love with amusements, beguiled by the notion that life can be frittered away in idle pastimes. He warns that all humans must be accountable for their time because they are apt at any hour to enter on "an exact and eternal retribution." And, whatever humans do, they must do all to the glory of God. Sprague allows that recreation is needful but only for the "more successful discharge of duty." To that end, a change of pace becomes critical. Simply changing from one task to another can recharge one's energy.

Amusement must be refreshing but certainly not trifling, however. Sprague tells the young female reader that there are four criteria by which to judge the legitimacy of amusements. She must ask herself, first, can God accompany me in it? Second, will the activity make me unfit for serious thought or hazard my soul for eternity? Third, when in the final hour of death, will I look back on this amusement with pain or pleasure? Finally, will the activity better fit me to fulfill my duties?[62]

With such an extreme emphasis on duty and eternity, Sprague could offer no approval for mixed dancing. He objects to it not just because it wastes time: "Everyone knows that it brings the sexes together in circumstances, to say the least, not the most favorable to the cultivation of female delicacy."[63] He seems most concerned about the common practice of the sexes dancing together at balls and assemblies. If a group of girls wished to dance for themselves, he had no objection.

Although similar to Sprague's manual in its emphasis on Christian stewardship of time and on daily piety, Harvey Newcomb's (1803–63) book, *The Young Lady's Guide to the Harmonius Development of Christian Character,* adds to a Christian's duties the stewardship of one's health. Newcomb was motivated by his evangelical fervor: "The services which God requires of us, as laborers in his vineyard, are such as to call for vigor of body and strength of mind. A feeble state of health, other things being equal, must be a hinderance in the divine life." Since a Christian's body, mind, and spirit belong to God, the individual is obligated to use all lawful means to preserve health to the end of glorifying God.[64]

Although Newman was a conservative clergyman, he recognized that the education for women then in vogue had an insidious effect on their health: "There is a great and growing evil in the education of ladies of the middling and higher classes, at the present day. The tender and delicate manner in which they are bred enfeebles their constitutions, and greatly diminishes their usefulness in every station of life. Many of them are sickly, and few of them are able to endure the slightest hardships." He contrasts the education of the higher classes with that of working girls who, for the most part, possessed vigorous constitutions. Despite his prescription of "at least two hours every day in exercise in the open air," Newcomb excludes any discussion of dancing from his instructions. Nor does he recommend any specific kind of exercise.[65] In Newcomb's frame of reference, the true Christian lady simply orders her life so as to steward both health and time. He calculates the total cost of wasting "ten minutes at a time, six times in a day." For a lifespan of seventy years and having subtracted the first ten years, Newcomb shows that the series of ten-minute losses amount to a cumulative total of five years lost. The lady's goal must be to glorify God and to be able to give a good accounting of her life at the final judgment.[66]

The Ideal for the Lady

Although the advice from clergymen counseled Christian values exclusively, the ideal for the lady, whether formulated by women or men, required that she place Christian convictions and attendant character traits at the core of her values. Compared with the two contrasting models of the true gentleman and the "man of fashion," the literature from the era suggests that the only model for women prescribed adherence to what Barbara Welter has called the "four cardinal virtues" of piety, purity, submission, and domesticity.[67] However, as demonstrated by the advice of Sprague, Newcomb, and other clergy opposing dance, interpretations of piety and purity varied in degree. The early evangelicals urged a strict adherence to duty and stewardship—all focused on the goal of reward through eternity. Vain and frivolous amusements such as dancing held no place in such a value system. By contrast, etiquette writers assumed a piety and purity in ladies but held that decorum, grace, and skill in the polite arts—including dancing—were also important. According to their ideal, the lady was to be accomplished but not affected. Though fashionable and beautiful, she was also to pay attention to her health. Moderation and self-control completed the picture.

Although a strong literary tradition, extending back to the Middle Ages and even classical times, told the gentleman how to behave, the ideal for the lady begins to emerge in full relief only in the 1830s. Less ancient traditions feed this model, including the seventeenth-century English piety and civility books, such as Richard Allestree's *The Ladies Calling* and Richard Brathwait's *The English Gentlewoman*. Eighteenth-century English evangelical fervor transplanted to this country reinforced emphases on personal piety and the stewardship of time and money, as noted in the writings of George Whitefield and Hannah More. On the other hand, the European courtesy tradition—with its stress on civility and polite accomplishments—also contributes to the development of American rules of etiquette. The resulting tensions in the ideal for the lady recall contrasts between sixteenth-century ideals for the gentleman and for the Christian.

As the nineteenth century progressed, the picture of the lady would become more distinct, but the tensions would remain as evangelicals increased in number and power. In 1839 a Congregational cleric, Dana Goodsell

(1803–76), previewed that power with his gripping rhetoric and imagery. Goodsell told parishioners in Plainfield, Massachusetts, that life was a slender thread. He asked them to imagine attending a ball and suffering a ruptured blood vessel. Then he put the question: How will you fare at the final judgment? "The divine mercy, which spares you, as you hang suspended over the burning gulf, may go out at any moment, and you fall to rise no more!"[68]

Notes

1. William Lyman, *A Discourse Delivered at East Haddam, Second Society, Dec. 24, 1800; at a Public Lecture* (New London, Conn.: Samuel Green, 1801), 4; Kiah Bayley, *Fashionable Amusements Inconsistent with the Design and Spirit of the Gospel, Contrary to the Express Commands of God, and in Many Respects Productive of Evil, a Discourse Delivered February 5, 1804* (Wiscasset, Me: Babson and Rust, 1804), 17, 11.

2. Lyman, *Discourse,* 16, 5–12; Bayley, *Fashionable Amusements . . . A Discourse,* 21–23, 19.

3. Francis D. Nichols, *A Guide to Politeness; or, A System of Directions for the Acquirement of Ease, Propriety and Elegance of Manners* (Boston: Lincoln and Edmands, 1810), 6–7.

4. Ibid., 6–8.

5. Ibid., 24, 44–45.

6. Jacob Ide, *The Nature and Tendency of Balls, Seriously and Candidly Considered, in Two Sermons, Preached in Medway, the First Dec. 21: the Second Dec. 28, 1818* (Dedham, Mass.: H. and W. H. Mann, 1819), 2.

7. Ibid., 3–5, 8, 10.

8. The historian William McLoughlin includes the first three decades of the century in the Second Great Awakening. For a brief review of the revival and a short discussion of Emmons, see Sydney E. Ahlstrom, *A Religious History of the American People* (Garden City, N.Y.: Image Books, 1975), vol. 1, 491, 498–500, 505–7.

9. Information on Ide comes from the American Antiquarian Society's author-authority file, HO–JE. For Bayley, see Arthur T. Hamlin, *Kiah Bayley, Founder of Maine Institutions* (Newcastle, Me.: Lincoln County Publishing Company, 1986). Handwritten on the front of Bayley's personal copy of *Fashionable Amusements* is the following: "Dr. Emmons with the cordial respects of the Author" (photocopy provided by Colby College, Waterville, Maine).

10. *The Works of Nathanael Emmons with a Memoir of His Life,* ed. Jacob Ide (Boston: Crocker and Brewster, 1842; rpt., New York: Garland, 1987), vol. 5, 596. Emmons's specific references to balls come only in his works from the nineteenth century. His eighteenth-century writing makes no reference to either balls or dancing, though his overall theology certainly proscribes amusements. His 1822 sermon

"The Guilt of Taking Pleasure in Other Men's Sins" gives the only other specific reference to balls or dancing that I have found among his works. Again, he directs his attack at parents: "Parents who allow their children to attend balls and haunt taverns are more guilty than their children that do these things" (*Works,* vol. 6, 355). For further distinction regarding even the appearance of evil, see his 1821 sermon "The Avoidance of Apparent Evil," in *Works,* vol. 6.

11. Ahlstrom, *Religious History,* vol. 1, 516–17.

12. Stephen Elmer Slocum Jr., "The American Tract Society: 1825–1975" (Ph.D. diss., New York University, 1975), 38–44. The Andover founders depended upon voluntary effort by interested people to circulate their publications. Under vigorous leadership, the organization achieved a circulation of nearly 500,000 by 1823 and in the same year, by an act of the Massachusetts legislature, became officially known as the American Tract Society. Soon, however, men in New York envisioned a truly national organization, larger than the Boston association. By May 1825, the New York Religious Tract Society merged with the Boston association to form the American Tract Society, headquartered in New York City. The group, now based in Garland, Texas, has operated continuously since that time.

13. *Fashionable Amusements,* 2d ed., no. 73 in series by New England Tract Society (Andover, Mass.: Flagg and Gould, 1816), 1–3, 9.

14. Ibid., 9–10.

15. *The Works of Hannah More* (New York: Harper, 1841), 385–86, 389–90, 393; Bayley, *Fashionable Amusements . . . A Discourse,* 20, 26–27. In her complete work on female education, written in 1799, More laments the custom of women's having hours "at home" during which large numbers of people would call. She also decries the evening parties and balls that caused women to neglect domestic duties and robbed them of health and energy. Further, More denigrates the practice of having daughters displayed at balls for the purpose of procuring desirable husbands. Underlying her arguments is an emphasis on the stewardship of time required of all Christians.

16. Cited in Thomas Charlton Henry, *An Inquiry into the Consistency of Popular Amusements with a Profession of Christianity* (Charleston, S.C.: William Riley, 1825), 117–20.

17. *Essay on Dancing, in a Series of Letters to a Lady, Wherein the Inconsistence of That Amusement with the True Spirit of Christianity Is Demonstrated* (Philadelphia: Thomas and William Bradford, and J. W. Campbell, n.d.), 15, 19–21, 23, 30; Henry, *An Inquiry,* 93. Information in the card catalog of the American Antiquarian Society, which notes that the publisher John Wilson Campbell was in Philadelphia *only* in 1814 and 1815, suggests the *Essay on Dancing* dates from about those years.

18. *Presbyterian Historical Almanac* (1861), s.v. "Penney, Joseph." Ahlstrom reports that, from 1800 to 1837, Presbyterian membership increased from 13,470 to 226,557 (*Religious History,* vol. 1, 559). After graduating from the University

of Dublin, Penney emigrated to the United States and settled in Rochester, New York, where he preached against dancing in the First Presbyterian Church on 20 December 1829. Representing the southern migration of Presbyterians from their founding presbytery in Philadelphia, Henry assumed leadership of the Second Presbyterian Church in Charleston following his graduation from Princeton Theological Seminary.

19. Henry, *An Inquiry,* 98–99, 103, 146–47, 85.

20. Ibid., 101, 106–7, 113–14, 142.

21. Ibid., 163, 166.

22. Joseph Penney, *The House of Mirth* (Rochester: E. Peck, 1830), 7–9.

23. Ibid., 3–5; Henry, *An Inquiry,* 91.

24. Ahlstrom, *Religious History,* vol. 1, 556. See also Whitney R. Cross, *The Burned-over District* (Ithaca: Cornell University Press, 1950).

25. Ahlstrom, *Religious History,* vol. 1, 557; Charles Grandison Finney, *Lectures on Revivals of Religion,* ed. William G. McLoughlin (Cambridge, Mass.: Belknap Press of Harvard University Press, 1960), xlvi.

26. Finney, *Lectures,* 403–4, 406, 417; Charles C. Cole Jr., *The Social Ideas of the Northern Evangelists, 1826–1860* (New York: Columbia University Press, 1954), 101.

27. Finney, *Lectures,* 458, 153–54, 366.

28. William G. McLoughlin, *Modern Revivalism* (New York: Ronald Press, 1959), 118.

29. Charles G. Finney, *Hindrances to Revivals* (Boston: Willard Tract Repository, n.d.), 7.

30. Ahlstrom, *Religious History,* vol. 1, 525. Both Baptists and Methodists relied on common men with little education as their ministers. Both denominations proved very successful on the frontier. Among the Baptists, a local man who felt a call to preach could be confirmed by neighbors; they could gather a church congregation without waiting for a seminary graduate to come out from the east. In a different system, the Methodists divided the wilderness and a westward-moving population into circuits and laid down a strict discipline for circuit-riding ministers as well as for individual churches. For a brief discussion about the uneducated clergy in the early republic, see also Nathan O. Hatch, *The Democratization of American Christianity* (New Haven: Yale University Press, 1989), 18.

31. Ahlstrom, *Religious History,* vol. 1, 525.

32. Barton Warren Stone, *The Biography of Elder Barton Warren Stone, Written by Himself: With Additions and Reflections by Elder John Rogers* (Cincinnati: J. A. and U. P. James, 1847), 39–41.

33. Excesses in movement behavior have been known since before the Reformation. During the Middle Ages, chroniclers on the continent reported periodic outbreaks of "dance" mania. Some biblical translations record that Saul prophesied and "danced." See E. Louis Backman, *Religious Dances and Popular Medicine,* trans.

E. Classen (London: Allen and Unwin, 1952; rpt., Westport, Conn.: Greenwood, 1977), 170–258.

34. *A Few Reflections upon the Fancy Ball, Otherwise Known as the City Dancing Assembly* (Philadelphia: G. R. Lilibridge, 1828), 3–4.

35. Ibid., 4–5, 8, 14–15, 9.

36. For background on Jeter, see William E. Hatcher, *Life of J. B. Jeter, D.D.* (Baltimore: H. M. Wharton and Company, 1887), especially 196–98. For the text of the Revolutionary War resolution, see Norman Arthur Benson, "Itinerant Dance and Music Masters of the Eighteenth Century" (Ph.D. diss., University of Minnesota, 1963), 207.

37. Jeremiah Bell Jeter, *A Discourse on the Immoral Tendency of Theatrical Amusements* (Richmond: Wm. MacFarlane, 1838), 5 (first quote), 12 (second quote), 11 (third quote), 9 (fourth quote), 13, 15.

38. Slocum, "American Tract Society," 61–62, 68–72.

39. *A Short and Hasty Essay in Favour of Dancing and Musick* (Concord, Mass.: J. T. Peters, 1817), 8.

40. Ibid., 12, 4.

41. [Saltator], *A Treatise on Dancing; and On Various Other Matters, Which Are Connected with That Accomplishment; and Which Are Requisite to Make Youth Well Received, and Regulate Their Behaviour in Company. Together with Lessons, the Figures of Country Dances, and Cotillions* (N.p., 1807), i–iv.

42. Ibid., 57 (first quote), 62 (long quote), 71–72.

43. Ibid., 61 (quote), 83.

44. G. Oliver, *A Vindication of Rational Amusements* (Hull, England: Myrton Hamilton, 1818), 4, 6. The English evangelical opposition to dancing also circulated in this country in the form of George Burder's *Lawful Amusements* (Baltimore: George Bourne, 1808). His *Village Sermons* appeared in an American edition in 1803. Both Burder and his mother had been converted by Whitefield. With no formal education, Burder began preaching in 1776 and was later ordained by the Congregational church in Lancaster. Subsequently, he became instrumental in forming the Religious Tract Society of London. See the *DNB*, s.v. "Burder, George."

45. "Salem Assembly," Dec. 1810, broadside, Massachusetts Historical Society, Boston.

46. J. Hammond Trumbull, *The Memorial History of Hartford County, Connecticut, 1633–1884* (Boston: Edw. L. Osgood, 1886), 588.

47. E. H. Conway, *Le Maitre de Danse or, The Art of Dancing Cotillons: By Which Every One May Learn to Dance Them without a Master . . .*, 2d ed. (New York: C. S. Van Winkle, 1827), 3–4.

48. Richard H. Shoemaker, *A Checklist of American Imprints 1820–1829, Title Index,* comp. M. Francis Cooper (Metuchen, N.J.: Scarecrow, 1972).

49. *Encyclopaedia Americana,* 1829–33, s.v. "Dancing."

50. Arthur M. Schlesinger, *Learning How to Behave* (New York: Macmillan, 1946), 18.

51. *Ladies and Gentlemen's American Etiquette with the Rules of Polite Society; to Which Is Added Hints on Dress, Courtship, Etc.,* By an American (Andover, Mass.: J. D. Flagg, [182?]), 51–56.

52. *The Laws of Etiquette, or, Short Rules and Reflections For Conduct in Society,* By a Gentleman (Philadelphia: Carey, Lea, and Blanchard, 1836), 22, 172.

53. Ibid., 176–77 (long quote), 181 (short quote).

54. *The Young Lady's book: A Manual of Elegant Recreations, Exercises and Pursuits* (Boston: Bowen, and Carter and Hendee, [1830]), 24 (first quote), 398 (second quote).

55. Ibid., 396 (first and second quotes), 411. The same chapter on dancing also appears in *My Daughter's Manual, Comprising a Summary View of Female Studies, Accomplishments, and Principles of Conduct* (New York: Appleton, 1838).

56. *The Young Lady's Own Book: A Manual of Intellectual Improvement and Moral Deportment,* by the Author of the Young Man's Own Book (Philadelphia: Key and Biddle, 1833), 148–50.

57. [Eliza Ware (Rotch) Farrar], *The Young Lady's Friend,* By a Lady (Boston: American Stationers' Company, 1837), 148–49 (quotes), 162, 176–77, 198–99.

58. *A Manual of Politeness, Comprising the Principles of Etiquette, and Rules of Behaviour in Genteel Society, for Both Sexes* (Philadelphia: W. Marshall, 1837), 207 (quote), 23–24, 74.

59. Farrar, *Young Lady's Friend,* 362–66 (including first quote), 368 (second quote); *American Women Writers,* ed. Linda Mainiero (New York: Ungar, 1980), s.v. "Farrar, Eliza Ware Rotch."

60. *My Daughter's Manual,* 282–85 (including first quote), 287 (second quote), 216 (third quote).

61. William Buell Sprague, *Letters on Practical Subjects, to A Daughter,* 3d American ed., rev. and enl. (New York: Appleton, 1834), 125.

62. Ibid., 126 (first quote), 127 (second quote), 130–32.

63. Ibid., 134.

64. Harvey Newcomb, *The Young Lady's Guide to the Harmonius Development of Christian Character,* 11th ed. (Boston: Wm. J. Reynolds, [1843]), 172.

65. Ibid., 180 (first quote), 179 (second quote).

66. Ibid., 228–29.

67. Barbara Welter, "The Cult of True Womanhood: 1820–1860," *American Quarterly* 18 (Summer 1966): 151–75.

68. Dana Goodsell, *A Discourse Delivered in the First Congregational Church in Plainfield, Mass., February 10, 1839* (Concord, Mass.: David Kimball, 1839), 18–19.

6

The Evangelical Mainstream and Radical Reformers: 1840–60

It is the duty of the State and the Church to provide Public Amusements.

Edward Everett Hale, 1857

So, if any of you think you can honor God in a round of demoralizing amusements, and thus prepare for the retributions of eternity, I think very differently.

G. L. Foster, 1848

In the middle decades of the nineteenth century, mainstream American Protestant clergy confronted professing Christians throughout the settled states with the issue of amusements, including the question whether believers could lawfully dance. An unprecedented number of books dealing with the issue rolled off urban presses from Jackson, Michigan, south to St. Louis, and east to Richmond. Ministers preached on the subject from Alabama and South Carolina north to Connecticut. The question engaged the attention of all evangelical denominations, drawing published opinions and clear consensus from the Disciples of Christ, Methodists, Baptists, Lutherans, and Episcopalians, as well as from the always vocal Presbyterians and Congregationalists.

The amusement question pertained to the major entertainments of the day—theater, cards, novels, horse racing, the circus, and dancing. Ballet as well as social dance drew the ire of clergymen. In 1843, a transplanted easterner, the Reverend Henry Ward Beecher (1813–87), warned young men in Indiana about the evils of the modern city, as a part of his lectures on moral and spiritual dangers facing the country. Recalling Puritan frugality and Calvinist purity, he thundered: "We cannot pay for honest loans, but we can pay Elssler hundreds of thousands for being an airy sylph!"[1] Beecher's indictment of Fanny Elssler, the European Romantic ballerina, contrasted with the enthusiastic reception given the dancer by many easterners, including congressmen, who found her enchanting.

As a representative of mid-Victorian America, Beecher typified the confident Protestant minister who considered himself both guardian of truth and arbiter of morality. The historian Charles C. Cole observes that the words of America's clergy often carried "the forcefulness of law." When addressing the issue of whether or not Christians could engage in amusements in general or dancing in particular, most ministers displayed what Cole calls "a remarkable amount of intolerance."[2] An analysis of their opinions, published and pronounced in the two decades prior to the Civil War, also reveals an outspoken and nearly universal concern for the morality, decorum, and health of middle- and upper-class women. The rush of antidance sermons came in direct response to the pervasiveness of the art.

The Population and Dancing at Midcentury

America's population in the 1840s and 1850s expanded westward as the frontier edged beyond the Mississippi. Native-born settlers were joined by waves of immigrants, a phenomenon that continued until the first decades of the twentieth century. The new Americans swelled the ranks, not only of the total population, but also of particular denominations and churches. For example, the Lutheran church experienced marked growth with the influx of German immigrants.[3] By 1850, the Roman Catholic church had 3 million members in America, followed by the Methodists, at 1.25 million, and the Baptists, with 1 million. Presbyterians counted about three-quarters of a million members, while Lutherans and Congregationalists each numbered approximately a quarter million members. Of the total United States and territorial population in 1850, about 25 percent of the people belonged to churches.[4]

Urban Growth and Theater Dance

The nation had primarily a rural, agrarian population for the first half of the century, but a major change occurred in the 1850s. The historians Samuel Eliot Morison and Henry Steele Commager document that decade as the time when the country's population as a whole increased by 36 percent, whereas the population of towns and cities of eight thousand or more increased some 90 percent.[5]

Larger population centers became the places where increasing numbers of people could be entertained via public, commercial enterprise. Cities and towns supplied the space, facilities, communications, and transportation systems necessary to support theaters, whether for dance or plays; concerts; lectures; tent shows; the circus; and horse racing.[6] Such facilities and productions required large amounts of money, hence proximity to banks or wealthy individuals. Attracting an audience depended on advertising, which, in turn, required printing presses and newspapers. In antebellum America, where steamboats and railroads carried passengers in local or regional travel, mainly east of the Mississippi, and where the telegraph was not yet widely available, advertising an event such as Fanny Elssler's American tour required months of advance planning and mailing, in addition to reliance upon local newspapers and broadsides. Elssler's European fame was so great that the *New York Morning Herald* had included regular reports on her activities for several weeks prior to her New York arrival. When she eventually landed, the public was ready for her.[7]

America could claim no ballet companies or studios of its own, although foreign ballet stars had come from Europe for short tours since the late eighteenth century. However, Elssler's American tour of 1840 and 1841 became the single most important event of its kind until the twentieth century. She performed to rave reviews in New York, Philadelphia, Washington, Baltimore, Boston, Richmond, Charleston, New Orleans, and Providence. Elsslermania in New York became so great that products were named after her. At the time of her opening, tickets changed hands several times and far exceeded their original cost. Although preachers such as Beecher condemned her from the pulpit, former president John Quincy Adams applauded her dancing; President Martin Van Buren invited her to the White House; and Congress recessed to see her. In staid Boston, Ralph Waldo Emerson and Margaret Fuller disagreed over the impact of Elssler's dancing. Emerson called the experience "religion"; Fuller said it was "poetry."[8]

The popularity of theater dance extended beyond ballet and Fanny Elssler. The mid-nineteenth century witnessed the advent of a new American genre based on vernacular dance and music. Blackface minstrelsy began in the late 1820s and became enormously popular from the 1840s until the later decades of the century. It reached its height as a uniquely American entertainment in the 1860s, when the country possessed about one hundred companies playing nothing but minstrel shows. Minstrelsy's popularity coincided with the rise of the "common man." The form emerged as an institution at a time when the rapid expansion of America's population meant that culture would inevitably divide into high-brow and low-brow—the elite and the popular. By the 1850s, audiences in large cities could choose from among drama, opera, symphonic music, melodrama, the circus, minstrelsy, and variety shows.[9] Most theater dance like Elssler's occurred in eastern cities. Minstrel shows played well in urban centers of the North and East. However, a few historians have identified the beginnings of a performance tradition as far west as Salt Lake City, Utah, and Portland, Oregon, and as early as the first half of the nineteenth century.[10] But the great concentration of both theater dance and ballroom dance at that time occurred east of the Mississippi.

Couple Dances

The advent of couple dances contributed in no small measure to the popularity of the art among its devotees and to the opposition waged by its detractors. Although the waltz came to this country from Europe earlier in the century, its widespread popularity is not reflected in the etiquette books, dance manuals, and antidance sermons until after 1840. The polka, another extraordinarily popular new dance, made its Paris debut in the early 1840s and soon spread to the United States. These two new dances contrasted dramatically with established favorites, the country dances, cotillions, and quadrilles. The latter two forms required four couples in a side-by-side position to form a square; country dances were longways dances with partners opposite one another. Dancing then proceeded in set figures and refrains. Although usually cued by a caller or prompter, these dances demanded that everyone in the square know the figure and the chorus. The group figure dances invited no individual inventiveness but required a certain degree of skill on the part of all participants in order for the dancing to be enjoyable.

In contrast, the new dances permitted individual couples to travel around the ballroom, governed by their own skill, the originality of their patterns, and the tempo and rhythm of the music. Though each man had to lead so as to synchronize with the flow of dancers, he retained his own independence in determining steps and patterns. The style of a Viennese waltz added the sensation of vertigo as dancers whirled first in one direction for eight measures and then in the reverse direction for the next eight measures. At a tempo of probably fifty-four to sixty measures per minute, the waltz would have provided dancers with an exhilaration that contrasted dramatically with the more sedate pleasure of traditional group figure dances. For a young lady to whirl around a dance floor in the arms of a young man, as the closed dance position required, to the romantic strains of a Viennese waltz, would have been unlike anything else she had experienced.

Dance masters who wrote instructional manuals continued the tradition of their predecessors—to present dancing as orderly, rational, and aesthetic.[11] In 1847, Charles Durang, a Philadelphia dance master, published *Durang's Terpsichore,* in which he actually repeats the claims for dancing made by the Boston writers Saltator and Francis D. Nichols forty years earlier: "Dancing deserves the attention of the enlightened, as a *necessary accomplishment;* it is a natural exercise, tending to promote the exhilaration of the mind, and the dissemination of good feeling and rational enjoyment, among all classes of our society." Durang declares that dancing also serves as a "preservative to health" because it is physical exercise. Nonetheless, participation must be circumscribed by "prudence and temperance."[12] Moreover, he does not advocate dancing for everyone. Noting that an individual must possess some physical prerequisites, Durang advises that unless one can perform with some success and avoid appearing clumsy or ridiculous on the dance floor, it is far better to remain a spectator than to venture forth with a partner. In particular, he mentions that those who are "incurably ill-shaped, unconquerably heavy, or insensible to any graceful motion" ought not attempt dance lessons.[13]

Advising on quality of ballroom performance, Durang affirms that light and graceful motion as well as elegant yet natural carriage are important. However, an aesthetic performance was incomplete without good manners. Durang continued the emphasis on developing American standards, a view that appeared in etiquette manuals after 1820. He advocates that Americans conform to that "which the good sense of our most polished society may from time to time adopt." To merely envy Paris and London society implies a "national deterioration in Republicans of our intelligence" and also deprecates our dignity. Americans can legitimately acknowledge the European tradition as "alma mater in many of the arts" but must go beyond that to establish their own standard of behavior. Yet, in the European tradition that descended from the Renaissance, Durang suggests that manners derive from morals, and he declares unequivocally that good dancing and good behavior are inseparable: "they must go hand in hand, to impart pleasure and to secure a just moral result—therefore, it is wiser to invest the embellishments of the art with the graces of refined manners; (which indeed are the ornaments of it.) Thus will dancing become a rational, and necessarily an innocent amusement; worthy of a place among the other elegant arts."[14]

Despite such views, those who proscribed dancing and amusements preached a host of arguments in opposition. For the first time in this country, antidance voices became so numerous, yet so in agreement, that arguments can be clearly categorized.

Amusements Pro and Con

Those who wrote against dancing within the larger context of amusements constituted the mainstream of evangelical Protestant clergy, a group that crossed denominational lines but excluded the more liberal Unitarians and the numerous sects in existence. Sydney Ahlstrom characterizes this evangelical mainstream as emanating from the Reformed tradition's theological doctrines; it had a Puritan outlook, advocated a personal, experiential faith, and tended "toward Arminianism, perfectionism, and activism." He observes further that, despite the fact of the constitutional separation of church and state, this Protestant block enjoyed an influence and confidence tantamount to that accruing to a "formal establishment."[15] Clergy pronounced their opinions with all the assurance that the Congregational minister Gustavus L. Foster (fl. 1840s and 1850s) displayed to his church in Jackson, Michigan, when he declared the impossibility of honoring God and preparing for eternity while engaging in a "round of demoralizing amusements." He confidently predicted that those who disagreed with his stand would learn at the judgment day who was right.[16] Foster, like most of the evangelical dance opponents, seemed prompted to preach on the subject of "fashionable worldly amusements" because they fascinated his parishioners. His views typify mainstream opinions and rely upon a centuries-old theological dualism.

In his writings, Foster divides humankind and human desires into two categories—the carnal and the virtuous. Those in the latter category attempt to "hush appetite and passion" by giving conscience and reason control over behavior. Worldly amusements fall into the category of the carnal, though Foster does not condemn them out of hand. When amusements serve to give participants "new power for more important duties," and when a person "violates no physical law, or any such other law as may be attached to him, because of his intellectual and moral nature," then Foster finds them appropriate. However, he draws a line tightly around those amusements that are "manifestly demoralizing in their influence." That includes horse racing, gambling, theater, and "those most reprehensible dancing scenes." Whether the dancing occurs at villages or in a bar-room, he calls them a "promiscuous assembly" often started by a "herd of profligate young men." Foster condemns a second classification of amusements, not as "absolutely demoralizing," but as having a "powerful tendency in that direction." The "fashionable and well conducted balls" would be an example of such an amusement.[17] Other clergy delineate different categories and descriptions but most include playing cards, the theater, and the circus under amusements to be indicted; some commentators also impugn the reading of novels.[18]

Foster's division of human desires into the carnal and the virtuous follows other Pauline dualities that undergirded arguments against amusements. Preaching to Presbyterians in St. Louis in 1847, the Reverend William Potts (1802–52) relied on Paul's exhortation to avoid the "unfruitful works of darkness" (Ephesians 6:11). The duality of light and darkness contrasts virtuous and profitable human activities with those considered wicked and wasteful. In Potts's view, the latter includes "fornication, uncleanness, covetousness, filthiness, foolish talking & jesting." Typically, the evangelical clergy cast the amusements of society into the same category. Works of darkness, according to Potts, issue from the dark part of the soul, destroy conscience, and distract the mind from communion with God. More specifically, they "remove the natural, shrinking modesty of the female mind, and thus destroy the outworks of female virtue."[19]

Another common duality—the tension between being worldly or being godly—encountered earlier but repeated in the middle decades of the nineteenth century, relies on Paul's command, "Be not conformed to the world" (Rom. 12:2). Bishop William Meade (1789–1862) of the Protestant Episcopal church wrote from Virginia in 1855 that Christians in baptism renounced the "devil and all his works," the "pomps and vanities of this wicked world," and the "sinful lusts of the flesh." In Meade's view, modern amusements, thus, were interdicted by baptismal vows.[20] Similarly, the Reverend Franklin Wilson (1822–96) admonished Charleston Baptists in 1856 that their chief duty as humans was to glorify God. The goal in life is labor, not pleasure. The entire life of a Christian is to be sanctified.[21] Thus, godliness and worldliness, the eternal and the temporal, the spirit and the flesh, the church and fashionable society—all point to the fundamental notion, held by mainstream evangelicals, that the Christian must be distinct from the worldling.

The practical implications of this notion meant that one should avoid all amusements that were blatantly cruel and immoral. All amusements with strong tendencies to or with effects that produced evil or the appearance of evil were likewise to be avoided. Any activities that "unfit the mind for the duties of life" also became proscribed. Finally, any amusements that detracted from the pursuit of holiness and spirituality became interdicted.[22] Theodore Ledyard Cuyler (1822–1909), a Presbyterian cleric in New York City, phrased the criteria for legitimate recreation in the following terms: "whatever makes your body healthier, your mind happier, and your immortal soul purer, is Christian recreation." Preferring the term "recreation," he declined the label "amusement" on the ground that it meant only "pleasure for its own sake and ultimate end."[23]

Of course, not all Americans held to the evangelical code for amusements. Frederic W. Sawyer (1810–75), a Boston lawyer, wrote *A Plea for Amusements,* which appeared in 1847 and again in 1857. Commenting on the general tenor of church members' views in his day, he observed: "I apprehend that a careful observer would find that the piety of most Christians is measured, in a great degree, by the near approach that they make to the ascetic state. The more they withdraw themselves from the pleasures and amusements of the world, the higher they rise in the estimation of the church. The more they disrelish earthly joys,—the less they can see that is lovely in the world,—the higher are they set in the scale of piety."[24]

More specifically, Sawyer argued that the heterosexual partnering in dances provided a most salutary benefit on American men, who, in effect, were civilized by women. When properly taught and practiced, dancing softens and refines the manners, a necessary quality for that "respectful and delicate intercourse between the sexes" deemed essential for their highest good. In Sawyer's opinion, dancing and women could even be credited with civilizing western culture.[25]

Perhaps the most liberal view of amusements and their place in society was advanced by Edward Everett Hale (1822–1909), when he spoke "Before the Church of the Unity" in Worcester, Massachusetts, on 16 December 1855. Hale was a Congregational minister, author, and, later, chaplain of the U.S. Senate. When his ideas are contrasted with the views of contemporary evangelicals, Hale ranks with urban reformers—even those of the early twentieth century—in his forward-looking proposal that both government and church should plan carefully for the recreational needs of citizens. Undergirding that view is his assumption that both rest and work are important: "God is not pleased with heads throbbing, or hands trembling, because they have overwrought in his service." Hale attacked the popular notion that all necessary recreation could occur at home. He contrasts a play at the theater with the same one read at home, and questions the quality of a Beethoven symphony rendered only on a "poor thin piano at home." Recognizing the socioeconomic realities of the era, Hale emphasizes that only the rich and the educated can supply entertainment in their own houses. The poor and the "ignorant" must resort to public amusements. The saloon may provide the only social life for the illiterate worker.[26] Thus Hale urges: "Let the law of the State take that ground, that the public ought to provide public entertainment and oversee it, just as it provides public education and oversees it, and all our great questions, as we call them, about the influence of dancing, and the influence of music, and the influence of the drama in such things, would become very little questions of detail."[27] Despite Hale's radical views, public amusements remained essentially a matter of commercial enterprise for decades. Private amusements—in the sense of those enjoyed within a small group, select group, or family—remained the norm for the 1840s and 1850s. Most dancing fell into this category.

Arguments against Dancing

In Sawyer's 1847 *Plea for Amusements*, he writes that no one knows just how the hostility began, "But in whatever way the prejudice against dancing first arose, it is certain that such a prejudice exists, and that it has existed for centuries." He also observes that dancing has been "frowned down" more than "talked down": "It has not been so much traduced, as an amusement, by what the religious portion of the community have said against it, as by what they have not said. It has been banished from their fire sides, more by half-expressed doubts and misgivings as to the propriety of it, and by innuendos and ominous shakes of the head, when the subject has been brought forward, than by any positive objections that have been raised."[28] Since Sawyer wrote from Boston, it is possible that his observations proved correct for that area. It is also likely that parents and elders conveyed their opposition by "innuendos and ominous shakes of the head." Particularly on the subject of immorality, mid-Victorian Americans would have shrunk from precise and graphic language. However, antidance writers are quite clear in designating the kind of dancing they oppose.

The Kind of Dancing Opposed

The vast majority of evangelicals decried dancing as amusement, but they specified more particularly "modern dancing" or "fashionable dancing." The Reverend William Potts provides a concise and comprehensive indictment that typifies the position of many authors. He objects to stage dancing, fancy balls and masquerades, public balls, and private dancing parties in homes. Though few writers name particular dances, their descriptions make clear that the waltz and polka drew the particular wrath of opponents. Asa D. Smith (1804–77) told his Brainard Presbyterian Church in New York City in 1847 that the proscribed dancing meant "dancing as all the world know it to be practised in fashionable circles—'promiscuous dancing,' as some have termed it, or as engaged in by the sexes in company. We mean the mingling of the sexes at full-blown balls."[29] Another Presbyterian cleric, John McDonald (1807–47), characterized balls as "a worldly assembly, at which men meet in merriment to dance." More succinctly, he called them one of the "world's sacraments." Similarly, assemblies were gatherings of men and women to dance, "for the sake of procuring and imparting pleasure."[30] Almost universally, dance opponents took care to distinguish the dancing referred to in the Bible from that which they opposed in their own day. In addition, clerics pointed out that they did not denigrate dancing as purely a physical exercise. What they did indict was dancing and occasions for dancing that served no other purpose than enjoyment and pleasure.

Some authors assumed a more philosophical tone and pointed out that they did not interdict dancing in theory or in itself. In 1849, B. M. Palmer (1818–1902) instructed his Presbyterian parishioners in Columbia, South Carolina, that, though not wrong in the abstract, "what if it be wrong in the concrete? . . . but what if it be sinful in its inseparable adjuncts?" For Palmer, all "corporeal actions" considered by themselves were "wholly indifferent and devoid of moral character." Yet people's motives for physical activity had to be considered, as did the evil consequences of the activity: "It is against the dance as a recognised social pleasure, with all its adjuncts of large assemblies, levity, dissipation, revelry, forgetfullness of God and duty, that the Church in every age has levelled its censures and pointed its warnings."[31] Just the year before, Jonathan Townley Crane (1819–80) had made the same point with his parishioners in the New Jersey Conference of the Methodist Church: "Measured movements of the body, or dancing, like measured movements of the vocal organs, or language, can not be judged of in the mass, but the moral character of each class of it must be determined, and its lawfulness or expediency ascertained, by considering its design and its general results." Despite his own lack of experience in dancing, Crane remained confident of his views. In the preface to his book, he tells the reader that many learned essays have been written on capital punishments. "It is not needful, either to dance, or to be hung, in order to be able to come to a conclusion touching the expediency of the performance."[32]

Thus, dance opponents, working either from hearsay or from actual experience, decried dancing in its concrete and contemporary practice by American society, rather than in its essence or according to abstract theory. However, the practice decried was that engaged in by the middle and upper classes. Subsequent arguments about women, health, and stewardship make clear that the published antidance sermons of this era did not aim at those who danced in working-class saloons and/or brothels.

Charges of Immorality

The concrete elements that seemed to arouse the ire of midcentury evangelicals pertained to the heterosexual nature of fashionable dancing and to the closed-dance position of the waltz and the polka. In his exposition of the general rules of Methodism, published in Louisville in 1851, the Reverend Moses M. Henkle (1798–1864), spelled out the inherent evil in the group figure dances as well as in the embrace and performance of the waltz: "The artfully arranged *pantomime,* the *turns,* the *touching* passes, the advance and retreat, the oft repeated grasp, and pressure of the hand, the swimming waltz performed in each other's embrace, all these have a natural language, more eloquent in its appeal to the passions than its translation into words could be." Henkle considered sex the critical attraction in dancing, sensual pleasure the appeal. Dress, music, drink, and dancing all strike the "passions and animal appetites." Even music is designed to stir the passions. As a consequence, Henkle declares that a young girl attending a ball will inevitably be diminished in her purity and innocence. More serious, he charges that many of the worst marriages have been contracted in the ballroom.[33] Others predict that the "indecent dances involving personal liberties between the sexes, which would be unsafe and indecent any where, become fashionable, and finally indispensable." Though the anonymous author of *Southey's Dream* makes no further clarification about specific dances or specific liberties, the popularity of the waltz and the polka makes clear that these dances were the author's target.[34]

Elaborating on the theme of female purity, John F. Mesick (fl. 1846–74), pastor of the German Reformed Salem Church in Harrisburg, Pennsylvania, told his parishioners in 1846 that the nature of the modern dances was such that "their movements, attitudes and evolutions are repugnant to a natural sense of propriety, and inconsistent with that unsullied purity of mind which we consider inseparable from the individual to whom we would yield the homage of our hearts."[35] Pointing out that the gross immodesty of the fashionable dances found ladies abandoning themselves "without a blush or a sigh" to improprieties they would object to anywhere else but in the ballroom, Franklin Wilson asked Baptists whether both men and women were not endangered. "Will not the sacred barrier of modesty be rudely shattered, and the way prepared for an easy descent to the depths of actual vice?"[36]

Most dance opponents of the era concentrate on men's unlicensed proximity to women at balls. Their charges invariably refer to men "who have no just claims to intimacy" taking liberties with female partners, that is, dancing with women who were neither daughters nor sisters. Palmer spells out his concern in terms that identify the waltz as the villain: "How comes it that, even in communities where the Gospel lifts its voice, and therefore virtue has a sure abode, the waltz so extensively prevails? A species of dance I do not hesitate thus publicly to denounce as undisguisedly licentious. The liberties, too, taken in the dance are such as can hardly be safe, even when sanctioned by the sacred laws of kindred and of tender friendship."[37] Knowing that humans are essentially depraved and fallen, Palmer feared the fleshly enticements of the dancing scene. Décolletage, physical motion, the "electric touch of the hand," the glaring lights and giddy confusion of sounds—all produced a danger as great as a "smoking brand to a magazine of powder." Though he probably did not dance himself, Palmer's description of the delights of a dance conveys an idea of what the waltz must have seemed like to youth perhaps starved for excitement and diversion: "And there are pleasures which intoxicate and madden, set the blood on flame, and consume while they delight. The dance is of this latter kind—it fascinates with a peculiar charm, and hurries its votaries along with a wild delirium, too much intoxicated to perform the sober duties of life, and too far maddened to heed the warnings prophetic of their speedy ruin."[38]

Concern about the intensity of attraction and the immorality of the dance position was so great that Edward Duffield Neill (1823–93), a Presbyterian preacher in St. Paul, Minnesota, preferred his daughter experience the physical manifestations of a religious ecstasy rather than have strange men familiarly placing their hands on her waist: "If there was to be a choice, let me see the female shouting under religious feeling, and moaning wildly in consequence of the agony from sin, or leaping with the joy from forgiveness, in preference to her being seen in a ball room, extravagantly dressed, ready to dance with any one, and searing her own conscience by indulging in all the vanities of life."[39]

Though the preponderance of allegations about the immorality of dancing applied to fashionable social dancing and balls, a few authors specifically refer to stage dancing. Potts links stage dancing with Herodias and Salome in the Bible and categorically labels it one of the "unfruitful works of darkness." Yet in a second reference to theater dance, he implies that the performer is always "a woman from a foreign theater" in a European city. Crane declares that Paris produced the "professional dancing girls of our own day" and quotes Longfellow on the low virtue of a "mere dancing girl" in a short skirt. Her only skill appears to have been the dubious feat of being able to raise one foot to the shoulder while twirling on the toes of the other foot.[40] Since both Crane and Potts published in 1848, it seems likely that they referred back to Fanny Elssler, who toured from Paris at the beginning of the decade.

Other than the alleged immorality of the closed dance position and its indelicate effects on female dancers, the most serious charges by dance opponents refer to women in the role of seducer. William Calmes Buck (1790–1872), pastor of the Baptist church in Greensboro, Alabama, places women in the mold of the temptress Eve when he denounces the ballroom atmosphere: "Extravagance, excess and riot, reign here; and it is the special object of the female amateur so to attire herself as to display her person in the most attractive (not to say voluptuous) manner possible." He further claims that the "laws of female modesty" simply do not apply in the ballroom.[41] Both dances and dresses put ideas into the minds of men that lead to "the society of persons, an association with whom ought to exclude them from the presence of delicate and refined, not to say, Christian, ladies." Delicacy forbade mentioning the word "prostitute." But in a passage that was graphic for the period, Crane claims that dancing is used by the "most wretched of females, as a mode of advertising their profession, and of inflaming the passions of their miserable victims." Equally blatant, Beecher decries "strumpet-dancers" who get money that should pay off the national debt.[42]

Thus, charges of immorality place women in two roles. On the one hand, they, like Eve, appear as temptresses—on stage and when wearing revealing dress in the ballroom. On the other hand, pure women were cast as victims when subjected to the embrace of strange men in the dance. Closely related to charges of immorality are the allegations that dance attracts a "promiscuous assemblage," undesirable companions "remarkable for their laxity in morals."[43] Most of the emphasis falls on undesirable men, but the concern pertains to women as victims.

Undesirable Companions

Henry Ward Beecher warned the young males of Indiana about the men of pleasure who corrupted youth. "Those who run the gay round of pleasure cannot help dazzling the young, confounding their habits, and perverting their morals." More specifically, the "bad company" included "all the idle, the dissipated, the rogues, the licentious, the epicures, the gluttons, the artful jades, the immodest prudes, the joyous, the worthless, the refuse." Emphasizing the seriousness of urban temptations, Beecher warned that the youth possessed the same passions as did those evil and idle libertines.[44] The Reverend Jesse Winecoff (1816–73), Lutheran pastor at Selinsgrove, Pennsylvania, told his congregation in 1850 that the several evils associated with dancing included "wicked company, idle and injurious conversation, swearing, intemperance, midnight revelry, quarreling, lasciviousness." Both his and Beecher's characterizations of undesirable company suggest that the worldly, the idle, and the intemperate constituted the questionable as well as the downright immoral.[45]

Mrs. F. E. Garnett, the only known female author among dance opponents of these decades, told Baptists and other readers in 1858 about the particular dangers to women who entered the ballroom. Those ladies put themselves forward as equals with male gamblers and drunkards. To have such men clasp the waist of a lady, as required in the waltz and polka, surely proved unthinkable to Mrs. Garnett as well as to the evangelical clergy.[46] The book *Modern Dancing,* by Charles Carroll Bitting, D.D. (1830–98), a Baptist minister, was published in Richmond the same year that Mrs. Garnett's book appeared in Louisville. Echoing her themes, Bitting wrote that at the fashionable dances, the "unsophisticated novice" fraternizes with the "practiced libertine." The gambler and the "debauched" caress the "pure" and the "innocent."[47] An anonymous author publishing in Hartford, Connecticut, in 1847 summed up the perspective on dancing with the comment that it could even be considered a "highly desirable enjoyment for young persons" if the participants and other tendencies could be controlled. But such control proved difficult when "any man of respectable appearance" with the price of admission could attend a public ball.[48]

Because literature on the reform of ballrooms and dance halls does not emerge until the early twentieth century, the degree to which public balls actually existed earlier is simply not known. Undoubtedly, there were public dance halls and/or saloons where dancing occurred. In her research on prostitution and reform, Barbara Meil Hobson has documented "dance halls" in Boston in 1820. But, they are cited in a configuration with brothels and gambling houses. All were places frequented by prostitutes and located on Southac Street, an infamous place in Boston.[49] The term "public ball" would not be applied to dancing in such places. By contrast, etiquette books of the era used the term to refer to a subscription event where not everyone was known to all participants. However, as the later discussion on etiquette will show, rules for polite society carefully protected the virtue of young ladies at such events.

Therefore, dance opponents' objection to undesirable companions pertained in all probability to men of some refinement and wealth, who may have gambled and drunk liquor to some degree and who circulated outside a woman's circle of immediate family and friends. In large cities, gentlemen even had access, by the late 1850s, to a guide to seraglios that catered to wealthy men.[50] Thus, those men labeled as undesirable companions at public balls may have been fine gentlemen but not Christian gentlemen. Though listed separately in antidance arguments, the category of undesirables also included those who taught dancing.

Dance Masters of Questionable Character

For the first time in American antidance literature, dance masters came in for their share of concentrated character assassination as part of the opposition to dance. Previously, isolated references had denigrated a dance master; by midcentury collections of indictments ranged from the brief to the lengthy, but all impugn the moral character of teachers. Jesse Guernsey, D.D. (1822–71), a Congregationalist pastor, writes in an 1850 sermon to the First Church in Derby, Connecticut, that those "who have made dancing, for the amusement of others, the business of their lives" possess a "vicious character." Potts calls them "godless."[51] Typically no explanation and no evidence follow such allegations. Thus, the reader is never sure whether or not the author refers to a local teacher or merely to general hearsay. As with other charges against dancing, allegations against teachers cross both geographical and denominational lines. Nathan Lewis Rice, D.D. (1807–77), preaching to Presbyterians in Cincinnati in 1847, observed that those who arranged the steps for modern dances were not known for their "prudence and modesty." In far stronger terms, Mesick told his Harrisburg congregation that dance "tutors" were the "very refuse of foreign cities; men destitute of either stability or principle; who, on account of their profession, are not esteemed worthy of an introduction into the social circle of the families by whom they are employed." Parents, therefore, encountered great danger when entrusting their children to such men. Similarly, Palmer declared that men of "low-birth," "ill-breeding," and "loose morality" were totally unfit to educate "even the heels of Christian children." Dance masters constituted nothing but a class of vagrants, for the most part "graduated in the pot houses and kitchens of Paris."[52]

In a clear example of the common strategy employed by dance opponents to push their case, John Rogers (1800–1867), elder of the Church of Christ in Carlisle, Kentucky, and certified to preach by Barton W. Stone, among others, indicted dance masters in the early 1840s on historical evidence only. Quoting the "celebrated Rollin," otherwise unidentified, Rogers labeled dance teachers as "a set of degenerated mortals." Assuming that the said Rollin was correct in his imputation, Rogers expanded on the evil: "that as dancing-masters are a set of light-headed, light-heeled, irreligious and degenerated mortals, it is most dangerous, and wicked to commit the care of our children to them."[53] The reader never knows whether Rogers had ever encountered any dancing master face to face.

By contrast, seven years after Rice's discourse in Cincinnati, the Reverend Samuel Ramsey Wilson (1818–86) told Presbyterians there that the "immodest waltz" was taught by French Monsieurs and Mesdames but he otherwise omitted any explicit moral or immoral attribution.[54] Although teachers of other nationalities had been known in the country since the eighteenth century, French dance masters drew more than their share of invective. Given that the evangelical clergy themselves would not have had first-hand experience with dance teachers, it seems likely that Wilson's unequivocal dismissal of dancing as taught by the French derived from hearsay. The eagerness with which evangelicals denigrated foreign teachers displayed a pious chauvinism. In Alabama, for example, Buck denounced a dancing master as a "French infidel or wandering mountebank, of infamous morals and perverted habits." If nothing else condemned the modern dance, in his opinion the character of its teachers would stamp it with infamy.[55]

Wine and Strong Drink

Concern about temperance had resulted in the formation of sundry societies devoted to the cause since the early nineteenth century. Maine passed the first state prohibition law in 1846. During the next decade, thirteen more states passed similar laws. In such a climate, charges that alcohol contributed to the immoral atmosphere of balls and assemblies are to be expected.[56] It is surprising, however, that so few of the antidance treatises speak to this alleged evil. Those that do address the topic merely note drinking as an undesirable element. For example, Buck wrote in 1857 that the ballroom was a "nocturnal revel, where drinking and cards compete with the dance." Similarly, in identifying the associated evils of the modern dances, Mesick specified wine and strong drink. The concern crossed denominational lines; the Methodist Henkle and the Baptist Franklin Wilson echoed the remarks of the German Reformed pastor.[57]

The most illuminating exposition on the evils of drinking and dancing comes from the Congregational pastor Jesse Guernsey, who feared for the morals of young men seduced by drink more than for the well-being of young women:

> The fact is worthy of notice in this connection, that the amusement of the ball-room, and the patronage of the bar-room, have to a considerable extent, been fashionable and unfashionable together. A few years ago, the dance had extensively grown into disuse; and such was the state of public sentiment respecting it, that you could rarely find a person of respectable standing in society, who would risk his respectability by attendance at a ball. Just then, too, a young man of character, would as soon have thought of cutting off his right hand, as of calling at a public house for aught that could intoxicate. Now, the dance is again becoming popular; the ball-room is again becoming the rallying place of gaiety and fashion: and now, too, (singular coincidence, is it not?) . . . it is no uncommon thing for young men to be seen bowing at the shrine of Bacchus.
>
> The coincidence is not so very remarkable after all, if we but remember that the amusement of the ball-room, hardly ever fails to secure a flourishing business to the barkeeper.

Guernsey's fear—one shared by many other evangelical clergy—was that one drink would eventually lead to drunkenness. Typically, those who experienced conversions at churches and revival meetings were asked to take a pledge of abstinence. According to Guernsey, many later forgot the pledge when they entered the ballroom, where the first drink pushed them "upon that downward way which ends in a drunkard's grave."[58]

Thus, the aversion to wine and strong drink in the context of dancing applied to the "ball-room" and to men. Whether or not men actually became intoxicated is not clear. To what degree clergy feared for women's drinking also is not clear. However, Foster explicitly voiced that concern, telling readers the term "ladies" did not apply to those who drank:

> *Ladies,* did I say? Originally this term signified "a distributor of bread among the poor;" but how shockingly some of the best terms have been applied!
>
> *Two women to one man revelling around a herd of decanters in this day!* And can it be possible that some of the former as well as the latter became intoxicated? Has it come to this; that while men who care for the good morals of the town, are doing all they can to suppress the ravages of intemperance—to dry up the tears of human woe—that women are lending a helping hand to such as are at least reckless of the public good, for the sake of paltry gain?[59]

Chauvinistic Assumptions

Midcentury evangelicals believed that one of the evil aspects of dancing derived from its impious origins, its associations with "heathenism," and its popularity in the "godless capitals of the Old World," such as Paris, which possessed a notoriously immoral people. It was understood that, historically, dancing had been cultivated only by people outside polite society, namely, slaves and courtesans.[60] Thus, Henkle explained to southern Methodists that dancing never taught refinement: "So far from being peculiar to a high state of refinement, it is, and, from the earliest dawn of history, ever has been, the universal attendant on every degree of barbarism, even the very lowest. There is no people so imbruted, so ignorant, so rude, as not to be addicted to the *accomplishment* of dancing." The "unintellectual" character of dancing disposes it peculiarly "to the tastes, condition, and morality, of barbarous people, who neglect mental and moral culture, and look for enjoyment, only, to animal appetites and passions." Henkle seeks to prove his point by asserting that blacks dance better and also learn faster than whites. Citing no evidence and no examples for such claims, he concludes that dancing remains merely an "*animal affair.*"[61]

A contemporary Methodist, Bishop Thomas Asbury Morris (1794–1874), confirms that Henkle's notions of barbarism and dancing were not unique. Morris's *Miscellany* of essays and sketches, published in Cincinnati in 1854, declares that dancing is a "barbarian practice" and that heathen nations possess much more dancing than Christian countries. Explaining this alleged fact, Morris states: "The lower people are degraded by ignorance and sin, the more they are devoted to this sort of dissipation." As further evidence, he observes that dancing rises to popularity in this country when revivals and religion are in a state of decline.[62]

The Episcopalian bishop William Meade linked historical and biblical incidents with Protestant-Catholic tensions and with the questionable reputation of dancing. Outlining the historical progress of dancing in Western culture, he points out that nothing could have been more immodest even in ancient culture than the "half-dressed female performers on the stage" who engage "in an unnatural use of their limbs." Like sixteenth-century reformers, he recalls to the reader the example of Salome and John the Baptist in the Bible as well as the dictum of Cicero, whom Meade quotes as remarking: "Scarcely any sober person dances, unless he is deranged." Meade also chronicles some of the church fathers against dancing. Further, he asserts that wherever "the Romish Church prevails," dancing occurs on Sundays, thus breaking a commandment. Given such a history and the fact that dancing was never enjoined as a part of either Jewish or Christian worship, Meade feels under no obligation to restore it to the church as per the Old Testament examples of religious dancing.[63]

Other authors of several denominations mix aspersions to dancing's un-intellectual character with historical and contemporary French immorali-ty. Charles Porterfield Krauth (1823–83) discoursed on the subject to mem-bers of his Evangelical Lutheran church in Winchester, Virginia, in 1851. He explained that "a reading and intelligent population never is a dancing one. The highest refinement of all countries, and especially of our own, is separating itself more and more from the practice." Further, he points out that dancing is inimical to virtue. Though he gives no source for his claims, Krauth confidently maintains that: "In our cities the dance is the known companion of the worst forms of vice—the prelude, preparation and attendant of the vilest orgies of the dregs of the worst part of the popula-tion."[64] Echoing the virtue theme, Potts declares fancy balls and masquer-ades to be the products of the "depraved cities" of southern Europe and France, hence the results of all the Old World "corruptions." Smith cites Egyptians dancing before their gods and Greek bacchanalian orgies, along with the dancing of "the ignorant and degraded African," to establish that dancing carries no refinement and no redeeming value.[65]

Based on his reading of *Putnam's Magazine* and a New York paper edited by a French nobleman, Buck called Paris the "polluted fountain" from which rose all forms of vice, including the modern dance: "The popular dances of this country are all of Parisian origin and mold; and, unfortunately for the purity of our people, some of the most lewd and corrupting forms of French dances are the popular and fashionable dances of this country." After impugn-ing the French in general and Paris in particular, Buck elaborated on their immorality by claiming that less than one-third of the births in that city were legitimate, a result he ascribed to their "licentious dances and concomitants." Yet Paris led the world of fashion in dressing and dancing.[66] He assumed the comparison spoke for itself. Echoing Buck, Crane also names Paris as the "grand propaganda of dancing, folly and Atheism," though he credits the Reverend Dr. Baird as the source for the statistic on illegitimacy.[67]

Vain and Harmful Exercise

Women and their attire drew the regular fire of evangelical clergy on the grounds of humility and Christian stewardship. Crane states the case suc-cinctly: "We object to the dance, because a wanton waste of the means of doing good is a positive sin; and dancing leads to unnecessary expenditure. The dance, and the ultras of dress and fashion, are sworn companions." Expanding on the theme, Rice points to the lack of prudence, perhaps im-moral character, of "Madam Fashion" who governs women at balls: "Ladies who attend such places, must dress *fashionably;* and we certainly know that Madam Fashion is not one of the most prudent ladies, particularly when she displays her taste *on special occasions.*[68] While complaining about imprudent dress and the waste of money on clothes, clerics do not state what constituted modest and prudent attire. Nor do they denigrate hair ribbons, hoop skirts, type of fabric, quality of accessory, or the like. Their criticisms simply are not specific. Nonetheless, dance opponents agreed that dancing fostered a taste for or love of personal display and show.[69]

Thus, women's dress was targeted on counts of both excessive cost and excessive exposure of their bodies. To spend money on clothes and needless ornamentation that could be better spent on "doing good," as Crane noted, was a "positive sin." In addition, dance opponents also argued that the emphasis on fashion and female display fostered a love of vanity and other undesirable traits. Mrs. Garnett agreed with the male clergy and charged that dancing "excites envy, and cherishes a spirit of competition, not in intellectual excellence, but superior elegance in dress and movement."[70]

Women's dressing and dancing also became criticized as a health hazard. Though most authors do not discuss women's health in particular, there seems to be more concern for women than for men. Mrs. Garnett again echoes the arguments of male opponents. Allowing that humans need exercise, she favors those kinds that carry no moral danger, for example, walking, riding, jumping, and the "skipping rope." Further, dancing generates an excitement that makes the young forget good health measures; they ride home from late night dances in cold air, when they are sweaty and damp. Then they get insufficient sleep. Elaborating on these points, others declare that dancers usually participate to excess, so the activity is followed by exhaustion, not the renewal that a wise physical recreation should produce. Bitting warns that dancing only exercises certain muscles, that it overheats the body, and that the exertion is so great that sleep becomes impossible. Potts talks about the unnatural excitement that also prevents sleep and agitates the system. Winecoff concludes that dancing does not promote health but is instead "a successful *destroyer* of health."[71]

In a comprehensive assessment of dancing's harmful effects, Krauth makes several key points. Morning, he asserts is the best time to exercise, but people dance in the evening. Exercise should be at regular intervals, but dancing evenings take place on no fixed basis. Exercise should also be taken in the open air, but dances are held in crowded, overheated, and ill-ventilated rooms. Exercise should be moderate but dancing is carried to excess. He argues that constitutions are taxed to the limit; latent heart disease is worsened; and consumption is acquired, especially for the young female. In fact, he states that she might exhaust her "vital energy" in one winter of dancing. Rice also asserts, "No one acquainted with facts of frequent occurrence, will deny, that the health of many young females is destroyed by excessive exertion on such occasions."[72] Mesick goes further and claims that "many an untimely death has been the dreadful penalty incurred by exposure on such occasions," especially for women who tend to wear low-cut gowns best suited to summer. The combination of overheated rooms and dancing to exhaustion, along with rich food consumed late at night and entry into chill air without proper clothes, regularly and inevitably, in the minds of many dance opponents, produced disease and death. Franklin Wilson coined the epitaph to this line of reasoning: "The dance has proved to them [ladies] the herald of death, and the ball-room the gate of the grave."[73] The reality of death focused many arguments on the wise or rational use of time.

Trivial and Irrational Activity

The evangelicals viewed time as a gift from God. With a Last Judgment awaiting all Christians at the end of their lives, how time was to be spent became a critical factor in all decision making. Worship and glorification of God were paramount in importance. Thus, regular Bible reading, prayer, meditation, and church attendance were preeminent among daily duties. Work and family responsibilities also carried great importance. In addition, performing acts of Christian charity useful to the improvement of society and Christian brethren became personal responsibilities. To fit oneself for these tasks and in keeping with the belief that humans were created in the image of God, evangelicals emphasized the development of mental faculties in the individual. "Mens sana in corpore sano," Juvenal's second-century dictum, did not mean that body and mind held equal importance in Christian valuing.[74]

The preeminence of reason and of utility meant that dancing could claim no logical place of importance in the evangelicals' value system. Without explaining, they simply labeled dancing "irrational and undignified," because it possessed "nothing in itself, or object or effects, worthy the dignity and interest of a rational and immortal being."[75] Their rationale evolved from the apparently obvious. Because dancing is an observable physical activity and because writers assumed a separation of body and mind, they had to conclude that dancing was *only* a physical activity. Mrs. Garnett reasoned: "The mind is not employed in it at all. Not a single power that is peculiar to man is called into requisition—not one." She observed that both monkeys and dogs can dance and concluded that dancing, therefore, "is certainly not a rational exercise. It is purely animal, and as such is of the flesh—fleshly." Edward Neill reached his conclusions about the imputed mindlessness of dancing, based on his own observations or the reported observations of people who danced. He decided that people who frequented dancing assemblies were unable to entertain themselves in any more fitting way. "Where men and women are highly cultivated, they are not forced to such shifts to make an evening pass away." To be "highly cultivated" meant to engage in the "higher and more rational pleasures of the community." Further, it is "improper" that Christians should engage in any recreational activity that does not "strengthen the mental powers." While drawing elevates and music refines, dancing only makes the mind "giddy." Others concluded, though without telling readers how they arrived at their conclusions, that dancing induced "mental vacancy," "dissipation," and/or "trifling conversation."[76] Such arguments reinforced the chauvinistic assumptions that "barbarous" people, heathens, and blacks were not rational beings.

In a more complete analysis, Guernsey explained that the nonutilitarian and unintellectual nature of dance and the ballroom make them worthless and wasteful for the Christian:

> But in the dance there is nothing, absolutely nothing that serves to give nourishment and strength to the mind. It never suggested a great thought; it never gave to the human soul an impulse in the direction of greatness. No soul enkindling truth did it ever communicate, no glowing aspirations after knowledge did it ever inspire. I have yet to see the man, and I apprehend the world has yet to see the man, who will even pretend to believe that he is intellectually richer and nobler for having shared in the amusement of the ball-room.[77]

Henkle claimed that prior to, while attending, and after a ball, the participant's mind was filled with "fascinating frivolities." Such a mind-set opposes a return "to sober study, or rational labor." Finally, he concludes: "It is much easier to play the dancing dandy, than to earn distinction by ploughing glebes of classic lore, or mastering the difficulties of a profession." Moreover, he knows of instances where a "successful *debut* in the ballroom, has rendered a young man utterly worthless for ever after."[78]

A related argument derives from the only Catholic treatise of this era. *Balls and Dancing Parties from the French of Abbé Hulot*, "By A Young Man," was issued from a Boston press in 1857. The original French came from the pen of Henri-Louis Hulot (1757–1829), canon and grand-vicar at Rheims in the later years of his clerical career. Hulot's commentary on the absurdity of what dancers look like, especially without music, dramatically calls to mind the views of Petrarch. In Hulot's description:

> What, in fact, can be more laughable than to see dancers advance, fall back, bend the body, jerk it up again, and whirl around like birds struck on the head? If music had not lent the charm of its harmony to cover the folly and absurdity of danc- ing with an appearance of sense and propriety, and if people could only see the movements of dancers performed in silence, they could not help exclaiming with the greatest Roman orator, Cicero, that *He who dances must be drunk or mad.*[79]

In a contemporary and related view of the meaningless character of danc- ing, Crane puts down the purported "accomplishment of dancers." Those who advocated dancing called it an accomplishment needed in polite soci- ety. In refuting that position, Crane recites what he considers the dubious talents of dancers. "They have learned to perform certain unmeaning mo- tions, regulated by the senseless squeak of a fiddle. They have learned how to lift up first one foot, then the other; now to make a scrape in this direc- tion, now in that. They have learned the important secret how to perform certain complicated maneuvers, which have, in themselves, neither mean- ing nor utility. And this is the sum total of the noble art of dancing."[80] In effect, dancing did nothing to fit the Christian for eternity.

Foe to Piety

For many dance opponents, life and time were identical, and the Christian owed both to God. Thus, Buck could declare that to rob God of our time is tantamount to murder. Such an adamant position derived from a con- ception about the importance of personal spiritual life and preparation for eternity, coupled with an anxiety about the shortness of earthly life, which, therefore, permitted no time for amusement. Hence, modern dancing was a "waste of time and substance, an injury to enlightened conscience and the spirit of piety, practiced without reference to the glory of God, and a prep- aration for death and judgment."[81]

Yet, not only personal and individual time but group and societal time loomed as important. For centuries, dance advocates had argued that the passage from Ecclesiastes, "a time to dance and a time to mourn," granted permission for dancing. And for centuries, opponents had held that the passage did not legitimate dancing. During the nineteenth century, evan- gelicals again worried because the "judgments of God are abroad in the earth," and the power of the Holy Spirit seemed withdrawn from the church. In 1854, on the eve of the Civil War, Samuel Wilson called Presbyterians to attend to the seriousness of the times and forgo frivolous amusements such as dancing:

> Christians, I turn to you and ask, is this a time to dance? Look out upon the world; listen to the sounds of lamentation, and mourning, and woe that are borne to our ears upon every breeze. . . . Are not the clouds big with the wrath of an angry God? Are not famine, and pestilence, and grim-visaged war stalking over the face of the earth; and is not one commercial disaster after another filling the nations with perplexity, and sending consternation into every community? And the Church of Jesus Christ, alas! what shall be said of it. Divided more and more; distracted, corrupted; forsaken of her children; the sport of the profane, and the song of the drunkard. And shall we make merry? Is this a time to dance, when the threatening hand of a jealous God is stretched out over the nations, and his Holy Spirit is with drawing from the church? Surely, rather is it a time to turn to the Lord "with fasting, and with weeping, and with mourning."

Wilson's words must have struck some positive chord, for the Presbyterian Board of Publications issued the same text under a new title, *A Time to Dance,* probably within two years after its initial delivery, in 1854, at the First Presbyterian Church of Cincinnati.[82]

Although Wilson warned Christians about the seriousness of the time in which they lived, many evangelicals reminded readers and listeners about the Last Judgment awaiting them. Dance opponents generally agreed that dancing and the ballroom proved a "sad preparation for death," an event that might come in the next hour. Bitting told Richmond Baptists in 1858 that people who engaged in ballroom dancing in fact danced on a slender thread over a terrible abyss. Like Dana Goodsell's rhetoric from 1839, Bitting's imagery evoked Jonathan Edwards's famous sermon. Bitting warned,

> The infatuation of frivolous pleasures is great as that of danger, and it may be, that when called out in the next set, dancing on the very verge of that pit whose quenchless fires hiss with the vengeance of an angry God, a more terrific plunge awaits you who are dancing on a more slender thread, and over a more terrible abyss. Is it profitable; is it wise; is it safe, to spend time in such trivialities, when death and eternity are so near, and perdition just beneath? Answer on your knees, in your privacy with God, and in remembrance of the judgment.[83]

Responsibility to Weaker Christians

A fundamental Pauline precept about regulating behavior carried conservative interpretations for dance opponents. "So then, if food makes my brother sin, I will never eat meat again so as not to make my brother fall into sin" (1 Cor. 8:13). In explaining that freedom in Christ permitted them to do many things, Paul warned of each individual's personal responsibility to watch out for the welfare of weaker Christians. "Be careful, however, not to let your freedom of action make those who are weak in the faith fall into sin" (1 Cor. 8:9).

Albert Barnes (1798–1870), the well-known Presbyterian evangelist, told readers of the *American National Preacher* for January 1844 that the Pauline freedom did not pertain to the permissibility of dancing. Rather, the issue was whether or not it was "consistent and proper for professing Christians to engage in amusements" such as dancing and whether or not it was proper for Christian parents to train children in ballroom behavior. Even though a Christian is theoretically free to dance, Barnes argued that dancing served no purpose with which any Christian ought to be concerned, that is, dancing does not prepare for eternity, grant grace, help one understand the Bible, promote personal prayer and piety, or the like. Elaborating on Paul's warning, the anonymous author E.Y. wrote in *Dancing, as a Social Amusement,* the American Tract Society publication from the late 1840s, that, even though Christians may have time, leisure, and money for dancing, the further question remains for them: "Is it expedient?" That is, will dancing edify the participant? Will it bring harm or danger to others? Even though one person could dance with impunity, if that example brought harm to weaker brethren, then the true Christian was obliged not to make a fellow believer fall into sin.[84]

Ideal for the Christian

The Pauline preachment "Be not conformed to the world" (Rom. 12:2) received almost universal quotation in antidance treatises throughout the centuries and enjoyed renewed popularity during the middle nineteenth century. Clear distinctions between people of the world and people of God often eluded dance opponents in their writing. Many simply counted those who circulated in fashionable sets as "worldlings." Others stated that people of the world made the pursuit of pleasure their sole aim and/or focused on the present rather than eternity. Mesick explained differences a bit more fully. Using the duality of light and darkness, he observed that the difference between the two kinds of people was as perceptible as the difference between night and day, darkness and light. He pointed more specifically to ultimate focus: "No man deserves the name of Christian, no man can indulge a good hope of salvation, unless his faith in Christ is productive of non-conformity to the world; a stand which is indispensable to his separation from a perishing race and his incorporation into the Kingdom of Heaven."[85]

Adversaries also argued that church members who danced proved ineffective witnesses to the nonbeliever. Christians were supposed to be a "peculiar people," those whose light would shine before others with "garments even unspotted from the world." Dance opponents regularly state that Christians who danced failed in this mission. According to Rice, "one of the chief reasons why the moral influence of individual christians, and of the church upon the unconverted is not greater, is to be found in their conformity to the world."[86]

Thus, the ideal Christian experienced personal conversion, possessed a soul focused on heaven, and desired no more of worldly pursuits. Personal holiness became a goal obtainable only through constant checks on sensual, fleshly desires and through daily communion with God via prayer and Bible reading. The subject of eternal salvation became all absorbing. The proper biblical guide to follow was Paul's admonition: "Well, whatever you do, whether you eat or drink, do it all for God's glory" (1 Cor. 10:31). This ideal was widely held and forcefully presented by the mainstream clergy.[87]

In addition to invoking the basic authority of the Bible, mid-nineteenth-century evangelicals introduced historical precedent in the form of testimony by early church fathers as well as opinions of contemporaries. John T. Brooke, for example, commenting on the credibility of the American Tract Society, stated that the society "is sustained by Christians of every Evangelical denomination, and is, therefore, the fairest representative that can be found of sound Protestant sentiment, upon any point, of doctrine, or practice pertaining to the 'common salvation.' "[88] Other clergy stressed that the general sentiment of all evangelical denominations prevailed against dancing and balls. Presbyterians also cited the authority of that denomination as a body, noting that as early as 1818 the General Assembly had officially pronounced against dancing. Some clerics declared that contemporary changes in the influence of religion also gave weight to their opposition. In 1847, Smith observed: "There has hardly been a time, for forty years past, when the reviving influences of God's Spirit have been so generally withdrawn, as at the present period; and just at this time is there an almost unprecedented passion for dancing—not confined to the world, but making inroads upon the church. As religion declines, dancing flourishes! And who does not know that the reverse is true? Who ever knew dancing parties and balls to abound in a powerful revival of religion?"[89] Franklin Wilson, a Baptist, wrote several pages on "The Dance and The Revival." Morris, a Methodist bishop, concluded that "the more people pray, the less they feel like dancing; and the more they dance, the less they pray, or love praying."[90]

The importance of salvation for eternity, coupled with the shortness of this life, induced many clergy to employ fear and threat. Bitting, for example, closed his treatise on *Modern Dancing* with this exhortation: "Friend, when you take the next dance, remember that one hour may see you in another world, and ere you take the first step, think whether it will lead you into heaven or into hell." Foster warned his readers: "Sin is progressive: 'first the blade, then the ear, and then the full corn in the ear.'" By his estimate "thousands" had entered the ballroom with innocent intentions and then exceeded all bounds of respectable society, finally to be ejected from polite society, "fit subjects only for the world's moral dung-hill." Commonly, temperance people believed that the first drink led to alcoholism. Applying the same logic and psychology to dancing, Morris asserted: "Vice is progressive, in no cases more so than in drinking, gambling and dancing." Consequently even an innocent parlor dance, held in the controlled environment of home and under parental supervision, was off-limits. Some declared that it was difficult to contain private dancing: "It becomes more and more fascinating, until it chafes under restraint and plunges into the rushing stream of pleasure." Others evaded the issue by asserting that there were other amusements and exercises available with no attendant evil effects or consequences; therefore, clerics instructed Christians to participate only in those activities where no potential danger lurked.[91]

Critics of the Evangelicals' Stance

Although most clergy argued for complete abstinence from dancing, not all ministers agreed with such a stringent view. Those who criticized the evangelicals cannot be automatically deemed atheists and agnostics. Nor can they be characterized as unqualified dance advocates. Further, the known opinions all raise different objections to the mainstream evangelical view.

In 1856 Oliver Johnson (1809–89) presented a paper entitled "Amusements: Their Uses and Abuses" to the Pennsylvania Yearly Meeting of Progressive Friends. He points out that if dances were held more frequently, less time and cost would be devoted to their attendance and less sleep lost due to excessive participation. Further, more beneficial physical exercise would be gained. Johnson quotes the Unitarian leader William Ellery Channing, in the latter's "Address on Temperance," delivered in Boston, 28 February 1837: "'It is to be desired, that dancing should become too common among us to be made the object of special preparation as in the ball; that members of the same family, when confined by unfavorable weather, should recur to it for exercise and exhilaration; that branches of the same family should enliven in this way their occasional meetings; that it should fill up an hour in all the assemblages for relaxation in which the young form a party.'"[92] Channing also urged dancing as one of several innocent amusements that, when offered to the public, would serve to curb temptations to intemperance. He argued that the first means for suppressing vice is to afford people the opportunity for "innocent pleasure." That is, unlawful pleasures could be prevented by furnishing the possibility of lawful pleasures such as dancing, music, and theater.[93]

The Presbyterian cleric James L. Corning (1828–1903) urged the church to develop a new attitude toward amusements in general, one that avoided a strategy of straight condemnation. He pointed out that preachers focused on the evil of amusements such as dancing but neglected to preach on attendant evils: "late hours, gluttony, extravagant display, hypocritical etiquette, these are never right and never can be." In Corning's view, dancing in its "most objectionable form" is still the least of the evils connected with fashionable parties:

> Why, I have sat beside a professing christian woman in one of the beautiful parlors of a fashionable metropolitan avenue, whose jewelled neck and ears and fingers and dazzling brocade, as much as said to the assembled guests, "none of your dresses cost as much as mine;" and then I have seen her go into the supper-room and eat enough to make a swine have gripes of conscience, and then come out, obese, and panting for breath, made marvelously religious by sandwiches and champaigne [sic], and wind up the farce with a pious discourse on the sin of dancing!

Thus, in Corning's view, the evangelicals focused on some obvious evils but not on the "deadly" sins or behaviors.[94]

A still different criticism pointed to Presbyterian church discipline. George Hornell Thacher (1818–87), writing under the pseudonym Clericus, vigorously attacked the Albany Synod of the Presbyterian Church for making dancing a case for church discipline and excommunication. The synod's action, which occurred in 1843, left church members only two choices if they were caught dancing or teaching their children to dance: they could submit to the synod's authority or be excommunicated. While not advocating "balls or worldliness," Thacher objected to the synod's peremptory action on the grounds of an important principle. Ecclesiastical courts, he asserted, had no right to make dancing or not dancing a condition of church membership. "Because if church courts take it into their heads to force the conscience of a layman in regard to one thing, not in itself wrong, they may in a thousand other things. Where is the limit to this power? Where will they stop?"[95]

Sounding like a modern civil libertarian, Thacher also attacked the one-issue people in his era. Echoing Corning, he writes with biting sarcasm that, among the growing list of evils against which such men inveighed, "is that most awful of all awful iniquities that ever cursed the earth—an evil, which, to judge of the importance they attach to it, is likely to bring in its train, wars, pestilences, and famines, and other dire calamities, like the merchant's goods, too numerous to mention: we mean the evil of occasionally dancing for amusement. Compared with this, heathenism, with all its degradation, its cruelty and its crimes, is as nothing."[96] With similar sarcasm, Johnson echoed the sentiment that evangelical clergy focused on the easy and the obvious instead of attacking the more serious evils in society, such as slavery.[97]

The views of Thacher, Channing, Corning, and Johnson appear to stand out in the contemporary context, as do the published opinions of Hale on the need for government and church to plan and organize public amusements for all classes of society. Other views that contrasted with those of the evangelical dance opponents came from the etiquette books of the era. Though some of these manuals were written by European authorities, such publications increasingly came from American men and women. While favoring dance, these etiquette authorities cannot be categorized as unqualified dance enthusiasts. They set clear and strict limits on male-female behavior at balls, and they expressed concern for women's health.

Views on Etiquette and Health

The title of an 1849 book, *Etiquette at Washington; Together with the Customs Adopted by Polite Society in the Other Cities of the United States,* hints at the true nemesis of antidance writers, namely fashionable society, which was thought to be the real villain behind amusements. "These persons affect to consider themselves the first class of people, and superior to all others. The ground of their superiority is, that they are addicted to expensive self-indulgences, which imply wealth. The real bond of union among them is the pursuit of pleasure."[98] By contrast, the anonymous author of the 1849 *Etiquette,* a "Citizen of Washington," wrote precisely to assist those elevated to wealth and property in understanding the rules by which American society conducted itself. He found nothing objectionable in such elevation. As a commercial society and democratic republic, America provided the opportunity for people to achieve upward mobility. Yet the acquisition of mere money did not in itself qualify persons for refined society. "Courtesy is a distinctive characteristic of gentility; and stiffness and hauteur of the want of it."[99]

Similar advice appeared in a number of other books from the era, many of which carried the words "American" or "Republican" in their titles. However, the European tradition still was in evidence. Charles William Day, whose borrowed name was Count Alfred D'Orsay, authored *The American Ladies and Gentleman's Manual of Elegance, Fashion and True Politeness* (1850), which appeared first under another title in London (1836) and then in this country in numerous editions, with various titles, beginning in 1843. Like the "Citizen of Washington," Day also points out that people rise rapidly in a mercantile society and "it rarely happens that the polish of their manners keeps pace with the rapidity of their advancement." Concern with becoming the right kind of person for polite society manifested itself in at least thirty-six new books in the 1840s and thirty-eight more in the next decade. The total exceeded the number of such publications in any previous period of American history.[100]

Behavior at Balls

Etiquette writers demonstrate that a concern for guarding the respectability of persons admitted to public balls remained paramount. Public assemblies were usually managed by a board, whose duty it was to guard admission. The "Citizen of Washington" admitted, though, that such a plan did not guarantee that all persons would demonstrate civility and the desired quality. However, writers generally agreed that the lady could refuse a dance with a stranger if she did so politely.[101] Men were told not "on any account" to ask a "strange lady" to dance, or they would be considered "impertinent." Day stressed that no two people should be introduced unless it had been previously understood as agreeable to both. As a further safeguard, the anonymous author of *True Politeness* (1847) counseled ladies to go with a party of friends to "ordinary public balls." In that situation, they would not have to depend upon the master of ceremonies for introductions to male partners, since, "in spite of his best efforts, objectionable individuals will gain access to such." *True Politeness* also urged the lady never to go too early to public balls and to avoid being seen at them on a frequent basis. Finally, etiquette authorities continued to agree that ballroom acquaintances did not extend beyond the assembly. That is, no man could recognize a lady on the street after a ball unless she chose to acknowledge him first. If she nodded or bowed to him, he might then be permitted to raise his hat to her. If, however, he wished to meet the lady further, he had to seek formal intro-duction.[102] Thus, rules of the fashionable world carefully circumscribed the behavior of ladies and gentlemen at public balls.

Even the rules for dancing the allegedly immoral waltz prescribed that a distance be maintained between the sexes. Decorum decreed that men never danced without wearing gloves. Thus, bare skin could not touch bare skin. Conventions also ruled that "the lady should be led through the figure with the utmost possible delicacy. Her partner has the privilege of taking her hand for this purpose, but he should not abuse the privilege. He should simply touch and not grasp it; and in waltzing, particular care should be taken to avoid pressing her waist. It ought only to be touched with the open hand."[103] Finally, any touching of partners had to be gentle; crushing holds were com-pletely *gauche*. Day advised gentlemen not to press the lady's waist in the waltz "lest you leave a disagreeable impression not only on her *ceinture*, but on her mind."[104]

Given the restrictions on introductions in addition to the discreet dis-tance and gentleness decreed for the closed dance position, it is difficult for the modern reader to understand why the evangelicals became so incensed about the supposed immorality of the couple dances. Their viewpoint be-comes more comprehensible seen in the context of Victorian values. The Victorian code developed with a general distrust of the body. Daily dress completely covered it; women's fashions distorted it. The code carefully guarded sexual activity as well, even in marriage. The typical male on the eve of his wedding had seen only the face and hands of his bride except perhaps for the glimpse afforded by décolletage at a ball. Physical contact had been limited to a formal kiss on the hand, unless knees had touched daringly under a table. Further, marriage manuals commonly recommend-ed sex only once a week and told the couple not to undress in front of each other. Thus, touching even within the bonds of marriage, was restricted by prevailing rules for health and morality.[105] In this context, the closed dance position seemed a total breech of decorum and morality, for the lady danced with the man's hand on the small of her back. The position appeared like an embrace.

To embrace one's dance partner, when that person was not a spouse or close kin, aroused the righteous wrath of dance opponents. But the popu-larity of the couple dances made the action common. Moreover, it was con-sidered in bad taste for husbands and wives to dance with each other at balls except perhaps for the first set. The "Citizen of Washington" stated that they could enjoy each other's company at home; other writers give no rationale for the rule.[106] The temptations of the closed dance position were accentuated by other mores. Any lady a man danced with was to have homage paid her as though she were a queen and he the faithful servant. The manual of *True Politeness* strongly reminded the lady of this fact and told her, in effect, to lean on the man and expect service from him. In return for such service and protection, the lady civilized the man by her presence. She also beautified the environment by her appearance.[107]

Miss Leslie's Behaviour Book (1859) told the reader straightforwardly that the gentleman wanted his partner to make a perfect appearance on the dance floor and to entertain him with a bright mind as well: "Even the most humane man, whatever may be the kindness of his heart, would rather not exhibit himself on the floor with a partner *ni jeune ni jolie,* who is ill-drest, looks badly, moves ungracefully, can neither keep time to the music nor understand the figure, and in fact has 'no dancing in her soul.' If, with all the rest, she is dull and stupid, it is cruel for any kind friend to inflict her on a gentleman as a partner. Yet such things we have seen." Although Miss Eliza Leslie (1787–1858) allowed that no lady could be truly ugly if she possessed at least an "intelligent eye" and a "good humored mouth," a woman so unlucky as to have a deformed figure "has no occasion to exhibit the defects of her person by treading the mazes of a cotillion, or above all, in going down a country dance." Brutally, the author repeated the fact or rumor that young men say a lady who is ugly or misshapen and insists on dancing a waltz or polka deserves the penitentiary. Any lady so unfortunate as not to be blessed with perfect form and a beautiful face should make herself a scintillating conversationalist instead. The true lady cultivated self-knowledge. When suspecting herself to be deficient in all the necessary qualifications of the ballroom, she ought to be wise enough to give up dancing. Ladies "verging 'on a certain age' " ought to do likewise.[108] With such a premium placed on beauty of face and figure in the ballroom, it is small wonder that women spent many hours preparing themselves to be properly coiffed and dressed before making their appearance.

Though beauty reigned on the dance floor, a lady's moral qualities remained important in all aspects of life. A true lady would never sully her mind with impure thoughts, even when dancing the tantalizing couple dances. The anonymous author of *The Habits of Good Society* (1860) acknowledged that the waltz and polka could be made "very indelicate" but hastened to add that any dance could. That is, the thoughts and behavior of the dancers can make any dance moral or immoral, but the dance itself is value free—simply physical body movements. Thus, evangelicals, when imputing impure thoughts to women or to men dancers, invested the dance itself with moral attributes. The author of *Good Society* chastised the clergy for such attribution and, thereby, for following "in the steps of the Romish Church" on the continent. Attributing evil or immoral thoughts to young dancers insulted them: "But it is a gross insult to our daughters and sisters to suppose them capable of any but the most innocent and purest enjoyment in the dance, while of our young men I will say, that to the pure all things are pure. Those who see harm in it are those in whose mind evil thoughts must have arisen. *Honi soit qui mal y pense.*"[109]

Women's "Sphere"

The emphasis on morality derived in part from a fundamental notion about the role of women in antebellum America. In effect, males relegated them to a pedestal, from which females were to dispense moral virtues, religious duties, refinement, and beauty. While men built businesses, ran railroads, invented machinery, and sullied themselves in politics, women's "sphere" remained the home. Ladies were supposedly not unequal in rights or function, merely different in role and purpose. The *Ladies' Vase* of 1843 explained:

> Instead of seeking hopelessly, and in direct opposition to the delicacy of her sex, to obtain for her political privileges; instead of bringing her forward as the competitor of man in the public arena; we would mark out for her a sphere of duty that is widely different. In the domestic circle, "her station should be at man's side, to comfort, to encourage, to assist"; while, in the christian temple, we would assign her an ennobling, but a feminine part,—to be the guardian of the sacred and spiritual fire, which is ever to be kept alive in its purity and brillancy on the altar of God.

Elucidating further the assignment of religious duties to women, the author points out that women have many trials to bear and therefore need the support of Christianity. Religion is their only "elevating" and enduring principle in this temporary world. It permits them to rise above the sordid and the "degrading" as well as the sorrowful.[110] When women thrust themselves into such places as men worked in and ran, they departed from their "Heaven-appointed sphere," according to the Baptist cleric Daniel Clarke Eddy (1823–96) in *The Young Women's Friend* (1857). Exalting the benefits of the God-given sphere for women, Eddy points out that home is "woman's throne, where she maintains her royal court, and sways her queenly authority." Thus, the relationship of male to female as of servant to queen in the ballroom applied in the home as well, where piety ranked as woman's crown.

God designed her for piety; it would be her comfort not only on this earth but in the hereafter.[111]

By their superior Christian moral example, women could dispense civility even beyond the sphere of home. The lady who possessed rank and fortune as well as time could engage in charitable activity, which extended her virtues "far beyond the mansion where she presides, or the cottage which she protects."[112] When women were thus assigned a queenly role in the sphere of hearth and home and when they were considered to be the superior moral sex, endowed by God with piety, then any activity that threatened women meant a threat to the character of future generations and, ultimately, to the well-being of the country. The threat of dancing applied to women's physical health as well as to their purity and piety.

Women's Health

Both male and female authors traced women's role as healer in the home to a divine decree. Perhaps none was more vocal in this than Catharine Beecher (1800–1878), the sister of Henry Ward Beecher. In her *Letters to the People on Health and Happiness* (1855) she declares, "Woman is the Heaven-appointed guardian of health in the family, as the physician is in the community." Though her duties were not as extensive or complicated as the man's, they were nonetheless as important. Beecher urged that all women consider such a calling to be part of their profession and to train for it. Like the evangelical clergy, Beecher understood that "Providence" had set women apart for the "chief responsibility of sustaining the family state, in all its sacred and varied relations." Her views were not unique. In 1837 the American Physiological Society, founded in Boston, resolved that women as wives and mothers were second only to God in the physical, mental, and moral development of the human race.[113]

Yet despite this heaven-endowed task, Beecher found that middle-class women of her generation fell into the category of the chronically ill. Many, in fact, considered their perpetual state of distress to be the norm. Based on her own statistics gathered from "about two hundred different places in all the Free States," Beecher concluded that "the standard of health among American women is so low that few have a correct idea of what a healthy woman is." Twentieth-century historians have corroborated Beecher's findings and documented the fact that illness proved the norm more than the exception for the Victorian lady who was disenfranchised from all but domestic and religious duties.[114]

Causes of illness included more than a narrowly circumscribed set of responsibilities and challenges. Beecher understood that domestic duties precluded women's exercising in the open air. She also acknowledged that the "pernicious customs of dress" militated against women's engaging in any kind of vigorous physical activity that could build up their cardiovascular endurance and muscular strength. Her description of the end results of corseting plus layers of long skirts and petticoats presents the picture of a lady unduly encased and exposed at the same time. By the midcentury's prevailing rules of fashion, "one half the body is subjected to extreme changes from heat to cold, while the other portion is compressed by tight girding, heated by accumulated garments, pressed downward by whalebones, and by heavy skirts resting over the most delicate organs." Beecher labeled the model figure in fashion plates as "miserable," an ideal that depicted "the distortions of deformity and disease as models of taste and fashion."[115]

When this mode of dress was combined with décolletage for evening balls and when the lady danced excessively in overheated rooms, ate rich food late in the evening, and then went out into chill air for the homeward ride at a very late hour, she surely become susceptible to colds, perhaps pneumonia. Ladies trussed as styles demanded could not be physically conditioned or active beyond walking and dancing, even if their domestic responsibilities permitted. Twentieth-century students of health and wellness understand that a fit body must be exercised; that strength, flexibility, and endurance not used are lost rapidly. However, in the nineteenth century only a few exceptional individuals such as Beecher and some later physical training directors advocated exercise for women.[116] More commonly, the cure for female complaints was total rest.

Etiquette writers who warned ladies against tight lacing sounded only somewhat concerned about the state of female health; they stopped short of any radical recommendations for reform. The *Ladies' Vase*, for example, seemed more concerned about aesthetic qualities than about health restrictions caused by the corset. The author noted, "Few circumstances are more injurious to beauty than the constrained movement, suffused complexion, and labored respiration that betray tight lacing." Moreover, a too-small waist produced a disproportionate figure, something inimical to the laws of symmetry. Emily Thornwell's *Lady's Guide* gave the reader five pages of information on the physiological harm achieved by overly tight lacing, but followed with aesthetic implications of the practice. In addition to constricting the lungs, crushing internal organs and the like, tight lacing caused blood to rush to the face, neck, and arms when the lady exercised in a heated room. The effects proved displeasing to Thornwell just as they had to the anonymous author of the *Ladies' Vase*. Thornwell wrote, "Young ladies at parties frequently become so suffused from this cause, that they present the appearance of a washerwoman actively engaged over a tub of hot suds. Tight lacing also causes an extreme heaving of the bosom, resembling the panting of a dying bird."[117] Although Thornwell warned that stays too tightly laced produced dangers to health, the young female reader concerned with making a good impression at parties and balls got the clear message that she ought to be concerned first and foremost with tight lacing's dire consequences to her appearance.

Etiquette books of the period shed light on one further argument of the evangelicals. To the modern reader, the author who argued that dancing occurred too late in the evening and resulted in too much lost sleep might seem like the proverbial "old fogy." However, social authorities told the nineteenth-century reader that proper arrival hours at the ballroom varied from 9:00 P.M. to midnight. *Etiquette at Washington* recommends arriving between 9:00 and 10:00 P.M. *How to Behave* says that 10:00 P.M. is early enough to go to a ball.[118] Late arrival at balls in addition to vigorous dancing until the early morning hours could have proved harmful to delicate constitutions. Florence Hartley warned the 1860 reader that many young ladies did not watch their health. That is, they never left the ball until "utterly exhausted." Then they slept late the next morning, "scarcely touching breakfast, that most important meal." Hartley reminded the young lady of her era that maintaining good health was a duty. Her rationale appears to have been the fact that women in her day were less fit than their mothers or grandmothers had been. To help remedy the situation, Hartley prescribed one and one-half hours of exercise daily in the open air, as well as prudent dressing, eating, and sleeping. Acknowledging that dancing in overheated rooms often harmed the female, Hartley recommends a walk of four to five miles per day for the young woman in full vigor.[119]

The modern reader, perusing the etiquette books and Beecher's writings, understands that the evangelical clergy no doubt were correct in their charges that dancing proved a health hazard to women. Tight lacing, overdressing on the bottom half of the body and underdressing on the top half, coupled with infrequent—if any—exercising between balls, could hardly have produced a fit person. But dance opponents very likely drew their conclusions merely by observing contemporary behavior. That produced a line of reasoning both circuitous and self-fulfilling in nature: The fact that ladies were chronically ill proved that they were born with delicate constitutions. Since they were so delicate, they ought to be kept as hothouse flowers, not overtaxed either mentally or physically. Often ladies became ill, and perhaps died, following excessive exercise and exposure at balls. Therefore, dancing proved an obvious deterrent to good health. In effect, the sum of social role and fashionable dress, along with inadequate fitness knowledge and practice, wrought little but physiological havoc on the well-being of middle- and upper-class Victorian women. In fact, Beecher concluded at midcentury: "I think I can show also that if a plan for destroying female health, in all the ways in which it could be most effectively done, were drawn up, it would be exactly the course which is now pursued by a large portion of this nation, especially in the more wealthy classes."[120] It was to those classes that contemporary literature spoke in depicting the feminine ideal.

The Ideal for the Lady

The antidance treatises and the politeness books portrayed contrasting, though not mutually exclusive, ideals for the mid-nineteenth-century lady who belonged to society's leisure class. Neither kind of literature spoke to working women, immigrant women, or pioneer women. The ideals essentially followed the models depicted during the first four decades of the century, though by the 1840s and 1850s the pictures had emerged in fuller detail. On the one hand, the true lady upheld religion, morality, motherhood, and family. On the other hand, the lady in society displayed perfection in beauty, grace, and refinement. Antidance books depict the ideal in Christian behavior as a lady who remained pure, protected, and pious. Etiquette books portray a lady who appeared an ornamental queen of society, a woman who could accept or refuse dances and introductions at her whim, though she was to be guided by genuine courtesy and pure morality. Dance opponents regularly mentioned the "delicacy" of females, but the image bespeaks a combination of innocence, modesty, and frailty rather than sickness exclusively.[121] Since etiquette authorities spoke to those who went out in society and danced, their readers presumably enjoyed more than minimal health and vigor. To go out to dancing parties at nine or ten in the evening and then dance until the early hours of the morning, all the while looking lovely and appearing gracious, surely required at least moderate stamina. Although dance opponents supported the notion of good health, they did not prescribe practice to that end except in speaking generally against the unhealthy aspects of dancing. However, some etiquette writers warned specifically about the tightly laced corset and the need for regular walking and adequate rest. Neither set of writers counseled anything so radical as total dress reform and regular, vigorous exercise for ladies.

These contrasting ideals for the midcentury lady represent differences in degree that for centuries had distinguished the ideal for the gentleman and the ideal for the Christian. The nineteenth-century lady, according to dance opponents, was to focus on religion to the exclusion of worldly vanities. The ideal for the lady set forth by etiquette authorities depicted a female who followed the precepts of morality, grounded in Christianity, but who also displayed the beauty, charm, grace, and skill required in the polite world frequented by the middle and upper classes.

Dancing beyond the Mainstream

In marked contrast to the fashionable ideal, women of the several utopian sects that flourished at midcentury provide a picture of females sufficiently healthy to work and to enjoy dancing. Those radical religious groups and communitarian societies that approved dancing provide a context for further clarifying the arguments of dance opponents, particularly as those arguments pertained to women.

The pre–Civil War years were rife with reform movements of one kind or another. Women's rights advocates met at Seneca Falls, New York, in 1848. The next year Amelia Bloomer introduced dress reform for women.[122] Sylvester Graham and others urged dietary reform for all. Benevolent societies worked to aid widows and orphans and to spread temperance. Not least, religious revivals of the early decades of the century had produced a fertile climate for the burgeoning utopian settlements of one kind or another.[123] Three of these developed theologies wherein beliefs surrounding sexual activity intertwined with notions of perfectionism to permit and promote dancing. The Shakers, the Oneidans, and the Mormons stand out in dramatic relief from those who embraced the prevailing Victorian morality and evangelical opposition to dance.

The Shakers

Formally known as the United Society of Believers in Christ's Second Appearance, the Shakers aimed at perfection and freedom from sin through control of the passions and total subjugation of the sexual impulse. Although their movement originated in England during the latter eighteenth century, the Shakers experienced their period of greatest vitality between 1830 and 1850, when they totaled some six thousand members in nineteen American communities.

A primary emphasis on work as well as worship characterized the Shaker settlements, which, in effect, became little oases in the secular world. The 1814 covenant drawn up for the settlement at Pleasant Hill, Kentucky, for example, illustrates the signers' degree of separation from mainstream society. These individuals testified that they had freely agreed to dissolve all ties to the flesh and to the world. By contrast, those who later deserted Shaker communities were said to be "going to the world." Simple dress combined with simple living, on a daily basis, produced a routine in which productivity and group meetings left no time for amusements. Besides producing their own food, supplies, and furnishings, members contributed to the larger mercantile world.[124] Worship provided the renewal necessary for return to work.

The dance in Shaker worship evolved from an individualized, spontaneous activity to a formally choreographed choral art. Henri Desroche points out that dancing during the late eighteenth and early nineteenth centuries corresponded to the spontaneous and frenzied activity reported at frontier revivals such as the famous Cane Ridge camp meeting. In time, and perhaps inevitably, the dance became formalized and ritualized by particular leaders. Whether spontaneous or formal, involuntary or voluntary, Shaker dancing served as a personal release for individual members. Restrained on every front by rigorous taboos against normal physical and social interaction with the opposite sex, as well as against amusement and playfulness, the natural human desires to play, love, and create could find release in the songs and dances of the worship service. The more specific purposes of dancing were to mortify and to shake off the lusts of the flesh and pride of the spirit.

An open and simple meetinghouse permitted ample space for group dancing. Although men and women danced simultaneously, members of one sex did not touch the other. Choral dancing prevailed—in circles, lines, and squares—but with each sex in separate formations. Simple, repetitive steps with rhythmic arm and hand motions produced a dancing beneficial to the participant, rather than movement specifically choreographed for the aesthetic satisfaction of viewers.[125]

A contemporary description of a Shaker worship service comes from Charles Nordhoff, a nineteenth-century traveler to communal societies. Having visited several of their settlements in the 1870s, Nordhoff provided a composite picture of a Shaker worship service on Sunday morning. According to his account, seats were arranged only along the walls of the meetinghouse. When the people had assembled for worship, they stood in ranks, the men facing the women, and the elders of each sex in the front of their respective formations. After a hymn and brief address by the eldress, the participants broke rank, with a separate square formed by some who began a hymn that engaged the rest and resulted in marching, perhaps with clapping. Nordhoff described variations that include reforming ranks, speaking by men and/or women, singing, and dancing, though the latter he labeled "being a kind of shuffle." Occasionally, one of the number came to the front, bowed to the elder and eldress, and then began to whirl—"a singular exercise" continued for a "considerable time." According to Nordhoff, the person who whirled may be "deeply moved" or "in some tribulation of soul." When the members of a group marched and danced, they kept their hands in front of their bodies in a kind of gathering-in motion; he called it "gathering a blessing." When any individual asked for prayer, that person reversed the motion as if to draw his or her hands toward the body. Nordhoff reported all the movements performed "with much precision and in exact order," with the music very quick and rhythmic. Although there was no instrumental music, he found that singers kept time "admirably."[126]

Some visitors to the Shaker services considered the dancers inspired, dramatic, and graceful, but others, such as Horace Greeley, thought the dancing was closer to the disordered movement of kangaroos or penguins. Popular opinion, as conveyed in the "Imbert Lithograph copied by Currier and others," deemed the movement ridiculous.[127] Most Americans, in fact, had no experience of dancing in worship. The "dancing exercise" or ecstatic outbursts documented at frontier revivals were anathema to traditional Protestants. Similarly, the dance in worship as practiced by African Americans and native Americans would have existed outside the sphere of acceptability for mainstream evangelicals. The uniqueness of Shaker dancing, coupled with the radical nature of Shaker religious beliefs, provided no means by which the evangelical denominations could accept and approve dancing.

The Oneida Community

Although evangelicals could perhaps look with tolerance on the Shaker doctrine of celibacy, they could by no means approve the reverse approach to sexuality established by John Humphrey Noyes and his followers. Twentieth-century readers may well associate the Oneida, New York, community with a product—Oneida silver plate. Noyes's nineteenth-century contemporaries, however, viewed his community primarily in terms of its system of "complex marriage," something interpreted by outsiders as adultery or free love.[128]

Noyes had been converted under Charles G. Finney in 1831, had studied at Andover Seminary and at Yale, and had been licensed to preach. Following a short period in the ministry, and after he had developed exceptional theological views, Noyes announced in 1834 that he was "radically perfect" and, thus, unable to sin. Yale revoked his license, but Noyes continued to spread his views. He believed in total freedom from sin and that the millennium had begun when Christ reportedly came in 70 A.D. He felt that communal living was the only logical arrangement for saints equally yoked in faith and love, and he was committed to the notion that his views had to be actualized before the Kingdom of Heaven could finally arrive in all its glory. Noyes organized his community in 1841; its life extended for thirty-two years.[129]

The Oneidans gained the most notoriety over the system instituted in 1845, wherein, theoretically, every woman was married to every man. Sexual intercourse was thus possible and practiced among all members of the community with any person of one's choice, although some limits were placed on the age of partners. To the believers, the system provided a solution to the larger culture's problems of adultery, prostitution, divorce, and the like.[130] Moreover, women gained freedom from unwanted pregnancy by the practice of male continence.

Although the community of Oneida was clearly male-dominated, women also achieved freedoms in dress and recreation. They wore the bloomer costume and rid themselves of corset, petticoat, crinoline, and bustle. Unrestricted movement permitted them to learn baseball in the 1850s and swimming in the next decade.[131] By midcentury, they also danced for recreation. Constance Noyes Robertson, in her story of the Oneida Community from 1851 to 1876, tells about the values placed on dancing:

> Dancing which at this period was sometimes frowned upon by the godly of the outside world was extremely popular in the Community. Beginning in 1855 . . . they made a point of teaching everyone, both old and young, and after that first lesson . . . they danced whenever they could. Everyone enjoyed it, from the babies and the children . . . watching in the gallery to all the grown-ups who took part. . . . it was urged that dancing be made an ordinance of worship and edification, not a "mere pleasure-seeking affair." Dancing was for the earnest and thoughtful as well as the young and giddy. All amusements were good "so long as the spirit of improvement has place."

The Oneida *Circular* for 8 November 1855 reported that the first dancing lesson occurred in a hall sufficiently large to accommodate thirty to forty couples at one time. "Floor-masters" who knew how to dance instructed the novices in steps, rhythms, bows, and curtsies. The *Circular* for 14 June 1860 reported that the young and talented dancers were warned against excess and against any behavior that would make it unpleasant for the older and less experienced dancers to enjoy themselves. By the same token, less accomplished dancers were urged to improve their skills. Oneidans valued amusements that provided the greatest participation for the greatest number in the community, thereby promoting "universal fellowship." From that perspective, they found dancing superior to ball playing and similar games.[132] Despite the urging by some to make dancing an "ordinance of worship," it retained a strictly recreational and social role in the community.

The Mormons

Originating with a revelation to Joseph Smith from the Angel Moroni in 1830, the Church of Jesus Christ of Latter-Day Saints officially organized on 6 April that year in Palmyra, New York. The intent was to restore the Church of Christ, based on new revelations, in those latter days. With the addition of converts and after migrations to Ohio, Missouri, and, finally, Illinois, the believers, under the guidance of their "Prophet," received a charter from the Illinois legislature in 1839 to build their own settlement, Nauvoo—"city of beauty and repose."[133]

In his analysis of Mormon recreation, Rex Skidmore describes a positive view of amusement and dancing among the early saints of Nauvoo. The city charter permitted settlers to license and regulate their own theatrical entertainments. In addition to a theater, the city also had a dance hall. Private dancing occurred as well in the home of Joseph Smith on Christmas and New Year's of 1843. Mormons were restricted from frequenting public halls in the gentile world, for fear they would mix with undesirable company. However, dancing in a wholesome environment, under proper supervision, was deemed normal and healthy recreation. Reportedly, several Nauvoo musicians even organized themselves into a "Quadrille band" for accompanying dances.[134]

In October 1844, following the death of the "Prophet," Joseph Smith, Brigham Young issued a warning to the people that it was not then a time to dance but rather an occasion to mourn and to pray. But if Young had any notions about the inadvisability of dancing per se, they apparently dissolved in the light of a "divine revelation" received 14 January 1847, when the Saints were wintering in Omaha on their way west. Skidmore reports that verse twenty-eight of the revelation enjoined the believers to praise the Lord in singing, music, and dancing. From then on, the people believed that they had received "divine" approval for wholesome recreation. Not surprisingly, activities such as music, recitations, and dancing proved popular evening entertainment on the migration across the plains. In fact, Mormon leaders considered such amusement a necessary step in building and maintaining "morale" if the people were to endure the hardships of travel as well as the loss of their original "prophet" and the persecution that drove them from Nauvoo.[135]

The first band of Mormons reached Salt Lake City in April 1847. From the time of their permanent settlement, dancing played a vital role in their lives. By 1850, the Bath House, the first facility for amusement, had been erected and was used primarily for dancing. By 1853, the Social Hall was built and remained a recreational building for several decades. Skidmore posits that it was the first such facility erected by a church in this country. The degree of popularity of dancing is evidenced by the fact that dancing schools multiplied within the community shortly thereafter. Several buildings served as schools by day and dancing academies by evening. By the winter of 1854–55, dancing was being taught in practically all nineteen school buildings in the territory. Karl Wesson, in his study of a century of Mormon dance, reports that between 1850 and 1890 the people considered dancing a necessary part of all celebrations. According to Skidmore, group figure dances were the norm; the church did not approve of couple dances such as the waltz and polka.[136]

Despite the opposition to dancing in the "sectarian world," the Mormons pursued their own course of planning and providing recreation for their people. Early warnings by leaders about avoiding "bad" company and having dances in a wholesome environment indicate that some in the church were concerned about possible incipient evils. Despite such concerns, Brigham Young maintained a positive view of dance, although he cautioned participants about purity of motive: if they could not serve God with a "pure heart" when dancing, they should not dance.[137]

In general, evidence suggests that the Mormons in Salt Lake City maintained a moderate stance regarding the permissibility of dancing. Aware of possible evils, they did not abolish the activity but chose to regulate it. By this action they differed dramatically from the evangelical dance opponents who argued that a policy of moderation in dancing was just as dangerous as a policy of moderate drinking. But, regardless of how well conducted their dances were, the Mormons, like the Shakers and Oneidans, proved so radical in theology that they could not have served as advocates for dance in a manner acceptable to mainstream denominations.

Notes

1. William G. McLoughlin, *The Meaning of Henry Ward Beecher* (New York: Knopf, 1970), 20; Henry Ward Beecher, *Lectures to Young Men on Various Important Subjects* (Cincinnati: Wm. H. Moore, and Salem: John P. Jewett, 1846), 248. It would be impossible to ascertain the precise number of books like Beecher's that, in whole or in part, opposed amusements and dancing. However, a comprehensive search has revealed fifteen extant publications between 1840 and 1849 and an additional twenty-four books in the following decade.

2. Charles C. Cole, *The Social Ideas of the Northern Evangelists 1826–1860* (New York: Columbia University Press, 1954), 13, 16.

3. Sydney E. Ahlstrom, *A Religious History of the American People* (New York: Image Books, 1975), vol. 2, 208–9, and vol. 1, 627–28. From approximately 143,000 immigrants in the 1820s, the totals per decade increased to over 2.5 million by the 1850s.

4. E. S. Gaustad, *The Rise of Adventism* (New York: Harper and Row, 1974), xiii.

5. Samuel Eliot Morison and Henry Steel Commager, *The Growth of the American Republic* (New York: Oxford University Press, 1952), vol. 1, 502; Russel Nye, *The Cultural Life of the New Nation* (New York: Harper, 1960), 124.

6. Athletic contests, with the exception of boxing, racing, walking, and spontaneous as well as sporadic baseball games, did not exist. The rise of club, town, and collegiate teams in organized competition occurred after the Civil War. Although larger towns and cities provided more opportunity for access to amusements, travelling theater companies and showboats took some kinds of performances to smaller towns and rural areas after 1830 (Nye, *Cultural Life*, 194–95).

7. Ivor Guest, *Fanny Elssler* (Middletown, Conn.: Wesleyan University Press, 1970), 128.

8. Ibid., 185, 129–33, 136–37, 146.

9. Russel Nye, *The Unembarrassed Muse: The Popular Arts in America* (New York: Dial, 1970), 166; Robert C. Toll, *Blacking Up: The Minstrel Show in Nineteenth-Century America* (New York: Oxford University Press, 1974), 4.

10. See, for example, Jennifer P. Winstead, "Tripping on the Light Fantastic Toe: Popular Dance of Early Portland, Oregon, 1800–1864," in *American Popular Entertainment*, ed. Myron Matlaw (Westport, Conn.: Greenwood, 1977): 229–40; and Debra Hickenlooper Sowell, "Theatrical Dancing in the Territory of Utah, 1848–1868," *Dance Chronicle* 1, no. 2 (1977–78): 96–126.

11. See, for example, Charles Durang, *Durang's Terpsichore: Or, Ball Room Guide* (Philadelphia: N.p., 1848). Elias Howe, *Howe's drawing-room dances* (Boston: Ditson, 1850), and Henri Cellarius, *The Drawing Room Dances* (New York: Dinsmore, 1858), both instruct the reader in the intricacies and music of the polka, waltz, mazurka, and quadrille, with additional commentary on fancy dances, cotillions,

and contra dances. However, neither author emphasizes the extended apology for dancing with instructions on etiquette that Durang does. Durang also distinguishes between private or ballroom dancing and theater dancing, which permitted "scientific steps and elevated movements" (29). His *Terpsichore* first appeared in Philadelphia in 1847. Two subsequent editions were published in 1848 and 1856. The author of at least four other books on dancing, Charles Durang (1796–1870) was the son of John Durang, America's first native male dancer to gain acclaim for his work on the stage.

12. Durang, *Terpsichore*, 8, 5.

13. Ibid., 24–25.

14. Ibid., 25, 26, 30, 178, 161–62, 180.

15. Ahlstrom, *Religious History*, vol. 1, 568–69.

16. Gustavus L. Foster, *Fashionable Amusements: A Sermon Preached in the First Congregational Church of Jackson, Michigan* . . . (Detroit: Garrett and Geiger, 1848), 22.

17. Ibid., 5, 9–13.

18. Beecher, *Lectures*, 224; N. L. Rice, *A Discourse on Dancing Delivered in the Central Presbyterian Church, Cincinnati* (Cincinnati: Holland and Hitchler, 1847), 5.

19. William S. Potts, *A Sermon on Certain Popular Amusements of the Day* (St. Louis: Keith and Woods, 1848), 1, 6.

20. William Meade, *Baptismal Vows and Worldly Amusements* (New York: Protestant Episcopal Society for the Promotion of Evangelical Knowledge, 1855), 3, 12.

21. Franklin Wilson, *Popular Amusements: Or, How Far May a Christian Indulge in Popular Amusements?* (Charleston, S.C.: Southern Baptist Publication Society, 1856), 6–7.

22. Ibid., 10–13, 15–16.

23. T. L. Cuyler, "Sermon On Christian Recreation and Unchristian Amusement," *The Pulpit and Rostrum: Sermons, Orations, Popular Lectures, Etc.*, no. 1 (New York: E. D. Barber, 1858), 11–13.

24. Frederic W. Sawyer, *A Plea for Amusements* (New York: D. Appleton, and Philadelphia: George S. Appleton, 1847), 29.

25. Ibid., 211–12, 215.

26. Edward Everett Hale, *Public Amusements for Poor and Rich: A Discourse Delivered Before the Church of the Unity, Worcester* . . . (Boston: Phillips, Sampson, 1857), 6–8.

27. Ibid., 15.

28. Sawyer, *Plea*, 206, 199–200.

29. Potts, *Popular Amusements*, 9–12; Asa D. Smith, *Dancing as an Amusement for Christians: A Sermon, Delivered in the Brainerd Presbyterian Church, New York* . . . (New York: Leavitt, Trow, 1847), 5.

30. John McDonald, *May I Go to the Ball?* (Philadelphia: Presbyterian Board of Publications, n.d.), 19, 24; Abbé Hulot, *Balls and Dancing Parties Condemned by the Scriptures* (Boston: Patrick Donahoe, 1857), 9.

31. B. M. Palmer, *Social Dancing Inconsistent with a Christian Profession and Baptismal Vows: A Sermon, Preached in the Presbyterian Church, Columbia, S.C. . . .* (Columbia, S.C.: Office of the South Carolinian, 1849), 11–12.

32. J. Townley Crane, *An Essay on Dancing* (Cincinnati: Swormstedt and Poe, 1854), 9, preface.

33. Moses M. Henkle, *Primary Platform of Methodism or, Exposition of the General Rules* (Louisville: Southern Methodist Book Concern, 1851), 252–53, 249–50.

34. *Southey's Dream, or the Three Visible Kingdoms,* By A Layman Of Maryland [1851], 14.

35. John F. Mesick, *A Discourse on the Evils of Dancing; Delivered . . . Before the Congregation of The German Reformed Salem Church of Harrisburg* (Harrisburg: Theo. Fenn, 1846), 8.

36. F. Wilson, *Popular Amusements,* 20.

37. Rice, *Discourse,* 13; Palmer, *Social Dancing,* 21–22.

38. Palmer, *Social Dancing,* 21, 15.

39. Edward D. Neill, *Michal, or Fashionable Dancing, an Undignified Amusement for a Christian . . .* (St. Paul, Minn.: Combs, 1859), 13–14. Considering that Neill came from the traditional mold of college graduate and conservative Andover Seminary training, his anxiety over dancing must have been extreme to prefer the ecstatic release of religious enthusiasm so horrifying to mainline Presbyterians and Congregationalists.

40. Potts, *Popular Amusements,* 10, 14; Crane, *Essay,* 66–67.

41. W. C. Buck, *May Christians Dance, Attend Theatres, Circuses, or Play Games, Etc.?* (Nashville, Tenn.: South Western Publishing House, 1857), 19.

42. *Southey's Dream,* 14–15; Crane, *Essay,* 104; H. W. Beecher, *Lectures,* 248. Crane's graphic reference to dancing and prostitution is the only such reference from the antidance literature of the middle decades. Crane's assertion seems to have been based on earlier historical discussion and on reference to contemporary Paris. He makes no specific reference to dance and prostitution in America. Beecher's charge undoubtedly aimed at Fanny Elssler, but the aspersion casting her as a "strumpet" derives from the long-held notion, carried from Europe, that stage dancers were immoral people. Just how prevalent stage dancing was in the middle decades is not known. Minstrelsy was on the rise, as was vaudeville or variety theater, but, as mentioned earlier, no ballet companies existed in this country. By contrast, more specific data exist about the extent of prostitution. For example, female moral reform societies had organized by the 1830s, and a comprehensive survey of two thousand prostitutes in New York City had been undertaken by William Sanger in 1858. See David Pivar, *Purity Crusade: Sexual Morality and Social Control, 1868–1900* (Westport, Conn.: Greenwood Press, 1973), 1–43.

43. Potts, *Popular Amusements,* 11; F. Wilson, *Popular Amusements,* 20; Buck, *May Christians Dance?* 18.

44. H. W. Beecher, *Lectures,* 249, 241–42.

45. Jesse Winecoff, *A Discourse on Modern Dancing* (Gettysburg, Pa.: H. G. Neinstedt, 1850), 13.

46. Mrs. F. E. Garnett, *Dancing: Religion and Revelry* (Louisville: Kentucky Baptist Book Concern, 1858), 94.

47. C. C. Bitting, *Modern Dancing* (Richmond: Printed by H. K. Ellyson, 1858), 14.

48. *Dancing: Its Influence on the Character and Example of the Christian* (Hartford, Conn.: Edwin Hunt, 1847), 21; Potts, *Popular Amusements,* 10–11.

49. Barbara Meil Hobson, *Uneasy Virtue: The Politics of Prostitution and the American Reform Tradition* (New York: Basic Books, 1987), 13–14.

50. A *Directory to the Seraglios in . . . All Principal Cities in the Union* was published in 1859. See David Pivar's analysis, *Purity Crusade,* 31–32, 47.

51. Jesse Guernsey, *A Discourse on the Evils of the Dance Delivered in the First Cong. Church, Derby, Conn.* (Birmingham: T. M. Newson, 1850), 8; Potts, *Popular Amusements,* 14.

52. Rice, *Discourse,* 12; Mesick, *Discourse,* 8; Palmer, *Social Dancing,* 11.

53. John Rogers, *A Discourse on Dancing; Delivered in the Christian Meeting-House, in Carlisle, Ky.,* 4th ed. (Cincinnati: J. A. James, n.d.), 17. Rogers probably refers to Charles Rollin (1661–1741), the French writer and historian. Rogers probably quoted from Rollin's history of ancient peoples, including the Greeks, a book that came out in many editions.

54. Samuel R. Wilson, *Dancing: A Discourse on the Fashionable Amusement of Dancing, Delivered in the First Presbyterian Church, Cincinnati* (Cincinnati: Ben Franklin Steam Printing Establishment, 1854), 17.

55. Buck, *May Christians Dance?* 20.

56. Ahlstrom, *Religious History,* vol. 1, 517–18, and vol. 2, 347. In 1826 an American Society for the Promotion of Temperance originated in Boston. One in Connecticut followed shortly thereafter.

57. Buck, *May Christians Dance?* 19; Mesick, *Discourse,* 9; Henkle, *Primary Platform,* 251–52; F. Wilson, *Popular Amusements,* 20–21.

58. Guernsey, *Discourse,* 9–11.

59. Foster, *Fashionable Amusements,* 18.

60. Joseph F. Tuttle, *Shall I Dance?* (Philadelphia: Presbyterian Publication Committee, n.d. [between 1856 and 1862]), 18–19; S. R. Wilson, *Dancing,* 17.

61. Henkle, *Primary Platform,* 258–59.

62. T. A. Morris, *Miscellany: Consisting of Essays, Biographical Sketches, and Notes of Travel* (Cincinnati: L. Swormstedt and A. Poe, 1854), 142–43.

63. Meade, *Baptismal Vows,* 14, 30–37.

64. Charles Porterfield Krauth, *Popular Amusements: A Discourse Delivered in*

the Evangelical Lutheran Church, Winchester, VA . . . (Winchester, Va.: Republican Office, 1851), 7, 13.

65. Potts, *Popular Amusements,* 10; Smith, *Dancing as an Amusement,* 6–7.

66. Buck, *May Christians Dance?* 16–17.

67. Crane, *Essay,* 66. The statistic seems the same for Buck and Crane, though Crane says one-third of births were of uncertain parentage, and Buck claims fewer than one-third were legitimate.

68. Crane, *Essay,* 112; Rice, *Discourse,* 13.

69. Neill, *Michal,* 13; *Dancing: Its Influence,* 7; McDonald, *May I Go to the Ball?* 23; Tuttle, *Shall I Dance?* 19; Morris, *Miscellany,* 141.

70. Meade, *Baptismal Vows,* 37; Garnett, *Dancing,* 91.

71. Garnett, *Dancing,* 55, 82; Meade, *Baptismal Vows,* 38; Bitting, *Modern Dancing,* 10; Potts, *Popular Amusements,* 13; Winecoff, *Discourse,* 12.

72. Krauth, *Popular Amusements,* 11–12; Rice, *Discourse,* 7.

73. Mesick, *Discourse,* 6; Crane, *Essay,* 115–18; Palmer, *Social Dancing,* 10; F. Wilson, *Popular Amusements,* 18.

74. James Leonard Corning, *The Christian Law of Amusement* (Buffalo: Phinney, 1859), 68–69.

75. P[hilip] Anderson, alias "Honestus," *An Answer to Certain Queries on the Subject of Dancing* (Richmond: C. H. Wynne, 1857), 91; Morris, *Miscellany,* 141.

76. Garnett, *Dancing,* 140; Neill, *Michal,* 7–8, 11–12; Henkle, *Primary Platform,* 243–44; Mesick, *Discourse,* 9; *Dancing: Its Influence,* 8. Mrs. Garnett's claim that both monkeys and dogs can dance recalls the sixteenth-century references by Calvin and Daneau, which compared dancing to the antics of goats and monkeys. See chapter 2, above, for a discussion of their views.

77. Guernsey, *Discourse,* 6.

78. Henkle, *Primary Platform,* 244–45.

79. Hulot, *Balls and Dancing Parties,* 12. See chapter 1, above, for discussion of Petrarch's views.

80. Crane, *Essay,* 76–77.

81. Buck, *May Christians Dance?* 5; Bitting, *Modern Dancing,* 11; Alfred Bryant, *Ought Christians to Dance?* (Chicago: S. C. Griggs, 1855), 27; Rice, *Discourse,* 23; Anderson, *Answer to Certain Queries,* 54. Anderson's quote omits the commonly used adjective "sad" before "preparation."

82. S. R. Wilson, *Dancing,* 29–30. The treatise by Wilson, *A Time to Dance,* no. 172 (Philadelphia: Presbyterian Board of Publication, n.d.), must not be confused with the publication under the same title and number that was issued from the press of the American Tract Society, probably about 1833. Wilson's treatise, with his name on the title page, was a reprint of his 1854 sermon published under the title *Dancing: A Discourse.* In June 1985 the cataloguer at the Presbyterian Historical Society in Philadelphia expressed the belief that *A Time to Dance* was probably published in 1855 or, at least by May 1856.

83. Tuttle, *Shall I Dance?* 17; Bitting, *Modern Dancing,* 23, 13.

84. Albert Barnes, "On Dancing," *American National Preacher* 18, no. 1 (1844): 14, 16–17; E.Y., *Dancing, as a Social Amusement by Professed Christians, or Their Children,* no. 491 (New York: American Tract Society, [1847?]), last page.

85. *Dancing: Its Influence,* 6–7; Mesick, *Discourse,* 4–5.

86. Cuyler, "Sermon on Christian Recreation," 5; Rice, *Discourse,* 4.

87. McDonald, *May I Go to the Ball?* 9.

88. John T. Brooke, *A Little Thing Great; Or, The Dance and the Dancing School. Tested, in a Few Plain Sermons . . .* (New York: Robert Carter and Brothers, 1859), 72.

89. Smith, *Dancing as an Amusement,* 11, 16.

90. F. Wilson, *Popular Amusements,* 57–63; Morris, *Miscellany,* 143.

91. Bitting, *Modern Dancing,* 23; Foster, *Fashionable Amusements,* 14; Morris, *Miscellany,* 140; Tuttle, *Shall I Dance?* 21; F. Wilson, *Popular Amusements,* 25.

92. [Oliver Johnson], *Amusements Their Uses and Abuses* (New York: By the author, 1856), 13–14.

93. William Ellery Channing, "Address on Temperance," *The Works of William E. Channing, D.D.* (Boston: American Unitarian Association, 1893), 109–10.

94. Corning, *Christian Law,* 101, 36–37. It was easy to target behaviors such as going to the theater, dancing, or playing cards, since these actions were all readily observable. It was somewhat more difficult to identify envy, lust, gluttony, anger, sloth, jealousy, and pride in others. Popularly known since the Middle Ages as the seven deadly sins, they do not appear in the catalog of evils recited by American dance opponents.

95. Clericus [George H. Thacher], *A Letter to the Synod of Albany, on the Subject of Dancing . . .* (Albany: Joel Munsell, 1847), 4, 15; idem, *Progressive Democracy in Religion* (Schenectady: Riggs, 1848), 6–7.

96. Thacher, *Progressive Democracy,* 4–5.

97. Johnson, *Amusements,* 3 (unnumbered).

98. *Etiquette at Washington, Together with the Customs adopted by Polite Society in the Other Cities of the United States,* 2d ed., rev. and enl. (Baltimore: J. Murphy, 1850); *Southey's Dream,* 10.

99. *Etiquette at Washington,* 52, 91.

100. [Charles William Day], *Etiquette: Or, A Guide to the Usages of Society with a Glance at Bad Habits* (New York: Wilson, 1843), 4; Arthur M. Schlesinger, *Learning How to Behave* (New York: Macmillan, 1946), 18.

101. *Etiquette at Washington,* 55, 58; [Day], *Etiquette,* 28.

102. *The American Letter-Writer, and Mirror of Polite Behaviour* (Philadelphia: Fisher, 1851), 224; [Day], *Etiquette,* 5; *True Politeness: A Hand-book of Etiquette for Ladies,* By an American Lady (New York: Leavitt and Allen, [1847]), 38, 35; *Etiquette at Washington,* 60; *How to Behave: A Pocket Manual of Republican Etiquette and Guide to Correct Personal Habits . . .* (New York: Samuel R. Wells, 1872 [c. 1856]), 94.

103. *Etiquette at Washington,* 59.

104. [Day], *Etiquette,* 29.

105. Stephen Kern, *Anatomy and Destiny: A Cultural History of the Human Body* (New York: Bobbs-Merrill, 1975), 110–11.

106. Durang, *Terpsichore,* 169; *How to Behave,* 94; *Etiquette at Washington,* 69.

107. *True Politeness,* 40–41.

108. Eliza Leslie, *The Ladies Guide to True Politeness and Perfect Manners; Or, Miss Leslie's Behaviour Book* (Philadelphia: T. B. Peterson, 1864), 319–20, 321–22. The several editions of *Miss Leslie's Behavior Book* testify to the fact that the book was widely read. After a first edition in 1853, five more appeared by 1864.

109. *The Habits of Good Society: A Handbook for Ladies and Gentlemen . . . [from the Last London Edition]* (New York: Rudd and Carleton, 1860), 233. This book appeared anonymously in London in 1859. Despite the claim about Catholic opposition on the continent, I have not discovered Catholic antidance publications in America for this time period.

110. *Ladies' Vase; or, Polite Manual for Young Ladies . . . ,* By a American Lady (Lowell, Mass.: N. L. Drayton, 1843), 145, 190.

111. [Daniel Clarke Eddy], *The Young Woman's Friend; or, The Duties, Trials, Loves and Hopes of Woman* (Boston: Wentworth, 1857), 23, 26–27. True to his vocation as a Baptist minister, Eddy instructed the young lady about the ideal for Christian character; his book came out in five editions by 1866.

112. *The Young Ladies Guide to Gentility and Useful Knowledge* (Philadelphia: Evans, 1857), 23–24.

113. Catharine E. Beecher, *Letters to the People on Health and Happiness* (New York: Harper, 1855), 186, 188; Regina M. Morantz, "Making Women Modern: Middle-Class Women and Health Reform in Nineteenth-Century America," in *Women and Health in America,* ed. Judith W. Leavitt (Madison, Wis.: University of Wisconsin Press, 1984), 347. For an analysis of Beecher's thought with respect to women's roles, see Susan Hill Lindley, "Woman's Profession in the Life and Thought of Catharine Beecher" (Ph.D. diss., Duke University, 1974).

114. C. Beecher, *Letters,* 122. See, for example, Jane Stephens, "Breezes of Discontent: A Historical Perspective of Anxiety-Based Illnesses among Women," *Journal of American Culture* 8, no. 4 (Winter 1985): 3–9; Ann Douglas Wood, "'The Fashionable Diseases': Women's Complaints and Their Treatment in Nineteenth Century America," in *Women and Health in America,* ed. Leavitt, 222–38.

115. C. Beecher, *Letters,* 107.

116. Wood, "'Fashionable Diseases,'" 225. Emma Willard, founder of Troy Female Seminary, and Mary Lyon, founder of Mount Holyoke Seminary, both advocated regular exercise for women. Early doctors and physical training directors who devised rest and exercise programs for women will be discussed in chapter 8. Catharine Beecher urged that women who did not get sufficient exercise through housework should engage in calisthenics and have access to "gymnastic assembly rooms" (*Let-*

ters, 187). Her most comprehensive publication on the subject appeared in 1856 under the title *Physiology and Calisthenics for Schools and Families* (New York: Harper, 1859); three later editions came out in the 1860s. Chapter 1, "Physical Education," includes exercises for feet and legs. She recommends six pliés in each of the five ballet positions, though her command is "Sink." She does not mention the words "ballet" or "dance." Although Beecher advocated a relatively wholesome program of health reform for women, she did not recommend abandoning corsets nor urge wearing the new pant suit developed by Amelia Bloomer (see note 122, below).

117. *Ladies' Vase,* 83; Emily Thornwell, *The Lady's Guide to Perfect Gentility, in Manners, Dress, and Conversation, in the Family, in Company . . . and in Gentlemen's Society* (New York: Derby and Jackson, 1859), 133.

118. *True Politeness,* 35; *Etiquette At Washington,* 66; *How to Behave,* 92.

119. Florence Hartley, *The Ladies' Book of Etiquette and Manual of Politeness . . .* (Boston: G. W. Cottrell, 1860), 266–67, 270, 281.

120. C. Beecher, *Letters,* 7, 10–11, 85. Beecher had elaborated on this generalization in her 1846 treatise *The Evils Suffered by American Women and American Children: The Causes and the Remedy* (New York: Harper, 1846). In her *Letters,* Beecher declared that the plan destroying female health encompassed mental as well as physical harm, and it applied particularly to middle-class single women of more than average talents. Knowing that good health required sufficient exercise to the whole person, Beecher observed that the "great majority of American women have their brain and nervous system exhausted by too much care and too much mental excitement in their daily duties," while another class suffered from too much time with too little to satisfy their intellectual and creative talents. For Beecher, the latter derived from "want of some worthy object in life, or from excesses in seeking amusements" (108). Her writing indicates that she was no ardent devotee of dancing, yet she understood the value of amusements in moderation. She observed that the fear of excess in amusements led many in her day to "shun altogether what requires only to be taken in moderation. From a want of just views on this subject there has been too often a marked line of separation between those who seek amusements and those who avoid them" (85).

121. A variant ideal in the nineteenth-century literature, according to Regina Morantz, describes the female as "weak, sickly, dependant, and ornamental" (348). However, that ideal actually combines elements of the two that emerge from the dance opponents and the etiquette authorities.

122. In 1849 Amelia Bloomer introduced the first bifurcated garment for women, a pant worn under a skirt, designed to permit greater freedom of movement. The garment did not enjoy immediate popularity. For example, in July 1851, a "Bloomer Ball" was held in Lowell, Massachusetts, evidently the first practical effort in the town to introduce the new garment; as Charles Cowley's *History of Lowell* reports, "the ball was a success, but the costume was not a success" (2d rev. ed. [Lowell, Mass.: Sargeant and J. Merrill and Son, 1868], 141).

123. Winthrop Hudson, "A Time of Religious Ferment," in *The Rise of Adventism*, ed. E. S. Gaustad (New York: Harper & Row, 1974), 9.

124. Louis J. Kern, *An Ordered Love: Sex Roles and Sexuality in Victorian Utopias* (Chapel Hill: University of North Carolina Press, 1981), 100; Daniel MacHir Hutton, *Old Shakertown and the Shakers* (Harrodsburg, Ky.: Harrodsburg Herald Press, [1936?]; 12th ed. enl. and rev. by Jane Bird Hutton, 1981), 28.

125. Henri Desroche, *The American Shakers from Neo-Christianity to Pre-Socialism* (Amherst: University of Massachusetts Press, 1971), 117–20; Edward Deming Andrews, *The Gift to Be Simple* (New York: Dover Publications, 1962), 144–46. Andrews's book contains the most complete analysis of extant Shaker song and dance.

126. Charles Nordhoff, *The Communistic Societies of the United States* (1875; rpt., New York: Schocken Books, 1971), 143–44.

127. Andrews, *Gift*, 156; Edward Deming Andrews, *The People Called Shakers* (New York: Oxford University Press, 1953), 149.

128. According to Louis J. Kern, Noyes was arrested on charges of adultery in Putney, Vermont, in 1847 (*An Ordered Love*, 207).

129. Ibid., 213, 208, 246; Gaustad, ed., *Rise of Adventism*, 11.

130. L. Kern, *An Ordered Love*, 233.

131. Ibid., 274, 264.

132. Constance Noyes Robertson, ed., *Oneida Community: An Autobiography, 1851–1876* (Syracuse: Syracuse University Press, 1970), 188, 194–95, 141.

133. L. Kern, *An Ordered Love*, 143. Though a prospering place by the 1840s, neighboring critics apparently were outraged by the reported practice of polygamy. When Smith decided to run for president in 1844, the action drew opposition. In June of that year, both he and brother, Hyrum, were dragged from jail and murdered at nearby Carthage, Illinois, where they had been held on charges of polygamy. Following the violent death of the "Prophet," the community split into two groups. One went to Missouri for settlement. The members of the other group, under the leadership of Brigham Young, trekked across the Plains to their ultimate settlement in Salt Lake City.

134. Rex Skidmore, "Mormon Recreation Theory and Practice: A Study of Social Change" (Ph.D. diss., University of Pennsylvania, 1941), 15–18, 22–23.

135. Ibid., 28–31.

136. Ibid., 39, 44–45; Karl Wesson, "Dance in the Church of Jesus Christ of Latter Day Saints, 1830–1940" (M.A. thesis, Brigham Young University, 1975), 38, 41.

137. Skidmore, "Mormon Recreation Theory," 35–36, 45; Wesson, "Dance in the Church," 40–41.

7 Conservatives, Liberals, and the City: 1865–89

> If evil and good are mingled it is easier to denounce the
> mixture indiscriminately than to stop and separate the
> good from the evil, and then approve the one and
> condemn the other.
>
> Washington Gladden, 1866

> The whirlpool of the ballroom drags down the life, the
> beauty, and the moral worth of the city. In this whirlwind
> of imported silks goes out the life of many of our best
> families. Bodies and souls innumerable are annually
> consumed in this conflagration of ribbons.
>
> T. DeWitt Talmadge, 1872

After a wartime hiatus in published criticism, dance opponents from towns
and cities across the country resumed their production of sermons and books
against amusements in general and dance in particular.[1] The steady stream
of both printed opposition and etiquette books in the quarter century following the Civil War indicates that dancing remained enormously popular. No radically new kind of social dance was introduced, yet the dance con
troversy showed few signs of abating. Evangelicals held steadfast against the
evils of the waltz and other "round dances"; the majority disapproved of the
"square dances" as well. Dance opposition grew in a broader geographical
area, but published criticism of denominational opposition to dancing also
appeared.

Significantly, the adversaries of dance put forth no new substantive arguments. They firmly opposed dancing on the same grounds that had been
cited during the middle decades of the century, despite major changes in
population, immigration, Protestant denominations, and cultural values, as
the country shifted from an agrarian to an urban base. In addition, new
physical training authorities began asserting that women were not, by nature, frail and delicate creatures who might be harmed by dancing. Yet amidst
such turmoil, staunch adversaries stood firm against amusements. Thus, the

mainstream evangelicals of the middle decades became the conservative evangelicals of the postwar decades.

The Urban Context

Sydney Ahlstrom calls the rise of the city the "major social trend" of the post–Civil War era. There were great migrations to the cities from American farms and from across the Atlantic. Between 1881 and 1890, well over five million immigrants made the ocean voyage seeking a new start; they constituted the largest entry into this country for any decade during the nineteenth century. These immigrants represented a variety of countries and religious beliefs, the influx of which dramatically affected the growth and status of some denominations such as the Lutheran church and threatened the position of authority traditionally held by the older and larger Protestant denominations. The difficulty the latter groups faced was, in Ahlstrom's words, that "evangelicalism was no longer calling the tune—or more accurately, that fewer people were heeding the call."[2] Although major Protestant groups tripled their combined membership between 1860 and 1900, the Roman Catholic church, already the largest affiliation at midcentury, quadrupled its membership during the same period. Simultaneously, traditional evangelical denominations faced dissent from within. On one end of the spectrum, extreme liberals left the church while more moderate liberals assailed the inerrancy of the Bible and pushed the new social gospel. On the other end, conservatives who were troubled by the inroads of liberalism began to congregate, eventually to evolve into the fundamentalists of the twentieth century.[3] Faced with an array of religious beliefs and opinions among the people, many clergy in the cities began to accommodate their doctrines and delivery to a message that would bring in larger Sunday morning audiences.

Among those whom Ahlstrom calls the "Princes of the Pulpit," Henry Ward Beecher (1813–87) retained enormous popularity throughout his forty-year career at Plymouth Congregational Church in Brooklyn Heights, New York. Called to the church in 1847, he soon attracted up to 2,500 people weekly. After 1850, volumes of his collected sermons, prayers, and lectures appeared in print annually throughout the country. For example, his *Lectures to Young Men on Various Important Subjects,* which was issued first in 1846, reappeared throughout the century, though sometimes under different titles.[4]

T. DeWitt Talmadge (1832–1902), a clear rival to Beecher among New York clergymen, presided at the pulpit of Central Presbyterian Church in Brooklyn beginning in 1869. With a tabernacle that seated 5,000 people and as the author of sermons published in 3,500 papers, in this country and abroad, Talmadge can legitimately be called one of the most popular preachers of the period. "A master of sensational rhetoric" and a good storyteller, though he was sometimes "careless with facts,"[5] Talmadge represented the new era of dance opposition that would culminate in the early twentieth century with the vernacular and sentimental rhetoric of the well-known preachers Billy Sunday and John Roach Straton. Talmadge stood hard and fast for the inerrancy of Scripture and against the evils of society, as the titles of his books demonstrate—*The Abominations of Modern Society* (1872) and *Social Dynamite; or, The Wickedness of Modern Society* (1889). Chapter titles of the latter publication highlight some of the perceived problems of the era: "Intemperance," "Divorce," "Profanity," "Drunkenness and the Social Evil," "Dancing," "Society Women," "Fashion's Follies," "Sins of the City," "Lies," and "Spoils."[6]

It is not clear whether sensational preaching and writing simply brought crowds, money, and personal fame or whether it brought genuine conversions to the gospel of Christ. William G. McLoughlin suggests that Beecher, Talmadge, and others of that ilk "thought it their duty to outshine the secular amusements which competed with their church services."[7] Whatever the motives of these preachers, the rise of the city and massive immigration meant that urban evangelism was the order of the day.

The acknowledged master among the evangelists was Dwight Lyman Moody (1837–99), a shoe salesman turned preacher. His revivals suited the era of P. T. Barnum and the titans of industry. Moody remained "the greatest figure in American Protestantism" from 1875 until his death. His popularity tells much about the mindset, taste, and educational level of middle-class and rural-born Americans, the audiences to whom conservative dance opponents spoke and wrote.[8]

With no formal college or theological training, Moody remained, in Richard Hofstadter's words, "immensely ignorant—even of grammar." He read only the Bible and considered it the answer for all questions and issues.[9] In an era when the critical intellectual questions facing the church revolved around the problem of how to reconcile Scripture and science to deal with the dilemmas of an urban-industrial society, Moody and the conservative dance opponents preached a simple and sentimental Christianity.

Dance Opponents React to the City

Reflecting the simplistic answers applied to complex problems that Moody's sermons propounded, the Presbyterian cleric William Carson (1846–1936) told the Lane Seminary Club of Cincinnati in 1889:

> We live too fast. The spirit of restlessness is in the air. Every book and page and paper bears the impress of an awful intensity. Life is cut short in the midst of its blooming years by wanton revels, excitement, hilarity and dissipation. What we need most is the serene and joyful spirit of our Saviour, the sweet cordial of hope eternal, that will soothe the feelings it inspires, that will cool the flame of an excited life, allay its all consuming thirst, and bring light and peace and rest and happiness and heaven.[10]

Giving a more specific comparison with previous practices, an anonymous treatise disseminated by the American Baptist Publication Society lamented: "We live in an age when nothing is considered settled. The opinions of those who have gone before us pass for little. The decisions of the past are challenged for re-investigation, and in some places this question of dancing is put forward to be considered." The author observes that he could recall the time when the question of Christians dancing was not even up for consideration. If anyone was caught dancing, the person would be regarded as sinning and would "be dealt with accordingly."[11]

Not surprisingly, dance opponents became concerned about the degree to which their particular denominational memberships were affected by the changing urban life and values. Although many wrote to Christians or church members in general, Hiram Mattison (1811–68) in 1867 appealed specifically to Methodists on the evils of cards, chess, billiards, bowling, dancing, dominoes, and the theater. He opened with the acknowledgment:

> It is commonly reported among us, and we partly believe it, that some of you Methodists who were once poor and unknown, but have grown rich and prominent in the world, have left the narrow way in which you walked twenty or thirty years ago, have ceased to attend class-meetings, seldom pray in your families or in prayer-meetings, as you once did, and are now indulging in many of the fashionable amusements of the day, such as playing chess, dominoes, billiards, and cards, dancing and attending theatres, or allowing your children to indulge in them. Others, it is said, who do not practice those things themselves, apologize for them; and some not only indulge in them, but even have bowling alleys and billiard tables in or near their dwellings, and have dancing in their parlors whenever their children or company desire it.[12]

Mattison's charge that newly rich Methodists had forsaken their earlier, more stringent life styles holds the ring of truth when one recalls that the postwar years saw the general rise of the nouveau riche. Large, ornate houses and other displays of wealth made it altogether possible that many families indeed had their own recreational equipment and facilities. The ostentation became a hallmark of those who prospered from the laissez-faire capitalist system.[13]

Preaching in Milford, Michigan, in 1884, the Reverend Charles S. East-man (1841–1931) told Methodist church-goers that the "spirit of extravagant display. . . has been stimulated and developed more through the influence of the Dance than any other single factor." In support of his claim, he told parishioners that ladies' ball gowns cost from $3,000 to $8,000. Further, "It is reported that two recent balls in the city of New York cost in toilets and appointments over $800,000, a sum larger than the annual income of the strongest missionary society in America." Though his evidence may or may not have been accurate, Eastman spoke as no lone Methodist critic.[14]

Concern about the spread of amusements and dancing motivated other Methodist clergy north and south to speak out against perceived evils. Jonathan Townley Crane (1819–80) had written an essay specifically against dancing in 1849. In 1869 his book *Popular Amusements* came out. Danc-ing was criticized there, along with horse racing, theater, baseball, cards, chess, billiards, social gatherings, and novel reading. In his introduction to the book, Bishop E. S. Janes observed: "Recently the advocates of popular amusements have been both bold and insidious. They have used the pul-pit, the press, and so-called 'Christian Associations' to propagate their views."[15] Similarly, the Reverend John G. Jones (1804–88) in 1867 pub-lished *An Appeal to All Christians Especially the Members of the Methodist Episcopal Church against the Practice of Social Dancing*. Though the substance of his book had been presented in a series of articles in 1852, Jones reports that he revised and enlarged the earlier pieces for his book. He believed there was a special need for a "calm and scriptural discussion" of the subject due to the "extraordinary efforts" being made to entice young church members into the ballroom. Active in the Mississippi district of the Methodist church all his life, Jones held views that reflect the popularity of amusements in the southern states.[16]

An equally strong concern about changing values emanated from Chris-topher Rhinelander Robert (1802–78), a Presbyterian businessman and philanthropist in the North. He wrote, "I have been a church member nearly half a century, and I have never known the tone of spirituality so low as it has been for ten years, or over." In earlier decades, he continued, Presbyte-rians and members of "kindred denominations" were not seen at the opera, theater, balls, or dancing parties. Then, at almost the same time that pro-fessional singers were introduced into the church services, Christians began to attend balls. Lamentably, by the seventies, professing Christians even hosted dancing parties, including "not infrequently," some of the "most objectionable" dances.[17]

The Conservative View of Amusements, Dance, and Health

Those conservative evangelicals of the postwar decades who wrote against dancing, almost without exception, argued against the practice as carried out in their day. They objected not to dance or dancing in the abstract, but to the perceived evil associations of the balls and dancing parties of "modern society." Heightening the denigrating impact, the Reverend Hiram Collins Haydn (1831–1913), a Presbyterian clergyman, denounced the dance of "modern civilized society." His essay deserves attention because its publication by the American Tract Society in 1880 represented the consensus of conservative opinions. Haydn's treatise also won the title of "Prize Essay" on the responsibilities of Christians with respect to amusements, in a contest sponsored by the trustees of Dartmouth College in 1878. The contest was held every two years to ascertain the best writing estimated to counteract worldly influences. Haydn's measured, philosophical approach to the evils of dancing contrasts with the blatant and more sensational denunciations of Talmadge, who railed against the "abominations" of society. In Haydn's words: "The question is not whether, in any conceivable circumstances, dancing may be justified. Such a proposition calls for no serious discussion. To take certain measured steps to music, in itself considered, may be a harmless thing. . . . The good or evil of it must therefore be a thing of times, associations, methods, and degree—which condition the dance as we know it."[18]

What Haydn and the other adversaries objected to specifically were the evils of the "round dances." In the postwar years, the term was applied to the waltz, polka, shottische, and other dances that used the closed dance position and required dancers to progress around the room as individual couples. In essence, the round dances were deemed evil because of the face-to-face position of partners. Typically, opponents such as Haydn also objected to the square dances on the grounds that they led to the round dances. However, the Reverend William Cleaver Wilkinson (1833–1920), a Baptist opponent, in an 1869 essay reprinted numerous times and widely quoted into the twentieth century, criticized all dance as a "social institution." His concern lay with the way respectable people and "no inconsiderable proportion of accepted Christians" practiced dancing.[19] For some conservative or orthodox clerics, such perceptions meant that Christians had no choice but to maintain a clear posture separate from the people of the world.

Charles G. Finney

Lamenting the worldliness and the "fast age" of contemporary society, the famous revivalist and president of Oberlin College, Charles Grandison Finney (1792–1875), again entered the fray concerning amusements. Finney and the Reverend C. F. W. Walther, a Lutheran leader and theologian, merit individual attention because they argue from a more theoretical basis than do many of the antidance authors of the period and also because they invoke an uncommon point of view in the post–Civil War decades. At a time when Beecher, Talmadge, and others attempted to gather audiences via popular appeal and sensational delivery, Finney and Walther stood hard and fast for a narrow biblical view of the Christian life. Recalling the pronouncements of George Whitefield and sixteenth-century Calvinists such as Christopher Fetherston, Finney declared, "A spiritual mind cannot seek enjoyment in worldly society."[20]

In his 1873 essay "Innocent Amusements," Finney did not merely make assertions about the best way to live the Christian life; he also laid out a morality argument that, in effect, concluded that virtually no amusements could be considered innocent. The line of reasoning led critics to attack Finney for promoting an ascetic life that permitted no rest, recreation, or amusements at all. Finney, in a note to the editor published at the end of his tract, points out that he supports all recreation and amusement engaged in for "health and vigor of body and mind with which to promote the cause of God." The key to Finney's reasoning lies in the motive of the individual participant. He argues that all human acts of an "intelligent" nature (presumably not reflexive in nature) are moral and must be, therefore, either right or wrong. The moral character of an act does not reside in the act itself but in the agent's motive. Further, no act of a moral agent can be considered innocent that is not in accord with the "law and gospel of God." The biblical criteria Finney puts forth are the "great commandments" to love the Lord with all one's heart and to love one's neighbor as oneself. In addition, he relies strongly on Paul's admonition: "Whether ye eat or drink, or whatsoever ye do, do all to the glory of God." Thus, even the biological necessities of eating and drinking can be considered sinful if engaged in for the sake of merely satisfying one's appetite. A moral agent, in Finney's view, eats and drinks with innocence only when doing so to build health and strength to serve God. Extending that reasoning to amusements, he argues, "Therefore, no amusement is innocent which is engaged in for the pleasure of the amusement, any more than it would be innocent to eat and drink for the pleasure of it." His ultimate conclusion follows: "Nothing is innocent unless it proceeds from supreme love to God and equal love to man, unless the supreme and ultimate motive be to please and honor God." Accordingly, only those amusements can be considered innocent that are engaged in for the sole purpose of serving and honoring God "more than anything else that we can engage in for the time being."[21]

Judging by his introduction to the manuscript on amusements, Finney apparently intended to clarify and set to rest some of the questions about the issue. That he failed in his intent is evident from the fact that the question of amusements continued to be raised for decades following the publication of his writing. Moreover, contemporary readers of his tract probably were as troubled as the modern reader in ferreting out clear guidelines for their own behavior. The fault lies primarily in two areas. First, Finney pronounces general statements almost with the force of law. Yet he makes no specific applications for the reader. He declares that none but "benevolent amusements" can be considered innocent but he makes no specific reference except to fishing and hunting—both activities not then considered in the forefront of the amusement question. Finney allows that fishing and hunting for amusement are not innocent, but the same activities for the sake of producing food for health with which the better to serve God would be innocent. For the average young man or woman who wished to dance or go to the theater, his reasoning left many gaps of omission. Second, Finney's reliance on the morality of motive as the critical criterion for determining the rightness or wrongness of an amusement assumed that humans can easily and clearly discern their motives for participating in sundry activities. He discusses nothing with respect to the very human activity of doubting one's own motivations.

C. F. W. Walther

Carl Ferdinand Wilhelm Walther (1811–87) was as firm as Finney in his views about the correct pathway for the Christian life. His book on dance and theatergoing, *Tanz und Theaterbesuch,* appeared two years before the end of his life, the result of a half century of preaching and theological study. Whereas Finney's views written in the 1870s may not have influenced vast numbers of readers, Walther's influence carried considerable weight among a substantial portion of America's Lutherans. Ahlstrom calls him "probably the most influential figure in nineteenth-century Lutheranism in America," and by 1870 the Lutheran church numbered 400,000 members, making it the fourth largest Protestant denomination in the country.[22]

Like Finney, Walther stresses that the true Christian is marked by a complete change in consciousness toward reality and self. Like the apostle Paul, he or she becomes dead to the world. However, Walther hastens to add what the apostle also points out, namely, that it is God who works the transformation in the Christian via the Word.[23] Walther expresses a serious concern for the fact that young people in his church desired to be more worldly. Rather than acquiescing, he urges the narrow path of abstinence from dancing and theater.

Walther, like antidance writers universally since the Reformation, relies on the authority of the Bible to undergird his assertions. He carefully points out that there is no mention of couple dancing in the Bible. In addition, Walther invokes the authority of "our beloved Luther." Some might argue that Luther approved of dancing, Walther says, because the reformer declared that it was no sin to dance at weddings if it was done decently; but Walther hastens to note that the dances of the nineteenth century were not those to which Luther referred. Further, he states that Luther did object to the turning couple dances of his day, which were imported from France to Germany.[24]

What reveals Finney and Walther as very conservative, compared with other dance opponents of their day, is their emphasis on the need for Christians to be "heavenly minded," that is, separate from the world in consciousness, inclinations, and behavior, as well as in their stress on biblical authority. Finney's and Walther's treatises could well have been written a half century or more earlier. Neither man admits of any moderation in the path of abstinence from amusements and the ways of the world. Neither speaks to the need for regular exercise or to women's health in particular. Their confidently expressed assertions give no guidance to a questioning mind that might wonder why carefully regulated dances had to be avoided. One suspects that, for Finney, Walther, and many others of the era, the unspoken horrors of possible sexual immorality lurked too deeply to be addressed.

Particular Evils and Dual Roles of Women

The specific evils that conservative evangelicals found in dancing related to its perceived immorality; in turn, these allegations derived from assumptions about the way women should behave. Although both points appeared central to the arguments of adversaries from 1840 to 1860, language and example become more explicit in the postwar years.

The most graphic description of the "indecent" position employed by some in the waltz comes from the pen of Jonathan Townley Crane: "It is a shameful, revolting spectacle to see a young girl whirling around in the arms of a man who perhaps an hour ago was an utter stranger to her, her head leaning upon his breast, and their whole persons in closest contact." Whether or not he had actually seen this pose goes unclarified. Obviously, the closed dance position proved "offensive" because women were to be pure and protected.[25]

The offense to delicacy and refinement, the language and qualities that were highly valued in the middle decades, gives way to "passion and nothing else" by 1869 in Wilkinson's book. In the *Dance of Death,* published in San Francisco in 1877, the journalist Ambrose Bierce (1842–1914?) charges that the "modern waltz is not merely 'suggestive' . . . but an open and shameless gratification of sexual desire and a cooler of burning lust." Further, he declares that "perfect dancers" find the waltz "an actual realization of a certain physical ecstasy which should at least be indulged in private, and, as some would go so far as to say, under the matrimonial restrictions." Later he flatly asserts: "The privileges of matrimony relieve the necessity for the dance." The remark—which may or may not have originated with Bierce— became sufficiently popular to find its way into the writing of twentieth-century dance opponents. Similarly, another of Bierce's pronouncements was seized upon by later detractors because of its vivid imagery and sensationalism. With no acknowledgment of authorship and no evidence to prove the truth of the claim, Bierce indicted the dance hall in a remark he quoted: "'The dancing hall is the nursery of the divorce Court, the training ship of prostitution, the graduating school of infamy.'" Bierce does not specify what he meant by the "dancing hall"—whether it was a public hall rented for a private party or a private hall or a commercial establishment open to anyone for the price of admission or a drink. However, Eastman and other sources specify a variety of places where dancing occurred,

> ranging from the bestial dance of the city dive to the wildering [*sic*] dance of the glittering palace of sin . . . to the barbaric magnificence of the dance of metropolitan millionaires, and even the quadrennial inaugural dance with which a great nation humiliates itself upon the enthronement of its Chief. For it is true that dances of high and low degree are distinguished from each other by no essential principle, but mainly by the rank and reputation of their participants.[26]

It is in the antidance treatises of the postwar years that authors first speak about alleged evils of dancing and balls in language that specifically mentions prostitution, brothels, and divorce. The Reverend J. R. Sikes (1832–95), pastor of the English Evangelical Lutheran Church in Ashland, Pennsylvania, preached in 1867 about the origins of dancing in Paris and the "wretched females" there, concluding: "This at least shows that brothels and ball rooms are akin to each other." However, he declined to describe further "facts" for fear of astonishing and shocking the virtuous females in his congregation. A few clerics alleged or implied that women as well as men drank at balls, became inflamed by passion and succumbed to ultimate "ruin."[27] Females who became prostitutes and/or pregnant were referred to as "fallen women" or "abandoned" girls. Most of the claims about such behavior continued to state generalizations without proof or with unidentified substantiating "evidence." A common claim that was widely quoted even into the twentieth century appeared first in Haydn's essay of 1880. He quotes an unnamed New York City police chief as declaring, "'Three-fourths of the abandoned girls in New York were ruined by dancing.'" In 1882 the Reverend Samuel Milton Vernon (1841–1920), a Methodist pastor in Indianapolis, used the same quote but cited its source as the *New York Journal of Education*, though with no date.[28]

The amassing of statistical evidence probably reflected the mounting concern among nineteenth-century reformers about how to deal with prostitution as a social evil. Far from new, the problem was exacerbated as America became more urbanized and the population exploded with increasing numbers of immigrants. Though subsequently refuted, the popular theory of the day, which dance opponents preached, held that seduction was the "primary cause of prostitution."[29] Starting from that assumption, one could then logically argue that dancing parties and balls, particularly public gatherings, provided opportunity for young women to be ensnared and started on the road to "ruin." Such thinking gained further credibility when bolstered by the commonly held assumption that sin is progressive. Conservative dance detractors from several denominations regularly advised their readers and listeners that Christians should avoid evil from the start. Just as one drink inevitably led to drunkenness, so the square dances led to round dances, the parlor dances to balls. Though perhaps harmless in themselves, square dances and parlor dances shouldn't be indulged in because the lesser evil inevitably led to the greater evil. A longer descent into sin began with a "social party" and moved gradually downward through "picnic croquet and dance" to ultimate "ruin."[30]

In addition to abstinence urged by male clerics, the other solution to the problem of wicked dancing lay in urging pure and pious women to assume responsibility for upholding the moral tone of society. Haydn declared unequivocally that it fell to Christian women to guard the moral ground: "if Christian mothers and daughters who do love the things that are pure, lovely, and of good report, will not, upon its obvious merits, arise and banish this style of dancing from good society, it will probably never be done."[31] Reinforcing earlier notions that women effect a civilizing influence on men, Sylvester F. Scovel (1835–1910), a Presbyterian minister and later the president of Wooster College, elaborated on these responsibilities when he decried dancing and French fashions, which he asserted made women no longer "'decorus, modest and womanly.'" He said, "Here, then, emerges the plain question: Will the women of free America hold, willingly or undesignedly, the place of a force for popular corruption? Will they constantly exhibit spectacles from which the good turn away grieved, especially when they find the wicked encouraged by them and hastening their own ruin? *Will* they betray their high mission, received from God, at the silly and profane behest of the most corrupt civilized nation on the globe?" Although Scovel enjoined young men to a life of purity and Christian self-denial, he, like other dance opponents of the era, placed the responsibility for morality on women. In his view, if women refused to dance, there would be no problem.[32]

When women did go to balls, where a spirit of pride, vanity, and personal display was fostered, they were viewed as perpetrators of evil. It was alleged that women squandered lavish sums of money on dresses and parties to keep up with others or to attract personal admiration. Such money, opponents declared, could be better used to help the poor. But casting women in the role of vain spendthrift actually carried two indictments. On the one hand, they spent too much money on clothes and personal appearance, thus succumbing to the sin of pride and becoming guilty of poor stewardship. On the other hand, women visually seduced men by their fashionable dress. Typically, dance opponents did not attempt to discuss degrees of intentionality on the part of women. In his book *The Upas Tree, or Dynamite in Dancing Exposed,* the Baptist evangelist William Evander Penn (1832–95) avers in his preface that he had preached this message for the past seven years, before "not less than one hundred thousand people." His indictment claims "it is simply a fact that many of the girls and women are dressed in such a way and manner as best and most successfully to excite the baser passions of men." Such had been the fashion for forty years. As a consequence: "This fruit alone has sent hundreds of thousands of men, women and girls to premature graves, dishonored graves, felons' cels [*sic*], and to an endless hell. That this semi-nude condition, in which many girls and women are seen in the dance, has been productive of a vast deal of sin and crime, no honest man certainly will deny."[33]

Opponents did not characterize the men allegedly seduced as either Christian gentlemen or men of suspect reputation. But concern about the undesirability of ballroom partners and dance masters remained high. In this context women were cast as pure and innocent. A lengthy and comprehensive diatribe on the subject by the Presbyterian minister George C. Heckman (1825–1902) represents the conservatives' fears. Referring first to the "indolent, dissolute" and morally "bankrupt" character of dancing masters, Heckman continues:

> Women must take such partners as the accident of the dance brings them, even though it throws them into the hands and arms or under the gloating, sensual gaze of the dissipated and licentious; for Fashion—child of Sin and Death—will embrace incarnate corruption, though reeking with the filth of bar-room, theatre or brothel, if only it comes with cold and gay attire or respectable social connections. The rules of this social amusement will allow a man guilty of every crime which should make women loathe him and banish him from all respectable company to take liberties with the person of wife and sister and daughter which under no other circumstances than marriage would be permitted to the man of purest morals or closest friendship.[34]

Dance detractors thus placed women in blatantly conflicting roles with respect to the morality of dancing, on one hand idealizing them as the divinely endowed guardians of society's moral tone, but on the other indicting them as seducers of hapless males. The clergy believed that the round dances and the balls of the era contributed to the ultimate downfall and "ruin" of pure women. However, in keeping with middle-class Victorian values, antidance treatises expressed no concern for the spiritual or social welfare of "fallen" or "ruined" women. Neither do they allude to any opportunity for an amended life for such women.[35] Similarly, the treatises devote very little attention to those women of lower socioeconomic status who danced on the stage in theaters and in concert saloons.

Stage Dancing and Working Women

Considering the vehemence with which opponents objected to dancing as a fashionable amusement, it is somewhat surprising that they did not object strenuously to dance as theater art or entertainment. Previous decades would have found little dance and few women on American stages; but in the post–Civil War years the rise of the city ushered in musicals, vaudeville, and the female chorus line. For example, the celebrated musical theater extravaganza called *The Black Crook* opened in New York City in 1866, ran for over a year, and was revived during the remainder of the century. A sequel called *The White Faun* opened in 1868.[36] *The Black Crook* may have introduced the female chorus line to a vast number of theater-goers, but the idea likely originated in what came to be known as "honky-tonks," where women served as hostesses, sang, and danced. Larger establishments had choruses of six to twelve girls and called their performances "ballet." One claim cites "hundreds" of such commercial enterprises—labeled "honky-tonks" or "free-and-easies"—by the 1870s and 1880s. The research of Kathy Peiss on working women and their amusements shows there were over two hundred of these "concert saloons" in New York City even by the 1860s—along Broadway, the Bowery, and the waterfronts. They catered to male audiences. Ladies attending would have risked damaged reputations, because it was the waiter-girls who "were greatly responsible for causing polite society to brand concert-saloons as scurrilous and indecent."[37]

Undoubtedly, ministers vocally decried the alleged immoral behavior and scanty costumes of female dancers, as well as their onstage appearances, but authors of books opposing dance seldom brought up these performers. Only Crane and the English reformer, preacher, and author John Ashworth (1813–75) mention "dancing girls." Ashworth's book, published in Philadelphia in 1866, tells of a dancer named Annie who went from performing on the public stage to eventual sickness and ruin. In 1869 Crane declared that "a dancing girl, however loudly her fame may be trumpeted by the newspapers, finds her professional reputation every-where a bar to her reception into good society."[38] His view may have reflected social class distinctions in addition to a disdain for the stage.

Nancy Ruyter points out in her analysis of American dance in this era that dancers in the theater "probably without exception" came originally from theater families, from the urban poor, or from farm families. Some got temporary spots in touring shows, but others won more secure jobs, primarily in the cities. Many dancers, then as now, undoubtedly held other jobs on the side—perhaps as factory workers, waitresses, or "hostesses."[39] Any thought of such work by middle- or upper-class women would have fallen outside the bounds of respectability. Thus, since clergymen targeted the dancing and balls of fashionable society, most may have thought it unnecessary to write against theater dance or the dance of the "honky-tonks" because few if any of their parishioners engaged in it.

The disrepute of both stage dancing and ballroom dancing was closely linked to the dance opponents' valuing of mind over body and intellectual education over physical education. For example, Bostwick Hawley, a trustee of Wesleyan University and president of the Board of Education in Saratoga Springs, New York, extolled the satisfactions and virtues found in pursuit of the "higher" pleasures—education, good conversation, reading, "doing good . . . and religious worship." Dancing, by contrast, required "little intelligence" and no skill other than in the feet.[40] Showing the viewpoint to be widespread, John H. Morley's (1840–1923) sermon on 29 January 1882 to the Congregational Church in Winona, Minnesota, lauded a "cultured mind" as opposed to "nimble feet." Similarly, Eastman told his parishioners that dancing was scarcer in society as one moved "upward" through the "successive ranks of intelligence, morality and religion." By contrast, dancing was more common as one moved "downward" to the gin palace, beer garden, theater, and "house of infamy."[41] In such places, questions of morality mixed with issues of women's health.

Health Issues and Women

As opponents continued to denounce dancing on the grounds of health, they targeted ballroom dancing exclusively. The degree to which they may have feared the spread of venereal disease is not known; very few references to it can be found in the antidance literature. But the issue engendered a good deal of public concern in the postwar era.[42] However, the conservative evangelicals focused their opposition on the exertion to the female system that dancing caused. Mattison didn't consider that regular dancing could provide healthful exercise and in 1867 pointed out that the problem was worse for the "delicate" female. "Every dancer knows that after a night spent in the ballroom it takes two or three days for the system to recover its wonted elasticity and spirits." Preaching the same year, Sikes decried the "excessive exercise" at dances and avoided any acknowledgment that "excessive" is a comparative term. In 1888 Heckman still called dancing an "unnatural" and "violent" exercise for women. These arguments suggest that conservative clergy remained unaware of the research on women's physical capacities by medical men of the era. Nonetheless, it is likely that infrequent, vigorous exercise, taken in overheated, poorly ventilated rooms while wearing ballroom dress, did indeed cause colds, contribute to consumption, and possibly result in eventual death for some females. But the proof offered by one Disciples of Christ minister, James William Lowber (1847–1930), remains typical of the testimony of dance opponents: "We have known many instances of ruined constitutions induced by exposure at the dance; and I have preached sermons at the funerals of girls that had been killed by the modern dance."[43]

The fact remains that the physical problem affecting most women, with respect to exercise, resulted from the era's clothing styles. The majority of women still encased themselves in corsets, which, when combined with several layers of outer garments, made any exertion but walking virtually impossible. Although a few medical men began studies to ascertain the physiological capacities of women's strength and endurance, dance opponents do not mention such investigations. The views of these doctors separate them from the conservative opponents.

Piety versus Worldliness

In shoring up their arguments against dancing, innumerable ministers declared that only worldly people danced; no dancer ever attended prayer meetings and became active in church. In a typical claim, Henry M. Tenney (1841–1932) told his First Congregational Church in Cleveland, around 1889, that after nineteen years in the ministry, "I have uniformly found that the prevailing influence of these forms of amusement has been very decidedly against an earnest Christian life, and very strongly in opposition to those revival efforts which seek the immediate conversion of souls."[44] To those people who, like Tenney, had argued for decades that dancing was sinful because it detracted from revivals, the Congregational cleric Washington Gladden (1836–1918) pointed out very logically that any "absorbing interest" could similarly detract from revivals. Finney had made the same point decades earlier. Although some clerics argued with force that the aim of a Christian life was holiness and usefulness, to which dancing did not contribute, others used rhetorical questions and threats to persuade readers and listeners to turn from dancing. Sikes, for example, told his Pennsylvania Lutheran congregation that, of course, they did not want to die in a ballroom. Pushing his cautionary remarks further, he pointed out that the sick and dying did not call for a dancing master but for a minister of the gospel.[45] The rhetorical question or statement was typically used with no follow-up, thus leaving the reader or listener with an apparently logical argument against dancing.[46]

Concern for spiritual life and growth ultimately came down to a theology, propounded in previous decades, emphasizing the primary aims in life as worship and work. Amusements and other diversions distracted one from pursuing those two essential goals and, therefore, held no value and were essentially sinful. An accountability to God for use of time, money, behavior, and speech followed inevitably from the total transformation of one's being, as a consequence of a personal conversion experience. Moderation and prudence proved right guides for living. Within this framework, health was to be maintained and recreation became a necessity to that end. However, recreation or amusement had to function only to renew one for return to work, that is, it had to build up body, mind, and soul.[47] Anything that detracted from that goal was disapproved as a legitimate amusement for Christians.

Disapproval of dancing came to parishioners in several ways: from the pulpit or in conversation; in print, as the antidance literature testifies; and, more seriously, in the form of church discipline. Not all denominations invoked a discipline procedure, but the practice had been known as far back as the sixteenth century in the French Reformed church. In this country, the Presbyterians had a long tradition of using discipline, which, by mid-century, had begun to trigger some outspoken criticism.

Cases of Discipline: Criticism of Tradition

In "The Conception of the Christian Life Prevailing in the Presbyterian Churches of the South during the Nineteenth Century," William D. Blanks points out that dancing constituted a greater problem for the denominational boards and assemblies than did any other popular amusement of the era. Dancing could and did occur in private homes and many Presbyterians had difficulty in finding it such a wicked sin, a fact that led to numerous disciplinary cases. These became most frequent in the decade of the seventies. As early as 1818, the general assembly of the denomination had pronounced dancing a danger to Christians. Blanks reports that the statement was read again and again in subsequent decades to remind churchgoers about the immorality of dancing. But the 1865 general assembly admitted that many churches had been lax in administering discipline to members found guilty of dancing.[48] Blanks concludes that there is "no reason to believe" that discipline was applied universally or with the same effectiveness throughout the denomination. For instance, the Rev. Robert G. Thompson expressed public disapproval of Chicago officials when he published his *Pleas Before the Synod of Chicago* in October 1868. Thompson reports that there were forty-two offenders who admitted dancing. Most promised to abstain in the future; Thompson took issue with the treatment of four who justified their dancing on the grounds of its being an innocent amusement.[49]

In the cases of church discipline applied in the South, a great number involved an offense by a church elder.[50] Frank E. Block, deacon of the Atlanta church, defended himself in a treatise in 1878, providing insight into what many Presbyterians of the day probably thought and felt about the purported evils of dancing and the denominational action against it. The

Presbyterian church had accused Block on two counts. First, he had held an "entertainment" in his home at which dancing was not only permitted but encouraged. Second, he had thereby encouraged violation of church laws and tempted other, younger, church members to sin. In his defense, Block maintained that he had grown up in a Christian home where dancing had been considered desirable if engaged in "at the proper time, with proper persons." Block also asserted that the Bible nowhere proscribes dancing. Since the Bible served as the basis for church law, he contended that he had broken no law. He asserted that the real evil lay not in the dance but in the dancer: "I deny that dancing begets or conduces to lust, except in the mind of the foul debauchee. . . . It depends entirely upon the man, and his evil purposes and inclinations."[51] Here, he implies continuation of the antebellum notion that the "delicacy" of women meant they were to be pure and protected.[52]

According to Block, the Presbyterian ministers in Atlanta, without exception, saw no harm in dancing per se. He joined them in contending that the harm lay in abuses, not in the dance itself. In fact, Block even declared that three-quarters of all church members held the same opinion. But, in his view, such distinctions were of less consequence than the motives for opposition to dancing. "But I protest against the whole principle which underlies this subject. It is that spirit of fanaticism, which, while its design may be good, is sure to end in evil."[53] Block argued, as had George Thacher in the 1840s, that the issue of dancing fell to individual liberty of conscience. He contended that dancing proved no more an occasion to sin than did any other kind of heterosexual association. In his final plea to the synod, Block touched at the root of antidance fervor in the century. "In our abhorrence of evil and our desire to benefit men, we admit no middle ground, but rush to positions unwarranted alike by reason and by revelation. Let the principle be once admitted and liberty of conscience is destroyed."[54] Block was not alone in his appeal to reason and clear discernment; similar strong protests also came from people in other denominations.

The Liberal View of Amusements, Dance, and Health

Since the late fifties when Edward Everett Hale had called for the church and government to provide amusements in proper context, the notion had been slowly growing among clergy from several denominations, in different part of the country, that the church had taken a wrong stand in preaching total abstinence from dancing. The known extant writings cited here represent an appeal to reason rather than emotion, and a concern for individual liberty rather than uniform moral prescription. Though the clerics see some good in dancing, they do not give it unqualified support.

Washington Gladden and Other Clergy

Washington Gladden, writing in 1866 from his Congregational parish in North Adams, Massachusetts, called the policy of abstinence "a stupendous failure." Addressing the liberty of conscience issue that Block had invoked, Gladden declared: "The new and better doctrine of Christian liberty in the use of things innocent must now be preached. . . . If the grace of Christ is sufficient to keep a man honest and truthful amidst the temptations of trade, doubtless it is sufficient to keep him sober and steady amidst the temptations of amusement. Our religion ought to be able to control us in all our conduct; if it does not it is because we have got the wrong kind of religion."[55] Acknowledging that human beings need amusements or recreation for physical and mental well-being, Gladden expressed the radical notion that an individual could glorify God in play as well as in work or worship. In opposition to those who preached that any evil must be resisted from the outset, he urged careful discrimination between the amusement and its abuses, plus moderation with respect to participation. Thus, he argued that simply because bad men abused bowling, billiards, cards, and theater-going, this should not deter good men from moderate use of such activities. "If you set out with the determination to deny yourselves everything that is abused, you will find that your possessions and enjoyments will be few." To counteract the conservative policy of proscribing amusements, Gladden introduced the equally radical notion that young people could be trusted with the truth: "It is high time that we had made the discovery that all young people who are not imbecile are fit to be trusted with the truth in regard to this whole subject. There is a right way and a wrong way of using these amusements and they can easily discern between them."[56]

When applying such liberal views to dancing, however, Gladden retrenched a bit. He had "no doubt" that the round dances then in practice were "essentially wrong." Waltzes and polkas were a "moral abomination." Presumably, he refers to the closed dance position required in those dances, though he leaves the reader in doubt about the point. However, like mainstream evangelicals from the previous era, Gladden asserts that the round dances' "low origin" in the "dens of infamy in Paris" also made them immoral. Unequivocally, he declares: "No respectable woman ought to engage in them." But with respect to other kinds of dancing, Gladden maintains his more liberal stance. Echoing William Ellery Channing's views preached in 1837, Gladden argued for the benefits of parlor dancing undertaken in moderation. He considered the "simple square dances" to be not only free of sin but "excellent," and recommended that they be "allowed and encouraged by Christian people." Although balls and parties where dancing continued late into the night were an abuse of dancing, they were not evil in themselves. The wrong lay in the dissipation, not in the dancing. Gladden declared that if the same people in the same room indulged in the same excesses as at balls—overeating, drinking, keeping late hours and promiscuous company—but marched up and down the hall all night instead of dancing, "their sin would be just as great" as if they had danced.[57]

Echoing the criticism Gladden and Block directed toward the church's stand on amusements, Marvin Richardson Vincent (1834–1922), pastor of First Presbyterian Church in Troy, New York, spoke out in 1867 in the publication *Amusement a Force in Christian Training.* He indicted the church for "signally" failing in the regulation of popular amusements by concentrating on alleged evils and forgetting to develop the inherent good in amusements. Vincent flatly asserts that the abuses in dancing are not inseparable from the amusement itself. Further, he clarifies that what is amusement to one person becomes toil to another. Like Gladden, he also points to the fine distinction between dancing and marching to music: "Youth must not dance, but they may march to music in company, and go through calisthenic exercises, involving a good deal more motion than dancing. But if people may march to music and be guiltless, it is very hard to see how skipping to music converts the exercise into sin."[58]

Speaking from the same discriminating point of view, C. H. W. Stocking, an Episcopalian, preached in Chicago in 1873 that the abuses in balls and dancing parties were to be decried but the parlor dances approved. In his published sermon, Stocking concentrates on the Christian's response and points to the issue of individual taste and liberty, which Gladden and Block also affirmed. He acknowledges the validity of total abstinence for any individual who chooses that path, but warns that a blanket proscription becomes problematic when people "insist on binding the consciences of others, and are constantly assuming the ermine and exercising the functions of the judge. Not content with their own self-denials, they lay their fellows under the ban of their prohibition, and when you have aggregated individual prejudices, you have created what we call public religious opinion, that often defeats the very ends it is intended to subserve." To those who argued that the truly pious Christian inevitably must choose total abstinence, Stocking replied that moderate social participation in no way countermanded the spirit of true piety. "Every expedient for making home attractive by the introduction of games and dancing will be a point gained in the interests of morality."[59]

In 1874, the Unitarian cleric Octavius Brookes Frothingham (1822–95) wrote from New York and reflected the earlier advocacy by Hale, who recognized social class distinctions in society. Frothingham's chief complaint was that the supply of amusements was inadequate to meet the demand. They are the "luxury of the few, not the food of the multitude." The changed urban life of the 1870s meant that the vast majority of men and women needed amusement: "Undeveloped, uncultivated, unelastic, and unpliable, limited in thought, confined in sentiment, constrained in feeling, narrow in sympathy, with few outlooks into a world of beauty, with few amenities or social beguilements, with the smallest means of access to the genial elements of life, the most inadequate remedies for the dullness of their daily pursuits; they instinctively, if not consciously, demand artificial recreation. They must have it, or they sicken and droop." Frothingham's advocacy of amusements foreshadows the early twentieth-century theory of amusements as the opiate for the masses. He understood that labor was not the problem, "but to have no relief from labor is." Frothingham saw amusements as a solution for the masses who had little variation in their work or daily lives, though he made no pretense that existing amusements met his requirements for the "perfect recreator."[60]

The publications by Gladden, Vincent, Stocking, and Frothingham all represented serious, didactic writing, in contrast to *The Parson on Dancing* by J. B. Gross, which bespeaks a unique perspective on several counts. Partly satirical, partly whimsical, yet still partly serious, the 1879 book came from the pen of a defrocked Lutheran cleric in Pennsylvania. As such, the writing merits more attention.

The Case of J. B. Gross

The most liberal view of dance to be printed during the postwar decades came from the pen of the Reverend Joseph B. Gross (d. 1891), a Lutheran minister from Wilkes Barre, Pennsylvania. *The Parson on Dancing,* published by J. B. Lippincott in Philadelphia, stands as one of several books authored by Gross and printed by the company. But, as the only known prodance treatise by a nineteenth-century clergyman, it immediately elicits curiosity about his motives in writing. One's curiosity is further piqued by the fact that Gross was struck from the roster of the Pennsylvania Ministerium in

1878; his celebration of dance appeared the next year. Careful reading suggests that Gross wrote because he took personal and rhetorical delight at poking holes in the antidance arguments of conservatives.[61] His "Invocation" sets the tone: "HAIL Terpsichore, Sweet Goddess of the Dance: Art-Divine! Grace of Manners and Innocent Joys are thy Charming Gifts, Gentle Muse, and not in the Rhythism [sic] of Motion, but only in a Bad Heart, or a Vicious Tongue, is the *Guilt of Sin*. Then hail, Terpsichore, Sweet Goddess of the Dance, all hail! Bigots may scowl, Hypochondriacs—Horror-Stricken, may sigh, Dancing is, nevertheless, an Amusement as Old and as Universal as the Human Race."[62]

Gross's reasoning is in dramatic contrast to that of Finney, Walther, and other conservative evangelicals. In the preface, Gross acknowledges that dancing is judged positively or negatively "in a great measure" depending upon the "intelligence and moral culture" of the persons who speak out about it. He hints, as did Gladden, that many critics failed to sort good from evil. Clearly, Gross aimed at the more intelligent, if not intellectual, reader. The thoroughness of his analysis, the sources quoted, and the language employed all speak to that point. For example, when analyzing the role of dancing in the oft-quoted case of Salome and John the Baptist, Gross observes: "Instigated by her libidinous mother, whose proud and revengeful disposition stood out in bold relief on this joyous yet tragic occasion, she unthinkingly as well as, most likely, unconscious of evil, 'asked John Baptist's [sic] head in a charger.'" The excerpt is typical of his style and tone. He relies for authority on encyclopedias in addition to well-known historical authors such as Plato and Locke.[63] His analysis includes a definition of dancing, discussion of its contemporary manifestation, detailed coverage of its ancient pagan heritage, and an equally detailed exposition of the Old and New Testament verses on dancing. That Gross aimed to point a finger at the dance detractors of his day is clearly evident from his attacks on the typical reasons for opposing the activity. That he took delight in so doing is evidenced not only by his language, sources, and thorough, clear logic, but also by his reference to "principles no less novel than they are erudite," which desire "respectful notice in these mirthful pages."[64]

Gross speaks of dancing in its global sense as both art and amusement.[65] To those who asserted the undesirability and mere physicality of dancing because it was popular among "heathenish" people, Gross declared: "The fact that we dance, does not make us barbarians simply because barbarians too dance." Nor does that fact make dancing in civilized culture a "Barbarous and Sinful Pastime."[66] Combating the numerous claims that dancing

injures the health of participants, Gross makes his claims with straightforward reasoning that recalls the same logical assertions by Richard Mulcaster and Martin Luther in the sixteenth century. In Gross's words, "the abuse
of a practice or institution, which is not in itself reprehensible or deleteri-
ous . . . by no means . . . furnishes a valid argument for its condemnation
and disuse." He echoes Luther's opinion that the gluttony of some people
offers no good reason for abstaining from food. In addition, not only is
dancing beneficial to health, it also provides proper social refinement when
engaged in intelligently and in moderate circumstances. Quoting Locke on
its social value, Gross seems to delight in adding the additional support of
Ruskin, apparently quoted in the Philadelphia *Weekly Times,* on a point that
Gross states will no doubt startle the "morose votaries of asceticism." To wit:
" 'music and *precise dancing* are, after all, the only safeguards of morality.' "[67]

Gross concludes that dancing clearly belongs among the liberal arts as
an important part of education. Yet, his advanced notions probably pertain
to the use of dance in the church. After chronicling the dancing of Old
Testament Hebrews, Gross queries: "The Hebrews . . . habitually and ap-
provingly worshipped God in the dance, and why should it not be proper
to introduce the dance into the Christian Church, as a leading and holy
element in the cultus of the New Testament? *Unto the pure all things are pure!*
Titus, first chapter and fifteenth verse."[68]

The next American clergyman known to advocate dance in the church
was the Reverend William Norman Guthrie, who wrote in 1923. Between
the time of Gross and that of Guthrie, a host of other advocates would have
to break down the arguments against dancing. Those among them who
researched the physical capacities of females made enormous contributions
toward a more informed view of women's physical health and stamina.

Health and Physical Training Authorities

The advocacy of health and exercise in America gathered adherents by the
1880s. As cities grew, opportunities for outdoor activities decreased. Larger numbers of people no longer had the benefits of daily exercise through
the regular performance of farm duties, which caused outspoken medical
doctors and physical training directors to press the need for regular, graded
calisthenics for both sexes. This recommendation stood in marked contrast
to the accepted practice of prescribing inactivity—total rest—for allegedly
sick females. The new exercise programs required a radical transformation
in women's dress as well as in their lives.

Despite numerous warnings about the ill effects of tight lacing, most women regularly followed the dictates of fashion and artificially reduced their waists to alarmingly small sizes. Robert Tomes, an author and physician, commented with incredulity in 1874 that it is "marvelous" to note that women still persist in this practice "which they all must know to be at the risk of their lives." Mary Joanna Safford's (d. 1916) book on *Health and Strength for Girls* (1884) portrayed the typical young girl as encased in a "laced, boned and steeled jacket." Further encumbered by many thicknesses of clothes around the midsection and hampered by narrow-heeled shoes, the girl could in no way engage in vigorous physical activity. According to Safford, the "growing taste" for sufficient "strength to do what one chooses and so have a 'good time'" had not yet reached the young school girls. She indicates a growing fashion for exercise among older ladies and young women.[69]

Even while Safford was publishing her observations, male authorities were carrying on long-term research. Dio Lewis (1823–86), a health reformer and gymnastic authority, wrote in the *North American Review* for December 1882. After two decades of teaching, Lewis reported that women simply did not think they practiced tight lacing: "In forty years' professional experience with the wearers of corsets, we cannot now recall a single confession, even from those who had reduced their waists [by] from ten to fifteen inches." Conversation with several corsetmakers confirmed his testimony; fashionable ladies and their imitators regularly purchased corsets that were from three to ten inches smaller than their waists. In addition to criticizing restrictive corsets, Lewis indicts tight shoes, high heels, and long, heavy skirts combined with unequal distribution of garment weight over the female body. Based on his own teaching experience, Lewis found that women were so encumbered they could do no exercise beyond "gentle" walking or dancing, and would function best by resting:

> As to exercise in the gymnasium, the observation of thirty years in ladies' seminaries leads to the conviction that girls in corsets seriously endanger their welfare when they try to exercise beyond gentle walking and dancing. All attempts at free arm or leg work must prove mischievous. For many years we have cautioned corseted women against the gymnasium, and have seriously urged easy-chairs and lounges. The advice given by Dr. Edward Clarke, and repeated by thousands of doctors to their lady patients, to lie down as much as possible, and periodically spend a week in bed, is, if a corset be worn, not only wise and merciful, but indispensable.[70]

Such testimony to the harmful effects of prevailing fashion and to the ensuing physical limitations on women makes it easy to see why dance opponents, observing only what they saw about them, logically assumed that females constituted the weaker sex. When women were too restrained by steel and whalebone to exercise, cardiovascular capacity diminished and muscles atrophied. Prolonged bed rest merely accentuated the physiological decline.

Evidence about the extent to which female weakness prevailed comes from a famous neurologist, Dr. Silas Weir Mitchell (1829–1914). Writing in 1877, Mitchell reports:

> Nothing is more common in practice than to see a young woman who falls below the health-standard, loses color and plumpness, is tired all the time, by and by has a tender spine, and sooner or later enacts the whole varied drama of hysteria. As one or other set of symptoms is prominent she gets the appropriate label, and sometimes she continues to exhibit only the single phase of nervous exhaustion or of spinal irritation. Far more often she runs the gauntlet of nerve doctors, gynaecologists, plaster-jackets, braces, water-treatment, and all the fantastic variety of other cures.

Mitchell prescribed prolonged bed rest and no activity at all for women with the symptoms he described. Over a period of six weeks to two months, their diet was to be reduced to nothing but skim milk. They were kept in a dark room, with no activity—not even reading, sewing, or writing—and were stimulated only by massage or electricity. Mitchell then eventually brought the patient back to a full diet; and, after a fortnight, the patient might have someone read to her. The modern reader is horrified at the thought of such a prescription, with its consequent physical and psychological debility. In his day, however, Mitchell gained international fame for his "rest cure."[71]

Happily, not all doctors favored the "rest cure." James Caleb Jackson (1811–95), a doctor, minister, and author, became active in health reform during the 1840s and through the 1860s. In 1859 he founded a periodical called *The Laws of Life*, which carried in the April 1866 issue an analysis of dancing's benefits and ills. Jackson cites women's attire among the evils of dancing as practiced. It inhibited natural circulation, and the irregular or nonroutine exercise of a ball caused great fatigue. Though he himself participated in a group meeting weekly for two hours of "recreative dancing," in a well-lighted and ventilated hall, he fully agreed with the harmful health effects of dancing as practiced by the great majority of people.[72]

Comparative analysis of physical capacity in women came from Dio Lewis and also from Dr. Dudley Sargent (1849–1924), a physician and a Harvard physical training director. Not content merely to extol the benefits of regular exercise, by the 1880s both Lewis and Sargent reported in popular periodicals about experiments they had conducted that established that women were not, by nature, the weaker and more delicate sex. As a reformer and a man of science, Lewis regularly inquired about and observed the health status of women outside the Victorian middle class. He states that his findings confirm that immigrant women and Native American women, as well as those from Africa and Asia, did not possess health or physical condition inferior to that of their male contemporaries. Experiments conducted at his Lexington and Boston schools also gave evidence that women could be better gymnasts than men. His female subjects could do a full gymnastic schedule, dance three nights a week, and walk five to ten miles on Saturdays with no ill effects—when they abandoned their corsets, put on healthy dress, and adopted sound habits with respect to rest and diet.[73]

Similar results were published by Sargent, based on his work as physical training director at Harvard's Hemenway Gymnasium. Reporting on his anthropometric studies and historical research, Sargent wrote on the "Physical Development of Women" in Scribner's Magazine (1889) and decried the use of the corset. He declared that the garment's restriction accounted for the failure of the female "to realize her best opportunities for development." Further, he denounced the long skirts that kept women hampered for "three thousand years." During exercise, a woman should wear a skirt only to the knee or "the bloomer costume, such as is now in use in the college gymnasia for women." Concerned with science, health, exercise, and the well-being of both sexes, Sargent spoke out with no regard for the importance of fashion and with full scientific conviction that women could improve their physical condition. In what was probably one of the earliest pronouncements of a basic conditioning principle, Sargent declared: "Muscles grow large and vigorous from use, and from disuse become weak, flabby, and relaxed."[74]

Clearly, the proponents and followers of the "rest cure" had not heeded this fundamental law of use and disuse. Nor had the conservative dance opponents paid attention to Lewis's and Sargent's research on the physical strength capabilities of women. However, dance masters and etiquette writers continued to urge the health benefits of dancing as one of several values surrounding the art. Even so, one prominent teacher lamented a decline in graceful dancing.

Dance Masters

Writing on the values of the art in 1867, the dance master Lawrence De Garmo Brookes quoted from historical and scholarly sources equally as prestigious as those Gross cited. Like dance masters from earlier decades, Brookes was more than merely literate and skilled in dancing. In *Brookes on Modern Dancing,* he cites many ancient writers and then quotes several paragraphs from Sir Thomas Elyot on dancing's developing the virtue of prudence. Following Elyot's example, Brookes also cites the Roman physician Galen on the health benefits of dancing. For his nineteenth-century readers, Brookes presses the "Sanitary Advantage" theme in an attempt to persuade the reader that dancing provides important and contrasting values to counteract the "over mental education" then so highly stressed, particularly for young ladies. Although Brookes gives rules for ballroom behavior, he clearly emphasizes the advantages of family dancing, just as Gladden and other liberal clergy did. But, unlike some earlier dance masters, Brookes declares that older people can also benefit from learning the art; he testifies to having taught an eighty-year-old man who enjoyed dancing immensely and found it a most "beneficial exercise for himself."[75] Brookes's emphasis on the health value of dancing was not unique in the era but it did cast him as one of the more liberal spokespersons for dancing when compared to evangelical opponents.

Corroborating the view of clerics who stated that dancing had become more popular, even among church members, the dance teacher William B. DeGarmo (fl. 1865–84) tells us that "most fathers and mothers, including the majority of clergymen, send their daughters to dancing schools." He published his remarks in *The Dance of Society,* which appeared in four editions between 1875 and 1884.[76] In 1885 the well-known dancing master Allen Dodworth (1817–96), whose career had spanned fifty years in New York City, also acknowledged the popularity of dancing even as he lamented the decline in the gracefulness of his students. The round dances did not require the serious instruction and practice of former years. He also noted that a lack of space on the dance floor contributed to "positions of indelicacy": "The dancers are in constant collision, all feeling it to be a necessity to shrink into the smallest possible space—until positions of indelicacy become no longer offensive. It may be truthfully asserted, that our young people of to-day are as virtuously and modestly inclined as those of any period; and when space is sufficient, fashions of indelicacy in dancing are soon abandoned."[77]

Fully aware of the opposition to dancing, Dodworth affirms his belief that "to make pleasant motions to good music cannot be *sinful.*" He proposes in his book that parents and friends ought to organize weekly dances on the local YMCA premises so that young people might gather in well-supervised surroundings for an evening of enjoyable sociability. "The community could be taught by example that extravagance of expense, suppers, late hours, and other dissipations, have no necessary relation to dancing." Thus, like Gladden and others who urged the well-supervised parlor dance, Dodworth gives no unqualified approval to the balls and extravagant dancing parties of his era. He sees the benefit in dancing and urges that the good not be thrown out with the bad. He further corroborates the claims of dance opponents that many of the round dances came from Paris, and he explains that the popularity of the polka in Paris of the 1840s meant that dancing masters had to use many ballet girls to help teach the new dance. Yet, according to Dodworth, their training did not fit them for the task of teaching "manners and motion." Clearly, Dodworth was a dancing master from the old school, which considered morality, manners, and good dancing inseparable as well as essential for those who wished to appear to advantage in polite circles. Observing the society of his day in New York, he decried the coarseness and brutality present everywhere.[78]

Testimony to Dodworth's concern for the importance of moral education and the good name of dancing comes from his instructions to dance masters. Heading the list of qualifications for a teacher of dancing is "A good moral character," followed by "A liberal education." Then, commenting on the deficiencies of America's educational system, he declares:

> We have schools, academies, colleges, and universities . . . where morality is secondary to theology. We want schools or places where the practice of moral conduct, especially in all the little incidents of young life, is made the primary and dominant duty of the time and place.
>
> Our ordinary education rests too much upon the theory that the multiplication table teaches the Golden Rule. Children are talked at about right doing, but have we not too much telling and not enough practising?[79]

According to Dodworth, dancing that was well taught could help to fill this vacancy and instruct the young in moral virtue in a way that was fun while also providing the opportunity for practicing, not merely listening to talks about rules.

Etiquette Authorities

Those who prescribed behavior in the polite world also would exert tight control on manners and morals. Some, such as the leading social arbiter Sarah Josepha Hale (1788–1879), agreed with those clergy who contended that great abuses in amusements did not logically argue for abolition or abstinence. Hale placed dancing first and foremost in a category of activity that had been too much abused and too little evaluated for its benefits.[80] Unlike Dodworth she concluded that responsibility for the decline in the value of dancing lay at the feet of Christian parents. If they had not banned it from their homes, dancing would not have become so degraded. Had they given up music in the same way, she continues in her book *Manners,* that art would have become equally depraved. Hale reaffirms that women are the moral guardians of society and country: "Woman is the natural guardian of the moral virtues: if she become shameless in her amusements, the inner world of home will soon be corrupted. No republic can be sustained where the moral virtues are dishonored in the social life of a free people." Consequently, the responsibility falls to mothers to rear daughters who will set the proper tone at balls.[81]

Hale's 1868 book summarized the code she had propounded for more than three decades when she reigned as the leading female authority on good conduct. Her advocacy of dancing as a beneficial and desirable accomplishment marks her as a liberal compared with the conservative evangelical clergy who strongly opposed dancing. Yet her qualified approval of all dancing places her in the ranks with Gladden, Vincent, and the liberal clergy who urged parlor dancing but lamented the excesses of balls and large parties. Hale's attitude about women's role in society clearly marks her as no radical. She asserts that Christians must be examples to the world when she discusses the traditional importance of women's controlling morality and virtue. Commenting on her day, she observes there is "so little to mark any outward distinction between the Church and the world."[82] The statement could have come from the pen of any number of evangelical clergy who counted themselves dance opponents.

By the 1880s other women became popular as etiquette authorities, some continuing to claim authority until well into the twentieth century. Mary Elizabeth Sherwood (1826–1903) wrote *Manners and Social Usages* in 1884; it appeared in several editions through 1918. Her information on balls remains essentially the same throughout this thirty-four-year period. Like Hale, she believed that women as wives and mothers held the responsibility for managing social situations and for tempering the coarse and vulgar tendencies of men. Society was to be led by those who traditionally had possessed talent and money, not by the nouveau riche.[83] Similarly, Clara Bloomfield-Moore (1824–99), writing under the pseudonym of Mrs. H. O. Ward, established in the title of her etiquette book the notion that the privileged class ought to set the rules for the polite world. Her *Sensible Et-*

iquette of the Best Society appeared in its twentieth revised edition in 1878; it became the most popular book of its kind after Sherwood's. Like Hale, Bloomfield-Moore observes that she writes only about those rules suited to the people of a "republic." Typically, she also ascribes to women the duty to "do all in their power toward the formation of so high a standard of morals and manners that the tendency of society will be upward instead of downward, seeking to make it in every respect equal to the best society of any nation."[84] A third woman who established herself as an authority on manners was the daughter of Samuel Gridley and the famous Julia Ward Howe. Florence Marion Howe Hall's (1845–1922) book *Social Customs,* which appeared in several printings between 1881 and 1911, conveyed the author's belief that etiquette helped to fill the gaps left by formal legislation, aiding the preservation of order in a society beset by the problems of immigration and the growth of cities and industries. In effect, she sought to have manners serve as a subtle means of social control, an important factor in an era of unprecedented urban problems.[85]

These women and other authors from the period not only provide traditional guidance on how to behave; they give detailed instructions for the conduct of balls, addressing topics such as the desirable number of musicians and floor preparation. The new prescriptions on how to plan for balls indicate the increasing popularity of dancing and of large parties. Some authorities actually agreed with dance opponents about the attendant excesses. Robert Tomes (1817–82), a physician and author whose *Bazar Book of Decorum* proved popular in the seventies, observed that the young cultivated dancing as though "there was nothing so necessary to mankind as dancing." As a physician, he approved the health benefits of the activity, but he failed to see the necessity of "dancing the German from midnight to four o'clock in the morning, six days out of the seven of each week." Such excess he labeled "dabauchery, not social enjoyment."[86]

Extravagance in frequency and cost of balls applied also to the size of such gatherings. A crowd of five hundred was not uncommon. However, such a multitude usually could not be accommodated in one's own home. Authorities warned against overcrowding in hot and poorly ventilated rooms. Consequently, many people began to hold balls in "public rooms." Hall graphically describes the need for a change of venue: "We have therefore adopted the custom of giving private balls at public assembly-rooms; and for the dancers this is infinitely more agreeable than trying to dance in crowded parlors, where the heat and the great crowd of non-combatants destroy all the pleasure for the young people."[87]

Those who constituted the "non-combatants" included chaperones, still necessary for all unmarried young ladies. Etiquette writers warned that the practice of giving balls in public rooms presented the potential for careless chaperonage, especially in cities, "which are now largely populated by irresponsible foreigners." Yet, mothers of the young ladies were not always invited to dances in private houses. "In small cities, or in good, quiet, sober-going Boston, such a custom is less dangerous than in a place like New York, where the immense foreign population has necessarily had its effect on manners and customs." At dances where there were no chaperones, but especially at gatherings in public rooms, the hostess was to assume responsibility for watching over the young single ladies.[88]

A female at eighteen and a male at twenty-one were considered old enough to go out in society, but they were clearly told how to behave toward each other, and those instructions also applied to drinking. Bloomfield-Moore advised young men to limit their champagne to two glasses, ladies to one glass. Hall counseled young women that it was sometimes wiser to avoid the supper table late in the evening unless they were prepared to run into males who could not hold their liquor. No one, of course, was to allow liquor to affect his or her speech or behavior in any way. Nonetheless, Sherwood records that sometimes young men did drink too much and behaved in an unseemly fashion. Nonetheless, by 1884, she reports she found such "breaches of decorum" to be rare. The most stringent instructions came from Eliza Lavin's *Good Manners* (1888), which declared that the proper hostess withheld wine from young men and carefully checked the names of strangers submitted to the hostess for invitations. Moreover, she dropped from the guest list "any young woman who displays a penchant for staircase flirtations." The proper hostess understood that such principles constituted "the safeguard of society."[89]

Instructions for male-female relationships perpetuated some of the older traditions but appeared to be more relaxed, as the reference to "staircase flirtations" indicates. The term did not even appear in earlier etiquette books. Proper introductions of gentlemen to ladies remained *de riguer*, however, and gentlemen were told not to dance with anyone to whom they had not been formally introduced. There was some relaxation of the rule that introductions at a dance did not allow a man to assume acquaintanceship with a woman outside of the ballroom, though a few authorities noted that the rule still applied in Europe and in America. Ladies were permitted to walk about the ballroom with their partners after a dance, but they were not to dance more than two dances with the same partner. Young ladies were further advised not to accept invitations for every dance; the fatigue would be too great and the heated faces induced by such nonstop activity would be "too unbecoming." In fact, the general time allotted for balls could, in itself, induce fatigue if one stayed the full evening. Authorities generally agreed that it was not fashionable to arrive before 9:30 or 10:00. Suppers could be served all evening or only at a time designated by the hostess—sometimes not until midnight. Dancing then continued until at least 1:00 A.M., often later.[90]

A further indication of the relaxation in rules came from Bloomfield-Moore, who saw no harm in clergymen dancing: "The sooner that we recover from the effects of the Puritanical idea that clergymen ought never to be seen at balls, the better for all who attend them. When it is wrong for a clergyman to go, it is wrong for any member of his church to be seen." By contrast, evangelical dance opponents regularly told listeners and readers that even non-Christians opposed the idea.[91]

Since the "best society" set the rules for balls and dancing parties, and since such rules were to some degree always being altered as society changed, etiquette books would always be on the cutting edge of prescribed social rules and roles. Thus, because of their dance advocacy, etiquette authorities could be labeled liberal, compared to conservative evangelicals. But, measured against the general range of society, etiquette writers would inevitably be considered only moderately liberal or perhaps even conservative. The concept of maintaining social control via rules decreed by the "best society" meant that countervailing ideas and behavior would not be tolerated. Thus, etiquette writers of the post–Civil War era adhered to traditional notions of Christian courtesy and morality. They maintained that true courtesy was exemplified by the Golden Rule and that good manners were inseparable from those good morals that derived from biblical principles.[92] Etiquette authorities continued to promulgate the notion that women were to govern social situations, civilize men, and safeguard the morality of family, society and country. Yet, as society changed, social arbiters had to keep up with the times by formulating new rules for new subjects such as divorce, swimming, use of cosmetics, and riding in a taxi. Urban circumstances were gradually reshaping the lady's person and role.

The Ideal for the Lady

As social rules metamorphosed and research on women's health mounted, the monolithic ideal for the lady inevitably began to erode. Conservative male clergy who opposed dancing portrayed a lady who could be both victim and temptress on the dance floor. As pure and pious partner, she could succumb to the charm and passion of the male who embraced her in the waltz. Such entrapment would be facilitated by the music, lights, and fashions presented at a large ball. However, the lady herself might become the perpetrator of evil by dressing and adorning her person so as to attract admiring male glances and, ultimately, appeal to men's baser passions. Because dance opponents do not discuss degrees of intentionality, they thus cast the middle- or upper-class Victorian lady in a dual role, as both innocent victim and potential temptress. Protection of the pure lady proved paramount for the dance opponents, as shown by their abundant arguments speaking to the evils of the new "round dances" and undesirable companions at public balls. Their allegations that dance contributed to a gross waste of money cast women as victims of fashion and worldly conventions who succumb to pride, vanity, and careless stewardship. Because women were at the same time indicted for potentially seducing men by their attire, conservative male clerics who opposed dance left men free of responsibility for maintaining morality at dancing parties and balls. It was women who were held responsible for the moral tone of home, family, and society; they were still to be pure, pious, submissive, and domestic.

By contrast, etiquette books indicate some loosening of restrictions on male-female behavior, and they tend to indicate an equal responsibility for both men and women to follow the rules of good behavior. Although some, like Hale, reaffirmed that women were to set the moral tone for a party, etiquette writers also emphasized general rules of decorum and civility that effectively distinguished polite society or the "best" society from the lower classes.

New perspectives on the role of women came from those few medical men and women who conducted research on the physiological capacities of females. Their findings pointed to a woman potentially strong and healthy if she discarded her fashionable corset and dress and engaged in regular, vigorous exercise. In their view, dancing could be totally healthy and enjoyable. Even though some traditional physicians prescribed the "rest cure" for sick females, the ideal for the lady had begun to evolve from the standard in the antebellum era. As urban school systems, commercial amusements, and job opportunities all expanded, the traditional "lady" would evolve further into the "new woman" of the twentieth century.

Notes

1. Altogether a total of 49 known antidance treatises exist for the period 1865–90. The five years following the Civil War saw the production of 11 books. The seventies found 20 more in print, and the eighties another 16. Two undated books are likely to have been written in this period as well. These totals do not reflect the subsequent editions of many volumes. The treatises issued from pens and pulpits of all denominations except the Roman Catholics and smaller Protestant groups. The more densely settled eastern half of the country, from the Atlantic to the Mississippi, produced most of these publications, with antidance books published in the urban centers of New York, Philadelphia, Cincinnati, and Chicago. Yet sermons and books of local clerics were also published in small towns, such as Hollis, New Hampshire; Harrison, Ohio; Bedford, Indiana; Fulton, Kentucky; Milford, Michigan; and Winona, Minnesota. Opposition literature also appeared from presses west of the Mississippi—in Kansas City, Dallas, and San Francisco. Since dance opponents wrote didactic treatises aimed at persuading readers to change their behavior, the proliferation of published opposition during this era testifies to the expanded popularity of the art.

2. Sydney Ahlstrom, *A Religious History of the American People* (Garden City: Image books, 1975), vol. 2, 191, 208, 216, 189.

3. *Eerdmans' Handbook to Christianity in America* (Grand Rapids, Mich.: Eerdmans, 1983), 283, 286; Ahlstrom, *Religious History,* vol. 2, 274–75.

4. William G. McLoughlin, *The Meaning of Henry Ward Beecher* (New York: Knopf, 1970), 28; Ahlstrom, *Religious History,* vol. 2, 196. See chapter 6, above, for discussion of Beecher and Ellsler. *Popular Amusements* (1896) duplicates the lecture on that topic from the 1846 edition, including the dated indictment against money spent to see Fanny Elssler perform on stage.

5. *The Wycliffe Handbook of Preaching and Preachers,* ed. Warren W. Wiersbe and Lloyd M. Perry (Chicago: Moody Press, 1984), 95.

6. Thomas DeWitt Talmadge, *Social Dynamite: or, the Wickedness of Modern Society* (St. Louis: Holloway, 1889). Interestingly, Talmadge's catalog of evils in "modern society" recalls Phillip Stubbes's equally vivid depiction of perceived abuses in sixteenth-century England. In both instances, dancing found its place among the worst of alleged urban ills. See discussion of Phillip Stubbes in chapter 2, above.

7. William G. McLoughlin, *Modern Revivalism* (New York: Ronald Press, 1959), 326–27.

8. Ibid., 166; Richard Hofstadter, *Anti-intellectualism in American Life* (New York: Knopf, 1963), 107; William G. McLoughlin, *Revivals, Awakenings and Reform* (Chicago: University Press, 1978), 144.

9. Hofstadter, *Anti-intellectualism,* 108.

10. William Carson, *History of Dancing, An Address Delivered by Rev. W. Carson, A.M. before the Lane Seminary Club* (Harrison, Ohio: Walter Hartpence, 1889), 8.

11. *Dancing: Social Dancing for Purposes of Amusement—Is the Practice Consistent with the Christian Profession and Life?* (Philadelphia: American Baptist Publication Society, no. 110, n.d.), 1, unnumbered.

12. Hiram Mattison, *Popular Amusements: An Appeal to Methodists, in Regard to the Evils of Card-Playing, Billiards, Dancing, Theatre-Going, Etc.* (New York: Carlton and Porter, 1867), 3, unnumbered.

13. Mark Twain called the postwar decades—marked by corruption at the highest levels of government—the "Gilded Age." His novel *The Gilded Age, a Tale of Today* appeared in 1873, coauthored with Charles Dudley Warner.

14. Rev. C. S. Eastman, *May Christians Dance?* (Milford, Mich.: Official Board of the M. E. Church of Milford, n.d.), 5. Margaret Macmillan's analysis of the Methodist denomination in nineteenth-century Michigan indicates that the clergy regularly preached against the evils of drink, cards, tobacco, and dancing in fundamental terms, illustrated with emotional examples. See Margaret Burnham Macmillan, *The Methodist Church in Michigan: The Nineteenth Century* (Grand Rapids, Mich.: Eerdmans, 1967), 290.

15. Rev. Jonathan Townley Crane, *Popular Amusements* (Cincinnati: Walden and Stowe, and New York: Phillips and Hunt, 1869), 13.

16. John G. Jones, *An Appeal to All Christians Especially the Members of the Methodist Episcopal Church, against the Practice of Social Dancing* (St. Louis: P. M. Pinckard, 1867), iv. See also the southern view held by the Disciples of Christ Church on dancing and amusements, in David Edwin Harrell Jr., "Sin and Sectionalism: A Case Study of Morality in the Nineteenth-Century South," *Mississippi Quarterly* 19, no. 4 (1966): 157–70.

17. C. R. Robert, *The Mixed Multitude, Ancient and Modern*, 2d ed. (New York: Geo. F. Nesbitt, 1877), 15, 7, 13–14.

18. Rev. H. C. Haydn, *Amusements, in the Light of Reason and Scripture* (New York: American Tract Society, 1880), 7, 117–18.

19. Ibid., 124; William Cleaver Wilkinson, *The Dance of Modern Society*, 3d ed. (New York: Funk and Wagnalls, 1884), 7–8, 22–23. Wilkinson's ideas first appeared in *Baptist Quarterly* 1, no. 4 (Oct. 1867): 465–87. Essentially the same content then was expanded into a book, the first edition of which appeared in 1869. Several editions and printings appeared into the twentieth century.

20. Charles G. Finney, "Innocent Amusements," 16 Jan. 1873 (Finney Papers, Box 7, Oberlin College Archives), 6; Charles G. Finney, *Innocent Amusements* (Boston: Willard Tract Repository, n.d.), 13. An unpublished manuscript dated 16 January 1873, in Finney's hand, indicates that he wrote even at a late stage of his life (age eighty-one) because letters to him clearly suggested that the issue had not been put to rest. In Finney's view, the issue would not be resolved until it had been more fully discussed. He attempted to remedy perceived deficiencies in the polemic with his 1873 manuscript and with an article published by Willard Tract Repository of Boston.

21. Finney, *Innocent Amusements,* 28, 4–6.

22. Ahlstrom, *Religious History,* vol. 2, 218; Frank S. Mead, *Handbook of Denominations in the United States* (Nashville: Abingdon Press, 1951), 114. The East Coast and especially the Pennsylvania Ministerium had been the dominant Lutheran center until about 1840. By that time a number of Germans had settled in St. Louis; their ranks included a large cadre of confessional Lutherans from Saxony, one of whom was C. F. W. Walther. He soon emerged as the leader of what came to be known as the Lutheran Church—Missouri Synod. Formed in 1847, that body emphasized pietism, confessionalism, and the German language. Whereas those in the eastern half of the country tended to approve a moderated confessional stance and to use the English language, Walther held fast for what he considered to be a strict, orthodox Lutheran fellowship. By World War I, the Missouri Synod had become the largest single synod within the Lutheran church in this country. Ahlstrom credits "the intellect, erudition, piety, and personality" of Walther as the force behind such tremendous growth. Walther's book opposing dance would, therefore, have served as an authoritative guide for generations of Missouri Lutherans. (Ahlstrom, *Religious History,* vol. 2, 217.)

23. C. F. W. Walther, *Tanz und Theaterbesuch* (St. Louis: Lutherischer Concordia Verlag, 1885), 6, 9.

24. Ibid., 13, 15–17. In a letter to his wife, dated 28 July 1545, Luther objected to the dances in which women and maidens were bare "in front and back." That is, the women's skirts flew up due to the turning of couples. Apparently the Leipzig city council prohibited such dancing in 1511, as did the University of Wittenburg in 1540. See *Luther's Works,* 50, "Letters III" (St. Louis: Concordia Publishing House, 1959), 279.

25. Crane, *Popular Amusements,* 90.

26. Wilkinson, *Dance of Modern Society,* 64; William Herman [Ambrose Bierce], *The Dance of Death* (San Francisco: [H. Keller], 1877), 50, 87, 101–2; Eastman, *May Christians Dance?* 3. Commercial dance halls have been documented in New York from the 1860s. They ranged from "sailor dance-houses," which varied in quality but some of which were vile dives, to Harry Hill's Dance-House. Opened in the late fifties, by 1869, the latter drew men from all walks of life, including "members of Congress and of the Legislature." It appears to have been a type of early taxi-dance hall; a private door admitted the one hundred women free of charge. Though not paid by Harry Hill, they were clearly the attraction for male customers. House rules decreed that each man had to dance and then treat his partner to a drink at the bar following each dance. The women, mostly young girls, were "of a superior class" and well dressed but "started on the road to ruin." See Matthew Hale Smith, *Sunshine and Shadow in New York City* (Hartford, Conn.; J. B. Durr, 1869), 228–29, 435–45, 631–34.

27. Rev. J. R. Sikes, "A Time to Dance," *A Sermon on Dancing,* 2d rev. ed. (York, Pa.: Office of the Teachers' Journal, 1879), 10; Mattison, *Popular Amusements: An*

Appeal, 12; Sylvester F. Scovel, *Popular Corruption, An Address Delivered Before the Students' Christian Association of Washington and Jefferson College* (Pittsburgh: Published by the Association, [1866?]), 25; Rev. S. M. Vernon, *Amusements in the Light of Reason, History and Revelation* (Cincinnati: Walden and Stowe, and New York: Phillips and Hunt, 1882), 113, 118, 121.

28. Haydn, *Amusements, in the Light of Reason and Scripture,* 123. The quote appears in the same decade in Rev. Henry M. Tenney, *Popular Amusements* ([Cleveland? 1889?]), 14; Vernon, *Amusements in the Light of Reason, History,* 121. Whether or not the statistic from a New York police chief derived from personal opinion or systematic study is unknown. Large-scale studies on prostitutes began appearing at least by 1858; for example, Barbara Meil Hobson cites the survey of two thousand prostitutes done in 1858 by William W. Sanger. See Hobson's historical analysis, *Uneasy Virtue: The Politics of Prostitution and the American Reform Tradition* (New York: Basic Books, 1987), 85–109.

29. Although twentieth-century researchers have clarified the motivation for entry into nineteenth-century prostitution, an 1859 essay pointed to the same root cause—low wages. Caroline Dall, an author and a leader in the women's rights movement, described the extent of women's dependency and plight in her book, the first chapter of which was titled "Death or Dishonor." She wrote, "Seven thousand eight hundred and fifty ruined women walk the streets of New York—five hundred ordinary omnibus-loads. They are chiefly young women under twenty, and the average length of the lives they lead is just four years. . . . What drives them to it? The want of bread." See Caroline H. Dall, *"Women's Right to Labor"; or, Low Wages and Hard Work* (Boston: Walker, Wise, and Company, 1860; rpt., *Low Wages and Great Sins,* ed. David Rothman and Sheila Rothman, New York: Garland, 1987), 15. Sanger's 1858 survey of two thousand prostitutes in New York City determined that 61 percent were immigrant women. Hobson's current research affirms that, at midcentury in Boston and Philadelphia as well, immigrant prostitutes outnumbered those born in this country. Hobson concluded that entry into prostitution was "a natural outgrowth of women's social dependencies and weak economic position." See Hobson, *Uneasy Virtue,* 85–109.

30. Jas. H. Brookes, *May Christians Dance?* (St. Louis: J. W. McIntyre, 1870), 138; Rev. Arthur T. Pierson, *The Ethics of the Dance* (Boston: Watchword, 1887), 9; Rev. George C. Heckman, *Dancing as a Christian Amusement* (Philadelphia: Presbyterian Board of Publications, 1879), 9–10; James Laird, *A Sermon on Guides in the Choice of Amusements* (Hollis, N.H.: J. C. Hildreth, 1873), 14; Anna Bartlett Warner, *Tired Church Members* (New York: Robert Carter, 1881), 49–50; Harrell, "Sin and Sectionalism," 157. Warner is the only woman author of antidance treatises known during this period; however, she published extensively in other areas, especially children's fiction. See *American Women Writers,* s.v. "Bartlett, Anna Warner."

31. Haydn, *Amusements, in the Light of Reason and Scripture,* 124.

32. Scovel, *Popular Corruption,* 15.

33. W. E. Penn, *The Upas Tree, or Dynamite in Dancing Exposed* (St. Louis: C. B. Woodward, 1890), 28–29. The first edition of this book probably appeared in 1884.

34. Heckman, *Dancing as a Christian Amusement,* 20–22. Similar expressions can be found in: Crane, *Popular Amusements,* 103; Brookes, *May Christians Dance?* 80, 140; Laird, *A Sermon,* 13; and Wilkinson, *Dance of Modern Society,* 75.

35. In her analysis of prostitution for the period 1820–60, Barbara Meil Hobson writes: "Although the image of fallen woman as innocent victim became literary convention, it did not negate the deep-seated prejudice and condemnation of society toward sexually deviant women. The Victorian code, which dictated that a woman who abandoned her virtue had no place in society, was firmly planted in the middle-class system of values." By contrast, Hobson cites the social-class background of managers and executive committee for the New England Female Moral Reform Society from 1836 to 1860. About two-thirds of the members were from the lower middle and lower classes. The primary objective of the society was to protect "virtuous women" but also to "rescue their fallen sisters." See Hobson, *Uneasy Virtue,* 72, 54–55.

36. *The Black Crook* opened in September 1866 and continued until January 1868, for a total of 475 performances. A stint in 1870 added another 122 performances and the following year 57 more. An 1872 revival ran for twelve weeks. In addition, touring versions proved immensely successful. See a discussion of these shows in Troy and Margaret Kinney, *The Dance* (New York: Tudor, 1926), 231–34, and in Nancy Lee Chalfa Ruyter, *Reformers and Visionaries: The Americanization of the Art of Dance* (New York: Dance Horizons, 1979), 7.

37. Joe Laurie Jr., *Vaudeville: From the Honky-tonks to the Palace* (New York: Henry Holt, 1953), 10–16; Kathy Peiss, *Cheap Amusements: Working Women and Leisure in Turn-of-the-Century New York* (Philadelphia: Temple University Press, 1986), 141–42; Parker R. Zellers, "The Cradle of Variety: The Concert Saloon," *Educational Theater Journal* 20, no. 4 (Dec. 1968): 578–83. Zellers declares that as early as 1856–57 the concert saloon was a common sight along Broadway and the Bowery. By the 1860s such saloons had spread to major cities in the country. Peiss notes that efforts to attract women to the theater began as early as the 1860s and 1870s, but such audiences came primarily from the working classes to see the "variety" or "vaudeville" shows (142–45).

38. John Ashworth, *Strange Tales from Humble Life: A Dancer* (Philadelphia: Henry Longstreet, 1866); Crane, *Popular Amusements,* 97.

39. Ruyter, *Reformers and Visionaries,* 10.

40. Bostwick Hawley, *Dancing as an Amusement, Considered in the Light of the Scriptures, of Christian Experience and of Good Taste* (N.p.: N. Tibbals and Sons, 1877), 51, 55.

41. Rev. John H. Morley, *The Relative Place of Amusements: A Discourse Preached*

at the Congregational Church in Winona . . . (Winona, Minn.: Republican Steam Printing House, 1882), 9; Eastman, *May Christians Dance?* 17.

42. See, for example, the analysis by David Pivar, *Purity Crusade: Sexual Morality and Social Control, 1868–1900* (Westport, Conn.: Greenwood, 1973).

43. Only one of the antidance books mentions the work of the medical and physical training authorities who urged exercise for women. An undated anonymous publication by the American Baptist Publication Society, titled *Dancing: Social Dancing for Purposes of Amusement,* approved Dio Lewis's system but distinguished it from dancing for amusement. See section below in this chapter on "Health and Physical Training Authorities." Mattison, *Popular Amusements: An Appeal,* 15; Sikes, *A Sermon on Dancing,* 8–9; Heckman, *Dancing as a Christian Amusement,* 17; J[ames] W[illiam] Lowber, *The Devil in Modern Society* (Cincinnati: Standard Publishing Company, 1888), 6.

44. Tenney, *Popular Amusements,* 15–16.

45. Rev. Washington Gladden, *Amusements: Their Uses and Their Abuses* (North Adams, Mass.,: James T. Robinson, 1866) 26; Sikes, *A Sermon on Dancing,* 11–12.

46. The single most commonly employed example is the biblical story about Salome's dancing, which, opponents alleged, caused John the Baptist to be decapitated. Therefore, dancing was wrong for a Christian. The example appears in books after the Civil War (see Hawley, *Dancing as an Amusement,* 33) though it first appeared in literature prior to the Reformation.

47. Elder B. H. Carroll, *A Sermon on the Modern Social Dance* (Dallas: Texas Baptist Publishing House, 1877), 7; Tenney, *Popular Amusements,* 9–10.

48. William D. Blanks, "Ideal and Practice: A Study of the Conception of the Christian Life Prevailing in the Presbyterian Churches of the South during the Nineteenth Century" (Ph.D. diss., Union Theological Seminary, Richmond, Virginia, 1960), 234–35, 237–38, 242. According to Blanks's statistics, discipline cases involving dancing, for fourteen urban churches and forty-seven rural churches, totaled thirty-nine for the decade of the 1870s out of eighty-one for the entire century. The practice of discipline became less commonly used by the 1880s.

49. Robert G. Thompson, *Pleas before the Synod of Chicago* (Beloit, Wis.: N.p., 1869). See chapter 6, above, for discussion of George H. Thacher, who criticized church discipline in the Albany synod in the 1840s.

50. Blanks, "Ideal and Practice," 242.

51. Frank E. Block, *Defense of F. E. Block* (Atlanta, Ga.: N.p., 1878), 1–2, 10.

52. That postwar evangelicals still clung to the belief is demonstrated, for example, by the words of the evangelist George Pentecost (1842–1920) when he preached in Minneapolis in 1879: "Under no other circumstances than in a ball room would any pure minded and modest girl allow the same liberties taken with her person by half a dozen different men." See George F. Pentecost, *The Christian and the Ball Room, or, The Essential Evil of the Dance of Modern Fashionable Life* (Minneapolis: Johnson, Smith and Harrison, 1879), 9.

53. Block, *Defense,* 14–15. Blanks's contemporary analysis tends to support Block's assertions.

54. Ibid., 16. Following lengthy debate, the synod voted to sustain Block's appeal. The case marked a turning point in the exercise of church discipline. See Harvey K. Newman, "Notes and Documents," *Georgia Historical Quarterly* 67, no. 4 (Winter 1983): 503–11.

55. Gladden, *Amusements,* 29.

56. Ibid., 5, unnumbered, 17, 23.

57. Ibid., 24–26.

58. Rev. Marvin R. Vincent, *Amusement a Force in Christian Training* (Troy, N.Y.: Wm. H. Young, 1867), 21–23, 15.

59. Rev. C. H. W. Stocking, *Amusements: A Discourse Delivered in the Church of the Epiphany . . . The Chicago Pulpit,* part 3 (1873), 111, 113, 115.

60. O. B. Frothingham, *A Plea for Amusement* (New York: D. G. Francis, 1874), 26, 9, 12, 16.

61. By the time of his book's publication, Gross had been stricken from the rolls of the Lutheran ministry in Pennsylvania for a year, although he had been under suspension for the previous six years. The 1873 suspension had carried the proviso that Gross remain under indictment until such time as he "repent of his errors." Church records do not specify what constituted the alleged false teaching. Since Gross did not have a church of his own, it seems likely that his writing, rather than his preaching, proved to be the bone of contention between him and the Pennsylvania Ministerium. The probable target would have been Gross's book *The Doctrine of the Lord's Supper as Set Forth in the Book of Concord* (1873). It proved a counter-response to one by the Lutheran leader Charles Porterfield Krauth on a central doctrinal issue. Krauth sat on the committee that struck Gross, and Gross undoubtedly knew that Krauth had written his own antidance book in 1851. See chapter 6, above, for further discussion of Krauth.

62. Rev. J. B. Gross, *The Parson on Dancing as It Is Taught in the Bible, and Was Practiced among the Ancient Greeks and Romans* (Philadelphia: Lippincott, 1879; rpt., Brooklyn: Dance Horizons, n.d.), Invocation, unpaged.

63. Ibid., 91. Gross also quotes extensively from *Horatio Smith, Festivals, Games, and Amusements* (New York: Harper, 1847), the preface for which is dated 1831.

64. Gross, *Parson on Dancing,* 13.

65. In this opinion he concurs with those who wrote about dancing for the *Encyclopaedia Americana,* and who pronounced that dancing began as instinctive activity and then evolved into an art, becoming "much cultivated as an elegant amusement in the intercourse of society, and an elegant spectacle in public entertainments." The *Encyclopaedia Americana* carried the same text on dancing for volumes dated 1829–33, 1836, and 1857.

The ninth edition of the *Encyclopaedia Britannica* (1878) carried with it a four-volume supplement titled *Encyclopaedia Americana.* The latter, however, contained no article on dance. The piece on "Dance" in the *Britannica* reflects a more sophisticated view of dance as an expressive art, probably the result of the romantic ballet in Europe. Based on Gross's wide-ranging interests and general erudition, it seems probable that he would have known the 1878 *Britannica* text.

66. Gross, *Parson on Dancing,* 23, 24. In contrast to dance opponents who regularly called forth the oppositional arguments of Cicero and the early church fathers, Gross details the positive historical heritage of dancing in classical antiquity.

67. Ibid., 26–27, 34. See chapter 2, above, for a discussion of the views of Mulcaster and Luther.

68. Ibid., 85.

69. [Robert Tomes], *The Bazar Book of Decorum . . .* (New York: Harper, 1874), 82; Mary J. Safford and Mary E. Allen, *Health and Strength for Girls* (Boston: D. Lothrop, 1884), 36, 7–8. Safford's claim about increased interest in exercise and health is confirmed by the fact that at least five normal schools of physical training were operating by 1890. See Joanna Davenport, "The Normal Schools: Exploring Our Heritage," *Journal of Physical Education, Recreation and Dance,* 65, no. 3 (Mar. 1994): 28.

70. Dioclesian Lewis, "The Health of American Women," *North American Review* 135, no. 313 (Dec. 1882): 507–8. Lewis developed a new system of gymnastics and subsequently established the Normal Institute for Teacher Preparation, which opened in 1861 in Boston. He had attended Harvard Medical School in the 1840s and subsequently practiced medicine. My discussion of the corset controversy does not represent a thorough analysis of all the available evidence. A more complete discussion appears in Valerie Steele, *Fashion and Eroticism* (New York: Oxford University Press, 1985), 161–91. Though her analysis focuses primarily on evidence from England and France, it serves to illumine the points of view surrounding tight lacing.

71. S[ilas] Weir Mitchell, *Fat and Blood: and How To Make Them* (Philadelphia: Lippincott, 1877), 25–26, 41–42, 75ff. Mitchell's book appeared in another edition as late 1905. A second book with a similar title, *Fat and Blood: An Essay on The Treatment of . . . ,* appeared in an eighth edition as late as 1911. Twentieth-century researchers have described the psychological effects of the "cure" upon patients and the concomitant power of the male doctor over the prostrate female. See Barbara Ehrenreich and Deirdre English, *For Her Own Good* (Garden City: Anchor Books, 1979), 131–40.

72. James Caleb Jackson, *Dancing: Its Evils and Its Benefits* (Dansville, N.Y.: F. Wilson Hurd, 1868), 4, 12. The article, which appeared in *The Laws of Life* 9, no. 4 (Apr. 1866): 49–53, was later published in book form.

73. Lewis, "Health of American Women," 503, 505–6.

74. Dudley A. Sargent, "The Physical Development of Women," *Scribner's Magazine* 5 (Jan.–June 1889): 181, 183–84.

75. L[awrence] De G[armo] Brookes, *Brookes on Modern Dancing . . . With An Essay On Etiquette* (New York: N.p., 1867), 3–5, 8, 13.

76. W[illiam] B. DeGarmo, *The Dance of Society*. . . , 3d ed., rev. and corrected (New York: William B. DeGarmo, 1879), 13 (unnumbered). The book's title lists DeGarmo as secretary and treasurer for the Society of Professors of Dancing in New York. In 1865 he had been elected to the Paris counterpart of that organization (160). He is not to be confused with a William Burton DeGarmo, better known in biographical indexes for the era.

77. Allen Dodworth, *Dancing and Its Relation to Education and Social Life* (New York: Harper, 1885; new and enl. ed. with introd. by T. George Dodworth, New York: Harper, [1900?]), 1, 15, 10.

78. Ibid., 10–11, 16–17, 20–23. Dodworth began his teaching career in 1835 and regularly visited Europe to keep abreast of the newest developments in dancing. His lament about the quality of society and dancing in 1885 must be understood as a comparison of contemporary modes with the more decorous behavior of earlier decades. For a more complete perspective on his life and career, see Rosetta O'Neill, "The Dodworth Family and Ballroom Dancing in New York," in *Chronicles of the American Dance*, ed. Paul Magriel (New York: Henry Holt, 1948), 80–100.

79. Dodworth, *Dancing*, 271–72.

80. Mrs. [Sarah Josepha] Hale, *Manners; or, Happy Homes and Good Society All the Year Round* (Boston: J. E. Tilton, 1868; rpt., New York: Arno Press, 1972), 101.

81. Ibid., 104–5, 100, 285.

82. Ibid., 285.

83. *American Women Writers*, ed. Linda Mainiero (New York: Ungar, 1980), vol. 4, s.v. "Sherwood, Mary Elizabeth"; Mrs. John Sherwood, *Manners and Social Usages* (New York: Harper, 1884), 95–102.

84. Mainero, *American Women Writers*, vol. 1, s.v. "Bloomfield-Moore, Clara Sophia Jessups"; Mrs. H. O. Ward [Clara Bloomfield-Moore], *Sensible Etiquette of the Best Society: Customs, Manners, Morals and Home Culture*, 20th rev. ed. (Philadelphia: Porter and Coates, 1878), xii, xvii.

85. Mainero, *American Women Writers*, vol. 2, s.v. "Hall, Florence Marion Howe"; Florence Howe Hall, *Social Customs* (Boston: Estes and Lauriat, 1887), 1–9.

86. [Tomes], *Bazar Book of Decorum*, 89–90. Etiquette books told readers that four musicians were sufficient; pianist and violinist proved to be the mainstays of such ensembles. Musicians were to play both waltzes and quadrilles so that those who objected to the round dances could still participate and enjoy themselves. Ward, *Sensible Etiquette*, 200–201. Allen Dodworth explained that the German was introduced in New York City about 1844. At that time the quadrille was the fashionable dance, he says, but it was known as the cotillion. The German was known in Europe by the same name. To make a distinction, the latter became the "German Cotillion." Eventually the dance was called simply the "German." Dodworth states that the dance required a constant partner change and involved both round dances and figure dances. Dodworth, *Dancing*, 144ff.

87. Sherwood, *Manners and Social Usages,* 99–100; Hall, *Social Customs,* 130.

88. Sherwood, *Manners and Social Usages,* 100; Hall, *Social Customs,* 131.

89. Ward, *Sensible Etiquette,* 226, 202; Hall, *Social Customs,* 134; Sherwood, *Manners and Social Usages,* 101; Eliza M. Lavin, *Good Manners* (New York: Butterick Publishing Company, 1888), 282–83.

90. Ward, *Sensible Etiquette,* 217–18, 201, 204, 223, 224; Lavin, *Good Manners,* 275; [Tomes], *Bazar Book of Decorum,* 225; Sherwood, *Manners and Social Usages,* 97.

91. Ward, *Sensible Etiquette,* 220.

92. Hale, *Manners,* 4; Ward, *Sensible Etiquette,* xviii; [Martha Louise Rayne], *Gems of Deportment and Hints of Etiquette* . . . (Detroit: Tyler, 1882), 249; S. L. Louis [John A. Ruth], *Decorum: A Practical Treatise on Etiquette and Dress of the Best American Society,* 4th ed. (New York: Union Publishing House, and Chicago: Chas. L. Snyder, 1881), 16–17, 20–21.

8 Embattled Fundamentalists and the Rhetoric of Moral Panic: 1890–1929

Right dancing can . . . serve both as an awakener and a test
of intelligence, predispose the heart against vice, and turn
the springs of character toward virtue.

G. Stanley Hall, 1904

Don't go to that dance . . . it is the most damnable, low-
down institution on the face of God's earth. . . . It causes
more ruin than anything this side of hell.

Wm. A. "Billy" Sunday, n.d.

The historian Bernard Weisberger has observed that the evangelical crusades against smoking, drinking, and gambling enjoyed a "certain nobility" in the middle of the nineteenth century. These movements belonged to a general scheme for "improving all human institutions" and ushering in an era of "millennial righteousness." By the end of the century the same issues, including that of dancing, became part of a more complex and problematic social context. Although urban reformers urged the passage of social legislation to solve the problems, conservative and fundamentalist dance opponents still believed that mass evangelism would transform individuals first and society ultimately.[1]

Linking dance opposition with the virtues of pure women, noble mothers, and American patriotism, embattled turn-of-the century fundamentalist preachers and evangelists displayed a fervor that reflected the intensity of their struggle against the forces of "modernism." Continued urban growth, massive immigration, expanding public schools, commercial amusements, black migration north, ragtime music, radical new dances, radio, movies, women in the work force and in revealing dress—all converged to form a society in flux, one that engendered fear and anxiety among dance detractors. Faced with such tumultuous social change, adversaries advanced no new substantive arguments. But their old arguments, typified by the preaching of the popular evangelist Billy Sunday, became strident in tone and descended from the merely sentimental to the vernacular and vulgar in language. Many opponents exhibited a mind-set that the historian Richard Hofstadter has called the "one-hundred percent mentality." In Hofstadter's definition of the term, it referred to "a mind totally committed to the full range of the dominant popular fatuities and determined that no one shall have the right to challenge them."[2]

As dancing increased in popularity, adversaries targeted the latest manifestations of that popularity. Augmenting their claims with sensational statistics, they waged war against the new woman, the new dances, and the new dance institutions of the era—*thé dansants,* dance halls, dance bands, and public school dances. Understanding the adversaries' rhetoric of moral panic necessitates comparing their outlook with the contrasting views of contemporary educators, health authorities, and etiquette writers.

The Context: 1890–1909

In 1898 the Presbyterian cleric Robert P. Kerr (1850–1923) declared from Richmond, Virginia, that the guiding principle for Christian conduct was to "be moved ever by the dear love of Jesus." Kerr wrote *The Dance, the Card Table, the Theatre, and the Wine Cup* in opposition to those perceived evils in society, which some thought to be the "idols" of American culture. Kerr's fellow Presbyterian cleric T. Dewitt Talmadge (1832–1902) called such activities "social dissipations." J. M. Buckley (1836–1920), a Methodist clergyman, observed that the practices of dancing, attending theater, and playing cards provoked constant debate. For Buckley and for others, the distinctions between people of the world and people of God became clear; the former were governed by fashion, the latter by religion.[3] The debate engaged the black church as well.

A black Baptist in Virginia known only as A. Binga Jr. was new to the ranks of published clergy. In 1887 he reported on the "Past and Present Social, Moral and Religious Condition of the Colored Baptists of Virginia" and noted that both "dancing and gaming" were "struggling for birth and recognition in our social circles." Early in the new century, Binga published a short pamphlet on the question whether church members should be disciplined for attending balls and the theater. His opposition reflects the same Bible-based arguments that detractors had put forth for the nineteenth century. Binga's restrained style and tone fit more with the writings of mid-nineteenth-century opponents than with the strident and sensationalist rhetoric of early twentieth-century adversaries. Binga's stance also clearly reflects an evangelical position consonant with that of contemporaries who argued vociferously against worldly dancing and in favor of a personal encounter with Jesus Christ.[4]

Beginning at the end of the nineteenth century, two clear lines of development emerge within the ranks of modern revivalists. These help to explain changes in technique from the "pious soul-winning" of Moody to the "barn storming 100 percent Americanism" of Billy Sunday. On the one hand, the historian William McLoughlin points out that the American revivalist tradition has yielded the model of the "fervent exhorter"—the man with "no education and no formal theological training" but with a clear call to preach the simple gospel. On the other hand, the country has also supported the "evangelistic clergyman," a model descended from Jonathan Edwards and George Whitefield—men with college and seminary training plus "sufficient theological knowledge to entitle them to the doctor of divinity degrees," which many held.[5] Both kinds of revivalist appear in the ranks of dance detractors.

The "Fervent Exhorter"

Typical of the model of the "fervent exhorter" was Samuel Porter Jones (1847–1906). Among the one or two foremost men in a wide field of evangelists at Dwight L. Moody's death, Jones earned the title "the Moody of the South," as a result of his preaching at a Nashville revival in 1885. By the end of his career in 1906, Jones claimed he had converted 500,000 individuals out of a total audience of 25,000,000 listeners.[6] Though he wrote no book on dance opposition, his sermons and anecdotes carry denunciations aimed to spark an audience's attention. Jones, for example, had no time for dancing masters, particularly the French:

> Oh, if I have a contempt for a being in this universe that I cannot reach down to, it is a dancing-master. His only business is to go about through the community despoiling the spiritual interest of children and making them fall in love with giddy worldliness and foolishness that will damn them in the end. . . .
>
> If I was pastor here and had a sister in my church that sent her children to a dancing school, I would turn her out. Not the little children, but the old hypocrite of a mother.

His hyperbole perhaps amused audiences but served only to give dancing a bad name. He maintained that "there is not a family in the city of St. Louis where the father who trains his children for ball rooms and germans can lay his hands upon the head of his daughter and say: 'This daughter will die as pure as an angel.' " In Jones's frame of reference, a lady could not be a Christian and dance. She might dance and be a "perfect lady" but not a Christian. Neither could a gentleman be a Christian and play cards. Jones seemed equally assured of the fact that no town would hire a woman, otherwise qualified for a job, if potential employers knew that she was a "first class dancer."[7]

In the tradition of "theatricality" established by Jones, Milan Bertrand Williams (fl. 1889–1910) flourished as a midwestern itinerant evangelist in the late eighties and during the nineties. He was assisted by the neophyte evangelist Billy Sunday. After 1901, Williams mixed revival preaching with lectures on "sex problems" and, in McLoughlin's words, then "veered off into the perils of immigration and the virtues of the Anglo-Saxons."[8] By the teens of this century, Sunday expanded on the latter theme. Neither man had any time for dancing, not even the square dance.

Williams's 1896 publication *Where Satan Sows His Seed* gave the reader "Plain Talks" on the evils of modern amusements—dance, theater, cards, and wine. However, he considered dancing to be to "some extent" a greater evil than the other amusements. Whereas people who danced had been satisfied formerly with cotillions and country dances, "The blood of young America [now] is too hot for the square dance." According to Williams, devotees of the waltz found the square dance "insipid." He seemed convinced that dancing held an almost addictive delight for those who pursued it. In particular, he declared that dancing held more fascination for women than for men; the latter, he announced, also felt attractions to harlotry, profanity, liquor, and dishonesty. Those who countenanced dancing or the ballroom were counted not as their sister's keeper, but as her murderer. As proof of such claims, Williams offered what appeared to be overwhelming statistics. He declared that, according to the Women's Christian Temperance Union, the latest figures tallying the number of "fallen women" in the country showed a total of 500,000. Of that number, 375,000 said they had been ruined by dancing. Characteristic of the "fervent exhorter" at the century's end, Williams gave no source and no explanation of how his data were gathered.[9]

The "Evangelistic Clergyman"

Although his opposition to dancing points in the same direction as that of Jones and Williams, J. Wilbur Chapman (1859–1918), a Presbyterian, represents the other side of the traditional American evangelist. Chapman had worked with Moody, and when the latter died Chapman emerged as the major figure among revivalists. Educated at Oberlin, Lake Forest College, and Lane Theological Seminary, Chapman had served parish pastorates but continued in evangelistic work until he yielded popular leadership to Billy Sunday in 1912.[10]

In Chapman's 1904 publication *The Christian's Relation to Amusements and the World,* his objectivity and restraint contrast markedly with the approach of Jones and Williams. Chapman asserts that the sins connected with amusements are not the all-consuming evils some would make them to be:

> I am persuaded that all the sins of the church are not to be summed up under the heads of theater-going, card-playing, and dancing, for there may be some in the church who congratulate themselves that they have not been guilty of these things, while, on the other hand, they are quite as grievous sinners in the eyes of God. . . . I think the time has come when we ought, as ministers of the Gospel, let it be known that in our judgment there are many things quite as harmful and possibly more so than the indulgence in the so-called popular amusements. It might be more wicked to gossip than to go to the theater; it might be just as sinful to treat with indifference the character of another as to dance. Let us be right with God in all things rather than to be censorious about a few things.

While Chapman appears to be sensible in his recognition that the perceived behavioral sins connected with participation in amusements are not the most grievous in the world, he nonetheless speaks against dancing for the Christian on the grounds that first-hand testimony, from "all classes and conditions of people," has informed him of the many who have attributed their "downfall" to dancing.[11] Lurking beneath such traditional opposition may have been both a longing and a fear.

McLoughlin observes that both the evangelistic clergymen and the fervent exhorters shared a belief in the "old-time religion" and an opposition to "science, modernism and progressivism." The writings of William Bell Riley (1861–1947), a Minneapolis Baptist who headed the World's Christian Fundamentals Association, exemplify McLoughlin's claim. Riley focused not merely on soul winning but castigated sundry urban practices and beliefs, including dancing, divorce, and the "isms."[12] He saw the "city" as the critical problem of the age. "The great down-town district is more and more becoming a moral sink in which the souls of our daughters are being drowned daily."[13] His moral outrage seemingly knew no bounds when the Minneapolis police chief pointed to the evils of local dance halls: "When the chief of police of my own city says to a fairly representative company of people, 'The dance halls of our municipality are the devil's agency for the work of degraded men and the down-fall of unsuspecting girls, and the deeper condemnation of the scarlet woman,' it is time the public roused itself to a fresh consideration of this same public social custom." Riley's outrage probably emanated from his view that dancing was contributing to the breakup of the American family: "it is a fact that divorce courts are crowded more and more with the very men and women whose domestic fidelity has been destroyed through the unholy influence of the theatre, and the unjustifiable conduct of the dance."[14]

Such sweeping denunciations, when combined with exhortations to abstain totally from dancing, characterized the conservative and fundamentalist dance opponents of the era. Like Riley, they tended to see urban problems almost exclusively in a moral framework. They argued for individuals to mobilize toward improving the city. The need for urban evangelism could, therefore, be linked to urban improvement.

Charges against Dancing: Fallen Women and Other Evils

The two decades at the century's turning found couple dances such as the waltz still popular and continuing to draw the wrath of opponents. Writers denounced the "round dances," the "dances of modern society," or the "modern dances" even though the same dances had been "modern" for several decades. Since the introduction of the waltz early in the century and the polka during the 1840s, no dramatically new ballroom dance had arisen. Even though the older "square dances" proved less objectionable, particularly if done under the chaperonage of parents in a home, staunch adversaries continued to indict the whole of dancing on the grounds that sin is progressive. Square dances led to round dances, and the parlor dance led to the public, society dance.

Although theater dance did not come under widespread indictment, William Dallman (1862–1952), a pastor and later vice-president of the Lutheran Church–Missouri Synod, declared in 1894 that it was not always proper for women to dance, even if they did so alone. He declared dancing in ballet "a shameful thing. [The women] are not far from naked and dance before men for their amusement often in a very indelicate and suggestive position, as you can see from pictures and descriptions." Even long dresses did not necessarily make the dance acceptable. He noted that "the serpentine dances and skirt dances are danced in the longest dresses, and they are as nasty, lewd and indecent as anything can be." Dallman does not say why he found them so objectionable. Neither does he say where or if he actually saw such dancing.[15]

Allowing for no path of moderation, conservative and fundamentalist

opponents declared against dancing primarily on the grounds of its incidental characteristics. They continued themes from earlier decades. Charges
revolved around what some called the "locked" embrace of the closed dance
position. Turn-of-the-century authors pronounced as strongly as ever that
no pure-minded woman would permit a man who was not next of kin to
hold her close, as in the round dances.[16] The threat of such permissiveness
was widespread since men rarely danced with their wives, according to
Williams. Concerns about the breakdown of home, family, and marriage
appeared.[17] Adversaries declared that the appeal of dancing with the opposite sex was the real attraction. In other words, single-sex dancing would have
no devotees. More than one writer called modern dancing nothing more
than "hugging set to music," the purpose of which was "to fan the flame of
passion, to gratify as far as possible an unhallowed lust, to lead the unwary
into lascivious nets."[18] Although these arguments sometimes appeared in
restrained language, more commonly the fears led to the use of vivid and
excessive imagery. For example, W. L. Sanford, vice-president of the Baptist Young People's Union (BYPU), lamented in 1893 from Waco, Texas,
that no reformation of the dance was on the horizon: "Oh! if the liberties
permitted in the ball room were attempted in the parlor, there would be more
jealousy, and anger and strife, and bloodshed than a century of years could
blot out from memory."[19]

Pronouncements about the evil effects of the modern dance continued
to derive from dance opponents' view of women. These writers reaffirmed
the idea that females were either noble and pure or "fallen" and evil. According to Sanford, "whenever a woman submits to liberties to which her fine
sense of prudence warns her are wrong, she descends from the lofty throne
which man's veneration has erected for her in the temple of his heart, and
surrenders her dignity and self-respect, the fitting crown of noblest womanhood."[20] That many women were perceived to have descended from the
"lofty throne" is testified to by the recitation of a favorite statistic, first quoted
by Hiram Collins Haydn in 1880. A typical citation comes from a four-
page tract published by Don Carlos Janes (1877–1944), an evangelist in the
Church of Christ denomination. Attempting to substantiate the wickedness
of dancing, Janes writes: "The testimony of the chief of police of New York
City is that 'seventy-five per cent of the abandoned girls of that city were
ruined by dancing.' "[21]

Use of such statistics becomes increasingly frequent toward the end of
the century, an attempt to prove the degrading effects to which dancing led
women. By 1901 George F. Hall (1864–19?), a Christian minister in Chi-

cago, added more sweeping statistics to the charges against dancing. In his *Pitfalls of the Ballroom,* he decries the vast "army" of naive and sweet girls brought into the ballroom and then sold to the brothel. "There are 500,000 prostitutes in America today according to the best obtainable statistics. What an army of shame! What an array of moral turpitude! What a charge against our boasted civilization!" Readers do not learn the source of his statistic, but the size of such an "army of shame" obviously moved Hall to impassioned rhetoric. He viewed most ministers as weak and spineless when it came to the dancing question in particular and sin in general.[22] A perspective on national prostitution statistics appears in a 1909 publication by a Virginia Baptist cleric, William Wistar Hamilton (1868–1961). According to him, these "creatures themselves" declare that "of the five hundred thousand fallen women in the United States over three hundred thousand started from the ballroom, and that their average life of shame is but six years."[23]

Apart from dancing, a growing and heterogeneous urban population, coupled with industrial expansion, would, in itself, have increased the demand for prostitution. Greater numbers of women working, living on their own, and frequenting public amusements would have increased the pool of potential prostitutes. The rise of the pimp system has been clearly documented for this era. Moreover, the increase in public amusements facilitated more casual social contact between men and women. For example, Dr. E. L. Powell (1860–1933), pastor of the First Christian Church in Louisville, lamented in 1891 that young men and young women, seated side by side, watched *The Black Crook* without a blush: "It is only a few years ago that parents would not think of allowing their daughters to witness a ballet-piece like the 'Black Crook.' But that time has gone by, and young men and maidens sit together and witness almost nudity, without the droop of an eyelid."[24]

On the other hand, social mores would have prevented most middle- and upper-class girls from frequenting the theater and public dance hall. Rules of etiquette governing male-female behavior still prevailed in ballrooms and at elegant dance parties. Thus, to conclude that all dancing inevitably led to prostitution depended upon incomplete information at best and total distortion of facts, figures, and logic at worst. Yet, dance opponents do not speak of such exceptions. Neither are they troubled about the lack of information pertaining to geographical and random sampling for statistics employed. One senses that detractors were grasping for any possible argument to shore up their case. When logic and hard evidence did not obtain, rhetoric became increasingly embroidered with phrases chosen to catch an audience's attention. Thus, James Brand (1834–1899), a Congregational minister in Ohio, quoted Professor Amos R. Wells, who observed that dance, like Gaul, is divided into three parts; it is one-third esthetic, one-third physical, and one-third sensual. Concentrating on the latter, Brand continued, " 'The sensuality of the dance makes bold-eyed women of soft-eyed maidens; it makes swaggering rakes of pure lads; it changes love to flirtation and a game of flippant shrewdness; it makes applicable to manly America Tolstoi's terrific strictures on ignoble Russia. It never creates a Christian; it *discreates* a Christian and creates a sensuality.' "[25]

Although the perceived "sensuality" of the round dances drew the greatest number of attacks, accusations from previous decades were resurrected, though with less frequency. The majority of arguments were tied in some way to preserving women's purity and morality. For instance, scattered references continued to indict the character of dance masters in general and French teachers in particular.[26] The undesirable people at dances, particularly the male "libertines," also bothered some writers.[27] As always, opponents expressed concern about the association of dancing with drinking.[28] Women came under the usual indictment for their dress. According to Hamilton in 1909: "no pure woman can go clad as the dance seems to demand, without doing violence to modesty. This may be all right for ballet girls and variety shows and fast women, but does not betoken that modesty and refinement which every man admires and demands of his wife."[29]

Dance detractors by and large laid the responsibility for morality solely at the feet of women, leading an occasional voice to speak to the issue of a double standard. Hall, for example, actually attacked the prevailing double standard of morality but pointed to women for fostering it:

> There is no question . . . that dancing fosters a double standard of morals. . . . And a double standard of morals is one of the greatest curses of the age.
>
> Why is it that society promptly kicks out and down forever the girl whose sin is found out, while the male demon who debauched her is permitted to continue in the even tenor of his way? Where does such a code find its origin, or its reason to exist? Certainly not in the Word of God. Nor in an innate sense of justice. . . .
>
> The most bitter enemy to fallen woman is woman "unfallen." It ought not to be so. Let us get out of that rut. Let us call for sympathy everywhere for any body and everybody who honestly tries to reform.[30]

While Hall calls for a single standard of morality, suggesting an open, objective, and truly gospel-oriented state of mind, he elsewhere seems to contradict his words as he describes a "pert miss," taught by a "foreign" teacher: "Compare the natural grace of a pure girl taught by a pure mother, with the disgusting affectation and brazen effrontery of a pert miss, who is trained by a foreign dancing-master not to blush."[31]

Other charges in respect to women in previous decades—that they wasted both time and money on dancing—tended to be cited with less frequency in this period. However, William H. Allbright (1849–1907), in an 1891 sermon to the Pilgrim Congregational Church of Dorchester, Massachusetts, attacked the "charity ball" with special vigor. To pay as much for pew rent in church as for dancing parties struck him as a serious problem. But when the expense for such a ball ran so high that only five hundred dollars was netted for charity, priorities seemed out of order. Closely related to the issue of wasting time and money, a new charge claimed that dancing fostered a caste system in society. The Reverend Perry Wayland Sinks (1851–1940) told Chicago Congregationalists in 1896 that he saw tendencies toward a "revival of the hated caste and class distinctions of the old world; only in our day and in this country it is the distinction of 'sets' and 'cliques'—an aristocracy of pretense rather than one of birth." Corroborating Sinks's perception was the commonplace in antidance treatises and etiquette books, stated or implied, that people of the "best society" patronized dancing.[32]

Concern for morality also mixed with health issues for women. Though many men cited the old claim that the activity proved to be no good exercise, one new bit of "evidence" offered in this era resulted in a statistic that also became a favorite of subsequent writers. Preaching at the Wesley Methodist Episcopal Church in South Boston, the pastor, Rev. Dr. Charles Tilton, told listeners: "A careful calculator has estimated that in an evening's program from ten o'clock to two, a good dancer will cover close upon twelve miles."[33] When such a distance was covered by women wearing lowcut dresses in overheated and poorly ventilated rooms, followed by exposure to cold night air, it could be argued that dancing was indeed unhealthful exercise.

Adversaries vigorously reaffirmed the argument that dancing was not only unhealthy but also merely physical. Allbright, for example, wrote that dance attacks the feet. It is no temptation to a "one-legged person!" Presumably responding to theories of evolution, Sinks declared it was a shame that hours were "squandered on a laborious bodily exercise." Quoting an unnamed source, he asserts that, in dancing, " 'monkeys might be trained to display greater agility than we, and bear statelier gravity.' "[34] Extending the excessive rhetoric, Dr. Marion Palmer Hunt (1860–1944) declared in 1897 that some of the best dancers are the "untutored savages, the illiterate negroes and the patients in our lunatic asylums." Hunt's belief that "savages" and inmates of insane asylums made good dancers is reiterated in Hamilton's book over a decade later. Although racism is clearly evidenced, the context implies that the late nineteenth-century practice of invoking Cicero as a dance opponent helped to trigger the excessive statements.[35] The charges also suggest, in part, why conservatives felt increased fear when dancing invaded the public schools.

Among the adversaries' treatises, the earliest references to dancing in the schools come in the nineties. Hunt, for example, decried its spread into "Christian schools":

> Sad to say, dancing is now tolerated if not encouraged in many of our Christian schools. This evil is growing apace. It is encouraging to note that a protest that promises to check this evil is now voicing itself. A Christian school that even tolerates dancing . . . has become largely unchristian. Why should Christians put up the money to build, endow schools, and pay faculties and furnish pupils to have them taught to do that which all the creeds of Christendom denounce as evil and only evil and that has actually been the occasion of the fall of some two-thirds of the more than 200,000 prostitutes in our land.

His reference to the evil in schools pertains primarily to colleges though he declares that dancing had been introduced into high schools as well.[36] Opponents were chiefly concerned that the physical activity of dancing deterred students from pursuing mindful studies. In 1905, William Henry Bates (1840–?), a Presbyterian minister, declared what others felt, namely, that students' primary interest seemed to be "for the education of the wrong end of themselves."[37]

Toward the end of the century, writers also continued to reaffirm that dancing opposed spiritual growth. Surprisingly, dance opponents do not cite statistics in these arguments. No figures appear in the literature to indicate that dancing detracted from church enrollment and attendance. Nonetheless, opponents often stated extravagant claims to make their case. They tended to cast the dancing issue in language that suggested imminent peril to Christianity. The seriousness of their charges resulted in part from a fundamental notion that the Christian church served to civilize and stabilize American society: "The most depraved infidel that ever blasphemed the name of his Maker will not deny the broad, elevating civilizing influences of the church; the most pronounced man of the world will not deny that the virtue of the fireside, the peace and happiness of mankind, the existence of all free institutions, the stability of government itself, depend upon the perpetuity of the Christian church."[38] By far the greatest support for dance opposition came from the contemporary evangelical denominations who had attacked dancing for decades.[39] By contrast, etiquette authorities, most of whom also counted themselves Christians, continued to write as advocates of well-regulated dancing.

The Strict Rules of Etiquette Authorities

A sampling from the ever-increasing store of etiquette books reveals that several trends continued from previous decades. However, the demand for such books now extended beyond the large urban centers. Sara B. Maxwell (1837–1904), an Iowa author, drew from "recognized authorities" when compiling her *Manners and Customs of To-Day,* published in Des Moines in 1890. Acknowledging that etiquette authorities usually addressed city dwellers, Maxwell states her intention "to reach all classes," especially those with limited opportunity to learn the rules of civility. Her book and others of the era make it clear that balls and dancing continued as popular activities of the "best people" in society.[40] As in earlier decades, invitations told guests to come late—at nine or ten in the evening—although some authors wrote that arrivals might continue until the break of day when "attendance at other affairs has made an early appearance impossible." The time to leave could be as late as two or three in the morning. The lady always had the prerogative of deciding when to leave. Hostesses were to avoid overcrowding and provide good ventilation. Wise women had ready supplies to get female guests back on the dance floor in case of emergencies; "cologne, camphor and ammonia" could be used to revive those suffering from "sudden faintness." An astute hostess hired four musicians to play for dancing, though a fashionable ball required a full orchestra.[41] Attention focused on the dancing, which required careful floor preparation, and on the midnight supper. The latter was substantial and, according to one authority, "Champagne is always served."[42]

Female dance devotees who read the etiquette authorities learned that they should not dance too often with the same man; that they must be introduced to partners prior to dancing; that they should not walk around the ballroom by themselves; and that they certainly must not "sit with a man in obscure corners." Such behavior was both "ill-mannered and indiscreet." An indication of more liberal rules for women comes from a 1909 book stipulating that girls must be protected from untoward circumstances such as being out in a cab with a male escort and having the cab break down at 2:00 A.M. On the whole, the etiquette books still prescribe strict rules for behavior between the sexes with respect to introductions, accepting dances, chaperonage, and the like. Continuing the long-held belief that public events meant open admission, ladies were told absolutely to avoid public masquerade balls.[43]

Although the activities open to females were expanding in the early twentieth century, girls and women still needed to know how to dance and to protect their reputations. The author who styled herself a "Woman of Fashion" liberally decreed in 1909 that a girl must not sit out more than one hour with a young man. Nor should she dance more than seven times with the same man. To women who did not dance well, she advised giving up balls "at once." To compensate, they were to find their "own sphere and adorn that." Thus, vestiges of the earlier notion about women's proper "sphere" remained. An 1891 book that purported to serve as a "Practical Guide to Deportment, Easy Manners, and Social Etiquette" stated plainly that a wife "Owes first Duty to Home." Clearly, despite the alleged and actual sins of the "city," etiquette writers continued to maintain a strict code that protected females and held them up as the guardians of morality. In fact, the "Woman of Fashion" closes her chapter on chaperones with the line, "Shelter the girls."[44]

Social arbiters also retained a belief that manners and morals were inseparable, and both were necessary to Americans. Some writers still made explicit connections with religion. For example, Maud Cooke's (fl. 1890s– 1907) 1896 manual *Social Etiquette, or, Manners and Customs of Polite Society* told readers that, even though society was divided on the merits of dancing, "After all, 'the ball-room is a more fitting field for a display of the Christian graces than most Evangelical people are willing to admit.' "[45] Corroborating a similar viewpoint, a 1907 manual titled *Correct Social Usage* pointed out that "Society's etiquette expresses the soul's courtesy. It is the coin of the realm of good breeding, and the coin may be minted in each individual whenever the right molds are found." True etiquette also came from the heart; merely following correct rules could be "cold and lifeless," making individuals into nothing more than "mere social puppets." Such a command of correct behavior did not come with birth; it had to be learned. Since Americans' weak point was the exhibition of good manners, the author recommended that "the curriculum of the regular day school should be supplemented by the graceful exercises of the school for dancing and deportment." The ultimate goal became the ability to display good manners unselfconsciously.[46] The Unitarian minister Frederic Dan Huntington (1819–1904), later an Episcopalian bishop, even titled his 1892 book *Good Manners a Fine Art*. In it he links that art with Christianity, which in turn is the basis for morality, a commonly held view.[47] While the majority of etiquette authorities included dancing among the polite accomplishments necessary for good society, a few continued the minority trend from earlier decades that clearly opposed dancing because it was morally and spiritually objectionable.[48] Dance instructors did not, of course, agree with such a view. In fact, they were expanding their notion of dancing to encompass a more explicitly acknowledged expressive realm, a movement that appealed especially to women.

Developments in Dancing, Dressing, and Health

The 1890s gave rise to an increasing emphasis on the healthful and aesthetic qualities of dancing. Advocates of the Delsartean system of physical culture urged its advantages in improving posture and natural movement, providing light rhythmic exercise, and developing individual expressive qualities. Private schools of oratory and elocution, as well as women's colleges, adopted Delsartean content and techniques in the late nineteenth century. In the process, American Delsartism helped pave the way for the admission of dancing to public schools and colleges.[49]

Early and sustained efforts to incorporate healthful and expressive dancing into a school curriculum occurred at Harvard and in Dudley Sargent's private Normal School of Gymnastics. By the eighties and nineties, the value of gymnastics had become so widespread in colleges for both men and women that some observers, such as Sargent, saw a need to train teachers who could spread the value of physical training, including dancing, to other colleges, and, ultimately, to the public schools.[50] In 1894 Sargent invited Melvin Ballou Gilbert (1847–1910) to become an instructor in aesthetic dancing at Harvard's Summer School of Physical Training and at Sargent's own school. They called the course "Esthetic Calisthenics" to deflect criticism from dance opponents.[51]

According to Gilbert's biographer, Eugenia Everett, one of his former pupils called the course work a kind of " 'modified ballet' "; toe dancing and " 'the more intricate movements' " were apparently removed. Gilbert himself described aesthetic dancing as "systematically arranged exercises in the elementary principles of the art of dancing, coupled with a harmonized method of arm, head and body movements." An emphasis on mind-body unity aimed to achieve an expressive value that Gilbert believed should not be eclipsed by sheer physical virtuosity. Gilbert's "Esthetic Calisthenics" was the first course in the country to "disseminate" a dance technique formerly reserved for professional dancing girls who trained for the stage. Gilbert wrote about his philosophy of aesthetic dancing and its benefits to the whole person, and his essay on this topic appeared in 1903 in a book titled *Athletics and Out-Door Sports for Women.*[52] It heralded the new century's concept of a healthy, athletic woman. The notion was enlarged by writings of women doctors, by popular journals, and by the new psychology fostered by G. Stanley Hall.

Notable among the publications urging exercise for women was Dr. Anna Mary Galbraith's (1859–19??) 1895 book titled *Hygiene and Physical Culture for Women,*[53] which provided dramatic contrast to Dr. Silas Weir Mitchell's "rest cure." She observes that women had accepted ill health as natural to their sex, a point Catharine Beecher had noted some fifty years earlier. By contrast, Galbraith cites Dio Lewis's article on the health of African women and, presumably, draws on her own observations, made in Vienna, regarding the vigor of peasant women. Though an advocate of exercise, Galbraith points out that dancing involves only the lower limbs and is not controlled by frequency. Nonetheless, she asserts that dancing could be a profitable exercise were it performed in more hygienic circumstances. Her comments confirm the arguments of dance opponents. In Galbraith's words: "As it is, the dance takes place in an overcrowded, ill-ventilated room, the woman is not properly dressed to take any exercise at all, and it is carried to excess. Hence, women are carried out of the ballroom in a fainting condition, and, occasionally someone drops dead." Accordingly, Galbraith recommends dress reform for women and stresses the critical importance of regular exercise.[54]

In the 1890s even the *Ladies' Home Journal* was urging outdoor sports, divided skirts, and looser corsets. By the turn of the century, the increasing scope of physical activity for women included cross-country walking, swimming, skating, rowing, running, lawn tennis, field hockey, fencing, bowling, track athletics, and basketball. Though knee-length bloomers had become the accepted uniform for basketball, tennis might still be played in long skirts.[55]

Forceful arguments for an "artistic and sensible" street attire acknowledged the results of a symposium on women's dress that had appeared in *The Arena* for 1892. Participants had agreed that fashion heretofore ruled that woman be garbed simply to make herself appealing to men. They maintained, "Fashion says that the chief use of woman is to exhibit dry goods fantastically arranged on her person." Invoking the catechism and declarations about the "chief duty" of man, symposium participants argued that women had been forced to dress as though their "chief duty" in life was not service to humanity but merely to "'stand and wait.'" Participants angrily pointed out the double standard of morality that was created when one sex was clothed so as to reshape and accentuate body parts for the sake of eroticism and admiration:

> Woman is not hallowing her Creator's name, she is not glorifying her Maker, when she tacitly accuses Him of bad taste in the formation of her body, and by her clothing interferes with the normal working of His wonderful mechanism. To clothe human beings on the principle that the form of one sex is more immodest than that of the other, is to perpetuate a "double standard of morality." To emphasize the fact of sex, thrusting it constantly and conspicuously upon the attention, is to cultivate pruriency and vice in society.[56]

Although hemlines did not rise until after the first decade of the twentieth century and corsets still encased women wearing street clothes, the advent of the modern "athletic girl" represented the beginning of the eventual demise of detractors' arguments that dancing harmed women's health. Other developments revealed new insights about dancing as more than merely physical.

G. Stanley Hall's (1847–1924) pioneering work, *Adolescence,* which appeared in two volumes during 1904, points to a holistic view of human beings rather than the traditional mind-body dualism that dance opponents' stressed. His concept of the body emphasizes the importance of motor development with respect to the formation of character. The contrast of Hall's views with those of the dance opponents becomes dramatic when he cites the aesthetic proportions and physical condition of "unspoiled savages" and compares them with the bodily proportion and vigor of "civilized" people. "Their women are stronger and bear hardship and exposure, monthly periods and child birth better."[57]

Foreshadowing his later advocacy of dancing, Hall stresses the integration of physicality with intelligence and looks to the cultural past, to the expressive value of folk dances. He concludes that dancing may be, in fact, the "most liberal of all forms of motor education." Although he lauds national dances, Hall laments the deterioration in expressive quality of the contemporary ballroom dances, "too often stained with bad associations." For the sake of young people, adults needed to revive the dance to its full expressive potential.[58]

No one did more in the early years of this century to bring Hall's vision to fruition than Dr. Luther Halsey Gulick (1865–1918), a medical doctor, educator, and early leader in physical training. He not only wrote about the value of dance but actually implemented folk dance curricula into public schools. Following more than a decade of teaching in the YMCA Training School at Springfield, Massachusetts, Gulick moved into the New York public school system during the first decade of this century. As director of physical training, he coordinated curricular activities, including a model unit on folk dancing. Gulick also promoted folk dance festivals and wrote prodigiously on the value of dancing, athletics, play, health, and morality.[59]

The Context: 1910–19

The "New Physical Education" and Dance Curricula

Gulick's book *The Healthful Art of Dancing* was published by Doubleday in 1910. A pioneering analyst of dance, Gulick wrote at a time when America was dance-mad but largely ignorant of the activity as art. Espousing the same themes that Gilbert and Hall had sounded—the joy, health, beauty, and expressive value in dancing—Gulick pointed to the narrow concept that most people held: "In America we have so completely forgotten the deeper possibilities of the dance that the word in general use has come to have but one meaning, namely, a man and a woman holding each other and performing an exceedingly simple whirling movement of music set in four-four or three-four time."[60] His words suggest that most dance opponents merely reacted to the word "dance" and/or to the outward appearance of contemporary dancing.

Gulick, on the other hand, could not be satisfied with conventional ideas about dancing nor with the public's lack of concern for immigrant heritage. He lamented in 1910 that Americans had only emphasized immigrants' economic value and had not "understood, cared for, or even thought about the precious social heritage they might give us—a heritage of art, of story, of music, of the dance." Folk dancing, in Gulick's view, provided an important avenue for maintaining that critical "joy and happiness" vital to living. Americans lived, not in isolation as individuals, but in communities as social groups. Further, due to the steady stream of immigration, Americans had become a uniquely "cosmopolitan people." Since the nation's schools aimed to educate all the children of all the people, Gulick urged that folk and national dancing be part of the curriculum; such dancing provided social, moral, and aesthetic benefits for rich and poor, as well as for farm and city youth.[61] Gulick's philosophical analysis spoke to the expressive quality of dance in its essence:

Dancing is not only the most universal of the arts, but the mother of all art. Out of the rhythm of body-movements has grown the sense of rhythm and balance that underlies art as portrayed in music, sculpture, architecture, painting.

Dancing is a language, particularly of the feelings. Like other forms of language, it is a means, not an end; a vehicle, not a load, a possibility, not a value. It may express that which is good or that which is bad, the pure or the impure. The value lies in the "worth-whileness" of that which is said.

He went on to analyze dance in its imitative, symbolic, interpretative, and pure art forms—including the work of Isadora Duncan.[62]

Although Gulick's analysis of dance as an art was remarkable for 1910, he was not alone in his advocacy of dance in education. Gulick's friend and professional colleague Dr. Thomas D. Wood (1865–1951) published his views on physical education in 1910 in *The Ninth Yearbook of the National Society for the Study of Education*.[63] An apologist for a view that considered dance a desirable part of one's total education, Wood pointed out that recent developments in psychology and physiology had "shown the more vital and intimate interdependence between the different aspects of life, which are called physical, intellectual, and moral." Echoing Hall, Wood declared, "Motor sensation is the great cornerstone in the foundation of human education." Acknowledging this fact as well as the need for a new American program of physical education, Wood decreed that the proper subject matter of such curricula ought to be play, games, dancing, swimming, outdoor sports, athletics, and gymnastics. Dancing, uniquely, held expressive value. When it was taught "as a form of expression of worthy ideas and feelings," and connected with the other arts, then dancing contributed to total education most significantly. Its health and recreative benefits combined with its expressive values.[64]

Time was required for Wood's plans to be implemented in public schools nationwide. In the meantime, support for dance education came from contemporary teachers of the art. In 1914, Emil Rath published the first edition of his *Aesthetic Dancing*, in an attempt to "extend the work begun by the late Mr. Melvin B. Gilbert." With an eye to a larger cultural context, Rath suggests a "renaissance" of dance: "Dancing is rapidly becoming a universal and popular art-form of expression. In all countries there seems to be taking place a renaissance of dancing, a reawakening of the love for rhythmic movements."[65] Louis H. Chalif's (1877–19??) ballet primer, *Text Book of Dancing*, also appeared in 1914. Whereas Rath's work presented a modified ballet, Chalif's presented classical ballet, as well as a section on standard ballroom dancing.

Later editions included sections on Greek dancing and toe dancing. In addition, Chalif published books on folk dancing in the 1920s. His books were sold by the Chalif Normal School of Dancing in New York City. It was in New York that the author had been befriended by Luther Gulick and hired to teach dancing in the local public schools during the first years of this century. His private studios represented the early American development of ballet as an art taught mainly in that venue rather than in the public schools.[66] In yet another approach to dance education, Elizabeth Burchenal (1877–1959), who worked first under Gulick in the New York City schools and continued in the system until 1916, originated the American Folk Dance Society the same year. She also organized and served as the first chairperson of another national group, the Playground and Recreation Association's Folk Dance Committee.[67] Though many other individuals subsequently contributed to the growth of dance education in the country, Burchenal, Chalif, Rath, Gulick, and Wood led early twentieth-century educational efforts, both public and private, to teach American girls and boys the joys of rhythmic motor expression in a context that was both healthful and moral.

A surge of legislation requiring physical education in the public schools coincided with publications and curricula produced by these early leaders. After 1914 states increasingly passed laws favoring the broad program of physical activities that Wood recommended. Such laws gained adherents, in part, as a result of the new objectives formulated for American public schools. By 1918 the seven "Cardinal Principles of Secondary Education" were enunciated. Striving to achieve the goals of "ethical character," "health," and "worthy use of leisure," physical education proponents pushed their curricula, including dancing, for both boys and girls.[68]

New Dances and the New Woman

As school leaders and reformers expanded their ideas about dance and education, the new century also saw radical developments in popular dancing. In every way the new dances of the immediate pre–World War I era differed dramatically from the ballroom traditions of the previous century. Ragtime music from New Orleans and St. Louis, with its syncopated rhythms and stop-time beat, upstaged the popularity of the staid waltz, with its regular metrical markings. The black tradition also brought in torso, hip, shoulder, and head movements. The turkey trot, grizzly bear, Texas Tommy, and similar new dances allegedly were spawned in "red-light districts" with thriving saloon–dance halls. Adversaries believed that the dances represented a new low in social dancing.[69]

Changes in urban living and in class distinctions fostered the unprecedented popularity of dancing between 1910 and 1914. The need for urban recreational centers for masses of people meant that enterprising capitalists increasingly opened dance halls and dance academies. Working-class women and men tended to frequent the new public dance halls, and members of the middle and upper classes enjoyed the growth of cabarets after 1910. The context fostered a new permissiveness that enabled both sexes to view dancing and to enjoy drinking in each other's company. During the pre–World War I years, exhibition dancing gained more devotees, and urban cabaret owners responded by adding dance floors for their customers. Eventually even conservative hotels opened dance floors, including roof gardens, and the long afternoon tea dance immediately became fashionable. The glamour and excitement surrounding the new urban institutions attracted respectable young women with no chaperones even though many watchful mothers and moralists decried the development.

Although Irving Berlin's popular song of 1911, "Everybody's Doin' It Now," was a response to the grizzly bear, the title's claim applied to dancing in general during the prewar years. F. Leslie Clendenen of St. Louis titled his 1914 instructional manual *Dance Mad.* Statistics from the era suggest that dancing was indeed as popular in Milwaukee or Springfield as in Chicago and New York. The new dances had no rigid form, could be learned quickly, and did not require perfect performance, making public dance facilities attractive to those who had both the urge to try them and the price of admission. Boundaries that had previously separated blacks from whites, men from women, and upper from lower classes began to erode as more women patronized public dances and the black population of northern cities rose dramatically.[70]

With the exception of the tango, from Latin America, the dances all derived from American culture. Fittingly, an American couple became the public's hero and heroine. The popularity of Vernon and Irene Castle signaled a general consensus that the new dances ought to be adorned with respectability. Posture, style, and etiquette may not have been seen in the average dancer of the era, thus helping to give the new dances a bad name, but the Castles changed the look of the tango and other new forms. They displayed skill, elegance, and propriety in their dancing and brought a new feminine ideal to the American performance scene.

Irene Castle embodied the "New Woman"—the twentieth-century successor to the modern, athletic girl of the nineties and the turn of the century who had exercised and danced in her gymnasium bloomers and middy blouse. But Castle, ever the athletic ingenue, was chic as well as respectable in her dress. She presented a "natural" figure rather than one that was corseted and artificial. She bobbed her hair but still wore a hat. Her skirts didn't touch the floor but she kept her legs together when she danced; she executed no high kicks as the ballet girls did on stage. She danced with skill but under the direction and tutelage of her husband; she was not a single, professional woman nor was she just a dancing girl on stage. Her image of chic plus propriety helped to make her performance of the new dances acceptable, despite their unsavory origins. Castle herself declared that she and Vernon got their " 'new dances from the Barbary Coast. Of course, they reach New York in a very primitive condition, and have to be considerably toned down before they can be used in the drawing room.' " Moreover, Irene Castle was obviously healthy. Her dancing performances distinguished her dramatically from the mid-nineteenth-century women who considered invalidism to be normal. Not only did Castle perform, she also taught and wrote about manners and model dancing.[71]

The 1914 book *Modern Dancing,* the title page of which gave "Mr. and Mrs. Vernon Castle" as the authors, contained information about dance position, steps, styling, and etiquette. The book was not only an instructional manual but an apologia for the new dances. The introduction, by Elizabeth Marbury, who urged the Castles to open their "Castle House" in New York City, points out that dancing offered no more temptations than other modern pastimes: "Surely there cannot be as great moral danger in dancing as there is in sitting huddled close in the darkness of a sensational moving-picture show or in following with feverish interest the suggestive sex-problem dramas." Marbury recommended that dancing be presented as "healthful exercise and as a fitting recreation." Moreover, it was the "women of every city" whom she charged with responsibility for opening up dance halls for young people, where they "can dance to good music under refined supervision." The Castles declared that the new dances could be graceful and elegant, if they were well executed. They also observed that the evil seen could well reside in the mind or eye of the viewer: "The vulgarity of a dance lies always as much in the mind of the dancer as in the steps, and a suggestive dance is inevitably the outcome of an evil thought, or a lack of knowledge of the finer and better way to dance."[72]

Contemporary etiquette books confirmed the popularity of dancing and urged the kind of refinement the Castles displayed. Florence Howe Hall's (1845–1922) *Good Form for All Occasions* (1914) recommended the new *thé dansant* as a convenient way for receiving friends and giving the debutante her "coming out" party. But Hall cautioned guests against a possible encounter with whirling "dervishes": "While the present tango craze lasts this will sometimes be difficult. With old and young spinning about the room like so many dancing dervishes, the visitor must thread her way warily between the couples, lest she be run down as by a motor-car."[73] Although wanting to protect the lady's reputation, Hall approved the "tango and other new dances" as modified—presumably by the Castles:

> When . . . first introduced, there was a great deal of unfavorable criticism of the method of holding the partner, and of the "shaking and wiggling" motions of the body. The latter was a consequence, it is said, of the slow movement of the music. This rendered it difficult to dance without a swaying accompaniment. By making the tempo a little more rapid it has been found possible to eliminate the last feature, and good dancers have proved that the tango, one-step, and the like can be executed well and gracefully without holding the partner too closely. It is evident that the new dances have been greatly modified, and that they will not be given up at present.[74]

Other new trends in dancing are reflected in Hall's advice that ladies should not refuse to dance with a man who "breaks in" unless her partner refuses to let her go. Stag lines were appropriate, though only at private parties and subscription affairs where people would be known to each other. Since public dances accepted anyone who paid admission and "no one under the age of Methuselah is immune from the present craze for dancing," Hall still felt the need to protect women from undesirable companions.[75] Yet the new custom of "stag" lines and "breaking in" signaled an increased casualness in male-female relations. The new moving picture show, which permitted both sexes to sit cozily together in the dark, pointed to the same liberalization of social custom. Altogether, clothes, dances, balls, dance halls, and commercial amusements contributed significantly to the emergence of an American woman in transition.

No longer were females kept completely in their "sphere" at home, excluded from colleges or universities. No longer did the average middle-class woman consider physical and mental debilitation to be expected of her gender. The second decade of the century saw modern women working outside the home in a variety of jobs.[76]

With better health and more appropriate clothing, they displayed more athletic interest. As early as 1909, nearly half the midwestern colleges and universities had intercollegiate sports for women. Even in some high schools, girls participated in athletic contests, notably basketball and field hockey, and also in dance. By 1920 most youth remained in school well into their teen years, which meant that the majority of American girls probably experienced some kind of dancing in their physical education programs.[77]

A further indication of women's new confidence in their own goals and interests comes from divorce statistics of the era. Mary P. Ryan reports that by the 1920s, one in six marriages ended. After the turn of the century, women increasingly cited as the cause of their divorce the failure of the marriage to provide for their personal fulfillment.[78]

To many observers in the country, the new woman seemed out of control. When females could earn their own money, they could take public transportation to public amusements and mingle as well as dance with any manner of "undesirable" companions. They could learn new ideas and values, aspire to new roles and circumstances. Prominent among the vocal upholders of traditional roles for women were the fundamentalist clergy. Within this cadre of spokesmen, no one shouted louder, to bigger audiences, than did the man who called himself "God's mouthpiece"—William A. Sunday.

New Adversaries and New Allegations

"Billy" Sunday (1863–1935) began as a baseball player in Iowa and evolved into the twentieth century's premiere "fervent exhorter." With a high school education, a religious conversion, a gift of gab, and a sense of theatricality, Sunday became the most prominent evangelist in America between 1906 and 1918. When his biographical sketch was written for *Who Was Who in America,* he had reportedly preached to more people—estimated at eighty million—than any other single man in the history of Christianity. Daily newspapers reported the number of converts at his revivals as avidly as modern sportswriters print baseball statistics.

Sunday appealed to the average man and woman in America. He embodied a popular male ideal—anti-intellectual, athletic, Anglo-Saxon, midwestern, and rural. He entertained audiences with coat off, tie thrown away, and sleeves rolled up. His energy, physical gyrations on the speaker's platform, and gifts of oratory demonstrated to all present that he embodied a "real, he-man" brand of Christianity. After he was converted, Sunday gave up all the stereotypical male vices—drinking, cursing, smoking, and chasing women. He gave proof to the notion that a conversion transforms the individual. In Sunday's case, the transformation was moral, not intellectual. According to the historian Richard Hofstadter, the emergence of the "one-hundred percent mentality" can be traced in Sunday. Such a mind-set tolerated "no ambiguities, no equivocations, no reservations, and no criticism."[79] Sunday's sermons linked dance opposition, prohibition, patriotism, pure women, motherhood, and morality. He preached a fundamentalist religion and a fundamentalist Americanism. His successes, as measured by audience attendance, indicate that the majority of American men and women probably agreed with his ideas. Between 1906 and 1918, Sunday held "city-wide revivals" in ten of the country's top fifteen most populous cities. With continued success, Sunday came to believe that he had a divine mission to lead America against all forces of evil then assaulting the country. Dancing and the modern woman constituted part of that evil.[80]

Sunday's "Plain Talk to Women" amounted to a series of exhortations aimed at praising marriage and motherhood while denigrating any other female endeavor. His language reveals the descent into the vernacular and vulgar that attracted audiences in the early part of the century: "Don't you go with that young man; don't you go to that dance. . . . I say, young girl, don't go to that dance; it has proved to be the moral graveyard that has caused more ruination than anything that was ever spewed out of the mouth of hell." Sunday believed his words had to be strong to counteract the attractions pulling the contemporary young girl away from her true, Christian role:

> I believe there is something unfinished in the make-up of a girl who does not have religion. The average girl today no longer looks forward to motherhood as the crowning glory of womanhood. She is turning her home into a gambling shop and a social beer-and-champagne-drinking joint, and her society is made up of poker players, champagne, wine and beer drinkers, grass-widowers and jilted jades and slander-mongers—that comprises the society of many a girl today. She is becoming a matinee-gadder and fudge-eater.[81]

Not content to lambaste single women, Sunday charged that married women who shrank from maternity did so for the love of "fine garments" and opportunities to flirt at social functions. The great goal in life for women should be to marry and have children. Sunday had no time for "society women" who abdicated such responsibilities. However, he cautioned young girls against marrying "infidels" or the wrong men; such a fate proved worse than remaining an "old-maid." Confident in the goal he had set, Sunday declared, "All great women are satisfied with their common sphere in life and think it is enough to fill the lot God gave them in this world as wife and mother." Continuing the biblical frame of reference, Sunday told female audiences that, with Jesus, they could save the world, but on the side of the devil, they would "damn" it. It remained for women to choose the high path to purity and morality. Reiterating the nineteenth-century formula that women plus homes equaled power and satisfaction, Sunday stratified the several planes of power, telling females that they could hold the country's destiny in their hands: "Our homes are on the level with women. Towns are on the level with homes. What women are our homes will be; and what the town is, the men will be, so you hold the destiny of the nation." Extending their power to encompass the whole of western culture, Sunday asserted that the "downfall" of their gender proved the ruin of Greece and Rome. It followed, therefore, that American women had to stand as the last bastion of civilization. "The virtue of womanhood is the rampart wall of American civilization. Break that down and with the stones thereof you can pave your way to the hottest hell, and reeking vice and corruption."[82]

Sunday's "Plain Talk to Women" as well as his unpublished sermon on "Amusements" demonstrate the truth of Hofstadter's characterization that Sunday evinced the "one-hundred percent mentality." The sermon on "Amusements" survives in notes only, suggesting that Sunday gave the talk so frequently and warmed to it so easily that a full prepared text was unnecessary.[83] To Sunday, dancing and cards were even greater enemies to society than the saloon. Though his reasoning is not clear on the point, dancing apparently posed the greater evil because of its immoral character. Indicting the old "round dances" as well as the modern dances of the twentieth century, Sunday declared that even in the square dance, the position of "corners" was such that it could not be "tolerated." In sum, dancing proved to be a "HOT-BED" of "IMMORALITY" that he denounced "UNFLINCHINGLY."[84]

Sunday's "success" in changing listeners' attitudes can be measured to some degree by the converts, or "trail-hitters," who came forward to shake his hand, making public their declaration for Christianity. Sunday's all-time record number of converts was reached in the 1917 ten-week New York City campaign, when a total of 98,264 was tallied. According to McLoughlin, Sunday himself claimed that he had preached to 100,000,000 people, even in the days before radio and sound amplification, and the estimate may not have been far off. In the twenty most successful rallies of Sunday's career, he attracted a grand total of 593,004 "trail-hitters." Considering that Sunday held "almost 300" revivals during a career spanning four decades, his impact on the American public becomes immense. But, following the New York campaign, Sunday's light began to fade. It was observed that, "From sinful New York, a revivalist could only go downwards." American society was changing; no subsequent big-city revivals were held for the next thirty years in this country.[85] Yet Sunday was not an anachronism in his own time. Plenty of lesser-known "fervent exhorters," "evangelistic clergy," and local parish pastors preached the same themes; they simply did not command the national recognition that he did. Their publications against dance, however, made them potent in their own day and their messages accessible in later decades.

The books published between 1910 and 1919 that opposed dance, in whole or in part, present a breadth of opposition from around the country and from several denominations. Compared with the nineteenth century there was a marked decline in Presbyterian and Congregational authors and a rise in Methodist writers. Known antidance publications from this decade total eighteen books, from sixteen authors; these include six Methodist and three Lutheran writers. The latter were part of the increased immigration from Scandinavian countries in the later nineteenth century, many of whom settled in the rural Midwest.[86]

Most of the antidance treatises mention dancing and/or amusements in their titles, indicating that the issue remained as vital for many Christians as it had been in the 1840s and 1850s. However, the focus had shifted slightly. Formerly the question had been whether or not any participation in amusements was permissible. In the twentieth century, the issue became which commercial amusements were allowable. Those targeted as questionable were dancing, theater, cards, and movies.

Arguments against dancing concentrated on its performance as a purely social activity. No antidance books of the period mention folk dance, aesthetic dance, or theater dance, despite the research, books, and programs that expanded people's ideas about dance during the first decade of the century. The adversaries' concentration on only one kind of dancing indicates that opposition followed traditional patterns. Opponents also tended to be insular in their argumentation. For example, the 1913 book by Warren A. Candler (1857–1941), a Methodist bishop, was titled *Theater-Going and Dancing Incompatible with Church Membership*. It is largely a reprint of an 1872 address by the Episcopal clergy of Virginia to their parishes; it appeared anonymously but has been attributed to C. W. Andrews. Candler is listed as the compiler for the 1913 book but his preface is dated 1884. He included in the volume statements by church boards and bishops from several denominations during the 1860s and 1870s. Similarly, *The Devil in Modern Society*, a 1918 publication by a Disciples of Christ minister, James William Lowber (1847–1930), is merely the tenth edition of a book first published in 1888.[87] Although the book has some additional content beyond that of the first edition, the essay on dance remains exactly the same despite a thirty-year difference in time and radical changes in style of dancing, ladies' social roles, and women's dress.

The consistent use of generalized terms such as "the dance," "modern dance," or the "round dances," conveys to readers the impression that all dance fell under indictment. For instance, when Carl Edin Nordberg (1880–1926), a Lutheran minister, spoke to the young people of his church in Marinette, Wisconsin, in 1914, he confidently declared that "it is quite generally conceded among serious Christian people that all our modern dances must be classified among sinful amusements." His subsequent mentions of "the modern round dances" such as the shottische and the waltz, as well as the unhealthful environment produced by hot air and "gaslight," suggests that Nordberg's references were passé by the time of the book's second edition in 1922. The new dances might not have been popular in Marinette in 1914, but they surely would have been widely practiced in Minneapolis by the time the second edition was produced by the Augsburg Publishing House. Nordberg was not alone in his anachronistic references.[88]

Authors' reliance upon prior context, statistics, language, and arguments becomes most obvious in accusations pertaining to the immorality of dancing. The Reverend Gulbrand G. Belsheim (1871–1930) of Mason City, Iowa, told ministers assembled in 1914 for the state's District Pastoral Association of the Evangelical Lutheran Church that "the dance is the leading feeder of the divorce court, the brothel or house of illfame, our houses of correction and homes of rescue." Adding more power to his attack, Belsheim provided "Statistical Evidence" by quoting from William Dallman (1862–1952), whose 1894 book was titled *The Dance:*

> "It is a startling fact, but a fact nevertheless, that two-thirds of the girls who enter dancing schools are ruined before the year is out, and that three-fourths of all outcasts among women had a man's arm about them for the first time when they were young girls at a social dance. I know of a select dancing school where in the course of three months eleven of its victims became brothel inmates. Of 200 brothel inmates with whom I talked personally, 163 regarded the dancing school and the ball-room as the direct cause of their downfall. There are in San Francisco 2,500 bad women. Prof. LaFloris says: I can safely say that three-fourths, or 1,875 of these women, were led to their downfall thru the influence of dancing."[89]

Although Belsheim acknowledges Dallman, without giving the date of his book, Dallman had taken the quote directly from T. A. Faulkner but had not cited the latter's book, *From the Ball Room to Hell,* which appeared in both 1892 and 1894.[90]

Faulkner's professional credentials included a presidency of the Dancing Masters' Association of the Pacific Coast and proprietorship of a Los Angeles dancing academy. According to the title page of one book, his publications had circulated by "the million," though most were published by the author. The vast majority of Faulkner's charges pertain to the immorality of dancing as that had been demonstrated by the number of women who "fell" into a life of sin due to the ballroom or dance hall. His statements and statistics seemed worth quoting since he was a converted—hence, former—dancing master. For instance, he maintains, "It has been proven by facts and statistics from every source that the most amorous woman makes the best dancer." Further, "No woman can waltz virtuously and waltz well." Worse yet: "You will generally find that a prostitute is a perfect dancer." Connecting prostitutes and their clients with liberal churches who approved dancing, Faulkner characterizes dives on the Barbary Coast in San Francisco: "A girl must be able to dance well, before she is taken into those dance houses by her owner and her body sold to whoever will buy. Eighty per cent of the thousands of the denizens of the underworld have been members of some church where dancing was permitted."[91]

The decade also gave rise to more extravagant claims about the evils of dancing than ever before. In an era that brought vast audiences to hear Billy Sunday's vernacular oratory, the accusations by the contemporary Baptist evangelist Mordecai F. Ham (1877–1961) hardly seem surprising.[92] In 1914, speaking to a revival meeting at Palestine, Texas, Ham declared that dancing held its followers "in a bondage more relentless and stupefying than either strong drink or narcotic drugs." Yet the evil was not solitary in effect. Dancing aroused male passion to the point that the only relief was to ruin daughters or visit a brothel. The ultimate consequence of the latter was, in turn, to spread venereal disease. Further, Ham cites a physician who alleges a causal connection between insanity and the "modern eccentric dances."[93]

Although charges about the immorality of dancing dominated opposition arguments, concerns about health still appeared. Opponents focused on the ill-ventilated environments, thinly clad participants, late hours, and excessive dancing. In 1912, the Methodist cleric William Milburn Dye (1868–1960) claimed that statistics showed "habitual dancers die at an average early age, men 31, and women 27."[94] Statistics of a different persuasion appeared around 1912 in a publication by Florence Ethel Smith, formerly a student at Moody Bible Institute, then musical director for the evangelist Joel A. Smith. As the only known female dance opponent of this era and genre, Smith expressed particular concern for women's health and morality: "It has been carefully calculated that the distance covered by a good dancer in one evening's program of twenty waltzes, four polkas and two quadrilles is twelve miles. How horrified a mother would be if she thought her daughter would have to walk twelve miles after 9:30 P.M. and in the arms of a young man all the way. And yet I hear mothers say, 'it is such a lovely exercise.'"[95] In sharp contrast, the moderate Congregational cleric Richard Henry Edwards (1877–1954) objected to dance halls, in part, because there was so little dancing; commonly, ten- to twenty-minute intermissions after three or four minutes of dancing left time for inappropriate behavior.[96]

Undoubtedly, the spread of dancing in school physical education programs prompted publications by Bishop Matthew Simpson Hughes (1863–1920) of the Methodist church and Harry Benton of the Disciples of Christ church. Writing in 1917, Hughes declared that contemporary newspapers reported the rapidly growing practice of incorporating dances in schools throughout the country. However, neither Hughes nor Benton specifies the kind of dance program they indict, whether it be in a formal school curriculum, an after-school club program, or an evening recreational-social event like a prom. Benton spells out the ultimate fear when he charges that 70 to 75 percent of the country's "fallen" women descended to that condition by dancing. How, he queries, can the public schools aid the white slave market and contribute to diseases that are the "most odious and foul of all the diseases known to man?"[97] To shore up their positions, both men point to the mere physicality of dancing. Hughes writes in moderate terms that the "affiliations of the dance as we have seen it are not intellectual." By contrast, Benton carries his charges to the extreme, alleging that often a person of "subnormal intelligence is a perfect dancer," and then declaring that the "dance upsets the intellect."[98]

Both men clearly saw the schools as centers for intellectual development and as guardians of the nation's morality. Both strongly reiterate claims by Billy Sunday and other dance opponents that emphasize the need to protect "womanhood" in order to maintain the purity and stability of home and nation. However, Benton again displays the excess characteristic of the "one hundred percent mentality." His opening salvo reads, "The Public School Dance Is Un-American," followed by "Motherhood Endangered." His extrapolations knew no bounds. After pointing out health hazards to women that allegedly accrued from dancing, Benton declares that public school dancing means "Taxation without Representation." He argues that because dance curricula cost money, and because the schools are tax-supported, in part by Christians who do not want dancing, holding public school dances amounts to unfair taxation. Christians should not be assessed for "that which has no place in education and which a Christian cannot enjoy or partake of, but which he loathes." Eventually some parents even took such claims to court.[99]

This notion contrasts dramatically with the more global view of dancing propounded by Gulick, Wood, and others, who lauded the aesthetic, social, and ethnic values in dancing well taught in the schools. Demonstrating that dancing had become a regular part of many school and recreation programs, a report by Edward W. Stitt, district superintendent of schools for New York City, told readers of the *Tenth Yearbook of the National Society for the Study of Education* that a carefully regulated curriculum of dance classes could improve the social skills and appearance of young men at the same time that it provided healthful recreation for both sexes. Stitt's survey found that such farflung cities as St. Louis, Milwaukee, Cleveland, Pittsburgh, and Holyoke, Massachusetts, among others, had by the first decade of the century begun successfully to use school buildings for city recreation programs. Such a use demonstrated, in effect, the kind of public, governmental support for recreation first urged by Edward Everett Hale in the mid-nineteenth century. By 1911, the New York City program encompassed clubs, gymnastics, game and library rooms, study rooms, and "mixed dancing classes." Stitt pronounced the first year's experiments—which were begun with extremely careful supervision by a "woman principal" and with no intent to draw large numbers to the classes—a complete success: "There was a gratifying improvement in the general appearance of the young men. The association with the young ladies not only developed a higher social tone, but also led the young men to be very careful about clean collars, neat neckties, polished shoes, and everything that pertains to correct personal appearance."[100]

The school recreational programs that Stitt described further emphasize the different strategies for attending to the problems of twentieth-century urban society. Urban reformers and school leaders who saw the good in dancing believed that government and schools, as well as private associations, had to bring their collective resources and authority to bear in alleviating the massive problems of cities. They focused attention on the common good and public welfare. On the other hand, fundamentalist dance opponents still tended to stress that urban ills could best be resolved through reforming individuals by Christian conversion. In 1914, Billy Sunday, riding what McLoughlin calls the crest of a reaction against the "social gospel," pronounced, "We've had enough of this godless social service nonsense."[101] However, Sunday sometimes became impatient with the slow pace of indi-

vidualized reform. In those moods, as McLoughlin points out, Sunday urged
"'a law preventing any boy or girl over twelve years of age from attending
dancing schools'" and another one "'providing that nobody should be allowed to dance until after they were married,' and then only with their spouses."[102] Although such ideas were not enacted into law, the ultimate legisla-
tive victory for Sunday and the fundamentalists came with the Eighteenth
Amendment to the Constitution, which brought prohibition. Taking effect
on 16 January 1920, the law heralded a new decade that also saw the end
of mass urban revivalism, as Sunday had championed it, and the beginning
of technologies that would further transform American habits and tastes,
especially for music and dancing.

The Context: 1920–29

Changes in dancing, from Broadway to ballrooms, suffused the country as
music entered homes via radio, movies became "talkies," and cars transported
people to dance halls, ballrooms, hotels, clubs, cabarets, and speakeasies.
Toward the end of the decade, Charles Lindbergh flew the Atlantic nonstop, and Americans named a dance after his feat. So popular did dancing
remain that fundamentalist clergy and evangelists continued to voice their
strong opposition to it, though their ultimate battle with the "modernists"
concerned quite another issue, the teaching of evolution in the public
schools, a dispute that culminated in the famous Scopes trial. The decade
proved the period of greatest controversy between the two camps. Dancing
was simply one of the evils the fundamentalists thought threatened the country, thanks to "flappers," jazz, and advancing technology.

New Technology

It is difficult to overestimate the impact of the phonograph and radio on
America, particularly after World War I. According to Russel Nye, a historian of popular culture, the production and sales of phonograph records
became a business in the 1890s and a "big business" during the war years.
Nye points out that the Victor Record Company pushed its assets from
thirteen million to twenty-three million dollars between 1913 and
1915. Now Americans could enjoy popular music anytime, regardless of
their ability to play the piano, read music, or sing. The expanding market
meant that musicians, arrangers, and song writers were in growing demand.[103] Further, the development of large bands and orchestras added a
whole new sound to the American music and dance scene. Paul Whiteman,

who organized a band after World War I, became known as the "King of Jazz" by the twenties. He commanded a $25,000 salary for six nights—reputedly the largest fee paid to a dance band at that time—when he played the opening engagement at the Trianon Ballroom in Chicago in 1922.[104] A well-known rival sound, developed in the middle twenties, came from the band of Guy Lombardo. He began with a Cleveland radio station in 1923 but gained resounding acclaim when he started playing over Chicago's new station, WBBM, in 1927. Lombardo reported that the local telephone company complained because no one was making calls during the band's broadcasts on Saturday nights.[105] Eventually advertising its playing as the "sweetest music this side of heaven," Lombardo's band endured perhaps longer than any other big band in the nation—more than fifty years.

Radio gave more Americans more dance music than did the Victrola. Commercial broadcasting began 2 November 1920 from station KDKA in Pittsburgh. Eighteen months later, there were 220 stations on the air. By 1922, some 3,000,000 homes had radios. Three years later, estimates put the country's listening audience at 50,000,000. In its first decade, radio beamed into every third home in the nation.[106] Thus a turn of the dial could bring listeners news, political conventions, variety shows, sports events, and the ubiquitous dance music.

Then, in 1927, another breakthrough in mass media appeared. Al Jolson sang on the moving picture screen in *The Jazz Singer.* The addition of sound to the movies would soon spawn the movie musical and spread dancing to an ever-increasing public audience. Thus, radio and "talkies" began and expanded in the twenties as a prelude to a decade when the nation became acclimatized to popular music and dancing. But in the twenties, radio also became a new tool for a few churches.

Radio provided the perfect vehicle for preachers to enter homes across the nation. Probably no clergyman proved more skillful in the early days of radio than the Reverend John Roach Straton (1875–1929), who was pastor of Calvary Baptist Church in New York City by 1918. By 1923, Calvary Baptist operated the country's first church radio station. Straton became known via print and radio throughout the country for his sensational attacks on the alleged "evils" infiltrating the nation. Not surprisingly, Gregory Mason, in the *American Mercury,* dubbed Straton the modern day "Savonarola."[107] His book *The Dance of Death, Should Christians Indulge?* appeared about 1920, followed by *Fighting the Devil in Modern Babylon* in 1929.[108] The two books attacked a society turned from God to mammon.

Although prewar dance devotees had flocked to commercial dance halls and hotels, dancers of the twenties could also satisfy their passion for the latest fad dances at any of the growing number of glamorous ballrooms, clubs, cabarets, and speakeasies. Just as radio transformed Americans from musical participants to listeners, the availability of closed cars and ready cash permitted aspiring dancers to become avid participants on a nightly basis and helped to transform male-female relationships. A car meant a getaway from parental supervision and privacy with the opposite sex. Writing in 1928, the sociologist Robert Cooley Angell reported on his study of American undergraduate campus life and noted the dramatic impact of the automobile on heterosexual relations: "The ease with which a couple can secure absolute privacy when in possession of a car and the spirit of reckless abandon which high speed and moonlight drives engender have combined to break down the traditional barriers between the sexes. What is vulgarly known as 'petting' is the rule rather than the exception in all classes of society."[109] The enclosed car also permitted young people to sneak a drink from a flask. The association of dancing with drinking, driving, parking, and petting clearly contributed to fears about the immorality of the "modern dance." Yet other technology also had a major impact on gender relations.

Movies as well as magazines that focused on sex and true confessions garnered the attention of twenties' consumers. Angell speaks of the "highly sexed motion picture." Frederick Lewis Allen describes advertisements and films that emphasize kissing, necking, and petting—all in an atmosphere of allure, brilliance, and pleasure. Both Angell and Allen judge the movies a contributing factor to the change in women's social roles and the rules applying to them. Russel Nye's much more recent assessment of the film industry's impact on American culture points to its establishment at the beginning of the decade as the major form of dramatic entertainment for the public. Vaudeville died in its shadow, while the legitimate stage attracted smaller and more elite audiences. In Nye's words, "movie houses simply drew away audiences by millions."[110] Thus, it would be hard to minimize the impact of motion pictures on the country's mores, tastes, and values.

New Fashions and New Dances

Altered social roles and rules were perhaps most clearly expressed in women's behavior and dress. Although *Vogue* displayed spring styles of 1919 that showed merely an ankle below skirts, thereafter hemlines seemed to rise with the stock market. Despite some subsequent dips in both hems and stocks, by 1927 women wore dresses at knee level. The prewar trend toward slimmer and straighter figures continued, as fashion decreed that the ideal feminine form was no longer amply endowed, as it had been in the late Victorian and Edwardian eras, but rather boyishly slim, unencumbered by steel and whalebone. Allen notes, for example, that in a short three-year period, from 1924 to 1927, sales for corsets and brassieres "in the department stores of the Cleveland Federal Reserve District" fell by 11 percent.[111] Corsetless girls turned down their hose and rolled the tops rather than cinching them with garters and straps. The display of limbs permitted by raised hems and dropped hose proved shocking to dance opponents, who equated the wearing of corsets with the preservation of chastity. Reports that women left their corsets at coatcheck rooms before dancing only reinforced the notion that the "modern dances" defiled American "womanhood." The Baptist cleric J. W. Porter (1863–1937) declared in 1922, "Many young men have gone so far as to refuse to dance with a woman who has on her corset."[112] To women who wore the new styles, the ease of movement permitted must have been a welcome new freedom. Short hair, short skirts, short sleeves, free waists, and few undergarments meant that the "flapper" could swing, swivel, and kick in a way that her 1912 sister could only have imagined.

The new dances of the decade further exaggerated the previously dramatic movement and rhythmic styles, which had in turn distanced the ragtime era from the days of the Victorian waltz and the shottische. They often appeared on stage before invading the dance hall, hotel, or cabaret. Some survived longer than others. Fad dances, first known in the ragtime era, had become a permanent fixture in American popular culture. The shimmy, Charleston, black bottom, and varsity drag captured the public's fancy for a while. Partners did not stand in an upright position facing one another and move gracefully around the floor to an even beat, as they had in the old round dances. Nor did dancers in the twenties cling or drape themselves over their partners, as had earlier dancers who bounced vertically in unison to a rapid one-step. The new dances required performers to bend and kick, swivel or sway their hips, shake their shoulders, and swing their arms—perhaps holding onto a partner at arm's length, or perhaps not touching one another at all. Energetic, rhythmic, vigorous, and sexy—the fad dances owed a debt to America's black heritage and to the choreography of popular Broadway shows.[113]

American popular culture of the decade derived much from the blacks who streamed out of the South, bound for the North, during the teens of this century. The population of Harlem, for example, quadrupled between 1914 and 1930. As blacks brought their music and dances with them, Harlem became the mecca for entertainers. Nightspots such as the famed

Cotton Club played to white audiences who made the nightly trek uptown from downtown Manhattan to hear the great names in music—among them Duke Ellington and Cab Calloway. Dancers displayed their talents not only in clubs but in the equally famous Savoy Ballroom, which opened on 12 March 1926. They also appeared on Broadway and toured. The 1921 show *Shuffle Along* became the first black musical to play coast to coast in white theaters and helped to popularize tap dancing. The famous black tap dancer Bill "Bojangles" Robinson was supposedly "discovered" in *Blackbirds of 1928* and went on to Hollywood film fame.[114] The Black Renaissance lasted for the decade. During that time, money, cars, ballrooms, theaters, clubs, radio, and dancing dramatically liberated some blacks in the entertainment world as well as some women in their social roles.

According to the historian Paula Fass, dancing and smoking proved to be emblematic of a woman's liberation in the 1920s. Although respectable middle-class women did not smoke, the habit became increasingly popular during the decade, particularly among college women. Such behavior emerged as another area in which there was an erosion of the standards that once held women morally superior to men. The twenties' girl who not only smoked but also wore makeup further broke down barriers. As women enjoyed the freedom to ride alone in cars with men, they also found dancing a popular pastime for social recreation. To the young, dancing did not seem objectionable; it seemed "almost compulsory." Corroborating the point, Angell called dancing "perhaps the most popular diversion of all," based on his survey of undergraduate college students in 1928.[115]

Despite greater freedom in dancing, dressing, and smoking, the formalities and conventions decreed by etiquette authorities of the 1920s did not evaporate. Emily Holt's *Encyclopaedia of Etiquette* provides an example of how social rules were adapted over the first two decades of the new century. Originally published in 1901, the book appeared in numerous revised and enlarged editions through 1926. By the twenties, the topic of "Balls and Dances" still occupied an entire chapter of fifty-eight pages devoted to details of invitations, dress, hostessing, facility preparation, orchestra, servants, supper, arrivals and departures, and accepting or refusing a dance. The question of chaperones for young ladies still merited some attention, although Holt advised, "To line a drawing room on the occasion of an informal dance with sober, elderly ladies is . . . to promote nobody's welfare or pleasure." Holt declared that, on the whole, the term "ball" had gone out of fashion except for very large and very elaborate public evening affairs. The term "dance," which had formerly meant only an informal event, was used in its place to designate "an affair no matter how elaborate, provided only that it be private, and not public." The practice of "cutting in" meant that even if a lady started a dance with one partner, she might finish with another. However, decorum still required that the gentleman not leave a lady stranded in the middle of the floor alone after a dance and that he ask for a dance with courtesy and civility.[116]

In describing the correct dance position, Holt omitted discussion of distance between partners but warned dancers to behave with a sense of propriety for the setting and never to "emulate" stage dances:

> The modern dances have been freely criticized because of the objectionable method of holding the partner, and also because of the "shaking and wiggling" motions of the bodies of the dancers. It is said that these swaying movements were necessitated by the tempo of the music. However this may be, these dances have now won acceptance if not approval, and it has been demonstrated that they can be performed gracefully and without giving offense to the most squeamish chaperon, when, as is now customary, the dancers remember what is fitting and forbear to emulate the abandon of stage performers.[117]

In the twenties, dancing, high-school activities, commercial amusements, and cars all facilitated the opportunities for youth of both genders to socialize together, presumably getting to know one another well. And although marriage seemed to be the goal for most females, statistics do not suggest that more marriages were ultimately happy and stable. Ryan reports that the divorce rate exploded 2,000 percent between 1867 and 1927. One out of six marriages ended in divorce by the twenties.[118] Thus, dance opponents did not fail to shout loud and long that divorce, prostitution, and a decline in the valuing of traditional "womanhood" all resulted from the immoral "modern dance."

New Language, Old Themes

The rhetoric of moral panic continued from the teens through the twenties in strident tones, sensationalist verbiage, and the usual specious reasoning. At least twenty extant publications that opposed dance in whole or in part appeared during the twenties, making that decade the third highest in number of such publications.[119] Denominational shifts meant that the greatest outpouring of invective came from Baptists, Methodists, and Disciples of Christ or Christians. For the first time since the early nineteenth century, no Presbyterians wrote books against dancing; similarly, Congregational clergy evidenced no interest in continuing the polemic, if one judges by the extant oppositional books or pamphlets. As in the earlier decades of the century, attacks came from parish clergy and itinerant evangelists who, although not speaking to the massive audiences that had been attracted by Billy Sunday, preached to multitudes in smaller gatherings and reached many more via the small tracts and pamphlets sold for a few cents per copy.

Upset by the popularity of the "modern dance," opponents encouraged the fear that the very stability of the country was threatened. The Reverend J. W. Porter, a Southern Baptist, leveled his attacks in 1922 with supreme confidence that the primary enemy of the nation was the "ballroom": "The wave of licentiousness, now sweeping over the country, and threatening the very foundations of our civilization, is due in large measure to the ballroom. The decline of social ideals, and the lowering of Christian standards have led to the downfall of other nations, and will, if unchecked, be the ruin of our own country." The evangelist C. F. Weigle declared dancing to be a "moral cancer eating at the vitals of the nation."[120] By 1929 the country looked so bad to John Roach Straton, peering out from his New York City Calvary Baptist pulpit, that America seemed to be nothing less than a "modern Babylon" overseen by the devil.

The specific "evils" that dancing presented purportedly emanated from the "embrace" of the "modern dance," the "round dance," or the "public promiscuous dance." Rarely precise in naming the particular dances they attacked, detractors almost always resorted to a generic denunciation. The fact that some mentioned the waltz in particular makes the modern reader wonder about the degree to which opponents kept in touch with the popular dances. The closed dance position of the waltz did not at all resemble positions assumed in the Charleston or the black bottom, for example. Whether or not adversaries actually saw dancers "hugging" to music with "no daylight" between the bodies, they nonetheless continued to level such charges with regularity.[121]

When male lust, modern dances, "voluptuous music," and liquor all combined on the public dance floor, opponents declared that the resulting temptations led to even greater social evils. Girls allegedly surrendered to or were captured by "white slavers."[122] If male dancers did not succeed in seducing their female partners in vacant rooms near dance halls or in back alley strolls, then the men themselves frequented red light districts. That behavior, in turn, led to the spreading of intense and abnormal sexual urges and deadly diseases. Close fraternization with partners other than spouses also supposedly spawned jealousy and infidelity. Divorce, even murder, resulted. Porter charged that "liquor and the dance-hall are responsible for fifty percent of the murders of America."[123]

Whereas nineteenth-century opponents used restrained language until the late eighties and nineties, dance opponents of the twenties spoke plainly. Lee Ralph Phipps (1878–1964), a Methodist minister, stated unequivocally that at a certain point the "modern dance" ceased to be merely a physical exercise and became "a form of intercourse between the sexes." Even more dramatic was the evangelist Harry Vom Bruch's charge that the evils of the masquerade ball led to sibling incest, which was revealed only when the male and female removed their masks following the act of intercourse.[124] Sensational rhetoric attempted to make more vivid the point that moderation in dancing was no option. The evangelist Melvin Morris, of the Maryland Baptist Union, declared, "Moderation in Dancing is damnation in baby clothes!" Echoing Mordecai Ham a decade earlier, Clovis G. Chappell (1882–after 1949), a Methodist minister, charged that only drug addiction held its victims in such a tight grip. He asserted, "Whether you are a dancer or not a dancer, you must agree with me that nothing short of the dope habit holds its habitues in so tight a grasp."[125]

Dramatic statistics also continued to be cited in popular arguments against dancing. Straton, Phipps, and Porter, for instance, again brought up the statistic first quoted among dance opponents by Hiram Collins Haydn in 1880, that three-quarters of the abandoned girls in New York City met their ruin through dancing.[126] One of the new indictments using statistics, including sweeping and specious numbers, appeared in tandem with mixed metaphors and grammatical errors. Harry O. Anderson, a Christian evangelist from Oakland, California, writing around 1928, cited the number of "soiled doves" who had become a "great army" of shame:

It is said that there are 5,000 girls lost every twelve months in the city of Chicago. With each passing year 5,000 girls slip out of sight never to be seen again by parents or loved ones in the city of Los Angeles. In a century over 7,000,000 girls are lost in a life of shame and sorrow. It is estimated that 600,000 girls, soiled doves, travel up and down, in and out, wandering to and fro as a great army. They have been ensnared into a life of sin. Six hundred thousand soiled doves. A careful survey of all of these girls was made and they are asked to tell frankly the cause that lead them into this life. This survey revealed that 68% or 375,000 attributed their downfall to the **modern day dance**.[127]

Inevitably, T. A. Faulkner remained a popular source for similar arguments. His testimony as a "converted dancing master" served to authenticate his charges. A new book containing his 1893 and 1916 publications appeared in 1922 and thereby helped to spread his ideas to the contemporary reader.[128] At least seven authors of antidance books in the decade quoted Faulkner as an authority. Writers in the twenties also favored the graphic quotation attributed to Dr. Frank G. Richardson in the nineteenth century to the effect that the dance hall served as the "nursery of the divorce court, the training ship of prostitution, the graduating school of infamy."[129]

Despite the radical changes in social roles for women, fundamentalists continued to view with horror the decline in that "indefinable something we call womanhood."[130] A clear sense of moral panic appears in one writer's comparison of America with ancient Rome, where immorality proved the "great sin" of the nation.[131] Some authors voiced additional concern about the assault on morality and womanhood supposedly perpetrated by the public school's sponsorship of dances. Both Vom Bruch and Morris claimed that thousands of girls met their ruin that way. Morris's assertion further displays the syntactical collapse often found in these twentieth-century writings: "The dance takes 50,000 young people out of the high schools every year. In one city alone during one year over one hundred high school girls became mothers through the dance."[132] According to Lamphear, the tremendous number of illegitimate births proved the "principal indictment against the Modern Dance in our Public Schools." Others argued that dancers did not make good students. Dancing and study were incompatible; like oil and water they could not be mixed. Though not always clear in their writing, opponents usually linked such arguments to women and fears of immorality, rather than to men.[133]

The feud over teaching evolution in the schools perhaps served to maintain the uninformed, chauvinistic, and racist claims that lunatics, blacks, and trained monkeys always proved to be the best dancers. However, the diffusion of black dance and music via the stage and radio may also have contributed to such claims. Lamphear phrased his view with sweeping confidence and no evidence: "The fact is that the world over, among savage or civilized, and in all ages, dancing is one of the strong indications of the predominance of the animal passions over the intellectual faculties. Inferior intellectuality and an over-developed animalism inevitably create the demand for the Dance as a social pastime." In addition, the southern roots of some dance opponents seem to have accounted for racist attitudes. For example, Chappell wrote, sarcastically: "Here is a pastime in which the very finest performers are trained monkeys. In our Southland the negro is also an artist. And among the white people some of the best dancers in the world are in the lunatic asylum."[134] Antidance books do not detail more specifically the association of blacks with modern dances and music, but a racist attitude clearly was intertwined with the fear of dancing's alleged immorality in the early twentieth century.

Taking another tack, many opponents still pressed a strong antidance argument by alleging its harmfulness to health. Authors in the twenties continued to focus on minimal clothing, lack of sleep, and unhealthful environment; but they shored up their claims with statistics that had been presented in the teens. At least five writers stressed that an average dancer would travel ten to sixteen miles in the course of four hours or an evening's dancing. The clear implication is that covering so many miles in one evening harmed the health of women in particular.[135] In an era when physical education leaders in colleges and universities had been making substantial progress in understanding the process of physical conditioning, fundamentalists were either unaware of or blind to such information. In the absence of clear reasoning and logic, extravagant indictments of the "modern dance" held sway.

The decade's antidance books also renew allegations that dancing harms spiritual life and growth. In typical sensationalist fashion, Straton pronounced that "spiritually speaking, dancing Christians are dancing corpses."[136] He continued to expound the old idea that reform of society must come about through individual conversion. In his 1929 publication *Fighting the Devil in Modern Babylon,* he echoed Billy Sunday's denunciation of "this godless social service nonsense." Straton declared, "I believe in salvation as the only source of true social service." Anderson reached back even further, speaking to readers in 1928 in a manner that would have been familiar to Kerr and his contemporaries of the 1890s: "The question is not whether you should do this or do that, and not do this and do that, and other negations but the question is, 'what would Jesus do?'"[137]

Signs of Impending Change

Despite some continuity in the methods and ideas of both conservative and fundamentalist clergymen and evangelists from 1890 to 1929, the cultural developments of the twenties boded no return to nineteenth-century values. The expansion of technology, commercial amusements, Prohibition, and universal public schooling, among other advances, had forever altered the American social landscape. In the process, the voices of Billy Sunday and other dance adversaries had lost their appeal for many listeners. Ahlstrom provides pertinent examples of issues on which the liberals gained ascendance as conservatives lost ground, including "new attitudes toward recreation":

Even as modern religious ideas steadily advanced or as concern for social issues increased, the churches tended to lose their capacity to shape and inform American opinion. The debacle of Prohibition functioned both as evidence and cause of the churches' loss of authority in a culture where urban values became primary. The decline of the Puritan Sabbath despite strenuous campaigns in its behalf, the emergence of new attitudes toward recreation despite old Puritanic suspicions of play, and the expansion of the amusement industry served meanwhile to weaken the disciplinary aspects of church membership. Modern thought and social change were slowly bringing down the curtains on the "great century" of American evangelicalism.[138]

At the end of the decade, the impact of the closed car, radio, movies, leisure time, and increased wealth was pervasive. Dance halls grew in number and elegance across the country. Dance music on radio entered homes across the land. The development of sound in films heralded the advent of the movie musical, with dancing galore, in the decade to come. Well-taught and regulated dancing took its place in the formal school curriculum of physical education; by 1930, thirty-six states had passed legislation requiring physical education for all schoolchildren and youth. At the college level, not only was dancing popular as a social-recreational activity, but the first major in dance had been instituted at the University of Wisconsin, Madison. Moreover, despite the protestations of John Roach Straton, some churches sponsored recreation, even dancing, for their youth.[139]

Perhaps the most radical of all prodance attitudes within the Protestant church at that time were expressed by a Protestant Episcopal cleric in New York City. The Reverend William Norman Guthrie (1868–1944) was something of a maverick dance advocate, a twentieth-century counterpart to the Lutheran minister J. B. Gross, who had urged dance in worship services as early as 1879. On 8 January 1923 Guthrie read a paper, later published, before "the Club," an organization of clergy in the diocese of New York. He titled his work *The Relation of the Dance to Religion*. Speaking to an educated audience, he assumed his listeners had read the *Encyclopedia Britannica* on dance and were familiar with its historical development. Guthrie analyzed contemporary dance and then put before his audience a vision of "expressive dance," with its possibilities for church worship. His view of dancing, which actualized the expressive powers of human nature, also recalls the earlier, similar advocacy of Luther Gulick and G. Stanley Hall. For Guthrie, the present need for dance was imperative: "It seems to me there is nothing more tragic in the present moment for us civilized men than the almost complete loss of our natural and spiritually necessary bodies. They are not organs of soul-expression any more, these poor paralyzed limbs of ours!"

Elaborating on the physical degeneration wrought by modern, urban-industrial life, Guthrie told his listeners that human beings needed to recapture their bodies as a "divine plastic language once more." Although folk dancing proved beneficial, he thought that only "expressive dance" provided the most complete possibilities for expression. He argued that such dance would prove the "salvation" of the body. As a step in the process of restoring the dance to its rightful place in the culture, Guthrie's church, St. Mark's in the Bouwery, on 8 December 1922, held an hour and a half "Rhythmic Pictorial Oratorio," which received "rapt attention." The acceptance was so positive that another such dance event was planned in the future.[140] By midcentury, those like Guthrie who maintained a high opinion of the body and believed in the value of dance as an aid to worship had organized themselves into the National Sacred Dance Guild.

Notes

1. Bernard Weisberger, *They Gathered at the River* (Boston: Little, Brown, 1958), 227. I am indebted to my former colleague at St. Olaf, Dr. James Aune, for the phrase "rhetoric of moral panic," which I believe characterizes the tone of conservative and fundamentalist antidance rhetoric in this era.

2. Richard Hofstadter, *Anti-intellectualism in American Life* (New York: Knopf, 1963), 118–19.

3. Robert P. Kerr, *The Dance, the Card Table, the Theatre, and the Wine Cup* (Richmond: Presbyterian Committee of Publication, 1898), 23; G. W. Samson, *Idols of Fashion and Culture; or, Lusts Bowed to and Served Through Social Customs Fostered by Fashion, Veiled by Culture* (Boston: James W. Earle, 1891), 238–39; T. DeWitt Talmadge, *Sin: A Series of Popular Discourses* (Chicago: Rhodes and McClure Publishing Company, 1897), 281; J[ames] M[onroe] Buckley, *The Amusements Prohibited by the Methodist Episcopal Church* (New York: Eaton and Mains; Cincinnati: Curts and Jennings, [1896?]), 4, 7.

4. Binga's writings are the only ones identifiably by a black author that I have encountered. See A. Binga Jr., *Sermon and Address* (Richmond: Johns and Company, 1887), 3–15; idem, *Binga's Addresses on Several Occasions*, 2d ed. (N.p.: 190?), 5–12. During the two decades from 1890 to 1909, at least forty treatises appeared in opposition to dance and amusements.

5. William G. McLoughlin, *Modern Revivalism* (New York: Ronald Press, 1959), 364–65.

6. Ibid., 282, 290, 305; *Appleton's Cyclopaedia of American Biography*, s.v. "Jones, Samuel Porter." After his own dramatic conversion from drink in 1872, Jones entered the Methodist Episcopal Church South and began to preach one week later.

7. *Sam Jones' Sermons* (Chicago: Rhodes and McClure, 1896), 142–43, 139, 309.

8. McLoughlin, *Modern Revivalism*, 389–90. Over 8.5 million people landed in this country between 1901 and 1910, many of them from Eastern Europe, in contrast to the predominantly Western European and British immigrants of earlier decades. The century's first decade, in fact, witnessed the greatest influx of immigrants of the entire Atlantic Migration. To the rural American with "homespun," small town values, the hordes of "foreigners" proved threatening. See the breakdown of immigration figures by decade, from 1821 to 1970, in Sydney E. Ahlstrom's, *A Religious History of the American People* (New York: Image Books, 1975), vol. 2, 208.

9. M[ilan] B[ertrand] Williams, *Where Satan Sows His Seed, Plain Talks on the Amusements of Modern Society* (New York: Fleming H. Revell, 1896), 49–51, 98–99.

10. McLoughlin, *Modern Revivalism*, 377–78, 388.

11. J[ohn] Wilbur Chapman, *The Christian's Relation to Amusements and the World, a Sermon . . . Delivered in Atlanta, Georgia* (N.p., n.p., [1904?]), 8–9, 12.

12. *Dictionary of American Biography*, s.v. "Riley, William Bell." Riley came to the First Baptist Church in Minneapolis in 1897. In 1902 he founded Northwestern Bible Training College. By 1919 Riley became leader of the conservative churchmen and head of the World's Christian Fundamentals Association.

13. William B[ell] Riley, *Messages for the Metropolis* (Chicago: Winona Publishing Company, 1906), foreword, 74.

14. Ibid., 35–36.

15. William Dallmann, *The Dance* (Baltimore: Lutheran Publication Board, 1894), 5. His reference likely pertains to the new dancing of Loie Fuller, "La Loie," of European fame, and her imitators. Wearing a skirt made of yards of material, Fuller manipulated the fabric skillfully under lights to create an unusual vision of light and motion. Whether or not the phenomenon could properly be labeled dancing is another question. However, the *Encyclopedia Americana* for 1904 (the original spelling of "Encyclopedia" in the title was changed the year before) clearly designates the genre of "skirt dancing."

16. William Edward Biederwolf, *The Christian and Amusements* (Chicago: Winona Magazine, 1907), 32; G. B. Ilsley, "The Attitude of the Church toward Amusements," No. 3 in *Baptist Sermons I–J* (Rochester, N.Y.: American Baptist Historical Society, [1881–1900], 13ff; J[ames] Monroe Hubbert, *Dancers and Dancing: A Calm and Rational View of the Dancing Question* (Nashville: Cumberland Presbyterian Publishing House, 1901), 28–31, 34; Wm. Wistar Hamilton, *Worldy Amusements: How to Decide or, The Benefit of the Doubt* (Philadelphia: Griffith and Rowland Press, 1909), 63.

17. Williams, *Where Satan Sows His Seed,* 121; G[eorge] J. Pfefferkorn, *Ist Tanzen Sünde?* (Chippewa Falls, Wis.: N.p., 1901), 54–56; Talmadge, *Sin,* 282.

18. Williams, *Where Satan Sows His Seed,* 92–93; George F. Hall, *Pitfalls of the Ballroom* Chicago: Laird and Lee, 1901), 63; Hubbert, *Dancers and Dancing,* 30.

19. W. L. Sanford, *The Dance* (Waco, Tex.: Baptist Standard Print, 1893), 5.

20. Ibid., 6.

21. Don Carlos Janes, *Dancing* (Louisville: N.p., n.d.), 3. At least twelve anti-dance books published between 1890 and 1909 contain that statistic. Without exception, they do not cite the investigator, the year in which the data were gathered, or the total number of women upon which the percentage was figured.

22. Hall, *Pitfalls of the Ballroom,* 92, 10–12.

23. Hamilton, *Worldly Amusements,* 69.

24. Dr. E. L. Powell, *Perils of the Church in the World of To-Day* (Louisville: Guide Printing and Publishing Company, 1891), 7. Kathy Peiss's analysis of working women and leisure in New York between 1890 and 1920 clearly establishes the popularity of public dance halls for young working girls. Dance styles and rules for behavior, according to Peiss's research, were far more casual than the rules stipulated in etiquette books of the same decades. In her discussion of "Cheap Theater," Peiss implies confirmation of Powell's statement that men and women sat side by side. She writes: "Many commentators point out the intimacy and sense of community of these theaters, suggesting the cohesive cultural role they played in working-class neighborhoods." Peiss found that, according to one audience survey in 1910, 60 percent of the vaudeville viewers came from the working class; one-third were women. See Kathy Peiss, *Cheap Amusements: Working Women and Leisure in Turn-of-the-Century New York* (Philadelphia: Temple University Press, 1986), 140, 143. See also Barbara Meil Hobson, *Uneasy Virtue: The Politics of Prostitution and the American Reform Tradition* (New York: Basic Books, 1987), 141–47.

25. James Brand, *The Young Christian and the Popular Dance* (Chicago: Advance Publishing Company, 1892), 20–21. Hamilton also quotes Wells in his 1909 *Worldy Amusements,* 122. Amos Russel Wells (1862–1933), a Congregational minister, achieved renown as editor of the *Christian Endeavor World* and author of ninety volumes of sermons, essays, stories, and poems. Under Wells's leadership from 1891 to 1927, the periodical became one of the most widely read in the field of religious journalism.

26. *Sam Jones' Sermons,* 142–43; Pfefferkorn, *Ist Tanzen Sünde?* 23; T. A. Faulkner, *From the Ball Room to Hell and the Lure of the Dance* (LaCrosse, Wis.: The Light, 1922), 21. This volume is a compilation of two earlier books. *From the Ball-Room to Hell* was first published in 1892. *The Lure of the Dance* came out in 1916.

27. Pfefferkorn, *Ist Tanzen Sünde?* 24–25; Hamilton, *Worldly Amusements,* 68; Chester Fairman Ralston, *A Candid Consideration of Troublesome Questions* (Gloversville, N.Y.: [Daily Leader, 1906]), 37.

28. Pfefferkorn, *Ist Tanzen Sünde?* 46. Pastor of the Evangelical Community

in Chippewa Falls, Wisconsin, George Pfefferkorn (18??–19??), charged in 1901 that dancing led to drinking, a view not as implausible as it first sounds. Pfefferkorn pastored a German population that commonly used alcoholic beverages at parties. Local dance halls typically did not have water available, but saloons were nearby. Since dancing makes people thirsty, they had no choice but to consume the liquor.

29. Hamilton, *Worldly Amusements,* 64.

30. Hall, *Pitfalls of the Ballroom,* 176–77, 181.

31. Ibid., 47.

32. William H. Allbright, "The Christian and the Dance," *Pilgrim Series* 3 (Mar. 1891): 34–35; Perry Wayland Sinks, *Popular Amusements and the Christian Life* (Chicago: Bible Institute Colportage Assn., 1896), 26.

33. [Charles Tilton], *Modern Dance Denounced* (Texarkana, Ark.-Tex.: Baptist Sunday School Committee, n.d.), 6.

34. Allbright, "Christian and the Dance," 28; Sinks, *Popular Amusements,* 27–28; W[illiam] W. Gardner, *Modern Dancing: In the Light of Scripture and Facts* (Louisville: Baptist Book Concern, 1893), 79.

35. M. P. Hunt, *What's the Harm in Dancing Anyway?* ([Louisville]: N.p., [1897]), 28; Hamilton, *Worldly Amusements,* 63. Hamilton's quotation of Cicero, who had been out of vogue since the sixteenth-century dance enemies cited him, declares that no man could possibly dance unless he was either drunk or mad.

36. Hunt, *What's the Harm,* 29–30; see also Hall, *Pitfalls of the Ballroom,* 20–21.

37. [William Henry Bates], *The Worldly Christian's Trinity: Cards, Theatre, Dance* [Boston: Watchword and Truth, 1905], 31; A[dna] B[radway] Leonard, *The Modern Dance* (New York: Eaton and Mains; Cincinnati: Curts and Jennings, [1896–1900]), 5.

38. Brand, *The Young Christian,* 9; Sanford, *The Dance,* 3.

39. Brand states he corresponded with "nearly" one hundred prominent pastors and laymen on the subject. He reports, "A very large proportion of the replies are squarely against the practice of dancing by church members" (23–24).

40. Sara B. Maxwell, *Manners and Customs of To-Day* (Des Moines: Cline Publishing House, 1890), 7–8. According to Arthur Schlesinger's count, five or six new books appeared each year between 1870 and 1917. Women's magazines also expanded the sources of information on correct social behavior. See Arthur Schlesinger, *Learning How to Behave* (New York: Macmillan, 1946), 33–34.

41. Daphne Dale [pseud. for Chas. F. Beezely], *Our Manners and Social Customs: A Practical Guide to Deportment, Easy Manners, and Social Etiquette* (Chicago and Philadelphia: Elliott and Beezely, 1891), 223; Emily Holt, *Encyclopaedia of Etiquette* (New York: McClure, Phillips and Company, 1901), 133; Maud C. Cooke, *Social Etiquette or Manners and Customs of Polite Society . . .* (Chicago: National Book Concern, 1896), 241–43, 247.

42. Holt, *Encyclopaedia of Etiquette,* 133; Maxwell, *Manners and Customs,* 161;

Mrs. Frank Learned [Ellin Craven], *The Etiquette of New York Today* (New York: Frederick A. Stokes Company, 1906), 40.

43. Dale, *Our Manners,* 226–27; Holt, *Encyclopaedia of Etiquette,* 154; *Correct Social Usage: A Course of Instruction in Good Form, Style and Deportment by Eighteen Distinguished Authors,* 9th rev. ed. (New York: New York Society of Self-Culture, 1907), 172–73; *Etiquette for Americans: By a Woman of Fashion,* new and rev. ed. (New York: Duffield and Company, 1909), 193, 195; Cooke, *Social Etiquette,* 258. Despite a changing culture, authorities continued to philosophize about the need for polite behavior—subsumed under a discussion about the importance of manners and morals for Americans in general and women in particular. The 1909 publication titled *Etiquette for Americans* "By a Woman of Fashion," tells readers that the book was prompted by the current demand for an "up-to-date manual of American etiquette." Pointing out that social rules change with the times, the author mentions that golf and motoring, for example, were unknown when earlier etiquette books appeared. Not only did new activities require new rules for appropriate behavior, but formerly popular activities changed in their mode of presentation, again necessitating an alteration of earlier rules. A measure of that change with respect to dancing is suggested by the fact that the 1909 author did not write a special section on dancing and balls as had customarily appeared in earlier manuals. Instructions for dancing are subsumed under "Invitations" and "Chaperones," for example. New topics in 1909 included smoking, telephoning, sports, motoring, and "financial dealings with women." See *Etiquette for Americans,* 1, 9, 66–67, 191–95.

44. *Etiquette for Americans,* 193, 195, 201; Dale, *Our Manners,* 41.

45. Cooke, *Social Etiquette,* 255.

46. *Correct Social Usage,* 9, 13, 26, 17, 31–32, 34.

47. F. D. Huntington, *Good Manners a Fine Art* (Syracuse: Wolcott and West, 1892), 11, 19. Despite his positive view of the body and its importance in display of manners, Huntington does not advocate dance. However, this lack of endorsement cannot necessarily be construed as opposition to dance. The substance of his book is philosophical rather than prescriptive. He treats concepts rather than particular activities.

48. See, for example, G[eorge] H[enry] Sandison, comp., *How to Behave and How to Amuse: A Handy Manual of Etiquette and Parlor Games in Two Parts* (New York: The Christian Herald, 1895), 73.

49. Nancy Lee Chalfa Ruyter, *Reformers and Visionaries: The Americanization of the Art of Dance* (New York: Dance Horizons, 1979), 18–27; C. W. Hackensmith, *History of Physical Education* (New York: Harper and Row, 1966), 356–57. Authorities like Steele Mackaye and especially Genevieve Stebbins taught the Delsarte system to actors and public speakers as well as the general public. Stebbins's book, titled *The Delsarte System of Expression,* appeared in six editions between 1885 and 1902.

50. Although Oberlin College introduced calisthenic drills for women as early as 1847, the biggest surge in this area came from the women's colleges after 1865 when Vassar became the first to erect a gymnasium (Hackensmith, *History of Physical Education,* 372–74).

51. Eugenia Everett, "Melvin Ballou Gilbert: Turn-of-the-Century American Dance Educator" (M.F.A. thesis, York University, 1983), 24–25, 58, 60. During his tenure at these two schools, and later at the Boston Normal School of Gymnastics and Wellesley College, Gilbert taught hundreds of teachers the art of dancing. Beginning as a ballroom teacher in Portland, Maine, Gilbert progressed to the presidency of the American Society of Professors of Dancing from 1892–98, the study of ballet, and the development of his course in aesthetic dance. Gilbert's influence was enlarged by the publication in 1890 of his book on *Round Dancing.* In it, Gilbert says that he made no attempt to overcome the dance opponents "as that work is being accomplished, by the exemplification of effects, produced by the exalted position which dancing justly holds in society, and by its having become one of the indispensable accomplishments of our young society people." See M. B. Gilbert, *Round Dancing* (Portland, Me.: By the author, 1890), 12.

52. Everett, "Melvin Ballou Gilbert," 58–59; Melvin Ballou Gilbert, "Dancing, Aesthetic and Social," in *Athletics and Outdoor Sports for Women,* ed. Lucille Eaton Hill (New York: Macmillan, 1903), 56, 65–67.

53. Anna Mary Galbraith, *Hygiene and Physical Culture for Women* (New York: Dodd, Mead, 1895. The substance of her 1895 book reappeared in 1911 under the title *Personal Hygiene and Physical Training for Women;* it subsequently appeared in several editions from W. B. Saunders between 1911 and 1925. Galbraith's credentials were impressive, as her biography in *Who Was Who in America* attests; she did postgraduate medical study in Vienna and Munich followed by hospital work in Philadelphia and New York. In addition, she was a Fellow of the New York Academy of Medicine, a member of the American Medical Association, and medical examiner for the Presbyterian Board of Foreign Missions.

54. Galbraith, *Hygiene and Physical Culture,* xxvii–xxix, 70, 77. See discussion of Dr. Silas Weir Mitchell in chapter 7, above.

55. Mary P. Ryan, *Womanhood in America from Colonial Times to the Present,* 3d ed. (New York: Franklin Watts, 1983), 212. Hill, *Athletics and Outdoor Sports for Women,* has chapters on these several sports. Accompanying pictures show women in knee-length bloomers for both basketball and aesthetic dancing, although they played golf and tennis in floor-length skirts.

56. Frances E. Russell, "Symposium on Women's Dress," *The Arena* 6 (1892): 500–501.

57. G. Stanley Hall, *Adolescence: Its Psychology and Its Relations to Physiology, Anthropology, Sociology, Sex, Crime, Religion and Education* (New York: D. Appleton, 1907) vol. 1, 132, 168–69.

58. Ibid., 214.

59. From 1886 to 1903 Gulick served as director of physical training for the YMCA Training College in Springfield, Massachusetts. Beginning in 1903, he served a three-year term as director of physical training for the New York City schools. At the same time, he also served as president of the American Physical Education Association. In 1906 he helped to found the Playground Association of America and served as its first president from 1906 to 1909. Concurrently, and until 1913, Gulick also headed up the Department of Child Hygiene with the Russell Sage Foundation. By 1916, Gulick encouraged the formation of the American Folk Dance Society. Through these several leadership roles, Gulick advocated the development of curricula in schools and community agencies to include dance, sports, and games. His biographer, Josephine Dorgan, said of Gulick: "No religious missionary has been more sincere in his aim to gather to Christ than Luther Gulick in his twofold object of educating for character and bringing to Jesus." One of Gulick's longstanding contributions was the creation of the YMCA delta emblem. See Ethel Josephine Dorgan, "Luther Halsey Gulick, 1865–1918" (Ph.D. diss., Teachers College Columbia University, 1934), 26, 37, 143; *Dictionary of American Biography*, s.v. "Gulick, Luther H."; and G. S. Hall, *Adolescence,* vol. 1, 138.

60. Luther H. Gulick, *The Healthful Art of Dancing* (New York: Doubleday, Page, 1910), 5.

61. Luther H. Gulick, *Folk Dancing: Illustrating the Educational, Civic, and Moral Value of Folk Dancing* (New York: Department of Child Hygiene, Russell Sage Foundation, [1912]), 7–9.

62. Gulick, *Healthful Art of Dancing,* 4–5. Gulick discussed Duncan's dancing under the heading "Emotional Interpretation" and concluded that he had never seen anyone with more facial expressiveness combined with control of the entire body (221–22). Antidance treatises do not mention Duncan.

63. Wood served as director of physical education and college physician at Stanford University from 1891 to 1901. From Stanford, Wood continued his career at Columbia University until 1932 in a similar capacity. Arthur Weston, *The Making of American Physical Education* (New York: Appleton-Century-Crofts, 1962), 150.

64. Thomas Denison Wood, "Physical Education," *The Ninth Yearbook of the National Society for the Study of Education,* Part 1, *Health and Education* (Chicago: University of Chicago Press, 1910), 80, 82, 103.

65. Emil Rath, *Aesthetic Dancing* (New York: A. S. Barnes, 1919), foreword. Rath served as director of the Normal College of the American Gymnastic Union in Indianapolis. The "renaissance" of dance was surely aided by touring performers. By 1914, Anna Pavlova, the famed Russian ballerina, had toured the United States. In the same year two American artists, Ruth St. Denis and Ted Shawn, formed the Denishawn Company; they spread the idea of American modern dance to cities around the country during the next decade and a half. As early as 1909–10, St. Denis had performed as a solo dancer in seventeen cities of the United States. For a discussion of dance as fine art, motivated by the Russian ballet touring in con-

temporary America, see Troy and Margaret West Kinney, *The Dance: Its Place in Art and Life* (New York: Frederick A. Stokes Company, 1914).

66. Dorgan, "Luther Halsey Gulick," 94; Louis H. Chalif, *The Chalif Text Book of Dancing*, 3d ed., rev. and enl. (New York: By the author, 1916).

67. Burchenal served as executive secretary of the girls' branch of the Public School Athletic League of New York City, where she introduced folk dancing between 1905 and 1916. She was an organizer of the Archive of American Folk Dance, beginning in 1929. See *Who's Who of American Women*, s.v. "Burchenal, Elizabeth."

68. Weston, *The Making of American Physical Education*, 74; R. Freeman Butts, *Public Education in the United States from Revolution to Reform* (New York: Holt, Rinehart, and Winston, 1978), 194.

69. An article from 1927 lends credibility to the assertion that the turkey trot, grizzly bear, and Texas Tommy came from cabarets and dance halls in San Francisco's Barbary Coast. Actresses reportedly were introduced to these dances in a social context in San Francisco, and they subsequently brought them to the Broadway stage about 1911–12. See H. E. Cooper, "Rag on the Barbary Coast," *Dance Magazine* 1–17 (Jan. 1924–Dec. 1927): 31, 60.

70. F. Leslie Clendenen, *Dance Mad, or, the Dances of the Day* (St. Louis: Arcade Print Company, 1914). For a fuller discussion of the new century's fad dances, their popularity with blacks, and the gradual crossing of social boundaries between blacks and whites, see Lewis A. Erenberg, "Everybody's Doin' It: The Pre–World War I Dance Craze, the Castles, and the Modern American Girl," *Feminist Studies* 3, nos. 1–4 (Fall 1975–Summer 1976): 155–70. A modified version of Erenberg's article is included as a chapter in his subsequent book, which discusses urban social, commercial, and amusement changes in turn-of-the-century New York. See Lewis A. Erenberg, *Steppin' Out: New York Nightlife and the Transformation of American Culture, 1890–1930* (Chicago: University of Chicago Press, 1984). The entry of blacks into white society was augmented from the teens on by the tremendous exodus from the South to the North—especially to New York City. Lynn Fauley Emery quotes Department of Labor statistics in 1916 stating that 350,000 blacks migrated northward in an eighteen-month period. She reports, "Harlem grew from a community of 50,000 in 1914 to 80,000 by 1920 to 200,000 by 1930." See Lynne Fauley Emery, *Black Dance in the United States, 1619 to Today*, 2d rev. ed. (Princeton: Princeton Book Company, 1988), 221.

71. Erenberg, "Everybody's Doin' It," 163–66.

72. Mr. and Mrs. Vernon Castle, *Modern Dancing* (New York: World Syndicate Company, 1914), 22–24, 32–34, 134.

73. Florence Howe Hall, *Good Form for All Occasions* (New York: Harper, 1914), 24. The daughter of Samuel Gridley and Julia Ward Howe, Hall established her reputation as an etiquette authority by 1887 with her book *Social Customs*. She was essentially conservative and confined her writing to the social patterns of the upper middle class. See *American Woman Writers*, s.v. "Hall, Florence Marion Howe."

74. Hall, *Good Form,* 161–62.

75. Ibid., 164–66, 158.

76. Ryan, *Womanhood in America,* 230, 204–5. In 1870, the majority of women working outside the home were employed as household servants; by 1920, only one in four was so employed. During the 1910s, white-collar jobs for women rose by 64 percent, surpassing manufacturing jobs as the main area of the work force where women held jobs. According to Ryan, the new jobs were considered to be an example of "upward mobility," a new experience for women. Between 1890 and 1920 women built a national organizational network that Ryan terms almost as "sophisticated in its own way as the corporate business world." During the same decades, the number of professional women increased at a rate almost triple to that of men.

77. D. B. Van Dalen and Bruce L. Bennett, *A World History of Physical Education,* 2d ed. (Englewood Cliffs, N.J.: Prentice-Hall, 1971), 451. The authors report, for example, that as early as 1905 the Marshall, Michigan, high school girls basketball team won the state championship and were greeted upon their return home by bonfires, ten thousand Roman candles, and crowds of people, including the superintendent and ex-mayor.

78. Ryan, *Womanhood in America,* 244.

79. Hofstadter, *Anti-Intellectualism,* 118–19.

80. William G. McLoughlin, *Billy Sunday Was His Real Name* (Chicago: University of Chicago Press, 1955), 46–47.

81. "A Plain Talk to Women," in *Billy Sunday Speaks,* ed. Karen Gullen (New York: Chelsea House, 1970), 107, 111.

82. *Billy Sunday Speaks,* ed. Gullen, 109, 111–13.

83. Examination of his notes indicates that he merely reiterated the same old themes and sometimes the same old language that had been previously preached. For example, he repeats Milan B. Williams's declaration that to "Sow the Dance" means to "Reap the Brothel"; he also reiterates the common characterization that dancing was nothing more than a "hugging match set to music."

84. Billy Sunday, "Amusements" (n.d.), Folder 3, Box 9 of Sermons in the *Sunday Papers,* Billy Graham Center, Wheaton College, Wheaton, Illinois.

85. McLoughlin, *Modern Revivalism,* 415. McLoughlin's figures for Sunday's twenty most successful revivals indicate that four of the twenty cities came from his 1916 campaign: Trenton, Baltimore, Kansas City, and Detroit. Statistics for the sermon on "Amusements," from September to November 1916, indicate that the yield of "trail-hitters" was good though not outstanding. Some sermons yielded a bit more, some fewer. See Billy Sunday, *Sunday Papers,* Folder 11, Box 10; Weisberger, *They Gathered at the River,* 266–67.

86. Of the known antidance publications from this decade, three were issued from Louisville, two came from Chicago, and four were printed in New York City. The remainder appeared from towns and cities in Indiana, Ohio, Tenessee, Illinois, Kentucky, Wisconsin, Iowa, Texas, and Oregon. The preponderance of writing from

cities other than New York or Chicago suggests there was some consensus of values considered "American" and "Christian" as opposed to a great diversity of ideas and customs brought in by waves of immigrants.

87. W[arren] A[kin] Candler, comp., *Theater-Going and Dancing Incompatible with Church-Membership* (Nashville: Publishing House of the M. E. Church South, 1913). The book first appeared with nearly the same title, *The Incompatibility of Theater-Going and Dancing with Membership in the Christian Church.* It was issued as "An Address of the Clergy of the Convocation of the Valley of Virginia, to the People of Their Respective Parishes" from Philadelphia in 1872. The acknowledged author was the Episcopal cleric C. W. Andrews. The other example from the teens, repeating an earlier edition, comes from J[ames] W[illiam] Lowber, *The Devil in Modern Society,* 10th ed. (Cincinnati: Standard Publishing Company, [1918]). The first edition of 1888, which came from the same publishing house and city, is subtitled "Seven Sermons Preached in the First Christian Church, Paducah, Kentucky."

88. Carl E[din] Nordberg, *Modern Amusements: Talks to Young People,* 2d ed. [Minneapolis: Augsburg Publishing House, 1922], 5, 8–9.

89. G[ulbrand] G. Belsheim, *The Amusement Craze of Our Times* (N.p.: N.p., [1919]), 4, 5–6. See also Dallmann, *The Dance,* 30–31.

90. Faulkner's statistics found even wider circulation through subsequent editions, as well as through the publications of other authors during the second decade of this century. The eighth edition of Dallman's book appeared in 1921, thus exposing hundreds of Missouri Synod laity and clerics to the authority of Faulkner. The only known antidance book by an American Catholic priest, the Right Reverend Monseignor Don Luigi Satori (1843–?), appeared in 1910 under the title *Modern Dances* and includes evidence from Faulkner's books. See Rt. Rev. Mgr. Don Luigi Satori, *Modern Dances* (Collegeville, Ind.: St. Joseph's Printing Office, 1910), 16. In addition, nine other books published between 1911 and 1917 quote Faulkner and his statistics on "fallen women."

91. T. A. Faulkner, *From the Ball Room to Hell,* 36, 59; idem, *The Gates of Hell or Eastern Ball Room Unmasked* (Columbus, Ohio: Hussey and Faulkner, 1896), 52.

92. According to the *Annual of the Kentucky Baptist Convention for 1962,* two of Ham's "most notable successes occurred in the conversions of Billy Graham and Grady Wilson" (157).

93. M[ordecai] F[owler] Ham, *The Modern Dance: A Historical and Analytical Treatment of the Subject: Religious, Social, Hygienic Industrial Aspects as Viewed by the Pulpit, the Press, Medical Authorities, Municipal Authorities, Social Workers, etc.,* 2d ed. rev. and enl. (N.p., n.p. [1916]), 27–28. Apparently such tainting referred to a mental addiction. Ham quotes a Dr. S. Grover Burnett, former president of the University of Missouri Medical School, as saying that "many of the causes of insanity developed in the United States within the last few years may be traced to modern eccentric dances as a causal source."

94. William Milburn Dye, *Popular Amusements and Their Substitutes* (Louisville: Pentecostal Publishing, 1912), 9.

95. Florence Ethel Smith, *Dancing as a Modern Amusement* (Chicago: Christian Witness Company, n.d. [1912?]), 3.

96. Richard Henry Edwards, *Christianity and Amusements* (New York: Association Press, 1915), 67. This book followed an earlier detailed analysis of the contemporary recreation scene in American culture. See Edwards's *Popular Amusements, Studies in American Social Conditions*, No. 8 (New York: Association Press, 1915).

97. Matthew S. Hughes, *Dancing and the Public Schools* (New York: Methodist Book Concern, 1917), 4–5; Harry Benton, *The Public School Dance* (Eugene, Ore.: World Evangel, n.d.), 12–13.

98. Hughes, *Dancing and the Public Schools*, 11–12; Benton, *Public School Dance*, 7.

99. Benton, *Public School Dance*, 1, 4–5. In Benton's words: "Many public school students are Christians. Many come from Christian homes. True Americanism demands that we give these due consideration. . . . No school has a moral right to affront the home, parenthood and the church." In 1921 a California court held in favor of parents who did not want their children to dance as part of a physical education curriculum. The decision was based on the right of parents to control the principles inculcated in children. See Robert H. Bremner, ed., *Children and Youth in America: A Documentary History, 1866–1932* (Cambridge, Mass.: Harvard University Press, 1970–74), vol. 2, 936–37.

100. Edward W. Stitt, "Evening Recreation Centers," in *The Tenth Yearbook of the National Society for the Study of Education*, Part 1, "The City School as a Community Center." (Chicago: University of Chicago Press, 1911), 40–41, 46–47.

101. Billy Sunday, *Watchman-Examiner* 2, no. 33 (13 Aug. 1914) 1066; McLoughlin, *Modern Revivalism*, 399.

102. McLoughlin, *Billy Sunday Was His Real Name*, 141–42.

103. Russel Nye, *The Unembarrassed Muse: The Popular Arts in America* (New York: Dial, 1970), 326.

104. Nancy Banks, "The World's Most Beautiful Ballrooms," *Chicago History* 2, no. 4 (Fall–Winter 1973): 207. With a full orchestra, Whiteman produced a sweeter sound than the traditional and smaller black band and called it "symphonic jazz."

105. Guy Lombardo, with Jack Altshul, *Auld Acquaintance* (Garden City, N.Y.: Doubleday, 1975), 62. Further testimony to the acceptance of dancing and dance music comes from the fact that Guy Lombardo and his Royal Canadians played New Year's Eve at the Waldorf Astoria in New York City from 1929 on and at every Presidential Inaugural Ball for FDR and Harry Truman (173).

106. Paul Sann, *The Lawless Decade* (New York: Crown, 1957), 38–39. Another point of comparison is total annual radio sales. Between 1922 and 1929, they increased 1,400 percent, from $60,000,000 to $842,548,000. Radios and cars were

key factors in the decade's rising mass production and prosperity. See Frederick Lewis Allen, *Only Yesterday* (New York: Blue Ribbon Books, 1931), 165, 296.

107. Gregory Mason, "Satan in the Dance-Hall," *American Mercury* 2 (May 1924): 175; *Dictionary of American Biography*, s.v. "Straton, John Roach"; *The National Cyclopaedia of American Biography*, s.v. "Straton, John Roach." When William Jennings Bryan died, Straton assumed leadership of the fundamentalist forces.

108. John Roach Straton, *The Dance of Death, Should Christians Indulge?* (New York: Calvary Baptist Church, n.d. [1920?]) and *Fighting the Devil in Modern Babylon* (Boston: The Stratford Company, 1929). At least ten editions of the first book appeared; only one edition of the latter book came out.

109. Robert Cooley Angell, *The Campus: A Study of Contemporary Undergraduate Life in the American University* (New York: D. Appleton, 1928), 167–68. Whereas in 1919, barely 10 percent of the country's automobiles were enclosed, by 1927, almost 83 percent enabled driver and riders to brave any kind of weather. In 1919, between 6,000,000 and 7,000,000 passenger cars were in regular operation; by 1929 more than 23,000,000 ran on the nation's growing number of hard-surfaced roads. As Allen pointed out, the automobile became perhaps the "most potent statistic of Coolidge prosperity." See Allen, *Only Yesterday*, 100, 163.

110. Allen, *Only Yesterday*, 100–102, 107; Nye, *Unembarrassed Muse*, 373–74, 377–78. Already by 1920, Nye reports, Hollywood's payroll had reached 20,000,000 dollars. By 1926, top stars were drawing individual salaries ranging from 10,000 to 40,000 dollars per week. Nye counts 1926 as the industry's best year; some 20,000 theaters showed films, and new buildings under construction ran at the rate of 1,000 per year. Audiences totaling 7,000,000 people daily and 9,000,000 on Sunday saw 700 to 800 films in that year.

111. Allen, *Only Yesterday*, 104.

112. J[ohn] W[illiam] Porter, *Dangers of the Dance* (Louisville: Baptist Book Concern, 1922), 33. Allen makes the same point, referring to the modern young woman of the twenties: "Some of them, furthermore, were abandoning their corsets. 'The men won't dance with you if you wear a corset,' they were quoted as saying" (*Only Yesterday*, 89–90).

113. The shimmy, reportedly, developed from the shoulder-shaking of singer Gilda Gray. Mae West also claimed its invention. The Charleston first became a public craze following the 1923 musical, *Runnin' Wild*. Three or four years later the black bottom was seen in *George White's Scandals*. In 1927 the varsity drag appeared in a show titled *Good News*. See John Greene Youmans, "A History of Recreational Social Dance in the United States" (Ph.D. diss., University of Southern California, 1966), 101, 103, 107–9; Robert Darrell Moulton, "Choreography in Musical Comedy and Revue on the New York Stage from 1925 Through 1950," (Ph.D. diss., University of Minnesota, 1957), 39; Edward Thorpe, *Black Dance* (Woodstock, N.Y.: Overlook Press, 1989), 65–68. The foregoing references to the

origins of the Charleston and black bottom are standard. The different citations by Lynne Fauley Emery suggest the difficulties of determining accurate origins for vernacular dancing lost in the oral tradition. Emery provides sources that indicate that the Charleston first appeared in Irving C. Miller's production of *Liza* but did not become popular until the introduction of the hit song "Charleston" in *Runnin' Wild*. Emery also states that the black bottom first appeared in Miller's production of *Dinah* in 1924. See Emery, *Black Dance in the United States*, 224–28. See also the thorough discussion of such dances in a cultural context in Katrina Hazzard-Gordon, *Jookin': The Rise of Social Dance Formations in African-American Culture* (Philadelphia: Temple University Press, 1990).

114. Emery, *Black Dance in the United States*, 221–24. Bill Robinson had danced professionally in the theater since the 1890s and was fifty years old when he was reportedly "discovered." Marshall and Jean Stearns report that Robinson, perhaps more than any other tap dancer, helped critics to become more sophisticated in their understanding of tap; see their *Jazz Dance: The Story of American Vernacular Dancing* (New York: Macmillan, 1968), 156. Robinson also appeared in 1930s movies with, among others, the child star Shirley Temple.

115. In her essay on smoking and dancing as liberation symbols for the twenties' woman, Fass notes: "The ability to dance was both a sign of belonging to the world of youth and a necessary accomplishment if one wished to take part in the activities of that world." See Paula Fass, "Smoking and Dancing as Symbols of Liberation" in *Ain't We Got Fun? Essays, Lyrics, and Stories of the Twenties*, ed. Barbara Solomon (New York: New American Library, 1980), 172, 178–79; Angell, *The Campus*, 163–65.

116. Emily Holt, *Encyclopaedia of Etiquette*, rev. ed. (New York: Doubleday, Page, 1921), vol. 1, 141–44, 173–77. Schlesinger confirms the trend toward informality in the postwar years. In his chapter titled "Relax" he observes that "simplicity, common sense" and "spontaneity" returned to deportment. That fact did not, however, limit the publication of etiquette books. At least sixty-eight appeared from 1918 to 1929. (Schlesinger, *Learning How to Behave*, 51, 58.)

117. Holt, *Encyclopaedia of Etiquette* (1921 ed.), vol. 1, 179.

118. Ryan, *Womanhood in America*, 239, 244.

119. The output of antidance literature in the 1920s was surpassed in the 1850s by 24 books and in the 1890s by at least twenty-six books that, in whole or in part, inveighed against dancing.

120. Porter, *Dangers of the Dance*, preface; C. F. Weigle, *The Dance of Death* (Louisville: Pentecostal Publishing Company, n.d.), 12.

121. Clovis G. Chappell, *The Modern Dance: Three Sermons* (Nashville: Publishing House M. E. Church, South, 1923), 24; *The Dance: Fifty Statements Concerning Its Morality* (Chicago: Christian Witness Company, [1928?]), 6; Guy A. Lamphear, *The Modern Dance: A Fearless Discussion of a Social Menace* (Chicago: Glad Tidings Publishing Company, 1922), 35.

122. Weigle, *Dance of Death,* 13; Harry H. Vom Bruch, *The Carnival of Death or the Modern Dance and Other Amusements* (New York: Book Stall, [1920?]), 41–42. According to current historical research on prostitution, the term "white slavery" carried highly charged connotations in the Progressive Era, including the ideas that all women were potential victims and that an "underworld of European immigrants" operated an international network. See the discussion in Hobson, *Uneasy Virtue,* 142–43.

123. Lamphear, *Modern Dance,* 49–50; Straton, *Dance of Death,* 16–18; Clyde Lee Fife, *Fife's Revival Sermons* (Louisville: Pentecostal Publishing Company, 1922), 220; Porter, *Dangers of the Dance,* 35.

124. Lee Ralph Phipps, John Emory Roberts, and DeWitt Miley Phipps, *Popular Amusements: Destructive and Constructive* (Nashville: Cokesbury Press, 1925), 53; Vom Bruch, *Carnival of Death,* 57–58.

125. Melvin G. Morris, *The Devil's Ball, or the Modern Dance* (Baltimore: Old-Time Religion Company, 1920), 50; Fife, *Fife's Revival Sermons,* 223; Chappell, *The Modern Dance: Three Sermons,* 4.

126. Straton, *Fighting the Devil in Modern Babylon,* 34; Porter, *Dangers of the Dance,* 44; Phipps, *Popular Amusements,* 55.

127. Harry O. Anderson, *Should a Christian Dance?* (Oakland, Calif.: N.p., [1928?]), 4–5.

128. Faulkner's 1893 book was titled *From the Ballroom to Hell* and the 1916 publication appeared as *The Lure of the Dance.* Another contemporary dance master, J. Harvey DeHoney, published a kind of novel in 1929, the purpose of which seemed similar to Faulkner's, that is, to tell readers the evils of dancing. Moreover, DeHoney's book, published by the Independent Printing Company of Portland, Oregon, copied Faulkner's title almost verbatim. DeHoney's title reads *From the Ballroom and Dance Halls to Hell.* Subsequent dance opponents do not quote DeHoney.

129. Vom Bruch, *Carnival of Death,* 56; Straton, *Dance of Death,* 18–20; Lamphear, *Modern Dance,* 53; John L. Brandt, *What About the Modern Dance?* (Cincinnati: Standard Publishing Company, 1922), 11. Although first quoted in the antidance books by Ambrose Bierce in 1877, with no reference to origin, the phrase continued to serve 1920s dance opponents because it pointed to a breakdown in traditional values surrounding the importance of home, marriage, motherhood, and morality.

130. Vom Bruch, *Carnival of Death,* 51–52; Straton, *Dance of Death,* 34.

131. Lamphear, *Modern Dance,* foreword.

132. Vom Bruch, *Carnival of Death,* 39; Morris, *Devil's Ball,* 34.

133. Lamphear, *Modern Dance,* 57; Brandt, *What About the Modern Dance?* 6; Fife, *Fife's Revival Sermons,* 218–19; Porter, *Dangers of the Dance,* 51.

134. Lamphear, *Modern Dance,* 32; Chappell, *The Modern Dance: Three Sermons,* 12; Porter, *Dangers of the Dance,* 54. A similar accusation first appeared in the antidance literature in the 1851 book by Moses M. Henkle, a Southern Methodist, entitled *Primary Platform of Methodism,* and then in the 1897 publication

by a Baptist, Marion Palmer Hunt, *What's the Harm in Dancing Anyway?*

135. Vom Bruch, *Carnival of Death*, 33; Morris, *Devil's Ball*, 36: Lamphear, *Modern Dance*, 15; Chappell, *The Modern Dance: Three Sermons*, 12; Phipps, *Popular Amusements*, 50.

136. Straton, *Dance of Death*, 37; Morris, *Devil's Ball*, 47–49.

137. Straton, *Fighting the Devil in Modern Babylon*, ii; Anderson, *Should a Christian Dance?* 7.

138. Ahlstrom, *Religious History*, vol. 2, 404.

139. Straton, *Fighting the Devil in Modern Babylon*, 44–45. For a summary of dance developing in the Mormon Church, see Karl Wesson, "Dance in the Church of Jesus Christ of Latter-Day Saints, 1820–1940" (M.A. thesis, Brigham Young University, 1975). For a discussion of dance in physical education curricular and state legislation, see Van Dalen and Bennett, *World History of Physical Education*, 439–41, 464–65.

140. William Normal Guthrie, *The Relation of the Dance to Religion* (N.p.: N.p., [1923]), 1, 24, 26, 28, 31–32.

9 Urban Reformers and the Dance Hall: 1908–40

> In all of our large cities the two agencies run for
> commercial reasons which draw the largest number of
> young people are the theatre and the dance hall.
>
> Louise deKoven Bowen, 1911

When Louise deKoven Bowen (1859–1953), a prominent Chicago native representing the city's Juvenile Protection Association, spoke out against the evils of her city's commercial dance halls during the early decades of the twentieth century, she represented a new element in the annals of American opposition to dance.[1] Earlier opponents, as well as those contemporary with Bowen, had almost exclusively been clergy and evangelists, from the several American Protestant denominations, who wrote against the evils of dancing as practiced in their day. They had long objected to particular dances, balls, and large dancing parties, as well as to the context in which dancing occurred. These adversaries remained influential until after the midpoint of the present century.

At the end of the nineteenth century and during the first two decades of the twentieth century, however, there emerged a growing cadre of citizens concerned with the quality of urban life, especially as it affected young people. Motivated by what they saw around them—immorality, corruption, exploitation, and the devaluing of individuals, particularly women—male and female social reformers launched a sustained attack on the context in which dancing occurred, the rapidly increasing numbers of urban dance halls and academies.[2] Unlike most evangelical clergy who regularly urged abstinence from dancing, these public-spirited citizens argued, as had Washington

Gladden more than four decades earlier, that the good in dancing must be preserved and only the abuses abolished. To that end, they gathered data, amassed public opinion, and pushed legislation; after approximately three decades of effort, the dance hall became not only regulated but accepted by the majority of American citizens.

The investigations and advocacy of early twentieth-century urban reformers reflect a widespread paternalistic concern among the middle-class men and women who led the citizens' committees and associations aimed at cleaning up commercial dance halls. Their goal was to make cities places that could provide young people in particular with moral and healthful recreation.

The Need for Urban Recreation

The expansion of cities, one of the major social trends in the Gilded Age, intensified during the first part of the twentieth century. With western land effectively closed to homesteading, and with technology rapidly developing, immigrants found jobs in urban centers.[3] Masses of people packed into large cities produced crowded housing and sanitation problems. For the first time in America, the question of how and where vast numbers of citizens were going to spend their work-free time called for serious attention. The poor and the uneducated had to be assimilated and offered opportunities to become productive citizens, which posed new challenges for school officials, public health officers, and those reform-minded individuals concerned with a balanced way of life.

The focus on quality of life encompassed the need for play and recreation in healthful and moral settings. After three centuries in which stress had been placed on the primacy of work and worship, more than a few Americans were recognizing the importance of accommodating another vital dimension of human existence. They realized that public recreation should be provided for working-class people, as Edward Everett Hale had urged in the 1850s. Urban reformers urged two avenues of responsibility for public recreation, including dancing: city and state legislation for the regulation of commercial enterprises, and the use of school facilities and curricula for additional opportunities.

One of the most vocal activists of the period was Jane Addams (1860–1935), founder of the famous Hull-House in 1889, a settlement and education center amid Chicago's immigrant slums. Her 1909 publication *The Spirit of Youth and the City Streets,* which appeared in numerous subsequent editions through 1926, was a pioneering work in urban sociology. In it, Addams points out the particular evils that the modern city inflicted upon young men and women:

> Never before in civilization have such numbers of young girls been suddenly released from the protection of the home and permitted to work unattended upon city streets and to work under alien roofs; for the first time they are being prized more for their labor power than for their innocence, their tender beauty, their ephemeral gaiety. . . . Never before have such numbers of young boys earned money independently of the family life, and felt themselves free to spend it as they choose in the midst of vice deliberately disguised as pleasure.[4]

Young people, many of them from Europe or from American farms, were working in mindless factory jobs and needed some outlet to satisfy social and recreational cravings. Dancing provided a logical and inviting opportunity for young men and women to meet, mingle, and enjoy themselves. But working-class folk, who lived in what the New York reformer Michael M. Davis called "a nest of boxes tucked four stories in the air," had no private homes large enough for dancing, so they patronized the burgeoning numbers of commercial—and often disreputable—dance halls and "academies." Addams's observations of Chicago's dance facilities led her to the following conclusion: "One of the most pathetic sights in the public dance halls of Chicago is the number of young men, obviously honest young fellows from the country, who stand about vainly hoping to make the acquaintance of some 'nice girl.' They look eagerly up and down the rows of girls, many of whom are drawn to the hall by the same keen desire for pleasure and social intercourse which the lonely young men themselves feel." Addams and other reformers of the era felt empathy for youth who longed for a break in the monotony of routine lives and dull jobs, yet they reacted with horror and alarm at conditions in the dance halls of Chicago, New York, and other large cities.[5]

The Dance Hall Problem

The perceived magnitude of the problem in Chicago led the Juvenile Protection Association (JPA) to undertake an investigation of the city's dance halls in the winter of 1910–11. Statistics showed that an estimated 32,000 children went to the movies in Chicago but as many as 86,000 young women and men patronized dance halls some nights. According to Bowen, the dance hall served as an emotional outlet, a "safety valve for their surplus energy."

In 1911, the city had 306 licensed halls and "about 100 unlicensed." Prompted to investigate by a number of calls from concerned mothers, the JPA committee visited 278 dances and 328 halls between November 1910 and March 1911. They found that "saloon and vice interests" primarily controlled the city's dance halls. Moreover, the halls that adjoined saloons often had only saloon keepers and prostitutes for chaperones. Even when police were present, they did little to control the environment. Operators broke liquor laws by selling to minors, and the dance halls served as points of rendezvous for prostitutes. The majority of youth attending were boys from sixteen to eighteen and girls between fourteen and sixteen. Most boys showed signs of inebriation by midnight. With four to five minutes spent dancing followed by fifteen to twenty minutes of drinking, a high incidence of intoxication was hardly surprising. The committee concluded that "hundreds of young girls are annually started on the road to ruin, for the saloon-keepers and dance hall owners have only one end in view, and that is profit."

Though the JPA committee focused first on the moral context, members were equally concerned about health and safety. Bowen's report cites poor lighting, minimal fire protection, toilets for men accessible only through the bar, floors covered with "expectoration," and little or no ventilation in rooms filled with tobacco smoke, dust, and the aroma of sweat. The committee found that "girls frequently faint and are carried out or laid upon the floor, their clothing torn open and cold water thrown upon their chests."[6]

In addition to producing the JPA report, Bowen authored an article for *The Survey* in June 1911. At the same time, Jane Addams gave even wider circulation to the evils of the Chicago dance hall when she wrote a summary of the problem for the *Ladies' Home Journal* of July 1913. Their findings appear to have been sensationalized to some degree in a book titled *From Dance Hall to White Slavery: The World's Greatest Tragedy.* Published in 1912 and authored by "Investigators for the Metropolitan Press," the book consists of cases told as "thrilling stories of actual experiences of girls who were lured from innocence into lives of degradation by men and women engaged in a regularly organized WHITE SLAVE TRAFFIC." Bowen and Addams, as well as the president of the Chicago Board of Education, are quoted regarding the magnitude of the problem.[7]

Similar reports came from other cities. In New York, a health administrator, Michael M. Davis (1879–1971), reported in 1911 on an investigation of that city's commercial recreations that had been conducted under the auspices of the Department of Child Hygiene of the Russell Sage Foundation. In a booklet titled *The Exploitation of Pleasure,* Davis, like Addams, presses the point that "recreation within the modern city has become a matter of public concern; *laissez faire,* in recreation as in industry, can no longer be the policy of the state." The public problem with respect to the dance hall stemmed from the fact that young people no longer learned to dance in their homes or under the supervision of a private teacher of high repute: "When each of ten thousand girls could learn to dance in her home[,] society might have little concern with the matter; but when no more than ten of those ten thousand are able to learn to dance elsewhere than in academies commercially established and run for profit, the quality of these academies becomes a matter with which the state that cares for its citizens has every need to concern itself."[8] Writing from Baltimore in 1912 and focusing on the routineness of jobs and the limited amount of home space, M. S. Hanaw described the plight of a young working girl and boy:

> If we live through a day at the side of the average factory worker in this city, we learn that his hours are long, his work confining and tiresome, the sanitation of the shop poor, the salary poorer, and the "joy in labor" quite lacking. Following this same average worker out of the shop into the home, we find an atmosphere of gloom and narrowness, an under-supply of food, lifeless, uninteresting surroundings, little "home spirit," a restless desire for excitement of some kind after "the day of toil." The average home is inadequate to provide this. Space for the girl to entertain "the best beau," for instance, is out of the question; and so the girl turns to other avenues offered, outside the home, for the re-cre-ation [*sic*] of physical and mental powers and for social life.[9]

Maria Ward Lambin, in San Francisco, wrote about immigrant enculturation, the industrial city, and the dance hall: "The young working population of the cities, largely second-generation foreign-born, growing up in the increasingly tense atmosphere of industrial life, found dancing—even its degenerate forms—a more profound relief for tired nerves and overstrained attention than any so-called 'respectable' amusements. . . . Unfortunately, it was considered more 'American' to go to the saloon dance hall than to the foreign society hall."[10]

The discovery of evils in the dance halls of San Francisco, Baltimore, and New York replicated the findings of Bowen's committee in Chicago; all of these reports had resulted from on-site investigations. The reformers expressed concern about the immorality of the dance hall context due to the pervasiveness of liquor, prostitutes, and other undesirable customers. They were alarmed by the unhealthful sanitary conditions and poor lighting and ventilation. Objections to immoral dances, to obscene language, and the like figured in indictments of the dance hall but these issues did not appear to be of more or less concern than the other problems. In each instance, the seriousness of the context derived from the fact that young girls patronized dance halls. As Michael Davis pointed out, the great numbers of the population involved made the issue one of significant proportion:

> The social significance of these facts is apparent when we learn that the one hundred dancing academies of Manhatten are reaching, annually, not less than one hundred thousand individuals as paying pupils; and that 45% of these pupils are under sixteen, 90% under twenty-one. Practically all the young girls among the mass of the people pass during the period of adolescence through the education of the dancing academy. We have here an influence over the adolescent of New York which is of practically universal scope.[11]

A different type of reform concern also yielded statistics and a perspective about the dance hall problem. Those engaged in fighting the organized and commercialized vice of prostitution added their investigative studies to the published documents of the teens. An extensive and detailed analysis, *Commercialized Prostitution in New York City*, appeared in 1913 and in a revised edition in 1917. Among the places identified as catering to vice were the freestanding public dance halls; the dance halls that existed as part of an amusement park; the "concert halls," either freestanding or as part of an amusement park complex; and excursion boats. In the "concert halls," girls on stage, ostensibly there to sing and entertain, were typically prostitutes who were assisted by male waiters in securing their customers. The New York City report, introduced by John D. Rockefeller Jr., listed further evils of the unregulated dance hall context, including the presence of professional prostitutes, pimps, gamblers, pickpockets, minors, and purveyors of pornographic advertising cards, as well as the practice of suggestive or "tough" dancing. Yet this information was not entirely new. Many of the same contexts and threats to working girls had been identified in 1909 by the New York reformer Belle Israels. However, she included details about the excursion boats, as well as about saloon dance halls and the downtown dance academies, the latter of which were "infested with the 'spieler[s],'" young men hired to assist the dance teacher and attract young girls. As a further enticement, girls could get into the academies cheaper than men—for only ten cents.[12]

Reports from Cleveland, Kansas City, and Milwaukee in 1912 highlighted similar issues of dance halls in particular and the significance of the commercial amusement problem in general. The published findings for both Kansas City and Milwaukee came from Rowland Haynes (1878–1963), field secretary for the Playground and Recreation Association of America, another organization concerned about urban issues. Collectively such reports exemplify the spread and the spirit of urban reformers in the Progressive Era. They based their recommendations and actions on first-hand evidence, whether from surveys or on-site investigations.

These investigative reports and surveys indicate that dance facilities fell into several categories. Milwaukee, for example, had dance halls for the general public, for clubs, and for fraternal orders, as well as dance academies. The latter offered instruction in addition to sponsoring dances. Typically the halls for clubs or fraternal orders were rented for one evening at a time.[13] Davis singled out some New York City facilities as "great public places," such as the Grand Central Palace, in addition to the saloon dance halls, the club halls, and those places rented specifically for the purpose of a dance for profit. Academies were evaluated as those of the "better class" and those of a "lower type," with the former having more and better supervision for its activities.[14]

The popularity of these dance facilities is indicated by attendance figures reported in the recreation surveys. Haynes stated that the total attendance at dance halls and academies on a Saturday evening in Milwaukee in November 1911 was about 9,300 dancers and observers. For Sunday evening, 12 November, the crowd totaled approximately 3,600 to 4,100 customers. Fully two-thirds of them on both nights were between eighteen and twenty-five years of age. That number constituted about 14 percent of the city's total population for that age group. Haynes, who authored the Kansas City survey, reported that in that city the total weekly attendance of all dance halls amounted to 16,566 people. In the public dance halls, 65 percent of customers were between the ages of fifteen and twenty-five. Figures in the several reports from sundry cities do not permit exact comparative analysis. However, if the data for Milwaukee and Kansas City were typical, the high percentage of youth attending dance halls helps to validate the concerns expressed by the urban reformers. Drawing a contrast with the situation in public halls, Haynes was careful to comment on the dance hall activity of neighborhood ethnic groups in Milwaukee, primarily married couples who brought children as young as five years of age. Such dance events were, in Haynes's opinion, generally of a "high order." Where neighborhood control prevailed, instead of the commercial profit motive, a more benign environment existed. In the neighborhood setting, for example, drinking took place as part of the gathering of friends and family. By contrast, drinking in commercial dance halls was encouraged by operators who had no proprietary interest in the patrons.[15]

Although the recreation surveys for Milwaukee and Kansas City were intended to gather information pertaining to the whole scope of city recreation activities, Cleveland's report came from the dance hall inspector. Cleveland had previously studied the dance hall situation and decided to take municipal action to regulate dance facilities. A "self-constituted" committee had found in 1910 that numerous evils prevailed in these public establishments. For example, boys and girls from fourteen to eighteen years of age attended dance classes where liquor was sold on the premises. They were allowed to remain at the dance until 3:00 A.M. Prizes were offered to the girls who could drink the most liquor in an evening. Buildings had no proper sanitation facilities, and fire codes were disregarded. Unlighted halls and rooms provided places where patrons congregated and conducted themselves "in a reprehensible manner." No protection existed against "gangs of toughs and rowdies" invading the premises. Finally, police on duty did not attempt to correct such deficiencies, and some even tried to lead young girls "astray." As a consequence of these findings, Cleveland instituted a new ordinance to regulate dance halls and appoint a dance hall inspector to oversee implementation. Under the municipal law, 110 halls were licensed, though substantial improvements were required before a license could be obtained. A few new buildings were built to code, but several existing halls were refused licenses because of inadequate facilities or unfit environs. Nonetheless, Robb O. Bartholomew, the dance hall inspector who authored the 1912 report, lamented the closing of some thirty-two dance halls because their demise put an end to opportunities for neighborhood social gatherings:

> Here was offered the only opportunity for general gatherings of a social nature which were generally followed by dancing. The entire family participated in these dances, which would, but for the demoralizing surroundings, have provided the means by which the citizens living near them could have enjoyed the recreational and social life which is necessary to the well being and proper development of every normal citizen. These halls have been dismantled, and there are now no club houses for many thousands of Cleveland's citizens. One of the greatest means of making us better neighbors and therefore better citizens by bringing us together where our purposes are unified and stimulated for better things, has been temporarily stayed. Ought not the municipality provide for certain sections of the city halls where opportunities for participation in wholesome recreation would be offered to all members of the family?[16]

Bartholomew, like Addams, Davis, Hanaw, and others, advocated municipal responsibility for preventing social ills and uniting citizens in healthy recreation, thereby promoting some degree of social cohesion and control.

Citizenship, Schools, and Dancing

Concern for integrating the millions of new immigrants into an American citizenry became a factor in the rationale for recommending municipal and state responsibility for the recreational life of city dwellers. Haynes's Milwaukee report reveals that the purposes of a municipal recreation program included three aims: "To reduce delinquency," "To develop character," and "To make life worth living."[17] Hanaw's report from Baltimore gave a more telling and impassioned plea that the government provide recreation, including dance halls. In the introduction to the report, Belle Israels commented on such recreation: "We need simply to place safeguards around it. If we can adequately throw legal safeguards around commercialized forms of recreation, it is going to mean control of the entrance to the social evil." Yet, merely controlling the entrance of social evil was not the whole rationale. Hanaw put the city's larger responsibility in comparative terms:

> Surely the supervision of the recreations of the young is quite as important if not more important, than the supervision of the education of the young. I implore the community also to demand a further use of the public schools as valuable centers for public dances. It would hardly be possible to procure too many city halls to meet the needs of this popular form of recreation. . . . Aren't the schools the property of the people, and isn't dancing a normal desire of the young? If we care at all about the development of citizenship, let us consider what our city offers for amusements during the plastic years of the boy and girl.[18]

Testimony to the fact that Hanaw represented no lone voice in the wilderness comes from the fifty-seventh annual report of the Chicago superintendent of schools, in 1911: "In accordance with a general growing conviction that public school property as an investment is susceptible of yielding larger returns, the Board of Education authorized during the past year the opening of school buildings as social and recreational centers." The superintendent reported that city response was good. Nine centers opened, offering dancing, lectures, and other social activities. Subsequent reports from school officials indicated that the plan continued. The decision by the Chicago board of education affirmed a concern for the moral training and protection of youth. The superintendent's report of 1911 focused on a nationwide concern: "In recent times conditions that tend to start children and young people on the road to immorality have received unusual attention from many individuals and social organizations. Intelligent endeavor to substitute attractive and refined entertainment for an environment filled with temptation has been made here and there."[19] Some observers believed there had been a decline in "social and personal purity" of the country. Others argued the need for moral protection of youth because of a "belief that the pleasure-loving nature of the young must be recognized and planned for if they are to be guided into the paths of social morality during the formative years of life." With concern for both of these ends, the board of education appropriated ten thousand dollars in 1911 to help meet the demand for "moral social training in social centers, evenings, in ten school buildings."[20] The principle of free tax-supported schooling for all the children of all the people had been firmly established in the later nineteenth century; therefore, the use of school buildings for recreation was both logical and fiscally prudent.

Although the national outcry for public recreation had become more pronounced by the second decade of this century, early efforts had begun in New York City during the years when Luther H. Gulick served as director of physical training for the city's school system. The rationale behind New York's recreation program derived from concern about the increasingly crowded urban living conditions around the turn of the twentieth century. In a report published in *The Tenth Yearbook of the National Society for the Study of Education* (1911), New York's district superintendent of schools, Edward W. Stitt, noted that by 1910, census figures had indicated that 50 percent of America's population lived in crowded cities. He wrote, "It is a civic problem of great importance to determine just what recreative advantages should be provided by the cities for those who are forced to live in congested neighborhoods." Indicting the church for lack of attention to the public need for wholesome recreation, Stitt lauded the efforts of Jane Addams in Chicago and reformer Jacob Riis in New York. Stitt then went on to detail the progress in his system.

As early as 1901, eight schools had been opened for evening recreation and had an average attendance of 675. By the 1910–11 school year, the city intended to open thirty-eight schools as evening recreation centers each night except Sunday. Growing attendance figures had established both the need for and the success of the program. Stitt noted in 1911 that during the previous year, average nightly attendance had reached 12,985, with a yearly total of 2,165,457 men and women enjoying the opportunities that the recreation centers afforded them. "Mixed dancing classes" had been successfully introduced during the same year. Stitt wrote, "The principals and social workers confidently look upon these classes as furnishing the correct antidote to the evils resulting from the dance halls in congested districts, so often

run in connection with the lower order of liquor saloons." Additional ac-
colades and encouragement came from New York's mayor, William J.
Gaynor, who, according to Stitt, observed that it was the " 'duty of every
city to see that its young people dance in the right place. The gymnasiums
of public-school buildings are a safe place.' " Stitt reported that other cities
had begun similar school recreation programs, and more comprehensive data
gathered shortly thereafter provided proof of the growing national trend.
By 1914, authors of the survey *Recreation in Springfield, Illinois* reported that
"social dancing for young and old is taking place in over 200 school houses
scattered throughout the country."[21]

Dancing and Dance Hall Regulation

The call for cities and states to assume responsibility for quality recreation was
part of a move to educate people in citizenship and the wise use of leisure hours.
This made municipal and state regulation of dance halls a logical strategy once
observers had determined that dancing in a well-controlled environment met
the legitimate social needs and interests of young people. However, many
people looked at the new dances and music from the "ragtime revolution" of
1910 and the years following and wondered at the ultimate "good" in dancing. Dramatic changes marked twentieth-century dances compared with those
popular from preceding decades. The waltz, hailed as radical and exciting
seventy to eighty years earlier, looked staid and conservative by 1910.

The Dances and Music

Whether the dances or the music came first is difficult to determine. In the
end, it is a moot point. By the end of the first decade of this century, Americans heard and sang catchy tunes while trotting to the toe-tapping rhythms
of ragtime. Israel Baline, better known as Irving Berlin, gave the era its sig-
nature with "Alexander's Ragtime Band" in 1911. That musical heritage owes
much, of course, to the black tradition of composers out of St. Louis and
Kansas City, of whom Scott Joplin (1868–1917) may be the best known.
The other musical strand that fed into the music and dance of the early
twentieth century came from the New Orleans jazz players and composers
who moved up to Chicago in the teens and twenties, among whom Louis
Armstrong may be the most enduringly famous. When New Orleans jazz
and St. Louis ragtime diffused among whites as well as blacks, the new dances
that emerged made performers ecstatic and brought moralists up in arms.
    The commercial nature of the halls meant that whoever paid admission

got in, and men and women were closer together on the dance floor than ever before. Chaperones for ladies simply did not exist there. The formal distance between partners that was required in a proper waltz all but evaporated as girls clung to their partners. Couples pranced, trotted, pivoted, swayed, and swooped their way around the floor. The dancing madness of the pre–World War I years produced, according to one count, over two hundred new dances between 1912 and 1914.[22] The pervasiveness of dancing made this era the time "when America learned to dance," as Frederick Lewis Allen dubbed it in an article for *Scribner's* in September 1937.

The continued widespread popularity of dancing, coupled with the perceived immorality of the dances and the undesirable atmosphere of the dance hall, meant that reform remained a matter of public concern. Numerous articles critical of dance appeared in popular periodicals and in professional journals between 1910 and 1935. Specific charges invariably associated dancing with liquor, improper or immoral conduct, late-night hours, and undesirable clientele. Writers were divided about whether the real villain was the new, hot jazz or the slow, sensual jazz—but either kind was thought to inspire wicked, immoral dancing.

Most writers were deadly serious about the evils waiting to ensnare the young, particularly the unwary females. Ethel Mumford, for example, addressed mothers in an article called "Where Is Your Daughter This Afternoon?" which appeared in *Harper's Weekly* for 17 January 1914. Her special target was the *thé dansant;* even girls alone at a dance from four to seven in the afternoon alarmed her. Waltzing had given way to the tango, and girls of good breeding could be seen dancing "cheek by jowl with professionals whose repute is not even doubtful." Elaborating on the evils of the environment, Mumford generalized, "The whole dance-mad town has seemingly remained blind to the ever increasing incursion of the daughters of good families into the Tenderloin realm. The tango mania has been the cause of an amused shrug or two. Parents have not realized that the dance-halls have hailed the innovation of the *thé dansant* with delight, and that with widethrown doors, they are luring young girls into a worse environment than these same blind parents would dream could ever reach their little girls."[23]

Other writers, such as Gregory Mason, whose article appeared in *American Mercury* for May 1924, poked satirical fun at those who attempted to regulate dance hall behavior:

> Nearly always, however, the attempts to censor dancing are conceived in hysteria and carried out to absurdity. The beadles of Rochester had attempted to define

precisely the position which dancers may hold. The town fathers of Oshkosh have declared it black sin for prancing men and women to look into each other's eyes. Other extremists have even proposed the compulsory wearing of Sir Galahad belts of one inch daggers and electrically charged wires to make sin perilous and painful. Baseball masks would hinder cheek-to-cheek dancing. (One would have been appreciated by a lady I know, who, trying to draw back from a too proximate partner, found his inexpertly chewed gum entangled her hairnet!) Alas for the pure![24]

The Legislation and Reports

A slow but steady growth in city and state legislation to regulate dance halls occurred after 1912, with most municipal laws enacted after 1918. Louise DeKoven Bowen wrote a follow-up report on Chicago dance halls in 1917, stating that there were then 440 licensed halls but probably twice that number actually operating and many connected with saloons. The JPA believed that "fewer disreputable" halls existed than formerly but expressed discouragement that so little progress had actually been accomplished. In particular, the report cited the crowds of inebriates that made it impossible to keep order, let alone actually dance. Hall waiters and other employees assisted in getting youth intoxicated and then led them to houses of prostitution. Masquerade dances often found women dressed in male attire. Police on duty could not control the crowds, which could number as many as 1,800 people at a time, without calling in reinforcements. Obviously, health and sanitary facilities required additional attention with such huge gatherings.[25]

Although the Bowen report for Chicago decried the fact that more had not been done to improve the dance halls there, a 1920 report from Cleveland sounded a more positive note. That survey intended to assess conditions following the intensive 1910 Cleveland survey and the city's 1911 ordinance for regulation. According to the later report, the city had 115 licensed dance halls and eight licensed restaurants where dancing was permitted. Permits for dances usually numbered six thousand per year, with most events held between November and February. Improvements noted since the 1911 ordinance included careful inspection of dance halls, curtailment of liquor sales on dance hall premises, elimination of objectionable advertising, and maintenance of a "much higher standard of decorum." The Cleveland dance hall inspector had been appointed by the mayor and supervised forty deputy inspectors as well as two female chaperones, all of whom possessed police power and had to be present at all dances for which permits were issued. Nonetheless, the 1920 Cleveland report acknowledged the difficulty of regulating particular dances and of controlling solicitation by prostitutes. It further noted, "Auto parties which are the result of pick-up acquaintances at dances are growing to constitute one of a modern city's most serious social problems." However, the report indicated that the positive results of the early regulatory ordinance occurred in part due to the cooperation of the state association of dance teachers and the city's dance instructors—all of whom helped to raise the standards of dance halls. In addition, the dance teachers' association was preparing information which it intended to result in state regulation of dance halls. Minimum standards required the retaining of a dance hall inspector with adequate support staff; care in granting licenses; strict enforcement of rules; a high standard of decorum; 12:30 A.M. closings; and the exclusion of those under age eighteen after 9:00 P.M. unless they were accompanied by a parent or guardian.[26]

The issue of city control was aired nationwide by a story in *The Survey* of 29 January 1921. It discussed the results of a questionnaire sent to 400 cities. Of the 180 cities that replied, only 147 at that time possessed some kind of ordinance to regulate the dance hall. Great variation existed among the ordinances then in force. A subsequent article, in the *Literary Digest* for 26 February 1921, referred to the national survey and declared that unsupervised dancing in "promiscuous public gatherings" was "one of America's gravest problems."[27]

Despite some regulatory legislation, dance hall problems continued, as attested in the *Literary Digest* for 11 October 1924. Information in an article published there came from a survey and report done more than a decade after Davis's comprehensive analysis of New York City's problems with commercial recreation. Conducted and prepared under the leadership of Maria Ward Lambin, formerly the chief supervisor of dance halls in San Francisco, the 1924 New York report was published under the auspices of the Advisory Dance Hall Committee of the Women's City Club and the City Recreation Committee, chaired by Belle Israels Moskowitz. The *Literary Digest* account opened with a paragraph exonerating the dance hall as the only institution to blame for contemporary, illegal practices, pointing out that

> of the millions who dance every night in the public halls many pay part of the price with virtue. But it is not so much the fault of the dance-halls, we are told, as of conditions arising out of congestion and limited opportunity. People must play, and the dance-hall offers a universal pastime. Moreover, some of the evils found in the public dancing-places may be found also in the home of the so-called "better classes." The hip-flask is not more common in the public amuse-

ment places, we are told, than it is in private homes, and dancing may be equally as sensual on Fifth Avenue as over on Second or Third. Tho the report concerns itself with conditions in New York, they are by no means limited to that metropolis, for writers tell us that the evils are as characteristic of other large cities as of New York.

After placing the dance hall evils within the context of practices pervasive in society as a whole, the 1924 New York report concluded that " 'it would seem that the dance-hall is not in itself the cause, but rather an effect of conditions operating throughout our society.' "[28]

Proof of the continuing crowds invading dance halls and generating profitable business came in part from statistics in the 1924 report showing that New York City possessed 768 licensed halls. In Manhattan alone, 238 licensed places brought in a total of 6,113,604 dancers for the year. On the West Coast, San Francisco's infamous "Barbary Coast" had over 100 halls employing "over 2,000 girls" at the time the California Civic League conducted its survey in 1918. Closings and careful regulation followed. By 1922, 88 licenses were issued to public dance halls in San Francisco and 55 of those went to restaurants or hotels. According to the *New York World* in 1924, crowded urban conditions forced young people to dance in public places; they had no other place to get acquainted. Yet the builders of public dance halls did so for profit. A sampling of ballroom origins for the twenties clearly indicates that they were big and were being built around the country. Attendance figures for New York City and San Francisco indicated that people across the country were flocking to dance facilities in the late teens and twenties.[29] Thus, it was the great numbers of people in public, commercial dance halls, of varying quality, that still concerned urban reformers by the mid-twenties.

A comprehensive report on the dance hall situation in Pittsburgh appeared in 1925 from the recreation division of the city's Girls Conference, an organization of individuals from social agencies who were interested in "the girl problem of today." The report was made because social workers and others were allegedly ignorant of actual conditions in the halls. The writer, Collis Stocking (1900–1978), an economist with enough achievements to win him a place in *Who Was Who in America,* took pains to state in the introduction that there was no attempt to inject personal moral values into the report. The aim was merely to state the facts of the current situation. Statistics in the report indicate that, for the period between February and June 1925, Pittsburgh had a total of 155 licensed dance halls that brought in an aggregate of 1,886,690 patrons for the year. Weekly attendance for a fifty-week period amounted to 37,734. People from sixteen through forty-four years of age patronized the dance halls, but the ages most regularly represented were sixteen thorough twenty-five. Stocking also focused on the social class backgrounds of those who attended the dance halls and concluded that the quality of the dance hall was linked to both the wealth and social class of the patrons. The success of the public dance hall depended on the patronage of the working class—mill and factory hands, secretaries, mechanics, tailors, and the like. Stocking found that "the price in connection with the social atmosphere of the place is ordinarily effective in defining the type of patronage that is likely to be found." High standards seemed to result in a "relatively superior class of patrons."[30]

The social behavior of men and women at the dance hall, as described by Stocking, contrasted dramatically with the etiquette prescribed for behavior at balls during the nineteenth century and points to the democratization of American society as well as to radical changes in women's roles in the twentieth century. According to Stocking, "Sometimes more than a hundred youths under the age of twenty will congregate. They drink to excess, indulge in the most extreme styles of dancing, spend a great part of the intermissions in brazen petting parties and frequently there is a violent exchange of vulgar language on the part of both boys and girls." Despite the serious shortcomings of the dance hall in Pittsburgh in 1925, Stocking clearly favored retaining dance halls and concluded that they fulfilled a genuine social need for the age groups that frequented them.[31]

Elegance in the Twenties and Thirties

By the 1920s the popularity of the dance hall had resulted in an expansion of facilities from those that Davis and earlier writers surveyed at the end of the century's first decade. Stocking reports that, in addition to the traditional dancing academies and club halls, there were cabarets and restaurants, "road houses," the "boats," the "speak easy," "Negro Places," and the "closed hall."[32] Russel Nye's more recent analysis of the dance hall in the twenties adds to the list hotels and nightclubs. But it was the "dance palace" that proved to be the most popular or "most widely attended" type of public hall in that decade. The term "dance palace" sometimes applied to elegant amusement parks or outdoor pavilions with dance floors, as well as to the very large but more traditional ballrooms, many of which were ornately decorated and did indeed seem "palatial." Several of the latter acquired a national reputation. The famous Roseland ballroom in New York City, for example, opened on 31 December 1919. Among the show business personalities in attendance were Billie Burke, Florenz Ziegfeld, and Will Rogers. Facilities for dining and dancing as well as two bands performing during the night guaranteed continuous music and pleasure throughout the evening. Reportedly, receipts from the New Year's Eve opening totaled $18,000.[33] While Roseland drew white customers, its uptown counterpart, the Savoy ballroom in Harlem, catered mainly to black dancers.

The Savoy, a mecca for black musicians and dancers during the twenties, thirties, and forties, opened in 1926 and occupied an entire city block. Attendance at the Savoy testifies to the enormous popularity of dancing during the era. A *Life* magazine feature from the early thirties said the ballroom attracted some 500,000 paid dancers annually, and it had already been redecorated at a cost of $50,000. According to Barbara Engelbrecht's more recent account of its heyday, the Savoy could accommodate 3,500 to 4,000 dancers at one time; by 1951, when the ballroom reached its twenty-fifth anniversary, 15,000,000 dancers had stomped, shimmied, and swung on its floors, which had to be replaced "every three years." Englebrecht reports that by the anniversary year, an average of 700,000 customers had visited the Savoy each year.[34]

In Chicago, the Aragon and the Trianon achieved national renown for their palatial quality. On 5 December 1922, the latter ballroom opened with an elaborate decor and at a total estimated cost of $1,200,000. The grand march was led by General John J. Pershing, the World War I hero, and Mrs. Potter Palmer II, the society leader. Paul Whiteman, then "King of Jazz," began a six-night engagement on the opening evening. The staff included tuxedo-clad floormen who circulated to put an end to either improper dancing or displays of affection. The success of the Trianon prompted the owners, the Karzas brothers, to establish a second ballroom in 1926. Opening night for the Aragon, 14 July, brought out the elite of Chicago and a total attendance of 8,000. Both ballrooms regularly catered to the "better classes" of society though admission was to be had for the door price and correct dress. The nationwide popularity of these Chicago ballrooms began in 1927 when radio station WGN started live broadcasts first from the Trianon and then from the Aragon—billed as the "world's most beautiful ballrooms."[35]

By the thirties, other cities possessed equally well-known, large, and elegant dance facilities, including Frank Dailey's Meadowbrook in Cedar Grove, New Jersey, which, like the Aragon, had radio air time six nights a week. In Milwaukee, Devine's Million Dollar Ballroom drew a regular procession of name bands. The Palomar Night Club in Los Angeles, acknowledged as "the best-known dancing facility west of Chicago," drew 8,753 people to hear the bandleader Artie Shaw on 19 April 1939. In all of them, the decor and standard of behavior testified to the growing acceptance of dancing among much of society.[36] At the same time, however, one type of dance hall drew both customers and heavy criticism.

The Taxi-Dance Hall

Intended only for male patrons, the "closed" or "taxi-dance" hall appeared in the large cities of the Midwest and East by the mid-1920s. The *Literary Digest* of 22 March 1924 quoted Belle Israels Moskowitz as labeling it the "most disturbing" of the dance halls. Maria Ward Lambin recommended that it be abolished, for both girls and patrons were exploited. "The taxi girls take any fare who signals for them and pays the tariff," wrote John B. Kennedy in *Collier's* for 19 September 1925. His article, entitled "The Devil's Dance Dens," observed: "Dancing was once a diversion. Now it is a trade." Kennedy described the activity at a closed or taxi-dance hall and the life-style of the female dancers employed. So hot was the topic of dance halls and their control that *Collier's* advertised awards of ten, fifteen, and twenty-five dollars for the best writing on the topic submitted to the magazine. "What do you think of them and their influence on our young people? How should they be regulated?" asked the magazine ad.[37]

The most thorough analysis of both the social problems and the benefits associated with taxi-dance halls comes from Paul G. Cressey, a case worker and special investigator for the Chicago Juvenile Protection Association. Assigned in 1925 to report on the phenomenon, Cressey wrote a scholarly book on the subject, which was published by the University of Chicago Press in 1932. The initial assignment to investigate the "closed dance hall" came just a few years after the taxi-dance hall appeared in Chicago. According to Cressey, its parent was the "Barbary coast dance hall" where dancing was secondary to drinking. When that type of facility was finally abolished in 1913, the closed dance hall originated. It, in turn, sprang up in New York and later arrived in Chicago, where records on it by the Juvenile Protection Associated are dated from 1921.[38]

The name "taxi-dance" hall derived from the function of the girls or "hostesses" who worked as dancers for the male-only clientele. According to Cressey, "Like the taxi-driver with his cab, she is for public hire and is paid in proportion to the time spent and the services rendered." Ranging in age from fifteen to twenty-eight, the girls usually became taxi-dancers merely by chance.[39] Cressey found that many led double lives because they were afraid to tell their families about life in the dance hall: "The life of the taxi-dancer is one of these intermediate stages, and, like prostitution, it is an employment which can be of only short duration. The career of a taxi-dancer ends in her late twenties. It is a source of income only for the interim between later adolescence and marriage."[40] Not only was the career of short duration, it also produced enormous tension. Both personal and cultural conflicts beset the young, vulnerable girls who became taxi-dancers. Frequently, they responded by breaking all ties with family as well as other agencies of social control like the church. Often from immigrant homes or broken homes, the young taxi-dancers found themselves in a situation where they identified with unconventional, unstable, and out-of-the-mainstream male patrons.[41]

According to Cressey, the taxi-dance hall existed for the profitable exploitation of promiscuity, what he termed "intimate behavior upon the basis of casual association." Male patrons comprised a "polyglot crowd": Asians not accepted anywhere else; physically handicapped or atypical men scorned on other dance floors; older men who remained single for one reason or another; married men miserable in their wedlock; socially detached immigrants; and fugitives from justice or those fleeing from "local condemnation" of their conduct. Customers came from the ranks of the skilled and semiskilled craftsmen as well as from the group of commercial employments that required little special training. Only occasionally did Cressey find professional men or business executives in the taxi-dance hall. Thus, in general, the men represented the lower middle class.[42]

Summing up the social context for both girls and men, Cressey objectively analyzed the reasons for the rise and popularity of the halls: "In its catering to detached and lonely people, in its deliberate fostering of stimulation and excitement, in its opportunities for pseudo-romantic attachments, it may be seen as an epitome of certain phases of urban life. On the periphery of the respectable, tolerated but not condoned by the community, it gathers to itself those who have failed to find a place in the more conventional groups and institutions of the city."[43]

Recognizing that the taxi-dance hall contributed to promiscuous sexual behavior and that some girls found it to be a kind of "school" for learning the trade of prostitution, Cressey nevertheless pointed out the legitimate fulfillment of social needs for some groups of people. For the older, single man, the handicapped, the detached immigrant, and the Asian, the taxi-dance hall provided the only dance institution that made a place for them. He called it the only social situation in which they did not evoke a "tinge of pity, repulsion, or social condescension." Thus, Cressey asserted that any community plan to eliminate the taxi-dance hall must make appropriate provision for the social recreation of such minority groups.[44] He viewed the problem of the taxi-dance hall as nothing more than the problem of the large urban metropolis. The customers collectively presented "a panorama of the maladjustments typical of urban life."[45]

Although Cressey's detailed analysis dealt with Chicago, the problems there were probably no worse than those of many other large cities. The *Literary Digest* for 1 August 1931 carried an article about cleaning up New York City's "dives" and stressed the problems stemming from commercialized vice. The issue was seen as " 'greater in volume and more brazenly open than at any time in the last fifteen years,' " according to a report by the Committee of Fourteen, a voluntary board concerned with social problems. The report indicated that forty "dance palaces" had been studied in 1930 and all but three were taxi-dance halls. These establishments drew 35,000 to 50,000 men per week and employed 2,500 to 3,000 girls as dancers or "hostesses." According to the committee's report, the depraved moral atmosphere in which the girls worked was worse than anything seen in New York for many years. The *Literary Digest* reported one unequivocal conclusion reached by the Committee of Fourteen: " 'Experience both here and in other large cities proves that organized vice is back of our most serious troubles in crime.' " Finally, the committee noted there had been attempts to stifle its report.[46] The statement is not surprising. Prohibition did not end until 1932 and during its whole ill-fated period of enforcement, dancing, by association with liquor, would have been subject to the influence of criminal elements in the country.

The National Survey

By the last half of the 1920s, enough public outcry had been raised to prompt a national survey by the Department of Labor and a subsequent published report. According to *The Survey* for 15 October 1929, the recommendation of the government report was "Reform—don't attempt to abolish the dance halls."[47] The report itself, published under the byline of Ella Gardner, stated that the importance of the dance hall had come to public attention when the several recreation surveys were carried out during the early years of the century: "The investigations revealed that the public dance halls offered almost the only opportunity for this form of social recreation to many farm boys and girls who came to the towns for their amusements, to large numbers of young people who were working in industrial centers away from their parents and childhood friends, and to many city boys and girls whose parents through poverty or ignorance made no provision for the social needs of their children." Observing that the social problem presented by the public dance hall had to do with its value or danger to adolescents of fourteen to eighteen years, Gardner pointed to issues of admittance and safeguards. For the older adolescent, she asserted, the question was how to keep the dance hall from being a "demoralizing influence" and at the same time make it a "real recreational opportunity rather than a brighter form of boredom."[48]

Gardner and her team prepared their 1929 report using findings of the first national questionnaire on the topic, which was sent to all cities in the country with populations of 15,000 or more. Responses came in from 416 of the 500 cities surveyed. Twenty-five states sent copies of their state laws. In addition, Department of Labor officials visited fifteen cities in various parts of the country during 1925 and 1926. Findings indicate that by 1928, a total of 28 states had laws regulating the "operation of public dances and public dance halls." The regulatory legislation primarily concerned licensing, investigation of place and space, and affidavits regarding the character of applicants, posting of permits, minimum age of dancers, hours for minors, hours for closing, Sunday restrictions, lighting, conduct of dancers, type of dances permitted, and supervision by police or qualified matrons. Variation existed among the states; only six were reported to have "comprehensive" laws regulating dance halls. These state laws did not preclude city legislation, which the Gardner report also covered. Among the 416 cities responding to the survey, 240 possessed municipal ordinances regulating dance halls. However, in those cities with no dance-hall regulations, the "general powers of the police" were understood to include supervision of "public dance places." On the whole, the municipal ordinances had been enacted after 1918.[49] Despite the passage of significant numbers of state and municipal laws, Gardner acknowledged that the "chief problems" devolved to supervision of music, dancing, and public conduct; protection of minors; and control of the "after-the-dance rendezvous," particularly via cars. Her report noted further that the "closed halls" represented an extreme in "commercialization of the dance."[50]

Endurance Dancing

Competitions to see how long contestants could remain upright on the dance floor were another perceived evil associated with the dance hall. The *Literary Digest* for 5 May 1923 reported the growing attraction of endurance dancing. By the thirties, the contagion had spread to towns large and small.

People aimed to break records and become champions in what *The Survey* for February 1934 called America's manifestation of "dementia." The phenomenon raised concerns about young girls. The article said that "to social workers concerned with protective measures for young girls the spread and popularity of this extraordinary form of amusement is occasioning considerable anxiety." It went on to report that communities generally did not object to the contests because they brought in some money during the Depression years. Nonetheless, it said, "There are more of these marathons than most people realize and the morbid interest they attract is growing rather than diminishing."[51]

But, motivated by concern for young girls and women, just as early dance hall reformers had been, Mrs. Ruth Mix, chair of the Girls Protective Council, expressed concern for the girls who entered such endurance contests and often followed the marathons from one place to the next. Mrs. Mix's letter about the dangers of dance marathons appeared in the *Journal of Social Hygiene* for March 1936. Responding to her letter, the editors wrote:

> Mrs. Mix states that the Council is extremely interested this winter in certain danger spots which have been appearing in various communities during the depression. Among these the marathon is considered the most striking as well as the most elusive to control, as it brings a large amount of money to the town in which it is held, employs—if it may be called that—a number of people and is a recreation of sorts. "But," she asks, "is it not decidedly dangerous to the girls who participate? It is so emotionally stimulating that it takes away a desire for any honest work."[52]

Carol Martin's 1987 analysis of the phenomenon reports that, during their heyday, dance marathons ran "virtually everywhere"—in any kind of available space. Some drew small audiences of 200 to 300; others seated up to 5,000 spectators. Reportedly, an estimated 20,000 people found employment as promoters, contestants, and the several kinds of staff needed to run a contest. Although dance marathons began as simple contests where participants tried to set new records for staying vertical on the floor longer than others, they eventually evolved into exaggerated shows lasting six to twelve weeks, with contestants getting short breaks for rest and food each hour. They became a mix of dancing, swaying, and periodic walking races interspersed with singing and theatrics—anything to make a good show and draw an audience. Professional contestants mingled with amateurs out to make enough money to buy food. Promoters, emcees, and professional contestants, many of whom had their show business careers advanced by their participation in the marathons, worked together to involve the audiences actively in the spectacle. According to Martin, the daily narrative episodes drawn out around particular contestants held the audience's interest with the intensity of a radio soap opera.[53]

Not surprisingly, the popularity of dance marathons peaked in the thirties when many other forms of entertainment became too expensive for most Americans. Reportedly, the motion picture industry considered the marathons to be a threat. Some observers even suspected that objections to marathons were in fact initiated by theater managers. Yet, time would eventually run out on the success and appeal of the marathons. Martin observes that they were inevitably intertwined with the human turmoil of the Depression years and could never shake the association. They died "a slow death" in the late forties.[54]

The Issue Wanes

By the end of the 1930s, the problems of dance halls had, for all practical purposes, become a dead issue. The big bands and swing were in their heyday. A review of the popular periodicals indexed in the *Reader's Guide* shows that the topical heading of "Dance Hall" no longer existed, after more than two decades of inclusion. Moreover, the articles indexed under "Dancing" reveal the commercial success and acceptance of ballroom dancing. For example, the *Literary Digest* for 2 January 1937 headlined a "Bull Market in Ballroom Stepping" for Arthur Murray, by then an established commercial studio teacher. Unlike those who attended the dancing academies of the early part of the century, students at Arthur Murray's studios came from the professional ranks of society: "Of some 5,000 more or less current pupils, the largest percentage are editors and publishers. Lots of them will deny it, he says, but he can prove it by their registration cards. 'Name any ten best magazines or newspapers, and there will be a card of one of their executives in our file,' he says."[55] Obviously, the success of Arthur Murray represented some kind of change in the country's attitude toward dancing and places to dance. No single factor can be pinpointed that accounts for the change in attitude, but several can be highlighted.

Action taken to regulate the dance hall surely counts as an important step toward public acceptance. Despite wide variation among state laws, the content of the legislation spoke to the public health and welfare needs that urban reformers had concentrated on since the early part of the century, that is, health and sanitary conditions, supervision of minors, and the general moral environment. Passage of regulatory laws in twenty-eight states by the end of the 1920s, in addition to numerous municipal ordinances, meant that public information about dance halls had to have been disseminated. For the masses of people, dissemination of information probably came from personal observation as they attended dance halls that were better equipped, better decorated, and better regulated. Further, the enactment of such legislation also depended upon an assumption of the dance hall's importance. Any institution not worth saving is not worth regulating. The clearest exposition of such valuing by urban reformers came from Stocking's report in 1925 on the significance of the dance hall in Pittsburgh: "The puritanical tabu of dancing itself has gradually given way until now it is accepted as a recreation, by most social groups and practically all religious sects. The acceptance of the public dance is following in the wake as it becomes gradually divorced from the saloon and the house of debauchery as essential concomitants." Stocking held no doubt that the dance hall fulfilled a social need. In many instances, he declared, young people had no other place to meet. "Crowded home conditions, meager salaries and our late marrying age contribute a great deal towards the success of the public dance."[56] Like Cressey in his assessment of the taxi-dance hall, Stocking saw problems with the public dance hall but concluded that it fulfilled a genuine social need. In their views, the dance hall existed not as the leading source of social evils, but as a byproduct of urban living and human needs. Looking back from the 1970s, the popular-culture analyst Russel Nye concluded that between 1920 and 1940 the dance hall functioned as "one of the nation's most influential social institutions."[57]

Notes

An earlier version of this chapter was presented in a paper at the 1986 annual meeting of the Society of Dance History Scholars in New York City.

1. Louise deKoven Bowen (Mrs. Joseph Tilton Bowen) came from an old Chicago family, her grandfather having lived at Fort Dearborn. Her entry in *Who Was Who in America* shows Bowen was active in United Charities, woman suffrage, Woman's City Club, and Hull-House, among other endeavors. By 1926 she had amassed a record of fifty years in social service. Notable in the teens of this century were her efforts, on behalf of the Juvenile Protection Association, to clean up Chicago's dance halls. See her book *Growing Up with a City* (New York: Macmillan, 1926).

2. Dance halls had existed at least since the 1820s in urban areas. As cities grew, so did the number of dance halls and the number of people frequenting them. The expansion proved so great, with so many perceived attendant evils, that middle-class reformers launched the first widespread investigations and analyses of the dance hall problem during the pre–World War I years. For a detailed discussion of early dance hall reform efforts in New York City led by Belle Israels, see Elisabeth Israels Perry, *Belle Moskowitz: Feminine Politics and the Exercise of Power in the Age of Alfred E. Smith* (New York: Oxford University Press, 1987), 42ff; idem, " 'The General Motherhood of the Commonwealth': Dance Hall Reform in the Progressive Era," *American Quarterly* 37, no. 5 (Winter 1985): 719–33; and idem, "Cleaning Up the Dance Halls," *History Today* 39 (Oct. 1989): 20–26.

3. Sidney Ahlstrom, *A Religious History of the American People* (Garden City, N.Y.: Image Books, 1975), vol. 2, 208–9. The peak volume of Atlantic migration came in the decade from 1901 to 1910 when more than 8,790,000 people landed on American soil. The total surpassed the previous high decade of 1881–90 by some 3.5 million, according to Ahlstrom's figures.

4. Jane Addams, *The Spirit of Youth and the City Streets* (New York: Macmillan, 1910), 5–6. Alan Havig reports that Bowen did much of the research for Addams's book. See his analysis of recreation in "The Commercial Amusement Audience in Early 20th-Century American Cities," *Journal of American Culture* 5, no. 1 (Spring 1982): 1–19.

5. Addams, *Spirit of Youth,* 11–12; Michael M. Davis, *The Exploitation of Pleasure: A Study of Commercial Recreation* (New York: Department of Child Hygiene of the Russell Sage Foundation, 1911), 3. See also discussion of the larger context of commercial amusements in Richard Henry Edwards, *Popular Amusements,* Studies in American Social Conditions, No. 8 (New York: Association Press, 1915).

6. Louise deKoven Bowen, *Our Most Popular Recreation Controlled by the Liquor Interests* (Chicago: Juvenile Protection Association, 1911), 1–8; idem, "Dance Halls," *The Survey* 26 (3 June 1911): 384.

7. Bowen, "Dance Halls," 383–87; Jane Addams, "Public Dance Halls of Chicago," *Ladies Home Journal,* July 1913, 19; John Dillon and H. W. Lytle, *From Dance Hall to White Slavery: The World's Greatest Tragedy* (N.p.: Chas. C. Thompson Company, 1912). The vignettes in Dillon and Lytle's book tell almost exclusively about innocent working girls—rural, small-town, or immigrant young women who were victimized by city men. The quest for clothes, glamour, excitement, romance, and money, thought to be achievable via the dance hall and saloon, proved the usual way to ruin.

8. Davis, *Exploitation of Pleasure,* 3–4.

9. M. S. Hanaw, *Baltimore's Public Dance Halls* (N.p.: Fleet-McGinley Company, 1912), 5. Belle Lindner Israels wrote the introduction to this book.

10. Maria Ward Lambin (Mrs. James Rorty), *Report of the Public Dance Hall Committee . . .* (San Francisco: Center of the California Civic League of Women

Voters, 1924), 5–6. Lambin's view came as a historical perspective, expressed at the beginning of her report, on the condition of San Francisco dance halls in the 1920s. She served as "chief supervisor" of the dance halls at the time of the report.

11. Davis, *Exploitation of Pleasure,* 15. In his 1915 analysis, Richard Henry Edwards says "nearly" 600 dance halls ran on a profitable basis in New York (*Popular Amusements,* 16).

12. George J. Kneeland, *Commercialized Prostitution in New York City* (New York: Century Company, 1913 and 1917; rpt., Montclair, N.J.: Patterson Smith, 1969), 67–76; Belle Lindner Israels, "The Way of the Girl," *The Survey* 22 (3 July 1909); 491–92, 494–96.

13. Rowland Haynes, *Recreation Survey* (Milwaukee: Milwaukee Bureau of Economy and Efficiency, 1912), 11–13.

14. Davis, *Exploitation of Pleasure,* 14–15.

15. Haynes, *Recreation Survey,* 12–13; Rowland Haynes, *Recreation Survey of Kansas City: Annual Report of the Recreation Department of the Board of Public Welfare April 18, 1911–April 15, 1912* (Kansas City: Recreation Commission, 1912), 179, 205.

16. Robb O. Bartholomew, *Dance Hall Report* (Cleveland: N.p., 1912), 1–4. Cleveland is reported to have borrowed the idea of licensing dance halls from New York City. Other cities also planning to pass ordinances included Boston, Philadelphia, St. Louis, Indianapolis, Louisville, Minneapolis, Seattle, and the New Jersey cities of Elizabeth, Paterson, Newark, and Hoboken. See "The Common Welfare: Regulating Dance Halls," *The Survey* 26 (3 June 1911): 345–46. In her biography of Belle Israels Moskowitz, Elisabeth Perry details the difficulty encountered by Israels in having the New York State Assembly pass a licensing law. Initial efforts began in 1908 and regulation did not go into effect until March 1911. (See Perry, *Belle Moskowitz,* 48ff.)

17. Haynes, *Recreation Survey* (Milwaukee), 21.

18. Hanaw, *Baltimore's Public Dance Halls,* Introduction and 13.

19. *Fifty-seventh Annual Report of the Board of Education City of Chicago; Report of the Superintendent, 1911,* 22, 86–87.

20. Ibid., 87.

21. Edward W. Stitt, "Evening Recreation Centers," in *The Tenth Yearbook of the National Society for the Study of Education,* Part 1, "The City School As A Community Center" (Chicago: University of Chicago Press, 1911), 39–41, 46–47; Lee F. Hanmer and Clarence Arthur Perry, *Recreation in Springfield, Illinois* (Springfield: Springfield Survey Committee, 1914), 12. The figure of two hundred schools nationwide providing recreation further indicates that, when Bishop Matthew Simpson and the evangelist Harry Benton wrote in opposition to dancing in the schools, they were not opposing an isolated phenomenon. See chapter 8, above, for their views.

22. Marshall and Jean Stearns, *Jazz Dance: The Story of American Vernacular*

Dance (New York: Macmillan, 1968), 95. For insight into the questionable dancing styles of working-class women in New York City during the 1890s and the first decade of the twentieth century, see Kathy Peiss, *Cheap Amusements: Working Women and Leisure in Turn-of-the-Century New York* (Philadelphia: Temple University Press, 1986), 100–104. The sexual expressiveness of "spieling," or pivoting, and "tough dancing" particularly incited the horror of reformers. See also Edwards, *Popular Amusements,* 78–79.

23. Ethel Watts Mumford, "Where Is Your Daughter This Afternoon?" *Harper's Weekly,* 17 Jan. 1914, 28.

24. Gregory Mason, "Satan in the Dance Hall," *American Mercury* 2 (May 1924): 182.

25. Louise deKoven Bowen, *The Public Dance Halls of Chicago,* rev. ed. (Chicago: Juvenile Protection Association, 1917), 4, 5, 7, 9–10.

26. *Cleveland Recreation Survey: Commercial Recreation* (Cleveland: Cleveland Foundation Committee, 1920), 14, 80–83, 87–89, 90–95.

27. John J. Phelan, "Our Dancing Cities," *The Survey* 45, no. 18 (29 Jan. 1921): 631–32; "City Control of Dance-Halls," *Literary Digest* 68 (26 Feb. 1921): 32.

28. "New York's Dance-Halls," *Literary Digest* 83 (11 Oct. 1924): 33–34. The *Literary Digest* article echoed similar sentiments voiced by the San Francisco report on public dance halls. That report, issued under Lambin's name, stated that "relegated to the dive by religion and custom, the dance became the scapegoat for many of the social problems of the nineteenth century." See Lambin, *Report of the Public Dance Hall Committee,* 5–6.

29. "New York's Dance-Halls," 33–34; Lambin, *Report of the Public Dance Hall Committee,* 7, 14, 16–17. New ballrooms built in the late teens and twenties included the Trocadero at Elitch's Gardens, Denver, about 1917; Roseland, New York City, 1919; Graystone, Detroit, 1922; Trianon, Chicago, 1922; Roaring Twenties (built under the name Shadowland Casino), San Antonio, 1926; and Indiana Roof, Indianapolis, 1927. They accommodated from five hundred to several thousand people at a time, depending on the size of the floor and the band or other featured performers. See Lon A. Gault, *Ballroom Echoes* (N.p.: Andrew Corbet Press, 1989), for a description of each of those listed above.

30. Collis Stocking, *A Study of Dance Halls in Pittsburgh* (Pittsburgh: Pittsburgh Girls Conference, 1925), introduction, 10–11, 13, 15.

31. Ibid., 17–18, 28.

32. Ibid., 9, 19–20.

33. Russel B. Nye, "Saturday Night at the Paradise Ballroom: Or, Dance Halls in the Twenties," *Journal of Popular Culture* 7, no. 1 (Summer 1973): 16–17; Gault, *Ballroom Echoes,* 283–85.

34. Barbara Engelbrecht, "Swinging at the Savoy," *Dance Research Journal* 15, no. 2 (Spring 1983): 3, 5; "Life Goes to a Party," *Life,* 14 Dec. 193?, 64–67.

35. Nancy Banks, "The World's Most Beautiful Ballrooms," *Chicago History* 2,

no. 4 (Fall-Winter 1973): 207, 209; Gault *Ballroom Echoes,* 13–15, 17–18.

36. Gault, *Ballroom Echoes,* 46–48, 29–31, 51. Gault describes over 150 dance facilities, including historical facts and present-day status.

37. "Trotting to Perdition," *Literary Digest* 80 (22 Mar. 1924), 34; "New York's Dance-Halls," 33; John B. Kennedy, "The Devil's Dance Dens," *Colliers,* 19 Sept. 1925, 12, 51.

38. Paul G. Cressey, *The Taxi-Dance Hall* (Chicago: University of Chicago Press, 1932), 179–81, 186.

39. Ibid., 3, 72, 81.

40. Ibid., 82, 106.

41. Ibid., 72.

42. Ibid., xiv, 110–28, 141.

43. Ibid., 240.

44. Ibid., 265–66, 283.

45. Ibid., 288, 286.

46. "Cleaning Up New York's Dance Dives," *Literary Digest* 110 (1 Aug. 1931): 9–10.

47. "Reform, Don't Abolish Dance Halls," *The Survey* 63, no. 2 (15 Oct. 1929): 90.

48. Ella Gardner, *Public Dance Halls: Their Regulation and Place in the Recreation of Adolescents* (Washington, D.C.: U.S. Dept. of Labor, Bureau Publication No. 189, Government Printing Office, 1929), 1–2.

49. Ibid., 3, 9.

50. Ibid., 51, 34.

51. "Tripping the Long, Hard Fantastic for a Record," *Literary Digest* 77 (5 May 1923): 42–46; "Dance Marathoneers," *The Survey* 70 (Feb. 1934): 53.

52. "Are Dance Marathons Dangerous?" *Journal of Social Hygiene* (Mar. 1936): 169–70.

53. Carol Martin, "Dance Marathons," *TDR: The Drama Review* (Spring 1987): 48–51, 54.

54. Ibid, 61–62, 48. A graphic portrayal of the human degradation encountered in the marathons was enacted in the film *They Shoot Horses, Don't They?* starring Jane Fonda. The film was based on Horace McCoy's novel of the same title.

55. "Bull Market in Ballroom Stepping," *Literary Digest* 123 (2 Jan. 1937): 21–22.

56. Stocking, *Study of Dance Halls in Pittsburgh,* 25, 21.

57. Nye, "Saturday Night at the Paradise Ballroom," 15.

10 The Polemic Upstaged: 1930–69 and Beyond

It don't mean a thing if it ain't got that swing!
Irving Mills, 1932

The dance has become so prevalent that seemingly
most churches, preachers, teachers, and parents
have folded their hands and accepted defeat.
Robert Campbell, 1933

When the Baptist cleric Robert Campbell (1888–1954) wrote his book *Modern Evils* in 1933, it appeared to him that the great army of dance opponents had simply given up confronting the pervasive popularity of the "modern dance." To Campbell, that acceptance boded "moral and religious ruin" for the nation. Other Baptists concurred, but they did not stand alone. Norwegian Lutherans, who had been relatively absent from the fray until the second decade of the twentieth century, also agreed with Campbell's assessment. N. M. Ylvisaker (1882–after 1958), executive secretary of the Young People's Luther League, wrote that the dance was no longer a matter of pleasure or leisure: "In its effects it is proving to be one of the forces responsible for the moral degeneracy and delinquency of the youth of our land."[1] Unflinching in the face of the devil's perceived attacks on Christianity and conventional morality, Baptists and Lutherans produced most of the published arguments against dancing after 1930. The decline of interdenominational opposition suggests that "liberals" had gained ascendancy and/or that, as Campbell declared, preachers, teachers, and parents finally had "accepted defeat." While both viewpoints are true to some degree, a corollary also proved true. Very simply, other issues had upstaged the amusement question.

At least two major forces provoked the dramatic shift in attitudes after more than ninety years of fierce polemic over the permissibility of amusements in general and dancing in particular. One obvious event that upstaged the dancing issue was the stock market crash and the ensuing Great Depression. Sydney Ahlstrom, a historian of American religion, put the consequences succinctly and specifically: "As the fact of social catastrophe was gradually driven home to churchgoing America, Prohibition, Sabbatarianism, and the questions of personal morality occasioned by the rise of movies and 'ballroom' dancing yielded to larger issues."[2] Then, as Hitler rose to power in Europe, Americans once again became caught up in questions of war or peace, involvement or isolation. Personal and individual concerns inevitably gave way to matters of national safety.

Closely related to the fact that the dancing question was upstaged by life and death issues is the reality that commercial amusements had become embedded in American life. After the war, other factors triggered a decline in the popularity of ballroom dancing and eventually produced a whole new revolution in dance and music. By 1969, the last of the known antidance books appeared. To understand that gradual decline requires a brief review of the era in which dancing came to be accepted by the majority of Americans.

The Thirties and Forties: Media, Music, and Dancing

The significance of dancing to Americans of the thirties appears in Ahlstrom's analysis of the decade wherein "the times seemed out of joint":

> Despite the Depression, urban civilization continued to make its conquests. Jazz, dancing, feminism, and the Hollywood star system mocked the older moral standards, both Catholic and Protestant. Hard times notwithstanding, the automobile continued to transform traditional modes of living and loving. Sabbathkeeping was losing ground. All over the country racketeers and bank robbers seemed to prosper—even if Bonnie and Clyde and Dillinger were shot down. With millions hungry, the government was destroying livestock and ploughing under corn. WPA workers leaned on their rakes; hobos and tramps were everywhere; prosperity manifested itself very slowly. The times seemed out of joint.[3]

Perhaps nowhere was this disjuncture more apparent than in the dramatic contrast between daily life and the events portrayed in these successful movie musicals featuring the elegant dancing of Fred Astaire and Ginger Rogers.

Movies

Beginning in the peak years of the Depression, Fred Astaire teamed up with his most successful partner and brought the American public not only great dancing but romance, elegance, and humor—all for the price of admission to the silver screen. The best songwriters of the era, such as George Gershwin and Cole Porter, and the technology of talking pictures produced the new genre of the movie musical. Astaire's choreographic genius and the "magic" of his partnership with Rogers bailed RKO out of bankruptcy. The nine films they made together in the thirties all followed a formula. Fred pursued Ginger; she resisted his advances. Mistaken identities, confused messages, humor, and subplots with supporting characters ensued. Eventually, by his dancing, Fred overcame Ginger's resistance, and the two became a romantic duo. Long, swirling gowns and top hat, white tie, and tails became the pair's trademarks as they glided across shiny dance floors and swept up long staircases. Thin plots, one-dimensional characters, and humor that was corny by today's standards mattered little to audiences, who went to see the skilled, creative dancing of Astaire and Rogers. Not only did the duo make ballroom dancing decorous, elegant, and respectable, they added a dimension, combining it with tap dancing and even roller skating. In his solo performances, Fred created extraordinarily exciting and unusual numbers such as tap dancing in the engine room of a ship or dancing with three shadows in his tribute to Bill "Bojangles" Robinson. Set in glamorous places like New York and Rio, the films gave to Depression-weary movie-goers a feast of fantasy for a couple of hours.[4]

Movies became accessible to virtually everyone by the 1930s for the cost of twenty-five cents.[5] By 1939, about 65 percent of the country's population went to the movies at least once a week, a record far beyond the number who could see dancing live on stage.[6] Further testimony to the impact of films comes from statistics about popular songs. Formerly, popular music, by definition, had to attain that status via sales of sheet music and records. By the thirties, radio and film made far more pervasive intrusions into the American consciousness. D. Duane Braun cites 1936 as the year when 41 percent—a "formidable portion"—of popular music came from contemporary films. According to Braun, twenty-three of the top fifty-six tunes, as listed by *Variety* for that year, were brought to the public via movies.[7]

Eventually, the addition of color to films meant that audiences in the thirties and forties could see even more vivid representations of the creative, kaleidoscopic collages of Busby Berkeley, the incomparable tap dancing of stars like Eleanor Powell, or the astounding "flash" dancing of the Nicholas brothers. Individual stars as well as big production numbers were staples of Hollywood musicals following the success of Astaire and Rogers. Added attractions sometimes included the big bands then famous, such as those of Glenn Miller or Harry James.[8]

Americans who went to the theater and movies in the thirties and forties were exposed to a wide variety of dancing by men and women, blacks and whites. Gradually, productions moved from the strictly commercial to the more skillful and artistic. When George Balanchine choreographed for the 1936 Broadway musical *On Your Toes,* he made use of his Russian classical ballet training. And in the early forties, when Agnes De Mille choreographed *Rodeo* and *Oklahoma,* she combined her own notions of American modern dance and ballet with the country's western folklore, including renditions of cowboy postures and antics. No longer would dances be merely inserted into plots without regard for story line or character development. The art of dance was maturing.

Radio, Records, and Dance Bands

Although movies provided the most widespread visual exposure to and understanding of the several kinds of dancing prevalent in American culture, it was radio—the new invention of the 1920s—that popularized the dance music of the big band and swing era. Regular national programming in the 1930s served to spread the new sound of "swing" from coast to coast. Late in 1934 Benny Goodman landed a spot on a three-hour Saturday night program called *Let's Dance,* which was sponsored by Nabisco and originated from New York City. After the show ended in May 1935, Goodman decided to go on the road. In July of that year, he took his band on a six-week transcontinental tour. The tour proved less than successful until the band got to Los Angeles in August. With only tepid response from crowds, and under orders from ballroom operators to play "traditional" music, Goodman had finally gotten fed up and ordered his boys to play "their own" kind of music at the Palomar Ballroom in Los Angeles. Immediately, the Goodman sound drew thousands of teenagers out on the dance floor. They had been listening to his Nabisco broadcasts for the previous several months; the show came on early in California due to the time lag from East Coast to the West Coast. Almost overnight, his new sound made Benny Goodman the unrivaled "King of Swing."[9]

Progressing from the "sweet" and "hot" jazz music played by small combos of the twenties and early thirties, "swing" came from large bands that produced an ensemble sound. These groups played written arrangements, that is, they rehearsed rather than improvised. The musicians had to read music and respond as a group to the director's baton. But the lack of spontaneity that had characterized the small jazz combo did not imperil the popularity of the new sound. When Goodman and his band appeared in New York's Paramount Theater in March 1937, hundreds of fans—mostly teenagers—lined up before sunrise for the first morning show. Mounted police arrived by 7:30 A.M. to keep the enthusiastic crowd under control. Inside, when the band finally appeared on stage, exuberant youth danced in the aisles to the music of their hero. Though adored by the young, "swing" drew the skepticism of the "longhairs" who thought it could never be compared with really "good music." By 1938, Goodman proved the success of his new sound even to these doubters. On 16 January of that year, his band became the first jazz ensemble to play a concert in Carnegie Hall. So famous was that event that forty years later Goodman returned to play a celebration concert in honor of the 1938 "first."

In another groundbreaking move, Goodman brought the talented black pianist Teddy Wilson into both his large ensemble and the Benny Goodman trio in 1936. Later in the same year, he brought in Lionel Hampton to play in the Benny Goodman Quartet. According to James Lincoln Collier, a jazz historian, "nobody before had attempted obvious racial mixing in major locations where attention would be attracted." Goodman also relied on several musical arrangements by the black bandleader Fletcher Henderson. And, in a widely heralded "Battle of the Bands" series in 1937, Goodman's group played against the black band of Chick Webb at Harlem's famous Savoy ballroom.[10]

There are countless success stories of dance music and dance bands. These forms and musicians simply infiltrated American consciousness during the late thirties and early forties; band leaders, both white and black, became household names and popular idols. Musicians like Artie Shaw, the Dorsey brothers, Count Basie, and Duke Ellington made headlines all over the country. Demand for the dance music of the big bands was so great that one count listed over three hundred swing bands alone during the height of the craze.[11] In addition, many "sweet" bands like that of Guy Lombardo played music for the ever popular smooth dances. The periodicals *Down Beat* and *Metronome* tracked current tunes and bands with the detail and regularity of modern-day sports-page statisticians. In addition to these print periodicals, weekly radio shows played the current favorites.

Your Hit Parade began broadcasting in 1935 and continued for more than two decades, bringing to the listening public each Saturday night a program of popular songs and melodies. Other regular shows featured bands playing at ballrooms and hotels. National hookups and radios in almost every home, as well as in many automobiles, meant that the sounds of "swing" bands and "sweet" bands could be heard in Brush, Colorado, or Marshalltown, Iowa, just as easily as in Chicago or New York.

After Goodman's transcontinental tour in 1935, bands increasingly traveled cross-country as well as locally, to play in person for people's dancing pleasure. Even small-town dance halls and outdoor pavilions could attract a live band. It was not hard for dance enthusiasts to find at least one or two places to dance every week. In addition to community dance halls and amusement parks, college and university campuses held junior-senior proms, sorority and fraternity dances, and other special-event dances. Live band music was de rigueur for large dances. For smaller dances, records that were played on victrolas or the ubiquitous "jukeboxes" provided dancing any time, any place. Russel Nye reports that by 1940 there were a half million jukeboxes, or coin-operated, multirecord phonograph players, in every conceivable kind of commercial establishment. For a nickel they played music for dancing and listening when fans could not get to the big bands in person. By 1946, one tally found a jukebox for every five hundred people in New York City.[12]

Further testimony to the ubiquity of dance music, thanks to the availability of records and phonographs, comes from statistics showing that in 1927 sales of popular songs amounted to 107,000,000 records. By 1946, sales had reached about 300,000,000 records a year. Though not all popular tunes constituted dance music, some record companies specialized in the latter. For example, Decca Records, which originated in 1934, made dance records for thirty-five cents per platter, which, Nye says, sold "by the thousands." The older, established Victor Record Company, sold 900,000 dance records in 1936 alone, "accounting for 80 percent of its total output." Dance music meant not only big bands but big business.[13]

Swing Dancing, Smooth Dancing, Latin Dancing

By January 1937, the popularity of dancing in the country had risen to the level of a "craze," in the words of the *Literary Digest*. Evidence came from reports about the success of Arthur Murray's dance studios. The periodical reported, "To-day in his New York studios, 200 teachers are not enough to take care of the clamoring line of clients who want to learn to dance." So many businessmen had begun to take lessons that Murray had installed lockers and added showers to his establishments. Editors and publishers constituted the largest group of customers, then doctors. Altogether Murray studios pulled in about 5,000 pupils in 1937. The *Literary Digest* concluded the country had gone "dance-mad" when its writers learned that more than 16,000 dance schools existed in the country; there were over 120 of them in New York City alone. The *Digest* declared, "Statisticians report the least amount of dancing in the Midwest, due, they aver, to religious scruples and sparsely populated areas." Reports from dance schools around the country indicated that enrollments for 1937 topped figures for the past twenty years. The new year promised to bring a "dance-boom" rivaling that of the pre–World War I years. According to Arthur Murray, more than 650,000 people had enrolled for his "correspondence course" in learning to dance. Why the craze to learn? The *Literary Digest* credited the impact of musicals and movies: "Musical comedies and dance movies have more effect on audiences to-day than formerly, for such types of dancing, in modified form, are now incorporated in the modern ballroom, and those who frequent the better hot spots of the town are forced to know the more intricate steps. Hollywood has exerted unprecedented influence on ballroom dancing, and credit for this goes largely to the team of Rogers and Astaire."[14]

The predominance of "swing" and "sweet" bands meant that dancers enjoyed both swing dancing and smooth dancing. Some also performed the new Latin dances. Dancing to "swing" music produced variations on the Lindy-hop and the jitterbug. Some authorities suggest that the Lindy evolved into the jitterbug by the early forties. Others maintain that the Lindy was simply known more widely as the jitterbug.[15] Fundamentally, such dancing entailed an emphasis on rhythm and a breakaway position. Rather than dancing exclusively in the traditional face-to-face, or closed, position, partners stayed apart more, with only hands touching. They also remained in one spot on the floor rather than traveling around the room as in a waltz or foxtrot. Energy, coupled with acrobatic maneuvers, separated aerial Lindy-hoppers from the "floor" group. So popular was this kind of dancing that John Martin, the dance critic for the *New York Times,* offered the following description in 1943:

> Your true jitterbug is likely to do almost anything in the way of a dance step; he will go in for a bit of Lindy Hop and a touch of Suzy-Q; he will unwind his partner brusquely to arm's length and snatch her back again, swiveling his hips and turning his toes in and out the while, his face rapt and immobile. When he really gets going he may improvise all sorts of fantastic figures and even try a touch of acrobatics, to all of which his partner will respond with calm and cooperative agility. It does not matter what you do specifically; it is the spirit of the thing that makes or breaks you.[16]

Whatever its precise origins, that kind of dancing remained the property of a small group of devotees, reportedly those who frequented the Savoy ballroom in Harlem, until the music of Goodman hit the top of the nation's popularity charts. Langston Hughes had observed that some dancers at the Savoy, primarily a black ballroom, used to invent acrobatic stunts and "absurd things" purely for the entertainment of white spectators. In the early 1930s, *Life* said the Savoy was known for its "barbaric dancing" and that 15 percent of its clientele was white. Harlemites called the Savoy the "home of happy feet." Martin visited the ballroom early in 1943 and commented on the artistry of the black dancers:

> For real spectator entertainment, there is probably nothing within hailing distance of the Savoy Ballroom in Harlem, especially on a Tuesday night when the Four Hundred Club is in session. The white jitterbug is oftener than not uncouth to look at, though he may be having a wonderful time and dancing skillfully, but his Negro original is quite another matter. His movements are never so exaggerated that they lack control, and there is an unmistakable dignity about his most violent figures. The relation of partners to each other is almost casual; phrases are executed apparently independently at times and often in the midst of a dance a couple will separate without warning of any kind and walk out of the dance area. There is a remarkable amount of improvisation and personal specialty mixed in with the Suzy-Q and familiar Lindy-Hop figures; some of it is acrobatic and strenuous, some of it superficially erotic, and all of it full of temperament and quality.
>
> Of all the ballroom dancing these prying eyes have seen, this is unquestionably the finest.[17]

Even in the more sedate versions of swing, women were no longer draped over male partners, something the moralists had objected to in the fad dances of the ragtime era. Although smooth dances like the waltz and foxtrot brought partners into the traditional close "embrace," the dance music of the "sweet" bands conjured up romance more than erotic imagery. By the thirties, the tango had been around for two decades so that its close-partner position seemed less scandalous. In neither the rhumba nor the samba did partners dance quite so close; by 1942, about one-half of Arthur Murray's students throughout the country were trying to learn the samba.[18] However, youth in the thirties and early forties more often than not joined in group fad dances like the big apple and conga, or partner and solo dances like truckin', the Suzy-Q, and the shag.[19]

Women's attire allowed them to dance the new dances just as the twenties styles had enabled the flapper to Charleston and shimmy. Although hemlines dropped by 1933, they gradually rose over the next few years. By 1939, skirts again came approximately to knee level.[20] Wearing anklets and saddle shoes, the bobby-soxer or the jitterbug of the era could swing with abandon whether on the floor or in the air. When she wanted to dress up for the college prom or a sophisticated downtown date, she might wear a floor-length gown of soft, swishy fabric just like Ginger Rogers wore in the movies. Elegant women's fashions also featured a return to more natural contours that again showed a waist and bosom instead of the boyishly slim silhouette of the flapper. A sure sign of the increasingly relaxed rules for women's dress and behavior came with the advent of slacks or pants. For the Baptist cleric Robert Campbell in 1933, women in "trousers," as well as "modern dancing," constituted a major part of what he termed "modern evils."[21]

The Opposition

One of the most distinctive features of dance opponents' arguments after 1930 is their anachronistic character. The vast majority of detractors continued to denounce the "modern dance," a phrase opponents used in targeting their objections in the 1860s. Few authors bothered to name specific dances, and those who did often cited dances no longer in vogue. For example, the Baptist evangelist John R. Rice (1895–after 1959) in 1935 criticized the bunny hug, tango, two-step, and waltz in one sentence, as though they were all current dances. A few years later, the Christian evangelist A. G. Hobbs Jr. (1909–after 1958) argued against the "round dance," resurrecting a term in vogue during the 1840s when the waltz and polka first became popular.[22] Although the waltz, tango, rhumba, and conga are mentioned by two writers after 1930 who opposed dancing, adversaries during this era almost universally fail to indict the new swing dancing.[23] Neither do they argue against contemporary fad dances. Whether or not they were unaware of that kind of dancing is not clear. It seems likely that the beleaguered opponents in the thirties and forties tended to copy the terminology and arguments of earlier decades in an effort to sustain their own views. Unlike dance opponents in previous eras who cited contemporary clergy and evangelists as strong supporters of an antidance stand, adversaries in the 1930s and 1940s had little contemporary support. Thus, their publications fell back on authorities from the nineteenth century.[24] Their reliance on outmoded authorities also meant that dance detractors during the Depression and World War II depended heavily on out-of-date language and statistics. However, since they rarely used dates to identify writers, quotes, and statistics, their readers probably did not know that the supposed authorities held no current status and, perhaps, no veracity.

Lutherans and Baptists

To those few writers who argued strongly against dancing during the 1930s and 1940s, the "embrace" of the closed-couple dances, that is, the waltz or Latin dances, remained the specific target of wrath. Some Missouri Synod Lutherans stand out as particularly clear in their definitions and rationale for objections. Dr. John H. Fritz (1874–1953) spelled out in his *Pastoral Theology*, a staple for seminarians, that dancing in itself did not constitute an objectionable activity for Christians if one were merely to step or skip to music. However, he said, "*the promiscuous dancing of the sexes in the usual way in which dancing is practiced is sinful* because the naturally highly charged sex mechanism is apt to be unduly excited and the sex urge unduly stimulated."[25] In particular, Fritz cited the closed dance position often seen in public dance halls. However, he makes no allowance for carefully regulated dances; in fact, he does not even address the possibility. Moreover, he makes no reference to the open, breakaway positions of swing or to the nonpartner, group dances like the Suzy-Q and the conga. Using a broader circumscription for objectionable dancing, Dr. Paul E. Kretzmann (1883–1965) stipulated in the early forties that the term "modern dance" encompassed the form of dancing that "began with the waltz and has continued its course downward, as steps from the Barbary coast and from the African jungles were introduced." Kretzmann did not refer specifically to contemporary fad dances or to the jitterbug but he did allow "the average folk dance, in which rhythmic movement and pantomime are the chief consideration." He did not address the fact that many folk dances have couple positions that involve close bodily contact.[26]

In an analysis of the "Adiaphora," or concept of "things indifferent," which sixteenth-century reformers regularly employed in their arguments against dancing, Dr. Theodore Graebner (1876–1950) rejected the notion that dancing could be classed among "indifferent" or morally neutral activities. Speaking in 1934 to the Texas District Convention of the Missouri Synod Lutheran Church, Graebner declared "the modern dance is essentially the same wherever you go. Its origin is in the tango. . . . The waltz is decency itself compared with the modern forms of the dance." With one sentence, Graebner thus indicted all twentieth-century dances from 1912 on—with no regard for style, rhythm, couple position, or place of performance. In another global indictment, he asserted that: "All modern psychologists are agreed that dancing is an expression of the sex instinct in its lowest animal forms." The tone of these and other statements constitute clear continuation of the historical polemic rather than a scholarly analysis of a centuries-old theological concept. Graebner's subsequent use of quotes from the nineteenth-century adversaries Wilkinson and Faulkner further add to the impression that he began his discussion of dancing with a strong negative bias that no amount of objective analysis and current information would countermand.[27]

A descent into sheer polemic appears in *Lutheran Customs* by the cleric Marmaduke Nathaniel Carter (1881–1961). His assertions recall the typical late nineteenth- and early twentieth-century claims that rules for the parlor ought to prevail on the ballroom floor: "Can a little music give a young man a privilege he did not have without the music?" Continuing in this vein, Carter concludes that "the only young man who has that right [to embrace] is the young woman's husband. No husband? Then no encirclement till you get one."[28] Unlike his fellow Missouri Synod colleagues, Carter attacked "solo or interpretive" dancing on the basis of "what is being interpreted, and the amount of cloth that goes along with the process." Citing the biblical events of Salome's dancing and the subsequent beheading of John the Baptist, Carter felt free to extrapolate about the event, stating: "more than likely it was attended by the 100 percent undress that would have been permitted at little Herod's corrupt Oriental court."[29]

A similar indictment against the ballet came from the 1945 book *The Modern Dance on Trial* by Jesse Marvin Gaskin (1917–?), a Baptist minister in Tonkawa, Oklahoma. Gaskin's comments must be taken with a measure of doubt. Since America's major ballet performances then took place primarily in the East, Gaskin's exposure to that theater art form may have been via a local company or not at all. Whatever his experience of the ballet, he spoke with complete authority in denouncing it: "Sex and the dance are inseparable. The ballet, for example, loses its appeal when clothes are put on the dancer. It is the base, vulgar display of nudity that apeals [*sic*] to the cheap-minded admirer. The ballet dance violates Paul's injunction to dress modestly" (1 Tim. 2:9). Like Carter, Gaskin also cited the example of Salome. Extrapolating to his own era, Gaskin indicted Hollywood and the movies for popularizing dance: "Moral delinquency there exceeds that of ancient Babylon, or Sodom."[30]

Thus, the arguments from this period narrow to an almost exclusive focus on the immorality of dancing. Only two authors even suggest the possibility of one's health's being harmed.[31] Former issues of wasted time or squandered money do not appear at all. The overriding emphasis on the "embrace" of the

The Polemic Upstaged   331

"modern dances" led to continued strong protestations about dancing's harmfulness to America's youth. For example, the Norwegian Lutheran cleric Oscar Hanson (1908–after 1967) likened the temptations inherent in dancing to the hazards of fire: "Young people by the thousands in America are in pain and misery of body and soul because they have played with the fire of lust and temptation. Annually thousands of young men and women in America burn their bodies and souls with shame and disgrace, physical and spiritual ruin because of the modern dance." Writing in the 1940s, Hanson gave no current evidence for his assertions about the thousands who "burn with shame."[32] Continuing his exhortations, he linked morality with patriotism, as had Billy Sunday: "Can I as a loyal American endorse, approve, or have anything to do with a movement that is ruining thousands of young American men and women annually? The modern dance is a moral menace. It is a cancerous germ that is eating its way into the moral fibre of American youth. It is fire that burns the body, mind, and soul to a painful death of destruction. *Young America! Don't play with fire!*"[33] According to Hanson, young people could have all of their social and recreational needs fulfilled through the Lutheran church's youth organization known as the Luther League. Such an environment proved safe, whereas "the high school dance is the training ground for the ballroom, the night club, the rotten roadhouse."[34] Hanson's assertion suggests that high school dances were common, and statistics bear that out.[35]

Only Campbell refers to poor students who dance, and he disparages them with a racist attitude reminiscent of commentary from writers earlier in the century. "It does not take brains to dance. The negro in the back alley is often an expert in dancing. Those most often sent home from college . . . are usually the best dancers." As further proof that dancing involved no mindful activity, he revived the charge that even "lunatics" could dance.[36] In similar chauvinistic and racist language, Gaskin linked dancing with animal behavior and "heathens," particularly those in Africa or the South Sea Islands:

> The above quotations pointing out that dancing is an art among primitive animals, along with the fact that the best dancers in today's world are the most uncivilized people on earth, is [*sic*] convincing evidence that the dance is of heathen origin and is utterly pagan in nature. If you want to find a real dancer, go to Africa, or the South Sea Islands. There you will find folk who dance by nature. The only American who does not have to learn to dance is a negro; it is natural with him. Ask the missionary who has been to Africa and see what he says about the innate dancing nature of the negro.

The quotations Gaskin uses to prove his position supposedly establish the purely sexual nature of dancing among animals and, historically, among western Europeans. Sources for the quotations are not mentioned, nor are the qualifications of his "authorities."[37]

Although Campbell and Gaskin might be considered isolated individuals with racist attitudes, other interpretations suggest their viewpoints were more widely shared. In an article titled "Walter F. White and the Savoy Ballroom Controversy of 1943," the historian Dominic J. Capeci Jr. tells about the reason the Savoy had its license revoked for several months in spring and summer 1943 for violations of the city's administrative code. Although the ostensible grounds were health issues, many believed that the real reasons for closing the Savoy were race-related. Capeci argues convincingly that the temporary closing of the Savoy was prompted by anxieties about whites in Harlem and mixed dancing.[38] Such fears were related to the role and concept of white women.

Tradition and Change for Women

Dance opponents of the thirties and forties continued the position—prominent for more than a century among antidance writers—that the burden of morality fell to women. They told readers that men wanted wives, not just dancing partners. Without addressing the chastity of men, writers either explicitly or implicitly stressed the point that men wanted women who had the "charm of unspoiled virginity." Accordingly, Kretzmann advised girls to assist male relatives and friends to a sober and chaste behavior by exercising care in the degree to which they revealed their bodies to admiring male glances. He argued that the temptation to lust came most strongly through the eyes.[39] Baptists and nondenominational evangelists, as well as Lutherans, repeated the same themes. Excerpts from Campbell's declarations about women proved so appealing to the evangelist John Carrara a decade later that he incorporated many of them. He averred that

> a woman loses her modesty when dancing. One of the most beautiful phases of our national life is the reverence of our men for pure womanhood. Deep in the soul of the woman is born that inherent modesty for which the American woman is noted. The painted face, the brazen look, the plucked eyebrow, the indecent dress which we see now may attract men's eyes but never his heart. This woman places an impassable gulf between herself and the respect and affection of American gentlemen. God has linked courtesy and modesty together as He has linked the destiny of the man and the woman. When there are no longer any modest women in the world, there will be no more gentlemen.[40]

Campbell's portrait of a pure and true woman recalls that picture painted by writers of a century earlier when the "Cult of True Womanhood" first
became part of the American social code. In 1933 Campbell declared: "To
be a woman in the truest and noblest sense of the word is to be the best and
most admirable thing under the canopy of heaven. . . . A true woman is
estimated by the real goodness of her heart, the greatness of her soul, and
the purity and sweetness of her character."[41] If young girls did not understand the role and character to which they should aspire, their mothers were
to instruct them.[42] Given this general concept of women held by dance
opponents of the thirties and forties, their strong emphasis on the immorality of dancing is hardly surprising.

Pronouncements about the morality that women were to uphold, for the
good of homes and country, were perhaps motivated anew by the radical
changes in women's dress, behavior, and social roles. For example, William
Bell Riley, the noted Baptist fundamentalist leader of Minneapolis, preached
in 1934 against "The Ways of Women in Unsexing Themselves." Among
Riley's litany of evils, the listener heard denigrations of bobbed hair, trousers, "women's rights," "profane speech," explosions of temper, drinking, and
smoking. Riley, like Billy Sunday and others before him, also had no time
for "society matrons." In 1937 Minneapolis seemed hardly better than the
ancient city of Sodom due to the abundance of cigarette smoking, cocktail
drinking, and midnight dancing by society matrons.[43]

Typically, Riley and others also upheld the ancient notion of two kinds
of women, based on the story of Eve in Genesis. According to Riley's 1934
sermon, a Christian woman proved the ultimate in "character accomplishments" but a woman without Christ became nothing but "Satan's dupe" as
well as his "delight."[44] That the view was widely held is evidenced by dance
opponents' repeated use of statistics about "fallen" and "ruined" women.
However, Clara J. Jones (1900–?), a contemporary Lutheran social worker
in Fargo, North Dakota, brought out her own book of vignettes, *Shall We
Dance?*, which told the sorry plight of girls who had become "victims" of
the dance. Appearing first in the *Lutheran Herald* for 6 March 1934, Jones's
stories apparently found enough positive response to warrant a separate
publication in the form of a fourteen-page booklet. The clear message
throughout is that the sins of smoking, drinking, and dancing—particularly
at public balls—eventually lead to uncontrollable passion and pregnancy out
of wedlock. In Jones's words, "Step by step is the secret of those who fall."[45]

Like the dance opponents of previous decades who used the same themes
and arguments, writers in the thirties and forties usually did not address the

changing roles of women or attempt to discriminate among social forces that affected women's behavior.[46] In contrast to denunciations by dance detractors who alleged that dancing destroyed homes, led to divorce, and encouraged prostitution, even murder,[47] sociologists and historians of the 1930s point out that it was the severe economic problems of the Depression that led to dramatic changes in marriage, morality, and family. As Frederick Lewis Allen observed, the divorce rate dropped precipitously from 1.66 per thousand in 1929 to 1.28 per thousand by 1932. Reality dictated that to break up a marriage cost money. Though divorce statistics climbed again when times got better, a *Fortune* survey in 1937 showed that the majority of people were against "easy divorce." Similarly, the marriage rate fell between 1929 and 1932; to get married also cost money. Nonetheless, sex did not disappear. As one writer observed, "The huge sales of contraceptives—totaling, annually, according to various authorities, from an eighth to a quarter of a billion dollars, and transacted not only in drugstores but in filling stations, tobacco stores, and all sorts of other establishments—were certainly not made only to the married."[48] Thus, hard times, privacy in cars, sales of contraceptives, film romances, the heritage of the twenties—a host of factors— contributed to a freer behavior of men and women. Yet among all of the several forces affecting the social roles of women, at least for a time, perhaps none was more dramatic than World War II.

The effects of the war could be felt in almost every area of American life, from children buying war stamps and bonds in schools, to gas rationing, to blue and gold stars hanging in front windows signifying sons in service, to women working. Instead of presiding exclusively over home and family, available women were drafted for jobs vacated by men gone to war. "Rosie the Riveter" in head scarf and overalls became the patriotic model in advertisements. Women filled men's jobs in steel mills, shipyards, and on docks; they drove cabs and buses and served as mechanics, in addition to holding the usual clerical or desk jobs. Some joined the WACS or WAVES, and a few even ferried airplanes from one destination to another.[49] But most women served in myriad roles on the home front. Among other tasks, they rolled bandages for the Red Cross, tended victory gardens, and, not least, hosted servicemen in canteens and USO centers at home and abroad.

The War Years and Increasing Acceptance of Dance

For servicemen home from the front or on leave from their ships, dancing provided a way to meet girls, listen to music, exercise, or just "cut loose." The New York dance critic John Martin commented in 1944 that the town had "never seen so much strut and swing before." Where else but on the dance floor could guys and gals release pentup energy or forget war worries for a time, and in the process enjoy companionship with the opposite sex? Besides, the entertainment was cheap—no small factor if one was a private earning twenty-one dollars per month.[50] For many women, dancing and hosting servicemen became a patriotic duty.

Cognizant of the importance of providing for regular socializing, military bases held weekend dances for the men. For a marine who trained at Fort Bragg in South Carolina, along with 63,999 other men, Saturday night dances would have been the week's highlight.[51] If there weren't enough women nearby to serve as dance partners, others were imported. Men at San Luis Obispo in southern California apparently had the pick of the crop, according to an article titled "Dates for Defense," in *Colliers* for November 1941: "When you get 140 of southern California's prettiest debs, Junior Leaguers and young society matrons to ride 500 miles, pay their fares, dance five hours with 2000 soldiers and sit up the rest of the night in day coaches—that's something."[52]

The dramatic picture of more than a hundred young women traveling 500 miles in order to dance with men previously unknown to them stands in vivid contrast to the image conjured up by dance opponents in the thirties, who asserted that no pure woman should let a man put his arm around her unless the two had spoken marriage vows. In response to inquiries about the conduct of dances, *Recreation* magazine for September 1941 printed an article affirming that strict guidelines were maintained. Although rules for the Houston, Texas, recreation center seemed to circumscribe male conduct, the Sloane House YMCA in New York City checked girls recruited for dances with extreme care: they fingerprinted them.[53]

What did they dance? G.I. Joe and Rosie the Riveter anywhere in the country probably danced what they danced in New York City. Martin reported in January 1944 on the "Canteen," a night spot for service people in the "Big Apple":

> You'd be surprised how many kinds of dances you see, and well done, too. Rumbas and congas, of course, as well as foxtrots, jitterbugs and a few waltzes. They've got a recording at the Canteen of the "Parade of the Wooden Soldiers" and darned if the boys and girls don't break into an old-fashioned two-step, which was out of date before they were born, or funnier still, the polka, which even their mothers and dads didn't dance. Where did they learn them? They don't know.[54]

Although soldiers at a base in Lincoln, Nebraska, were introduced to the fundamentals of square dancing as part of their entertainment, it was swing music and dancing that held the top rank of popularity among American youth. When the Harry James Band played New York's Paramount Theater in June 1943, the audience was euphoric. James's appearance even caused riots in Times Square. According to "'Jive Bombers' Jamboree," an article in *Colliers* for June 5: "The New York Times and other sober publications found this behavior incomprehensible. Grave news writers found in the phenomenon something akin to the ecstatic impulse of the 13th century that sent thousands of small fry on the Children's Crusade, or to the exultant mass migration that inspired the legend of The Pied Piper of Hamelin. Psychologists thought the recent jitterbug jamboree was an expression of adolescent bewilderment brought on by the war."[55]

Military and patriotic organizations sponsored dances not only in New York, San Luis Obispo, or Fort Bragg, but also on college campuses. Many units of military trainees were stationed on college and university campuses so that the men could get their academic degrees and learn specialized fighting skills at the same time. Usually the trainees went from the campuses into service as officers, so they were top-quality students, carefully recruited for a particular branch of the armed forces. Though the impact of a military unit on a large campus might not have been great, the effect on a small campus would have been more noticeable. At least one Lutheran church historian credits the eventual acceptance of dancing by the church to this wartime phenomenon.

Writing in the early 1960s about the history of the Augustana Lutheran church, a denomination of Swedish background, G. Everett Arden observed:

> As the heirs of a pietistic tradition, the rank and file of Augustana clergy and laity traditionally looked upon dancing as an evil which true Christians must eschew. Though there were from time to time feeble efforts to change this position, the Church maintained an attitude of uncompromising opposition to dancing until after World War II. During the war, when military units occupied the campuses of the church colleges, dances were sponsored on school property by the military as a part of the regular recreational program. Though this provoked some opposition in the Church, dancing on the campus of church-related colleges was gradually accepted.[56]

In 1950, the Augustana Lutheran church issued a manifesto that left the question of dancing to the consciences of individual church members and to the judgment of the several college administrations. In a dramatic but realistic change of stance from the legalistic morality of earlier decades, when Carl Axel Lindwall (1868–1943) declared, "You cannot dance and be a child

of God," the mid-twentieth-century manifesto pointed out that "the problem of dancing is but one of the symptoms of the inroads of secularism upon
the Church. There are greater, more fundamental problems."[57]

Ironically, by the time that the Augustana church relinquished its formerly
strict opposition to dancing, the era of the big bands, Lindy-hopping, and
jitterbugging was on the decline. Never again would the couple dances, so
strenuously objected to, enjoy the popularity they had attained during the
decades from 1910 to 1945. One might also think that the dramatically
different roles assumed by women during the war would have defused the
opposition to dancing that had been based on assumptions about women's
frailty, superior morality, and special domestic role. But women were directed
back to hearth and home when veterans returned from service at the war's
end, and the published dance opposition continued, despite the decline in
the popularity of dancing. Tastes in music changed; many dance bands dissolved; and the advent of television caused many former dancers to sit at
home.

Postwar Decline, New Sounds, and Solo Dancing

The years immediately following the close of World War II witnessed a
decrease in big bands and ballroom dancing. Eight of the most successful
bands broke up in 1946. No one knows exactly why, but several factors are
pertinent. First, economic factors played a role. A 20 percent amusement
tax on dance halls and performances had been imposed to support the war
effort. It cost more to keep bands together, and ballroom owners had to
charge more to pay bands and the tax. Second, many men—prominent
musicians among them—did not come back from the war. Glenn Miller,
for example, lost his life in a flight over the English Channel just before
Christmas 1944. Third, new experiences always produce new sounds and
new rhythms. No art ever stays on a plateau; popular art, in particular, needs
to change to retain its status. Fourth, jazz music in this country pushed into
new dimensions during the forties with a variation known as "bop," which
was simply not danceable.[58] Finally, new music, radio, phonograph records,
and television were drawing people into different settings than the traditional
dance hall. Vocalists, in particular, came into prominence; they, rather than
the big bands, became the chief purveyors of popular music. Dancing to
vocal music did not hold the same attraction as dancing to the rhythm section of a large instrumental ensemble. Vocalists and the new jazz music of
the late forties and fifties favored listeners not dancers. Television favored

sitters as well. In 1947, there were 200,000 television sets in American homes; by 1951, there were 12,000,000. The total jumped to 20,000,000 a year later and the number continued to increase.[59] People seemed glad to be entertained at home, free of charge.

Some bands and some dances, of course, endured. The ever popular Guy Lombardo and his Royal Canadians continued to play New Year's Eve dates at the Waldorf Astoria in New York City into the 1970s. Harry James and his band toured Europe in 1970–71. Benny Goodman toured Asia in 1956 and then put together enough sidemen in 1978 to repeat his famous 1938 success at Carnegie Hall. Duke Ellington also made several international tours with his band and in 1970 became a member of the Swedish Royal Academy of Music. Nonetheless, the frequency of dates for dances severely diminished, as did the cross-country tours. Moreover, the large ballrooms disappeared at the same time. The famous Trianon in Chicago closed in 1954; its sister ballroom, the Aragon, held on for another decade. Changing urban conditions brought Harlem's Savoy ballroom to an end in 1958, though its downtown counterpart, Roseland, was going strong in 1967 and still operated, though on a limited basis, in the early nineties. However, the people who still went there to dance were not the youthful crowd but mainly those who had grown up with swing and the big bands.[60]

Just as the dance devotees grew older, so did the men who made the music. Some dance bands met their demise simply due to the natural aging, retirement, or death of the musicians. For example, the Dorsey brothers both died in the fifties; Glen Gray of the famous Casa Loma band died in 1963; and the popular drummer Gene Krupa passed away ten years later. Other leaders from the thirties and forties retired from directing their bands; for example, Artie Shaw made his final recording in 1954.[61] By the late fifties, other rhythms, sounds, and names rose to fame in the world of popular music and attracted new fans.

American Bandstand came on television in 1956 and reached some twenty million viewers daily—mostly teenagers. It became a forum for the latest in teen passions, both music and dances. Fats Domino, Bill Haley and the Comets, Elvis Presley, and others soon captured the popular market with the new sound of rock 'n' roll. Rockers using amplified guitars made the music and the beat louder and stronger than ever before. While adults danced to the latest Latin imports like the cha-cha and watched Arthur and Katharine Murray's dance parties on television, the real market for new music and dance lay with the teen set.[62] The tight pants and hip-swiveling of "Elvis-the-Pelvis" meant that torso movement in dancing was in for a while.

Not since the twenties had the hips been such a focus of attention. When the twist became popular, it seemed that dancers throughout country, at least the nongeriatric crowd, were shaking their hips. Grandparents and other oldsters considered the latest fad dances strange and wild compared to the Lindy and jitterbug—just as John Martin had predicted back in 1943: "Can you picture some possible agitation about the year 1960 to reject the hideous ballroom manifestations of the helicopter age and return to the charm and dignity of the jitterbug? Better check in your zoot suits, gang, just in case, and get ready to move on. Where do we go from here?" Martin's prediction came true in the alarmists' fears about the twist. In 1962 the cultural commentator Marshall Fishwick wrote that the dance drew "such descriptive epithets as barbaric, erotic, inhuman, and satanic." Continuing, Fishwick observed the cyclical nature of such denunciations. "I realized that I had heard a remarkably similar description myself once—when I learned how to jitterbug! So did my father, he admitted privately—when he did the Charleston."[63]

The early sixties produced a phenomenon in dancing unlike anything the country had experienced before. Indeed, the kind of dancing displayed had not been evident in any sizable manifestation since the ecstatic outbursts during the Middle Ages in Europe. Solo dancing was in, and individuals gyrated on the dance floor with no discernible acknowledgment of a partner. It mattered little if your "partner" faced you or turned away from you. A dancer's movements did not have to be synchronized with those of anyone else on the floor. Since movements were not codified by dance masters, no one needed lessons. Often dances changed so rapidly that what was "in" on one coast was "out" in the Midwest or on the other coast. The names of some dances—the monkey, fish, and pony—are reminiscent of the animal names given to ragtime fad dances. Others, such as the Watusi, the swim, and the surf, recall young people's interests in the sixties. The fears of moralists who had worried about close dancing in an earlier era were irrelevant to the dances of the sixties. No one touched. Nonpartner, solo dancing simply reflected the general maxim of "do your own thing."

Not only did the sixties manifestation of ballroom dancing shatter previous conceptions of that genre; other kinds of dance spread throughout the country and thereby extended the meaning of the word "dance." In 1965 Congress funded a new organization called the National Endowment for the Arts. One of the major programs funded by that agency involved tours by dance companies. Additional assistance to local sponsors came from numerous new state arts boards. With federal and state monies, towns, colleges, and other types of local sponsors were finally able to bring modern dance companies into the hinterlands. Performers and choreographers previously seen only in large metropolitan centers came to Iowa City, Iowa; Northfield, Minnesota; and numerous other towns, both large and small, throughout the country. Performances and dance instruction given through master classes served to teach the country that the label "dance" meant more than just ballet or ballroom dancing.

With money for the arts flowing more freely than ever before in the country's history, the study of dance became increasingly popular as an independent discipline in colleges and universities. Schools developed majors in dance, which complemented majors in music or theater. Though most of these programs emphasized the genre of modern dance, many schools also taught ballet classes; some even offered a major in ballet. Folk, ethnic, and ballroom dancing courses appeared in many curricula as did choreography, production, history of dance, music for dance, and the like. By the seventies, serious theater dance, primarily modern dance and ballet, had firmly established itself around the country.

In the face of such widespread and radical acceptance of American dance, one might expect that the traditional antidance polemic would have vanished. However, although few antidance books were printed, those that did appear suggest that enclaves of opposition remained entrenched in isolated pockets of the country. In reviewing the extant literature from the end of World War II until 1970, the question to focus on becomes: Did the opponents keep up with the latest trends in dancing? In view of the popularity of the new solo dances, did opponents still allege the former primary argument that dance was a temptation to immorality?

Diminished Opposition

Despite the fact that in 1933 the Baptist clergyman Robert Campbell had declared that too many teachers and preachers had accepted dancing—or, perhaps because of that perceived acceptance—Baptists continued to produce antidance books into the 1960s. The degree to which such publications diminished in general can be learned by comparing the postwar output with the number of publications issued from the time of the Depression through World War II. During the sixteen years from 1930 through 1945, a total of thirteen books or pamphlets, opposing dance in whole or in part, can be identified. Another five probably date from this period but their exact years of publication cannot be verified. By contrast, the twenty-four years from 1946 through 1969 yielded only fifteen such publications, one of which was the eighth edition of Graebner's book, first published in 1935. Although Lutherans produced two of the writings in the early fifties, the remaining opposition came from Baptists, Disciples of Christ, and, in one case, a Nazarene. In 1969, the last identified antidance book examined for the present study was published.

The absence of such books in the seventies and eighties points clearly to the fact that dancing had finally become accepted or dramatically upstaged. Other problems occupied the attention of clergy and evangelists. The prolonged Vietnam conflict, draft dodgers, civil rights, drugs, pornography, abortion, and the homeless could all lay claim to having attracted more serious attention than the question whether or not individual Christians should indulge in worldly entertainment. Moreover, these and other issues that concerned American society at large stood apart from the problems that churches themselves faced—declining memberships, declining gifts, mergers, and the like.

The numbers and sources of antidance publications that did appear during the period from 1946 to 1970 suggest that the Baptist church, at least the Southern Baptist Convention, firmly and unwaveringly held the line against dancing. Similarly, the Missouri Synod Lutherans maintained a strong stand, at least through the fifties. The remaining publications could well indicate isolated individual, idiosyncratic views held by persons within the Christian Church and the Nazarene Church but not necessarily common to the denominations as a whole.

For the most part, the antidance books from this period represent a mix of anachronistic arguments. Given the fact that "modern dance" had become an established genre of theater performance by this era, those writers who continued to oppose the "modern dance" or "modern dancing" probably confused their readers. The intent of dance opponents was to argue against ballroom dancing as a heterosexual activity. More particularly, they wanted to argue against those dances that required the closed-partner position. However, their language did not always convey that intent. For example, in 1969 Wendell Wellman, of the Nazarene Church, objected to the "modern dance" on the basis of its increasing sensuality. He declared that the twentieth century had increasingly turned from the "waltz-type dances" to those of the "North American Creole or Negro, and the dances of the South American countries."[64] In light of such information, the reader of that era might have taken offense at an implied racial slur. Other readers might have understood Wellman to be referring to musical stage or jazz dancing. Far more confusing and inaccurate is the statement from a pamphlet by a Baptist evangelist, Homer Martinez, which was published in Fort Worth, Texas, about 1962. His loose reference to "the modern dance" leaves the reader with no clear understanding of what particular kind of dance or dances are objectionable:

> The modern dance which was believed to be of Bohemian origin was first introduced to France, in a Parisian brothel. From there it traveled to Germany where it gained entrance slowly because of the attacks upon such dancing by the more respectable people. The dance then came from Germany to America in 1795. Some of the earliest records of the dance in America inform us that the old fashion [sic] saloons along the coasts of California embraced this illegitimate offspring. Dime a Dance saloons were born. In these places, hired females would dance and drink with the sailors for money.[65]

Martinez employs the typical strategy of earlier polemicists, objecting to dancing on the grounds of alleged origin with no intervening analysis of changes in position, style, music, rhythm, and/or cultural context: "Take a good look at this 'egg's' life history. Its biography is rather unwholesome. Incubated in the muddy waters of Sodom and Gomorrah. Born in a brothel house in France, and reared as a child of questionable environment in the American beer joint. Do you think the social trash pickers of our day can pull it out of the garbage can, and clean it up enough for children, churches, and Christians? If you are born of God you already have your answer."[66] The blatant generalities and misstatements, cast in starkly contrasting terms and couched in crass vernacular language, remind the reader of "fervent exhorters" such as Billy Sunday and Sam P. Jones.

In similar fashion, Porter Marcellus Bailes (1888–1963), a Baptist minister, wrote from Tyler, Texas, in 1946 about the evils of the "modern dance." Though he did name particular dances—bunny hug, Charleston, truckin', jitterbug, rhumba, and foxtrot—some were no longer popular. However, like Martinez, Bailes indicted these dances on the grounds of their alleged origins. He wrote that "the steps of the dance make it dangerous" and maintained that they came from "the lowest dives of sin." Bailes further denounced dancing by reviving the charge that even the illiterate and the insane could master it.[67] Marion Edgar Ramay (1890–1981), a Baptist minister and author, wrote from Edmond, Oklahoma, in 1958 that "the modern social dance" was objectionable, also on the basis of historical evils that could not be dispelled. "It is a deep conviction of mine that anything that was ever sinful within itself, is sinful now."[68]

Theodore Graebner, a Missouri Synod Lutheran, displayed a lack of so-phisticated knowledge regarding social dances when in 1951 he indicted the "modern dance" as including "in effect the tango with variations." That included the two-step, foxtrot, and "other popular forms." Going beyond specific dances, he also considered under the term "modern dance" the syn-copated and jazzy music accompanying dancing, as well as the casinos, road houses, and night clubs that catered to a "mixed clientele." Interestingly, he did not mention or allude to the Lindy or jitterbug, despite their popular-ity in the late thirties and forties. However, he did not object to the square dance, forms of the ballet that emphasized grace, and tap dancing that emphasized rhythm, when these genres were circumscribed within the prop-er place and time.[69]

Other opponents from this period who display awareness of more than one dance genre vary in their approval. For example, Don Humphrey (1936–?), a Christian evangelist writing in 1963 from Great Bend, Kansas, said he objected to square dances, chorus lines, "tap dancing and such," as well as to mixed social dancing.[70] Perhaps the most scholarly approach was initial-ly taken by Charles Chumley (1918–?), a minister in the Disciples of Christ church. Writing sometime after World War II, Chumley quoted from the 1947 *Encyclopedia Britannica* for his definition of "dancing" and conclud-ed that "the meaning of the word 'dance' is very broad in its scope." De-spite the credible beginning, he later reverted to using the blanket term "the 'modern' dance" for particular objections.[71] Probably geographical location accounted for the different kinds of dance genre mentioned by William Orr, an evangelist and author, who wrote from California in 1960. In addition to indicting the Hollywood movie industry, Orr had no time for "home dances," square dancing, ballet, and tap, as well as "modern dance." Al-though Orr argued that the cheek-to-cheek and body-to-body contact of the latter made it "the Devil's territory," the other kinds of dances represented evil because they progressed into increasingly more serious situations where one might be tempted to sin or lead others into sin.[72]

The primary objection to dancing held by writers from the post–World War II years through the sixties was that it tempted people to immoral con-duct. The closed dance position was thought to be the fundamental feature guaranteed to arouse passion, or the "sex instinct." But the language of oppo-nents who wrote against other kinds of dances also suggested they feared sex-ual temptation. John Scott Trent, a Baptist minister, declared in 1958 that "dancing has taken our young people back to savagery, with all the debasing associations and moral perils of its pagan background." He targeted the then current rock 'n' roll. Writing two years later, Orr referred to that "strange sort of jungle music with the tempo calculated to make the dancers throw off any restraint and indulge to the full."[73] A pamphlet published in 1959 by the Christian Life Commission of the Texas Baptist General Convention, titled *Teen Talk about Rock 'n' Roll,* pointed to the same addictive qualities about the contemporary music of that era. A companion pamphlet, *Dancing,* from the following year stressed the immoral temptations to be avoided when teens were confronted with the atmosphere surrounding dances. "Where there is a great deal of dancing there is frequently also a great deal of drinking, heavy petting and 'going all the way' in sexual adventures."[74]

In contrast to the more reasonable language and tone of these *Teen Talk* pamphlets, several writers from the era resorted to citing "authorities" and statistics from previous periods. Both Ramay, writing in 1958, and Martinez, who published around 1962, quoted T. A. Faulkner, the former dancing master who converted to Christianity and began opposing dance back in the 1890s.[75] A casual reader, unobservant of language and simply skimming over the books, could well have assumed that T. A. Faulkner was a mid-twentieth-century dancing instructor. In a similar fashion, the evangelist Harley Lane, writing after 1950, cited Jane Addams's judgments against the modern dance and the "jazz music" that accompanied it.[76]

In general, these writers continued to declare that the safest path for a Christian was to abstain from dancing; they asserted that forms other than mixed social dancing constituted "incipient evils" or temptations. Associated evils such as alcohol and smoking created undesirable environments. Yet, in order to clinch his position, Humphrey pointed to the ultimate source of evil: "Dancing will never be right until we can regiment people's intelligence and be sure that they only think certain things. That is not likely to ever happen, so the only other alternative is to not dance."[77]

Other authors' objections to dancing during the postwar period reveal no new positions. Surprisingly, some of them resurrect arguments that had not been aired since well before the Depression years. Several writers, from Bailes in 1946 through Wellman in 1969, reintroduce the old notion that dancing constituted a health hazard because it took place during late night hours and in smoke-filled rooms. Lane maintained that the distance traveled in an evening's dance amounted to more than 19.4 miles. His source was an unidentified Frenchman who computed the figure based on an evening of dancing waltzes, quadrilles, and mazurkas—all popular dances during the latter half of the nineteenth century. The argument using the mileage statistic had not been popular among antidance writers since the early 1920s.[78] Using an even more anachronistic charge, Lane echoed arguments from the 1890s when he asserted that private dances suggested the presence of a "smart set" and exclusivity—"both of which are out of line in a democracy." Ramay announced that dancing created a "social caste system" between those who danced and those who did not.[79] Although these charges had not appeared since the end of the nineteenth century, during the teens Harry Benton had implied a similar line of reasoning in his objections to dancing in the public schools. A variant on that theme appeared in the reasoning of Ramay and Orr; they pointed out that when public school dancing was a required activity, it undermined the parental authority of those who did not want their children to dance.[80]

A strong emphasis on two factors undergirded the arguments against dancing and continued a trend from the Depression and prewar years. First, writers universally maintained that dancing mentioned in the Bible constituted no valid argument for participation in the "modern dance." As a corollary, implicitly understood, the Bible stood as the final and ultimate authority for the Christian with respect to his or her behavior. Second, writers stressed the earlier, prominent argument that to abstain from dancing was the only viable course for a Christian. Because of Pauline exhortations to be separate from the world, to avoid even the appearance of evil, and to avoid leading one's brother or sister into temptations, moderate participation proved no acceptable alternative. Arguments opposed social dancing, and nowhere do these publications even mention the possibility of dancing as a part of worship.

Dancing in the Church

Formal evidence that the public's understanding of dance and dancing had changed or would change came as early as the 1940 edition of the *Encyclopedia Americana*. Prior editions of this serial began with a definition that called dancing "a form of exercise or amusement in which one or more persons make a series of graceful movements in measured steps in accord with music." The new edition for 1940 began with: "Dancing is rhythmic movements of the body or parts of the body to express emotion or as a medium for religious exercise, amusement, or to convey an idea." This latter statement opened up the possibilities for dance and dancing by admitting that there could be dance in the church as worship, that not all dancing fell under the rubric of "amusement." In fact, the decline of widespread denominational opposition after 1930 was accompanied by a slowly growing awareness that dance could legitimately serve to enhance the worship experiences of parishioners.

From the 1920s through the 1940s, in performances, articles, and lectures, the American modern dancers Ruth St. Denis and Ted Shawn pioneered the concept of using dance in the church.[81] Gradually other adherents bolstered their efforts. By the mid-fifties, some thirty years after William Norman Guthrie told New York City clergy about dance performances in his church of St. Mark's in the Bouwery, sufficient interest and commitment had been generated to form the Eastern Regional Sacred Dance Association. The regional title was dropped by 1958 as membership in the organization expanded throughout the country, and the group came to be known as the Sacred Dance Guild, a national association that continues to the present. Members included not only dancers but clergy, religious education directors, musicians, and others interested in supporting creative arts in the church. A newsletter told members around the country of the dancing, choreographing, performing, writing, and lecturing of fellow performers. Early members had come primarily from Congregational, Unitarian, and Methodist denominations, but as membership expanded nationally, people from all denominations joined. The inclusion of dance into worship services came more slowly in some churches, such as the various Lutheran synods, than it did in others, for example, the Congregational, Presbyterian or Unitarian churches. Nonetheless, the very existence of an organization devoted to creating dance as art within the life and worship of American churches was testimony to the virtual end of the centuries-old polemic.

Excursus to the Nineties

The past three decades have witnessed increasing acceptance of dance in both social and concert settings. A few statistics can highlight the trend. Reporting in the National Endowment for the Arts *Cultural Post* in the fall of 1980, Livingston Biddle noted that during the preceding fifteen years, American dance companies had increased in number from 37 to 200. Community arts agencies had grown from 125 to nearly 2,000 in the same period of time. Acceptance of the arts, including dance, spread throughout the country. Biddle cited the most "dramatic example" to be the growth of dance audiences beyond the East Coast. Whereas in 1965 80 percent of dance viewers lived in New York City, by 1980 about the same percentage lived outside of it.[82] Benefiting from an unprecedented flow of funds to the arts in the sixties and seventies, Americans around the country saw ballet and modern dance presented on the concert stage by touring companies, courtesy of NEA's Dance Touring Program. Anna Kisselgoff of the *New York Times* wrote in the 3 March 1985 edition that in the quarter century preceding the mid-seventies, the dance audience had exploded from one million to twenty million people. By 1984, a Louis Harris survey had reported that attendance at dance performances numbered fifty-eight million.[83] In addition to live events, there were television performances funded by companies such as Exxon and Mobil, which facilitated the widespread dissemination of dance to the American public. Another measure of the increasing acceptance was the incorporation of many dance major programs into the curricula of public and private colleges and universities. The founding of the National Association of Schools of Dance in 1981, as the first accrediting body for dance curricula in higher education, was further testimony to the expansion of dance curricula.

Not only did dance mature as a fine art, but the kind of dance companies who performed on the concert stage also broadened. By the mid-eighties, Peter Maxwell's Ballroom Dance Theater was touring the country, as was a reconstruction of Lindy-hopping in the form of Mama Lu Parks Lindyhoppers, who performed to the musical accompaniment of the Harlem Blues and Jazz Band. Numerous American and foreign ethnic dance companies also traveled the country. A revival of interest in tap dancing resulted in part in the successful Jazz Tap Ensemble, which played on concert stages around the nation. Concurrently came a desire for traditional ballroom dancing. The rage over the show *Tango Argentino* proved to be only one measure of that nostalgia.

Though scattered reports from towns and schools around the country had indicated that partner dancing was replacing the 1960s vogue for solo or nonpartner dance patterns, a *Newsweek* feature of 2 July 1984 told readers that Americans had gotten into dancing in a big way: "Among the 2 million Americans who regularly trot out to two-step are the 300 elite members of the Washington Waltz Group and friends, who include Chief Justice Warren Burger and Justices Byron White and Lewis Powell." According to *Newsweek* reporters, the fashion did not limit itself to the nation's capital or to older folks:

Teen-agers are touch-dancing at proms. In San Francisco's Mission District at a club called Cesar's, men in flashy white or red suits swivel their partners in an elegant salsa. At a small continental restaurant in Coconut Grove, Fla., couples have been known to suddenly take to the floor and weave among the tables in a slinky tango. . . . At the elegant new Park Suite Hotel in Denver, some 200 people waltz and fox-trot every Friday night to big-band music; in San Francisco, an often young crowd jams the Hyatt Regency for afternoon tea dances.[84]

Demonstrating that the 1984 vogue was no aberration, the *Smithsonian* for March 1989 carried a ten-page feature on the revival of ballroom and swing dancing, under the title "Cheek to Cheek Is Doubly Chic, the Second Time Around."[85]

Whether Hollywood films fueled the dance fever or just capitalized on it is irrelevant. In fact, films like *Flashdance, Footloose,* and *Dirty Dancing* proved to be popular attractions. Both the titles and content of the latter two focused on the age-old American hostility to dancing. The films, as well as scattered newspaper reports, indicate that opposition to dancing had not totally ended. American antidance attitudes still survived in small enclaves of evangelical and fundamentalist strength.

Newsweek's feature on the 1984 dance boom reported that Mesquite, Texas, a city of eighty thousand or more and located near the border of Dallas, still heard preachers warning the community that "allowing dancing was just one step on the road to topless waitresses." The specific target of the Mesquite Ministerial Alliance was the town council, whose members had given a permit to a "steakhouse with a modest 800–square-foot dance floor."[86] On 14 August 1987, editors of the *Minneapolis Star and Tribune* reprinted a *Washington Post* article that reported similar antagonism in the small town of Anson, Texas. A 1933 law had forbidden public dancing in the town under penalty of fine. Dance advocates organized themselves into an action group named "Footloose," after the 1984 movie about a "campaign to legalize dancing in a fictitious town in Middle America." Supported by the Texas chapter of the American Civil Liberties Union, the "Footloose" defense of dancing apparently rested on the issue of individual rights.[87]

In the even smaller town of Purdy, Missouri, hostilities over dancing in the public schools fueled a court battle. An Associated Press report of December 1988 carried the story: "Longtime residents say Purdy always has banned social dancing in the schools. But U.S. District Judge Russell Clark ruled that the school board's written policy against dancing unconstitutionally promoted the values of those who oppose dancing for religious reasons."[88] The school board appealed the decision, and a three-judge panel from the Eighth Circuit Court of Appeals overturned the lower court's decision. On 17 April 1990, the *New York Times* reported that the United States Supreme Court had refused to hear a challenge by Purdy students and parents who wanted dances. The decision by the appeals court held that dancing was a "'secular' activity and that a prohibition against school dances could be defended as an appropriately 'neutral' policy, whatever the motivation behind it."[89]

Rural and small-town Americans have usually promoted the values held dear by conservative evangelical and fundamentalist Christians. Yet, some prominent and not-so-prominent institutions of higher education also continued to oppose dancing despite the liberal attitudes of the late twentieth century. For example, in 1986 Oral Roberts University maintained a policy "that social dancing of any kind is not permitted on campus. Members of the student body are prohibited from planning, sponsoring, or working at social dances of any kind off campus."[90] Liberty University, in Lynchburg, Virginia, prohibited dancing or attendance at a "bar, nightclub, disco or rock concert." The prohibition appears in the 1987 student handbook in a category of activities that receive reprimands and monetary fines, including possession or use of fireworks, obscene or abusive language or behavior, unauthorized possession of firearms, discharging a false alarm, and possession of pornographic material. The school's vice president for student affairs said in a letter of 28 April 1987 that, since the school's purpose was to "train Christian leaders," the institution followed a policy of being "separated from the world" in certain areas like dancing.[91]

Some colleges assumed a more moderate stance. Both Bethel College in St. Paul, Minnesota, and Taylor University in Upland, Indiana, maintained restrictions on social dancing but not on all kinds of theater dance. In the late eighties, a pamphlet titled *Community Life at Bethel* read: "Pursuant to educational and developmental programs, certain aspects of folk and ethnic dance, aerobic exercise and movement, and the use of choreography in theater and musical productions may be deemed appropriate. (See 1 Corinthians 10:31.)" Similarly, in the late eighties, a Taylor pamphlet, *Life Together,* told students: "Because a significant number of evangelical Christians view that social dancing is a morally questionable activity, social dancing is not permitted on or away from campus. However, acceptable forms of expression in the academic program may include sanctioned folk dance, ethnic games, and the use of choreography in drama, musical productions, and athletic events."[92]

Two institutions of higher education made the news a decade later because of actual and hoped-for relaxation of bans on dancing. Baylor University in Waco, Texas, the largest Southern Baptist school in the country, made headlines around the nation when its regents finally called an end to 151 years of no dancing on the campus. The headline in the *Saint Paul*

Pioneer Press for Saturday, 20 April 1996, read, "Baptist School Goes Foot-loose, Permits Dancing on Campus." Reprinted from the *Washington Post,* the article was accompanied by a three-column-wide picture of Baylor's president, Robert B. Sloan Jr. and his wife, Sue, reportedly doing a "jitter-bug" to the rhythmic beat of the Glenn Miller classic, "In the Mood." One week later the *Chicago Tribune* ran a two-column feature headed "Wheaton Students Keep Dancing Shoes in Closet." The college, located in Wheaton, Illinois, has maintained a no-dancing policy throughout its 136–year history. But in 1995 a survey of Wheaton's 2,200 students found two-thirds of them favoring either some relaxation of the ban or lifting the ban entire-ly. A faculty vote the same year showed an overwhelming majority in favor of relaxing the ban. Both faculty and students are currently required to sign a pledge of abstinence from drinking, smoking, gambling, and social danc-ing. Duane Litfin, Wheaton College's president, was quoted as, in effect, attempting to steer a course of moderation between long tradition and con-temporary desires. "Whatever we do, we're going to go slowly," he said.[93]

Other changes in recent years have occurred in the corporate worship practice of some Pentecostal and charismatic churches, that is, the inclusion of dancing in church services. Although the national Sacred Dance Guild has been active for several decades, those churches that have actively fostered dancing in worship, from midcentury on, tended to be the more liberal mainline denominations. Their emphasis on dance as art stressed training dancers to perform in carefully crafted choreographies. In recent years, some of the more conservative denominations have begun to favor spontaneous "spirit-filled" movement behavior. This new manifestation of an old phe-nomenon has also elicited variations on the traditional arguments of the dance polemic.

The March 1989 issue of *Charisma and Christian Life* contains a feature article on the extent and kind of dancing pursued within churches. Exam-ples from around the country point to both choreographed dance perfor-mance and spontaneous dancing. A report on the August 1988 International Conference of the Worship Symposium, which drew about three thousand people to the event in Orlando, Florida, indicates that one-third of partic-ipants were pastors who wanted to develop a ministry of dance in their churches. A further testimony to the extent of dancing and the newly res-urrected controversy comes from Dr. Ansley Orfila in *The Evangelist* for October 1987. He points out that in the "spirit-filled churches" there is spontaneous dancing, prompted by the Holy Spirit, but also intentional or planned dancing, a combination of "a dance performance, social dancing and worship dancing." He views the latter kind of dancing as an invitation to immorality even though it occurs in the church: "I believe that planned dance performances, especially involving men and women together, will inevitably lead to immoral thoughts or actions. The planned, choreographed, humanly taught dancing promoted today is a far cry from the dancing in the Spirit that Pentecostal believers have known for years." Orfila's argument rests on the point that the Bible gives no basis for "planned or choreographed dancing in the church."[94]

The issue of intentionality, thus, continues as a distinguishing factor in dance opposition as it has since the days of summas for confessors, but in a more complex fashion. Medieval summas referred to the corrupt or innocent intentions of dancers; arguments in subsequent centuries carried forward the same issue. Contemporary arguments like Orfila's point to the intentionality of the choreographer. Purpose or intention has always been a necessary element for the creative artist. For example, when applied to dance as art in the church, the conscious, intentional choices of the choreographer are critically important in creating the appropriate dance presentation for a congregation. The kinds of choices made—regarding subject matter, degree of literal interpretation, spatial design, and the like—distinguish the less mature works of art from those that are more mature. In addition, the intentional attitude of the dancers further enhances or negates the artistic and worshipful value of dancing for a congregation. By contrast, "dancing in the spirit" becomes not so much artistic performance to assist in congregational worship as random movement behavior beyond the conscious, intentional control of the mover. Carried to its logical conclusion, Orfila's argument points to the question whether art in general, as well as artistic dance in particular, should be incorporated into the worship experience of a church.

The position of Orfila and others that the Bible gives no basis for "planned or choreographed dancing in the church" leads to another continuing element in dance opposition: the authority of the Bible. Orfila's argument rests on the same premise as the arguments of historical adversaries who stated that dancing, as practiced in their day, was wrong because the Bible nowhere gave authority for the "modern social dance." Again, carried to its logical conclusion, Orfila's argument would prohibit from worship such things as organs, guitars, electric keyboards, choir robes, banners, and the like—a host of traditional and contemporary visual and aural aids not mentioned in the Bible but that help to create a worshipful and celebratory atmosphere.

The foregoing examples do not represent any comprehensive survey but they do indicate that, despite widespread acceptance of dancing, opposition to it still rests on the kinds of reasoning and some of the same premises that have been invoked for centuries. Styles in dancing, kinds of dances, particular genres, musical accompaniment, and women's roles have all radically changed since the Reformation. Nonetheless, the continuation of dance opposition over half a millennium suggests that some essential characteristics in dancing and in denominational traditions combined to fuel American antidance attitudes. In two summary chapters I will analyze these critical variables in the context of cultural change.

Notes

1. Clara J. Jones, *Shall We Dance?* intro. N. M. Ylvisaker (Minneapolis: Augsburg Publishing, n.d.), introduction.

2. Sydney E. Ahlstrom, *A Religious History of the American People* (Garden City: Image Books, 1975), vol. 2, 412. Questions of worldly amusements and individual morality inevitably became secondary to survival in times of national crisis. The point had been earlier evidenced by the fact that no known antidance books were published during the Civil War years.

3. Ibid., 415–16.

4. The nine films starring Astaire and Rogers were: *Flying Down to Rio,* 1933; *The Gay Divorcée,* 1934; *Roberta,* 1935; *Top Hat,* 1935; *Follow the Fleet,* 1936; *Swing Time,* 1936; *Shall We Dance,* 1937; *Carefree,* 1938; and *The Story of Vernon and Irene Castle,* 1939. Traditionally, *The Jazz Singer* is counted as the first movie to have sound. It opened 16 October 1927, with Al Jolson in the lead role. See Russel Nye, *The Unembarrassed Muse: The Popular Arts in America* (New York: Dial, 1970), 379.

5. Ralph K. Andrist, ed., *The American Heritage History of the 1920s and 1930s* (New York: American Heritage/Bonanza Books, 1987), 207.

6. Nye, *Unembarrassed Muse,* 384. For comparison with movie attendance, the record for *Oklahoma,* first produced on Broadway in 1943, was a total of 2,248 people. Prior record figures for many musicals of the previous two decades were 500 and 600 people. The advent of "talkies," followed by the Depression, drastically reduced the number of Broadway musicals produced in the early thirties. In effect, Hollywood became the new mecca for dance directors; over half the legitimate theaters on Broadway closed by 1932–33. According to Robert Moulton's analysis of the New York stage musical, eighteen of the twenty-one major tap dance directors in the city between 1925 and 1931, ultimately left for the West Coast. Fifteen of them were gone by 1930. See Robert Darrell Moulton, "Choreography in Musical Comedy and Revue on the New York Stage from 1925 through 1950" (Ph.D. diss., University of Minnesota, 1957), 57, 75.

7. D. Duane Braun, *Toward a Theory of Popular Culture: The Sociology and History of American Music and Dance 1920–1968* (Ann Arbor: Ann Arbor Publishers, 1969), 43.

8. See, for example, Glenn Miller and his band in *Orchestra Wives* (1942), Harry James and his band in *Springtime in the Rockies* (1942), and Benny Goodman and his band in *The Gang's All Here* (1943).

9. Albert J. McCarthy, *Big Band Jazz* (New York: Berkeley Publishing Corporation, 1977), 226–27.

10. James Lincoln Collier, *Benny Goodman and the Swing Era* (New York: Oxford University Press, 1989), 186–87 and 137; idem, *The Making of Jazz* (Boston: Houghton-Mifflin, 1978), 213, 261, 278.

11. Nye, *Unembarrassed Muse,* 337. Nye cites the tally of George T. Simon, a historian of the swing era. Following the height of the big bands, Hollywood made biographical films of Benny Goodman, the Dorsey brothers, and Glenn Miller.

12. Nye, *Unembarrassed Muse,* 329; Murray Schumach, "A Juke Box for Every 500 Persons," *New York Times Magazine,* 14 Apr. 1946, 31. The term "jukebox" reportedly derives from the Reconstruction era "jook"—a place where "lower-class African-Americans drink, dance, eat, and gamble." The jook house was the place that accommodated the emerging dance culture of freed black people. Music was provided by guitars—often called "boxes." However, some old-timers have recalled early electric guitars and coin-operated music boxes being called "juice boxes" because they were plugged into electricity. See an extended discussion of jook houses, including pictures and an African etymology of the word, in Katrina Hazzard-Gordon, *Jookin'* (Philadelphia: Temple University Press, 1990), 76–119.

13. Nye, *Unembarrassed Muse,* 329, 336.

14. "Bull Market in Ballroom Stepping," *Literary Digest* 123 (2 Jan. 1937): 21–22.

15. Marshall and Jean Stearns, *Jazz Dance: The Story of American Vernacular Dance* (New York: Macmillan, 1968), 328. Prior to writing his "Swing Story" for the *Atlantic Monthly* of February 1986, Robert P. Crease interviewed Albert Minns, then a sixty-four-year-old veteran swing dancer from Harlem. Crease reports that the Lindy-hop, which in its basic pattern extended for eight counts, came out of Harlem's ballrooms in the twenties, when men would swing their partners into breakaway positions and go into solo improvisations. The "solo hops" and the Lindbergh solo flight to Paris gave the new dance its name. The label "swing" appeared with the new sound of the thirties. According to Crease, dance studios today use the terms "swing," "Lindy," and "jitterbug" interchangeably. Dance sophisticates will generally consider swing to be the genre and jitterbug to be a variant of the Lindy, requiring only six counts for a basic pattern (Crease, "Swing Story," 77). Margaret Batiuchok calls "swing" and "jitterbug" generic terms but "Lindy" a specific dance. See Batiuchok, "The Lindy" (Master's thesis, New York University, 1988), 22–38.

16. John Martin, "From Minuet to Jitterbug," *New York Times Magazine,* 7 Nov. 1943, 16.

17. Lynne Fauley Emery, *Black Dance from 1619 to Today,* 2d rev. ed. (Princeton: Dance Horizons, 1988), 222; "Life Goes to a Party," *Life,* 14 Dec. 193?, 64; John Martin, "The Dance: Social Style—Looking at the Ballroom in Some of Its Aspects—Events of the Week," *New York Times,* 10 Jan. 1943.

18. Braun, *Toward a Theory of Popular Culture,* 59; "New Dance," *Time,* 9 Mar. 1942, 46.

19. John Greene Youmans, "A History of Recreational Social Dance in the United States" (Ph.D. diss., University of Southern California, 1966), 116–27.

20. Frederick Lewis Allen, *Since Yesterday: The Nineteen-Thirties in America* (New York: Harper, 1940), 135–39.

21. Robert Campbell, *Modern Evils* (New York: Fleming H. Revell, 1933), 91.

22. John R. Rice, *What's Wrong with the Dance?* (Grand Rapids, Mich.: Zondervan, 1935), 8; A. G. Hobbs Jr., *Is It Wrong to Dance?* (N.p., n.d. [after 1937]), 9–10.

23. John Carrara, *Enemies of Youth,* 2d ed. (Grand Rapids, Mich.: Zondervan, 1942), 69; J[udson] E. Conant, *Is the Devil in Modern Amusements?* (Chicago: Moody Press, 1936), 15–16.

24. The works of T. A. Faulkner remained enormously popular even though his 1922 publication consisted of reprints of his 1892 and 1916 books. See chapter 8 for discussion of his writings. Other nineteenth-century authorities cited include: Hiram Haydn (1880); James Brand (1892); James H. Brookes (1870 and 1898); Perry W. Sinks (1896); and William Cleaver Wilkinson (1869). The most recently published twentieth-century dance opponents cited were John Roach Straton and Harry Vom Bruch.

25. John H. C. Fritz, *Pastoral Theology,* 2d rev. ed. (St. Louis: Concordia Publishing House, 1945), 196–97.

26. P[aul] E[dward] Kretzmann, *That Vexing Question of Dancing and Related Subjects: A Symposium of Short Articles and Discussions* (St. Louis: N.p., [1942?]), 7.

27. Theodore Graebner, *The Borderland of Right and Wrong,* 3d ed. (St. Louis: Concordia Publishing House, 1935), 39, 43–45.

28. M[armaduke] N[athanial] Carter, *Lutheran Customs: A Popular Presentation of Some Practices of the Lutheran Church* (Chicago: N.p., n.d.), 47. According to the title page, Carter served at St. Philip's Lutheran Church in Chicago between 1928 and 1957. He died in 1961.

29. Ibid., 47. Carter's mention of interpretive dancing points up the fact that by the 1930s the term had generally been replaced by the genre title "modern dance," to distinguish that kind of expressive dance found in schools and colleges from the traditional, classical ballet.

30. J[esse] M[arvin] Gaskin, *The Modern Dance on Trial* (Shawnee, Okla.: Oklahoma Baptist University, 1945), 17–18.

31. Otis Gatewood, *Why It Is Wrong for Christians to Dance* (Nashville: World Vision Publishing Company, [c. 1942–45), 5, 10; Peter Person, *The Sunday School Teacher and Modern Amusements* (Minneapolis: Northwestern Sunday School Conference, n.d.), 6. Person's book was probably written about 1930.

32. Oscar C. Hanson, *Don't Play with Fire!* (Minneapolis: Augsburg, n.d.), 1–2. Hanson's booklet probably appeared between 1941 and 1948, when he served as executive secretary of the Young Peoples' Luther League. He joined others before him in quoting Faulkner and in citing the unnamed New York City police chief who declared that three-fourths of the abandoned girls in the city came to their ruin because of experiences in dancing. Hanson fails to mention when the statistics were gathered; the figures were first cited in the antidance literature by Hiram Haydn in 1880.

33. Ibid., 5.

34. Ibid., 12. On the same grounds of progressive temptation, Judson E. Conant (1867–1955), a Baptist minister, declared in 1936, during the height of the swing era: "The folk dances in our schools, under the camouflage of 'calisthenics,' are nothing but the appetizers for waltz and Tango. High school dances may easily be the road to moral ruin and hell, for they open the door to dancing schools and ballrooms." See Conant, *Is the Devil in Modern Amusements?* 15–16. Professor Peter Person (1889–19?), a faculty member of North Park College in Chicago, objected to high school dances apparently on the grounds that they were not well chaperoned. See Person, *Sunday School Teacher,* 6.

35. A few figures can convey an impression of the pervasiveness of dancing in the schools. By 1930 a total of 36 states had laws requiring physical education in their schools' curricula; dancing would have been a part of those programs under the widely touted "new" physical education urged by Thomas D. Wood and others. During the forties, dance in the public schools emphasized square dancing, folk dancing, and social dancing. A 1947 survey of American colleges, excluding teacher-training institutions, indicated that 42 percent of 526 colleges taught at least one course in the genre known as "modern dance," in addition to classes in folk, social, tap, and square dancing. See C. W. Hackensmith, *History of Physical Education* (New York: Harper and Row, 1966), 449, 477; Deobold B. Van Dalen and Bruce L. Bennett, *A World History of Physical Education,* 2d ed. (Englewood Cliffs, N.J.: Prentice-Hall, 1971), 504–5. The opposite point of view to that expressed by Conant and Person appeared in the March 1941 issue of *Recreation.* George Fairhead, superintendent of recreation in Danville, Illinois, wrote about the positive social control over young people that a well-run and well-chaperoned dance club could bring. His position represents a continuation of that idea established by urban reformers in the first two decades of this century. See chapter 9, above, for discussion of the benefits of supervised recreational dances in schools. See also George A. Fairhead, "A Social Dance Club," *Recreation* 34 (Mar. 1941): 721, 754.

36. Campbell, *Modern Evils,* 22–23, 27.

37. Gaskin, *Modern Dance on Trial,* 12–13. Authorities are Dr. L. T. Wallace, a professor of ethics at Ouachita College in Arkadelphia, Arkansas, and a W. A. Hudson, otherwise unidentified by Gaskin.

38. Dominic J. Capeci Jr., "Walter F. White and the Savoy Ballroom Controversy of 1943," *Afro-Americans in New York Life and History* (July 1981): 13–32. The initial complaint against the Savoy came from army, navy, and city health officials who alleged that 164 servicemen had contracted venereal disease from women they met at the ballroom. Such complaints had served to give ballrooms a bad reputation for decades. Walter White, executive director of the National Association for the Advancement of Colored People, also reasoned that a charge that "venereal women" were infecting servicemen could be levied against many public places. Capeci points out, "Isolating the Savoy smacked of racial discrimination, as did police concern over interracial dancing" (17). He cites one source that put the white clientele at 40 percent on some occasions, though when such a high percentage of integration occurred is not mentioned.

39. Kretzmann, *That Vexing Question,* 11–12.

40. Carrara, *Enemies of Youth,* 24 and Campbell, *Modern Evils,* 23–24.

41. Campbell, *Modern Evils,* 92.

42. Gerhard Mahler, *To Dance or Not to Dance* (St. Louis: Concordia Publishing House, n.d.), 16–17. Mahler's book probably was written between 1940 and 1946.

43. William Bell Riley, *Sermon Texts,* Box Sh–Z, "The Ways of Women in Unsexing Themselves," 23 Sept. 1934 and Box H–N "Lot's Wife-Sodom's Society Matron," 23 Sept. 1937, 12. Riley's papers are held in the Northwestern College Archives, Minneapolis, Minn.

44. Riley, "The Ways of Women," 18.

45. Clara J. Jones, "The Preventive Program in North Dakota," *Lutheran Herald* 9 (2 July 1935): 639.

46. Kretzmann proved an exception with his reasoning of the argument that *any* tempting physical contact between unmarried men and women was a sin against the Sixth Commandment: "Any physical contact, in fact, any form of communication by word, or glance, or picture, or gesture, or posture, which is apt to arouse or to strengthen carnal desires, whether that be in the home, in an auto, in a boat, on the dance-floor, or anywhere else, is sinful" (Kretzmann, *That Vexing Question,* 12).

47. Rice, *What's Wrong with the Dance?* 26, 31–37; Carrara, *Enemies of Youth,* 25; William Masselink, *I and the Children Thou Hast Given Me: A Treatise on Our Covenant Youth and Worldly Amusements* (Grand Rapids, Mich.: Eerdmans, 1931), 222.

48. Allen, *Since Yesterday,* 134, 132.

49. Mary P. Ryan reports that women workers, recruited from the ranks of housewives, totaled "no less than 75 percent of the new workers in the early 1940s."

In different figures, 8,000,000 women "entered the work force during World War II." See Mary P. Ryan, *Womanhood in America: From Colonial Times to the Present* (New York: Franklin Watts, 1983), 254, 256. By the wartime peak in July 1944, 19,000,000 women were employed, a 47 percent increase from March 1940. See Karen Anderson, *Wartime Women: Sex Roles, Family Relations and the Status of Women during World War II* (Westport, Conn.: Greenwood, 1981), 4.

50. John Martin, "The GI 'Makes with the Hot Foot,'" *New York Times Magazine,* 9 Jan. 1944, 14; Lucy Greenbaum, "Fighters with a Boogie Beat," *New York Times Magazine,* 27 Dec. 1942, 10–11.

51. Meyer Berger, "'Reck' Halls—and They're Filled," *New York Times Magazine,* 29 Mar. 1942, 14.

52. Jim Marshall, "Dates for Defense," *Colliers,* 8 Nov. 1941, 66.

53. "For Their Off-Duty Hours," *Recreation* 35 (Sept. 1941): 390–91; Greenbaum, "Fighters with a Boogie Beat," 10–11.

54. Martin, "GI 'Makes with the Hot Foot,'" 14.

55. Meyer Berger, "Jive Bombers Jamboree," *Colliers,* 5 June 1943, 18–19.

56. G. Everett Arden, *Augustana Heritage: A History of the Augustana Lutheran Church* (Rock Island, Ill.: Augustana Press, 1963), 366.

57. C.A.L. [Carl Axel Lindwall], *The Dance,* No. 3 in Highways and Byways to Destruction (Rock Island, Ill.: Augustana Book Concern, [1910?]), 5. Judy Belan, special collections librarian at Augustana College, dated the publication about 1910. Born in Sweden, Lindwall received degrees from Augustana College and Seminary and was ordained to the ministry in 1902. Among other professional responsibilities, Lindwall served as president of the Swedish Historical Society of America and on the governing board of Augustana College. For the church's mid-century statement on dancing, see "Resolutions: A Statement by the Augustana Lutheran Church on Dancing," Augustana Synod Minutes, 1950, 321–23.

58. Nye, *Unembarrassed Muse,* 337; Crease, "Swing Story," 78.

59. Nye, *Unembarrassed Muse,* 337, 384. According to Nye, the television screen affected not only dancers but moviegoers. Film attendance in 1957 decreased by half from that of 1947.

60. Nancy Banks, "The World's Most Beautiful Ballrooms," *Chicago History* 2, no. 4 (Fall–Winter 1973): 215; John Briggs, "The Savoy Era of Jazz Closes on Auctioneer's Brief Reprise," *New York Times,* 1 Oct. 1958.

61. Though a few bands like Shaw's later reemerged under new leaders, with rights to the music of the original band leaders, that phenomenon tended not to occur until the seventies and eighties.

62. Don McDonagh, *Dance Fever* (New York: Random House, 1979), 83–87.

63. Martin, "Minuet to Jitterbug," 17; Marshall Fishwick, "The Twist: Brave New Whirl," *Saturday Review,* 3 Mar. 1962, 8–10.

64. Wendell Wellman, *What's with Entertainment?* (Kansas City, Mo.: Beacon Hill Press, 1969), 19.

65. Homer Martinez, *The Case on Dancing* (Fort Worth: By the Author, [1962?]), 6.

66. Ibid., 6–7.

67. Porter Marcellus Bailes, *Is the Dance Dangerous?* (Grand Rapids, Mich.: Zondervan, 1946), 13, 16–17.

68. M[arion] E[dgar] Ramay, *What's Wrong with the Social Dance?* (Edmond, Okla.: N.p., [1958?]), 3.

69. Theodore Graebner, *The Borderland of Right and Wrong*, 8th ed. (St. Louis: Concordia Publishing House, 1951), 113–14. For the most part, Graebner's 1951 edition contained very little in the discussion on dancing that was different from that in his 1935 edition.

70. Don Humphrey, *What Makes Dancing Wrong* (Dallas: Christian Publishing Company, 1963), 6–7, 27–28.

71. Charles E. Chumley, *The Christian and the Dance* (Nashville: Charlotte Avenue Church of Christ, n.d.), 1, 3, 5. The book appeared after 1947.

72. William W. Orr, *The Christian and Amusements* (Chicago: Moody Press, 1960), 99, 105–9.

73. John Scott Trent, *Dancing: Right or Wrong* (Nashville: The Sunday School Board of the Southern Baptist Convention, 1958), 4–5; Orr, *The Christian and Amusements,* 101.

74. *Teen Talk about Rock 'n' Roll* (N.p.: Christian Life Commission of the Baptist General Convention of Texas, 1959); *Teen Talk about Dancing* (N.p.: Christian Life Commission of the Baptist General Convention of Texas, 1960), unpaginated pamphlet.

75. Martinez, *The Case on Dancing,* 11; Ramay, *What's Wrong with the Social Dance?* 12. Amazingly, Martinez chose to use a direct quote from Faulkner that displays the language of a by-gone era as well as syntactical problems: "Two-thirds of the girls who are ruined, fall through the influence of the dance." Ramay paraphrased Faulkner on the same theme, but did not quote verbatim.

76. Harley Lane, *Is Dancing Harmful?* (Louisville: Herald Press, n.d.),7, 11.

77. Humphrey, *What Makes Dancing Wrong,* 27.

78. Lane, *Is Dancing Harmful?* 4.

79. Ibid., 12; Ramay, *What's Wrong with the Social Dance?* 10.

80. Ramay, *What's Wrong with the Social Dance?* 10; Orr, *The Christian and Amusements,* 107.

81. See, for example, Ruth St. Denis, "Dance as Spiritual Expression," in *Dance, A Basic Educational Technique,* ed. F. R. Rogers (New York: Macmillan, 1941), 100–110; idem, "What Is the Religious Dance?" *Dance Observer* 17, no. 5 (May 1950): 68–69; idem, "Ruth St. Denis and the Divine Dance," *Dance Magazine* 22, no. 2 (Feb. 1948): 16. Ted Shawn first performed in the Interdenominational Church of San Francisco in 1917. Shortly thereafter he toured some thirty cities with his "Dance Church Service." See Margaret Fisk Taylor, *A Time to Dance* (Austin: The

Sharing Company, 1976), 138–39.

82. Livingston Biddle, "America for the Arts," *Cultural Post* 6, no. 3 (Sept.–Oct. 1980): unpaginated. Figures vary depending upon definition of dance company and source of data. See also Leila Sussmann's "Anatomy of the Dance Company Boom," *Dance Research Journal* 16, no. 2 (Fall 1984): 23–28.

83. Anna Kisselgoff, "Has the Dance Boom Run Its Course?" *New York Times Magazine,* 3 Mar. 1985, 1, 32.

84. "Breaking Out: America Goes Dancing," *Newsweek,* 2 July 1984, 51–52.

85. Alice J. Kelvin, "Cheek to Cheek Is Doubly Chic, the Second Time Around," *Smithsonian* 19, no. 12 (Mar. 1989): 84–96.

86. "Beating the Devil," *Newsweek,* 2 July 1984, 52.

87. "Town's 'No-Dancing' Stand Challenged," *Minneapolis Star and Tribune,* 14 Aug. 1987, 10C.

88. "Teens in Town That Once Banned Dance Kick Up Their Heels at 'Awesome' Event," *Minneapolis Star and Tribune,* 12 Dec. 1988, 3A. Two years earlier the AP had put out a news release stating that, despite a prodance rally, the school board had declined to change its hundred-year-old policy opposing school dances. The town of Purdy is located about forty miles southeast of Joplin and had a population of 930 people in 1986. See "School to Keep Ban on Dancing," *Minneapolis Star and Tribune,* 16 Apr. 1986, 11A. Thus, the struggle among town factions over school dances continued actively in protests and court appeals from, at least, 1986 until the Supreme Court decision in 1990.

89. "Supreme Court Lets Stand a Missouri Town's Ban on School Dances," *New York Times,* 17 Apr. 1990, 22A.

90. *A Guide to Student Life at ORU,* rev. ed., (Tulsa, Okla.: Oral Roberts University, 1986), 23.

91. *The Liberty Way,* handbook of student policies, (Lynchburg, Va.: Liberty University, 1987), 28; personal correspondence to author from Vernon Brewer, Vice-President for Student Affairs, Liberty University, Lynchburg, Va., 28 Apr. 1987.

92. *Community Life at Bethel* (St. Paul, Minn.: Bethel College, n.d.), unpaginated pamphlet; *Life Together: Expectations and Responsibilities for Community Life at Taylor University* (Upland, Ind.: Taylor University, n.d.), unpaginated pamphlet. An additional set of guidelines makes clear, however, that "all choreography must be reviewed and approved by the chief administrative officer in that area and communicated to the Administrative Cabinet" ("Taylor University Campus Programs Policy," unpaginated typescript).

93. Sue Anne Pressley, "Baptist School Goes Footloose, Permits Dancing on Campus," *Saint Paul Pioneer Press,* 20 Apr. 1996; Stacey Singer, "Wheaton Students Keep Dancing Shoes in Closet," *Chicago Tribune,* 26 Apr. 1996.

94. Paul Thigpen, "Praise Him with the Dance," *Charisma and Christian Life* (Mar. 1989): 51; Ansley Orfila, "Dancing in the Church," *The Evangelist* (Oct. 1987): 54.

Part 3

Critical Variables
and Cultural Context

11 The Nature of Dance and the Polemic in Reprise

Debate over movement, manners, and morals has constituted the core of the historical polemic against dance for the past five hundred years. Movement—physical body movement—is the essence of dance. These two elements—the human body and movement—have drawn the brunt of attacks against the essential nature of dancing. But, because dancing and deportment have traditionally been inseparable and because the former has been primarily a heterosexual activity pursued in leisure time, the historical debate has also concentrated on incidental characteristics of dancing relative to manners and morals of participants and viewers. Inevitably, discussions of appropriate or inappropriate behavior drew on assumed or assigned roles of social class and gender for any given decade or century, culture or subculture. At the middle and the end of the nineteenth century and in the twentieth century, issues of race entered the polemic as well. A longitudinal summary of the historical polemic can focus our understanding in two ways. First, arguments pertaining to the essential nature of dance can be clearly delineated from those pertaining to the incidental characteristics. Second, a longitudinal summary will highlight continuities and changes in the arguments, thus helping to clarify reasons why the antidance attitudes persisted for so many centuries.

Arguments against Essential Characteristics

When judgments of good and bad are levied against dancing, performance quality invariably invites evaluation. Early criteria set by ancient dance critics proved simple and straightforward. As Plato noted centuries ago in the *Laws,* "one man moves in an orderly, another in a disorderly manner."[1] Although perceptions of order and disorder can apply to choreographic structure, quality of performance is usually more obvious to the untrained viewing eye than is choreographic structure. Thus, dance adversaries, from writers in the pre-Reformation era to the Puritans in America, cited the disorderly movement of dancers as a strong objection to the art. Attacks evolved from an assumed ideal for the Christian, couched solely in terms of moral and spiritual behavior. Increase Mather reiterated for Bostonians of his day what ministers and theologians had propounded for centuries: "How often does the Scripture commend unto Christians, Gravity and Sobriety, in their behaviour at all times."[2] One could not be both sober and grave while simultaneously moving in disorderly fashion.

In the sixteenth century, as in Plato's day, disorderly dancing was equated with temptation to or actual sexual immorality. The notion derived from centuries-old views about human nature. By the middle of the fourteenth century, Petrarch repeated the belief from antiquity that uncontrolled movements and roving eyes bespoke an inner lack of control. When the idea of order evolved to a reigning concept in the Elizabethan era, the importance of displaying inner as well as outward control became paramount in the ideals conceived to define the gentleman and the Christian. The widely understood rationale undergirding the importance of order prescribed that God ruled over humans, and humans ruled over beasts. Among humans, mind or reason was to govern the passions. Disorderly dancing demonstrated the absence of reason, hence, rule by passion. When mind no longer governed passions and behavior, humans descended to the level of brute beasts. Not surprisingly, therefore, Reformed churchmen like John Calvin and Lambert Daneau charged that dancers resembled apes, goats, and monkeys. Other writers decried the fact that dancers looked "franticke" or mad. Dance critics from the time of Petrarch through Increase Mather's day, and then again at the turn of the twentieth century, also invoked Cicero's famous dictum that no man danced unless he was either drunk or mad. To Petrarch, disordered dancing looked totally absurd without the covering power or meaning that musical accompaniment supplied. Even more serious, opponents exhorted Christians to avoid the rioting and reveling, including dancing, that characterized the pagans. To Increase Mather, the Pauline condemnation of such orgies in Romans 13:13 served as an express biblical prohibition of "mixt" and disorderly dancing.

The gender-specific language of courtesy writers and early dance opponents should not be misconstrued by the modern reader. Prescriptions for the gentleman's behavior were precisely that; courtesy treatises reveal little instruction for the lady. The few details one does find clearly indicate that the ideal in dancing, manners, and morals was to follow the rule of order and reason. Among writings of dance opponents, the guide to be followed by both genders was the ideal for the Christian, repeated by Mather as sobriety and gravity. Women were cited for disorderly dancing more frequently than were men, according to council sanctions by the Medieval church and objections to dancing voiced by individual opponents. Nonetheless, dance detractors do not claim that women were more subject to rule by passion, hence disorder.

The charges against dance performance on the basis of its involving disorderly motion can be traced through the American writing of Increase Mather. Such claims are not explicitly made in subsequent American anti-dance treatises, with the single exception of *Balls and Dancing Parties from the French of Abbé Hulot.* When it was published by a Boston press in 1857, it carried a passage recalling accusations by Petrarch, Cicero, Calvin, and Daneau:

> What, in fact, can be more laughable than to see dancers advance, fall back, bend the body, jerk it up again, and whirl around like birds struck on the head? If music had not lent the charm of its harmony to cover the folly and absurdity of dancing with an appearance of sense and propriety, and if people could only see the movements of dancers performed in silence, they could not help exclaiming with the greatest Roman orator, Cicero, that, *He who dances must be drunk or mad.*[3]

The writing of the French canon Hulot falls within the stream of arguments coming from European authors and cannot have been intended to apply to American dancing, though those who republished the book in this country must have thought the arguments applied. In point of fact, the American book is from the fourth Paris edition of 1842.

It seems reasonable to conclude that the European arguments against dancing as disorderly movement were aimed at folk or country dancing rather than at courtly dancing or dancing by the upper classes. Given the instructions from dance manuals as well as the prescriptions for polite behavior and Christian morals from the courtesy literature, it seems unlikely that the prescribed courtly dancing would have been construed as movement resembling the antics of mad folk or animals. Moreover, Mather and most earlier opponents probably did not observe dancing in courtly or upper-class society. They may have written purely from hearsay rather than from first-hand observation. However, viewers' perceptions of order and disorder can vary. Listeners' perceptions of hearsay accounts can also vary. Ultimately, the accuracy of these early allegations regarding the disordered movement of dance remain beyond verification.

After Mather's writings, the argument against disorderly dancing disappears until the 1850s. Although the reprint of Abbé Hulot's book recalled sixteenth-century characterizations, the charges of a Methodist bishop indicate that perceptions of disordered movement became mixed with anti-intellectual and racist attitudes. In 1851, Bishop Moses Henkle told southern Methodists that the "unintellectual" character of dancing made it peculiarly disposed to the taste and morality of barbarous people. He asserted that blacks danced better than whites and concluded that dancing remained an "animal affair." Baptist Marion Palmer Hunt, preaching to Kentucky parishioners in 1897, denigrated dancing for Christians on the grounds that even "untutored savages, the illiterate negroes and the patients in our lunatic asylums" proved to be among the best dancers.[4] In the ensuing decades, as the music and dance of blacks diffused throughout white America and, still later, when rock 'n' roll became popular, the scattered references to dancing as pagan savagery that represented a return to primitive life clearly bespeak a racist and Euro-American chauvinistic view. In effect, the moving of hips and pelvis, shimmying and shaking, to jazz rhythms and syncopated sounds appeared quite disorderly.

The notion of dancing as disordered and immoral also relates to the fact that adversaries universally adhered to a Platonic and Cartesian hierarchical mind-body dualism. They were fortified by Pauline polarities of flesh and spirit as evil and good, transient and eternal. The fact that dancing is of the flesh, that is, corporeal movement, led opponents to imply or to openly declare that dancing was merely physical. By the early nineteenth century, attacks against dancing explicitly asserted that it had a trivial nature because it was only a mechanical art. As proof, critics referred to the conversation and atmosphere at balls and dancing schools as nonedifying. The mind was not elevated; nor were spiritual matters discussed. By the middle decades of that century, arguments alleged that dancing produced a mental vacancy; it contributed nothing to the higher pleasures of life. Dancing was not only irrational but undignified; first-hand observation proved that people of refinement and culture never danced. Opponents agreed that a cultured mind was more highly valued than nimble feet.

By the century's end, some critics reiterated the animal theme that had been loudly proclaimed in the sixteenth century and then stated briefly in the mid-nineteenth century by Mrs. Garnett. Her charges did not emphasize disorderly motion but rather spoke to the anti-intellectual character of dancing. She declared that monkeys and dogs could dance; therefore dancing was merely a physical activity. The popularity of such allegations carried into the twentieth century. The concurrent spread of dancing into public schools via the curricula as well as extracurricular activities added to the anti-intellectual attacks. Early twentieth-century opponents declared that good dancers never made good scholars. They did not make the argument gender specific.

The other charge pertaining to the human body and to performance quality seems to have applied more to women than to men. Both English and French seventeenth-century writers decried the artificial posture and carriage learned at dancing schools. They based their condemnation on Isaiah 3:16, which denigrates the ancient Israelite women for proud and vain walking. In Mather's words: "they did walk with stretched-out necks, and with wanton eyes, wailing and mincing as they go, and making a tinkling with their feet." But Mather did not inveigh against women. He was angry at the dance master who opened a school in Boston, and he borrowed the biblical passage as an argument from earlier opponents' attacks. His wrath did not fall on women in particular. After Mather, the only other opponent to allege the wickedness of such artificial posture was the Reverend John Phillips of Charleston in the late eighteenth century. He asserted that dance lessons contributed to "vain and idle amusements." The charge applied more to the waste of time involved in dancing than to a specific indictment of a particular gender.

The single antidance argument that was derived from dance structure also constituted a staple in the American arsenal of ammunition against dancing. The closed dance position, which was introduced with the waltz, provoked the wrath of clergy and evangelists from the 1840s to the 1960s, despite the fact that other dances became far more popular than the waltz in the present century. To adversaries, the closed dance position represented an embrace, the dances nothing more than hugging set to music. The proximity of male and female bodies fueled fears of immoral conduct to follow. Even when the Lindy and jitterbug became popular, with their open or breakaway positions, adversaries inveighed against the "modern dance" on the grounds that it permitted liberties with a lady that were nowhere else tolerated in decent society. Because of the closed dance position, many clergy and evangelists considered the "round dances" to be evil in themselves, or in their essence. However, the majority of critics concentrated their attacks primarily on the changing or incidental characteristics of dancing.

Arguments against Incidental Characteristics

In every century of opposition, adversaries have asserted that dancing is evil because of its fruits, effects, tendencies, adjuncts, and/or abuses. To make such claims, opponents first had to answer a basic question. In the language of sixteenth-century theologians, Is dancing evil in itself or a matter of "adiaphora"? That is, can dancing be considered morally neutral, something neither good nor bad in its essence? Most allowed that dancing, in essence, was legitimate; in a sense they had to. The Bible mentions dancing in a positive light on numerous occasions in the Old Testament. However, dance opponents circumvented this fact by universally distinguishing the dancing of biblical times from that practiced in the society of their day. They declared that biblical examples did not involve men and women moving together. By contrast, the "dance of modern society," with its face-to-face embrace, was essentially wicked and unfit for Christians. For those who aimed their attacks at the abuses or associations of dancing, the heaviest barrage of charges pertained to a fear of immoral conduct between male and female.

Fears of Sexual Immorality

Overwhelmingly, from the pre-Reformation era to the twentieth century, the primary fear that emerged concerning dancing was that it would lead to a breach of the commandment forbidding adultery. Sixteenth- and seventeenth-century clerics and theologians, especially those who wrote cases of conscience, argued that the commandment forbade all occasions for temptation to adultery, as well as the specific act itself. On those grounds, they argued, the Bible prohibited dancing as a heterosexual activity. During the Renaissance and Reformation, dance opponents regularly declared that temptation to lust entered particularly through the eyes, but the touching and musical accompaniment in dancing also provoked temptations. Regardless of which sense's stimuli evoked the most tempting carnal desires, opponents feared the end results. The next intense barrage of allegations pertaining to sexual immorality appeared about 1840 and continued for more than a century. Although scattered references to the immorality of dancing can be found in earlier American antidance publications, allegations poured forth as the waltz gained widespread popularity. Such charges coincided with the relegation of women to the realms of "piety, purity, domesticity and submission."[5] Later nineteenth- and early twentieth-century writers became as graphic as the sixteenth-century opponents had been, declaring that dancing fed brothels and led to prostitution, "social disease," divorce, murder, and insanity. For some, dancing proved as addictive as alcohol and other drugs. The popularity of dancing, combined with the pervasive belief that men could not control their passions, resulted in adversaries' assertions that hundreds of thousands of women succumbed to male seducers in the ballroom or dance hall, thereby becoming "fallen women," "soiled doves," and victims of "white slavers."

Dance opponents universally employed a twofold model of women. On the one hand, females were innocent and hapless victims of male passion gone out of control. On the other hand, they were evil seductresses, daughters of Eve. For centuries, females were understood to be agents of the devil. In the seventeenth century, William Prynne cited the Medieval sects known as the Waldenses and Albigenses, who declared that women were the devil's powerful agents. The example quoted most frequently came from the New Testament, the passage in which Salome danced so seductively that Herod agreed to grant her most fervent wish.[6] For centuries, the incident seemed proof positive to dance adversaries that the evils surrounding dancing and women were insidious. Despite the age-old models of Eve and Salome, however, American opponents did not revive the European theme of woman as temptress until the middle decades of the nineteenth century. Then allegations continued that women dressed and adorned themselves to seduce men. Although most females allegedly employed the arena of the ballroom for this purpose, William Meade, an Episcopalian bishop in Virginia, declared in the mid-nineteenth century that women danced on stage only "half-dressed." William Dallman, a Missouri Lutheran pastor, echoed the theme at the end of the century. The Methodist cleric Jonathan Crane asserted—in terms that were graphic for the 1840s—that dancing was simply an activity of prostitutes.

The issue of immoral women, as popularized between approximately 1840 and 1940, derived authority from the nineteenth-century practice of attributing superior moral qualities to American women. When women became relegated to hearth and home, men handed them the responsibility for maintaining moral virtue and practicing religious piety. Conventional wisdom held that if women fulfilled these roles, then youth would develop good character; homes would remain strong; and both town and country would stand as a Christian bastion. Given this context, the new "round dances" of the 1840s, with their close embrace, introduced a threat, not only to individual women, but to family, city, and nation. Not surprisingly, therefore, conservative evangelical and fundamentalist adversaries continued to proclaim the virtues of Victorian Christian morality, particularly sexual abstinence outside of marriage, well into the twentieth century. As more women appeared to digress from the nineteenth-century model, leaders such as Billy Sunday and William Bell Riley preached loudly, throughout the teens and into the thirties, against the "modern" girl and "society women." Their protestations arose along with increasing options for females to have the same basic opportunities as males, with whom they began to share the right to education, careers outside the home, economic independence, political power, and the freedom afforded by less restrictive clothing. Better health care, including more reliable contraceptives, increased the freedom of the twentieth-century woman and lessened the control over her by men.

Women dissatisfied with their traditional roles, and seeking to escape from male domination, threatened to break up home and family, but defiant children could do the same thing. These charges came up sporadically throughout the centuries. Sixteenth- and seventeenth-century opponents declared that the popularity of dancing tempted youth to defy parents. Early nineteenth-century evangelicals also charged that dancing enticed youth to defy parental authority and to become dissatisfied with home as a source of recreational satisfaction. As the popularity of dancing spread to the public schools in the twentieth century, scattered references—some appearing as late as 1960—claimed that the activity undermined parental control. Allegations were bolstered by the Fourth Commandment, which requires children to honor their parents. The issue was also related to anxieties about the morals and authority of dance teachers.

Allegations about the immorality of dancing schools and, by implication, dance masters, had appeared first in the early sixteenth-century writings of Juan Luis Vives. Charges continued during that century and in the seventeenth century in England, when French dancing masters in particular were little esteemed among the English. Increase Mather's famous "Arrow" was clearly aimed at a fleeing teacher, Francis Stepney. According to Mather, when the dance master proved wicked, the dancing, by association, became lascivious. A century later, the Reverend John Phillips of Charleston targeted dance masters in that city. After a hiatus of a few decades, accusations against dance masters returned with new intensity in the mid-nineteenth century, when the "round dances" became widely popular. Conventional wisdom held that the new dances came directly from Paris, and so French dance teachers again came in for their share of invective. Allegations from the era also recalled earlier claims that such men were not merely undesirable but ill-born, ill-bred, and irreligious. As a group, they constituted a class of vagrants. Opponents in later decades termed them "morally bankrupt." Not surprisingly, by the 1930s, such charges disappeared from the literature. By then, public schools were including dance instruction in their physical education programs and dancing had been widely popular in the country for at least two decades. Moreover, commercial, instructional enterprises like the Arthur Murray chain of studios proved highly successful by the later thirties.

For as long as adversaries had argued against dance teachers, they had also objected to the immoral environments in which dancing occurred. Critics regularly counted undesirable people as among the evils associated with dancing, although the kinds of people so labeled varied with the times. The issue first appeared in the pre-Reformation era. When court dancing proved popular in the fifteenth century, Aeneas Sylvius, later Pope Pius II, warned readers that the courts proved little more than dens of iniquity. Some sixteenth-century writers concurred. Idleness, avarice, and temptation to lust were thought to flourish there. In Puritan New England, early laws forbade dancing in taverns and with Indians on the grounds of maintaining civil order and preventing contact with "heathens." The issue of unsavory environments and evil companions surfaced again in full force by 1840 when allegations appeared that public dances involved contact with idle libertines, epicures, rogues, and dissipated, intemperate men. Early charges seemed to pertain primarily to males as undesirable companions. By 1890 and in the decades following, accusations implied that dance halls allowed prostitutes as well as pimps on the premises. Writers in the teens and twenties talked about "white slavers" recruiting their women in the dance halls. In particular, the "closed" or taxi-dance hall drew the wrath of opponents because of the way in which they victimized the hired female dancers. After 1930 the critical language moderated to references to a "mixed clientele."

In addition to the varied company found at public dances, environmental issues were a concern of twentieth-century urban reformers, clergy, and evangelists. Public outcry against dance halls was loudest between 1908 and 1940 when opponents targeted a host of health and sanitation deficiencies. Facilities and safety features taken for granted today—separate toilets for the sexes, drinking fountains, fire escapes, adequate lighting and ventilation—were eventually required once a comprehensive system of licensing was put in place. Public outcry in popular periodicals began to subside by the late 1930s, indicating that city, county, and/or state regulations had been passed and ultimately had worked for the common welfare.

Liquor was another evil linked with public dance halls, but the connection of drinking with dancing long preceded the twentieth century. Renaissance writers commonly associated dancing with feasting and drinking. Nineteenth-century opponents had inveighed against wine and strong drink consumed at dancing parties. Victorian etiquette manuals prescribed champagne for the requisite midnight supper at elegant balls. Typically, nineteenth-century antidance arguments implied that men drank too much; but protests about early dance halls included charges that men also persuaded or forced young girls to drink to excess. The licensing of sales of alcoholic beverages eventually was instituted in the twentieth century for the common good.

The alleged evils of the environment surrounding dance pertained to music as well. Like the association of drinking with dancing, the allegation that dance music was immoral had a long history. In the sixteenth century, dance opponents asserted that some rhythms served to make the mind effeminate. They also declared that some songs had "wanton ditties." In America, such charges were virtually absent from the literature until the early twentieth century. With the exception of the treatise by the Reverend Oliver Hart, a Charleston Baptist active in the late eighteenth century, concern about dance music did not emerge until the advent of jazz. In the early twentieth century, both hot jazz and slow, sensual jazz provoked outcry. Though opponents merely asserted the evil influence of dance music, with no further explanation, their anxiety undoubtedly evolved from a Victorian Christian moral code, with its traditional gender-role assumptions, as well as from traditional Euro-American opinions about the kind of music that was proper for dancing.

Two additional charges pertain to morality but are unrelated to the preceding configuration of objections. In the fourteenth century, Petrarch declared that dancing served to effeminate the mind. In the late sixteenth century, John Rainolds repeated the allegation in a lengthy diatribe against stage dancing and theater. Seeing boys or men on stage in women's clothing particularly outraged dance detractors. Explicit charges of effeminacy did not carry over to the American antidance treatises examined for this analysis. However, the notion may have been implied in some eighteenth-century criticism of the "fine" gentleman, the man who demonstrated brilliant manners and facade but little substance and moral integrity.

The more comprehensive and continuous accusation pertaining to morality derived from the belief that the origin and historical associations of dancing served to make the activity objectionable. As far back as the thirteenth century, the Waldenses had declared that the devil served as the beginning, middle, and end of dancing. Reformation-era opponents attributed this idea to the early church fathers. Increase Mather reiterated the belief that the devil had invented dancing and that heathens had subsequently patronized it. The idea lost currency, however, after appearing in some of the late eighteenth-century American antidance books. The theme of historical association reappeared with the advent of the "round dances" in the middle of the nineteenth century. Critics of that era proclaimed that dancing had begun among heathens and barbarians and had come to America via Parisian brothels. In the view of American evangelicals, any practice from France proved morally objectionable. The argument appears to have been less popular during the post–Civil War decades, but it achieved new status in the early twentieth century, when the tango, turkey trot, and other new dances were variously reported to have been borrowed from Paris, San Francisco's Barbary Coast, or New York City's slums. The force of the argument held that any activity with so wicked a background could not possibly be safe for decent Christians. Those who used the issue to attack dancing did not consider that an activity might be reformed despite its allegedly unsavory history.

Assumptions about women proved central to all of the objections based on moral grounds, either explicitly or implicitly. Because the historical polemic came largely from male clergy and evangelists, gender issues also arise when the moral dimension inevitably mixes with assumptions about stewardship and spiritual life. Fundamentally, the elements of money, time, and health became the critical points of focus.

Stewardship of Money

Questions about the use of money were general and to be inferred from European dance opponents' writings. In the ideal for the Christian propounded by Reformed churchmen, worship and work clearly held preeminence over play and pastimes such as dancing. Money could be used to help the poor instead of promoting personal pleasure or buying costly array. This notion carried through Mather's day in Boston and was revived during the Great Awakening in this country. Accordingly, George Whitefield rejoiced at the fruits of his Charleston sermons: "A vast alteration is discernible in ladies' dresses; and some, while I have been speaking, have been so convinced of the sin of wearing jewels, that, I have seen them with blushes, put their hands to their ears, and cover them up with their fans."[7] Although Whitefield rejoiced no less at the conversion of many "moral, good sort of men," most antidance criticism of Christian character and the related issue of financial stewardship seemed to point more to women.

Dance opponents first talk specifically about the correct use of money in the late eighteenth century when dance masters flourished in the larger cities, and a leisure class enjoyed dancing, music, and theater during their work-free time.[8] Almost forty years after Whitefield gave thanks that the Charleston ladies had put away their jewels, Oliver Hart admonished the city's Baptists about the same issue. His observations led him to declare that the money spent on ball gowns, lessons in dancing schools, and the like could be put to better use in relieving the sufferings of the poor and orphans. Forty years later, Jacob Ide in West Medway, Massachusetts, told his parishioners that the cost of a single ball could defray the expense of a common district school for a whole a month.

The argument about stewardship of money continued through the first decade of the twentieth century. Critics invariably pointed to the cost of women's dresses and jewels, as well as to the expense of hosting a ball with its requisite sumptuous repast, servants, orchestra, decorations, and the like; admonishments followed that such expenditures of money should be used instead to help the less fortunate in society. Moreover, if women stopped spending such excessive sums of money on appearance, they would be less subject to the worldly temptations of "fashion," vanity, covetousness, competition, jealousy, and the like. When women competed with each other for the admiration of men and to acquire future husbands for their daughters, concern for self replaced concern for God. The professed Christian then became indistinguishable from the "worldling."

Stewardship of Time

The squandering of time as well as money distinguished the person of the world from the true Christian. When worship and work were valued, it became questionable to spend time in an activity that produced no necessary goods or services. Courtesy writers and later etiquette authorities argued that dancing carried social and aesthetic significance, that the skills and carriage learned along with good dancing proved necessary to an attractive appearance and to successful performance in polite society. But opponents attributed no such ennobling purpose to dancing. Poise and grace, they argued, could be learned from good Christian mothers rather than dissolute dance masters. The moral hazards that accompanied dancing parties and lessons rendered them no fit recreation or healthful exercise for sober and grave Christians. As a merely physical art with no redeeming social, aesthetic, or health benefits, dancing thus was deemed an idle pastime. Sixteenth-century critics proved especially strong in their denunciations. Their ethic held that "Idleness" became the "mother and nurse" of all vice; an "unhonest pastime" like dancing provided the context for innumerable associated evils to flourish. Several opponents over the centuries reminded readers that all Christians must account for their use of time—their deeds and their talk—at the Last Judgment. Dancing, the ballroom and the dance master made a sad preparation for entering eternity. The argument about wasting time proved to be a staple among dance opponents well into the twentieth century.

In certain strife-filled periods, some critics placed the issue of time in a slightly different context. Sixteenth-century English clerics and divinity students declared that the times were too serious to be filled with idle pursuits. Considering the tensions and wars between Catholics and Protestants, the era demanded praying and mourning instead of playing and dancing. Similarly, John Cotton and Increase Mather told seventeenth-century New Englanders that, with the judgments of God abroad in the country and the church in such "Distress," it was no time to dance. Undergirding these exhortations to prayer and gravity lay the fundamental belief that the Christian must redeem time, that the whole of earthly life ought to be spent in preparation for eternal life. Activities like dancing turned the mind from God to self and from the eternal to the earthly.

Stewardship of Health

The maintenance of health could be supported biblically, according to dance opponents, but not all pastimes proved to be healthy or re-creative. Activities that harmed the body, wasted time, or appeared to be disorderly and immoral carried no health benefit. The issue remained current throughout the centuries. Sixteenth-century dance critics proved to be especially vocal antagonists, basing their remarks on their observations of contemporary behavior. They charged that dancers lost sleep, suffered indigestion and pain, and incurred broken legs. Moreover, those who became exhausted lay in bed for one or two whole days thereafter. To staunch Calvinists like Christopher Fetherston, such episodes proved dancing to be no fit exercise for health or recreation. In 1798, John Phillips in Charleston produced probably the most exaggerated allegation when he declared that some women suffered abortions because of dancing. Subsequent nineteenth-century arguments seemed to pertain more to the fact that women of the middle and upper classes simply did not possess good health in general, nor did social convention, medical doctors, and fashion permit them to take regular and vigorous physical exercise. Encased in tight corsets, yards of fabric, hoops, and bustles, the average middle or upper class woman found herself relegated to her house unless she took an occasional walk or carriage ride. When she went to a ball dressed in a low-cut gown and thin outer cloak, danced for hours in poorly ventilated rooms, ate a late-night supper, and then went home amid the "night damps and inclement air," she probably did contract colds, if not consumption, as dance critics alleged.

By the turn of the century, some enterprising person reportedly calculated the number of miles that an active dancer covered in one night. Opponents variously asserted in subsequent books that the average participant traveled anywhere from ten to nineteen miles during an evening of dancing. None of the writers reminded the reader that dancers rested between rounds of dancing, thereby minimizing danger to an underconditioned cardiovascular system. Rather, they implied that when "your daughter" covered such a distance in one evening, while lightly clothed and in the arms of a strange man, the activity must indeed be dangerous. The practice of using a statistic to unite both health and moral arguments continued late into the second half of the twentieth century. However, after 1930 most dance detractors used the more sensible argument that dancing proved unhealthful because it occurred in smoke-filled rooms and occasioned the loss of sleep.

Patriotism

Unlike the arguments based on health issues, criticism of dancing on patriotic grounds cropped up only occasionally. Nineteenth-century claims that dancing proved neither rational nor useful simply represented the aims of American school curricula from the beginning. Intellectual and vocational training guided subject matter development. By the teens of this century, extreme arguments brought patriotism into the polemic. The Christian evangelist Harry Benton charged that the inclusion of dancing in the public schools amounted to nothing less than taxation without representation, hence, dancing was un-American.

Benton's accusation recalls scattered earlier arguments based on the issue of American patriotism. Reflecting contemporary concern for the development of an American republic with its own identity, a citizen of Philadelphia wrote in the 1820s that dancing was not a good activity for the new nation since it came from European courts and was practiced by the aristocracy. The self-styled "Representative of Thousands" remains the only writer to use this argument throughout the history of American opposition to dancing. Variations on the antirepublican theme, which appeared in late nineteenth- and early twentieth-century antidance books, bespeak social class hostility. Writers of the era argued against dancing on the grounds that it fostered a "social caste system" and the development of "smart sets" and "cliques." Without further elaboration, the reader is left with the impression that an activity that favored only the few over the many was ipso facto un-American.

Other attacks were aimed at theater dancing, which could also be construed as un-American. Jeremiah Jeter, a Baptist clergyman, recalled to Virginians of the 1830s that the Continental Congress had passed a resolution against theatrical entertainments during the Revolutionary War. Such an enactment proved that the theater fostered traits that did not strengthen the new Republic. The same charges also recall the eighteenth-century laws against stage entertainments in Boston and Philadelphia, enacted on the grounds that such amusement did not perpetuate the desired traits of thrift, frugality, and industry. For early Americans these qualities went hand in hand with piety.

The Practice of Piety

Concern with spiritual life actually dated back to the pre-Reformation era. The early fifteenth-century English writer Fabritius declared that dancing broke baptismal vows by enabling people to consort with the devil. Sixteenth-century Calvinists such as Christopher Fetherston observed that dancing profaned the Sabbath. He argued that the Lord's Day ought to be spent in worship, visiting the sick, feeding the hungry, clothing the poor, and similar good works. Increase Mather implied that parents who sent their children to a dancing master abrogated the vows they took when their offspring were baptized, in which they promised to rear them in the true faith. He then heralded an argument popular in various forms in the nineteenth century: an activity not sanctified by prayer was sinful. Eighteenth-century evangelists and clergy who preached during the Great Awakening summoned readers to renewed levels of piety by their declarations that a personal conversion experience so transformed the individual that he or she had no further desire for amusements such as dancing. The notion continued through the Second Great Awakening of the early nineteenth century. By the middle decades, some evangelical clergy alleged that dancing and balls proved harmful because they drew people away from revivals. Critics observed that when dancing flourished, revivals waned. Despite the fact that Charles G. Finney declared that any engrossing activity could produce a similar negative effect on the popularity of revivals, the argument continued throughout the century. Adversaries regularly repeated that dancing enticed people to more worldly, hence transient, pleasure. By contrast, the true and mature Christian ought to concentrate on things that endured for eternity. That is, the true Christian had to live in the world but he or she was to be distinct from the "worldling."

Precisely how that life was to be pursued is never clearly explained in the antidance books. The point they stress is that dancing was inevitably an activity popular among people of the world. Before and during the Reformation, opponents exhorted Christians not to dance because dancing occurred among Pagans, in Bacchic rites, in English masques, and in entertainments by worldly folk on Sundays. Increase Mather considered dancing among the "vain and profane" customs of the world. By the eighteenth and nineteenth centuries, however, dancing was considered one of the fashionable amusements of society. Thus, to be separate from the world meant standing apart from the popular customs of contemporary culture. The Bible verse commonly quoted to sustain this argument comes from Paul's epistle to the Romans in chapter 12, verse 2: "Do not conform yourselves to the standards of this world but let God transform you inwardly by a complete change of your mind." Whatever else that notion implied, the adversaries of dance clearly understood it to mean abstinence from dancing, cards, theater, horse racing, novels, and movies.

Thus, the vast majority of American antidance arguments derived from incidental characteristics surrounding the act of dancing, those perceived or actual effects or dependencies, not universally constant, but associated with the activity from time to time and place to place. Attacks on both the essential nature of dance and its incidental characteristics can be collapsed into two basic categories, the moral and the spiritual. Nowhere do adversaries object to dancing on aesthetic grounds. By contrast, courtesy and etiquette writers, as well as dance masters, invariably lauded the social and aesthetic value of dancing, while simultaneously holding to Christian moral standards. Their views highlight social-class distinctions between dance advocates and adversaries, as well as differences of degree between the ideal for the Christian, preached by dance opponents, and the ideal for gentle folk, held up by courtesy and etiquette authorities.

Social Class, Manners, and Motion

Because dancing is by nature a leisure art, those who cultivated it comprised the upper ranks of society. They possessed both time and money to spend on instruction, practice, and performance. Beginning with Italian dance manuals from the middle fifteenth century, instructions testify to the early maturation of dancing as a popular courtly pastime carried to the level of a finished art. In later centuries, when the popularity of fine dancing spread well beyond court and aristocratic circles and when middle-class well-to-do folk aspired to the style and activities of the upper classes, etiquette authorities and dance masters continued to urge dance lessons as a requisite accomplishment for entrée into the polite world. Though America developed her own authorities in the nineteenth century, the European tradition, wherein dancing held both aesthetic and social significance, still carried authority. As late as 1896, Maud C. Cooke emphasized the truth of Alexander Pope's dictum: "'They move easiest who have learned to dance.'"[9]

Although courtesy and etiquette writers from the Renaissance to the twentieth century regularly lauded the value of dancing, their approval was not unqualified. Because the ideal for the gentleman held that he was to serve as a moral and spiritual example for the common folk, sixteenth-century courtesy writers such as Richard Mulcaster, Sir Thomas Elyot, and Roger Ascham lauded only that dancing which was fashioned according to order, reason, proportion, and harmony. Ill-timed, unseemly, and disorderly dancing carried no aesthetic, social, or health value. The ideal held true for later centuries of courtesy and etiquette authorities as well. In fact, the nature of etiquette demands such a standard. It prescribes behavior considered to be society's best in terms of polite conduct. Although good manners can demonstrate merely the superficial mastery of social conventions, most authorities from the Renaissance to the twentieth century assumed that polite conduct emanated from the heart. Manners evolved from morals. Morality, in turn, derived from Christianity.

American dance teachers such as Allen Dodworth in the later nineteenth century, who continued in the tradition of Renaissance dance masters, also assumed an ordered, moral and aesthetic dancing. To both groups of authorities, abuse of dancing or a decline from the ideal did not warrant abolishing dance, as most adversaries argued. Rather, readers of etiquette books and dance manuals were advised to watch their own conduct carefully. Regulation, supervision, and moderation proved watchwords for etiquette writers and dance masters, who qualified the kind of dancing appropriate for the well-bred.

Given the standard of good court dancing or ballroom dancing as an orderly and moral activity for those in polite society, gracefulness became the aesthetic criterion by which performance quality was judged. To move gracefully denoted a skilled performance based on control, which came, not with birth, but with instruction and practice—perhaps daily over a period of years. Fifteenth-century dance manuals spelled out criteria precisely. The ideal in court dancing demanded mastery of the art's essential characteristics—balance, movement through space, timing, and effort. Such consummate skill, effortless to the point of appearing nonchalant, produced that well-ordered, smooth, and light quality of motion labeled as graceful. Obviously, only those persons with time and money could pursue the skills of good dancing. Common folk had only infrequent holidays or Sundays in which to indulge their desire for music and dancing. Their performance could never achieve the polish and perfection required at court or on the assembly hall floor. Thus, the aesthetics of dance performance derived from and depended upon the criterion of social class. As a consequence, good dancing became a part of the European ideal of polite conduct that continued to be of importance through the nineteenth century in this country.

However, as early as 1885, Allen Dodworth lamented the decline in the gracefulness of his students as well as the decline in dance masters qualified to teach both "manners and motion." With the advent of the "round dances" in the middle of the century, serious lessons no longer proved as necessary as in the days of the minuet. Steps and figures did not constitute so formidable an obstacle as in former times. Couples could whirl around the floor on their own; if one of the pair misstepped, only the partner suffered, rather than seven other dancers in a set of quadrilles or an entire audience watching a duo perform a minuet. Moreover, the new round dances fit the more democratic spirit of the century.

After the turn of the twentieth century, fad dances of the ragtime era proved even more capricious. All decorum and good breeding appeared to have vanished as "modern" women turkey-trotted, danced the grizzly bear, and later Charlestoned and Lindy-hopped—often as not with young men whom they had just met at the public dance hall. The democratization of dancing continued to spread as the public ballroom and big bands became ubiquitous during the 1930s and 1940s. Both the pervasiveness of dancing and the demise of prescribed formality coincide with the gradual decline in and end of extensive printed opposition to dancing after the thirties.

The cultivation of fine dancing as an art for close to five hundred years suggests that the arguments of dance opponents cannot be understood solely in moral and religious terms. Antidance attitudes throughout the centuries probably reflected some element of social class criticism. The case seems particularly strong from the late eighteenth through the early twentieth century in American writing, when stewardship of money regularly appeared as an issue in the antidance books. For example, George Whitefield's attacks against "fine" ladies who wore costly jewelry could indicate class criticism as well as attacks on those who embraced a "lukewarm" version of Christianity. Charges throughout the later nineteenth century appear to reflect an element of social class hostility as well as a concern for Christian stewardship. To declare that money spent on clothes, dance lessons, and balls could be better used to relieve the sufferings of the poor assumes a commonality of values among Christians with no concern for individual taste, enterprise, and gain. Similarly, arguments based on stewardship of time could also point to social class criticism, since only the leisure classes had time to spend on lessons, dancing parties, and balls, until the twentieth century. Assertions that good manners could be best learned from pure, Christian mothers, rather than dance teachers, seemingly carries more than a hint of antagonism toward the upper classes. However, the degree to which adversaries intentionally injected social class criticism into their arguments against dancing could only be verified on an author-by-author basis, wherein the totality of that person's theology, preaching, and writing was taken into account. Moreover, authors of antidance books were not, as a group, primarily concerned with social and aesthetic matters. Their attention focused on spiritual growth and moral behavior. That fact points to the critical difference in degree of emphasis between the dance adversaries and the dance advocates.

Writing and preaching to professing Christians, opponents prescribed what constituted the behavioral ideal for the Christian. By contrast, courtesy authors and early American etiquette authorities addressed the ideal for the gentleman and lady. Later etiquette writers, through the turn of the twentieth century, told readers what kind of behavior the "best" people in society displayed. Thus, clergy and evangelists stressed spiritual and moral growth, while courtesy and etiquette writers emphasized social and aesthetic development. Dance opponents regularly urged professing Christians to be separate from the fashionable amusements of the world, but courtesy and etiquette authorities typically expected Christian morality to undergird polite manners and motion in society. For the latter group, good breeding stemmed from Christian courtesy and observance of the Golden Rule. While the vast majority of dance critics saw no value in dancing because of its alleged evils and abuses, nearly all of the courtesy and etiquette writers approved well-regulated and well-performed dancing, because of its social and aesthetic values and assumed Christian moral foundation. Therefore, the critical difference in degree of emphasis between the dance adversaries and dance advocates depended on how narrowly they understood their Christian commitment and the particular prism through which they looked at the world. Yet, that difference in degree of emphasis does not fully explain the question, Why did opponents see dancing so exclusively in moral and spiritual terms? Answers will be explored in the final chapter.

Notes

1. Plato, *Laws,* 7:816.

2. Increase Mather, "An Arrow Against Profane and Promiscuous Dancing Drawn out of the Quiver of the Scriptures" (Boston, [1685]; rpt. in *The Mathers on Dancing,* ed. Joseph E. Marks III, Brooklyn: Dance Horizons, 1975, 35.

3. Abbé Hulot, *Balls and Dancing Parties Condemned by the Scriptures, Holy Fathers, Holy Councils, and Most Renowned Theologians of the Church* (Boston: Patrick Donahoe, 1857), 12.

4. Moses M. Henkle, *Primary Platform of Methodism, or, Exposition of the General Rules* (Louisville: Southern Methodist Book Concern, 1851), 258–59; M[arion] P[almer] Hunt, *What's the Harm in Dancing Anyway?* ([Louisville?]: N.p., [1897]), 28–29.

5. These were identified in the nineteenth century as the cardinal virtues to be displayed by true ladies. See Barbara Welter, "The Cult of True Womanhood: 1820–1860," *American Quarterly* 18 (Summer 1966):151–75.

6. See the accounts in Matt. 14, Mark 6, and Luke 3.

7. *George Whitefield's Journals (1737–1741),* intro. Wm. V. Davis (Gainesville, Fla.: Scholars' Facsimiles and Reprints, 1969), 444.

8. At the beginning of the century, Cotton Mather, in an address on the death of the schoolmaster Ezekiel Cheever, laments that parents would pay to send children to a dancing school but would not adequately compensate a schoolmaster. See the discussion in chapter 3, above, where this is first mentioned.

9. Maud C. Cooke, *Social Etiquette or Manners and Customs of Polite Society* (Chicago: National Book Concern, 1896), 253.

12 Aesthetics, Morality, and Gender

Because dancing is so obviously an art,[1] one searches for an explanation as to why adversaries throughout five centuries failed to see any aesthetic or social value in it, instead attacking it as an immoral activity and as a worldly pastime that imperiled spiritual growth. No simple answers present themselves. But a combination of factors pertaining to social class, vocation, biblical authority, and gender can illuminate the issue.

Adversaries and Aesthetic Awareness

As didactic writing, the antidance literature opposed what authors saw or understood to be going on in their respective societies. Although adversaries rarely tell the reader the experiential basis for their opposition, biographical data suggest that few, if any, of the Renaissance opponents would have seen the art of courtly dancing. In America, neither Increase Mather nor Cotton Mather gives any indication that he actually saw examples of polished dancing. George Whitefield saw dancing in taverns but probably not any examples of more refined dancing at balls, given the nature of his extensive travel and preaching. Though a few of the nineteenth-century clergy and evangelists comment that they had been to a ball or tried dancing once upon a time, the vast majority say nothing about their own experience with dancing. In all probability, they wrote from spoken or printed hearsay. Both the antidance books and etiquette manuals imply that eighteenth- and nineteenth-century Americans thought it inappropriate for a minister to attend a ball or dancing party. Very likely, twentieth-century elegant dance palaces would have been similarly avoided. Thus, it seems probable that the majority of detractors had no first-hand encounter with dancing as a courtly, ballroom, or stage art. The social class and cultural backgrounds of dance adversaries serve to substantiate the point.

Although European gentleman of the upper ranks in society, beginning in the fifteenth century, would have learned the art of dancing as a requirement of their social class, clergy and theologians would not have been subject to the same strictures. Few of them would have been invited to court or great houses to witness such dancing. As adviser to Catherine of Aragon in England, Juan Luis Vives could have been so positioned, but he would have been an exception. Moreover, dance opponents' identity as clergy in Puritan England of the late sixteenth and seventeenth centuries would have precluded their attendance at stage plays where dancing occurred as a theater art. American male dance opponents would have fared no better in terms of exposure to the social and aesthetic values of dance.

The ideal American male has been revered as woodsman, trapper, soldier, statesman, businessman, financial tycoon, and athlete but never as actor, musician, poet, painter, or dancer. With the election of Andrew Jackson to the presidency in 1824, a decades-long era began in which the "common man" was virtually deified. The model did not esteem intellectual or aesthetic acumen. Even after dancing entered public school curricula in this century, those who taught it have been primarily women and those who enrolled, mainly girls. Men and boys went instead to the playing fields. There, as in politics, business, and war, they encountered issues of morality but not of aesthetics. Outside of members of the upper socioeconomic class, which sponsored dancing assemblies, concerts, and the like, the typical American male has had little or no exposure to the realm of art, aesthetics, and dance. Consequently, American evangelical and conservative clergy, as primarily middle-class males, very probably lacked both the experience and the training needed to even consider the social and aesthetic significance of dancing. When that point is combined with an understanding of their vocation, a clearer comprehension of why they persisted in attacking the art of dancing on moral and spiritual grounds comes into focus.

Adversaries as Evangelical and Conservative Clergy

The particular identity and calling of dance opponents derives from their place in European and American church history. Although the origins of dance opposition within Christianity can be traced to the early church fathers, the American tradition of antidance attitudes emanated from the evangelical and anti-Catholic fervor that ignited during the Reformation. The writing and sermonizing of leaders such as Luther and Calvin inevitably led to the formation of denominations and sects that held the Bible as more authoritative than the centuries-old tradition and dogma of the Roman church. A new zeal for living a pious and moral life resulted in continental Calvinists and English Puritans' exhorting Christians to the need for repentance and reform. Antidance writings were published as a part of such preaching and exposition. Adversaries aimed to persuade readers that a profession of Christian belief required an amended life lived daily in that commitment.

Sustaining the centuries of American opposition to dance depended in part upon our long tradition of awakenings and revivals. Ministers and evangelists took seriously their calling to exhort people to follow their ideal for the Christian life. This strong commitment seems to have derived from the American character of the clerics and from their evangelical fervor. In his analysis of the pietistic perfectionism that he argues lies at the core of the American character, William G. McLoughlin explains that a basic tension was experienced by those who settled here; there was, on the one hand, a concern to "maintain perfect moral order" and, on the other hand, an equally serious desire to achieve "perfect moral freedom." When judged by their arguments against dancing, adversaries fell into the category of those primarily driven by a zeal to maintain "perfect moral order." Yet their further dilemma was how to balance, in McLoughlin's words, "personal responsibility for purity and social responsibility for order."[2] The nearly unanimous response of American adversaries was to stress personal moral reform and purity, which, they assumed, would ultimately lead to social reform and the maintenance of order.

By the mid-nineteenth century their virtually universal emphasis on individual repentance and reform, as well as daily piety, impelled opponents to tell readers that all the "evangelical" denominations opposed dancing. In effect, that meant Congregationalists, Presbyterians, Baptists, Methodists, Disciples of Christ, Lutherans, and Episcopalians—denominations that proved to be mainstream in the middle of the century. Later in the century a spirit of liberalism began to invade the American church. Those who continued to inveigh against dancing came from the ranks of conservative clergy and evangelists who still argued that the way to reform city and nation was to begin by converting the individual sinner. In McLoughlin's terms, "personal responsibility for purity" took precedence over "social responsibility for order."[3] Well into the twentieth century, fundamentalists continued to preach that message at urban revivals. Conservative Lutherans and Baptists also carried the same dance oppositional stance into the second half of the twentieth century.

Interestingly, the adversaries' call for repentance and a reformed Christian life, without dancing, did not reach out to everyone. Obviously, itinerant evangelists such as George Whitefield and Billy Sunday spoke to whomever would listen to them. But the majority of antidance publications were aimed at parishioners of a particular congregation, a particular denomination, or professing Christians in general. Clearly, there were people who danced who did not fall into any of these three categories. For example, people danced in saloon–dance halls as early as the 1820s in Boston. People also danced on stage in theaters. But dance opponents who were evangelical and conservative clergy did not write to or about such individuals; instead they argued against the dancing of the polite world, that is, the dances of "modern society." When dance halls became ubiquitous and dancing democratized, critics objected to the dancing in those places as well, directing their attacks at the "modern dances." The critical fact seems to have been that social or ballroom dancing proved more of a threat to the moral and spiritual life of greater numbers of church members or professing Christians than did stage dancing or dancing practiced in saloons and brothels. One might then ask: Was dancing only bad when practiced by middle- and upper-class church members or professing Christians? The answer is no, but dancing by this latter group of people was certainly a more serious offense than dancing by non-Christians. The professing Christian who danced not only allegedly broke commandments and baptismal vows but also set a bad example for others and, therefore, lost the power to witness effectively to nonbelievers.

Thus, American adversaries wrote against dancing in modern society as a part of their identity and calling to exhort Christians to right living, in the sense of personal moral purity and piety, just as sixteenth- and seventeenth-century European clergy had exhorted professing Christians to amend their lives. Balls, assemblies, and dancing parties posed a threat to the evangelical clergy's ideal for the Christian, to the immortal soul of the churchgoer who danced, and to the authority of the church in society. Attraction or addiction to dancing bespoke an attachment to the world and its transient pleasures rather than a conformance to biblical standards of personal purity, moral order, and preparation for eternity.

American adversaries confined expressions of their opposition to the published and spoken admonitions of individual clergy and evangelists, as opposed to collective social or legal action. They focused their writing and preaching on the individual churchgoer or professing Christian, who had both time and money to dance. This strategy contrasted dramatically with that of early twentieth-century urban reformers who published investigative reports, wrote in popular periodicals, and organized politically to pass legislation for effective regulation of dance halls.[4] The only known collective action by clerical opponents appeared in the form of church discipline, determined by some synods and/or denominations and meted out to individual church members who, by dancing, broke church or synod rules. Whereas the urban reformers aimed at social freedom and justice, the evangelical adversaries aimed at personal morality and piety.

The vast number of extant antidance publications were penned by white, male, middle-class Protestant clergy and evangelists. Only one such publication by an African-American clergyman, of the late nineteenth century, has come to light. More may eventually be found, but it seems probable that any existing antidance denunciations aimed at African Americans remained in the oral tradition until well into the twentieth century. The extent of a Catholic tradition of published dance opposition remains an open question; only one such publication from the nineteenth century is known. But statements in the literature examined suggest the existence of a tradition. No known published antidance book or tract was aimed at Native Americans or Jews.

Advocates among the Clergy

Although the vast majority of American clergy argued against dancing in parlors as well as public halls, a few allowed it in certain circumstances because of its positive social value. How do we account for the fact that not all clergy assumed an oppositional stance against dancing? Moreover, how do we explain why some clergy actually advocated dance and dancing? Critical points of distinction depended, first, on whether clergy viewed dancing as an activity with some redeeming social value or as an immoral pastime, utterly beyond any redemptive value. Second, dance advocates among the clergy tended not to hold broad or absolutist views about the nature of sin and temptation. Finally, a changing cultural context affected individual clergymen's views on both of the above points.

Even Martin Luther had argued that, since dancing was not essentially sinful, well-chaperoned dances could prove both enjoyable for young people and beneficial as an occasion for single men and women to meet each other. Though he decried the turning dances, wherein women's skirts flew up, he did not condemn all dancing. The key point that seemed to separate Luther and later moderates from the conservative opponents depended on their view of abuses in dancing. Conservatives saw abuses as so great or dancing itself as so full of temptation that abstinence proved the only safe path to follow. Luther, however, had pointed out that if the principle of abuse by some meant abstinence by all, then gluttony by some would mandate fasting by everyone. Adversaries ignored his line of reasoning. Their concern with individual sexual restraint and the threat of sexual misconduct seemed to override any other possible benefit that dance might have.

Even though the Unitarian cleric William Ellery Channing spoke out in favor of moderate dancing as early as 1837, the greater split between conservative evangelicals and the more liberal ministers began in the post–Civil War decades, when the midcentury union of evangelical denominations was losing power. Like Luther, the Congregationalist Washington Gladden, in 1866, held that abuses in dancing did not make the art wrong in essence. For Gladden the "square dances," indulged in under proper circumstances, could be healthful and recreational; however, the "round dances," because of their closed dance position, proved essentially wrong. The activities of two other clerics highlight an even greater split between their own views and those of conservative adversaries. In *The Parson on Dancing* (1879), the Lutheran J. B. Gross advocated dance in worship. He arrived at this recommendation based on historical and anthropological evidence about dancing as art and amusement. Not until 1923 did the next known dance advocate among the clergy appear in print. By the time that William Norman Guthrie spoke to the Episcopal diocese of New York, theater dance as an expressive art had been pioneered abroad and at home by Isadora Duncan, Ruth St. Denis, and Ted Shawn. Thus, the changing context of American culture and denominational response to such changes, in addition to the advent of dance as a theater art and the increasingly pervasive spread of social dancing, are all events that help to explain why the pool of dance detractors decreased dramatically after the 1930s.

The few clergy from earlier decades and centuries who were willing to publish their views on the positive values of dancing as a healthy social recreation and/or as an expressive art may have been guided by objective observation, logic, and/or a lack of fear in going against majority views. Their individual personalities and psychological profiles, as well as theological positions, surely also affected their moderate stance. Their positions were devoid of the common evangelical and conservative tenet that sin is progressive, that is, the idea that one drink will lead to alcoholism, and parlor dances will lead to public dances, which will, in turn, lead to prostitution. Clearly, these few clerics who could see some social and aesthetic value in dancing held differing notions about biblical authority and interpretation.

Adversaries and the Authority of the Bible

Since its formulation into a canonical Old and New Testament, readers have held diverse views about the Bible. Some call it the inspired word of God; others see it as a good book. Some stress the content of the Old Testament; others emphasize the New Testament. From the Reformation era to the twentieth century, adversaries regularly based their denunciations of dancing on selected portions of the Bible, not on all of it. Their selective use and interpretation of the Scriptures presented one constant model or ideal of how to live the Christian life. The ideal also asserted that the Bible forbade dancing.

Although it is simple to exhort people to follow the Bible and to find in it all the answers to questions about daily living, the actual practice of ferreting out specific answers to particular questions proves difficult for areas like art, amusements, and dance. In fact, the Bible does not make specific pronouncements about most particularities in life. Accordingly, each individual reader usually is free to develop his or her own interpretation about the meaning of a Bible verse. Generally, however, the task falls to theologians, clergy, and evangelists to explain the "correct" or valid interpretation. Dance adversaries derived their authority from an exegetical tradition involving both Old and New Testaments and developed by sixteenth- and seventeenth-century Protestant clergy and theologians.

The Old Testament, as the chronicle of the Jewish people prior to the time of Christ, presents an odyssey of both faith and law. The leaders of the Jews acted in faith that the Messiah would come at some future moment, but in the meantime they lived daily by the laws God gave them to insure life, health, order, and obedience. The Ten Commandments from the book of Exodus provided the cornerstone for such living. Three commandments in particular were cited by dance opponents. The Sixth Commandment prohibits adultery, but sixteenth- and seventeenth-century theologians explained its meaning to forbid any temptation to or occasion for committing adultery, fornication, and the like, as well as the specific acts themselves. Almost as prominent in the lexicon of European dance opponents was the Third Commandment, which enjoins Christians to make the Sabbath day holy. Dancing on the Lord's Day profaned the Sabbath and was thus prohibited by the Bible. The Fourth Commandment, which instructs children to honor their parents, served as authority to oppose dancing for the sixteenth-century Lutheran homiletician Andreas Gerardus Hyperius. For him and for some later writers, the attraction of dancing proved so strong that youth were led to defy parental authority imposed against it. Since the Ten Commandments do not specifically prohibit dancing or other pastimes, and because they provide general guidelines for moral and spiritual conduct, sixteenth- and seventeenth-century Protestant theologians and ministers wrote innumerable "cases of conscience" and "*loci communes*" to help the average pastor or parishioner make correct application of the commandments to daily living.

These and later writers regularly dismissed the several Old Testament verses portraying dancing as a commonplace activity among the ancient Israelites. The commands in Psalm 149:3 and 150:4 to praise the Lord with music and dancing were universally ignored by the dance opponents. They explained to their readers that the Bible presented dancing as a single-sex activity engaged in for religious celebration and praise. Both the kind of dancing described in the Bible and the motivation for it were distinguished from that dancing popular in the adversaries' time. By that caveat, opponents intended to exclude the Bible, once and for all, as an authority for validating the practice of modern, social dancing.

The Old Testament Scripture with which dance advocates regularly confronted their adversaries is from Ecclesiastes 3:4. "There is a time for every purpose under heaven . . . A time to mourn and a time to dance." Unlike other biblical passages, this one required more exegesis to prove that it did not legitimate the practice of dancing in modern society. Attempts varied by author and century. The important issue to recall is that dance opponents attempted to ignore, dismiss, or explain away any Bible verse that seemed to portray dancing in a positive light. That task proved much easier when they consulted the New Testament.

As the record of Jesus' birth, life, and death, the four gospels of Matthew, Mark, Luke, and John together contain only four references to dance or dancing. Some translations about the prodigal son returning home to a party mention dancing. Two other passages establish dancing as neither positive nor negative. However, the example of Salome dancing before King Herod proved to be the favorite of dance opponents. In every century, they declared that the incident offered proof positive that dancing was unlawful for the Christian.

Because the Pauline epistles in the New Testament do not mention dance at all but, instead, carry numerous exhortations to right living, they evoked a different kind of exegesis from adversaries. Paul's letters, plus the books of Timothy and Titus, instruct and admonish the new Christian in how to lead a holy and moral life, pleasing to God. But, like much of the Bible, they appear as generalizations, advising simply, "Whatever you do, whether you eat or drink, do it all for God's glory" (1 Cor. 11:31) or "Avoid immorality" (1 Cor. 6:18). In order to apply biblical proscription to the dancing of their day, adversaries relied heavily on such passages. They concentrated particularly on admonitions to be separate from the world; avoid doing things that belong to darkness; remember that your body is the temple of the holy spirit; give no offense to fellow Christians; do not lead a brother or sister to stumble and fall into sin; and do all to the glory of God. To make such generalizations relevant to dancing, opponents explicitly or implicitly used a syllogistic format. For example: Paul says in Romans 12:2, "Do not conform yourselves to the standards of this world"; dancing and balls belong to the people of this world; therefore, Christians must avoid dancing and balls.

In their zeal to convert individuals to a devout Christian life, adversaries throughout all centuries typically employed the following strategy. First, they relied on the authority of the Ten Commandments and Pauline generalizations as prescriptions for moral and spiritual living and as the basis for their denunciation of dancing. Second, they applied Bible verses selectively. Paul's admonition, "Do not conform yourselves to the standards of this world," applied to amusements but not vocations. Thus, readers learned to separate from the practices of worldly people in the matter of dancing and balls, but obsession with one's business affairs apparently carried no similar censure. Similarly, Paul's advice to avoid "every kind of evil" was applied to dancing, but not to the appearance of greed by making too much money. Third, adversaries interpreted Bible verses narrowly and absolutely. Almost universally, they selected one verse as their authority for a particular pronouncement and then interpreted the meaning of that passage in syllogistic fashion applied to dancing. They did not take into account the larger context in which the verse appeared, nor did they see the role of Paul as teacher, not law-giver. Most adversaries gave no analysis of the complexity of meaning that a passage might engender. For instance, Paul's admonition to avoid any action that might cause a fellow believer to stumble and fall into sin was applied absolutely to dancing. However, to follow such advice in a thorough-going manner could ultimately lead to avoidance of all activity except moderate sleeping and eating, for any human action could, based on interpretation and a fellow Christian's psychological makeup, conceivably cause him or her to fall into sin. Fourth, adversaries often reinforced by threat. They warned readers that life was short and sins were serious; at death, a final judgment would follow. Accordingly, they exhorted readers to take account of all idle deeds as well as idle words. Some told readers that if they had any doubts about the permissibility of dancing, they must heed that doubt, because the Bible says: "He that doubteth is damned." Others coerced by asking rhetorical questions like: "What if you died on a ballroom floor?" or "Who seeks a dance master in their final hour?" Given this legalistic use of Scripture and the dance opponents' heavy reliance upon historical authority, it was almost inevitable that critics over centuries would evolve a code morality.

Adversaries, Code Morality, and Order

When a generalization is presented in syllogistic fashion and pronounced authoritatively by a member of the clergy, the effect upon reader or listener is that a teaching becomes transformed into a law. In effect, the American adversaries' code of morality stipulated that the behavioral Ideal for the Christian meant that he or she was to be separated from the fashions and amusements of the world—dancing, theater, cards, the circus, horse racing, drinking, novels, and movies. The ideal was portrayed as moral righteousness informed by personal piety: go to church, maintain an individual prayer life, visit the sick, feed the hungry, and the like. Admonitions to "Avoid" and to "Do" emphasized behavior. The ideal did not speak to inner thoughts, desires, and attitudes.

In their antidance writings, evangelical and fundamentalist opponents emphasized sins, not sin, as a catalog of behaviors to avoid. They do not talk about sin as a trait or disposition. Although the Bible refers to sins as behavioral acts, as in the Ten Commandments, it also refers to sin as a trait, the most obvious example of which may be pride, in the Genesis story of Adam and Eve. One reason for dance critics' emphasis on sins as behavioral acts may have been to facilitate interpretation. It is easy to see the observable act of dancing or to see a supposed den of iniquity like a dance hall. It is easy to denounce what is visible and verifiable. To see and denounce pride, envy, greed, or sloth is difficult. Such traits or dispositions are not clearly discernible. Thus, ease of identification and popularity of denunciation may have helped to account for a code morality among those dance opponents who lacked theological training. A more complex analysis has been applied to other clergy.

Among the "strongly confessional" churches, led by clergy trained in colleges, universities, and seminaries, several factors may have combined to maintain a morality code. In *Centennial Essays: Augustana Lutheran Church 1860–1960,* Emmer E. Engberg assesses reasons why this Swedish Lutheran church long maintained a posture of legalism with respect to the evils of dancing, theater, cards, and the like. Though applied to one particular synod of one denomination, his analysis bears helpful insights for understanding the dance opponents as a whole. First, Engberg asserts the common-sense truth that neither people nor institutions easily separate themselves from past tradition. The importance of tradition to antidance writers can be judged by the fact that in every historical period analyzed, writers cited prior authorities to shore up their cases. That the weight of tradition dies hard can be further observed, for example, in a 1987 comment from the dean of students at Wheaton College in Illinois: "Wheaton College is an evangelical Christian liberal arts college and our guidelines on dancing reflect the tradition of many evangelical denominations and churches." Second, Engberg points out that Augustana Lutherans were convinced that it was the task of the church to save humans from the consequences of their "inherent weaknesses and evil tendencies." They could do this by proscribing activities that were not necessarily sinful in themselves, but that led to sin. This strategy characterized the majority of adversaries who argued that dancing was so evil in its tendencies that there was no hope of reform or of moderate participation. Third, Engberg observes that humans appear to have been born not only with "evil tendencies" but with "codifying tendencies." That is, "Whether in state or church, man has displayed an amazing willingness to subject himself to a drillmaster, or to become one. He is, by nature, a legalist. *It simplifies his religion.*"[5] Indeed, Washington Gladden had made the same point a century earlier. Code morality provides a clear list of "Don'ts" to follow. Subtleties and nuances of ethical thought and moral behavior do not enter in.

When an individual or personal behavioral code is preached to a subculture, and heeded by the listeners, the effect can be that order on the whole is maintained and control is held by the people who propound the code, in this case white male clergy and evangelists. Although American dance opponents do not talk about maintaining order in individuals and in society, that mo-tive seems implicit. The tone and substance of later nineteenth- and early twentieth-century arguments—charging that the dance contributed to divorce, prostitution, venereal disease, the development of the modern woman, and the breakdown of the family—all implied that adversaries felt threatened by massive cultural reorientation, a shifting of social roles and rules, as well as an emergence of female voices of authority. It was a fact of urban life that wom-en were increasingly out of the home, hence out of control. At the same time, commercial amusements were gaining customers, and denominations were becoming more liberal as they assessed what was really important. Fewer clergy and evangelists preached the historical code morality, and fewer people heed-ed the preaching. A changing society had forced a changing church.

Gender-Based Morality and Theology

Can the foregoing analysis sufficiently explain why dance opposition per-sisted on moral and religious grounds so tenaciously for centuries? I think not. Two points are central to understanding fully the adversaries' motives in arguing as they did. First, recall that the dance opponents, almost with-out exception for several centuries, were male. This point should be reex-amined in light of the fact that opposition concentrated on moral and spir-itual arguments. Second, the most extensive opposition to dancing over centuries focused on the alleged or actual sexual immorality—even the temp-tation to sexual immorality—of dancing or its environment. Such charges concentrated on the male and female dancing partners and their relation-ship to each other on the floor and/or following the dance.

Dance opponents cast women as either pure and pious or fallen and sin-ful. If the former, they were to be protected from the dance. If the latter, they were associated with dancing, either as victims of its evils or as perpe-trators of its evils by their role as temptress, "taxi-dancer," or prostitute.[6] Reliance on a code morality that preached abstinence from dancing was one means of controlling male passions. Casting responsibility for morality on pure and pious women and urging them to avoid dancing was another way to achieve the same end. The persistence with which evangelical and con-servative dance opponents preached against the art on the ground of avoiding any temptation to sexual misconduct and on the ground that sin is progres-sive suggests more than a hint of a gender-based fear. Over the centuries, adversaries' citations of Salome's dancing as proof of the art's unlawfulness further confirmed this fear.

The objections to dancing based on charges that it is "merely" physical or mechanical imply a typical hierarchical mind-body valuing, one conceived by men. Dancing and balls were not uplifting; conversation proved trivial; hence they were a waste of time because neither mind nor spirit was edified. Even animals danced. When the pagan Cicero declared that no man danced unless he were drunk or mad, the assertion seemed especially true to male Christian clerics. An exclusive emphasis on strict rationality, a fear of the passions and the physical body, and an effort to control by avoiding temptation all bespeak a traditional authoritarian theology and morality. Resorting to a strategy of threat and fear in trying to get parishioners to avoid dancing served to reinforce that traditional authoritarianism.

Would the antidance tradition have existed if the adversaries had been female? Would the arguments have been different? The fact that the issue of ordination for women is fairly recent makes the possibility of finding an answer even more daunting. Yet, just posing the questions can jar our thinking. Perhaps we can say only that, had women clergy been the adversaries of dance, they might have looked at dancing through another prism and entered into a discussion about grace rather than viewing the art only from the perspective of a legalistic morality.

What About Grace?

The dance opposition that was ignited with new fervor in the Reformation and that was carried directly to America began in a context that emphasized salvation by grace through faith. Salvation by grace, in the writings of Luther, stood in opposition to salvation by law and works. Ironically, dance opposition ended during the twentieth century in an unexamined tradition based on law and morality. Had the adversaries of dance followed the more difficult path of perceiving dancing within the social, aesthetic, and theological context of grace, the end result could have been radically different.

It cannot be accidental that the noun "grace," since antiquity, has carried both a theological and an aesthetic meaning. The ancients considered the Three Graces as maidens who favored the arts.[7] To the Greeks a favor was pleasing. One could not have a pleasing life without the gods' favor. Thus, we say today, "By the grace of . . . ," to indicate our good fortune. Grace in its theological dimension connotes good will, in contrast to a right or obligation, as the ground of concession. The contrast with contracts and law is obvious. Luther understood the grace of God, which alone justifies the sinner, to be a free, utterly unmerited divine gift. By definition, "gift" connotes that which cannot be earned. The notion of "gift" also applies in artistic performance.

The image of the Three Graces held artistic currency in the Renaissance as three virgins gifted in dancing. Botticelli painted them poised and balanced, suggesting ordered and effortless motion. The poet Sir John Davies celebrated them as models of morality. In his long poem *Orchestra* the three women dance with all due modesty and decency—and, of course, with grace. From the fifteenth century to the present, "graceful" has been the single adjective most often used to describe good dancing. It connoted that performance which bespoke practiced order and control—balance, timing, skill, beauty, and charm—the very qualities that dance masters hoped to instill in their students. Graceful dancing is, after all, a reference to quality of performance, to that which is first of all pleasing to the eye rather than right or wrong according to moral law.

In the antidance literature, the absence of grace in its theological and aesthetic dimensions, coupled with the presence of law, is striking. The fruits of the law are fear and retribution. The law can produce justice but not joy. By contrast, a positive affirmation of life flows from the concept of grace. The Greek word *charis* and the Latin *gratia,* as the roots of grace, stand in dramatic contrast to fear and retribution. A gift brings thanksgiving, joy, celebration. And dancing, in its essence, is celebration. It is testimony to God's creation—a human being with an infinite capacity for expression and joy in motion.

Notes

1. I use the term "art" in both broad and narrow senses. All dance is art, as opposed to science, for example. Different dance genres—ballet, ballroom, ethnic, modern, tap—hold varying degrees of potential for being called "fine art" in the traditional sense of that term.

2. William G. McLoughlin, "Pietism and the American Character," *American Quarterly* 17, no. 2, part 1 (Summer 1965): 165.

3. Ibid. I am using the denominational labels in a global sense here. There were certainly groups within denominations that represented less of an "evangelical" and more of a "churchly" persuasion. For example, the former German-based United Lutheran Church in America proved more hospitable to dancing on the campuses of church colleges in the early twentieth century than did the old Swedish and Norwegian Lutheran synods.

4. An examination of dance opposition within a particular city and decade might

reveal such organized group efforts aimed at cleaning up the city. But the antidance books, treatises, and tracts reveal no evidence of such collective action.

5. Emmer E. Engberg, "Augustana and Code Morality," in *Centennial Essays Augustana Lutheran Church 1860–1960*, ed. Emmer Engberg, Conrad Bergendoff, and Edgar M. Carlson (Rock Island, Ill.: Augustana Press, 1960), 126–27; reference to tradition at Wheaton College from personal correspondence to author from Sam Shellhamer, dean of students, 31 Mar. 1987.

6. Notions of women as evil seducers or temptresses derived from adversaries' biblical interpretation. In the beginning—in Genesis—Eve obeyed the devil and tempted her male companion. Pre-Reformation opponents cited early church fathers who declared that the devil was the beginning and end of the dance. That notion held through Increase Mather's day. In addition, fear of woman and her body, as well as seeing woman in the role of the devil's agent, carries a long history in Western European Christian tradition. For a detailed historical analysis of Christian patriarchal dominance, see Rosemary Radford Ruether, *Sexism and God-Talk* (Boston: Beacon Press, 1983), 72–115.

7. Aglaia, or Radiance; Euphrosyne, or Joy; and Thalia, or Festivity, first appeared in the ninth-century writings of Hesiod.

Appendix

A. Bible Verses on Dance
B. Known European Adversaries
   of Dance
C. Lesser-Known Adversaries
   Mentioned in the Text

A. Bible Verses on Dance

Chapter/Verse	*Good News Bible* (unless noted otherwise)	Other Translations
OLD TESTAMENT REFERENCES		
Exodus 15:20	The prophet Miriam, Aaron's sister, took her tambourine, and all the women followed her, playing tambourines and *dancing*.[b]	KJV & RSV[a] agree
Exodus 32:19	Moses came close enough to the camp to see the bull and to see the people *dancing*, he became furious.	KJV & RSV agree
Judges 11:34	When Jephthah went back home to Mizpah, there was his daughter coming out to meet him, *dancing* and playing the tambourine.	KJV & RSV agree
Judges 21:21	When the girls of Shiloh come out to *dance* during the feast, you come out of the vineyards.	KJV & RSV: "to dance in the dances"
Judges 21:23	The Benjamites did this; each of them chose a wife from the girls who were *dancing* at Shiloh and carried her away.	KJV agrees; RSV: "dancers"

Chapter/Verse	*Good News Bible* (unless noted otherwise)	Other Translations
1 Samuel 10:5–6	At the entrance to the town you will meet a group of prophets coming down from the altar on the hill, playing harps, drums, flutes, and lyres. They will be *dancing* and shouting. Suddenly the spirit of the Lord will take control of you, and you will join in their religious *dancing* and shouting and will become a different person.	KJV & RSV: "prophesying"
1 Samuel 10:10 & 13	Suddenly the spirit of God took control of him, and he joined in their *dancing* and shouting. . . . When Saul finished *dancing* and shouting, he went to the altar on the hill.	KJV & RSV: "prophesied" and "prophesying"
1 Samuel 18:6	Women from every town in Israel came out to meet King Saul. They were singing joyful songs, *dancing* and playing tambourine and lyres.	KJV & RSV agree
1 Samuel 19:19–24	Saul was told that David was in Naioth in Ramah, so he sent some men to arrest him. They saw the group of prophets *dancing* and shouting, with Samuel as their leader. Then the spirit of God took control of Saul's men and they also began to *dance* and shout. When Saul heard of this, he sent more messengers, and they also began to *dance* and shout. . . . As he [Saul] was going there, the spirit of God took control of him also, and he *danced* and shouted all the way to Naioth. He took off his clothes	KJV & RSV: "prophesying" and "prophesied"

	and *danced* and shouted in Samuel's presence.	
1 Samuel 21:11	"Isn't this David, the King of his country? This is the man about whom the women sang, as they *danced*."	KJV & RSV: "sing . . . of him in dances"
1 Samuel 29:5	After all, this is David, the one about whom the women sang, as they *danced*.	KJV & RSV same as above
1 Samuel 30:16	And when he had taken him [David] down, behold, they [raiders] were spread abroad over all the land, eating and drinking and *dancing*, because of all the great spoil they had taken from the land of the Philistines and from the land of Judah. (RSV)	GNV: "celebrating," instead of "dancing"; KJV agrees
2 Samuel 6:5	David and all the Israelites were *dancing* and singing with all their might to honor the Lord. They were playing harps, lyres, drums, rattles, and cymbals.	KJV: "played . . . on all manner of instruments"; RSV: "making merry"
2 Samuel 6:14	David, wearing only a linen cloth around his waist, *danced* with all his might to honor the Lord.	KJV: "played . . . on all manner of instruments"; RSV agrees with GNV
2 Samuel 6:16	As the Box was being brought into the city, Michal, Saul's daughter, looked out of the window and saw King David *dancing* and jumping around in the sacred *dance*, and she was disgusted with him.	KJV & RSV: "leaping and dancing"
2 Samuel 6:21	David answered, "I was *dancing* to honor the Lord, who chose me instead of your father and his family to make me the leader of his people Israel. And I will go on *dancing* to honor the Lord and will disgrace myself even more."	KJV: "therefore I will play before the Lord"; RSV: "make merry"

Chapter/Verse	*Good News Bible* (unless noted otherwise)	Other Translations
1 Kings 18:26	They [prophets of Baal] shouted "Answer us, Baal!", and kept *dancing* around the altar they had built.	KJV: "And they leaped upon the altar which was made"; RSV: "limped about the altar"
1 Chronicles 13:8	. . . while David and all the people *danced* with all their might to honor God. They sang and played musical instruments—harps, drums, cymbals, and trumpets.	KJV: "played before God with all their might"; RSV: "making merry"
1 Chronicles 15:29	As the Box was being brought into the city, Michal, Saul's daughter, looked out of the window and saw David *dancing and leaping* for joy, and she was disgusted with him.	KJV: "dancing and playing"; RSV: "dancing and making merry"
Job 21:11	Their children run and play like lambs and *dance* to the music of harps and flutes.	KJV & RSV agree
Psalms 30:11	You have changed my sadness into a joyful *dance;* you have taken away my sorrow, and surrounded me with joy.	KJV & RSV: "mourning into dancing"
Psalms 87:7	They *dance* and sing, "In Zion is the source of all our blessings."	KJV: "singers" and "players on instruments"; RSV: "singers and dancers"
Psalms 149:3	Praise his name with *dancing;* play drums and harps in praise of him.	KJV: "praise his name in the dance"; RSV agrees with GNV
Psalms 150:4	Praise him with drums and *dancing.*	KJV & RSV agree
Ecclesiastes 3:4	He sets the time for sorrow and the time for joy, the time for mourning and the time for dancing.	KJV & RSV agree
Song of Songs 4:1	How beautiful you are, my love! How your eyes shine with love behind your veil. Your hair *dances* like	KJV & RSV: "hair is as a flock of goats"

a flock of goats bounding down the hills of Gilead.

Song of Songs 6:5	Your hair *dances* like a flock of goats bounding down the hills of Gilead.	KJV & RSV same as above
Song of Songs 6:13	*Dance, dance* girl of Shulam. Let us watch you as you *dance*. [Footnote gives "come back, come back" as alternative.]	KJV & RSV: "Return, Return"
Isaiah 13:21	Ostriches will dwell, and there satyrs will *dance*. (RSV)	KJV agrees; GNV: "wild goats will prance"
Jeremiah 31:4	Once again you will take up your tambourines and *dance* joyfully.	KJV & RSV: "go forth in the dance of the merry makers"
Jeremiah 31:13	Then the girls will *dance* and be happy, and men, young and old, will rejoice. I will comfort them and turn their mourning into joy, their sorrow into gladness.	KJV & RSV: "rejoice in the dance"
Lamentations 5:15	Happiness has gone out of our lives; grief has taken the place of our *dances*.	KJV: "our *dance* is turned into mourning; RSV: "*dancing* has been turned to mourning"

NEW TESTAMENT REFERENCES

Matthew 11:17	We played wedding music for you, but you wouldn't *dance!* We sang funeral songs, but you wouldn't cry!	KJV & RSV agree
Matthew 14:6	On Herod's birthday, the daughter of Herodias *danced* in front of the whole group.	KJV & RSV agree
Mark 6:22	The daughter of Herodias came in and *danced*, and pleased Herod and his guests.	KJV & RSV agree
Luke 6:23	Be glad when that happens and *dance* for joy, because a great reward is kept for you in heaven.	KJV & RSV: "leap for joy"
Luke 7:32	They are like children sitting in the marketplace. One group shouts to	KJV & RSV agree

Chapter/Verse	*Good News Bible* (unless noted otherwise)	Other Translations
	the other, "We played wedding music for you, but you wouldn't *dance!*"	
Luke 15:25	On his way back, when he came closer to the house, he heard the music and *dancing*.	KJV & RSV agree

a. KJV = King James Version; RSV = Revised Standard Version
b. Italics added to facilitate comparison with KJV and RSV

B. Known European Adversaries of Dance

The following list gives the name, birth and death dates, nationality, religious denomination, and vocation or primary intellectual activity of known European adversaries of dance considered germane to this research. Information about these individuals was gathered from the sources consulted for the text of this book. The letter within parentheses at the end of each brief entry indicates whether the person was cited by Prynne (P), by Increase Mather or Cotton Mather (M), or in the courtesy bibliographies (C).

Aeneas Silvius de Piccolomini (1405–64)—Italian/Catholic; became Pope Pius II in 1458 (P).

Agrippa, Henri Cornelius (1486–1535)—German/Catholic; scholar/soldier; held degrees in law and medicine (P).

Alesius, Alexander (1500–1565)—Scottish/Lutheran; a divine; professor at Frankfurt and Leipzig (P).

Allestree, Richard (1619–81)—English/Anglican; a Royalist divine; in 1663, chaplain to the king; provost at Eton College (C).

Alting, Johan Heinrich (1583–1644)—German/Reformed; professor of theology at Heidelberg and Groningen (M).

Ames, William (1576–1633)—English/Puritan; a divine; professor of theology and then rector at Franeker, Holland (P, M).

Andrewes, Lancelot (1555–1626)—English/Anglican; bishop; one of the divines to prepare the King James Version of the Bible (P, M).

Antoninus de Forciglioni (1389–1459)—Italian/Catholic; a Dominican and reformer; archbishop of Florence; canonized in 1523 (P).

Aretius, Benedictus (1505–74)—Swiss/Reformed; professor of logic at Marburg; professor of theology at Bern (M).

Astesanus de Asti (d. c. 1330)—Italian/Franciscan; frère mineur, author of a popular summa for confessors (P).

Babington, Gervase (1550–1610)—English/Anglican; bishop of Llandaff, Exeter, Worcester (P, M).

Beard, Thomas (d. 1632)—English/Puritan; a divine, schoolmaster, and author (P, M).

Becon, Thomas (1512–67)—English/Anglican; a divine; vocal early Puritan and Marian exile to Strasbourg (P).

Bolton, Robert (1572–1631)—English/Puritan; a divine in Broughton, Northamptonshire; author of widely popular religious writings (P, M).

Brant, Sebastian (1458?–1521)—German/Catholic; poet and lawyer; his *Ship of Fools* made him famous in Europe (P).

Brathwait, Richard (1588?–1673)—English/Anglican?; poet and author; royalist sympathizer (C).

Brinsley, John, the Elder (fl. 1633)—English/Puritan; a divine and schoolmaster (P, M).

Bucer, Martin (1491–1551)—Alsatian/Reformed; a divine and theologian; known as the "Strasbourg Reformer"; spread Calvin's thought to England (P).

Bullinger, Heinrich (1504–75)—Swiss/Reformed; a divine and theologian; known as the "Zurich Reformer"; spread Calvin's thought to England (P).

Byrd, or Bird, Samuel (fl. 1580–1605)—English/Anglican?; a divine at St. Peter's, Ipswich; M.A., Oxford, 1605 (P).

Calvin, John (1509–64)—French/Reformed; a reformer and theologian at Geneva; established Geneva Academy, 1559 (P, M).

Clamanges, Nicholas de (c. 1360–1437)—French/Catholic; a Christian humanist/theologian; rector, University of Paris; papal secretary at Avignon (P).

Clavasio, Angelus de (1411–95)—Italian/Franciscan; vicar general of his order; moral theologian; author of a popular summa for confessors (P).

Coignet, Matthieu (1514/15–86)—French/Reformed?; a diplomat, lawyer, and courtier under the Valois; suspected of holding Calvinist beliefs (C).

Daneau, Lambert (1530–95)—French/Reformed; a divine; professor of theology at Geneva and at the University of Leyden (M).

Dod, John (1549?–1645)—English/Puritan; a divine in England; fellow at Cambridge (P, M).

Downham, or Downame, John (d. 1652)—English/Puritan; a divine in England; received B.D. from Cambridge (P, M).

Durham, James (1622–58)—Scottish/Convenanting; a divine; professor of theology at Glasgow (M).

Elton, Edward (15??–1624)—English/Puritan; a divine at Bermondsey, 1605–24 (P, M).

Erasmus of Rotterdam (1466–1536)—Dutch/Catholic; member of the Augustinian order; a humanist scholar (P).

Fabritius, Alexander, or Carpenter, Alexander (fl. 1429)—English/Catholic; his *Destructorium Vitiorum* earned renown in the fifteenth and sixteenth centuries (P, M).

Fenner, Dudley (1558?–1587)—English/Puritan; a divine in England and Holland; considered a leading exponent of Puritan theology (C).

Fetherston, Christopher (fl. 1583–1616)—English/Puritan; received a B.A. from Queen's College, Oxford, 1583–84; translated some of Calvin's writings (P).

Field, John (15??–1588)—English/Puritan; a divine at Aldermary Church, London; earned an M.A. at Oxford (P).

Flacius (Flach) Illyricus, or Francowitz, Mathias Flagh (1520/21–75)—Illyria/Lutheran; a professor of theology at Jena; wrote an ecclesiastical history (P).

Gosson, Stephen (1554–1624)—English/Puritan; an actor and playwright who became a divine; altered his view of theater and dance (C).

Hiperius, or Hyperius, Andrew Gerard (1511–64)—Belgian/Lutheran; a divine; homiletician; professor at Marburg (P).

Holcot, Robert of (d. 1349)—English/Catholic; a Dominican; Oxford Doctor of Theology and lecturer; revered among students at home and abroad into the sixteenth century (P).

Hollyband, Claudius (alias of Claude de Sainliens) (fl. 1566–1597)—French/Reformed; language teacher and the author of an early French-English dictionary; emigré in London (C).

Humphrey, or Humfrey, Laurence (1527?–1590)—English/Puritan; president of Magdalen College, Oxford; a Marian exile to Zurich and Basel (P).

Junius, Francis (1545–1602)—French/Reformed; a divine and a professor of theology at Heidelberg and at Leyden (M).

Lakes, Osmund (1544–1621)—English/Anglican; a fellow at Kings College, Cambridge; a divine (P).

Langhecruys, Jean van (1530?–1604)—Belgian; a professor of belles-lettres and law at Louvain, Flanders (P).

LaPrimaudaye, Pierre de (1545–after 1603)—French/Reformed; a courtier under Henry III and Henry IV; an author (C).

Lavater, Louis (1527–1586)—Swiss/Reformed; a canon and then head pastor in Zurich (M).

LeJeune, Father Jean (1592–1672)—French/Catholic; a member of the Oratory of Jesus; preached throughout France; led life of mortification and sanctity (M).

Le Maçon (Masson, or Massonius), Robert, La Fontaine (fl. 1562–1603)—French/Reformed; pastor at Orleans and of the French Church in London; edited Vermigli's *Loci Communes* (P, M).

Lovell, Sir Thomas (d. 1567)—an English peer (P).

Marlorat, Augustin (1506–64)—French/Reformed; a divine, he was active in establishing the French Reformed church; a martyr of Rouen (P, M).

Mulcaster, Richard (1530?–1611)—English/Anglican?; headmaster, Merchant Taylors School and St. Paul's School; an author (C).

Musculus, Wolfgang (1497–1563)—German/Lutheran; a divine at Augsburg; a professor of divinity at Bern (P).

Northbrooke, John (fl. 1570s)—English/Anglican?; a divine at or near Bristol; author of early treatise opposing theater (P).

Pellican, Konrad (1478–1556)—Alsatian/Reformed; a divine and professor of Greek and Hebrew at Zurich (P).

Perkins, William (1558–1602)—English/Puritan; a professor and famous preacher at Christ College, Cambridge (P, M).

Petrarch, Francesco (1304–74)—Italian/Catholic; a humanist scholar and poet (P).

Piscator (Fischer), Johann (d. 1626)—German/Protestant; a professor of sacred literature (P).

Polanus von Polansdorf, Amandus (1561–1610)—German/Reformed; a professor of theology at Basel (M).

Prynne, William (1600–1669)—English/Puritan; a pamphleteer; earned a B.A. at Oxford in 1621 (M).

Puteanus, Erycius (1574–1646)—Belgian/Catholic; chair of ancient history at Louvain (P).

Rainolds, or Reynolds, John (1549–1607)—English/Puritan; a scholar and president at Corpus Christi College, Oxford (P, M).

Ravanel, Pierre (d. 1680)—French/Reformed; a divine at Sauzet; an author (M).

Rhabanus (Hrabanus, or Rabanus), Maurus (784?–856)—German/Catholic; a Benedictine; abbot of Fulda; archbishop of Mainz (P).

Rivet, André (1572?–1651)—French/Reformed; a divine at Thouars; professor of theology at Leyden and at Oxford (M).

Simler, Josias (1530–76)—German/Reformed; a divine and professor of New Testament at Zurich (P).

Stubbes, Phillip (fl. 1581–95)—English/Puritan; a pamphleteer (P).

Taffin, Jean (1529–1602)—Dutch/Reformed; a divine in Heidelberg, Haarlem, Amsterdam; court chaplain to Prince of Orange (C).

Tilenus, Daniel (1563–1633)—German/Reformed; a divine and professor at Sedan, France; defender of Arminians in their struggle against Calvinists (M).

Ussher, James (1581–1656)—Irish/Anglican; archbishop at Armagh; professor of divinity at Dublin (M).

Vegio, Maffeo (1406/7–58)—Italian/Catholic; a churchman and a humanist educator (P).

Vergil, Polydore (1470–1555)—Italian/Catholic; a churchman and a humanist scholar; sent to England as papal official, 1502; signed renunciation of papal supremacy, 1536 (P).

Vermigli, Pietro Martire (1500–1562)—Italian/Reformed; professor at Oxford, Strasbourg, Zurich (cited as "Peter Martyr," P, M).

Vives, Johannes Ludovicus, or Juan Luis (1492–1540)—Spanish/Catholic; a scholar; a counselor to Catherine of Aragon in England (P, M).

Voet, Gisbert (1589–1676)—Dutch/Reformed; a theologian and author (M).

Walther (Gualther), Rudolph (1519–86)—Swiss/Reformed; a divine at St. Peter's, Zurich (P).

Williams, Griffith (1589?–1672)—English/Anglican; a rector in London and Carnavon; a bishop in Ireland (P).

Zepper, Wilhelm (1550–1607)—German/Reformed; a divine; professor of theology and president of the University of Herborn (P, M).

Zwinger, Theodore (1533–88)—Swiss/Reformed; a physician and a professor of moral theology and medical theory at Basel (M).

C. Lesser-Known Adversaries Mentioned in the Text

The following individuals are dance adversaries mentioned in the text, but their names do not appear in standard reference works such as the *Dictionary of American Biography, Who Was Who in America, Appleton's Cyclopaedia,* or *The National Cyclopaedia of American Biography.* Information about them was derived from the sources consulted in the preparation of this book.

Allbright, William Hervey (1849–1907)—A Congregationalist, Allbright was a pastor in Dorchester, Massachusetts.

Anderson, Harry O. (18??–after 1920s)—Anderson may have been an evangelist and a member of the Disciples of Christ.

Bailes, Porter Marcellus (1888–1963)—Bailes received his B.A. from Furman University. A Southern Baptist, he served as pastor of churches in Kentucky, South Carolina, Florida, and Texas. He was an author and was at one time vice president of the Southern Baptist Convention.

Bates, William Henry (1840–?)—An author and a pastor in New York and Missouri, Bates was a Presbyterian who had received a B.A. from Hamilton College and further training at Auburn Theological Seminary.

Bayley, Kiah (1770–1857)—Bayley was a Dartmouth-educated Congregationalist pastor who served in Maine and Vermont. He was a member of the first Board of Overseers for Bowdoin College and a founder of the Bangor Theological Seminary.

Belsheim, Gulbrand G. (1871–1930)—An Iowan with a medical degree, Belsheim belonged to the Evangelical Lutheran Church. He practiced as a physician in Iowa and Minnesota until 1903. Following his seminary training, he held pastorates in Iowa and Virginia from 1906 to 1925, when he again practiced medicine.

Benton, Harry (1873–1974)—Benton was a pastor in the Disciples of Christ denomination, serving churches in Oregon and Washington. He was a professor at the Eugene Bible University and served as editor of *Church and School and World Evangelism.*

Binga, Anthony (18??–19??)—Little is known about Binga, an African American who was pastor of the First Baptist Church in Manchester, Virginia, in the 1880s.

Bitting, Charles Carroll (1830–98)—Bitting graduated from high school in Philadelphia and eventually became a Southern Baptist minister, serving congregations in Virginia and Maryland. He was secretary of the Sunday School Board of the Southern Baptist Convention. Bitting was awarded an honorary D.D. from Furman University.

Brand, James (1834–99)—A Congregationalist who was trained at Yale and at Andover Seminary, Brand was an author and pastor, serving in Ohio. He was a trustee of Oberlin College and received an honorary D.D. from Iowa College.

Brandt, John Lincoln (1860–1946)—Born in Perry County, Ohio, Brandt became a member of the Disciples of Christ. He was a pastor in Ohio, Indiana, Missouri, and Colorado. In addition to writing some books, Brandt became a lyceum and chautauqua lecturer.

Bryant, Alfred (1807–81)—Born in Springfield, New Jersey, Bryant was a Presbyterian who had received his theological training at Princeton Seminary. Ordained in 1836, he served congregations in Indiana and Michigan. Bryant died in Lansing, Michigan.

Buck, William Calmes (1790–1872)—The Virginia-born Buck was ordained in the Southern Baptist church in 1812. Between 1820 and 1866 he served as pastor to churches in Kentucky, Mississippi, and Alabama. He was vice president of the Southern Baptist Convention, an author, and the editor of the *Baptist Banner and Western Pioneer.*

Campbell, Robert Clifford (1888–1954)—A Southern Baptist, Campbell graduated from Carson-Newman College. After further education at the Southwestern Baptist Theological Seminary, he was a pastor in South Carolina, North Carolina, Texas, and Arkansas. He was an author and also served as vice president of the Southern Baptist Covention.

Candler, Warren Akin (1857–1941)—Born in Georgia, Candler became a Methodist minister, educator, and author. He served as bishop of the Methodist Episcopal Church South beginning in 1898.

Carrara, John (1913–after 1955)—Carrara was described as a "devout Romanist for several years," although he is thought to have become a Baptist. He was an evangelist and author.

Carson, William (1846–1936)—A Presbyterian pastor from Massachusetts, Carson received an M.A. from Blackburn College. In addition he studied at Lane Theological Seminary and Union Theological Seminary. He served churches in Ohio and Indiana.

Carter, Marmaduke Nathaniel (1881–1961)—Born in Hanover County, Virginia, Carter belonged to the Lutheran Church—Missouri Synod. He was a pastor in Chicago as well as an author.

Chappell, Clovis Gilham (1882–after 1949)—Chappell was a Methodist minister in Alabama, Mississippi, North Carolina, Oklahoma, Texas, and Washington, D.C. He had attended Duke University and Harvard, and was awarded honorary D.D. degrees from Duke and Centenary College in Louisiana. Chappell wrote numerous books, which were published between 1921 and 1945.

Chumley, Charles E. (c. 1918/19–after 1956)—Chumley was a pastor who is thought to have belonged to the Disciples of Christ.

Conant, Judson E. (1867–1955)—Born in Jackson, Michigan, Conant graduated from high school in Albion. Ordained as a Baptist pastor in 1893 in Superior, Wisconsin, Conant served congregations in Michigan, Wisconsin, and Illinois.

Dye, William Milburn (1868–1960)—Dye was a Methodist minister in Tennessee, Virginia, West Virginia, New York, Idaho, Colorado, Missouri, and Kansas. He died in Daytona Beach, Florida, after having been affiliated with the Methodist Church since 1893.

Eastman, Charles S. (1841–1931)—Although born in Joliet, Illinois, Eastman received his ministerial training in Canada. He was a pastor in Ontario as well as in Michigan. Ill health caused him to retire in 1901; he died in Cleveland, Ohio.

Faulkner, T. A. (18??–after 1922)—A former Los Angeles dancing master who had served as president of the Dancing Masters' Association of the Pacific Coast, Faulkner was converted to the antidance point of view and became widely quoted by clergy and evangelists.

Fife, Clyde Lee (d. 1959)—Thought to be a member of the Disciples of Christ, Fife was ordained in 1909. He was an author, evangelist, and preacher in Kansas City, Missouri, for several years. He died in Abilene, Texas.

Foster, Gustavus L.—Foster was a Congregationalist who served as a pastor in Michigan in the 1840s and 1850s. At the First Congregational Church of Jackson, Michigan, he preached against dancing.

Gardner, William W. (1818–90s)—A Baptist and a graduate of Georgetown College, Gardner was ordained in 1844. He became a pastor in Kentucky, a professor at Bethel College, and an author.

Garnett, Mrs. F. E. (18??–after 1858?)—The author of *Dancing: Religion and Revelry,* Mrs. Garnett may have been a Baptist and may have lived in Kentucky.

Gaskin, Jesse Marvin (1917–??)—Gaskin studied at Oklahoma Baptist University, where he earned a B.A., and at Crozer Theological Seminary in Pennsylvania. A Southern Baptist, he was an author and a pastor in Oklahoma. He received honorary D.D. degrees from the Oklahoma School of Religion and from Oklahoma Baptist University, which he served as trustee from 1967 to 1971.

Gatewood, Otis (1911–after 1950)—A member of the Disciples of Christ, Gatewood graduated with a B.A. from Abilene Christian College in 1936. He became a missionary to Germany after World War II.

Goodsell, Dana (1803–76)—Goodsell, a Congregationalist, had a varied career. He studied at Princeton Seminary and became a pastor in Massachusetts. He was perhaps an agent of the Tract Society or the Sunday School Union in the West and the South. Prior to the Civil War, Goodsell was a businessman in North Carolina. He died in Philadelphia.

Gross, Joseph B. (1800/10?–1891)—A member of the German Evangelical Lutheran Church, Gross was ordained by the Pennsylvania Ministerium in 1827. He served as a pastor in Pennsylvania and New York between the 1840s and 1865 but was suspended by the Ministerium in 1873, when he lived in Easton, Pennsylvania. He was also the author of several books.

Guernsey, Jesse (1822–71)—Born in Watertown, Connecticut, Guernsey was a Congregationalist. He is known to have been a pastor in Connecticut during the period 1849–57. He died in Dubuque, Iowa.

Hall, George Franklin (1864–1914)—Born near Clarksville, Iowa, Hall received his undergraduate education at Drake University and earned a Ph.D. at Ruskin University in 1903. An author as well as a pastor, he served congregations in Kansas and in Chicago. He was probably a member of the Disciples of Christ.

Ham, Mordecai F. (1877–1961)—A Baptist and evangelist, Ham is credited with the conversion of Billy Graham.

Hamilton, William Wistar (1868–1960)—Hamilton, a Southern Baptist, earned a B.A. from King College, Bristol, Tennessee, a Th.D. from Southern Baptist Theological Seminary, and was awarded an honorary D.D. by Georgetown College in Kentucky. He was a pastor in Virginia, West Virginia, Kentucky, and Louisiana and served as president of the Southern Baptist Convention from 1940 to 1942. Hamilton also wrote several books between 1908 and 1940.

Hanson, Oscar Conrad (1908–after 1967)—A member of the Norwegian Lutheran Synods, Hanson was a pastor in South Dakota, an evangelist, and the executive secretary of the Young People's Luther League. He received a B.A. from Augustana College in South Dakota and a seminary education from Luther Seminary in St. Paul, Minnesota. Pacific Lutheran College granted Hanson an honorary D.D. in 1950.

Haydn, Hiram Collins (1831–1913)—After earning a B.A. from Amherst College and attending Union Theological Seminary, Haydn became a Presbyterian pastor in Connecticut and Ohio. He was also an author. Wooster College awarded him an honorary D.D. in 1878.

Henry, Thomas Charlton (1790–1827)—A Presbyterian, Henry graduated from Middlebury College in 1814 and studied at Princeton Seminary. He was a pastor in Pennsylvania, Kentucky, and South Carolina. Henry was awarded an honorary D.D. by Yale University in 1824. He died in Charleston during a yellow fever epidemic.

Hobbs, A. G., Jr. (1909–??)—Hobbs was an evangelist, an author, and a member of the Disciples of Christ.

Hubbert, James Monroe (1850–1934)—Born in Cassville, Missouri, Hubbert attended Union Theological Seminary. He was a Presbyterian pastor in Illinois, Tennessee, and Missouri. He served as dean of Cumberland Theological Seminary in Missouri, and as a church official in Philadelphia from 1907 to 1921.

Hughes, Matthew Simpson (1863–1920)—Hughes, from West Union, Virginia, was a Methodist who had been converted at a camp meeting in Loveland, Ohio. He joined the Iowa Conference in 1887 and became a bishop in 1916. Hughes died in Cleveland.

Humphrey, Don (1936–?)—Born in Mammoth Springs, Arkansas, Humphrey may have been a member of the Disciples of Christ. He was an evangelist and author.

Hunt, Marion Palmer (1860–1944)—Hunt attended William Jewell College and the Southern Baptist Theological Seminary. A pastor in Missouri and Kentucky, he served as the secretary of the Southern Baptist Convention and on its hospital committee.

Ide, Jacob (1785–1880)—A Congregationalist, Ide was educated at Brown and at Andover Seminary. He was a pastor in West Medway, Massachusetts, from 1814 to 1880. He also served in Maine and New Hampshire. Ide was a trustee of Amherst College during 1839–63. He received an honorary D.D. from Brown University in 1837. Ide wrote several books and edited *The Works of Nathanael Emmons.*

Ilsley, G. B. (1839–1923)—Born in Limerick, Maine, Ilsley studied at Colby College, which later awarded him an honorary D.D., and at Newton Theological Seminary. A Baptist, he was a pastor in Maine, where he was also a school superintendent. Ilsley wrote about the Baptist church in Maine.

Janes, Don Carlos (1877–1944)—Janes may have been a member of the Church of Christ and an evangelist. Born in Ohio, he also wrote several tracts or booklets. He died in Louisville, Kentucky.

Jeter, Jeremiah Bell (1802–80)—Jeter gained wide acclaim as editor of the *Religious Herald.* A Baptist, he was a pastor in Virginia and Missouri. His longest tenure seems to have been in Richmond, Virginia. He was a native of Bedford County, Virginia.

Jones, Clara Josephine (1900–??)—A social worker as well as a missionary to China, Jones was also an author. She belonged to the Norwegian Lutheran Synods.

Jones, John Griffing (1804–88)—Jones belonged to the Methodist Church South and was admitted to the Tuscaloosa, Alabama, Conference in 1824. A pastor in Mississippi all his professional life, Jones wrote *A Complete History of Methodism As Connected with the Mississippi Conference.*

Laird, James (1833–74)—Laird studied at Oberlin College and at Andover Seminary. He was a Congregationalist pastor in Vermont and New Hampshire. He died, probably while serving the church in Hollis, New Hampshire.

Lamphear, Guy A. (fl. 1906–29)—Lamphear was an evangelist, probably a Methodist.

Lane, Harley (19??–after 1950)—Lane may have been a Methodist and an evangelist. His writing was published by *The Herald Press,* Louisville.

Leonard, Adna Bradway (1837–1916)—Born in Mahoning County, Ohio, Leonard was a pastor and was a member of the Methodist General Conference eight times. He served as corresponding secretary of the Missionary Society from 1888 to 1912. He died in Brooklyn, New York.

Lindwall, Carl Axel (1868–1946)—The Swedish-born Lindwall was a member of the Swedish Lutheran Church. He attended Augustana College and Seminary in Illinois, which later awarded him an honorary D.D. Lindwall was a pastor in Chicago from 1909 to 1940.

Lyman, William (1764–1833)—A Congregationalist, Lyman was educated at Yale. He was a pastor in Connecticut and New York and a home missionary in western New York. He wrote books that were published between 1801 and 1807. He received an honorary D.D. from Princeton University.

Mahler, Gerhard (1897–1971)—A graduate of Concordia Seminary in St. Louis, Mahler was a member of the Lutheran Church—Missouri Synod. He was a pastor in Wyoming, Nebraska, and New York. Mahler served as editor of the *St. Louis Lutheran* from 1945 to 1952.

Martinez, Homer (19??–after 1952)—Martinez was an evangelist who may have been a Baptist.

Masselink, William (19??–after 1953?)—Masselink wrote about youth and entertainment. He may have been a pastor, although his denomination is not known.

Mattison, Hiram (1811–68)—A Methodist born in Herkimer County, New York, and converted in 1834. Mattison was both an author and a pastor who served congregations in New York and New Jersey. He was instrumental in building Trinity Methodist Church in New York City. Mattison died in Jersey City, New Jersey.

McDonald (also MacDonald), John (1807–47)—McDonald was a missionary to Calcutta as well as an author. He may have been a Presbyterian.

Mesick, John F. (fl. 1840s–1870s)—Mesick was a German Reformed pastor in Harrisburg, Pennsylvania, during the 1840s. In addition to his sermon against dancing, he had three other publications to his credit.

Morley, John H. (1840–1923)—A graduate of Williams College, Morley, a Congregationalist, also attended Andover Seminary. He was a pastor in Iowa, Minnesota, Vermont, and Massachusetts, and was superintendent of the Congregational Home Missions in Minnesota, 1884–99.

Morris, Melvin G. (fl. 1920s)—Morris was a Baptist who was an evangelist with the Maryland Baptist Union Association.

Morris, Thomas Asbury (1794–1874)—A Methodist pastor in Ohio, Kentucky, and Tennessee, Morris had been born in West Virginia. He was elected a bishop in 1836 and presided over conferences in Texas, Arkansas, Tennessee, and Oklahoma.

Neill, Edward Duffield (1823–93)—A Presbyterian, Neill was educated at Amherst College and Andover Seminary. He was a pastor in Minnesota, a state superintendent of public instruction in Minnesota, chancellor of the University of Minnesota, and president of Macalester College in St. Paul, serving in the latter post from 1874 to 1884. Neill was also an author.

Nordberg, Carl Edin (1880–1926)—Nordberg was a native of Norway who was a member of the Lutheran Free Church. He earned an M.A. from the University of Minnesota and studied at Augsburg Seminary. Ordained in 1905, he was a pastor in Minnesota and Wisconsin and an author.

Orr, William W. (fl. 1950s)—Thought to have been a Baptist, Orr was an author, a conference leader, and a radio minister.

Penn, William Evander (1832–95)—Penn served as a Confederate major in the Civil War. A Southern Baptist who was dubbed "The Texas Evangelist," he was the first full-time Baptist evangelist and first lay evangelist. Penn was also a lawyer and was known for his revivals, hymns, and books.

Penney, Joseph (1790–1860)—A Presbyterian who studied at the University of Dublin, Penney emigrated in 1822. He became a pastor in New York and New Jersey. He served as president of Hamilton College, wrote a book on education, and had several sermons published.

Person, Peter P. (1889–after 1941)—Born in Cooperstown, New York, Person belonged to the Evangelical Covenant Church. He received an undergraduate degree from the University of Chicago, an M.A. from Northwestern University, and an Ed.D. from Harvard. He became a professor at North Park College, Chicago, and an author.

Pfefferkorn, George J. (fl. 1860s–1901)—A member of the German Evangelical Association, Pfefferkorn was a pastor in Chippewa Falls, Wisconsin.

Phillips, John (fl. 1780s and 1790s)—For a time, Phillips is known to have been a Methodist and a pastor in Charleston and, perhaps, on Long Island. He appears to have been something of a maverick in the denomination. He had a few publications to his credit, dating from the late eighteenth century.

Phipps, Lee Ralph (1878–1964)—A Methodist, Phipps was licensed to preach in 1902; he was a pastor in New Jersey and Pennsylvania. He retired in 1945.

Porter, John William (1863–1937)—Born in Somerville, Tennessee, Porter was a Southern Baptist. He studied at the University of Mississippi, Lebahan University, and the Southern Baptist Theological Seminary. Ordained in 1891, he served as a pastor in Tennessee and Kentucky.

Potts, William Stephens (1802–52)—A Presbyterian trained at Princeton Seminary, Potts became a pastor in St. Louis. He was president of Marion College in Missouri from 1835 to 1839.

Ralston, Chester Fairman (1870–1955?)—Ralston graduated from Oberlin College and Seminary. A Baptist, he was a pastor in Ohio and New York. He received honorary D.D. degrees from Colgate University and from Carson-Newman College, Jefferson City, Tennessee.

Ramay, Marion Edgar (1890–1981)—Ramay was a Baptist and earned a B.A. from Baylor University. He was educated further at Southwestern Baptist Theological Seminary and also earned a law degree. He served pastorates in Texas and Oklahoma but was known for his revivals at the church in Edmond, Oklahoma. Ramay also wrote several books on doctrinal subjects. He was president of the Baptist General Convention in 1948. Oklahoma Baptist University conferred upon him an honorary D.D.

Rice, John R. (1895–after 1959)—A Baptist, Rice graduated from Decatur Baptist College and attended Southwestern Baptist Theological Seminary. He was a pastor and evangelist. Bob Jones University awarded him an honorary D.Litt. degree in 1945.

Rogers, John (1800–1867)—Born in Clark County, Kentucky, Rogers was a member of the Church of Christ. He was a pastor in Carlisle, Kentucky, and an elder and evangelist in Ohio, Indiana, Illinois, Missouri, Virginia, Maryland, and Pennsylvania. He wrote a biography of the early nineteenth-century evangelist Barton W. Stone.

Sanford, W. L. (fl. 1890s)—Sanford was a Southern Baptist and vice president of the Baptist Young People's Union in Texas.

Scovel, Sylvester F. (1835–1910)—Scovel graduated from Hanover College and from New Albany Theological Seminary. He was a Presbyterian pastor in Indiana, Ohio, and Pennsylvania and became president of Wooster College in 1883.

Sikes, James R. (1832–95)—Born in McLeansville, North Carolina, Sikes entered the ministry in 1860 and served as a Lutheran pastor in Pennsylvania, New York, New Jersey, Ohio, and North Carolina. He died in Gibronville, North Carolina.

Sinks, Perry Wayland (1851–1940)—Sinks was a Presbyterian and a Congregationalist. He studied at Hillsdale College in Michigan as well as at Oberlin Seminary, Boston University School of Theology, and Potomac University. Ordained in 1874, he was a pastor in Florida, Ohio, Maryland, and New York. Sinks was also an author.

Smith, Florence Ethel (18??–after 1920)—A student at Moody Bible Institute in 1895, Smith was a Presbyterian. She worked as musical director with the evangelist Joel A. Smith and was also a missionary in Chile.

Tenny, Henry M. (1841–1932)—Born in Hanover, New Hampshire, Tenny was a Congregationalist. He received a B.A. from Amherst College and studied at Union Theological Seminary. He graduated from Andover Seminary in 1867. Tenny was a pastor in Massachusetts, Minnesota, and Ohio. Amherst awarded him an honorary D.D. degree.

Tilton, Charles E. (18??–19??)—Tilton was a Methodist who served as pastor of the Wesley Methodist Episcopal Church in South Boston.

Trent, John Scott (19??–after 1963)—After studying at Mississippi College, Southern Baptist Theological Seminary, and New Orleans Baptist Theological Seminary, Trent became an evangelist with the Baptist Foreign Missions and a pastor in Birmingham, Alabama. He was a Southern Baptist.

Vom Bruch, Harry W. (fl. 1920s)—Vom Bruch was a Baptist who was educated at the Moody Bible Institute in 1914. He became an evangelist.

Weigle, C. F. (1870?–19??)—His denominational affiliation is not certain, but Weigle is known to have been an evangelist active around the 1920s.

Wellman, Wendell (?–after 1969?)—Wellman was a Nazarene who was apparently an author as well as an evangelist-pastor.

Williams, Milan Bertrand (fl. 1890–1910)—An evangelist in the Midwest, Williams served as a secretary of the Young Men's Christian Association. In the 1890s he was sometimes assisted by Billy Sunday.

Wilson, Franklin (1822–96)—Trained at Brown University and Newton Theological Seminary, Wilson was a Baptist pastor in Baltimore. He edited several periodicals in the 1850s and 1860s. Wilson also served as executive secretary of the Maryland Baptist Union Association. He was awarded an honorary D.D. by Columbian College, Washington, D.C.

Winecoff, Jesse (1816–73)—Winecoff was a member of the Evangelical Lutheran Church. He was a pastor in Pennsylvania and Maryland between 1840 and 1873. He died in Lavansville, Pennsylvania.

Index

The Abominations of Modern Society (Talmadge), 195

Adams, John Quincy, 143

Addams, Jane, 293–95, 299, 301, 344

"Address on Temperance" (Channing), 167–68

An Address To Persons Of Fashion, Relating To Balls . . . (Hill), 84, 89

Adolescence (Hall), 251

adultery, 37, 50, 114, 272, 368, 389–90. *See also* Ten Commandments

Aeneas Silvius de Piccolomini (Pope Pius II), 11, 371

Aesthetic Dancing (Rath), 253

African Americans: dance opponents among, 237–38, 387; dances of, 96, 159, 180, 327, 341; education of, 86; influence of, on dance, 73, 254, 269–70, 302–3; migration of southern, to North, 236, 255, 269; at revivals, 95, 96; whites' assumptions about, 158, 162, 245–46, 274–75, 331–32, 366

Agrippa, Henri Cornelius, 13–15, 19, 39n2

Ahlstrom, Sydney E., 118, 146, 194, 200, 275–76, 321

Albigenses sect, 10, 369

"Alexander's Ragtime Band" (Berlin), 302

Allbright, William H., 245

Allen, Frederick Lewis, 268, 269, 303, 334

Allestree, Richard, 62, 88, 135

Ambrose (early church father), 13, 37

The Amendment of Life (Taffin), 29

American Antiquarian Society, 112

American Bandstand (TV program), 338

American Baptist Publication Society, 196, 231n43

The American Chesterfield, 128

American Folk Dance Society, 254

The American Ladies and Gentleman's Manual of Elegance, Fashion and True Politeness (Day), 170

American Mercury, 267, 303–4

American National Preacher, 165

American Physiological Society, 174

American Revolution, 98, 121, 377. *See also* Continental Congress

American Tract Society, 106, 121–22, 133, 165, 166, 198

Ames, William, 44nn49, 50

Amusement a Force in Christian Training (Vincent), 212

amusements: controversy concerning, in

nineteenth century, 141–42, 146–49; evils associated with, 85, 112, 117, 168, 201–5, 239, 394; kinds of, proscribed by clergy and evangelists, 94, 112, 141, 146–47, 196–97, 236, 237, 239, 261, 392, 393; laws regarding, in Philadelphia, 79, 81; among Mormons, 182–83; in the Oneida community, 182; opposition to, 111, 133–35; private, 149, 167–68, 219, 221, 241, 296; public commercial, 149, 202, 236, 243, 261, 276, 294–99, 302–14, 321, 394; and social class, 148–49, 205–7, 213, 254–55, 293–97, 305–7, 311–12; support for, 124–25, 167–77, 191n*120,* 210–25, 240. *See also* dance; dance halls; stage plays

"Amusements" (Sunday), 260

"Amusements: Their Uses and Abuses" (Johnson), 167

Anatomie of Abuses (Stubbes), 32

Anderson, Harry O., 273, 275

Andrews, C. W., 261

Andros, Governor Edmund, 64, 65

Angell, Robert Cooley, 268

Angelus Carletus de Clavasio, 7

Anglican Church, 90–91, 124–25

animals (dancers likened to). *See* dance: as absurd activity

Anson (Texas), 348

Frère Antoine Estienne Mineur, 42n*32,* 43n*35*

Antoninus de Forciglioni, 10–11

An Appeal to All Christians Especially the Members of the Methodist Episcopal Church against the Practice of Social Dancing (Jones), 197

Aragon Ballroom (Chicago), 308, 338

Arbeau, Thoinot, 20, 24, 25, 39n*2*

Arden, G. Everett, 336

The Arena, 250

Armstrong, Louis, 270, 302

"An Arrow Against Profane and Promiscuous Dancing" (I. Mather), 3–4, 47, 49–55, 59, 78, 370

"The Art of Living in London" (Peacham), 60

Asbury, Bishop Francis, 94–96

Ascham, Roger, 25, 27, 379

Ashworth, John, 206

assemblies: in colonial America, 73–82, 98, 101n*35;* condemnation of, 84–86, 89,

108, 112, 134, 386; in eighteenth-century America, 119–20, 125–27; popularity of, 96, 107, 127; rules for, 77–78, 82, 125–26, 128–29. *See also* balls

Astaire, Fred, 321–22, 326

Astesanus de Asti, 7, 8

athletic contests, 184n*6,* 257–58

Athletics and Out-Door Sports for Women (Gilbert), 250

attire, 57; and cross-dressing, 37, 80, 304; proper ballroom, 128; republicans' objections to courtly, 119–20; *women's:* as an incitement to lust, 43n*35,* 62, 68n*36,* 151–53, 204, 225, 251, 369; clergymen's lamentations about, 86, 116, 159–61, 168, 197, 204, 241, 244, 374; corsets, 130–31, 173–77, 191n*116,* 207–8, 215–18, 225, 250–51, 256, 269, 376; reform of, 178, 181, 215–16, 218, 250–51; twentieth-century changes in, 255–56, 268–69, 327–28. *See also* money

Augustana Lutherans, 336–37, 393

Augustine, 36

Aune, James, 277n*1*

automobiles. *See* cars

Azor, Juan (Azorius), 16n*13*

Backman, E. Louis, 5

Bailes, Porter Marcellus, 342, 344

Baird, Doctor, 159

Balanchine, George, 323

ballad opera, 77

ballet: in America, 184n*6,* 253, 254; in movies, 323; opposition to, 141, 241, 330; rise of, in France, 24–25; stars of, 81, 122, 141–44, 153; support for, 343

Ballet Comique de la Reine, 24

Ballroom Dance Theater, 347

ballroom dancing, 347–48, 386

ballrooms, 266–68, 307–9, 318n*29,* 337–38, 380, 384

balls: in colonial America, 65, 74, 76, 79, 82, 86, 92, 101n*35;* condemnation of, 57–59, 62–63, 84–86, 89–90, 93, 96, 108, 110–12, 134, 146, 149–52, 202–3, 386; condemnation of, as antidemocratic, 119–20, 169–70, 345, 377; as marriage market, 137n*10,* 151; musicians for, 222, 234n*86,* 247; popularity of, 96, 107, 110; public, number of, 154; rules for behavior at, 128–29, 170–73, 222–24, 243, 247–49,

270–71. *See also* assemblies; attire; money; time

Balls and Dancing Parties from the French of Abbé Hulot ("By a Young Man"), 162–63, 365, 366

Balthazar de Beaujoyeulx, 24

Baltimore (Maryland), 143, 296, 300

Bangor Theological Seminary, 111

baptismal vows (dance as violation of), 9, 10, 59, 108, 147, 377, 386

Baptists, 90, 91, 97, 118, 119, 121, 141; antidance views among, 151, 153, 154, 164, 240–41, 267, 271, 272, 320, 330, 332, 340–42, 385, 386; number of nineteenth-century, 142; training of ministers among, 138n30; on women's attire, 204

Baptist Young People's Union, 242

Barnes, Albert, 165

Bartholomew, Robb O., 299

basse danses, 12, 23, 39n2, 40n12

Bates, William Henry, 246

"Battle of the Bands" (1937), 324

Bayley, Kiah, 108, 110–13

Bayley, Mrs. Kiah, 111

Baylor University (Texas), 349–50

Bazar Book of Decorum (Tomes), 222

Beard, Thomas, 52

Beecher, Catharine, 174–77, 191n116, 250

Beecher, Henry Ward, 122, 141–43, 153–54, 174, 194, 195, 199

behavior: clergymen's emphasis on, 84–86, 92, 98, 392–93; and dance, 363; dance instructors' emphasis on, 82, 83, 106, 108–10, 145, 220, 363, 379. *See also* civility; etiquette; sin

Bellamy, Joseph, 97–98

Belsheim, Gulbrand G., 262

Benson, Norman Arthur, 64–65, 74–80

Bentham, Joseph, 60

Benton, Harry, 264–65, 345, 376

bergerette (dance), 5

Berkeley, Busby, 322

Berlin, Irving, 255, 302

Bethel College (Minnesota), 349

Beza, Theodore, 27, 29

Bible, 43n35; citations of, as antidance authority, 15, 50, 52, 54, 58–59, 66n12, 89–90, 113, 121–22; dancing mentioned in, 52, 53, 93, 122, 150, 158, 163, 215, 368, 390, 401–6; golden calf worship in, 14, 28; inerrancy of, 194, 195; lack of prohi-

bitions against dancing in, 50, 90, 115, 201, 210; Protestants' reliance on authority of, 30, 37, 53–54, 63, 112, 166, 201, 210, 345, 385, 389–92. *See also* sin(s); Ten Commandments; *names of specific biblical figures*

Biddle, Livingston, 346

Bierce, Ambrose, 202

big apple (dance), 327

big bands. *See* dance bands

Binga, A., Jr., 237–38

Bitting, Charles Carroll, 154, 160, 164, 167

Blackbirds of 1928, 270

black bottom (dance), 269, 272

The Black Crook (musical), 205, 243

Blanks, William D., 209, 231n48

Block, Frank E., 209–12

Bloomer, Amelia, 178, 191nn116, 122

Bloomfield-More, Clara, 221–24

body: movement of, as essential characteristic of dance, 172, 363; notion that mind should rule, 21, 26, 38n2, 115, 206–7, 364–67, 395; as taboo subject, 171; as temple of Holy Spirit, 27, 29, 391; working together with mind in dance, 109, 124, 251, 253, 276–77; as work of art, 22, 37, 39n5, 40n13, 52. *See also* dance; exercise; health; rest

The Boke Named The Governour (Elyot), 23, 70

Bolton, Robert, 86

Book of the Courtier (Castiglione), 21–22

Boston (Massachusetts): assemblies in, 80, 82; ballet performances in, 143; dance masters in, 47–48, 50, 64–65, 79, 82; dance schools in, 48, 54, 55, 79, 367; growing sophistication of, 63; law against stage plays in, 81, 121, 377

Boston Gazette, 65

Botticelli, Sandro, 396

Boulson, Mr. (dance master), 76, 86

Bowen, Louise deKoven, 292, 295, 296, 304

Bradford, William, 56

Bradshaw, Charles, 82

Brainard, Ingrid, 12

Brand, James, 243–44, 354n24

Brant, Sebastian, 11–12, 14

Brathwait, Richard, 61–62, 88, 135

Brattle, Thomas, 64

Braun, D. Duane, 322

"breaking in" (to dances), 257, 271

Bridenbaugh, Carl, 82, 86

A Briefe Exposition With Practicall Observa-
tions Upon the Whole Book of Ecclesiastes
(Cotton), 66n*12*
Brooke, John T., 166
Brookes, James H., 353n*15*
Brookes, Lawrence De Garmo, 218–19
Brookes on Modern Dancing (L. Brookes), 219
Brooks, Lynn Matluck, 101n*35*
brothels. *See* prostitutes
Brownell, George, 76, 78–79, 100n*34*
Buck, William Calmes, 153, 156, 163
Buckley, J. M., 237
bunny hug (dance), 328, 342
Burchenal, Elizabeth, 254
Burder, George, 125, 139n*44*
Burger, Warren, 347
Burke, Billie, 308
Bussy-Rabutin, Count Roger de, 59–60

cabarets, 255, 266, 268, 307
Cady, Edwin, 83–84
California Civic League, 306
Calloway, Cab, 270
Calvin, John, 53; on animal nature of dance,
    27, 28, 51, 188n*76*, 364, 365; antidance
    views of, 27, 43n*47*, 92; influence of, 29,
    35, 67n*16*, 385
Campbell, Robert, 320, 328, 331, 332–33,
    340
Candler, Warren A., 261
Cane Ridge (Kentucky) camp meeting, 118–
    19, 179
Capeci, Dominic J., Jr., 332
Carnegie Hall (New York City), 324, 338
Caroso, Fabritio, 24
Carpenter, Alexander. *See* Fabritius, Alex-
    ander
Carrara, John, 332
cars, 266, 268, 276, 288n*109*, 305, 312, 334
Carson, William, 195–96
Carter, Marmaduke Nathaniel, 330
Casa Loma band, 338
Castiglione, Baldassare, 21–22
Castle, Vernon and Irene, 255–57
Catherine de Medici, 24, 31
Catherine of Aragon (queen of England), 13,
    384
Catholic Church, 8, 90; number of nine-
    teenth-century members of, 142, 194; op-
    position to dance by, 3, 4, 6–10, 13–15,
    34, 59–60, 162–63, 286n*90*, 387; support

for dance by, 3, 4, 8, 16n*13*, 24–25, 29,
    34–35, 51, 158. *See also* church councils;
    church fathers
Centennial Essays: Augustana Lutheran Church
    1860–1960 (Engberg), 393
cha-cha (dance), 338
Chalif, Louis H., 253–54
Channing, William Ellery, 167–69, 212, 388
Chapman, J. Wilbur, 239–40
Chappell, Clovis G., 273, 274
Charisma and Christian Life, 350
A Charitable Remonstrance Addressed to the
    Wives and Maidens of France (Frère Anto-
    ine Estienne Mineur), 43n*35*
Charles IX, 31
Charleston (dance), 269, 272, 327, 339, 342,
    380
Charleston (South Carolina), 74, 75–77, 79,
    80, 91, 93–96, 98, 143
Charleston Assembly of Dancing and
    Cards, 77, 80
chastity, 24
Cheever, Ezekiel, 63
Chesterfield, Lord, 83–84, 96, 128, 129
Chicago (Illinois), 292–95, 300–301, 304,
    308, 309
children: at dance halls, 295, 297–99, 312;
    dancing by, 44n*47*, 52, 53, 59, 165, 221;
    education of, 70–72, 86, 88, 99n*1*; par-
    ents' duty to, precludes dancing, 30, 53,
    60, 93, 95, 108, 155, 165, 168, 345, 370.
    See also schools
Children's Festival, 5
chorus lines (female), 205–6, 343
Christian, Francis, 75
Christian Church, 341
Christians: as dance opponents' audience,
    386–87; dancing's unlawfulness for, 4, 52–
    53, 96, 108, 141, 239, 240, 262, 344,
    345, 386; ideals for, 20, 28, 37–38, 61–
    64, 112, 165–67, 224, 364, 381–82, 385,
    392; and morality, 379; tensions between
    ideals for gentlemen and for, 70–105, 107,
    239, 364, 365
The Christian's Relation to Amusements and the
    World (Chapman), 240
Chrysostom, John, 9
Chumbley, Charles, 343
church councils, 4, 5, 9
church discipline, 53, 168–69, 196, 209–10,
    231nn*48, 49,* 237, 387

churches: changing history of American, 394; membership in nineteenth-century, 142; problems of twentieth-century, 341. *See also* Christians; church discipline; church fathers; clergy; Reformed churches; *specific denominations*
church fathers, 43n35, 166; dance opposition from, 4, 15n4, 158, 373
Church of Christ, 155
Church of Jesus Christ of Latter-day Saints. *See* Mormons
Cicero, 23, 109; on dance as absurd activity, 11, 13, 28, 51, 158, 163, 246, 364, 365, 395
cities: dance's association with, 32, 73, 83, 142–43, 194–97, 236; factors in rise of dance in, 63, 64, 107, 283n65; neighborhood social gatherings in, 298–99; and rise of dance in Renaissance Europe, 13; size of population living in, 301; and urban evangelism, 240–47. *See also* ballrooms; dance halls; urban reformers
"Citizen of Washington," 169–71
City Recreation Committee (New York City), 305
civility, 70–72, 75, 174; associated with dance instruction, 82, 83, 106, 108–10, 145, 220, 363, 379; as means of social control, 222; and morality, 248–49, 379; and social class, 70–73, 177–78, 225, 247. *See also* behavior
Civil War, 163–64, 193
Clark, Russell, 348
Clarke, Dr. Edward, 216
class. *See* social class
Cleate, Charles, 48
Clendenen, F. Leslie, 255
clergy: amusements proscribed by, 94, 112, 141, 146–47, 196–97, 236, 237, 239, 261, 392, 393; as authors of etiquette books, 128; critics of, 167–77; fears of, 394–95; gender of, 373, 387, 394–95; kinds of dancing opposed by, 386; lack of first-hand knowledge of dance by, 4, 89, 150, 156, 202, 272, 366, 383–84; lamentations about women's attire by, 86, 116, 159–61, 168, 197, 204, 241, 244, 374; prodance views of, 213–15, 276–77, 387–89; social class of, 384, 387. *See also* dance opponents; evangelists; money; piety; sin(s); time; *names of specific denominations and clergymen*

Clericus. *See* Thacher, George Hornell
Clete, Charles, 48
Cleveland (Ohio), 297, 299, 304–5
"closed dance halls." *See* dance halls: "taxi" or "closed"
Coke, Bishop Thomas, 94
Cole, Charles C., 142
A Collection of the Newest Cotillions and Country Dances (Griffiths), 83
College Pamphlets (Yale), 125
Collier, James Lincoln, 324
Collier's magazine, 309, 335, 336
colonial American dance, 82–90
Commager, Henry Steele, 142
Commercialized Prostitution in New York City, 297
Committee of Fourteen (New York City), 311
A Complete Christian Dictionary (Ravanel), 44n50
The Complete Gentleman (Peacham), 60
"The Conception of the Christian Life Prevailing in the Presbyterian Churches . . ." (Blanks), 209
Concerning the Use and Abuse of Dauncing (Le Maçon), 31
"concert halls," 297
"concert saloons," 206, 230n37
confession, 6–8
conga (dance), 327–29, 335
Congregationalists, 112; antidance views of, 106, 111, 114, 118, 119, 121, 122, 133–36, 141, 146–47, 155, 243–45, 385; dance supporters among, 148–49, 208, 346, 388; decline in dance opposition by, 261, 271; number of nineteenth-century, 142
Congress, 143
conservatism: and antidance opposition. *See* evangelists: conservative
Continental Congress, 80–81, 121, 377. *See also* American Revolution
contraceptives, 334
contra-dances, 82
conversion(s) (personal): of dance masters, 86; goals of, 114, 166, 377; by Samuel P. Jones, 238; as path to reformation, 265–66, 275, 385–86; Billy Sunday's, 258, 260
Conway, E. H., 126–27
Cooke, Maud, 248, 379
Coplande, Robert, 22

Corning, James L., 168, 169

Correct Social Usage, 248

cotillion (dance), 82, 100n*24,* 108, 126–27, 144, 234n*86,* 239

Cotton, John, 49, 51–52, 64, 66n*12,* 375

Cotton Club (Harlem), 270

Count Basie, 324

country dancing, 73, 76, 77, 80, 82, 108, 239, 365; as figure dances, 100n*24,* 126–27, 144; social class associated with, 13, 21

courtesy manuals: aesthetic emphasis in, 37–38, 123–25, 130, 374, 378; anti-dance views in, 29, 60–62; as influence on American etiquette books, 135; prodance attitudes of, 20–25, 27; rules for women in, 365. *See also* civility; dance manuals; etiquette

courtly dancing, 6, 12–14, 21–25, 365–66, 379, 380

Crane, Jonathan Townley, 150, 152–53, 159–60, 163, 197, 201–2, 206, 369

Crease, Robert P., 353n*15*

Cremin, Lawrence, 61, 62

Cressey, Paul G., 309–11, 315

Cromwell, Oliver, 56

Crowley, Robert, 33–34

"Cult of True Womanhood," 332–33

Cultural Post (National Endowment for the Arts), 346

Cuyler, Theodore Ledyard, 147–48

Dailey, Frank, 308

Dall, Caroline, 228n*29*

Dallington, Sir Robert, 29–30

Dallman, William, 241, 262, 369

dance: as absurd activity, 11–14, 27–36, 50–51, 158, 162–63, 245–46, 364, 365, 367, 395; abuses of, not an argument for its abolition, 26, 35, 41n*17,* 125, 211–12, 293; abuses of, so serious as to require abolition of, 28–29, 35, 210–11, 388; as addictive, 95, 239, 263, 273, 369; associated with worship, 5, 117–19, 152, 179–82, 215, 276–77, 345–46, 350–51, 388; behavior associated with, 5, 24, 28, 35, 49, 154, 239; church discipline for those who practice, 53, 168–69, 196, 209–10, 231nn*48, 49,* 237, 387; criticized for its origins, 157–59, 162, 211, 342, 343, 373; critics' lack of first-hand knowledge of, 4, 89,

150, 156, 202, 272, 366, 383–84; disorderly, 5, 13–14, 27–35, 38, 117–19, 180, 364–66; essential characteristics of, 172, 363; exposure to, by touring companies, 339–40, 346–47; as expressive art, 249–53, 261, 276–77, 345–46, 388, 389, 395–96; as first of progressively worse sins, 111, 167, 202–3, 241, 331, 333–34, 343–44, 348, 369, 389, 394; as graceful activity, 12, 19, 20–25, 38, 106, 122–27, 144–45, 321–23, 379–80, 395–96; as leisure activity, 7, 12, 21, 32, 36, 58, 95, 107, 123, 148–49, 162, 167–68, 275–76, 293–94, 300, 302, 311–12, 315, 363, 379, 381; life too serious for, 34, 47, 51, 54, 91–92, 95–96, 136, 163–64, 166, 364, 375; linked to rioting and reveling, 50, 59, 263, 364–65; miles covered by an evening's, 264, 275, 344, 376; as mindless exercise, 106, 111, 113, 118–19, 158–59, 161–62, 245–46, 264, 274, 331–32, 342, 366–67, 375, 395; in the movies, 321–23; as offense against church sacraments, 9, 10, 37, 59, 108, 147, 386; origins of, 214, 220; as personal freedom, 210, 211–25; popularity of, 96, 107–10, 126–27, 193, 220, 222, 237, 254–55, 268–72, 276, 294–99, 303–9, 317n*11,* 325–28, 386, 388; prevention of unlawful pleasures by tolerating, 168, 355n*35;* prohibited with Indians, 55, 371; prudence to be learned from, 23–24, 70, 72, 219; in Puritan New England, 48, 54, 55–56; sexual immorality associated with, 364, 367–73, 394, according to pre-twentieth-century sources, 4, 7–8, 13–15, 27–33, 57, 93, 151–53, 201–5, according to twentieth-century sources, 242–44, 262, 268, 272–75, 295, 296, 303, 329–32, 341, 343–44, 351, 367–68; social value of, 70–72, 109, 122–25, 215, 251, 265, 374, 378, 379, 382, 387–89; study of, as art form, 249–54, 276, 340, 346–47. *See also* assemblies; balls; country dancing; courtly dancing; dance opponents; folk dancing; mixed dancing; "round dances"; square dances; stage plays: dancing associated with; *names of specific dances*

The Dance (Dallman), 262

The Dance, the Card Table, the Theatre, and the Wine Cup (Kerr), 237

dance "academies," 292, 296–98, 307, 314

"The Dance and The Revival" (Wilson), 166
dance bands, 237, 266, 314, 322, 323, 325, 337, 380
dance floors, 255
dance halls: commercial, 167–68, 228n26, 254, 255, 266, 292–315, 316n2, 371–72; conditions in, 264, 295, 296, 299, 304, 371–72; criminal interests involved in, 295, 311; early, 386; endurance dancing in, 312–14; opposition to, 237, 240–41, 292–319; popularity of, 276, 294–99, 304–9, 317n11, 386; progression of evils associated with, 202, 274, 303–4, 309–11; regulation of, 293, 299, 302–7, 311–12, 314–15, 316n2, 317n16, 372; social class associated with, 243, 279n24, 293–95; "taxi" or "closed," 307, 309–12, 315, 371. See also ballrooms
Dance Mad (Clendenen), 255
dance manuals: advent of, 6, 12, 379; as guides to etiquette, 108–10, 144–45, 220, 365–66, 379, 380; importance of, 21; owned by dance masters, 74; as research source, 22–25, 126, 144; and spread of dancing, 107; twentieth-century, 253–56. See also courtesy manuals; specific titles
dance marathons, 312–14
dance masters: advent of, 6, 12, 374; character of, 53–55, 96, 122–24, 155–56, 205, 244, 245, 296, 367, 370–71; as church organists, 47–48; conversion of, 86; as dance opponents, 262–63; emphasis of, 82–90, 108–10, 126–27, 144–45, 218–20, 249, 365, 379; female, 74, 75; French, 48, 82, 155–56, 238, 244–45, 371; importance of, 21, 71; increase in, 57–58, 64, 73–76, 78–80, 82–85, 108; itinerant, 74–75, 107; no need for, for popular dances, 339, 380; and regulation of dance halls, 305. See also dance manuals; dance schools; specific individuals
The Dance of Death (Bierce), 202
The Dance of Death, Should Christians Indulge? (Straton), 267
The Dance of Society (DeGarmo), 219
dance opponents: biographical information on American, 413–22; biographical information on European, 407–12; blindness of, to dance aesthetics, 383–89; characteristics of American, 364–68, 394; decrease in, 321, 348; decrease in, during social cri-

ses, 98, 126, 193, 320–21, 352n2, 377; in eighteenth-century, 96–98; European, 3–18; factors in spread of, 44n50; mid- to late twentieth-century, 328–37, 348–49; number of works by, 226n1, 261, 277n4, 285n86, 289n119, 340–41; patriotic appeals by, 119–22, 169–70, 258–61, 264, 272, 331, 370, 376–77; themes of, 146–65, 363–82; urban reformers as, 292–93; women as, 113, 154, 263–64. See also clergy; dance; evangelists
"dance palaces," 307–9, 318n29, 337–38, 384. See also ballrooms
dance schools: behavior in, 109–10; closing of, in Concord, 122–23; increase in, 64, 75, 82; opposition to, 13, 32–33, 63, 367; proposed laws to prohibit, 266; spread of, 107–10; twentieth-century, 255, 314, 325–26. See also dance "academies"; dance masters; etiquette
Dancing (Texas Baptist General Convention), 344
Dancing, as a Social Amusement (American Tract Society), 165
Dancing: Social Dancing for Purposes of Amusement (anonymous), 231n43
"Dancing Exploded" (Hart), 91–94
Daneau, Lambert, 27–29, 36, 38, 51, 188n76, 364, 365
"Dates for Defense," 335
Davies, Sir John, 20–21, 23–24, 396
Davis, Michael D., 294–99, 305, 307
Day, Charles William, 170–71
Decca Records, 325
Deering, Thomas, 80
DeGarmo, William B., 219
DeHoney, J. Harvey, 290n128
Delsartean system (of physical culture), 249
De Mille, Agnes, 323
Denishawn Company, 283n65
Department of Labor, 311–12
Dering, William, 74
DeSainliens, Claude. See Holyband, Claudius
Desroche, Henri, 179
Destructorium Vitiorum (Fabritius), 9
devil: as associated with amusements, 85, 147; as associated with dancing, 9–10, 13, 27, 51, 59, 61, 92, 108, 373, 377
The Devil in Modern Society (Lowber), 261–62
"The Devil's Dance Dens" (Kennedy), 309

Devine's Million Dollar Ballroom (Milwaukee), 308
Dialogue agaynst light, lewde, and lascivious dauncing (Fetherston), 34
Dialogue Between Custom and Veritie (Lovell), 35
Dillon, John, 316n7
Dirty Dancing (movie), 348
Disciples of Christ, 141, 207, 264, 271, 341, 343, 385
"A Discourse on the Immoral Tendency of Theatrical Amusements" (Jeter), 120–21
The Divine Dramatist (Stout), 86
divorce: as associated with dance, 202, 240–42, 262, 272, 274, 334, 369; statistics on, 258, 271, 334
The Doctrine of the Lord's Supper . . . (Gross), 232n61
Dodworth, Allen, 219–21, 234n86, 379, 380
Domino, Fats, 338
Dorsey brothers, 324, 338
Down Beat, 324
dress. *See* attire
drinking: as associated with dance, 111, 151, 156–57, 167, 203, 223, 244, 372; breaking of link between dancing and, 315; and dance halls, 295, 296, 298, 299, 302–4, 311, 372. *See also* temperance
Duncan, Isadora, 253, 388
Durang, Charles, 145
Durang, John, 81
Durang's Terpsichore (C. Durang), 145
Dutch Calvinists, 90
Dye, William Milburn, 263

Eastman, Charles S., 197, 202, 207
Eddy, Daniel Clarke, 173
education: of children, 70–72, 86, 88, 99n1; dance an important part of, 106; of females, 113, 130, 137n15, 221. *See also* schools
Edwards, Jonathan, 56, 97, 98, 164, 238
Edwards, Richard Henry, 264, 317n11
Elizabeth I (queen of England), 19, 25, 31, 35
Ellington, Duke, 270, 324, 338
Elssler, Fanny, 122, 141–44, 153
Elyot, Sir Thomas, 70; as dance supporter, 19–20, 23, 25, 27, 37, 219, 379
Emerson, Ralph Waldo, 143
Emmons, Nathanael, 97, 111, 112

Encyclopaedia: Or, A Dictionary of Arts, Sciences and Miscellaneous Literature, 101n39, 123
Encyclopaedia Britannica, 232n61, 276, 343
Encyclopaedia of Etiquette (Holt), 270–71
Encyclopedia Americana, 101n39, 127, 232n65, 345
endurance dancing, 312–14
Engberg, Emmer E., 393
Engelbrecht, Barbara, 308
The English Gentleman (Brathwait), 61, 62
The English Gentlewoman (Brathwait), 61–62, 135
Enstone, Edward, 64–65, 76, 82
Episcopalians, 122, 141, 147, 158, 212, 248–49, 276, 385
Essay on Dancing (anonymous), 113
Essex, John, 74
Estienne, François, 27, 29
Etiquette at Washington ("Citizen of Washington"), 169–70, 176
etiquette books: authors of, 128; on clergy at balls, 384; code of behavior for dances in, 154, 220–25, 243, 247–49, 270–71, 307, 379, 381–82; numbers of, 127–28, 170, 280n40, 289n116; prodance attitudes of, 108–10, 125, 127–35, 169–77, 220–24, 374, 378; on public balls, 154; as research source, 144
Etiquette for Americans ("By a Woman of Fashion"), 281n43
The Evangelist, 350–51
"evangelistic clergyman" (revivalist style), 238, 239–41, 261
evangelists: conservative, 194, 198–209, 225, 258–61, 271–75, 320, 385–88; goals of, 236; liberal, 194, 210–25, 275, 320, 386, 387–89; themes of, 96–98, 242, 261, 363–82; urban mission of, 240–47. *See also* clergy
Eve (biblical figure), 61, 369
Everett, Eugenia, 249
"Everybody's Doin' It Now" (song), 255
excursion boats, 297
exercise, 376; dancing as, 150; recommended for nineteenth-century women, 131, 134–35, 160, 175, 190n116, 216, 225; recommended for renaissance women, 22; for twentieth-century women, 250, 275. *See also* dance; health; physical culture; rest
The Exploitation of Pleasure (Davis), 295–96
Exxon, 347

Fabritius, Alexander, 9, 377
fad dances, 269, 328, 339, 380
Fairhead, George, 355n35
Familiar dialogues on dancing, between a minister and a dancer (Phillips), 94, 95
Farrar, Eliza, 131–32
Farrer, L. E., 31
"Fashionable Amusements" (Bayley), 108, 110
Fashionable Amusements (anonymous), 112–13
Fass, Paula, 270
Faulkner, T. A., 262–63, 273–74, 286n90, 330, 344, 354n24
Fenner, Dudley, 36, 43n47, 44n50
"fervent exhorter" (revivalist style), 238–39, 258, 261, 342
Festival of Fools, 5
Fetherston, Christopher, 33, 34–35, 91, 95, 199, 375, 377
A Few Reflections upon the Fancy Ball, Otherwise Known as the City Dancing Assembly ("A Representative of Thousands"), 119–20
Field, John, 34
Field, Richard, 42n32
Fighting the Devil in Modern Babylon (Straton), 267, 275
Finney, Charles Grandison, 115–17, 181, 199–200, 208, 214, 378
The First Gentlemen of Virginia (Wright), 73
fish (dance), 339
Fishwick, Marshall, 339
Flagg and Gould (printers), 112
Flashdance (movie), 348
folk dancing, 6, 251–52, 254, 261, 277, 329, 349, 365
Footloose (movie), 348
Fortune magazine, 334
Foster, Gustavus L., 146–47, 157, 167
foxtrot (dance), 326, 327, 335, 342, 343
France. *See* dance masters: French; Paris
Frank Dailey's Meadowbrook Ballroom, 308
Frederick III (German ruler), 11
The French Littelton (Holyband), 31–32
French Reformed church, 29, 53, 67n16, 209
frequency (of dancing), 7, 8
Fritz, John H., 329
From Dance Hall to White Slavery (Dillon and Lytle), 295

From the Ball Room to Hell (Faulkner), 262–63
frontier: evangelizing of, 117–19, 179–80; expansion of, 142
Frothingham, Octavius Brookes, 213
Fuller, Loie ("La Loie"), 278n15
Fuller, Margaret, 143

Galbraith, Dr. Anna Mary, 250
Gale, George W., 115
Galen, 219
Gallini, Andrea, 123
gambling, 31
Gardie, Anna, 81
Gardner, Ella, 311–12
Garnett, Mrs. F. E., 154, 160, 161–62, 367
Gaskin, Jesse Marvin, 330, 331–32
Gaynor, William J., 302
gender issues (in dance), 363. *See also* clergy; men; women
The Gentleman in America (Cady), 83–84
The Gentleman's Calling (Allestree), 62
gentlemen. *See* men: ideals for; social class
George Whitefield's Journals, 1737–1741 (ed. Davis), 84, 86
German (dance), 222, 234n86
Gershwin, George, 322
Gilbert, Melvin Ballou, 249–50, 252
Girls Conference (Pittsburgh), 306–7
Girls Protective Council, 313
Gladden, Washington, 193, 211–14, 219–21, 293, 388, 393
A godly exhortation (Field), 34
Good Form for All Occasions (Hall), 256–57
Goodman, Benny, 323–26, 338
Good Manners (Lavin), 223
Good Manners a Fine Art (Huntington), 248–49
Goodsell, Dana, 135–36, 164
Gosson, Stephen, 32
grace. *See* dance: as graceful activity; Three Graces
Graebner, Theodore, 329–30, 341, 343
Graffenried, Madame Barbara de, 74
Graham, Billy, 286n92
Graham, Sylvester, 178
Gray, Glen, 338
Great Awakening, 84–86, 98, 373, 377, 385. *See also* Second Great Awakening
Great Depression, 314, 321, 322, 334, 340
Greeley, Horace, 180

Green, Joseph, 56
Green, Samuel, 49
Gridley, Samuel, 222
Griffiths, John, 82, 83
grizzly bear (dance), 254, 255, 380
Gross, Joseph B., 213–15, 219, 232n*61*, 276, 388
Guernsey, Jesse, 155, 156–57, 162
A Guide to Politeness (Nichols), 108–10, 126
"The Guilt of Taking Pleasure in Other Men's Sins" (Emmons), 137n*10*
Gulick, Dr. Luther Halsey, 251–54, 265, 276, 301
Guthrie, William Norman, 215, 276–77, 346, 388

The Habits of Good Society (anonymous), 172–73
Hackett, Theobald, 100n*34*
Hale, Edward Everett, 148–49; on publicly supported recreation, 169, 210, 213, 265, 293
Hale, Sarah Josepha, 220–22, 225
Haley, Bill, 338
Hall, Florence Marion Howe, 222, 223, 256–57
Hall, G. Stanley, 236, 250–52, 276
Hall, George F., 242–44
Hallam, Sarah, 75
Hallam Company (of England), 75, 77
Ham, Mordecai F., 263, 273
Hamilton, William Wistar, 243, 244, 246
Hammet, William, 94
Hampton, Lionel, 324
Hanaw, M. S., 296, 299, 300
Hanson, Oscar, 331
Harlem (New York City), 269–70. *See also* Savoy Ballroom
Harlem Blues and Jazz Band, 347
Harper's Weekly, 303
Harris, Louis, 347
Harry Hill's Dance-House, 228n*26*
Hart, Oliver, 91–94, 96, 97, 372, 374
Hartford (Connecticut), 82, 126
Hartley, Florence, 176
Harvard University, 249
Hawley, Bostwick, 206–7
Haydn, Hiram Collins, 198, 203, 242, 273, 354n*24*
Haynes, Rowland, 297–98, 300
health: of Africans, 250; dance as bad for, 25, 28, 33, 95, 142, 160–61, 176–77, 207–8,

217, 245, 262, 263–64, 275, 344, 375–76; dance as good for, 26–27, 38, 109, 127, 130–32, 145, 193, 215, 219, 225, 249–52, 256, 388–89; dance halls' threat to, 295, 296, 299, 304, 371–72; practices regarding, 215–18; of "uncivilized" people, 250–51. *See also* attire; exercise; rest
Health and Strength for Girls (Safford), 216
The Healthful Art of Dancing (Gulick), 252
Heckman, George C., 205, 207
Henderson, Fletcher, 324
Henkle, Moses M., 151, 156, 158, 162, 366
Henry, Thomas Charlton, 114–15, 119
Henry VIII (king of England), 13, 19, 38n*2*
Herbert, Lord (of Cherbury), 129–31
Herod (biblical king), 6
Herodias (biblical queen), 5–6, 52, 152
Hill, Sir Richard, 84, 89, 96
History of the Doctrine and Discipline of the Waldenses (Perrin), 9–10
Histrio-Mastix (Prynne), 3–5
Hitler, Adolf, 321
Hobbs, A. G., Jr., 328
Hobson, Barbara Meil, 154, 229n*28*, 230n*35*
Hofstadter, Richard, 195, 237, 258, 260
Hogrefe, Pearl, 38n*2*
Hollywood. *See* movies
Holt, Emily, 270–71
Holyband, Claudius, 31–32, 43n*35*
"honky-tonks," 206
hornpipe (dance), 82
Howe, Julia Ward, 222
How to Behave, 176
Hughes, Langston, 327
Hughes, Bishop Matthew Simpson, 264
Huguenots, 31
Huizinga, John, 10
Hulot, Henri-Louis, 162–63, 365, 366
humanist traditions, 11–13
Humphrey, Don, 343, 344
Hunt, Dr. Marion Palmer, 245–46, 366
Huntington, Frederic Dan, 248–49
Hygiene and Physical Culture for Women (Galbraith), 250
Hyperius, Andreas Gerardus, 30, 53, 390

Ide, Jacob, 110–13, 119, 374
Ide, Mary Emmons, 111
illegitimate births (as associated with dance), 159, 274, 333

immigrants: acculturation of, 296, 300; to Charleston, 76; dance masters characterized as, 155–56; effects of, on denominational growth, 142, 261; health of women, 218; numbers of, 316n3; and prostitution, 228n29, 290n122; scorn for, 239; social heritage of, 252; and urbanization, 194, 223, 236, 293. See also folk dancing
incest, 263, 273
Indians. See Native Americans
"Innocent Amusements" (Finney), 117, 199 200
insanity, 263, 369
Instruction of a christen woman (Vives), 13
International Conference of the Worship Symposium, 350
Isaac, Rhys, 73, 75, 97
Isaiah (biblical figure), 49
Israels, Belle, 297, 300, 305, 309, 316n2, 317n16

Jackson, Andrew, 384
Jackson, James Caleb, 217
James, Harry, 322, 336, 338
Janes, Don Carlos, 242
Jansenists, 60
Jarrett, Bede, 5
jazz, 266, 267, 302–3, 323–24, 337, 372
The Jazz Singer (movie), 267
Jazz Tap Ensemble, 347
Jeremiah (biblical figure), 47, 49
Jesuit stage plays, 24–25, 60
Jeter, Jeremiah Bell, 120–21, 377
Jews, 387
jig (dance), 73, 82, 85
jitterbug (dance), 325, 327, 335–37, 339, 342, 343, 350, 367
"Jive Bombers' Jamboree," 336
John de Burgh, 8
Johnson, Oliver, 167, 169
John the Baptist (biblical figure), 6, 52, 158, 231n46, 330
Jolson, Al, 267
Jones, Clara J., 333
Jones, John G., 197
Jones, Samuel Porter, 238–40, 342
Joplin, Scott, 302
Journal of Social Hygiene, 313
JPA. See Juvenile Protection Association
jukeboxes, 325
Junius, Francis, 50

Juvenal, 50, 161
Juvenile Protection Association (Chicago), 292–95, 304, 309

Kansas City (Missouri), 297–99
KDKA (radio station), 267
Kean, Thomas, 80, 81
Keller, Kate Van Winkel, 100n24
Kennedy, John B., 309
Kerr, Robert P., 237, 275
Kisselgoff, Anna, 347
Krauth, Charles Porterfield, 159, 160–61, 232n61
Krazas brothers, 308
Kretzmann, Paul E., 329, 332, 356n46
Krupa, Gene, 338

Ladies and Gentlemen's American Etiquette (anonymous), 128
The Ladies Calling (Allestree), 62, 135
Ladies' Home Journal, 250, 295
Ladies' Vase, 173, 175–76
lady (ideal). See social class; women: ideals for
Lady's Guide (Thornwell), 175–76
Lambin, Maria Ward, 296, 305, 309
Lamphear, Guy A., 274
Lancaster (Pennsylvania), 101n35
Lane, Harley, 344–45
Lauro (bassadanza), 40n12
Lavin, Eliza, 223
la volta (dance), 25
Lawful Amusements (Burder), 138n30
Law Gospelized; Or An Address To All Christians Concerning Holiness of Heart and Life (Whitefield), 86–89
laws: against dancing, 55–56, 80–81, 266, 348; against stage plays, 81–82, 121, 377; amusement, in Philadelphia, 79, 80–81, 377; requiring physical education in schools, 276
Laws (Plato), 364
The Laws of Etiquette (anonymous), 129
The Laws of Life, 217
Lectures to Young Men on Various Important Subjects (H. W. Beecher), 194
Le Jeune, Father, 59
Le Maçon, Robert, 31
Leslie, Eliza, 172
Let's Dance (radio program), 323
Letters on Practical Subjects, to a Daughter (Sprague), 133–34

Letters to the People on Health and Happiness (C. Beecher), 174

Levingston, William, 74

Lewis, Dio, 216, 217–18, 231n43, 250

Liberty University (Virginia), 349

Life magazine, 308, 327

Lindbergh, Charles, 266

Lindwall, Carl Axel, 336–37

"Lindy-hop" (dance), 266, 326, 327, 337, 339, 343, 347, 353n15, 367, 380

Literary Digest, 305–6, 309, 311, 312, 314, 325–26

Litfin, Duane, 350

Loci Communes, 30, 390

Locke, John, 70–72, 83, 96, 130, 131, 214

Lombardo, Guy, 267, 324, 338

Longfellow, Henry Wadsworth, 153

Lorenzo de Medici, 40n12

los seizes (dance), 5

Lovell, Sir Thomas, 33–35

Lowber, James William, 207, 261–62

Luther, Martin, 125, 385; burning of Catholic documents by, 7; dance opponents' citing of, 201; on grace, 395; tolerance of some dances by, 35, 36, 41n17, 44n47, 201, 215, 388; on turning dances, 25, 201, 388

Lutheran Customs (Carter), 330

Lutheran Herald, 333

Lutherans, 90, 141; dance opposition by, 154, 159, 199, 200–201, 208, 261, 262, 320, 332, 341, 385, 386; dance supporters among, 213–15, 336; Missouri Synod of, 228n22, 241, 329–30, 341, 343; Norwegian, 320, 331; number of nineteenth-century, 142, 200; Swedish, 79, 336–37, 393

Luther League. *See* Young People's Luther League

Lyman, William, 107–8, 112

Lyon, Mary, 190n116

Lytle, H. W., 316n7

magazines, 268

Magnalia Christi Americana (C. Mather), 57, 63, 64

Le Maitre de Danse or, The Art of Dancing Cotillions (Conway), 126–27

Mama Lu Parks Lindy-hoppers, 347

manners. *See* civility; courtesy manuals; etiquette books

Manners (S. J. Hale), 221

Manners and Customs of To-Day (Maxwell), 247

Manners and Social Usages (Sherwood), 221, 222

The Manner To Dance Bace Dances (Coplande), 22–24

A Manual of Politeness (anonymous), 131

manuals of pastoral care, 8–9

Marbury, Elizabeth, 256

marriage: dancing at celebrations of, 28, 52, 55, 56, 82, 201; mixed dancing as signifying, 20, 23–24; Noyes's views of, 180–81; as substitute for dance, 202, 273, 330; Sunday's view of, 259–60. *See also* divorce; men; women

Martin, Carol, 313–14

Martin, John, 326–27, 334–35, 339

Martinez, Homer, 342, 344

Mary, Queen of Scots, 31

Mason, Gregory, 267, 303–4

masquerades, 149, 248, 273, 304

Massachusetts Bay Colony, 55

Mather, Cotton: antidance views of, 56–60, 62–63, 96; on authorship of "Arrow Against Profane and Promiscuous Dancing," 49; on balls, 57–60; "Cloud of Witnesses" sermon by, 57–60, 91; lack of firsthand dance experience of, 383; literary style of, 90, 110; on singing, 64

Mather, Increase, 11, 29, 58, 66n8, 366, 367; antidance views of, 3–4, 8–9, 11, 13, 47, 49–55, 62–63, 78, 96, 364, 370, 375, 377, 378; "cloud of witnesses" cited by, 35–38, 58–59; on devil's association with dancing, 10, 92, 373; on education, 70, 72, 95; lack of first-hand dance experience of, 383; literary style of, 90, 110; on mixed dancing, 4, 20, 48–50, 52–54, 63, 365

Mattison, Hiram, 196, 207

Maxwell, Peter, 347

Maxwell, Sara B., 247

May poles, 49, 56, 79

mazurka (dance), 344

Mazzeo, Joseph A., 39n5

McDonald, John, 150

McIlvaine, Charles P., 122

Mackaye, Steele, 281n49

McLoughlin, William G., on evangelists, 117, 195, 238–40, 260, 265–66, 385–86

McNeil, John T., 16n6

Meade, Bishop William, 147, 158, 369

medieval traditions, 5–11
*The Memorial History of Hartford County,
   Connecticut, 1633–1884* (Trumbull), 126
men: as antidance leaders, 373, 387, 394–95;
   concerns about dance as undermining virtue of, 11, 141, 153–54, 157, 263, 272;
   dancing as part of training for gentle-, 62,
   70–72, 83, 96, 107, 109, 123, 128–29,
   265; effeminacy of, associated with dancing, 5, 9, 33, 372–73; of fashion *vs.* true
   gentlemen, 129, 135, 155, 178, 373; fears
   about undesirable, at balls, 151–55, 205,
   225, 244, 257, 371; ideals for, 20–22, 25,
   37–38, 59, 64, 83–84, 96, 128–29, 379,
   381, 384; lack of dance familiarity by
   American, 384; rules for dancing of, with
   their wives, 129, 171, 242; tensions between ideal for Christians and ideal for
   gentle-, 70–105, 107, 239, 364, 365
Merrill, Thomas F., 36
Mesick, John F., 151, 155, 156, 161, 165
Mesquite (Texas), 348
Methodists, 90, 118; on amusements, 237;
   amusements among, 196; antidance views
   among, 94, 141, 150, 151, 261, 264, 271,
   385; number of nineteenth-century, 142;
   opposition to views of, 125; support for
   dance in worship by, 346; training of ministers among, 119, 138n30
Metronome, 324
Michel, Artur, 25
Middlesex Gazette, 123
Miller, Glenn, 322, 337, 350
Mills, Irving, 320
Milwaukee (Wisconsin), 297–300, 308
mind. *See* body
Minns, Albert, 353n15
minstrelsy: blackface, 143–44, 186n42; medieval, 6
minuet (dance), 73, 77, 82, 380
Miss Leslie's Behaviour Book (Leslie), 172
Mitchell, Dr. Silas Weir, 217, 250
Mix, Ruth, 313
mixed dancing: church fathers' opposition to,
   5, 9; in community recreation programs,
   265, 301–2; mid-twentieth-century opposition to, 329, 341, 343, 348–49; nineteenth-century opposition to, 134, 149–
   53; partner no longer important in, 269,
   337, 339, 341; seventeenth-century opposition to, 4, 20, 37, 44n47, 48–50, 52–54,

57, 60, 63, 365; support for, 148. *See also*
   "modern dance"; "round dances"; schools
Mobil, 347
modern dance, 283n65
"modern dance" (dance opponents' phrase),
   241, 262, 271–75, 341–43, 367–68, 386
The Modern Dance on Trial (Gaskin), 330
Modern Dancing (Bitting), 154, 167
Modern Dancing (Mr. and Mrs. Vernon Castle), 256
Modern Evils (Campbell), 320
Modern Refinement (Lyman), 107–8
money (question of dance as wise use of), 92,
   93, 108, 110, 112–13, 120, 135, 159–60,
   197, 204, 208, 245, 330, 373–74, 381
monkey (dance), 339
Moody, Dwight Lyman, 195, 238, 239
Moore, Frank, 91
morality: code of, as antidance feature, 392–
   94; relation between manners and, 248–
   49, 379
morality plays (medieval), 5–6
moral reform societies, 112, 230n35
Moravians, 79, 90
More, Hannah, 113, 135, 137n15
Morison, Samuel Eliot, 142
Morley, John H., 207
Mormons, 178, 182–83
Morris, Melvin, 273, 274
Morris, Thomas Asbury, 158, 166
Morton, Thomas, 56
Moskowitz, Belle Israels. *See* Israels, Belle
motives (as factor in dancing's sinfulness), 7,
   8, 125, 172–73, 199–200, 210, 256, 351
Moulton, Robert, 352n6
Mount Vernon (Virginia), 75
movies, 236, 257, 266, 268, 276, 334; dance
   marathons perceived as threat to, 314;
   dancing in, 267, 276, 321–23, 326, 348,
   352n6; opposition to, 330
Mulcaster, Richard, 25–28, 35, 125, 215, 379
Mumford, Ethel, 303
murder, 272, 334, 369
Murray, Arthur, 314, 325–27, 338, 371
Murray, Katharine, 338
Murray, Walter, 80, 81
musicals, 205, 270, 321–23, 326, 352n6. *See
   also* movies: dancing in
My Daughter's Manual (anonymous), 132–33

Nashville (Tennessee), 238

National Association of Schools of Dance, 347
National Endowment for the Arts, 339–40, 346
National Synod at Dort (1578), 53
Native Americans: dance prohibited between colonists and, 55–56, 371; dances of, 180; health of women, 218; no antidance materials aimed at, 387; teaching of country dances to, 76
Nazarenes, 341
Neill, Edward Duffield, 152, 162
Newcomb, Harvey, 134–35
New England Female Reform Society, 230n35
New England Tract Society, 112, 113, 122
New London (Connecticut), 82
New Orleans (Louisiana), 143
Newport (Rhode Island), 82
Newsweek, 347, 348
"New Woman," 255–60, 268, 270, 307, 370
New York City, 78–79; ballet performances in, 143; dance halls in, 295–98, 305–6, 311; dance palaces in, 307–8; dance schools in, 325; Harlem, 269–70; recreation programs in, 301–2; stage plays in, 77, 80. See also Savoy Ballroom
New York Gazette, 78
New York Journal of Education, 203
New York Morning Herald, 143
New York Times, 326, 347, 348
New York World, 306
Nicholas brothers, 322
Nicholas de Clamanges, 10–11
Nichols, Francis D., 108–10, 123, 124, 126, 145
The Ninth Yearbook of the National Society for the Study of Education, 253
Nordberg, Carl Edin, 262
Nordhoff, Charles, 179–80
Normal School of Gymnastics, 249
North American Review, 216
Northbrooke, John: amusements frowned on by, 79; calls for reform by, 34, 91; on dancing and sexual immorality, 13–15, 19–20, 32, 39n2; on dancing schools, 33
Noverre, Jean Georges, 123
Noyes, John Humphrey, 180–81
Nye, Russel B., 266, 268, 307, 315, 325

Of the Vanitie and uncertaintie of Artes and Sciences (Agrippa), 13–15

Oklahoma (movie), 323
Oliver, G., 124–25
"one-hundred percent mentality," 237, 258–60, 264
Oneida community, 178, 180–83
On Your Toes (movie), 323
Oral Roberts University, 349
Orchesographie (Arbeau), 20
Orchestra (Davies), 20–21, 23–24, 396
Orfila, Ansley, 350–51
Orr, William, 343–45
D'Orsay, Count Alfred. See Day, Charles William
Th'overthrow Of Stage-Playes (Rainolds), 36–37
Owls, David, 55

pagans: as dance opponents, 4; dancing associated with, 61, 157–59, 162, 343, 365, 378; Indians as, 55–56; May poles associated with, 49
Palmer, B. M., 150, 152, 155
Palmer, Mrs. Potter, II, 308
Palomar Night Club (Los Angeles), 308–9, 323
Paramount Theater (New York City), 323, 336
Paris (France), 159, 220, 373
Parkes, Henry Bamford, 56
Parris Garden (London), 33–34
The Parson on Dancing (Gross), 213–15, 388
passion. See body; dance: sexual immorality associated with
"Past and Present Social, Moral and Religious Condition of the Colored Baptists of Virginia" (Binga), 237–38
Pastoral Theology (Fritz), 329
patriotism: dance opponents' appeal to, 119–22, 169–70, 258–61, 264, 272, 331, 370, 376–77; of dancing in World War II, 335, 336
The Patriot Preachers of the American Revolution, 1766–1783 (Moore), 91
Paul (biblical figure), 365, 391–932; on abstaining from appearance of evil, 121, 345, 391; on avoiding unfruitful works of darkness, 43n47, 147; on avoiding works of the flesh, 113; on dress, 116, 330; on glorification of God, 166, 199–200, 211, 391; on not conforming to the world, 114, 147, 165, 201, 345, 349, 378, 391;

on responsibility to weaker Christians, 164–66, 345, 391–92

Pavlova, Anna, 283n65

Peacham, Henry, 60

Peiss, Kathy, 206, 279n24

Pelham, Peter, Sr., 82

pelota (dance), 5

Penn, William, 79

Penn, William Evander, 204

Penney, Joseph, 114–15

Pentecost, George, 231n52

Pentecostals, 350, 351

Perkins, William, 36, 44n50, 60

Perrin, Jean Paul, 9

Perry, Elisabeth Israels, 316n2, 317n16

Pershing, John J., 308

Petrarch, Francisco, 11, 14, 28, 163, 364, 372

Philadelphia (Pennsylvania), 79–81, 86, 100n34; assemblies in, 80, 98, 119–20; ballet performances in, 143; stage plays in, 77, 121, 377

Philadelphia Assembly, 80, 98, 119–20

Phillips, John, 93–96, 367, 370, 375–76

Phipps, Lee Ralph, 273

phonographs, 266–67, 325, 337

physical culture, 249, 282n50

"Physical Development of Women" (Sargent), 218

Pierpont, Samuel, 80

piety (and separation from the world): clergymen's emphasis on, 51, 93, 96, 97–98, 110, 114–17, 121, 135, 147, 163–66, 173–74, 178, 199–201, 208–9, 246, 377–78; opposition to, 148; tract societies' emphasis on, 112–13

pilgrimages, 10

pimps, 243, 371

Pitfalls of the Ballroom (Hall), 243

Pittsburgh (Pennsylvania), 306–7, 315

Pius II (pope). See Aeneas Silvius de Piccolomini

"Plain Talks to Women" (Sunday), 259

Plato, 214, 364

Playground and Recreation Association of America, 254, 297–98

A Plea for Amusements (Sawyer), 148, 149

Pleas Before the Synod of Chicago (Thompson), 209

polka (dance), 144, 220, 335; etiquette involving, 172; Mormon distaste for, 183;

opposition to, 149, 151, 154, 198, 211, 241

pony (dance), 339

Poor of Lyons, 17n16

Pope, Alexander, 379

Popular Amusements (Crane), 197

Porter, Cole, 322

Porter, J. W., 269, 272, 273

Portsmouth (New Hampshire), 82

Potts, William, 147, 149, 152–53, 155, 159

Powell, Dr. E. L., 243

Powell, Eleanor, 322

Powell, Lewis, 347

prayer. See piety

Presbyterians, 90, 195–96; antidance views of, 106, 113–19, 121, 141, 150, 163–64, 166, 197, 198, 204, 205, 237, 239–40, 385; church discipline among, 209–10; as dance supporters, 168, 346; decline in dance opposition by, 261, 271; number of nineteenth-century, 142

Presley, Elvis, 338

Prohibition, 266, 275–76, 311, 321

prostitutes: association of dancing with, 13, 153, 154, 158, 202–3, 228n26, 240–41, 254, 262, 263, 272, 274, 334, 369; attire of, 43n35; breaking of link between dancing and, 315; and dance halls, 295, 296, 304, 305, 309–11, 371, data on, 184n6, 203, 229nn28, 29, 239, 242–43, 262–64, 273–74, 286n90, 297–99, 333; May poles associated with, 49

Protestants: as antidance leaders, 15, 19–44, 146–65; combined post–Civil War membership of, 194; as dance proponents, 24. See also Bible; Puritans; Reformed churches; specific denominations and clergy

Providence (Rhode Island), 82, 125, 143

Providence Assembly (Rhode Island), 82, 125

Prynne, William, 3–5, 7–11, 31, 37, 369

Pupilla Oculi (John de Burgh), 8

Purdy (Missouri), 348–49

Puritans, 90–91, 146. See also Protestants; Reformed churches; names of specific Puritans

Putnam's Magazine, 159

quadrille (dance), 344, 380; closed dance position contrasted with, 144; etiquette advice regarding, 128–30, 234n86; rise of, 127

Quakers, 79–80, 90, 167

Quintilian, 127

race issues (in dance), 363. *See also* African Americans; racism; whites
racism, 158, 162, 239, 245–46, 274–75, 329, 331–32, 366
radio, 236, 266–67, 276, 323, 337
ragtime music, 236, 254, 269
Rainolds, John, 36–37, 60, 372
Ramay, Marion Edgar, 342, 344, 345
Rankin, Hugh, 74–76, 80, 81
Rath, Emil, 253, 254
Ravanel, Pierre, 44n*50*, 50
Reader's Guide to Periodical Literature, 314
reason. *See* body: notion that mind should rule
Recreation in Springfield, Illinois, 302
Recreation magazine, 335
reform. *See* conversion(s); urban reformers
Reformation (antidance fervor in), 53–54. *See also* Protestants; Puritans; Reformed churches; *specific reformers*
Reformed churches, 27–31, 50, 53, 373; influence of, 146, 151. *See also* French Reformed church
The Relation of the Dance to Religion (Guthrie), 276
Religious Dances in the Christian Church and in Popular Medicine (Backman), 5
Religious Tract Society (London), 112
renaissance traditions, 11–13
"A Representative of Thousands," 119–20
republicanism (as basis for dance opposition), 119–20, 169–70, 345, 377
rest (as health cure), 215–18, 225, 250
revivals, 385; camp-meeting, 117–19; dance as rival to, 208, 378; dancing at, 117–19; early twentieth-century, 238–39, 258–60, 386; held by Finney, 115–17; held by Whitefield, 76, 91, 98, 106, 386; social dancing halted by, 126; and utopian communities, 178
rhumba (dance), 327, 328, 335, 342
Rice, John R., 328
Rice, Nathan Lewis, 155, 156, 159–61, 166
Richardson, Dr. Frank G., 274
Richmond (Virginia), 143
"Rightrate, Timothy," 123
Riis, Jacob, 301
Riley, William Bell, 240–41, 333, 370
Rivet, André, 44n*50*, 50
RKO, 322
Robert, Christopher Rhinelander, 197

Robertson, Constance Noyes, 181
Robinson, Bill "Bojangles," 270, 322
Rock, Judith, 60
Rockefeller, John D., Jr., 297
rock 'n' roll, 338–39, 344, 366
Rodeo (movie), 323
Rogers, Ginger, 321–22, 326, 328
Rogers, John, 155–56
Rogers, Will, 308
Rollin, Charles, 156
Roseland Ballroom (New York City), 307–8, 338
"round dances," 193, 241, 262; clergymen's anachronistic references to, 272, 328; evils associated with, 225; lessons not needed for, 219, 380; opposition to closed dance position of, 198, 211, 260, 368, 370, 388; origins of, 373. *See also* mixed dancing; "modern dance"; *specific couple dances*
Ruskin, John, 215
Russell Sage Foundation, 295
Ruyter, Nancy, 206
Ryan, Mary P., 258, 271

Sabbath: dancing on, 28, 33–34, 73, 158, 377, 390; decline in observance of, 276, 321; holiness of, 36, 57, 63, 112, 120, 390
Sacred Dance Guild, 276, 346, 350. *See also* dance: associated with worship
Safford, Mary Joanna, 216
St. Denis, Ruth, 283n*65*, 346, 388
Salome (biblical figure): Carter on, 330; as dance opponents' favorite example, 5–6, 231n*46*, 369, 391, 394; Daneau on, 28; Gaskin on, 330; Hart on, 92; Mather on, 52; Meade on, 158; Potts on, 152
salsa (dance), 347
Saltator, 106, 123, 124, 126, 127, 145
Salter, John, 76
samba (dance), 327
Sanford, W. L., 242
San Francisco (California), 296, 306
Sanger, William W., 228nn*26, 29*
Sargent, Dr. Dudley, 217–18, 249
Savannah Assembly (Georgia), 77–78, 125
Savoy Ballroom (Harlem), 270, 308, 324, 326–27, 332, 338
Sawyer, Frederic W., 148, 149
Schlesinger, Arthur, 127–28, 280n*40,* 289n*116*
Scholes, Percy, 55–56

Schoole of Abuse (Gosson), 32
"Schoolmen," 8–9
schools (public), 63, 236; community recreation programs in, 293, 300–302; controversies over dancing in, 237, 246, 264–65, 287n99, 331, 345, 348–49, 355n35, 370, 376; controversy about teaching evolution in, 266, 274; dance instruction in, 276, 367, 371, 384; exercise in, 249, 252–54, 257–58, 264–65, 274. *See also* dance schools; education
Scopes trial, 266
Scovel, Sylvester F., 204
Scribner's Magazine, 218, 303
Scripture. *See* Bible
Second Great Awakening, 111, 115–17, 377–78, 385
Sensible Etiquette of the Best Society (Ward), 221–22
separation from the world. *See* piety
Sewall, Samuel, 48, 56, 65
shag (dance), 327
Shakers, 178–80, 183
Shall We Dance? (Jones), 333
Shaw, Artie, 309, 324, 338
Shawn, Ted, 283n65, 346, 388
Sherlot, Henry, 48
Sherwood, Mary Elizabeth, 221–23
shimmy (dance), 269, 327
Ship of Fools (Brant), 11–12
Short and Hasty Essay in Favour of Dancing and Musick (anonymous), 122
shottische (dance), 198, 262
Shuffle Along (musical), 270
Sikes, J. R., 202–3, 207, 208
sin(s): as avoidable, 115, 392–93; dance as, 6–8, 62; motive as factor in determining whether dancing is a, 7, 8, 125, 172–73, 199–200, 210, 256, 351; progressive nature of, 111, 167, 202–3, 241, 331, 333–34, 343–44, 348, 369, 389, 394; seven deadly, 189n94. *See also* behavior; conversion
Sinks, Perry Wayland, 245, 354n24
Skidmore, Rex, 182–83
Slave Code, 86
slavery, 94, 169
Sloan, Robert B., Jr., 350
Sloan, Sue, 350
Slocum, Stephen, 122
Smith, Asa D., 149–50, 159, 166

Smith, Florence Ethel, 263
Smith, Hyrum, 192n133
Smith, Joel A., 263
Smith, Joseph, 182–83, 192n133
Smithsonian magazine, 348
social class, 363, 379; associated with different kinds of dance, 365–66, 380, 384, 386; codes of civility associated with high, 70–73, 177–78, 225, 247; of dance hall attendees, 254–55; of dance opponents, 384, 386; dance opposition as criticism of, 11, 12–14, 86–87, 150–51, 169–70, 245, 253, 377, 381; and dance palaces, 308–9; etiquette and courtesy manuals as guide to, 21–25, 37–38, 177–78, 221; fears about men of high, 153–55; of New England Female Moral Reform Society members, 230n35; and public amusements, 148–49, 205–7, 213, 254–55, 293–97, 305–7, 311–12
Social Customs (Howe), 222, 223
Social Dynamite (Talmadge), 195
Social Etiquette (Cooke), 248
Social Theories of the Middle Ages (Jarrett), 5
Society of Jesus. *See* Jesuit stage plays
songs (popular), 322, 324–25, 337, 372
South: ideal gentlemen in, 73–78; religion in, 90–91
Southey's Dream (anonymous), 151
The Spirit of Youth and the City Streets (Addams), 293–94
sports contests, 184n6, 257–58
Sprague, William Buell, 133–35
Springfield (Illinois), 302
square dances, 335; opposition to, 193, 239, 260, 343; support for, 212, 241, 343, 388
stage plays: benefits of, contrasted with balls, 120; clergymen's lack of familiarity with, 384; dancing associated with, 77, 80–81, 143–44, 186n42, 205–7, 241, 261, 349; dancing associated with, opposition to, 14, 36–37, 149–50, 152–53, 377; laws against, 79–82, 121; limited twentieth-century audience for, 268; opposition to, 4, 30, 31–33, 49, 60, 90, 120–21; and rise of cities, 143; support for, in Charleston, 75–77
Stagg, Charles, 74
Stagg, Mary, 74
stag lines, 257
Staples, Mr. (dance master), 80

Stebbins, Genevieve, 281n49
Stephens, Francis, 29
Stepney, Francis, 47–48, 54, 55, 78–79, 370
Stitt, Edward W., 265, 301–2
Stocking, Reverend C. H. W., 212–13
Stocking, Collis, 306–7, 316
Stone, Barton Warren, 118–19, 155
Stout, Harry, 86
Straton, John Roach, 195, 267, 272, 273, 275, 276, 354n24
Stubbes, Phillip, 32–33, 35, 79, 95, 226n6
Stubbings, F. H., 42n32
Summa Angelica, 7
Summa Astensis, 7
summas for confessors, 6–7, 9
Sunday, Billy (William A.), 239, 240; antidance views of, 236, 258–61, 331; audiences of, 386; rhetoric of, 195, 236–38, 258–61, 342; on social services, 265–66; on women, 259–60, 264, 333, 370
surf (dance), 339
The Survey (Department of Labor), 295, 305, 311–13
Suzy-Q (dance), 326, 327, 329
Swedish Lutherans, 79, 336–37, 393
swim (dance), 339
swing music, 314, 323–24, 326, 328, 329, 335–36, 348
Sylvester II (pope), 16n13

Tabouror, Jehan (or Jean), 38n1
Taffin, Jean (the Elder), 29, 34, 36
Talmadge, T. DeWitt, 193, 194–95, 198, 199, 237
tango, 255, 257, 303, 327, 328, 343, 347, 373
Tango Argentino (show), 347
Tanz und Theaterbesuch (Walther), 200
tap dancing, 270, 322, 343, 347
Taylor University (Indiana), 349
tea dances (*thé dansants*), 237, 255, 256–57, 303, 348
Teakle, Reverend, 73
Teen Talk about Rock 'n' Roll (Texas Baptist General Convention), 344
television, 337–38, 347
temperance, 112, 156–57, 167–68, 178. *See also* drinking; Prohibition
Ten Commandments: on adultery, 30, 37, 50, 56, 59, 67n16, 368, 389–90; dancing as breaking of, 10, 30, 117, 158, 368, 386,

389–90; on honoring parents, 370, 390; on keeping the Sabbath day holy, 30, 390
Tennent, Gilbert, 91
Tennent, William, 91
Tenney, Henry M., 208
Tenth Yearbook of the National Society for the Study of Education, 265, 301–2
Tentler, Thomas, 6–8
Testimony Against several Prophane and Superstitious Customs (I. Mather), 49
Texas Tommy (dance), 254
Text Book of Dancing (Chalif), 253–54
Thacher, George Hornell, 168–69, 210, 231n49
theater. *See* stage plays
Theater-Going and Dancing Incompatible with Church Membership (Candler), 261
Theater of God's Judgment (Beard), 52
thé dansants. See tea dances
Thomas de Vio (Cardinal Cajetan), 16n13
Thompson, Robert G., 209
Thornwell, Emily, 175–76
Thoughts Concerning Education (Locke), 70–72
Three Graces, 24, 395–96
Tilton, Dr. Charles, 245
time (antidance clergymen's emphasis on stewarding of), 28, 59, 62, 72, 92–93, 108, 110–13, 115, 133–35, 137n15, 161–63, 208, 245, 330, 367, 374–75, 381
A Time to Dance (American Tract Society), 121–22
A Time to Dance (Presbyterian Board of Publications), 164
Timothy (biblical figure), 391
Titus (biblical figure), 391
Tomes, Robert, 216, 222
towns (rise of dance in), 107–8, 142–43. *See also* cities
Traicte Des Danses, auquel est monstre qu'elles sont comme accessoires et dependences de paillardise (anonymous), 31–32, 43n35
Traite Des Danses (Daneau), 27–29, 38
The Transformation of Virginia, 1740–1790 (Isaac), 73, 75
Treatise of Daunces (anonymous), 31–32
Treatise on Dancing (Saltator), 106
Trent, John Scott, 343–44
Trianon Ballroom (Chicago), 267, 308, 338
truckin' (dance), 327, 342
True Politeness (anonymous), 170, 172

Trumbull, J. H., 126
turkey trot (dance), 254, 373, 380
turning dances, 25, 201, 388
twist (dance), 339
two-step (dance), 328, 335, 343, 347

Unitarians, 111, 146, 213, 346
University of Wisconsin (Madison), 276
The Upas Tree, or Dynamite in Dancing Exposed (Penn), 204
urban reformers, 265, 292–319, 355n35, 387. *See also* conversion(s)
utopian sects, 178–83

Van Buren, Martin, 143
Van Cleef, Joy, 55
Variety, 322
varsity drag (dance), 269
vaudeville, 184n6, 205, 268
Vautrollier, Thomas, 42n32
Vegio, Mapheo, 11
venereal disease, 207, 263, 264, 272, 369
Vermigli, Pietro Martire, 31, 59, 60
Vernon, Samuel Milton, 203
Victor Record Company, 266, 325
Village Sermons (Burder), 125
Vincent, Marvin Richardson, 212, 213, 221
A Vindication of Rational Amusements (Oliver), 124–25
virgins. *See* chastity; Three Graces
Vittorino da Feltre, 11
Vives, Juan Luis, 13, 20, 21, 33, 51, 370, 384
Vogue, 268
Vom Bruch, Harry, 273, 274, 354n24

Waldenses sect, 9–10, 17n16, 92, 369, 373
"Walter F. White and the Savoy Ballroom Controversy of 1943" (Capeci), 332
Walther, Carl Ferdinand Wilhelm, 199, 200–201, 214
waltz (dance), 335, 344, 347–48; closed couple position of, 127, 144, 151, 152, 154, 170–72, 198, 201–2, 242, 272, 327, 329, 367–68; etiquette advice regarding, 128, 171, 234n86; Mormon distaste for, 183; opposition to, 149, 151, 152, 154, 156, 193, 198, 201–2, 211, 239, 241, 262, 272, 328, 369; rise of, 127, 144
The Waning of the Middle Ages (Huizinga), 10
Ward, Mrs. H. O., 221–22

"A Warning to Youth" (Emmons), 111
War of 1812, 126
Washington, D.C., 80, 143, 169–70, 347
Washington, D.C., Assembly, 80
Washington Waltz Group, 347
Watusi (dance), 339
"The Ways of Women in Unsexing Themselves" (Riley), 333
WBBM (radio station), 267
Weaver, John, 74
Webb, Chick, 324
weddings. *See* marriage
Weigle, C. F., 272
Weisberger, Bernard, 236
Wellman, Wendell, 341, 344
Wells, Amos R., 244
Welter, Barbara, 135
Wesley, John, 76
Wesson, Karl, 183
WGN (radio station), 308
Wheaton College (Illinois), 350, 393
Wheeler, Thomas, 55
"Where Is Your Daughter This Afternoon?" (Mumford), 303
Where Satan Sows His Seed (Williams), 239
White, Byron, 347
White, Walter F., 332
The White Faun (musical), 205
Whitefield, George, 90, 94, 199; antidance views of, 70, 72, 84–86, 96, 108; lack of first-hand dance experience of, 383; revivals held by, 76, 91, 98, 106, 386; style of, 97, 238; themes of, 113, 135; on women, 86–89, 373–74, 381
Whiteman, Paul, 266–67, 308
whites (as dance opponents). *See* racism
white slavery. *See* prostitutes
The Whole Duty of Man (Allestree), 62
Who Was Who in America, 258, 306
Wilkinson, William Cleaver, 198, 202, 330, 354n24
Willard, Emma, 190n116
Willard, Reverend (Boston cleric), 48
William and Mary College, 74
Williams, Milan Bertrand, 239, 240, 242, 285n83
Williamsburg (Virginia), 73–75, 77
Wilson, Franklin, 147, 151, 156, 161, 166
Wilson, Grady, 286n92
Wilson, Samuel Ramsey, 156, 163–64
Wilson, Teddy, 324

Winecoff, Jesse, 154, 160
"Woman of Fashion," 248, 281n43
women: associated with evil, 5–6, 10, 43,
    153, 204, 205, 225, 369; attire of, as en-
    ticement to men, 10, 43n35, 62, 68n36,
    151–53, 204, 225, 251, 369; as authors of
    etiquette books, 128; as civilizers of men,
    148, 204, 224, 265; conservative clergy-
    men's assumptions about, 239; criticism of
    dancing of, really a criticism of social class,
    14, 86–87; as dance mistresses, 74, 75; as
    dance opponents, 113, 154, 263–64; dual
    views of, 61, 151–53, 201–5, 225, 242–
    47, 333, 369, 394; education of, 71, 88–
    89, 130; health problems of, due to danc-
    ing, 112, 131, 160–61, 174–77, 207–8,
    215–18, 245, 376; ideals for, 20, 21–22,
    24, 38, 59, 61–62, 83–84, 107, 129–36,
    177–78, 224–25, 332–34, 369, 381; ide-
    als for Christian, 84, 86–89, 107, 132–36,
    177, 239, 333; moral role of, 132–35,
    147, 151, 174, 177, 203–5, 221–22, 224,
    225, 244–45, 248, 260, 264, 332–33,
    369–70, 394; "new," 255–60, 268, 270,
    307, 370; proper sphere for nineteenth-
    century, 130–33, 173–74, 248; rules for,
    at assemblies and balls, 77–78, 128, 170–
    73; sins associated with dancing, 7, 367; as
    stage dancers, 205–7; in work force, 206,
    236, 243, 279n24, 293–94, 334, 356n49,
    394. See also attire; prostitutes

Women's Christian Temperance Union, 239
Women's City Club (New York City), 305
Wood, Dr. Thomas D., 253, 254, 265
World's Christian Fundamentals Association,
    240
World War II, 334–37, 340
Wright, Louis B., 73, 75
Wycliffe, John, 9

Yale University, 112, 125
Ylvisaker, N. M., 320
YMCA, 219–20, 252, 335
Young, Brigham, 182, 183, 192n133
The Young Lady's Book: A Manual of Elegant
    Recreations, Exercises and Pursuits (anony-
    mous), 130
The Young Lady's Friend (Farrar), 131–32
The Young Lady's Guide to the Harmonius De-
    velopment of Christian Character (New-
    comb), 134–35
The Young Lady's Own Book: A Manual of In-
    tellectual Improvement and Moral Deport-
    ment (anonymous), 130
Young People's Luther League, 320, 331
The Young Women's Friend (Eddy), 173
Your Hit Parade (radio program), 324

Zellers, Parker R., 230n37
Ziegfeld, Florenz, 308

Ann Wagner is professor of dance at St. Olaf College, Northfield, Minnesota, where she teaches courses in dance history
and ballroom dance. Formerly chair of the Department of
Dance, she is now chair of the Fine Arts Division at the college. She has published articles in *Design for Arts in Education; Proceedings, Society of Dance History Scholars;* and *History of Education Quarterly.* She is a contributor to the
International Encyclopedia of Dance.

University of Illinois Press
1325 South Oak Street
Champaign, Illinois 61820-6903
www.press.uillinois.edu